MANUFACTURING STRATEGY

MANUFACTURING STRATEGY

How to Formulate and Implement a Winning Plan

2ND EDITION

JOHN MILTENBURG

CRC Press
Taylor & Francis Group
Boca Raton London New York

CRC Press is an imprint of the
Taylor & Francis Group, an **informa** business
A PRODUCTIVITY PRESS BOOK

First published 2005 by Productivity Press

Published 2019 by CRC Press
Taylor & Francis Group
6000 Broken Sound Parkway NW, Suite 300
Boca Raton, FL 33487-2742

ISBN-13: 978-1-56327-317-9 (hbk)

Visit the Taylor & Francis Web site at
http://www.taylorandfrancis.com

and the CRC Press Web site at
http://www.crcpress.com

Text Design and Page composition by Typography Services

Library of Congress Cataloging-in-Publication Data

Miltenburg, John.
Manufacturing strategy : how to formulate and implement a winning plan / John Miltenburg.
p. cm.
Includes bibliographical references and index.
ISBN 1-56327-317-9 (alk. paper)
1. Production planning. 2. Production control. I. Title.

TS176.M5429 2005
658.5—dc22

2005000599

To Margaret

CONTENTS

PUBLISHER'S MESSAGE

If you are a manufacturing manager in a domestic or international company who hopes to take your company to the forefront of your industry, you need this book. In the revised edition of *Manufacturing Strategy: How to Formulate and Implement a Winning Plan*, John Miltenburg offers a sensible and systematic method for:

- Evaluating domestic and foreign factories in terms of the outputs they provide and the production systems they use,
- Evaluating your international manufacturing network in terms of the outputs it provides and the network design it uses, and
- Planning the appropriate manufacturing strategy to lead your market.

As one advance reader has told us, "It's like an MBA in a book" with a foundation firmly rooted in what has and hasn't worked in the field.

Part I of the book outlines the principles of competitive strategy of which manufacturing strategy is part. Different strategies apply to different industries, because industry structure and sources of competitive advantage differ. Within the same industry, companies can choose and succeed with different strategies provided they seek appropriate competitive advantages and target appropriate markets. Companies change positions in their industry by challenging competitors. Companies under attack use defensive responses to protect their positions. While challenges and responses are important for all companies, they are critical for domestic companies in globalizing industries.

Part II examines manufacturing strategy in a factory. The factory can be domestic or foreign and can belong to a company or a partner. Manufacturing strategy in a factory begins with the six manufacturing outputs: low cost, high quality, fast and reliable delivery; advance product features that give high performance; flexibility to change features, quantities, or delivery dates on request; and innovative new products. Determining which outputs win orders in the marketplace points the factory to production systems best suited to produce those results. Success with a particular production system depends not only on proper adjustment of the subsystems or levers in the production system, but also on an increase in overall capability in each lever. The JIT production system, with its kanban coordination and attention to zero defects and zero inventory, is a case in point. It requires not just adjustment of the levers, but also quantum improvement in capabilities.

Part III examines manufacturing strategy in international manufacturing networks. Principles of international competitive strategy are outlined first. The pattern of international competition varies among industries, industry segments, and vertical stages in an industry. International companies combine advantages created in domestic facilities with competitive advantages that stem from their network of worldwide activities. They adapt practices and strategies to cultures and customer needs in each country's market.

Manufacturing strategy for an international manufacturing network begins with the four network outputs: accessibility to markets, low cost factors of production, and advanced suppliers; cost avoidance or thriftiness realized from economies of scale and avoidance of duplication; mobility of products, processes, and personnel; and learning about cultures, customers, processes, and technology. Determining which outputs are important points the company to manufacturing networks best suited to produce those results. There are nine manufacturing networks—four are simple, five are complex. Each is appropriate for a different tradeoff between pressure for globalization and pressure for local responsiveness. Each disperses manufacturing activities in a different way. Success with a manufacturing network depends not only on proper adjustment of structural and infrastructural levers in the network, but also on an increase in overall capability in each lever.

Manufacturing networks use six types of factories: server, outpost, offshore, contributor, lead, and source. The first three, usually used in simple networks, have low levels of capability. The last three, usually used in complex networks, have high levels of capability.

Part IV examines how a company integrates manufacturing strategy for its factories and network with its business strategy.

Part V examines process improvement programs such as quality management, cycle time reduction, agile manufacturing, and reengineering, and advanced techniques such as six sigma, supply chain management, and enterprise resource planning systems, that companies use to change production systems and manufacturing networks and increase capabilities. This section also examines experience curves and the product life cycle, which are foundations for learning and improvement. A company makes improvements by focusing manufacturing, using improvement programs and advanced techniques, and investing in people and equipment. Evaluating proposed investments in manufacturing is part of making improvements. A systematic approach is examined that takes account of strategic concerns, such as whether an investment is consistent with business and manufacturing strategies, and economic concerns, such as the safety, profitability, and robustness of an investment.

Each chapter in Part VI examines a specific production system, exploring in depth the situations in which they should be used, the manufacturing outputs they provide, the lever adjustments required for success, and case studies of the production system at work.

Case studies from the Harvard Business School, the Ivey Business School, and elsewhere that may be used with this book and other material supporting this book are available on the Internet. Links to the web sites containing this information can be found at the publisher's web site (*www.productivitypress.com*).

Maura May
Publisher

ACKNOWLEDGEMENTS

Over the years many colleagues and friends, especially Ted Cambridge, Chun Hung Cheng, Philip Kirby, Robert Marshall, George Miltenburg, Walter Petryschuk, Randolph Ross, Martin Rudberg, Edward Silver, and Jacob Wijngaard have contributed advice, criticism, experience, and ideas—much of which has become part of this book. I am indebted to all of them.

I am also indebted to the many people who practice, research, write, and speak about manufacturing and strategy, especially Robert Hall, Robert Hayes, Yasuhiro Monden, Taiichi Ohno, Michael Porter, and Steven Wheelwright. Their work is the foundation on which the results in this book are built.

I wish to thank McMaster University and the DeGroote School of Business who have made it possible for me to teach, work, and write on this important subject.

Last, but not least, I wish to thank Maura May and Robert Cooper at Productivity Press for making this work so pleasant and for producing such a beautiful book.

CHAPTER 1

INTRODUCTION

A company's *business strategy* is the sum of the individual strategies of its component functions—manufacturing, marketing, finance, research and development (R&D), and so on. In a successful company, these strategies interlock to provide the company's maximum competitive advantage. No function is left out and no function dominates. In some companies, business strategy is dominated by nonmanufacturing functions, with the result being "thrown over the wall" to manufacturing. Manufacturing, often uncomfortable with strategic planning and trying to be all things to all people, delivers mediocre performance. This book helps manufacturing change this.

SITUATION 1.1

Water Heater Producer Faces Competition

TOP MANAGEMENT at a North American producer and distributor of commercial and residential water heaters worried that manufacturing could no longer provide what was needed to satisfy the company's customers.

Manufacturing provided what it had always provided:

- A range of products at a cost that had not increased in several years
- Quality levels as high as ever
- Standard lead times
- Standard conditions for scheduling, volume changes, and product design changes

However, what was satisfactory in the past was not sufficient today. A new competitor had entered the industry and was taking away market share by providing products with lower cost and faster delivery.

In many companies, personnel inside and outside the manufacturing function realize that manufacturing struggles to provide what the company needs to be successful. This is due to the increase in customer expectations and competitors' capabilities and also to outdated manufacturing capabilities. Manufacturing can meet market expectations only by realigning itself, making improvements, and increasing manufacturing capabilities. How to accomplish this is unclear to manufacturing managers and their staff advisers.

Manufacturing is complex. Large numbers of employees—skilled and unskilled, line and staff, flexible and inflexible—work in a network of domestic and foreign facilities. Formal and informal systems, good and bad practices, and old and new cultures coexist. Production sometimes consists of low volumes of highly engineered, customized products; sometimes medium volumes of high-performance products with short product life cycles; and sometimes high volumes of high quality, low cost commodities. Production processes are as varied as the products they produce. In the last 20 years, countless new techniques, technologies, and programs have appeared, each presented as the way to dramatically improve manufacturing capability. Companies need a manufacturing plan or strategy to bring structure into this complex environment.

Manufacturing changes slowly. It takes a long time to build new facilities, install new equipment, develop new suppliers, change operating procedures, train personnel, and close or move existing facilities. In comparison, customer requirements change quickly. New products appear, technology changes, economic conditions fluctuate, companies reorganize, new competitors emerge, and government regulations change. Manufacturing strategy keeps a slow manufacturing function aligned with a fast marketplace.

Manufacturing strategy can be considered the pattern underlying the sequence of decisions made by manufacturing over a long time period. When a formal manufacturing strategy exists, decisions follow a neat, logical pattern. When no strategy exists, the pattern is erratic and unpredictable. The essence of manufacturing strategy is to formulate explicitly how manufacturing decisions will be made so that manufacturing will help the company achieve a long-term advantage over its competitors.

Many managers are familiar with the distinction between effectiveness and efficiency. *Effectiveness* consists of doing the right things, whereas *efficiency* consists of doing things right. Manufacturing strategy focuses on effectiveness first, then on efficiency; that is, strategy seeks to ensure that the right things are done, then, that the right things are done well. It is not unusual to find manufacturers, without a strategy to guide them, doing the wrong things very efficiently.

SITUATION 1.2

Chip Maker Considers Options for Improving Manufacturing

SEVERAL LINE AND STAFF departments in a company that designed, manufactured, and distributed integrated circuit chips submitted proposals for improving manufacturing operations. These included proposals to implement new manufacturing technologies and improvement approaches such as computer numerical control (CNC) machines, just-in-time (JIT), kaizen, robots, six sigma, and supply chain management. Top management was bewildered by the many technologies and changes. Which were most appropriate? What were the benefits? In what order should they be implemented? How quickly should they be implemented?

Process for Formulating Manufacturing Strategy

Any process for formulating manufacturing strategy should do the following:

- Take into account customer requirements.
- Take into account competitors.
- Take into account manufacturing capabilities.
- Consider all options available to manufacturing.
- List the outputs that manufacturing will provide and specify, in detail, the optimal set of changes needed to accomplish them.

Companies use a variety of processes to develop manufacturing strategy.[1] These processes share enough common elements for a comprehensive, general process to be framed. Such a process is presented in this book. This process strikes a balance between difficulty of application and usefulness of results. The process is not so complex as to be impractical and not so simple that results are not useful.

The process can be used by domestic or international companies. It is equally applicable to large and small companies. Despite the considerable experience large companies have with strategic planning, most will find that this book's process provides richer insights than their current process. Small companies, often uncomfortable with any type of strategic planning, will find this process simple enough, and at the same time, rich enough to use for all their strategic planning.

The Process for Formulating Manufacturing Strategy

Automatic Generation of All Alternatives

This book outlines, in operational detail, a general process for formulating manufacturing strategy and developing an implementation plan. The process automatically generates all alternatives available to manufacturing and evaluates each in turn against the company's needs. This helps management explore the implications of alternative strategies.

Because no alternatives are overlooked, the outcome of the process is the best possible manufacturing strategy for the company. The process uses two comprehensive, easy-to-use worksheets: the manufacturing strategy worksheet for a factory (Figure 1-1) and the manufacturing strategy worksheet for a manufacturing network (Figure 1-2).

Conditions Under Which Popular Changes are Appropriate

During the process of formulating manufacturing strategy, three issues are examined:

- Where is manufacturing?
- Where does manufacturing need to be?
- What is the best way to move manufacturing from where it is to where it needs to be?

The answer to the last question is a list of changes that need to be made in manufacturing. These questions are applied to each factory in a company's manufacturing network, as well as to the network itself.

Many popular changes are discussed in Part V. These include benchmarking, improvement programs (such as quality management, cycle time reduction, agile manufacturing, kaizen, and reengineering), focusing manufacturing, soft technologies (such as six sigma, concurrent engineering, and supply chain management), and hard technologies (such as CNC and enterprise resource planning systems).

This book examines the strategic conditions under which popular changes should be used. The result is more than, "yes, it is appropriate" versus "no, it is not appropriate." The result is an understanding of the strategic conditions in which particular changes should be implemented, what

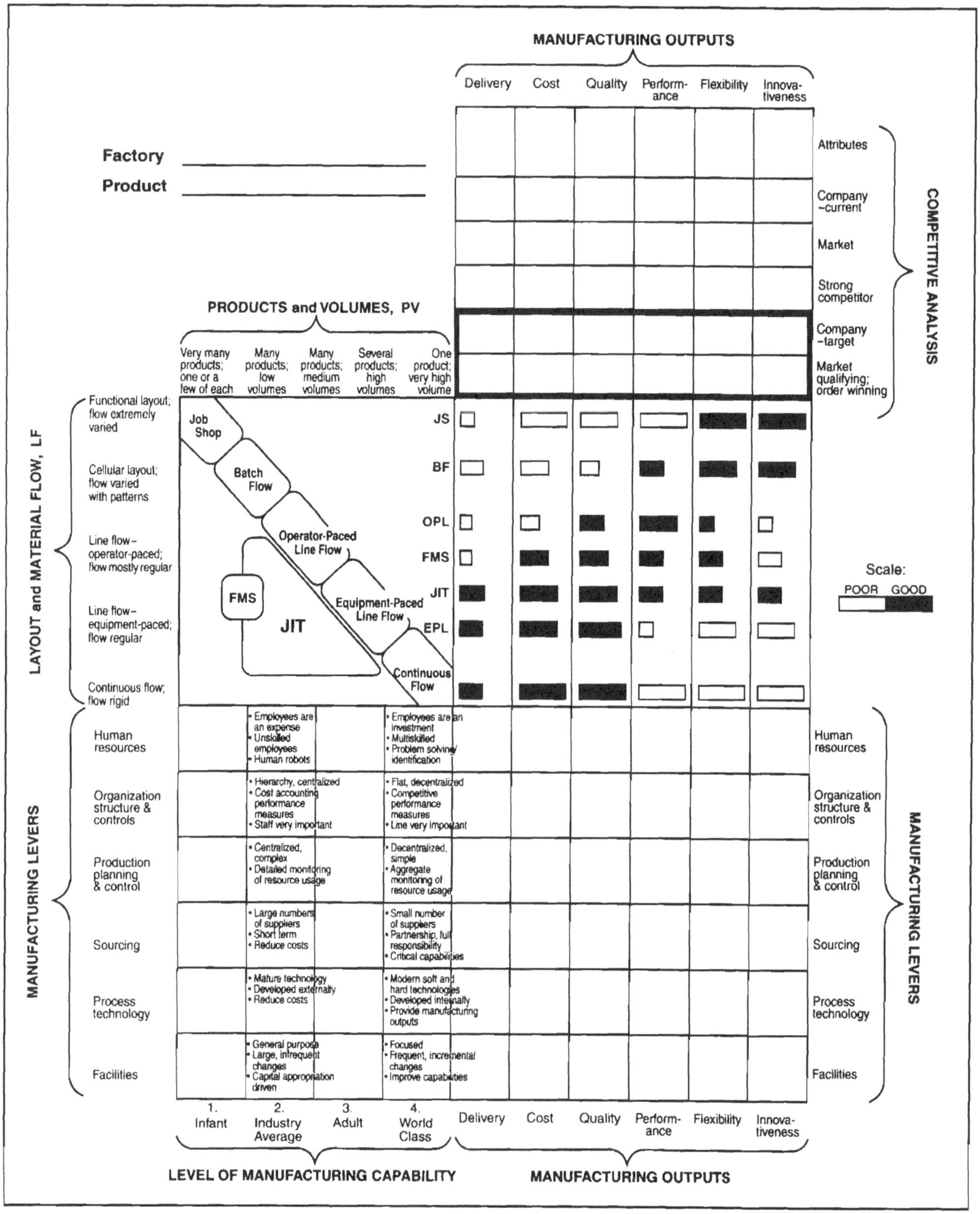

Figure 1-1 Manufacturing Strategy Worksheet for a Factory

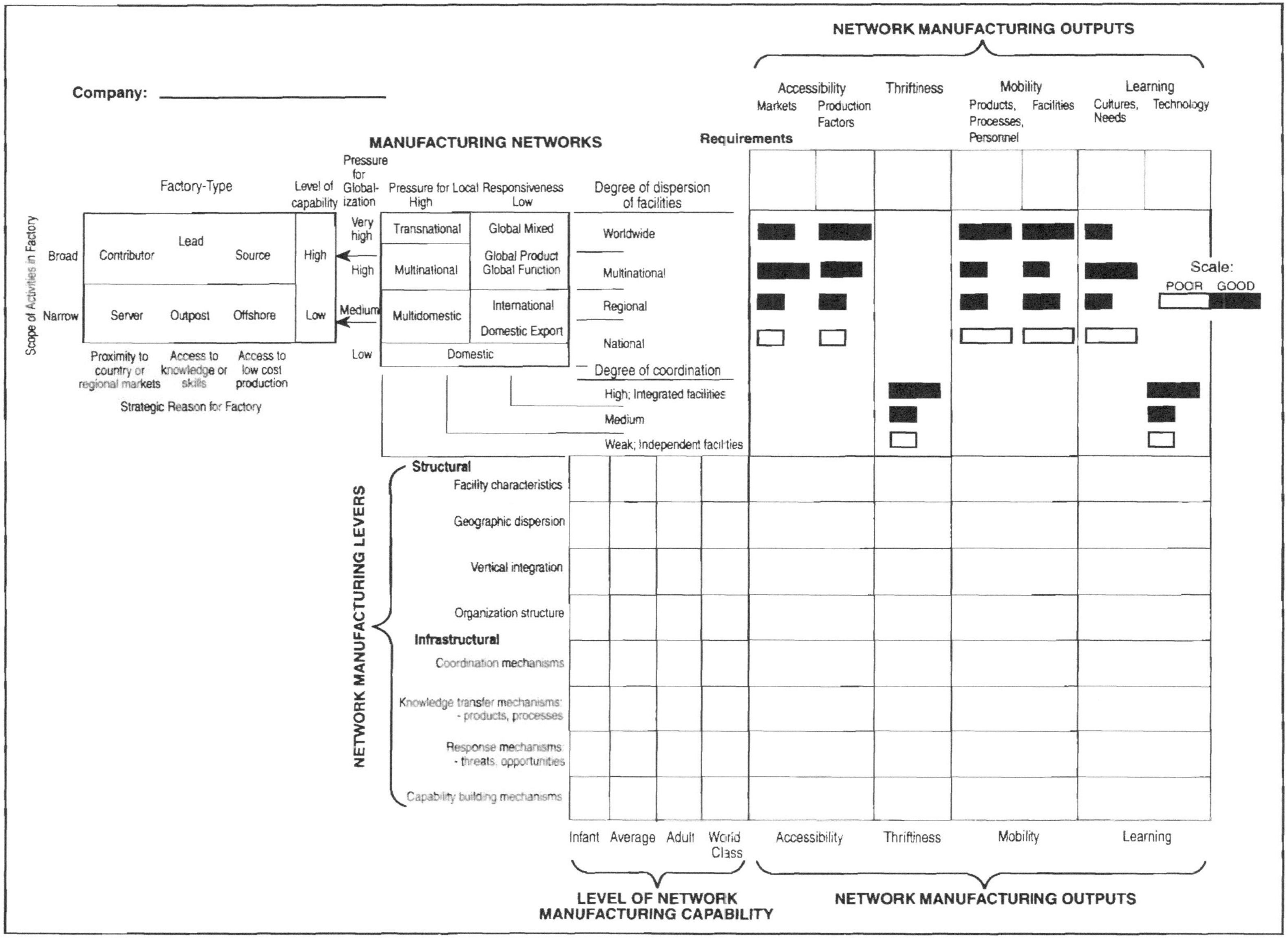

Figure 1-2 Manufacturing Strategy Worksheet for a Manufacturing Network

changes should be grouped together, and how changes should be organized for implementation.

Common Language

This book gives managers the skills needed to formulate and implement an optimal manufacturing strategy for their domestic or international company. An important outcome is the rich manufacturing strategy paradigm that is developed. Vocabulary, definitions, relationships, and so on, are developed to deal with manufacturing problems at both strategic and operational levels. The paradigm facilitates discussion among manufacturing managers, many of whom have long been uncomfortable with strategic issues. It also makes communication clearer between manufacturing managers and those outside of manufacturing, who will now have a better appreciation of what manufacturing can and cannot do.

How This Book is Organized

This book is organized into six parts:

- Principles of strategy
- Manufacturing strategy in a factory
- Manufacturing strategy in an international network of factories
- Manufacturing strategy and business strategy
- Programs used frequently in manufacturing strategy
- Seven production systems for focused factories

Part I: Principles of Strategy

Chapters 2 and 3 outline the principles of business strategy and competitive strategy. Different industries use different strategies because industry structures and sources of competitive advantage vary. Companies in an industry choose particular strategies to gain competitive advantages in their market segments.

Companies change their industry positions by challenging competitors. Companies use a variety of challenges to gain competitive advantage and increase profitability. Companies under attack use defensive responses to protect their positions. Challenges and responses are important for all companies. They are critical for domestic companies in globalizing industries.

Part II: Manufacturing Strategy in a Factory

Chapters 4 to 7 present the process for formulating manufacturing strategy for a domestic or foreign factory. The factory can belong to a company or a partner. The process has five elements:

1. What can a factory provide? (Manufacturing Outputs)
2. How does manufacturing provide what is required? (Production Systems)
3. What parts of a production system can be adjusted? (Manufacturing Levers)
4. Does manufacturing have sufficient capability for what is required? (Manufacturing Capability)
5. What outputs should manufacturing provide and at what levels? (Competitive Analysis)

Each element interacts with every other element. Interactions are displayed on the manufacturing strategy worksheet for a factory (Figure 1-1). Of the many possible interactions among elements, usually only five or six apply to a particular situation. The worksheet identifies and analyzes the important interactions.

Part III: Manufacturing Strategy in an International Network of Factories

This part of the book examines manufacturing strategy for international companies with networks of domestic and foreign factories.

Chapters 8 and 9 outline the principles of international competitive strategy. The pattern of international competition varies among industries, industry segments, and vertical stages in an industry. A range of patterns exists, beginning with multidomestic competition and ending with global competition. International companies combine competitive advantages created at their home base with advantages obtained from their network of worldwide activities. International companies do not manage worldwide activities with "one-size-fits-all" practices.

Chapters 10 to 12 present the process for formulating manufacturing strategy for an international network of factories. The process has four elements:

1. What can an international network of factories provide? (Network Outputs)
2. How does a company organize its domestic and foreign factories? (Manufacturing Networks)
3. What parts of a network can be adjusted? (Network Levers)
4. Does a network have sufficient capability for what is required? (Network Capability)

Each element interacts with every other element. Interactions are displayed on the manufacturing strategy worksheet for a network (Figure 1-2). Of the many possible interactions among elements, usually only five or six apply to a particular situation. The worksheet identifies and analyzes the important interactions.

There are nine international manufacturing networks. Four are simple; five are complex. Factories in a manufacturing network are divided into six types: server, outpost, offshore, contributor, lead, and source. The first three have low capability levels and are common in simple manufacturing networks. The last three have high capability levels and are common in complex networks. It is difficult to transform a factory with a low capability level into one with a high capability level. It is many times more difficult to transform a simple network with low-capability factories to a complex network with high-capability factories.

Part IV: Manufacturing Strategy and Business Strategy

Chapter 13 examines how companies integrate manufacturing strategies for factories and international networks with their business strategies.

Part V: Programs Used Frequently in Manufacturing Strategy

Chapters 14 and 15 describe popular programs for increasing capability, and changing production systems and manufacturing networks. These include benchmarking, improvement programs (such as quality management, cycle time reduction, agile manufacturing, kaizen, and reengineering), focusing manufacturing, soft technologies (such as six sigma, concurrent engineering, and supply chain management), and hard technologies (such as CNC, robots, and enterprise resource planning systems).

A company gains experience as its products move through their product life cycles (Chapter 16). This gives a company an opportunity to learn and improve product designs, production systems, and manufacturing networks. Improvements do not occur automatically. A company makes improvements by:

- Focusing manufacturing
- Using improvement programs
- Investing in people and processes

Focus is most important. Manufacturing cannot be successful for long unless factories are organized into factories-within-a-factory, with each focusing on a limited number of products, activities, and customers.

Confusion and frustration often surround the process of evaluating investments in manufacturing. Chapter 17 outlines an evaluation process that considers all strategic and economic concerns.

Part VI: Seven Production Systems for Focused Factories

Each chapter in this section examines a specific production system, treating in more depth the situations in which it should be used, the manufacturing outputs it provides, the adjustments required for success, and case studies of the production system at work. This part of the book is a reference to consult as necessary during the formulation of manufacturing strategy.

Case Studies and Other Resources

Case studies from the Harvard Business School, the Ivey Business School, and elsewhere that may be used with this book and other supporting material are available on the Internet. Links to websites containing this information can be found at the publisher's website (www.productivitypress.com) and the author's website (www.degroote.mcmaster.ca).

Endnotes

1. The following articles, books, and cases describe processes some companies use to develop manufacturing strategy.
    - Etienne-Hamilton, E., *Operations Strategies for Competitive Advantage: Text and Cases*, Dryden Press: New York, Chapter 3, 1994.
    - Fine, C., and Hax, A., "Manufacturing Strategy: A Methodology and an Illustration," *Interfaces*, Vol. 15, No.6, pp. 16–27, 1986.
    - Garvin, D., *Operations Strategy: Text and Cases*, Prentice Hall: Englewood Cliffs, New Jersey, 1992.
    - Hax, A., and Majluf, N., "The Corporate Strategic Planning Process," *Interfaces*, Vol. 14, No.1, pp. 47–60, 1984.
    - Hayes, R., and Wheelwright, S., *Restoring Our Competitive Edge: Competing Through Manufacturing*, Wiley: New York, 1984.
    - Hill, T., *Manufacturing Strategy: Text and Cases*, Irwin McGraw-Hill: Boston, 2000.

Part I

PRINCIPLES OF STRATEGY

CHAPTER 2

PRINCIPLES OF COMPETITIVE STRATEGY

Whether in a small domestic company with one factory, a medium sized international company with several regional factories, or a large global company with a sophisticated network of factories, managers who craft manufacturing strategy face a seemingly overwhelming number of possibilities. By the end of this book, these managers will make choices with confidence and ease. In this chapter, we start at the beginning—with business and competitive strategy—of which manufacturing strategy is a part.[1]

A company's *business strategy* is the plan management uses to stake out a market position, attract and please customers, conduct operations, compete successfully, and achieve organizational objectives.[2] A company's business strategy states, "Among all the possible plans and actions, we will move in this direction, focus on these markets and customer needs, compete in this fashion, allocate our resources and energies in these ways, and rely on these particular business approaches."

Closely related to business strategy is the *business model*, which is a company's plan for earning profits. A business model calculates the revenue-cost-profit implications of a business strategy. It estimates the revenue streams, cost structure, profit margins, and earnings that will be generated by a company's product offerings and competitive approaches. It answers the question, "Does the business strategy make economic sense?"

A mature company making acceptable profits has a "proven" business model. For example, Microsoft's business model requires its commercial customers to pay licensing fees for each copy of each software package their employees use. Microsoft is profitable, so this business model is proven. A new company that is losing money has an "unproven" business model. For example, one Microsoft competitor offered its commercial customers a suite of desktop and server software, training, support, and maintenance for $100 per year, per employee. This competitor is losing money, so this business model is unproven.

A company's *competitive strategy* is a subset of its business strategy. While business strategy addresses all strategic issues facing a company, competitive strategy focuses on a company's plan for competing successfully against competitors.

A winning competitive strategy is grounded in *competitive advantage*. A company has competitive advantage whenever it has an edge over competitors in attracting customers and defending against competitive forces. Many routes to competitive advantage exist, but the most basic route provides customers with superior value; namely, a good product at a low price, a superior product worth paying more for, or a best value product that attractively combines price and features.[3] A company cannot deliver superior value unless it organizes and performs activities more effectively than competitors and builds capabilities that competitors cannot easily match.

Industry Structure

Competitive strategy involves identifying a company's industry rivals. An *industry* is a group of companies producing products that compete directly with each other. Some examples include construction materials, farm equipment, medical imaging equipment, and steel.

Competitive strategy develops from understanding the level of competition in a particular industry. Five forces that determine this level of competition and a company's potential profits are[4]:

- *Threat of new competitors.* When profits rise, new competitors enter an industry. This brings additional capacity, which decreases prices.
- *Threat of substitute products.* The availability of substitute products limits prices.
- *Bargaining power of suppliers.* Powerful suppliers increase the cost of purchased materials.
- *Bargaining power of customers.* Powerful customers decrease prices for finished products.
- *Rivalry among competitors.* Tough competition decreases prices and increases costs such as marketing and new product R&D.

In industries where these forces are weak (such as defense contracting, health care, and pharmaceuticals), many companies earn good profits. In industries where one or more forces is intense (such as agriculture, apparel, and steel), few companies are profitable.

Each company must choose a position within its industry. Two elements help clarify a company's position: competitive advantage and competitive scope.

Competitive Advantage

Types of competitive advantage are divided into two categories: low cost and differentiation. *Low cost* is the ability to design, produce, and market a product for less than competitors. *Differentiation* is the ability to provide a product with better quality, features, and service than competitors. All successful strategies pay close attention to low cost and differentiation, while emphasizing one.

Low cost and differentiation differ in terms of the opportunities offered for competitive advantage. Low cost offers a company less opportunities. A company performs activities at the lowest possible cost to create a cost advantage over competitors. Differentiation offers a larger range of opportunities. A company tries to provide some combination of better quality, superior features, better service, faster delivery, and so on to satisfy customer needs.

Competitive advantage develops from how companies organize and perform activities. Companies create value by performing activities. The price customers pay for a company's products measures *value*. A company profits when value exceeds the cost of performing activities. To gain competitive advantage, a company may create comparable value but perform activities more efficiently than its competitors. This is low cost. Nucor Steel, one of the lowest cost producers of steel in the world, is an example. It performs steelmaking activities more efficiently than almost any other company.

A company may perform activities in a way that creates greater value. This is differentiation. 3M Company is an example. 3M organizes and performs activities—especially those related to new products—better than similar companies. This creates better products, sold for higher prices.

Value Chain

Activities are linked together in a value chain (Figure 2-1), and each has suppliers, owners, and customers. Suppliers provide inputs, owners use inputs to perform the activity, and customers consume outputs. Each activity contributes to value.

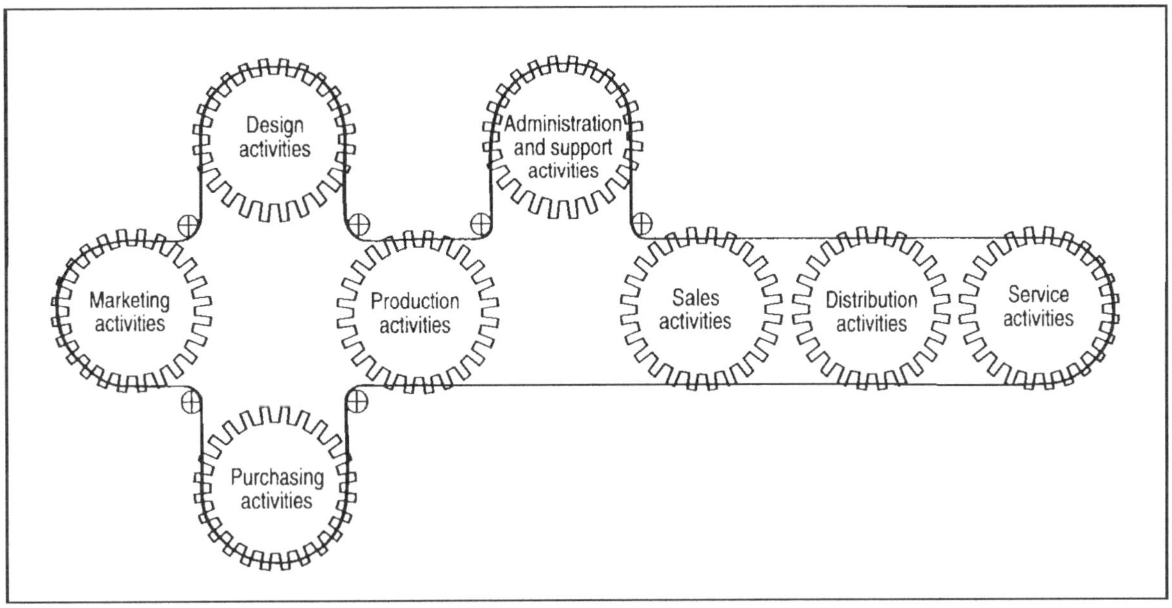

Figure 2-1 Value Chain of Activities

Strategy determines how a company organizes its value chain and performs activities. Companies gain competitive advantage when they find better ways to do this. For example, a manufacturer of construction equipment reorganized its activities for processing customer financing agreements. The original activities required input from three specialists and needed seven days to complete. The new activities required one specialist supported by a computer information system and only two hours to complete. This change helped the manufacturer differentiate itself from its competitors.

A company's *value chain* is a system of activities and linkages.[5] *Linkages* result from the affect of how one activity is performed on the cost or effectiveness of others. They create tradeoffs, which a company must resolve according to its strategy so competitive advantage is achieved. Outsourcing activities is one example. What products to outsource and what suppliers to use affect sales, manufacturing, and purchasing activities. How to perform these activities affects a company's ability to achieve low cost or differentiation advantages.

Linkages require a company to coordinate activities. For example, activities in sales, manufacturing, and distribution must be coordinated to achieve on-time delivery. Coordination requires a company to resolve tradeoffs that cross department lines. Japanese companies are particularly adept at coordinating activities between design and manufacturing. For example, they popularized concurrent engineering so new products are developed simultaneously with the manufacturing processes that produce them. Mitsubishi developed Quality Function Deployment and House of Quality in 1972 at its Kobe shipyard to coordinate design, manufacturing, and supplier activities.

Reorganizing the value chain by removing, reordering, or adding activities can produce a major improvement in competitive advantage. For example, Japanese camera manufacturers became industry leaders by creating value chains that combined single lens reflex camera technology with automated mass production and mass marketing. Kodak recently reorganized its value chain by adding digital technology, electronic photography, and high-resolution imaging to its silver-based film technologies.

Value System

A company's value chain is part of a larger stream of activities called the value system (Figure 2-2). The *value system* consists of the suppliers' value chains (who provide inputs), the company's value chain (that produces products), the distributors' and retailers' value chains (who distribute products to customers), and the customer's value chains (who use products in their own activities). Linkages connect activities in all value chains. Competitive advantage depends on how well a company manages the activities and linkages in the entire value system.

One example is the children's toy industry. Small companies purchase ideas for new products from independent inventors and entertainment companies. They hire outside specialists to design products. They contract manufacturing and packaging to factories in Asia who, in turn, subcontract labor-intensive work to other factories. Finished toys are shipped to commissioned wholesalers for distribution to retailers in major worldwide markets. Accounts receivable are subcontracted. Com-

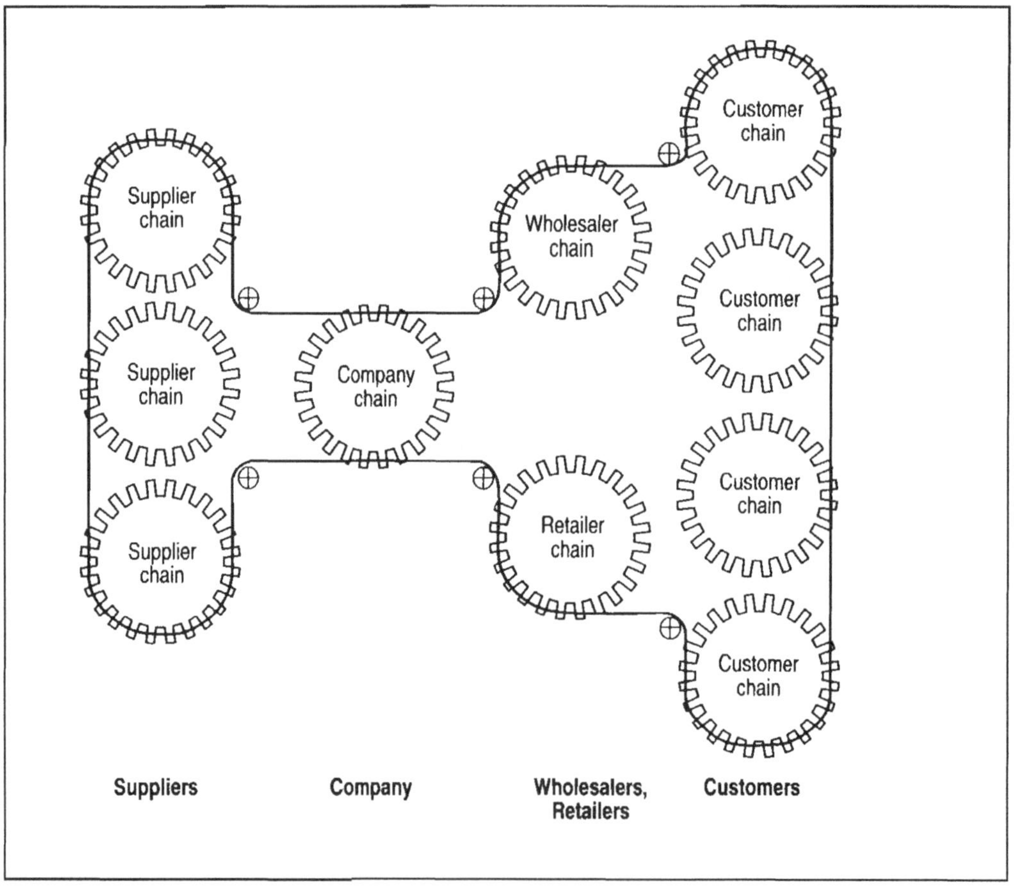

Figure 2-2 Value System

petitive advantage for the toy companies depends on how well they manage all the activities and linkages in this complex value system.

The value system helps identify the sources of low cost advantage. A company's *cost position* is the total cost of performing all activities relative to competitors. Low cost competitive advantage can result from any activity. Successful cost leaders can be low cost product developers, low cost manufacturers, low cost distributors, low cost marketers, or low cost service providers. They draw cost advantage from their value chain and those of their partners.

For example, prior to 1982, Toyota's Japanese operations were divided into two separate companies: Toyota Motor Manufacturing and Toyota Motor Sales. While Toyota Manufacturing took less than two days to manufacture a car, Toyota Sales needed between 15 and 26 days to take a customer order, transmit the order to the factory, schedule the order, and deliver the car to the customer. In addition to more time, Toyota Sales also incurred more cost. Overall costs at Toyota Sales exceeded the cost to manufacture the car at Toyota Manufacturing. Obviously, the value chain at Toyota Sales was a good place to create new sources of low cost competitive advantage. So in 1982, Toyota Sales and Toyota Manufacturing merged. All Toyota Motor Sales directors retired, and executives from Toyota Motor Manufacturing filled their jobs. Improvements began. Within five years, the time to perform order processing and distribution activities decreased to six days, and costs decreased significantly.[6]

The value system also helps to identify sources of differentiation advantage. Many linkages between a company and its customers exist, and each is a potential source of differentiation. The impact of a company's product on the customer's activity with it constitutes the most obvious linkage. A company creates value for its customers if customer's cost is lowered or customer's performance is raised. Consider, for example, a printed circuit board used by a customer in an assembly operation. It must be received into inventory, handled by assemblers, and repaired as part of the customer's product if it fails. How effectively each of these is executed can be a source of differentiation. Other sources are possible. The company's engineering group can assist the customer in product design, and the logistics group can assist the customer with just-in-time delivery.

Differentiation must be real. Some companies advertise their products as different and better, when, in fact, no sources of differentiation advantage exist, or they focus value systems on low cost. As a result, they waste time and money differentiating when there is no difference. Consider the decline of Cadillac as a force in the luxury automobile industry. Cadillac was the bestselling luxury automobile for so long that "Cadillac" became synonymous with "best." But Cadillac's value system languished, and Cadillac lost its sources of differentiation advantage. Accura, BMW, Lexus, and Mercedes improved their value systems, caught up to Cadillac, and raced by.

Competitive Scope

The second element that helps clarify a company's position in its industry is competitive scope. *Competitive scope* is the range of products a company produces, the distribution channels it uses, and the geographic areas and target markets where it sells. The most basic choice is between a broad and narrow scope. For example, Ford and Daimler-Chrysler have broad scopes; BMW and Korean car companies have narrow scopes. Ford and Daimler-Chrysler produce a wide range of automobiles; BMW focuses on luxury automobiles; and Korean car companies focus on economy automobiles.

Scope shapes the value system. By selecting a narrow market segment, a company can tailor each activity to the segment's needs and achieve lower cost or differentiation compared to broader line competitors.[7] For example, Swiss hearing aid producers focused on high amplification units for patients with severe hearing problems, achieving superior performance compared to less focused American competitors.

Alternatively, broad scope can lead to competitive advantage if a company shares activities across market segments. Japanese consumer electronics producers, such as Sony, Matsushita, and Toshiba, gain advantages from competing in related markets such as audio and video equipment. They use the same brand names, take advantage of common product and process technologies, and employ the same international supply and distribution networks.

Generic Competitive Strategies

A company positions itself to outperform competitors at meeting and exceeding customer needs. Companies conceive imaginative strategies to accomplish this. Many important differences among competitive strategies are revealed by determining whether a company's competitive advantage is drawn from low cost or differentiation and whether its competitive scope is broad or narrow (Figure 2-3). These choices help set a company's competitive strategy and position it within its industry.

Figure 2-3 shows five generic competitive strategies: cost leadership, differentiation, best value, focused cost, and focused differentiation. Four of these strategies are found in the shipbuilding industry[8]:

- Korean companies follow a cost leadership strategy. They build many types of ships with good, but not superior, quality, at a lower cost than Japanese competitors.
- Japanese companies follow a differentiation strategy. They build a wide variety of high quality ships at premium prices.
- Chinese companies follow a focused low cost strategy. They build standard, simple ships at lower prices than Korean competitors.
- Scandinavian companies follow a focused differentiation strategy. They build specialized ships such as icebreakers and cruise ships.

Many variations within each generic strategy exist. For example, there are multiple ways to differentiate and focus. A company must carefully decide the type of competitive advantage it seeks and the competitive scope in which it will operate, if it is to have any chance of achieving a competitive advantage. Figure 2-4 compares some characteristics of the generic strategies.

		Competitive Advantage		
		Low Cost		**Differentiation**
Competitive Scope	**Broad**	Cost leadership		Differentiation
			Best value	
	Narrow	Focused cost		Focused differentiation

Source: Adapted from Porter, *Competitive Advantage,* p. 12 and Thompson and Strickland, *Strategic Management,* p. 151.

Figure 2-3 Generic Competitive Strategies

	Generic Competitive Strategy			
Feature	**Cost Leadership**	**Differentiation**	**Best Value**	**Focused Cost and Focused Differentiation (Market Niche)**
Competitive Advantage	Lower costs than competitors	Ability to offer customers something different from competitors	Better products at same price or same products at lower price	Lower cost than competitors or something different from competitors in a market niche
Competitive Scope	Broad market	Broad market	Value-conscious customers	Narrow market where customer needs are distinctively different
Products	Good quality, basic produc	Superior products that create value for customers Many product variations	Good product with several upscale features	Features that appeal to needs of customers in market niche
Manufacturing Emphasis	Continuous search for cost reduction without sacrificing quality and essential features	Build features customers are willing to pay for Charge premium price to cover costs of differentiating features	Build product with several upscale features at low cost	Customize product to meet needs of customers in market niche
Marketing Emphasis	Good product at low price	Communicate key differentiating features to create reputation and brand image	Build reputation for value Under-price rival products with comparable features, or match price of rival products and provide better features	Communicate how product features meet special needs of customers in market niche
Strategy	Manage costs down in every area of the business	Constant improvement in product Use innovation to stay ahead of competitors	Develop capability to simultaneously manage costs down and add new, upscale features	Remain dedicated to serving niche customers better than competitors Do not dilute image by adding products to appeal to broad market

Source: Adapted from Thompson and Strickland, *Strategic Management*, p. 152.

Figure 2-4 Features of Generic Competitive Strategies

Cost Leadership Strategy

A company with a cost leadership strategy tries to perform its activities at the lowest possible cost, opening a cost advantage over competitors. Whenever a company has alternatives for achieving its cost advantage, it selects those difficult for competitors to copy. If competitors can copy a leader's low cost methods, the cost advantage is short lived.

Examples of companies that employ a cost leadership strategy are Black & Decker (power tools), Briggs & Stratton (small engines), Dell (computers), Lincoln Electric (welding equipment), Nucor (steel), and Whirlpool (home appliances).

Because of its innovative value system, Dell is the global low cost leader in the personal computer (PC) industry. Whereas many of its competitors manufacture PCs in volume and sell through independent wholesalers and retailers, Dell markets directly to customers, manufactures to customer order, and ships products within a few days of receiving an order. Its sell-direct strategy eliminates wholesaler and retailer costs. Its build-to-order strategy avoids misjudging customer demand and being saddled with obsolete components and finished goods inventory.

Nucor is the global low cost leader of steel products such as rolled steel, steel decking, and steel joists and girders. It has over $4 billion in annual sales and produces over 10 million tons. The company uses electric arc furnaces to melt scrap steel and iron ore. The molten steel flows into a continuous caster and rolling mill where it is shaped into steel products (Situation 24.1 in Chapter 24). This streamlined process eliminates many activities necessary in traditional integrated steel mills. Nucor selects plant sites that minimize shipping costs, take advantage of low electricity rates, and avoid unions. A nonunion workforce makes it easier for Nucor to organize improvement activities and use team-based incentive compensation systems, where workers and managers receive weekly bonuses based on team productivity. Maintaining a lean staff and allowing only four levels of management between the CEO and production workers keeps administrative costs low.

To achieve a low cost advantage, a company's total cost for the activities in its value system must be lower than competitors' total costs. At the same time, the company must produce features and provide services that customers consider important. The following are some of the key factors that affect costs.[9]

Cost of key inputs

The cost of performing activities partially depends on what a company pays for key resource inputs. Cost leaders locate factories in areas with low wage levels, energy costs, and taxes. Avoiding the use of union labor is important, not just to escape paying high wages, but also to escape union work rules that inhibit efficiency. Large companies use their bargaining power over suppliers to purchase large volumes of materials at low prices.

Economies of scale

Economies of scale arise whenever activities can be performed cheaper at large volumes and from the ability to spread certain costs (e.g., advertising, fixed production costs, and R&D) over a greater sales volume. For example, a company that sells a standard product worldwide can realize economies of scale as sales grow because it can spread fixed production costs over a larger sales volume. However, a company that produces differentiated products for each country market will not realize economies of scale because sales growth will require new products, which will require more R&D and fixed production costs.

Experience

The cost of performing an activity can decline over time due to the benefits of experience (Chapter 16). Sources of experience benefits include: employees performing activities more efficiently, debugging new technologies, studying competitors' products, studying workflows, making product design changes that enhance manufacturing efficiency, and benchmarking activities against similar activities at other companies. Experience also reduces the cost of building factories, other facilities, and programming computer systems.

Capacity utilization

Capacity utilization is important for activities with substantial fixed costs. Higher capacity utilization allows depreciation and other fixed costs to be spread over a larger production volume, thereby lowering fixed costs per unit.

Sharing resources

Sometimes, different business units and product lines share the same production processes and distribution facilities, share order processing and customer billing systems, utilize a common sales force, and so on. Sharing helps achieve economies of scale, generates experience benefits, and increases capacity utilization.

Vertical integration or outsourcing

Partially or fully integrating the activities of suppliers or distributors enables a company to bypass suppliers or distributors with considerable bargaining power. Other times, it is cheaper to outsource certain activities to outside specialists who, due to their expertise and volume, can perform the activities for less (Chapter 3).

Linkages between activities

When the cost of an activity affects how other activities are performed, costs can be reduced by seeing that linked activities are performed in a cooperative and coordinated fashion. For example, quality costs and inventory costs can be reduced when a company works cooperatively with key suppliers on quality practices, just-in-time delivery, electronic order processing, and the design of new products.

E-business technologies

Using the Internet for data sharing, online purchasing, and bill payment can reduce cost. For example, Singapore-based Advanced Manufacturing Online runs an Internet-based system where Asian customers and suppliers post orders and solicit price quotations. Customers shop for the best terms, and suppliers get quick and inexpensive access to customers. Teams of Ford designers worldwide use an online computer network to share ideas and create designs.

Costs in the wholesale-retail portions of the value system frequently represent 35 to 50 percent of the price that customers pay. Companies can reduce these costs by using the Internet to market products directly to customers.

First-to-market advantages and disadvantages

Sometimes, the first major brand in a market establishes and maintains its brand name at a lower cost than later arrivals (Chapter 3). New pharmaceutical products are an example.

Other times, such as when technology is developing fast, late entrants can benefit from waiting to employ cheaper and more effective second- or third-generation technology. Companies that follow, rather than lead, sometimes avoid costs that pioneers incur with path-breaking R&D and the opening up of new markets.

Managerial decisions

A wide variety of managerial decisions can drive cost up or down. Examples include either incorporating fewer or more features into products, shortening or lengthening delivery times, increasing or decreasing the number of distribution channels, and adding or cutting services. Low cost leaders often make large investments in technology to drive costs out of their value systems. Wal-Mart, for example, uses expensive, state-of-the-art technology throughout its value system. Its distribution facilities are highly automated; it uses online systems to order goods from suppliers and manage inventories; its stores have cutting-edge sales tracking and checkout systems; and it operates a satellite communications system that sends daily point-of-sale data to 4,000 suppliers.

A competitive strategy based on cost leadership is attractive when[10]:

- The product is a commodity readily available from many companies.
- There are few ways to achieve differentiation.
- Customers have low switching costs in changing from one company to another.
- Customers are large and have significant power to bargain down prices.
- Price competition among competitors is intense.

The biggest danger of a cost leadership strategy is excessive price-cutting, resulting in lower, rather than higher, profits. A cost leader has two options for increasing profits. It can be content with its current market share and use its low cost advantage to earn a higher profit margin on each unit sold, or it can use its low cost advantage to underprice competitors and attract price-sensitive buyers in greater numbers. Motorola likes the second option. According to a former CEO, "The only thing that matters is if the exponential growth of your market is faster than the exponential decline of your prices."

Differentiation Strategy

A company with a differentiation strategy seeks to be unique in ways that are valuable to customers. Companies differentiate themselves in many ways: broad product line (Campbell's Soup); engineering design and performance (BMW, Mercedes); prestige and distinctiveness (Chanel in women's fashion and accessories, Cross writing instruments, Ralph Lauren clothing, Rolex watches); product reliability (Johnson & Johnson in baby products); quality (Honda motorcycles, Michelin tires, Sony televisions); spare parts availability (Caterpillar); superior service (FedEx); and so on.

It is useful to organize types of differentiation into three categories:

- *Product features that lower a customer's total cost of using the company's product.* For example, supplying cut-to-size materials reduces a customer's materials waste. Providing just-in-time deliveries reduces a customer's inventory cost.
- *Product features that raise the performance a customer receives from the company's product.* Examples are providing greater durability, ease of use, and reliability; and making the product cleaner, safer, quieter, and more maintenance-free.
- *Product features that enhance customer satisfaction in intangible ways.* For example, Michelin tires satisfy customer desires for safety; Rolex and Gucci satisfy customer desires for status, image, and prestige.

How a company differentiates itself can change over time. For example, Xerox realized that its differentiated product would be copied as soon as its copier patents ran out, so it launched a strategy to become an industry leader in field service.

There are many sources of differentiation: product R&D activities that improve product design, add new features, or generate new products; process R&D activities that improve quality, enhance product appearance, or permit custom-order manufacturing; manufacturing activities that improve cycle time, reduce defect rates, or speed maintenance and repair; logistics activities that enable faster delivery, more accurate order filling, and fewer stockouts; and marketing and customer service activities that give quicker order processing, better credit terms, or superior after-sales support. Supplier activities are another source of competitive advantage. Toyota remains an industry leader in quality because of its superior suppliers and tough supplier certification program. All of these sources of differentiation are associated with unique capabilities and superior performance of value system activities.

A competitive strategy based on differentiation is attractive when[11]:

- The product is differentiated in many ways, and customers perceive these to have value.
- Customer needs and uses are diverse.
- Few competitors follow a similar differentiation strategy.
- Technological change and product innovation are fast-paced.

The pharmaceutical industry is an example of an industry where most of these conditions are satisfied.

Differentiation does not guarantee a competitive advantage. If customers see little value in the unique product features or competitors copy the features, differentiation fails. For example, Chrysler's unique 60,000 mile bumper-to-bumper warranty did not produce a lasting competitive advantage, because Ford and General Motors quickly copied it.

Best Value Strategy

A company with a best value strategy gives customers more value for their money by providing an average product at below average price or an above average product at average price. That is, a company satisfies customer expectations on product features and beats expectations on price, or it beats expectations on product features and satisfies expectations on price.

A best value strategy stakes out a middle ground between a low cost or differentiation advantage and between appealing to a broad or a narrow market (Figure 2-3).

Best value strategies work in market situations where customer diversity makes product differentiation the norm, and many customers are price sensitive. Customers in this market situation often prefer midrange products rather than the basic products of low cost companies or the expensive products of top-of-the-line differentiators. A company must have the resources and capabilities to produce midrange products at lower cost than competitors. Companies that don't have this (and most don't) should not follow a best value strategy because they will get squeezed between companies with low cost strategies and companies with differentiation strategies.

Toyota surprised everyone when it followed a best value strategy for its Lexus line of luxury automobiles.[12] In addition to its reputation for outstanding quality, Toyota is widely regarded as the automobile industry's low cost leader because of its outstanding skills in high volume manufacturing and its positioning of products in the low-to-medium end of the price range. Toyota used its cost and quality capabilities to build a best value strategy for Lexus. The company used its capability in making low cost cars to make luxury cars at lower costs than other luxury carmakers. It used its capability in making high-quality cars to make luxury cars with higher quality than other luxury carmakers. It also established a network of Lexus dealers to provide a high level of customer service. This combination of cost and differentiation (quality and service) was designed to draw price-conscious customers away from BMW and Mercedes and dissatisfied customers away from Cadillac and Lincoln.

Market Niche Strategies: Focused Cost and Focused Differentiation

A company with a focused strategy serves a particular market niche. A focused strategy based on low cost is possible if a market niche exists where customer needs are less costly to satisfy. A focused strategy based on differentiation is possible if a market niche exists where customers need special product features or services.

Focused low cost strategies are common. Manufacturers of generic products in apparel, building materials, food, and pharmaceuticals achieve low cost manufacturing, distribution, and marketing by making generic products similar to brand name products and selling them directly to retail store chains that need low cost generic products for their price-sensitive customers.

Focused differentiators like microbreweries, Porsche, and Haagen-Dazs target upscale customers willing to pay a premium price for products with world class features. Most markets contain a segment willing to pay a premium price for the finest products. Companies that design and manufacture products for industrial customers often follow focused differentiation strategies. AISCO Company is an example. AISCO designs and manufactures special purpose machines and material handling systems for a small number of companies worldwide that mine and produce aluminum, copper, and zinc.

Market niche strategies based on low cost or differentiation are attractive when[13]:

- A market niche large enough to be profitable emerges.
- Industry leaders lose interest in a market niche because of difficulty meeting customer's special needs in that niche.
- A company has the capability to serve the market niche and the resources to defend the niche against competitors (Chapter 3).

Market niche strategies are risky. Competitors may find effective ways to match the focused company in serving the market niche. Customer needs in the market niche may shift toward the product features desired in the broad market. When differences between customers in adjacent markets niches diminish, companies in adjacent niches become competitors.

Creating Competitive Advantage

Companies create competitive advantage by finding better ways to compete in their industry.[14] This is called *innovation,* and it comes from an accumulation of experience and learning. Innovation can be mundane and incremental or radical and breakthrough. It is manifested in product changes, process changes, new approaches to marketing, new forms of distribution, new definitions of competitive scope, and so on. Innovations shift competitive advantage when competitors fail to perceive the new way of competing or are unwilling or unable to respond.

External events, such as changes in product standards, environmental controls, regulations, and trade barriers, trigger innovation. New technologies, the development of new customer needs, the emergence of new market segments, and changes in the costs of inputs, such as labor, material, energy, equipment, and transportation, also trigger innovation.

New technologies create new possibilities for product design, production, marketing, delivery, and customer service. New technologies create new products and sometimes new industries. For example, Japanese companies used new electronics-based technologies to create new products and succeed in many industries.

Sometimes, it is hard for companies steeped in old technology to perceive the significance of new technology. For example, in the 1970s, most large integrated steel companies ignored new mini-mill steelmaking technology. Twenty years later, most integrated steel companies were struggling to survive, while mini-mill companies thrived. The leading U.S. vacuum tube companies all entered the semiconductor industry, but none succeeded. Newly started competitors, like Texas Instruments, succeeded with new value chains geared to the new technology.

New customer needs trigger innovation. Established companies may fail to perceive new needs or be unable to respond because meeting these needs requires significant changes in the companies' value chains. For example, Swiss watch manufacturers were slow to adapt to new customer preferences for inexpensive, disposable watches, for fear of undermining the Swiss image of quality and precision and because their factories were not suitable for mass producing low priced watches.

The emergence of new market segments triggers innovation. An example is the emergence of the furniture industry's home-office market segment. Some office furniture manufacturers perceived an underserved market segment of customers who needed small, inexpensive furniture for home offices. The furniture manufacturers designed standard products and manufactured them from inexpensive materials on high volume, automated equipment.

Significant changes in the cost of inputs, such as labor, material, energy, equipment, and transportation, trigger innovation. For example, in the 1950s, Japanese companies were competitive in simple manufactured products because of low labor costs. When their labor costs increased, they innovated by upgrading to higher value products. Today, Chinese companies are competitive in simple manufactured products because of their low labor costs. They will need to innovate in the future when their labor costs increase.

Sustaining Competitive Advantage

The sustainability of competitive advantage depends on the source of the advantage. Sources can be lower or higher order.[15]

- Lower order sources of competitive advantage are those that are easily copied by competitors, and so provide a short period of competitive advantage. Low labor costs and cheap raw materials are lower order sources because competitors can produce and source in the same location or find other low cost locations or sources. Another lower order source of competitive advantage is economies of scale from technology, equipment, or processes purchased from suppliers who also sell to competitors. In this situation, all competitors have the same technology and equipment, so no one has a competitive advantage.
- Higher order sources of competitive advantage are those that are not easily copied by competitors, and so provide a long, sustained period of competitive advantage. Higher order sources have a number of characteristics: They require advanced capabilities such as highly trained personnel, internal technical capabilities, close relationships with leading customers and suppliers, and sustained investment in facilities, R&D, and marketing. Higher order sources are associated with superior performance of value chain activities. Examples include proprietary process technology, product differentiation based on unique features, brand reputation based on cumulative marketing efforts, and customer relationships protected by high customer costs of switching companies.

The sustainability of competitive advantage also depends on the number of sources of competitive advantage a company possesses. A large number of sources make it harder for competitors to catch up. For example, Japanese small copier manufacturers possess several sources of competitive advantage: low manufacturing costs, advanced features, high levels of reliability, and extensive dealer networks.

Most importantly, the sustainability of competitive advantage depends on innovation generated by continuous improvement. Any advantage can be copied, so companies must create new advantages at least as fast as competitors copy old ones. In addition, sources of competitive advantage should be upgraded from lower to higher order. Japanese automobile companies entered foreign markets with small, inexpensive, average quality cars and competed on a low cost basis. Even while their cost advantage persisted, the Japanese companies upgraded. They built large modern factories to reap economies of scale. They became innovators in process technology, pioneering quality management, and just-in-time production, which improved product quality, reduced cost, and increased customer satisfaction. Then, they became innovators in product technology, incorporating new and better features into their products.

Creating and sustaining competitive advantage requires change, which is extraordinarily difficult, even for successful companies. Complacency is more natural. Successful companies are preoccupied with defending what they have. It is hard for them to destroy old lower order sources of competitive advantage, which may have led to success, in order to create new higher order ones. Often, it is easier for new companies, free from history and past investments, to innovate and become successful.

Moving Early to Achieve Competitive Advantage

Early movers gain competitive advantage from being the first to achieve economies of scale and the benefits of experience, establish brand names and customer relationships, and obtain the best suppliers, facility locations, and distribution channels.[16] Even when a competitor copies one of these sources of competitive advantage, the other sources remain. In this situation, early movers can sustain their competitive advantage for a long time. For example, Colgate, Procter & Gamble, and Unilever have been industry leaders in detergents since the 1930s; IBM has been a leader in computers since the 1950s.

Early movers gain the greatest competitive advantage in industries where economies of scale are significant and customers are reluctant to switch. In this situation, entrenched positions are difficult to challenge. For example, Alfa-Laval milk processing equipment, Allen-Bradley controllers, Coca-Cola, and Honeywell have been firmly entrenched leaders for generations.

Some cost leaders, first with a new product or process, exploit their advantage by lowering prices as quickly as possible to increase market share (Situation 16.5 in Chapter 16). Some even sell at an excessively low price or give their products away, expecting to earn profits in the follow-on market. For example, Toshiba did not earn back the investment it poured into its digital movie player through sales of the movie player. It expected to recover its money and more by selling spin-off products, such as high capacity audio players, storage devices for laptop computers, and other products that use related technology.

Like Toshiba, many cost leaders are not interested in being first with only one product. Instead, they want to be first with a technology that generates numerous related products that can be sold in a large number of markets around the world. The Walkman exemplifies how Sony squeezed every last product out of its innovation. Intel also wants to operate this way. Intel had long been content with its near monopoly position in providing microprocessors for PCs. All the while, its competitors worked to create less expensive microprocessors for non-PC applications such as smart identification cards, Internet-ready telephones, handheld computers, and digital cameras. Now this market is growing faster than the PC market, and Intel wants its share.

Not all early movers succeed. Among other things, early movers must correctly forecast industry trends. For example, Texas Instrument was an early entrant into electronic watches. It bet on light emitting diode (LED) displays and lost when liquid crystal displays (LCD) proved superior for inexpensive watches. It bet on electronic displays and lost when analog displays with quartz movements won for more expensive watches. A later entrant, Seiko, won when it moved quickly on LCD, analog, and quartz technologies, along with mass production and mass marketing.

Summary

A company's competitive strategy is a subset of its business strategy. While business strategy deals with all strategic issues facing a company, competitive strategy focuses only on a company's plan for competing successfully against competitors. A winning competitive strategy is grounded in sustainable competitive advantage. A company has competitive advantage whenever it has an edge over competitors in attracting customers and defending against competitors. There are many routes to competitive advantage, but the most basic route provides customers with superior value; namely, a good product at a low price, a superior product that is worth paying more for, or a best value product, which attractively combines price and features. Delivering superior value requires a company to organize and perform activities more effectively than competitors and build capabilities that competitors cannot easily match.

Different competitive strategies are appropriate for different industries because level of competition and sources of competitive advantage differ. Within the same industry, companies can choose and succeed with different strategies if they seek appropriate competitive advantages and target appropriate market segments. There are five generic competitive strategies: cost leadership, differentiation, best value, focused cost, and focused differentiation.

Creating and sustaining competitive advantage depends on innovation, which is, in large part, generated by continuous improvement.

ENDNOTES

1. The definitive work on competitive advantage is:
   - Porter, M., *Competitive Advantage: Creating and Sustaining Superior Performance*, The Free Press: New York, 1985.

   A substantial portion of this chapter draws on material from Chapters 1–4 in this book. This chapter also draws on material from:
   - Porter, M., *The Competitive Advantage of Nations*, The Free Press: New York, Chapter 2, 1990.
   - Thompson, A., and Strickland, A., *Strategic Management: Concepts and Cases*, McGraw-Hill Irwin: Boston, Chapters 3–10, 2001.
2. Thompson and Strickland, *Strategic Management*, p. 3.
3. Ibid, p. 149.
4. Porter, *Competitive Advantage*, pp. 5–7.
5. Porter, *The Competitive Advantage of Nations*, pp. 40–44.
6. Stalk, G., "Time—The Next Source of Competitive Advantage," *Harvard Business Review*, pp. 41–51, July–August 1988.
7. Porter, *The Competitive Advantage of Nations*, p. 44.
8. Ibid, p. 39.
9. These factors are from Thompson and Strickland, *Strategic Management*, pp. 153–157.
10. Ibid, pp. 161–162.
11. Ibid, pp. 166–167.
12. Ibid, p. 169.
13. Ibid, p. 171.
14. Porter, *The Competitive Advantage of Nations*, pp. 45–46.
15. Ibid, pp. 49–51.
16. Ibid, pp. 47–48.

CHAPTER 3

PARTNERSHIPS, CHALLENGES, AND RESPONSES

Chapter 2 outlines how a company builds competitive strategy on a foundation of sustainable competitive advantage and how its competitive strategy positions it in its industry. This chapter addresses how a company changes its position by forming partnerships with other companies and by challenging competitors. This chapter also examines how a company responds to competitor challenges.[1]

PARTNERSHIPS

Companies in most industries, virtually worldwide, use strategic partnerships. A company forms strategic partnerships to increase its competitive advantage in domestic and international markets, to help defend itself against competitor challenges, and to achieve some particular strategic goals, such as increased market share or increased profits. In addition, partnerships help a company bypass the slower and more costly process of building capabilities internally.

Sometimes, large differences in capabilities and resources exist between rival companies. When one company develops new products faster, achieves better quality at lower cost, or has more resources at its disposal to exploit opportunities, a rival company must move quickly to catch up. Often, the quickest way is with the capabilities and resources of a strategic partner.

Partnerships are a change from the past when most companies were content to go it alone, confident that they already had or could develop the capabilities needed for success. But globalization of the world economy, revolutionary advances in technology, and opportunities in new Asian, Latin American, and European markets (Chapter 9) have made partnerships an important element in a company's competitive strategy.

Alliances, mergers and acquisitions, and vertical integration are types of strategic partnerships.

ALLIANCES

Strategic alliances are cooperative agreements between companies that extend beyond normal company-to-company dealings but fall short of mergers and acquisitions in which companies have ownership ties.[2] Common reasons for forming alliances are to collaborate on new technology, develop new products, strengthen manufacturing weaknesses, improve supply chain efficiency, gain economies of scale in production or marketing, and acquire or improve market access. Today's average large company is involved in approximately 30 alliances compared to fewer than three a decade ago.

Some companies form alliances with competitors, distributors, and suppliers to gain efficiencies in supply chain management. For example, Volvo, Renault, and Peugeot formed an alliance to make engines for their large car models because none of them used enough engines to operate their own engine plant economically.

Alliances may utilize dealer networks for joint promotion of products, thereby economizing on distribution costs and improving access to customers. For example, Diageo (parent of Haagen-Dazs, Burger King, and Pillsbury) and Nestle (the world's largest consumer food company) created an alliance to distribute Haagen-Dazs ice cream and Nestle frozen desserts through the same distribution channel and to use the same display cases in retail stores. The alliance sought to reduce distribution costs and expand market access for the two products.

Alliances between domestic and foreign companies are used to penetrate foreign markets. For example, many companies formed alliances with Chinese companies to build market footholds in the fast-growing Chinese market. The Chinese companies help with government regulations, provide knowledge of local markets, give guidance on adapting products to suit Chinese consumer preferences, set up local manufacturing facilities, and assist in distribution, marketing, and promotional activities.

Alliances abound in the PC industry. Numerous companies specialize in microprocessors, printed circuit boards, monitors, disk drives, memory chips, software, and so on in North American, Asian, and European facilities. The only way a PC maker can secure a reliable supply of components is through alliances. Sometimes, these alliances are unusual. For example, Dell and IBM formed an alliance in 1999 when Dell agreed to purchase $16 billion of parts and components from IBM for use in Dell's PCs, servers, and workstations.[3] Dell determined that IBM's expertise and capabilities in PC components justified using IBM as a major supplier, even though IBM was a fierce competitor.

Alliances are helpful when close cooperation on new product development, production, or logistics is required. For example, Intel has alliances with numerous computer component manufacturers and software developers to simultaneously bring new products from all companies to the market, giving computer users the best performance from new computers that run on Intel's newest microprocessors.

Alliances are common in industries with rapid change. For example, the convergence of cable TV, telecommunications, and computer technologies generates new products and creates a need for alliances. Alliances of companies promoting wireless telecommunications systems compete head-to-head against alliances of companies promoting fiber-optic, line, and cable systems.

An alliance's value depends on how well the partners work together. For example, Merck and Johnson & Johnson formed an alliance to produce and market Pepcid AC, a stomach distress remedy.[3] Merck contributed the product, and Johnson & Johnson contributed production and marketing skills. The alliance succeeded; Pepcid AC became a bestselling remedy.

The best alliances have well-defined objectives. For example, Pratt & Whitney and the Aircraft Engines Division of General Electric aligned to develop and manufacture a new engine for a new Airbus airplane. Both of these fierce competitors make aircraft engines. However, they formed this alliance to compete against Rolls-Royce for the Airbus contract.

Alliances have risks. There is the danger of becoming dependent on another company for essential expertise and the danger that today's partner will become tomorrow's competitor. A company that aspires to be an industry leader or even a serious contender must, in the long run, develop its own capabilities in all sources of competitive advantage. Management should be careful that alliances do not distract it from this important duty.

Mergers and Acquisitions

A *merger* occurs when two, comparatively equal companies join to form a new company, often with a new name.[4] An *acquisition* occurs when one company purchases and absorbs another company. Ownership ties in mergers and acquisitions are more permanent than alliance ties. Companies use mergers and acquisitions when alliances cannot provide enough access to capabilities and resources.

Merging with or acquiring a competitor can dramatically strengthen a company's industry position and open new sources of competitive advantage. Combining operations fills resource gaps, allowing the new company to do things that the prior companies could not. Together, the companies have stronger technological skills, a more attractive lineup of products, wider geographic coverage, and greater financial resources to invest in R&D, capacity, or new opportunities. Combining operations may offer cost savings opportunities and even transform two high-cost companies into a company with average or below average costs.

Globalization stimulates companies into acquisitions to build market presence in countries where they do not currently compete. Nestle, Kraft, Unilever, Procter & Gamble, and other large food and consumer products companies made numerous acquisitions in a rush to establish their presence worldwide. Daimler-Benz merged with Chrysler to create a broader product line and a stronger global presence in the world automobile industry.

The race to establish strong positions in industries of the future stimulates companies to merge or make acquisitions to fill technology gaps. Intel made over 300 acquisitions in five years to broaden its technological base and position it as a major supplier of Internet technology products.

Mergers and acquisitions do not always produce the expected benefits. The skills needed to identify and make a merger or acquisition differ from the skills needed to make a merger or acquisition work. In most companies, management has an abundance of the first skill and a scarcity of the second. Combining the operations of two companies, especially large, complex companies, often meets with formidable resistance from employees. Conflicts exist in management styles and cultures. The expected cost savings, expertise sharing, and enhanced competitive capabilities usually take substantially longer than expected to realize, and sometimes, the benefits never materialize. For example, Ford paid a handsome price to acquire Jaguar but has yet to make the Jaguar brand a major factor in the luxury car market.

Vertical Integration

Vertical integration expands the company's value chain of activities backward into sources of supply or forward to final product users.[5] For example, a company can invest in facilities to produce components previously purchased from outside suppliers or open retail stores or a website to market its products directly to customers. A company vertically integrates by starting new activities in other parts of the value system or by acquiring a company already performing these activities.

Integrating backward produces a cost advantage when the volume needed is large enough to capture the same economies of scale as suppliers and when profit margins are sizable. Integrating backward produces a differentiation advantage when the company, by performing in-house activities previously outsourced, produces a better product or an improved level of customer service. Integrating backward lessens the company's vulnerability to costly, powerful suppliers. It also spares the company the uncertain dependency on suppliers for critical components and reliance on stockpiling, multiple sourcing, alliances, or substitute inputs.

Integrating forward also produces cost and differentiation advantages. In many industries, independent wholesalers, retailers, and sales agents handle competing brands of the same product. They have no allegiance to one company's brand and sell what earns the biggest profits. This frustrates a company's attempt to boost sales and market share, gives rise to costly inventory buildup and decreases utilization of capacity, and disrupts the economies of steady production. In such cases, a manufacturer may successfully integrate forward into wholesaling or retailing via company-owned distributorships, franchise dealer networks, a chain of retail stores, or direct Internet sales.

Choosing the best direction in which to integrate is not always easy. For example, America Online formed numerous alliances to integrate forward to end users of its Internet services. Then, Time Warner integrated forward by merging with America Online so that America Online could promote its publishing, movies, television, and music. The merger never produced the expected benefits. Both companies overlooked the need to integrate backward into companies that owned the high-speed cable lines and DSL connections to get access to customers who use the Internet.

Vertical integration has some serious disadvantages. It increases a company's capital investment, which increases business risk. Since a vertically integrated company has an interest in protecting its investments in technology and facilities, it may be slow to innovate (Chapter 2). Vertical integration poses problems of balancing capacity in each part of the value system. For example, in television manufacturing, the most efficient scale of production for making television screens differs from the most efficient scale of production for making printed circuit boards or power supplies. Backward and forward integration call for different management skills. Parts manufacturing, assembly operations, wholesale distribution, and retailing are different businesses that require different skills. Many above-average manufacturers, for example, are below-average distributors and retailers.

Some companies find vertical integration so burdensome that they follow a vertical de-integration strategy. They outsource activities formerly performed in-house and concentrate their energies on a narrower portion of the value system. This makes strategic sense when outside specialists can better perform an activity, and the activity is not a source of competitive advantage (Situation 3.1). Outsourcing gives the company flexibility against changes in customer needs, technology, and industry conditions.

Many advantages of vertical integration can be captured and many disadvantages can be avoided by developing alliances with world class suppliers and distributors. Relying on world class suppliers enables a company to obtain higher quality or lower cost components than internal sources can provide. Interacting with these suppliers helps a company innovate. For example, Metalurgica Romet SA is a world class supplier to Volkswagen. Volkswagen, Metalurgica, and other suppliers work together in a Volkswagen factory in Argentina. Volkswagen builds some parts of the car, such as the chassis and power train; Metalurgica builds doors; and other suppliers build other parts. Each company uses its own employees, equipment, and inventory. The arrangement enables Volkswagen to manufacture cars in half the time and at half the cost of a traditional factory.

The biggest danger of vertical de-integration is if a company contracts out too many activities or the wrong activities and loses its sources of competitive advantage. For example, Cisco outsources almost all manufacturing of its router and switching products to contract manufacturers in 37 factories worldwide.[6] Cisco avoids a loss of manufacturing capabilities by designing the production methods used by contract manufacturers. Then, Cisco uses the Internet to monitor factory operations around the clock. It knows immediately when a problem arises and gets involved when needed.

SITUATION 3.1

Deciding What to Outsource

OUTSOURCING WAS VERY POPULAR in the 1990s. Many companies outsourced activities in accounting, data processing, distribution, human resources, maintenance, parts manufacturing, payroll, purchasing, and customer service. Outsourcing easily cut costs and gained quick, short-term profits. Unfortunately, some companies outsourced too many activities, lost sources of competitive advantage, and struggled to compete ten years later.

Knowing what to outsource is the key to effective outsourcing. Figure 3-1 is a guideline to help companies understand what should, and should not, be outsourced. The decision to outsource a product depends on two factors: the general reason for outsourcing and the product-type.[7]

Company has		Product-type	
Capability	**Capacity**	**Modular**	**Integral**
No	No	Risky	Very risky
Yes	No	Good idea	Possibility
No	Yes	Risky	Bad idea
Yes	Yes	Possibility	Bad idea

Figure 3-1 Deciding What to Outsource: Is outsourcing a good idea, possibility, bad idea, risky, or very risky?

Two general reasons for outsourcing are capability and capacity. A company outsources when it does not have enough capability (knowledge, experience, or special equipment) or production capacity to produce the product in-house.

Two product-types are modular and integral:

- A *modular* product is comprised of interchangeable and independent components. Interfaces between components in a modular product are standardized. Personal computers (PCs) and bicycles are modular products. Bicycle manufacturers select a frame, wheels, seat, handle bar, gears, and bearings for a bicycle that meets a retailer's requirements for price, quality, and performance.

SITUATION 3.1

Continued

- An *integral* product is comprised of tightly related components customized for the product. Medical equipment, machine tools, and airplanes are examples of integral products.

Modular and integral are end-points on a continuum. All products occupy a position on the continuum that reflects the degree of modularity and integrality.

Figure 3-1 shows that capability is important and capacity is less important for modular products. If capability is "yes," then outsourcing for a modular product is a "good idea" or a "possibility." If capability is "no," then outsourcing is "risky." Modular products can be outsourced as long as a company has in-house capability. If a company does not have in-house capability, outsourcing is "risky" because competitors can use the same suppliers and copy the company's competitive advantage. IBM's early experience with PCs is an example.[8]

A PC is a modular product. In 1981, IBM entered the PC market. IBM did not have the capability to produce the product, but it had the capacity. IBM made the risky decision (Figure 3-2) to outsource most of the important components rather than wait until its own capability developed. Intel designed and built the microprocessor. Microsoft wrote the operating system. The PC was ready in 15 months, and by 1985, IBM had over 40 percent of the market. IBM's dominance was short lived, however. Competitors such as Compaq entered the market, used the same suppliers, and won market share away from IBM. By the late 1980s, IBM had developed its own capability and launched a new PC, the PS/2, which featured proprietary components and a proprietary operating system, but the new product never caught on. By 1995, IBM's market share dropped to less than 8 percent.

Figure 3-1 shows that capability and capacity are both important for integral products. If capability is "yes" and capacity is "no," then outsourcing for an integral product is a "possibility." In all other cases, outsourcing is "very risky" or a "bad idea." A company that produces integral products should have capability and capacity and should produce in-house. If a company lacks capability, it should develop or acquire it. If a company has capability, but not capacity, and decides to outsource, then the company should ensure that its suppliers do not leak knowledge to competitors.

Company has		Product-type	
Capability	Capacity	Modular	Integral
No	No	Risky	Very risky Toyota— Electronic systems
Yes	No	Good idea Toyota— Transmission components	Possibility
No	Yes	Risky IBM—Personal computer	Bad idea
Yes	Yes	Possibility	Bad idea Toyota—Engines

Figure 3-2 Deciding What to Outsource: Examples

To illustrate how to use this guideline, consider outsourcing decisions at Toyota for engines, transmission components, and electronic systems (Figure 3-2):

- Engines are an integral product. Toyota has capability and capacity. Figure 3-2 shows that outsourcing is a "bad idea." Toyota produces 100 percent of its engines in-house.
- Transmission components are a modular product. Toyota designs all components in its transmissions. It has capability but not capacity. Figure 3-2 shows that outsourcing is a "good idea." Toyota outsources 70 percent of production.
- Electronic systems are an integral product. Electronic systems are designed and produced by Toyota's suppliers because Toyota has neither the capability nor capacity. Figure 3-2 shows that outsourcing is "very risky," so Toyota maintains close relationships with these suppliers.

How Companies Challenge Competitors

A company launches a challenge against a competitor in order to increase the company's competitive advantage, market share, or profits, or to achieve other strategic goals, such as driving a competitor out of the industry.[9]

Challenges range in size from small to large to very large. An example of a small challenge is an apparel company that introduces a popular, seasonal design. This challenge is small because competitors can easily imitate the new design. An example of a large challenge is a pharmaceutical company that introduces an important new drug. An example of a very large challenge is a global company that sells its products in a particular country at very low prices over a long time period to drive domestic competitors out of the industry.

Challenges take time. That time is divided into three periods: buildup, benefit, and erosion.

- During the *buildup* period, which ranges from short to long, actions are taken, resources are deployed, and customers respond. For example, an ad campaign is launched, a price cut announced, and a new product introduced. If customers respond positively, new production capacity is brought online. Short buildup periods are preferred because the longer buildup takes, the more time competitors have to notice the challenge and respond.
- The results of a successful challenge are enjoyed during the *benefit* period. The length of the benefit period depends on how long it takes competitors to launch responses. The best challenges produce long benefit periods. A long benefit period gives a company time to earn above-normal profits and recoup the buildup costs.
- Competent competitors will not idly stand by and accept being outperformed without a fight. They counterattack with initiatives to overcome disadvantages faced. The *erosion* period begins when responses are launched. For example, Nabisco's A-1 brand was the king of steak sauces when Kraft launched a spicier sauce called Bulls Eye. The new product was very good. Nabisco responded aggressively. Within a few months, a similar product called A-1 Bold arrived on store shelves with a special promotional campaign. The response succeeded, and within a short time, Kraft discontinued its Bulls Eye product.

Seven important types of challenges are:

- Initiative to match or exceed competitor strengths
- Initiative to exploit competitor weaknesses
- Maneuver around a competitor
- Many simultaneous initiatives
- Guerilla offensives
- Preemptive strikes
- Cross-market subsidization

Initiative to Match or Exceed Competitor Strengths

It is difficult to challenge a competitor in its strong areas.[10] The challenge only works if the challenger can offer an equal or better product at a lower price and support the lower price with a low cost advantage. Without a cost advantage, the competitor responds with a price cut, and a war of attrition begins. Then, the challenger can only win if it has more financial resources.

Attacking a powerful competitor's strengths may be necessary when the competitor has a superior product and the challenger feels that it must seize a small piece of the competitor's strong competitive advantage. For example, Advanced Micro Devices, wanting to grow its PC microprocessor sales, attacked Intel head-on by offering a faster processor at a lower price. The company felt its survival depended on seizing a small piece of Intel's large market share. The company gambled that Intel would not respond by cutting its own price.

Initiative to Exploit Competitor Weaknesses

Challenges that exploit competitor weaknesses succeed more often than those that challenge competitor strengths.[11] Challengers usually attack competitors at their weakest points. If a competitor's product is weak in quality, features, or price, a challenger with a better product will target quality-conscious, performance-conscious, or price-conscious customers. If a competitor is weak in customer service, a service-oriented challenger will target frustrated customers. Challengers target customers in market niches and geographic regions where a competitor has a weak market share, is not working hard, or is ill equipped.

Maneuver Around a Competitor

Most companies avoid head-on challenges tied to aggressive price cutting, increased advertising, or costly efforts to out-differentiate competitors.[12] They prefer to maneuver around competitors to capture new or less contested markets, forcing competitors to try to catch up.

This can be done by introducing a new product that redefines the market and terms of competition. For example, Netscape Navigator, first marketed in 1994, created a new web-browser market and forced Microsoft and other competitors into catch-up mode. Introducing products with different features may better meet selected buyers' needs. For example, Lexus and BMW had great success with their luxury sport utility vehicles. Initiatives may be launched to build strong positions in geographic areas where competitors have little or no market presence. In many industries, this is in the less contested Asian, Eastern European, Latin American, and South American markets (Chapter 9).

Many Simultaneous Initiatives

Occasionally, a strong competitor launches a broad challenge involving multiple initiatives, such as new products, price cuts, increased advertising, free samples, and rebates, in most or all market segments.[13] The intent is to throw a competitor off balance, divert its attention in many directions, and force it to protect many market segments simultaneously. These challenges have the best chance of success when the challenger has an attractive product, and a strong brand name and reputation. Then, it can blitz market segments with innovative new products and advertising to entice large numbers of customers to switch.

Microsoft launched a multifaceted challenge in the mid-1990s to establish a strong Internet presence. In rapid succession, it introduced upgraded versions of Internet Explorer, incorporated Explorer in its Windows operating system, allowed Internet users to download Explorer for free, negotiated deals with Internet service providers to feature Explorer, created a cable Internet channel called MSNBC in a joint venture with NBC, formed alliances with numerous companies to provide content for the Internet and MSNBC, and put several thousand programmers to work on a variety of Internet-related projects such as adding Internet features to other Microsoft products and writing Internet software for cable modems and portable wireless devices.

In the 1980s, Honda launched a multifaceted challenge against Yamaha to regain its position as the world's largest and best motorcycle manufacturer (Situation 6.1 in Chapter 6).

Guerilla Offensives

A guerrilla offensive uses the hit-and-run principle to grab sales and market share whenever and wherever a company catches competitors napping. Guerilla offensives use the following tactics[14]:

- Offer a very low price to win a big order.
- Use short, intense promotions to steal customers from competitors. For example, offer a large discount for a short period of time.
- Launch special campaigns to attract customers from competitors hampered by problems. For example, promote quality when competitors have quality problems and guarantee delivery

times when competitors are about to have a labor strike.

Guerilla offensives are well suited to small companies lacking resources to mount other challenges against their large competitors.

Preemptive Strikes

A preemptive strike involves moving first to secure an advantageous position, which, once secured, cannot be threatened by competitors. There are many ways to do this[15]:

- A company acquires another company with exclusive control of valuable technology, giving it a hard-to-match technological advantage.
- A company secures exclusive access to the best raw material sources, the best suppliers, the best producers, or the best distributors. For example, DeBeers became the world's leading diamond distributor by purchasing the production of most of the important diamond mines.
- A company secures the best geographic locations, obtains the business of the most prestigious customers, or builds a unique and hard-to-copy image, such as Nike's slogan "Just do it" and its endorsement contracts with Michael Jordan and Tiger Woods.

Cross-Market Subsidization

An international company competes in many country markets around the world. A few of these country markets are profit sanctuaries for the company.[16] Profit sanctuaries are country markets in which an international company derives substantial profits because of its strong or protected market position. For example, Japan is a profit sanctuary for many Japanese companies because government trade barriers block many foreign companies from competing for large shares of Japanese markets.

In cross-market subsidization, an international company with multiple profit sanctuaries and ambitions for market leadership in a particular country or region attacks a domestic company for the purpose of driving it out of the industry. The international company cuts its prices in the domestic company's home market to grab market share from the domestic company. The international company subsidizes its razor-thin margins with healthy profits earned in its profit sanctuaries, something the domestic company cannot do. Prices decrease gradually over a decade or more as not to be too obvious and trigger protectionist government actions.

Cross-market subsidization works well for large international companies. Not surprisingly, it is a disaster for the small domestic companies it targets.

Choosing Whom to Challenge

It is never a good idea to attack a strong leader. The most likely outcomes are the squandering of valuable resources in a futile effort or a fierce and profitless battle for market share that ends with no change in the status quo.

A weak leader is a better target.[17] Signs of a weak leader are: unhappy customers, inferior product line, weak competitive strategy in terms of low cost leadership or differentiation, aging technology and outdated facilities, a preoccupation with diversification, and mediocre or declining profitability. Weaknesses provide many options for launching challenges. Attacks on weak leaders do not necessarily make the challenger the new leader. The challenger only needs to win enough sales from the leader to become a little stronger and a little more profitable.

Small competitors make attractive targets when challengers have resources and capabilities to exploit small competitors' weaknesses. Struggling competitors are favorite targets because they lack financial resources to withstand long, hard challenges. Domestic and regional companies, with relatively limited resources, are easy targets for large, predatory, international companies.

The type of challenge and the target depend on a company's resources and capabilities. Usually, a company organizes a challenge so its strengths target the competitor's greatest weaknesses.

How Companies Respond to Challenges From Competitors

In a competitive market, all companies face challenges from competitors. Companies develop defensive strategies to lower the risk of attack, to influence challengers to attack other companies, and to weaken the impact of any attack. Defensive strategy also helps companies protect their sources of competitive advantage from being copied. Protecting the status quo may not be enough. Sometimes, companies launch their own preemptive challenges.

Seven important ways companies respond to challenges are[18]:

- Block challengers
- Signal challengers that retaliation will be strong
- Defensive attack
- Defend domestic company against global competitors by using home country advantages
- Change domestic company to small multidomestic company
- Change domestic company to small global company
- Dodge global competitors

When industry or company profitability is very high, competitors are more willing to launch sustained challenges and combat strong defenses. Companies discourage these attacks, especially from new competitors, by keeping profits reasonable.

Block Challengers

A company can place the following obstacles in the path of would-be challengers[19]:

- Introduce new features or broaden the product line to close off market niches to would-be challengers.
- Participate in alternative technologies to reduce the threat of competitors attacking with better technology.
- Hire talented employees to broaden or deepen capabilities in key areas so the company can overpower competitors who try to copy the company's sources of competitive advantage. For example, Sony's extraordinary capability in consumer electronic technologies deters competitors from launching challenges.
- Discourage customers from trying competitors' products by lengthening warranty periods, offering free training and support services, providing coupons and free samples to customers most prone to experiment, or making early announcements about new products and price changes.
- Offer dealers and distributors volume discounts or better financing terms to discourage them from experimenting with other suppliers. Convince them to handle the company's product line exclusively to force competitors to use other distribution channels.
- Keep an economy priced product line to discourage competitors from attacking with lower priced products. For example, General Motors positions Saturn and Chevrolet as lower priced alternatives to Pontiac, Oldsmobile, Buick, and Cadillac. America Online acquired CompuServe and cut the price of CompuServe's service to position it as a lower price alternative. This blocked competitors using low price to entice America Online customers.

Signal Challengers That Retaliation Will Be Strong

The objectives of this defense are to dissuade challengers from attacking by alerting them that the resulting fight will cost more than it is worth, or to divert them to less threatening challenges. A company sends this signal by public announcements like the following[20]:

- Management will maintain the company's present market share.
- The company will match competitors' prices.
- The company will add production capacity to meet forecasted market growth.
- The company gives advance information on new products and technology breakthroughs. This gives would-be challengers cause to delay until they see the results of the announced actions.

A company can also make a strong retaliation to a weak competitor's challenge to show other competitors that the company is a tough defender.

Defensive Attack

An international company competes in many locations around the world, so it can choose where and how to respond to challengers. Sometimes, an international company attacks a competitor before the competitor launches a challenge. The attack may be in the country market where the competitor has its highest sales volume or best profit margins (profit sanctuaries) to reduce the competitor's financial resources for challenging the company in other country markets.

Defend Domestic Company Against Global Competitors By Using Home Country Advantages

Domestic companies face a difficult fight when large, opportunity-seeking, resource-rich global companies launch challenges to enter their markets.

If pressure for globalization in the industry is weak (Chapter 10) and a domestic company has competitive advantages well suited to the local market, a good strategy concentrates even harder on customers who prefer a local company and accepts the loss of some customers attracted to the global company. Many global companies aim their products at upper- and middle-income urban customers who view global brands as attractive and are willing to experiment with new products.

A domestic company should have the following home country advantages[21]:

- It is familiar with local customer needs and local product features.
- It has long standing relationships with customers.
- It may have a cost advantage because of simpler product design and lower operating, overhead, and transportation costs.

A domestic company uses these advantages to defend itself against a global challenger. For example, Bajaj Auto, India's largest manufacturer of motor scooters, defended itself successfully against a tough attack from Honda. In the early 1990s, Honda partnered with a local company and entered the Indian market to sell scooters and motorcycles on the basis of superior technology, quality, and brand appeal. Bajaj responded with several defenses.

- It launched a new, inexpensive scooter designed for India's rough roads.
- It invested in R&D to improve reliability and quality.
- It expanded an extensive network of distributors and roadside mechanic stalls.

Initially, Bajaj's market share dropped from 77 to 70 percent, and Honda's share rose to 11 percent. But the defense held, and ten years later, Honda withdrew from the Indian market.

Change Domestic Company to Small Multidomestic Company

If the pattern of competition in the industry is multinational (Chapter 10) and a domestic company has competitive strengths well suited for competing in other country markets, a good strategy is to enter these markets. Foreign sales increase profits and resources and improve capabilities.

These advantages help a company when large, resource-rich global companies launch challenges to enter its home market.[22]

For example, Jollibee Foods, a family-owned company with 56 percent of the fast food market in the Philippines, responded to McDonald's entry into its home market by upgrading service and expanding into new country markets. The company used its expertise in seasoning hamburgers with garlic and soy sauce and preparing noodle and rice meals with fish to win new customers in Hong Kong, the Middle East, and California.

Change Domestic Company to Small Global Company

Sometimes, a domestic company has such strong capabilities that it is able to transform itself into a small global company. For example, when General Motors outsourced production of radiator caps, Sundaram Fasteners of India pursued the opportunity and transformed itself from a domestic company to a small global company.[23] The company already had strong capabilities in quality. In 1999, its parent, Sundaram Clayton of India, won the Deming Prize for quality. Sundaram Fasteners purchased a radiator cap production line from GM, moved it to India, improved its capabilities, and quickly became GM's sole supplier of radiator caps. It built global distribution capabilities, learned about emerging technologies, and obtained QS 9000 certification.

Dodge Global Competitors

It is almost impossible to defend a domestic company against a determined challenge from a strong, resource-rich global competitor in an industry where pressure for globalization is strong (Chapter 10). In this situation, a domestic company has only two options[24]:

- Form a partnership with a global company.
- Focus on a market niche or a stage of the value system where the company's resources and capabilities provide it with competitive advantage.

For example, when the Russian PC market opened to foreign competition, Russian computer makers shifted to assembly of low cost PCs. When Microsoft entered the Chinese market, local software developers shifted from copying Windows products to developing customized Windows applications for Chinese markets.

Summary

Many companies form strategic partnerships to increase their competitive advantage and defend themselves against challenges from competitors. In addition, partnerships enable companies to bypass the slower and more costly process of building capabilities internally. Alliances, mergers and acquisitions, and vertical integration and de-integration are types of strategic partnerships.

Companies use a variety of offensive challenges to improve their industry position, secure competitive advantage, and increase profitability. Challenges can involve maneuvers around competitors or grand offences on many fronts. They can be guerrilla actions or preemptive strikes. Usually, the target of the challenge is a weak industry leader or a small or weak company. A company designs its challenge so its strengths strike the target's greatest weaknesses.

Defensive responses to challenges put obstacles in the path of challengers, strengthen the company's present position, and act to dissuade competitors from attempting to attack by signaling that the resulting battle will cost more to the challenger than it is worth.

The outlook for domestic companies in globalizing industries is discouraging. Sooner or later, resource-rich global companies will launch challenges in the home markets of domestic companies. Global companies' profit sanctuaries give them financial resources to mount strong and sustained challenges. These challenges include a long-term policy of cutting prices to seize market share and drive domestic companies out of the industry.

The best defense against challenges from global companies depends on the strength of the domestic companies' competitive advantage. If competitive advantage is strong and can be transferred abroad, domestic companies should expand to nearby countries and become small multidomestic companies. If the competitive advantage is very strong, domestic companies should transform themselves into small global companies. Domestic companies with strong local competitive advantage can compete against global challengers by focusing even harder on local customers. If none of this is possible, domestic companies should merge, be acquired by global companies, or shift their business to market niches.

ENDNOTES

1. This chapter draws substantially on material from:
   - Thompson, A., and Strickland A., *Strategic Management: Concepts and Cases*, McGraw-Hill Irwin: Boston, Chapters 3–6, 2001.

   It also draws on material from:
   - Porter, M., *Competitive Advantage: Creating and Sustaining Superior Performance*, The Free Press: New York, Chapters 13–15, 1985.
   - Porter, M., *The Competitive Advantage of Nations*, The Free Press: New York, Chapter 2, 1990.
2. Thompson and Strickland, *Strategic Management*, pp. 172–176; Porter, *The Competitive Advantage of Nations*, pp. 65–67.
3. These alliances are reported in *Business Week*, pp. 112–130, October 25, 1999.
4. Thompson and Strickland, *Strategic Management*, pp. 177–178.
5. Ibid, pp. 179–185.
6. "Meet Mr. Internet," *Business Week*, pp. 129–140, September 13, 1999; and p. 104, October 4, 1999.
7. This guideline is from Simchi-Levi, D., Kaminsky, P., and Simchi-Levy E., *Designing and Managing the Supply Chain*, McGraw-Hill Irwin: Boston, Chapter 7, 2003.
8. Chesbrough, H., and Teece D., "When Is Virtual Virtuous: Organizing for Innovation," *Harvard Business Review*, pp. 65–74, January–February, 1996.
9. Thompson and Strickland, *Strategic Management*, pp. 185–186.
10. Ibid, pp. 186–187; Porter, *Competitive Advantage*, pp. 513–532.
11. Thompson and Strickland, *Strategic Management*, p. 187; Porter, *Competitive Advantage*, pp. 533–535.
12. Thompson and Strickland, *Strategic Management*, p. 188.
13. Ibid, p. 188.
14. Ibid, p. 189.
15. Ibid, p. 190.
16. Ibid, p. 213.
17. Ibid, p. 191.
18. Ibid, pp. 191–193; Porter, *Competitive Advantage*, Chapter 14.
19. Thompson and Strickland, *Strategic Management*, p. 192; Porter, *Competitive Advantage*, pp. 489–494.
20. Thompson and Strickland, *Strategic Management*, p. 192; Porter, *Competitive Advantage*, pp. 494–497.
21. Thompson and Strickland, *Strategic Management*, pp. 219–220.
22. Ibid, pp. 220–221.
23. Ibid, p. 221.
24. Ibid, p. 220; Porter, *Competitive Advantage*, pp. 511–512.

PART II

MANUFACTURING STRATEGY IN A FACTORY

CHAPTER 4

MANUFACTURING OUTPUTS AND PRODUCTION SYSTEMS

Chapter 2 showed that a company has a competitive advantage when it has an edge over competitors in attracting and keeping customers. The most basic route to competitive advantage is to provide customers with superior value. Marketing professionals talk about four types of value: form, time, place, and possession. *Form*, *time*, and *place* are created in manufacturing by transforming raw materials into products in a timely manner and distributing products as required to customers. *Possession* is created in sales and finance by helping customers acquire products through activities such as advertising, pricing, and credit.

Manufacturing creates value in individual factories and in networks of manufacturing facilities. Part II of this book, beginning in this chapter, examines how manufacturing factories create value. Part III addresses how international networks of manufacturing facilities create value.

FACTORIES AND NETWORKS

A *manufacturing network* consists of distribution centers, manufacturing facilities, offices, research laboratories, and so on. Each manufacturing facility contains one or more macro factories. Each macro factory has a small number of micro or focused factories. A *focused factory* is a well-defined production system that produces most, or all, products in a product family. Situation 4.1 gives an example.

Capabilities at focused factories, facilities, and networks determine the form, time, and place value-types that manufacturing creates for its customers. The values are called the factory manufacturing outputs and the network manufacturing outputs. Factory manufacturing outputs are examined in this chapter. Network manufacturing outputs are examined in Chapter 11.

FACTORY MANUFACTURING OUTPUTS

To most managers, a factory provides its customers with "low cost, high quality products." While this view was suitable in the past, it is too simplistic and restrictive for most companies today. A factory provides six outputs: cost, quality, performance, delivery, flexibility, and innovativeness (Figure 4-2).

COST

Each product a factory produces has a *cost.* A low cost makes a low price possible and provides a

SITUATION 4.1

Macro Factories and Focused Factories in a Manufacturing Facility

CWM HAS AN INTERNATIONAL manufacturing network with facilities in North America and Europe.

- The manufacturing facility in Hamilton, Canada, consists of two macro factories, the North Plant and the South Plant (Figure 4-1).

Macro Factory	Focused Factory	Products	Production System	Worldwide Producer?
North Plant	Department 81	Disks	Equipment-paced line flow	No
	Department 10	Sweeps, shanks	Batch flow	Yes
South Plant	Shared Resources	Machined parts, sheet metal parts	Batch flow	No
	Seeding Department	Planters, drills	Operator-paced line flow	Yes
	Loader Line	Loaders	Operator-paced line flow	Yes
	Tillage Department	Tillage products	Operator-paced line flow	No

Figure 4-1 Macro and Focused Factories in a Manufacturing Facility

- The North Plant has two focused factories. One produces disks; the other produces two similar products, sweeps and shanks.
- The South Plant has four focused factories: a machine shop (shared resources) and three assembly departments, seeding, loader, and tillage.
- The six focused factories use three types of production systems: batch flow, operator-paced line flow, and equipment-paced line flow.

Three of the six focused factories are worldwide producers of their products. No other factories in the CWM network produce the same products.

better opportunity for profit than a high cost. While a straightforward concept, product cost can be difficult to measure accurately when manufacturing's large overheads need to be allocated. The more important cost is relative to the other manufacturing outputs, the more important it is to have a cost accounting system that measures it accurately.

QUALITY AND PERFORMANCE

Many nonmanufacturing people treat quality and performance as a single manufacturing output. For

Cost	Cost of material, labor, overhead, and other resources used to produce a product
Quality	Extent to which materials and activities conform to specifications and customer expectations and how tight or difficult the specifications and expectations are
Performance	Product's features and the extent to which the features permit the product to do things other products cannot
Delivery time and delivery time reliability	Time between order taking and delivery to the customer. How often are orders late, and how late are they when they are late?
Flexibility	Extent to which volumes of *existing products* can be increased or decreased to respond quickly to customer needs
Innovativeness	Ability to quickly introduce *new products* or make design changes to existing products

Figure 4-2 Factory Manufacturing Outputs: What a Factory Provides to its Customers

example, a Mercedes-Benz automobile is said to have outstanding quality. If this means that a Mercedes-Benz is designed and manufactured to exacting specifications, then we have the *quality* output. If it means that a Mercedes-Benz automobile has unique design features, such as a heavier frame, thicker upholstery, a more durable power train, a better audio system, and a deluxe coat of paint, then we have the *performance* output.

In manufacturing strategy, quality is associated with conformance to specifications and critical customer expectations. Performance is associated with features of the product that affect the product's ability to do things for customers that other products cannot. While separating quality and performance into two manufacturing outputs seems finicky, the distinction is important for good manufacturers. Tools and technologies that provide high levels of quality (such as statistical process control, six sigma, and standardization) often differ from those that provide high levels of performance (such as concurrent engineering and highly skilled workers). Differentiating between quality and performance allows us to design one production system for a McDonald's restaurant (where quality is important) and a different production system for a fine French restaurant (where performance is important).

Delivery

The delivery manufacturing output comprises delivery time and delivery time reliability. *Delivery time* is the amount of time a factory requires to supply a product to a customer. Usually, delivery times are well known and used to make delivery promises to customers when they place orders. Often, especially in busy times, manufacturing cannot meet all delivery promises, and customers might receive their orders later than promised. When this happens, delivery time reliability drops.

Customer expectations for delivery time and delivery time reliability have increased dramatically in recent years as a consequence of just-in-time manufacturing (Chapter 22) and supply chain management (Chapter 15). Customers now expect to be supplied frequently, quickly, and on time.

Flexibility and Innovativeness

Like quality and performance, many nonmanufacturing people treat flexibility and innovativeness as a single manufacturing output. Good manufacturers differentiate between the two.

To illustrate the difference, consider two manufacturers in the apparel industry: a factory that produces leather coats and a tailor of men's suits. A leather coat factory is flexible when it can easily change product mix and production volumes in response to fashion and season changes. This is *flexibility* because it is the ability to increase or decrease production of existing products. *Innovativeness* is the ability to produce new products. A tailor of men's suits is more innovative than flexible. A tailor can easily produce a suit for a new design or an unusual fit. It is more difficult, however, to double the number of suits produced in a month.

Differentiating between flexibility and innovativeness helps good manufacturers design and manage production systems that provide high levels of whichever output is most important to their customers.

History of the Factory Manufacturing Outputs

In the 1960s and early 1970s, most managers felt that manufacturing provided only two outputs to their customers: cost and quality. During the 1980s, delivery and flexibility were added to the list of outputs. This was a consequence of just-in-time, time-based competition, and flexible manufacturing systems. The initial definition of flexibility was too broad for manufacturing strategy purposes, so the definition changed. Those types of flexibility associated with existing products were called flexibility, and those types associated with new products and design changes to existing products were called innovativeness.

Something similar happened to quality. Definitions such as "quality is giving the customer what he or she wants" and "quality is meeting and exceeding customer expectations" were too broad to be useful in manufacturing strategy, so quality was redefined. Quality was associated with conformance to specifications and meeting critical customer expectations. Performance was associated with features of the product that affect the product's ability to do things that other products cannot.[1]

Figure 4-3 provides ways to measure the six manufacturing outputs. They are used in the competitive analysis element of manufacturing strategy (Chapter 6).

Tradeoffs and Competitive Advantage

Somewhat to the surprise of those in manufacturing and to the disappointment of those in marketing, no focused factory in the world can provide all six outputs at the highest possible levels. For example, it may cost a little more to have flexible workers or better machines. Standardizing product design may be necessary to achieve the lowest possible cost, even though it reduces innovativeness. Delivery may be longer if products with the newest high-performance features are required.

Figure 4-4 gives further evidence that tradeoffs must be made. Because they cannot provide all six outputs at the highest possible levels, these well-known manufacturers have chosen, either implicitly or explicitly, to provide a particular output at the highest possible level in the world while still providing other outputs at relatively high levels. The production systems used by these manufacturers are carefully designed and managed so that the required outputs are provided at the desired levels. The products produced are known for the high level at which a particular manufacturing output is provided. This competitive advantage is actively promoted in advertisements and other marketing activities.

Competing on Cost

Many commodities, such as structural steel shapes, chemicals, electronic devices, generic products, paper, and so on, are manufactured to standard specifications and sold under standard delivery terms. For these products, a customer's purchase decision is based exclusively on price. Consequently, cost becomes the most important manufacturing output, and low cost is the basis of competitive advantage.

Manufacturing Output	Measures
Cost	Unit product cost, unit labor cost, unit material cost Total manufacturing overhead cost Inventory turnover—raw material, WIP, finished goods Capital productivity Capacity/machine utilization Materials yield Direct labor productivity, indirect labor productivity
Quality	Internal failure cost—scrap and rework, percentage defective or reworked External failure cost—frequency of failure in the field Quality of incoming material from suppliers Percent defective Warranty cost as a percentage of sales Rework cost as a percentage of sales
Performance	Number of standard features Number of advanced features Product resale price Number of engineering changes Mean time between failures
Delivery	Quoted delivery time Percentage of on-time deliveries Average lateness Inventory accuracy Order entry time Master production schedule performance/stability
Flexibility	Number of products in the product line Number of available options Minimum order size Average production lot size Length of frozen schedule Number of job classifications in the factory Average volume fluctuations that occur over a time period divided by the capacity limit Number of parts processed by a group of machines Ratio of number of parts processed by a group of machines to total number processed by factory Number of setups Variations in key dimensional and metallurgical properties that the equipment can handle Is it possible to produce parts on different machines?
Innovativeness	Number of engineering change orders per year Number of new products introduced each year Lead time to design new products Lead time to prepare customer drawings Level of R&D investment Consistency of R&D investment over time

Adapted from Leong, G., Synder, D., and Ward, P., "Research in the Process and Content of Manufacturing Strategy," *Omega: The International Journal of Management Science*, Vol. 18, No. 2, pp. 109–122, 1990.

Figure 4-3 Measures or Attributes for the Manufacturing Outputs

Manufacturing Output	Product	Advertising Slogan
Cost	BIC pens	
	Commodities	
	Generic products	
	Steel bars and shapes	
Quality	Christian Dior	"A name synonymous with quality."
	Ford	"Quality is job one."
	JVC	"The perfect experience."
	McDonald's restaurants	
	Timex	"It takes a licking and keeps on ticking."
	Toyota	"There's quality and there's Toyota quality."
Performance	Acura car	"Precision crafted performance."
	Audi	"Never follow."
	Chrysler minivan	"We introduced the minivan. Then the competition caught up. We introduced the sliding fifth door. Then the competition caught up. We introduced the 60,000 miles, 5-year warranty. Then the competition caught up."
	Crest toothpaste	"Crest reduces cavities."
	Honda power equipment	"Honda engineering makes the difference."
	Honda Racing	"Performance first."
	Makita power tools	"More torque to do the job."
	Mercedes-Benz	"Engineered like no other car in the world."
	Philips	"Let's make things better."
	Tide detergent	"If it's got to be clean, it's got to be Tide."
Delivery	Airlines	
	Federal Express	
	Photo-finishing	
Flexibility	Clothing manufacturers	
	Furniture	
	Housing	
	Industrial equipment	
	Machine shops	
	Tool and die shops	
Innovativeness	3M	"3M-making innovation work for you."
	DuPont	"Better things for better living."
	Hewlett-Packard	"Invent."
	Seiko	"Innovation and refinement."
	Sony audio/video products	
	BASF	"The spirit of innovation. We don't make the products you buy. We make the products you buy better."

Figure 4-4 Products Well Known for a Particular Manufacturing Output

Competing on Quality

One of the major reasons for the success of McDonald's restaurants is that customers can rely on receiving identical products in every restaurant. Each product in the limited product line is produced to exacting specifications. Toyota automobiles are another example. All Toyota products are built to exacting specifications. Cost and delivery are also important but always give way to quality.

Competing on Delivery

As the following examples show, many manufacturers compete on the basis of delivery. A Westinghouse facility that produced custom-engineered electrical distribution equipment made delivery the most important manufacturing output for an important product family. Products were redesigned to be produced from modular components (somewhat reducing innovativeness). The components were stocked in inventory (somewhat increasing cost). When orders were received, the modular components were assembled quickly into final products and shipped to customers (significantly improving delivery time).

A North American manufacturer of cellular telephones, with a factory in an offshore, low-wage country, could not meet its customer requirements for fast, reliable delivery. The customers, large retailers, required fast delivery of medium quantities of cellular phones with special features. These manufacturing outputs could not be provided from an offshore factory, so the company moved its manufacturing operations to a new factory in North America designed to provide the highest possible levels of delivery and flexibility.

Competing on Performance

When discussing manufacturing outputs with a group of manufacturing managers, one Procter & Gamble manager stated that Tide detergent competed on the basis of performance. "Tide got clothes cleaner." It was designed with features that permitted it to do something other products could not.

Marketing professionals describe three kinds of product features: dissatisfiers, satisfiers, and exciters-delighters. *Dissatisfiers* are features that customers expect in a product. When missing, the customer is dissatisfied. *Satisfiers* are features that customers want. When present, customers are satisfied. *Exciters-delighters* are new features that customers do not expect. The presence of exciters-delighters excites and delights customers. All production systems must provide dissatisfiers and satisfiers. Only those able to provide a high level of performance provide the exciters-delighters.

It is not difficult to provide a high level of performance occasionally. However, it is difficult to provide a high level of performance year after year. One reason is that this year's exciters-delighters become next year's satisfiers, and this year's satisfiers become next year's dissatisfiers, so new exciters-delighters must be continually developed.

Competing on Flexibility

During a tour of the DAF engine and assembly factories, a DAF materials manager took two large brackets from different bins and asked whether members of the touring group could find any differences between the two brackets. Except for slight differences in the bracing and in the location of a few bolt holes, the brackets were identical. The materials manager went on to say that this was an example of why DAF needed more standardization of parts. Standardization would reduce the large number of different parts that needed to be stocked and controlled. It would also reduce the floor space used to store inventory. All of this would reduce costs.

Before commenting on the importance of standardization compared to other improvements that could be made, the group completed the tour. By the end of the tour, it was obvious that customers bought DAF trucks because the company provided an almost unlimited number of options. This allowed customers from all over Europe to obtain a truck perfect for their requirements. DAF was good at what it did. In 1987, it won the prestigious

"European Transport Truck of the Year" award. For manufacturing to provide such a high level flexibility, DAF might need many more part numbers than its competitors. The tour group concluded that while it is always important to guard against a proliferation in the number of part numbers, it was even more important to remember that DAF's competitive advantage was flexibility. DAF was too small to compete on the basis of cost in the standard transport truck business, where two giants, Mercedes and Volvo, dominated the market.

Competing on Innovativeness

Sony and 3M are two companies that compete by providing innovativeness at the highest possible level. Innovativeness is the ability to introduce new products and make design changes to existing products. Sony and 3M seem to be first in their industries to introduce new products. They make tradeoffs that favor innovativeness—so introducing new products is easy.

One example is Sony's introduction of the first home VCR in the early 1980s. At that time, the VCR was considered a complex electromechanical product. Sony's design staff and manufacturing staff designed and produced a product considerably larger than necessary from a design point of view. Although cost would increase, the larger size would make the product easier to manufacture, thus permitting the product to be brought to market sooner, which would give Sony a chance to gain a large market share before competitors responded with their own new products. It would also increase reliability (quality), which was necessary to win customer acceptance for the new product.

Competing on Several Outputs

It is almost impossible to provide more than one manufacturing output at the highest possible level in an industry. Most companies struggle to provide even one output at the highest possible level. Even companies with world class capability (Chapter 5) who may be able to provide more than one output at this level often decide to focus on one output. The Seiko Watch Company of Japan is an example. Seiko has a slogan, "innovation and refinement." Seiko supports the first part of the slogan with a steady stream of new products: most recently, the kinetic, kinetic auto relay, and the kinetic chronograph. The second part of the slogan qualifies the first part. "Refinement" describes the styling of Seiko's new products. What may appear as two outputs is actually one—innovativeness, narrowly defined.

Another example is Moen Company, one of the world's largest manufacturers of plumbing products. Moen has a marketing slogan, "Buy it for looks. Buy it for life." The first part of the slogan suggests that Moen provides a high level of innovativeness, and the second suggests a high level of quality. Moen supports the first part of the slogan with a steady stream of new products: the single-handle faucet, the washerless cartridge system, the swing and spray faucet, the lift faucet, the pressure-balanced shower valve, finishing technology, and so on. Moen supports the second part of the slogan with its "Lifetime Warranty." This limited warranty promises customers free parts if a Moen product fails. The customer calls a toll-free number, describes the problem, and is sent free parts. The author fitted his new home with Moen faucets because of this emphasis on quality. Ten years later, the faucets started to leak. The free parts didn't help, and faucets had to be replaced. Moen is actually providing a high level of innovativeness and an average level of quality. This is an example where manufacturing cannot provide what marketing is promising, and the result dissatisfies customers.

Competitive Advantage

The manufacturing outputs required by customers and the levels required change over time. For example, when Japanese companies entered the North American color television market in the 1970s, they changed the basis of competition from price to quality. High levels of quality characteristics, such as picture quality, sound clarity, and time without breakdowns, were required to win orders. North American manufacturers struggled to upgrade their production systems to provide the required levels of quality. Once they caught up, the Japanese companies dropped their prices and switched the basis of competition from quality back to price.

No focused factory in the world can provide all six outputs at the highest possible levels, so it is important to determine which outputs are most important to customers now and which will be important in the future. Meeting and exceeding these customer expectations is the factory's competitive advantage. As we will see, manufacturing strategy specifies the levels at which each manufacturing output will be provided and how the factory will accomplish this. This is called the *manufacturing* task.

Seven Production Systems

How does a focused factory provide the cost, quality, performance, delivery, flexibility, and innovativeness outputs to its customers?

The answer to this question seems obvious. It is seen each time we drive down the highway and pass factory and office buildings, with employees streaming in and out, suppliers making deliveries, and shippers moving finished products. We know that these buildings contain machines and processes, workers and managers, departments and control systems; everything working together to form a production system. We know that these elements work together, and each ineffective or overlooked element diminishes the production system. And we know that the production system provides the cost, quality, performance, delivery, flexibility, and innovativeness manufacturing outputs.

Both similarities and differences exist between the production systems used at different companies. Two factors have important effects on the similarities and differences: the type of product manufactured and the manufacturing outputs provided. For example, the production systems used at ISTC and Dofasco are very different. Each company manufactures a different type of product and provides different manufacturing outputs. ISTC manufactures railroad and subway cars. Dofasco is a fully integrated steel company. Because ISTC's products are highly engineered and custom designed for specific customer orders, the ISTC production system must provide high levels of innovativeness and performance. The production systems used by other manufacturers who also provide high levels of innovativeness and performance (such as manufacturers of machine tools and industrial packaging equipment and machine shops supplying parts in the aerospace industry) are very similar to ISTC's production system. Dofasco, on the other hand, produces large volumes of standard products on a production system that provides high levels of quality, cost, and delivery. Breweries, chemical plants, paper mills, and refineries all have production systems like the one at Dofasco.

It is not surprising that only a small number of different production systems exist (Figure 4-5). This has an important implication for manufacturing strategy.

A focused factory should use the production system most able to produce the mix and volume of products and provide the manufacturing outputs required by the factory's customers.

If a focused factory uses a different production system, it should change the production system to a more appropriate one, or at least recognize its vulnerability to a challenge from any competitor inside or outside the company, possessing a more appropriate production system.

There are seven different production systems. The product/volume-layout/flow (PV-LF) matrix

Production System	Product/Volume	Layout/Flow
Job shop	Very many products/ One or a few of each	Functional layout/ Flow extremely varied
Batch flow	Many products/ Low volumes	Cellular layout/ Flow varied with patterns
Operator-paced line flow	Several to many products/ Medium volumes	Line layout/ Flow mostly regular, paced by operators
Equipment-paced line flow	Several products/ High volumes	Line layout/ Flow regular, paced by the equipment
Continuous flow	One or a few products/ Very high volumes	Line layout/ Flow rigid, continuous
Just-in-time (JIT)	Many products/ Low to medium volumes	Line layout/ Flow mostly regular, paced by operators
Flexible manufacturing system (FMS)	Very many products/ Low volumes	Cellular or line layout/ Flow mostly regular, paced by the equipment

Figure 4-5 The Seven Production Systems

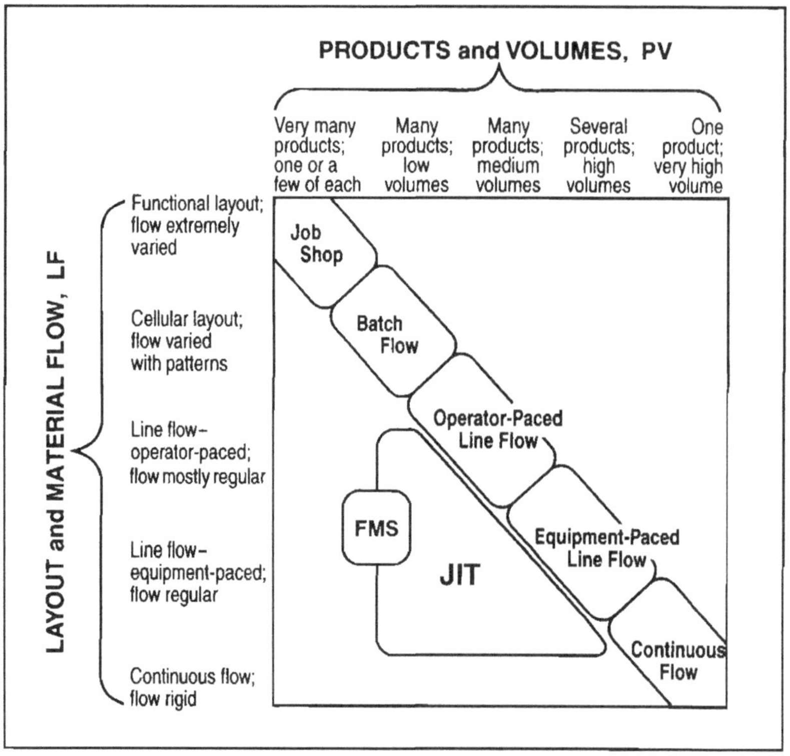

Figure 4-6 The Product/Volume-Layout/Flow (PV-LF) Matrix

in Figure 4-6 is a useful tool for analyzing similarities and differences among the seven production systems. The PV-LF matrix has four dimensions:

- Number of *products* produced
- Production *volume* of each product
- *Layout* or arrangement of equipment and processes used to manufacture the products
- *Flow* of material through the equipment and processes

The PV-LF matrix is an extension of the product-process matrix developed by Robert Hayes and Steven Wheelwright.[2] They found that many factory characteristics vary in accordance with two dimensions, product structure and process structure; and these dimensions also vary in accordance with the product life cycle (Chapter 16).

Products and Volumes

The products and volumes dimensions on the PV-LF matrix are shown across the top of the matrix (Figure 4-6) and are measured by asking the following product/volume question.

> *What products are manufactured, and in what volumes are they manufactured?*

The answer ranges from, "We produce whatever products our customers ask for, in whatever volume they want" to "We produce a very high volume of one product." These two answers anchor the range of possible answers to the product/volume question. Points along the range are:

- Very many different products produced in volumes of one, or a few, of each product
- Many different products produced in low volumes
- Many different products produced in medium volumes
- Several different products produced in high volumes
- One product produced in a very high volume

Manufacturers can easily answer the product/volume question. For example, one Tridon Company macro factory produced a family of hose clamps and a family of automotive electrical switches. The hose clamp product family consisted of a few products produced in very high volumes (tens of millions per year), while the electrical switch product family consisted of several different products produced in low volumes. The macro factory was organized into two focused factories, one for clamps and one for switches; and each used a different production system.

Layout and Flow

The layout and flow dimensions are shown on the side of the PV-LF matrix and are measured by asking the layout/flow question:

> *How are the equipment, processes, and departments arranged in the factory, and how does material flow from workstation to workstation as it moves through the factory?*

Factory Layout

There are three basic factory layouts (Figure 4-7):

- Functional layout
- Cellular layout
- Line layout

The particular layout a focused factory uses is determined by examining a standard factory layout drawing.

In a *functional layout*, equipment of the same type is located in the same area. For example, in a machine shop, lathes are in one department, shears in another, welders in another, and so on. Operators and supervisors work in one department and are highly skilled on the type of equipment in their department. Equipment and tooling are general purpose and can perform a wide range of operations.

In a *cellular layout*, different types of equipment and processes are located in the same department so

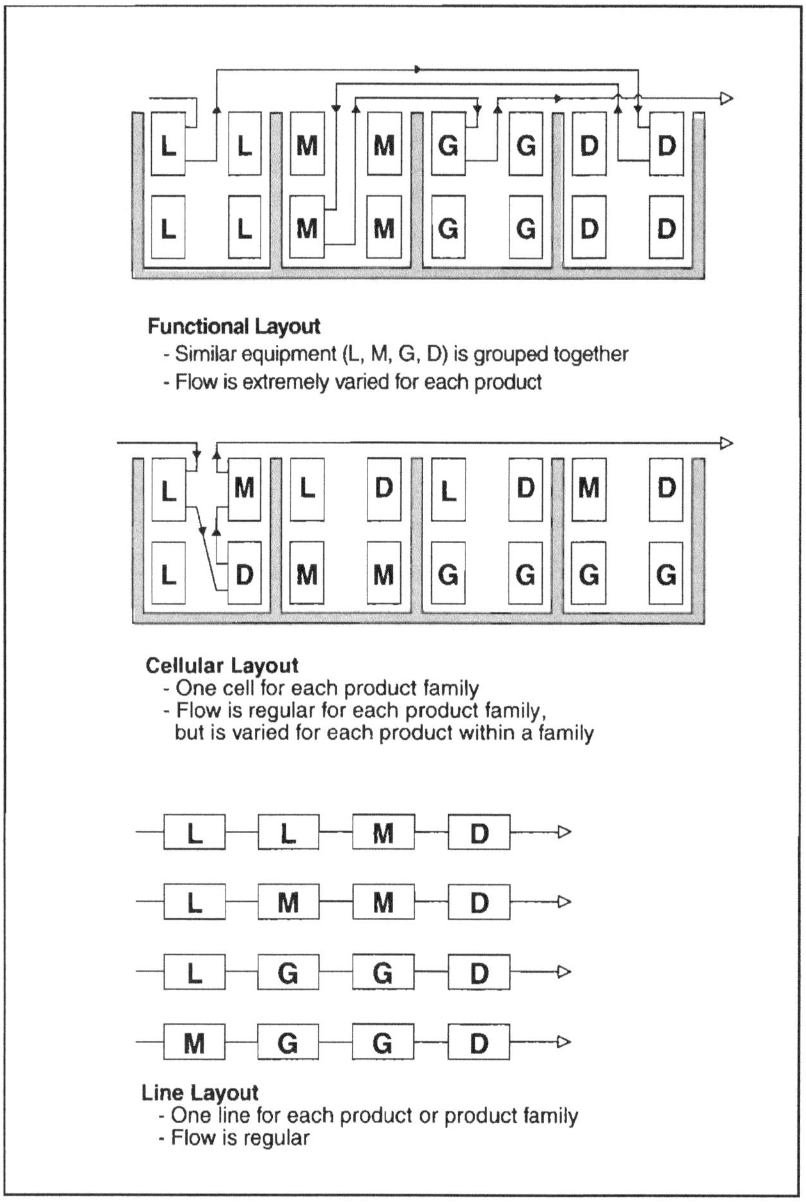

Figure 4-7 Basic Factory Layouts

that all operations required to produce any product within a relatively large product family can be performed in that department. Departments are often called manufacturing cells. Operators are trained to operate all equipment in their department. Equipment and tooling are general purpose because they are used to produce all products in a large product family; but it is often possible to specialize them slightly.

In a *line layout,* the different types of equipment needed to produce one product, or a small product family, are arranged into a line. Equipment and tooling are customized for the product or product family being produced. A line layout is appropriate when the production volume is high enough to fully utilize an expensive, dedicated line. Because equipment does most of the work, operators perform relatively simple tasks.

Material Flow

The particular material flow that a focused factory experiences is determined by walking through the factory. Starting at the unloading dock where purchased material is received, we walk through the factory, following material from workstation to workstation until we reach the workstation where a finished product is packaged and loaded for shipment to customers. The material flow depends on the layout, but for a particular layout, it can still vary somewhat. The range of factory layouts and material flows is shown in Figure 4-6.

When a factory is organized into a functional layout, the material flow is extremely varied. Depending on what operations need to be performed, the order in which they need to be performed, and the availability of equipment and operators, the material flow varies considerably from order to order. In a factory with a cellular layout, the flow is more regular because each product or product family is always produced in a particular department or cell. Within the cell, however, the material flow varies from order to order depending on necessary operations and workload at the machines.

Many companies use line layouts; thus, it is useful to separate lines into those where the pace or speed of the line is set by the operators and those where the pace is set by the equipment. With operator-paced line flows, the rate at which products are produced depends on the number of operators assigned to the workstations on the line, the speed at which they work, and how well they work as a team (Situation 4.2). The material flow in an operator-paced line flow is regular for the most part. There will be some variation when different products are produced and production volumes change.

An equipment-paced line flow is designed to run at one, or perhaps a few, speeds and produce a smaller number of different products than an operator-paced line flow. It is more capital intensive, less flexible, runs faster, and produces higher volumes. The material flow is regular. There may be slight variations when products are produced with different options. Traditional automobile assembly lines are examples of equipment-paced line flows. They run at speeds of approximately 50 cars per hour. There may be slight variations in the material flow when cars with different options, such as four- or six-cylinder engines, or two- or four-door models, are produced.

Some factories have material flows even more rigid than the equipment-paced line flow. They are called continuous flow lines. Compared to the equipment-paced line flow, the continuous flow line is more capital intensive, more highly automated, requires fewer operators, and allows fewer options to be produced. A continuous flow line

SITUATION 4.2

Operator-Paced Line Flow at Lincoln Electric

AN EXAMPLE of an operator-paced line flow is Lincoln Electric's factory in Lincoln, Nebraska. Materials flow from a long receiving dock on the north side of the factory, through the production lines, to a small storage and loading area on the south side. The production lines are designed so several different products can be produced on the same line by adjusting the line speed, assigning operators to different workstations, and using different tools and fixtures. Per-piece wage rates are paid to teams, rather than individual operators, to encourage operators to work together.

usually runs at an extremely high speed, 24 hours per day, seven days per week. It produces a very large volume of a single product. Often, the product is a commodity. Examples of continuous flow lines are continuous casting and rolling operations in steel mills, chemical plants, paper mills, and refineries.

Each production system corresponds to a unique set of values for the products, volumes, layout, and flow dimensions (Figure 4-6). This makes it easy for a focused factory to select the best production system.

Figure 4-8 describes other important characteristics of the seven production systems. The next section gives brief descriptions of each production system and the manufacturing outputs each provides.[3] Part VI of the book provides in-depth descriptions of each production system, useful for designing, operating, and improving production systems.

Job Shop Production System

A job shop production system produces a large number of different products in volumes ranging from one to a few of each product. A job shop production system has a functional layout. Equipment of the same type is located in the same department. Operators work in one department only and are highly skilled on the equipment in their department. Because many different products are produced in very low volumes, the equipment and tooling are general purpose. Material flow through a job shop varies considerably from job to job, and a great deal of material handling is required to move jobs from department to department. Jobs usually wait a long time for equipment to become available. Work-in-process inventory is high, and delivery times can be long (Chapter 18).

Batch Flow Production System

A batch flow production system produces fewer products in higher volumes than a job shop system. Products are produced in batches, which represent a few months of customer requirements. A combination of functional and cellular layouts is used. Cellular layouts are used when it is cost-effective to place different equipment into departments (called cells) to produce families of products. Because there are many products, the equipment and tooling are mostly general purpose. The material flow varies from order to order, although there are patterns of flow for product families and larger batches.

A special batch flow production system, called a linked batch flow production system, occurs when the number of equipment types is small, usually two or three. In this situation, equipment can be arranged in a line layout. The linked batch flow production system is important in processing industries especially chemicals, food, and pharmaceuticals. The linked batch flow production system is examined at the end of Chapter 19.

Line Flow Production Systems

In operator- and equipment-paced line flow production systems, equipment and processes are specialized and arranged into a line to produce a small number of different products or product families. A line flow system is appropriate when the product design is stable and the volume is high enough to make efficient use of a dedicated line.

Equipment-Paced Line Flow Production System

An equipment-paced line flow production system produces a small number of different products in high volumes. It is capital intensive and specialized. Operators perform relatively simple tasks at a rate determined by the line speed. For example, a J-car final assembly line in an automobile factory produces only J-cars in a limited range of options at a constant rate of 60 cars per hour (Chapter 23).

Production System	Product			Material		Equipment	Costs		Employees		Organization	
	Number	Variety	Volumes	Flow	Layout		Fixed	Variable	Staff	Line	Structure	Style
Job shop	Very many	Major differences	Very low	Extremely varied	Functional	General purpose, flexible	Low	High	Few	Highly skilled	Flat, decentralized	Entrepre-neurial
Batch flow	Many	Large variety	Low	Varied with patterns	Cells and functional	General purpose, some special-ization	Moderate	Moderate	Few	Multiskilled	Flat, decentralized	Entrepre-neurial
Operator-paced line flow	Several to many	Some variation	Medium	Regular	Line	Specialized, some flexibility	High	Low	Many	Multiskilled	Hierarchy, decentralized	Entrepre-neurial
Equipment-paced line flow	Several	Standard, with minor options	High	Regular	Line	Special purpose	Very high	Low	Many	Unskilled	Hierarchy, centralized	Bureau-cratic
Continuous flow	One or a few	Standard	Very high	Rigid	Line	Special purpose, highly automated	Extremely high	Very low	Very many	Few, unskilled	Hierarchy, centralized	Bureau-cratic
Flexible manu-facturing system (FMS)	Very many	Major differences	Low	Regular	Line and cells	Flexible, highly automated	Extremely high	Very low	Many	Few, unskilled	Hierarchy, centralized	Bureau-cratic
Just-in-time (JIT)	Many	Large variety	Low to medium	Regular	Line	General purpose, many specialized	Moderate	Low	Some	Multiskilled	Flat, decentralized	Entrepre-neurial

Figure 4-8 Some Characteristics of the Seven Production Systems

Operator-Paced Line Flow Production System

An operator-paced line flow production system is used when the number of different products is too high and the production volumes are too variable for an equipment-paced line flow production system. An operator-paced line is more flexible than an equipment-paced line and can be run at a variety of speeds. The speed depends on the particular product being produced, the number of operators assigned to the line, and how well the operators work as a team (Chapter 21).

Continuous Flow Production System

This production system resembles the equipment-paced line flow production system. However, it is more automated, specialized, capital intensive, and less flexible. It runs continuously, usually 24 hours per day, seven days per week, with little operator assistance. It produces one product or a narrowly defined product family at very high volumes. The product is often a commodity. This means product design is stable and standard, industry-wide specifications exist. This production system produces a product with the highest possible quality and the lowest possible cost (Chapter 24).

Just-In-Time (JIT) Production System

Before describing a JIT production system, it is important to distinguish between JIT techniques and a JIT production system. Many new and not-so-new techniques are called JIT techniques. Examples are kaizen, multiskilled workers, problem solving, pull production, setup time reduction, standardization, and statistical quality control. These techniques are also called "lean production" techniques and can be used to make improvements in all production systems (Chapter 15).

As we will see in Chapter 22, the JIT production system is much more than a collection of JIT techniques. It is a line flow production system with two important characteristics.

- It produces many products in low to medium volumes. The other line flow production systems cannot produce this mix or volume of products because the number of products is too high and volumes are too low.
- It forces continuous improvement by identifying wastes and compelling itself to eliminate the wastes. This leads to lower costs, improved quality, and faster delivery.

Flexible Manufacturing System (FMS) Production

An FMS production system consists of computer controlled machines, an automatic material handling system, and a computer system. An FMS runs unattended for long periods of time. The machines, material handling system, and computers are flexible, which permits an FMS to produce many different products in low volumes. For example, a Pratt and Whitney FMS in Canada produces 70 different products for the aerospace industry in volumes ranging from 30 to 1,000 units per year per product. Because an FMS is expensive, it is usually used in situations in which simpler, less expensive line flow production systems cannot be used (Chapter 20).

Craft, Mass, and Lean Production

The seven production systems can be organized into three groups: craft production, mass production, and lean production.

- Craft production
  - Job shop production system
  - Batch flow production system
- Mass production
  - Operator-paced line flow production system
  - Equipment-paced line flow production system

Continuous flow production system

- Lean production

JIT production system

FMS production system

This three-group categorization analyzes the differences between newer production systems (lean production) and older, traditional production systems (craft and mass production).[4] However, it is too general to be useful in manufacturing strategy.

Manufacturing Outputs Provided By Traditional Production Systems

The seven production systems were developed in different parts of the world at different times. There are two important reasons why all seven are useful today:

- Each production system is uniquely suited to produce a particular mix and volume of products.
- Each production system provides different levels of the manufacturing outputs: cost, quality, performance, delivery, flexibility, and innovativeness.

Figure 4-9 shows the levels at which each production system provides the manufacturing outputs when the production system is well managed. (Well-managed production systems are discussed in Chapter 5.) Black bars indicate high or good levels; white bars indicate low or poor levels. Long black bars indicate higher or better levels than short black bars. Long white bars indicate lower or poorer levels than short white bars.

This section examines the manufacturing outputs provided by the five traditional (craft and mass) production systems. The next section

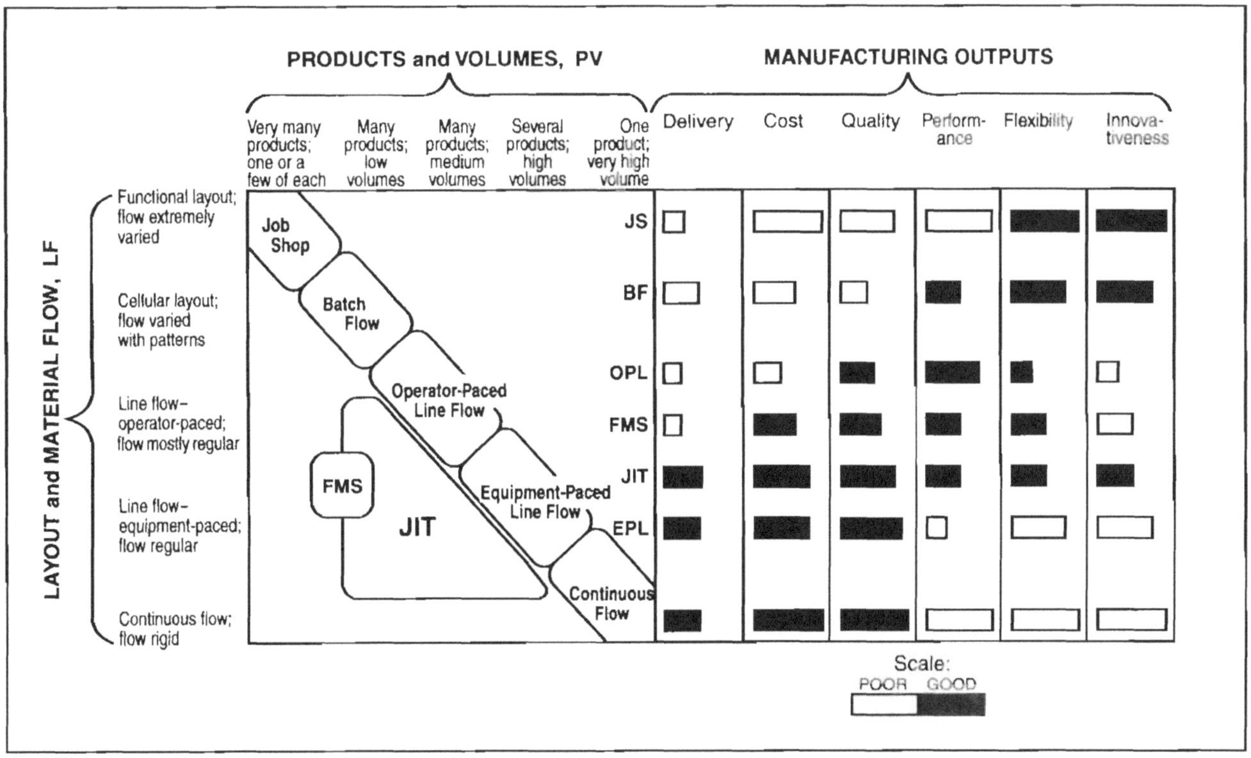

Figure 4-9 Manufacturing Outputs Provided by Well-Managed Production Systems

examines the manufacturing outputs provided by the two lean production systems.

Cost and Quality

Production systems near the bottom of the PV-LF matrix provide better levels of the cost and quality outputs than production systems near the top. Production systems, such as equipment-paced line flow and continuous flow, produce a single product or product family on specialized equipment with specialized tooling using relatively few operators. The specialization ensures that all product specifications are met, no matter how tight they are, so quality is high. Because the volume is high equipment utilization will be high. Consequently, cost is as low as possible.

Production systems near the top of the matrix (job shop and batch flow) produce many different products in relatively low volumes on general purpose machines with general purpose tooling. The quality of the products produced is good, otherwise customers would not buy them. However, the quality is not as high as it would be if the same products were produced on specialized machines with high volume tooling. The production volumes are too low to generate experience benefits (Chapter 16) or to justify significant improvement activity. The same reasoning applies to cost. The cost is reasonable, otherwise customers would not buy the products, but it is difficult for a job shop or batch flow production system to match the cost of a line flow production system that produces only a few products in high volumes on specialized equipment.

It is often impossible to produce the same product on production systems from opposite ends of the PV-LF matrix. For example, custom-engineered packaging equipment is produced to customer specifications in a job shop or batch flow production system. Because each order is different and the volumes are low, it is not possible to set up an equipment-paced line flow or continuous flow production system. All companies producing this product use a job shop or batch flow production system and therefore provide similar levels of the same outputs. Suppose, however, that one competitor sets up an equipment-paced line flow production system and produces a family of standard products in high volumes. If the standard product competes directly with any custom-engineered products, the competitor will have significant cost and quality advantages.

Flexibility and Innovativeness

Production systems near the top of the PV-LF matrix are able to provide better levels of flexibility and innovativeness than production systems

Situation 4.3

Flexibility and Innovativeness at a Clothing Manufacturer

A CLOTHING MANUFACTURER used a batch flow production system to produce an endless variety of dresses, shirts, skirts, pants, and jackets. Orders consisted of a garment type and a style, color, and size, and were produced in batches of 10 dozen garments. Batches flowed through a functionally organized factory, with a cutting department, sewing department, pressing department, and so on. Each batch was routed from department to department, and within each, to any available workstation until all required operations were completed. It was relatively easy for the manufacturer to change products and volumes and introduce new garment types, styles, and colors. The production system provided high levels of flexibility and innovativeness.

Situation 4.4

Not Enough Flexibility at a Chemical Factory

A COMPANY DEVELOPED a resin product with new advanced features not available in other resins. Then, the company built a continuous flow production system to manufacture the resin. Eighteen months later, the new features became standard features in the industry and were available in the resins produced by most of the company's competitors. The company could not introduce other new features into its product because of the high cost of converting its rigid, highly automated, continuous flow production system. Management should have anticipated the need to add new features and built a more flexible production system.

near the bottom. Production systems like the job shop and batch flow systems are designed to produce a wide variety of products in low volumes. Machines and tooling are general purpose, and operators are highly skilled. Consequently, it is easy to change volumes, make design changes, and introduce new products (Situation 4.3).

It is more difficult for an equipment-paced line flow or a continuous flow production system to change products and volumes, make product design changes, and introduce new products. The equipment and tooling are specialized for the product or product family being produced. Design changes and introduction of new products require major adjustments to the equipment and tooling (Situation 4.4). Consequently, these machine-oriented production systems provide less flexibility and innovativeness than the people-oriented production systems at the top of the PV-LF matrix.

Delivery

The shortest delivery time and the best delivery time reliability for a particular product are provided by the equipment-paced line flow and continuous flow production systems. Two reasons for this are:

- These production systems are dedicated to producing one product or product family. Equipment and tooling are specialized.
- These production systems operate at high speeds. They run for long time periods without stopping.

Production systems near the top of the PV-LF matrix provide good deliveries by expediting orders when necessary. However, expediting cannot be done all the time. Overall, production systems near the bottom of the PV-LF matrix provide better delivery than production systems near the top, but the differences are not as great as they are for the cost, quality, flexibility, and innovativeness outputs (Figure 4-9).

Performance

Manufacturers that consistently provide products with a high level of performance have production systems not excessively machine- or people-oriented. Well-managed production systems, which rely equally on the capabilities of machines and people, can best provide a high level of performance year after year (Situation 4.5).

A high level of performance requires a steady stream of new products, enhancements to existing products, and changes to equipment and processes. This is difficult for rigid production systems near the bottom of the PV-LF matrix. It is costly to change specialized, automated machines and tooling, retrain unskilled operators, change processes at suppliers, and stop high-speed lines for a few weeks to make changes. This can be done from time to time, but it cannot be done at the pace needed to provide a high level of performance year after year.

Production systems near the top of the PV-LF matrix have difficulty providing a high level of performance for a different reason. The production volume of any particular product is so low that the company cannot afford the design engineering resources required to design new, advanced features into the product, or the process engineering resources required to design new workstations and processes for producing new, advanced features. Situation 4.6 is an example.

Manufacturing Outputs Provided By JIT Production System

The long black bars in Figure 4-9 corresponding to the manufacturing outputs provided by the JIT production system are the reasons that companies are so interested in JIT. The JIT production system is examined carefully in Chapter 22. In this section, we summarize the reasons why it provides high levels of so many outputs.

JIT is a line flow production system, so it provides cost, quality, and delivery at the high levels associated with line flow production systems. JIT does this by utilizing all the capabilities of the equipment in the line. At the same time, the JIT production system, like the batch flow production system, is designed to produce many products in low to medium volumes. Consequently, flexibility and innovativeness are provided at the high levels associated with the batch flow production system. JIT does this by capitalizing on the exceptional skills of its workforce.

The JIT production system provides high levels of all manufacturing outputs, but it is the most difficult production system to design and operate. For example, it took Toyota more than 20 years to implement its JIT production system. Although many North American and European companies have successfully implemented several JIT techniques, far fewer successful implementations of a complete JIT production system exist. We will expand on this subject in Chapters 14, 15, and 22.

Manufacturing Outputs Provided By FMS Production System

An FMS production system is a line flow production system that produces a wider variety of products in lower volumes than other line flow production systems. An FMS production system uses expensive, flexible equipment and expensive computer hardware and software to form a physical line where many products can be produced in low volumes. The flexible equipment and computer system enable fast setups, rapid processing of very small batches of products, and continuous monitoring of quality.

Situation 4.5

Performance at a Clothing Manufacturer

THE MCG CLOTHING COMPANY produced socks, scarves, and clothing accessories in a factory located in Toronto, an expensive city for manufacturing. Rather than move manufacturing to another part of the world and produce standard products on a continuous flow production system, the company chose to stay in Toronto, use an operator-paced line flow production system, and compete on the basis of performance. They acquired the rights to produce prominent brands, such as Calvin Klein and Christian Dior, and produced attractive, fashionable products from expensive materials.

SITUATION 4.6

When a Production System Cannot Provide the Required Level of Performance

THE SUPERSONIC CONCORDE airplane competed on the basis of performance. It could cross the Atlantic in less than half the time it took a Boeing 747. To keep performance at a high level, R&D was needed on several new features:

- More economical, quieter engine
- Flatter wing that could quiet the sonic boom
- Smaller airplane that could cross the Pacific at the same cost-per-seat-mile as a Boeing 747

Only a batch flow or operator-paced line flow production system could support this high level of performance. However, the product volume was too low for these production systems. Air France and British Airways were the only customers, and they only had 14 Concordes. This volume was appropriate for a job shop production system. Unfortunately, a job shop production system does not provide a high level of performance.

Airbus, the present-day version of the British-French partnership that created the Concorde, could not provide the high level of performance that customers needed. In early 2003, Airbus told Air France and British Airways that it could not provide technical support for the Concorde at competitive rates. In October 2003, the Concorde was discontinued.[5]

Because FMS is a line flow production system, it provides cost, quality, and delivery at the high levels associated with line flow production systems. It also provides a high level of flexibility because it produces many products in low volumes. It provides a low level of innovativeness because introducing new products and making design changes to existing products require major changes to computer programs and fixtures (Situation 4.7).

SUMMARY

A manufacturing network consists of distribution centers, manufacturing facilities, offices, research laboratories, and so on. Each manufacturing facility contains one or more macro factories, which consist of a small number of micro or focused factories. A focused factory is a single production system that produces most or all products in a product family.

A production system provides six manufacturing outputs to its customers: cost, quality, performance, delivery, flexibility, and innovativeness. For each product, one or two outputs are provided at the highest possible levels in the industry, while the others are provided at high, but somewhat lower, levels. This gives sources of competitive advantage and recognizes that no single production system can provide all outputs at the highest possible levels.

There are seven different production systems:

- Job shop
- Batch flow
- Operator-paced line flow
- Equipment-paced line flow

SITUATION 4.7

When FMS is the Only Choice

AN FMS at the Perkins diesel engine factory in Great Britain produced 50 different products in volumes, averaging 13 units per day per product. The Pratt and Whitney FMS in Canada produced 70 different parts in volumes ranging from 30 to 1,000 units per year per product. These numbers of products and volumes would normally be produced on a job shop or batch flow production system. However, when very high levels of quality and delivery are required, the FMS production system is used. Neither the traditional line flow production systems nor the JIT production system can produce this mix and volume of products.

- Continuous flow
- Just-in-time (JIT)
- Flexible manufacturing system (FMS)

Each produces a unique mix of products and volumes. Each system provides a unique set of cost, quality, performance, delivery, flexibility, and innovativeness manufacturing outputs. One of the tasks of manufacturing strategy is to select the best production system for each product or product family, which the next two chapters describe.

ENDNOTES

1. For an interesting analysis of manufacturing outputs see, Roth, A., and Miller, J., "Manufacturing Strategy, Manufacturing Strength, Managerial Success, and Economic Outcomes," *Manufacturing Strategy*, Ettlie, J., Burstein, M., and Feigenbaum, A. (eds.), Kluwer Publishers: Dordrecht, The Netherlands, pp. 97–108, 1990.
2. Hayes, R., and Wheelwright, S., "Link Manufacturing Process and Product Life Cycles," *Harvard Business Review*, January–February, pp. 133–140, 1979.
3. Descriptions and characteristics of the seven production systems are adapted from Schmenner, R., *Plant and Service Tours in Operations Management*, New York: Macmillan Publishing Co., 1989.
4. This classification is from Womack, J., Jones, D., and Roos, D., *The Machine That Changed the World*, Harper Perennial Press, 1991.
5. "After Concorde," *The Economist*, pp. 59–60, Vol. 369, No. 8346, October 18, 2003.

CHAPTER 5

MANUFACTURING LEVERS AND CAPABILITY

A production system is divided into six subsystems (Figure 5-1):

- Human resources
- Organization structure and controls
- Sourcing
- Production planning and control
- Process technology
- Facilities

Human resources	Skill level, wages, training, promotion policies, employment security, and so on, of each group of employees
Organization structure and controls	Relationships between groups of employees in the production system. How are decisions made? What is the underlying culture? What systems measure performance and provide incentives?
Sourcing	Amount of vertical integration. What is the relationship with suppliers? How does the production system manage those parts of the value system it does not own?
Production planning and control	Rules and systems that plan and control the flow of material, production activities, and support activities such as maintenance and the introduction of new products
Process technology	Nature of the production processes, type of equipment, amount of automation, and linkages between parts of the production process
Facilities	Location, size, focus, and types and timing of changes

Figure 5-1 Manufacturing Levers: Six Subsystems that Comprise a Production System

These subsystems are called *manufacturing levers* to reflect the concept that each subsystem can be adjusted. Adjustments vary in size. Small adjustments are made to one or more levers to improve an existing production system. Large adjustments are made to all six levers to greatly improve an existing production system or change an existing one to a different production system. New manufacturing techniques or technologies (Chapter 15) are groups of adjustments to several levers.

The current position of a lever is the result of management decisions in the subsystem over a long time period. The current positions of the six levers completely determines:

- The type of production system
- How well the production system works
- The levels at which the manufacturing outputs are provided

This chapter examines each manufacturing lever, its level of capability, how levers interact with each other, and how they form a production system.

Six Manufacturing Levers

Human Resources

The human resources subsystem comprises the company's human resource policies for the production system in use. Decisions (or adjustments) made in this subsystem include:

- Mix of skilled and unskilled employees
- Number of job classifications
- Whether employees will be multiskilled
- Amount of training
- Level of supervision
- Policy on layoffs
- Promotion opportunities
- Responsibility and decision making given to employees
- Participation of employees in problem-solving and improvement activities

Organization Structure and Controls

This subsystem comprises the organization structure, control systems, reward systems, and culture. Decisions include:

- Whether the production system is a cost or profit center
- Whether the organization structure is flat or hierarchical
- Whether the production system is bureaucratic or entrepreneurial, centralized or decentralized
- Relative importance of line and staff
- Responsibility and authority at each level of the organization
- Measures to evaluate performance of individuals and departments
- Who is responsible for quality
- How managers are selected
- Use of teams

Sourcing

The sourcing lever focuses on relationships with suppliers and distributors. Decisions include:

- Amount of vertical integration
- Number of suppliers and distributors and their capabilities
- Whether supplier and distributor relationships are adversarial or partnerships
- Responsibility given to suppliers for design, cost, and quality
- Procedure for deciding whether a product will be produced internally or obtained from a supplier

Production Planning and Control

This subsystem consists of order entry, master production scheduling, materials planning, scheduling of machines and employees, controlling production on the factory floor, coordinating production support departments, and so on. Decisions include:

- Whether systems are centralized or decentralized
- Whether a push or pull control system is used
- Size of raw material, work-in-process, and finished goods inventories
- How information is gathered and used
- When maintenance is done
- How to schedule design changes and new products into production

Process Technology

The process technology subsystem consists of the machines, processes, and technologies used to produce products. Decisions include:

- Whether to develop technology internally or purchase it from external sources
- Whether technology is new or old
- Amount of automation
- Whether machines are general purpose or specialized
- Whether tooling is low or high volume
- Factory layout
- Whether layout and technology are static or continuously improving
- Quality practices

Facilities

The facilities subsystem includes the buildings within which production takes place, and production support departments such as material handling, maintenance, engineering, and tooling. Decisions include:

- Whether facilities are large or small
- Whether facilities are general purpose or specialized
- Location of facilities
- Capacity planning
- Capabilities of production support departments

Interactions Among Manufacturing Levers

Six manufacturing levers constitute a production system. The positions or arrangement of the six levers completely determines whether the production system is a job shop, batch flow, operator-paced line flow, equipment-paced line flow, continuous flow, JIT, or FMS.

Adjustments to the manufacturing levers should not be made in a haphazard way. When considering a possible adjustment, three characteristics of good adjustments should be checked.

Is the Adjustment Appropriate for the Production System?

Decisions in each subsystem must be appropriate for the production system. For example, human resources policies appropriate for a job shop production system are not appropriate for a JIT production system.

New techniques and technologies are sets of adjustments to the manufacturing levers. Of the many techniques and technologies available to a company, only those appropriate for the production system in use should be considered. For example, a manufacturer with a job shop production system hired a new manager whose previous experience was with an equipment-paced line flow production system. Any changes proposed by the new manager that draw on previous work experience should be checked to ensure appropriateness for the job shop production system.

Will the Adjustment Help Provide the Required Manufacturing Outputs?

Adjustments to a lever affect the manufacturing outputs provided by the production system. Of the many adjustments that can be made, those that most help the production system provide the required outputs should be selected. For example, suppose flexibility and innovativeness are the basis of competitive advantage for a focused factory with a batch flow production system. The factory is considering possible changes in the human resources area. Of the many adjustments that can be made to this lever, those leading to an increase in the levels of flexibility and innovativeness should receive highest priority. One such adjustment is a change to the incentive wage scheme to encourage operators to do rapid setups and produce products in smaller batches. Operators who avoid setups by producing in large batches could be penalized.

How Will the Adjustment Affect the Other Levers?

When making a decision in one subsystem, the implications of the decision on other subsystems should be considered. For example, changing the production planning and control subsystem may require changes in human resource policies (train employees and change job descriptions), sourcing (improve supplier deliveries), and organization structure and controls (adjust reporting procedures).

Figure 5-2 shows the relationship between the production system, the manufacturing outputs, and the manufacturing levers. When the six levers are set in the appropriate positions for the production system in use, the production system is said to be *well managed.*

Tradeoffs

It is not difficult to determine the current positions of the manufacturing levers in an actual production system. A walk through the factory that takes note of the types of machines, material handling procedures, maintenance practices, planning methods, information systems, routines of operators, activities of managers, attitudes of staff specialists, and so on, gives a good picture of where each lever is set.

When faced with choices about adjustments to a lever, many manufacturing managers say, "They

Situation 5.1

Prestige Furniture Inadvertently Changes Production Systems

Problem

Prestige Furniture Company manufactured high-quality furniture to customer specifications. A customer might bring in an antique furniture piece and ask that a reproduction be made. Another customer might ask for a furniture piece seen in a magazine. Company designers prepared drawings of the furniture, got customer approval for the drawings, and released drawings and a production order to the factory. The 30-year-old factory produced orders in a job shop production system.

A few years ago, the factory produced two identical sets of bedroom furniture by accident. No one knew what to do with the extra set. It was sold finally to an out-of-town furniture store for relatively high price. Soon thereafter, it became a common practice to produce one or more duplicate sets of furniture for many orders. All duplicate sets were sold to out-of-town dealers, so customers never knew that somewhere there were copies of their furniture.

The new practice was profitable. However, it made work in the factory more difficult. Some departments could barely handle the higher workload. Frequently, parts became mixed up, and some were even lost. The company made some changes to ease the difficulties. A small number of relatively unskilled employees were hired. A new parts identification system was implemented. Three high speed, mass production machines were purchased to increase capacity. Five simpler, labor-intensive machines were removed to make room for the new machines.

While employees agreed that changes were needed, many were uncomfortable with the new employees, new skills, new systems, and new machines.

Analysis

Before the practice of producing duplicate sets began, Prestige Furniture had a well-managed job shop production system (Figure 5-3). The new practice increased production volumes, which moved the company horizontally away from the diagonal of the PV-LF matrix. Adjustments were made to the human resources lever (new, unskilled employees), production planning and control lever (part identification scheme), and the process technology lever (new equipment). These adjustments and others began to change the job shop production system to a batch flow production system. More adjustments to the levers were needed to make the new production system a well-managed batch flow production system. From the employees' reaction to changes made so far, it appeared that adjustments to the human resources lever would be difficult.

In fact, the company never made the necessary adjustments for a well-managed batch flow production system. Production problems continued, and management spent most of its time "putting out fires." The levels of the manufacturing outputs were lower than they should have been. The situation was never corrected because there were no competitors to force Prestige Furniture to improve. The company was vulnerable to a challenge from any competitor with a well-managed job shop or batch flow production system.

Prestige Furniture should not have changed production systems. It was not necessary. Changing production systems is difficult, and the company did not have enough manufacturing capability to do it.

Instead, Prestige Furniture should have organized a small focused factory (Chapter 15) to produce small quantities of selected products on either a batch flow or operator-paced line flow production system. Products from the focused factory would be sold to retail chain stores, where cost and delivery time were most important. This strategy would have satisfied the company's desire for growth and given it two strong production systems instead of one weak one.

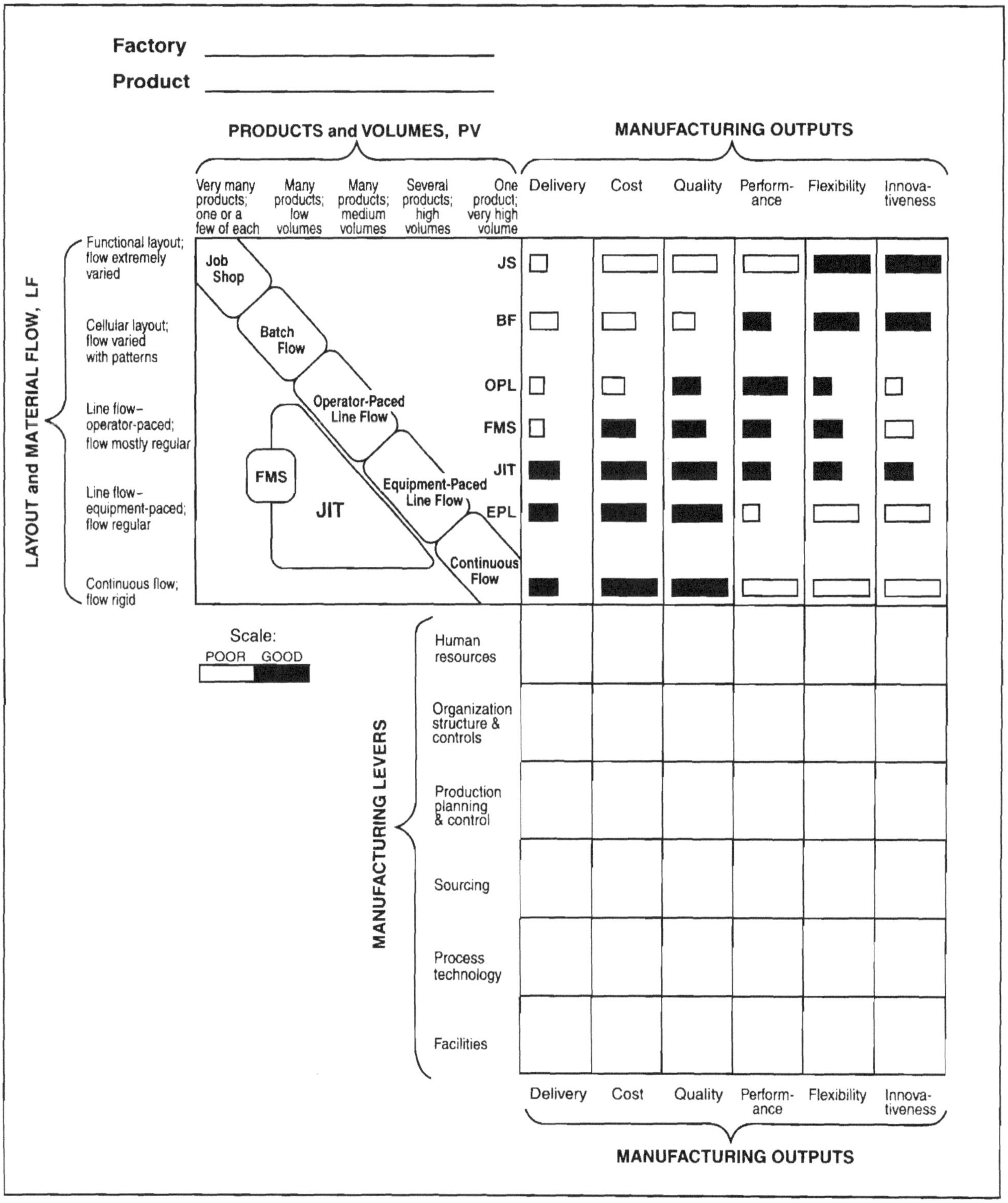

Figure 5-2 Relationship Between Production Systems, Manufacturing Outputs, and Manufacturing Levers

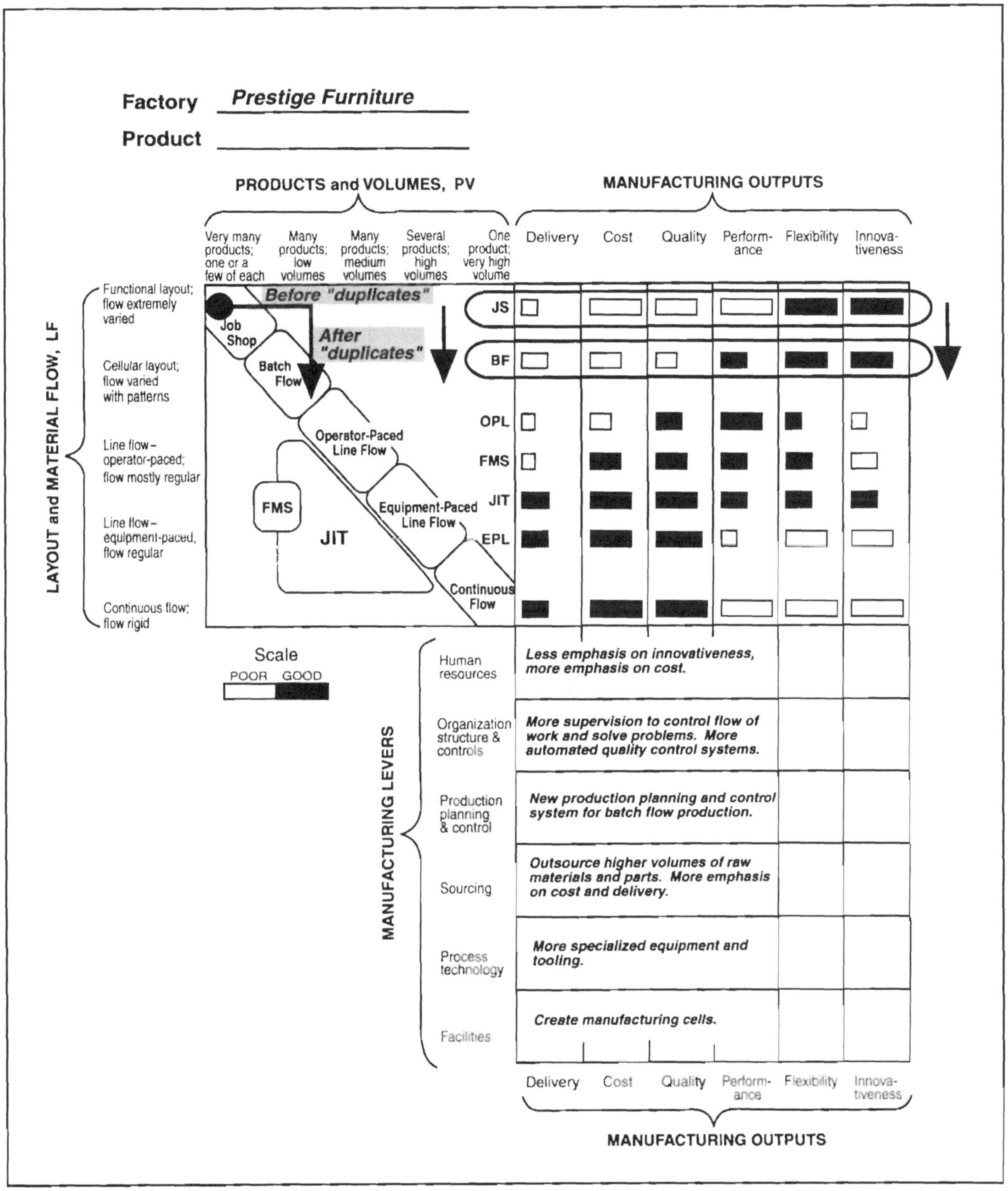

Figure 5-3 Analysis of Prestige Furniture's Implicit Decision to Change Production System

Situation 5.2

COR Sports Clothing Changes from Batch to Line Flow

Part 1
Problem

COR Sports Clothing was a medium-sized producer of sports clothing sold in wholesale and retail markets. The company had a reputation for innovative premium products with fine stitching, style, and colors, and fast, dependable delivery.

Manufacturing was done in a modern factory on equipment arranged in a functional layout. Cloth was cut in the cutting department; stitching was done in the large sewing department; and pressing and packaging were done in the packaging department.

Whenever inventory of a product (that is, size, style, and color) fell below 2 dozen pieces, a clerk wrote a production order to produce 10 dozen pieces. Bundles of 10 dozen pieces moved from department to department and from workstation to workstation until all operations were completed.

New products were designed on the recommendation of sales personnel, who were informed by wholesalers and retailers about the popularity of new styles and colors. COR could design, produce, and supply any new product within five business days.

According to the company's general manager, "Competition in the sports clothing business is cut-throat. It is essential to keep production costs down, despite increasing wage rates and rising material cost. It is also important to maintain quality of cloth and workmanship."

Analysis

COR used a batch flow production system. The company's competitive advantage was its flexibility and innovativeness. COR could quickly and reliably produce many sizes, styles, and colors of existing and new products. The general manager was very concerned about cost. Unfortunately, the batch flow production system probably cannot provide cost at the low level desired (Figure 5-4).

Part 2
Problem

The general manager decided to change the production system to reduce cost. A new line layout was implemented, patterned after a recently visited television assembly line. In the first weeks after the implementation, production flow was not as smooth as anticipated. Bottlenecks occurred at several workstations. Most of the problems disappeared when the size of the bundles was increased and a new procedure for releasing production orders was established.

The new production system improved efficiency and would have lowered cost had sales been large enough to use the factory's increased capacity. But sales were declining instead of increasing. Customers were reducing their orders. Panicky inquiries revealed that in the "standard" sports clothing business, COR was just one of many companies. Customers had bought from COR because of its variety, originality, and styling, and its fast, dependable delivery.

ANALYSIS

In an attempt to reduce cost, the general manager changed the batch flow production system to a line flow production system.

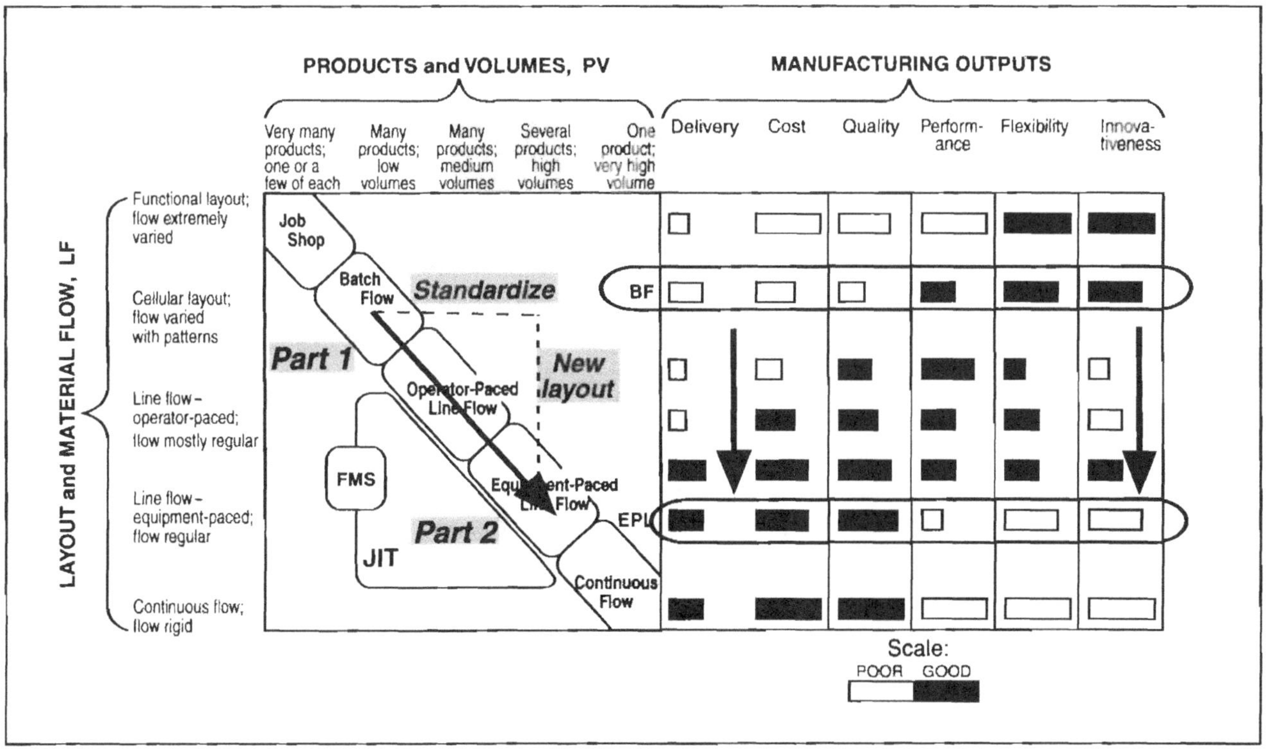

Figure 5-4 Analysis of COR Shirts

SITUATION 5.2

Continued

This required higher volumes of fewer products (Figure 5-4) and produced better levels of cost and quality. However, the levels of flexibility and innovativeness dropped, and since this was what customers wanted most, orders decreased.

PART 3

PROBLEM

At this point, the general manager had two options:

- If the line flow production system was kept, COR would have to find new customers and compete in the standard sports clothing business. This would require additional adjustments to manufacturing levers.
- If the production system was changed back to a batch flow system, COR would keep its old customers and continue in the custom sports clothing business.

The general manager selected the second option. The line was dismantled and the equipment was rearranged to form a batch flow production system.

ANALYSIS

The general manager should never have changed the production system. Improvements to reduce cost should have been made (Chapter 14), or a small focused factory (Chapter 15) to produce a small number of high volume, standard products on a line flow production system should have been organized.

always try to make the best decision." This implies that it is always possible to have the best. This belief is mistaken. Decisions almost always involve tradeoffs. For example, training employees to be multiskilled increases cost because of training expenses and higher wages; but it also increases flexibility and innovativeness. Some equipment is economical for producing small orders; other equipment is only economical for producing large orders. Production planning and control systems can be designed to minimize delivery time, setup cost, or finished goods inventory. Facilities can consist of a few large, general purpose departments or many small, specialized departments. Incentive wage plans can be designed to encourage different behaviors. Products can be designed to maximize performance or minimize cost.

DEFINING THE SUBSYSTEMS THAT CONSTITUTE A PRODUCTION SYSTEM

Figure 5-5 shows other ways of organizing subsystems within a production system. In each case, subsystems can be divided into two groups: structural and infrastructural. Each way of organizing subsystems has the following properties:

- *Comprehensive:* All manufacturing decisions fall within the subsystems.

- *Discriminating:* Complex manufacturing decisions can be broken into analyzable pieces, and each piece falls within one subsystem.
- *Reflective:* The subsystems are consistent with manufacturing's view of itself.

At superior manufacturers, structural and infrastructural subsystem groups are equally important, each subsystem is equally important, and each has a high level of manufacturing capability.

MANUFACTURING CAPABILITY

Improvements or changes are adjustments to manufacturing levers. Some companies have no difficulty making changes, even large ones. Other

Type of Subsystem	Skinner	Buffa	Hayes, Wheelwright, and Clark	Fine and Hax	This Book
Structural	• Plant and equipment	• Capacity and location • Product and process technology • Strategy with respect to suppliers and vertical integration	• Capacity • Facilities • Technology • Vertical integration	• Capacity • Facilities • Processes and technologies	• Facilities • Process technology • Sourcing
Infrastructural	• Production planning and control • Organization and management • Labor and staffing • Product design and engineering	• Strategic implications of operating decisions • Workforce and job design • Position of production system	• Production planning and control • Quality • Organization • Workforce • New product development • Performance measurement systems	• Product quality • Human resources • Scope of new products	• Production planning and control • Organization structure and controls • Human resources

Adapted from Leong, G., Snyder, D., and Ward, P., "Research in the Process and Content of Manufacturing Strategy," *Omega: The International Journal of Management Science*, Vol. 18, No. 2, pp. 109–122, 1990. The first four ways of organizing subsystems come from the following authors:

- Skinner, W, "The Focused Factory," *Harvard Business Review*, pp. 112–121, May–June 1974.
- Buffa, E., *Meeting the Competitive Challenge*, New York: Dow Jones-Irwin, 1984.
- Hayes, R., Wheelwright, S., and Clark, K., *Dynamic Manufacturing: Creating the Learning Organization*, New York: Free Press, 1988.
- Fine, C., and Hax, A., "Manufacturing Strategy: A Methodology and an Illustration," *Interfaces*, Vol. 15, No. 6, pp. 16–27, 1986.

Figure 5-5 Defining the Subsystems that Constitute a Production System

companies struggle to make small changes. Two factors have a major effect on a company's ability to make changes: top management's commitment and level of manufacturing capability.

Top Management

Significant changes cannot be made without the commitment and active participation of top management. Harley-Davidson Motorcycles had both when it turned itself around.[1] In 1981, AMF sold Harley-Davidson to a group of Harley-Davidson managers. High interest rates, a recession, strong competition from Japanese manufacturers, and quality problems combined to create a bleak outlook for Harley-Davidson. Nonetheless, by 1989, the company rebounded. Its share of the over 1,000 cc motorcycle market climbed from a low 16 percent to 25 percent. The levels of its manufacturing outputs were up: lower cost, better quality, and more reliable delivery time. Harley-Davidson improved its manufacturing capabilities by implementing a broad range of just-in-time and quality control techniques. Company leaders actively participated in the changes because they knew they would lose the company if they did not.

Manufacturing Capability

New manufacturing capabilities are built on a foundation of existing ones. The smaller this foundation, the harder it is to build on. When the level of manufacturing capability is low, anything beyond a few small changes is difficult. As the level of capability increases, more changes can be made at a faster pace.

The IBM RTP facility is an example of how a solid foundation of manufacturing capability makes it easier to implement new techniques and technologies.[2] The RTP facility uses almost every advanced manufacturing technique and technology: automatic guided vehicles, concurrent engineering, continuous flow production, employment security, flexible employees, flexible manufacturing systems, just-in-time, product standardization, robots, and training. It is easy to add more changes and techniques to a foundation this solid.

Overall Level of Manufacturing Capability

A high level of manufacturing capability is important for two reasons:

- Production systems with high levels of manufacturing capability provide high levels of the manufacturing outputs.
- Production systems with high levels of manufacturing capability make changes quickly and easily.

A measure of the overall level of manufacturing capability is given in Figure 5-6. The measure can take any value from 1.0 to 4.0. A value of 1.0 indicates an infant level of capability; 2.0 is an industry average level; 3.0 is an adult level; and 4.0 is a world class level.[3]

Harley-Davidson's overall manufacturing capability is near the adult level. IBM RTP is near the world class level. Companies with manufacturing capabilities near adult and world class levels can make numerous changes quickly and easily. Companies with infant or industry average levels of capability can only make small changes at a slow rate.

Infant Overall Level of Manufacturing Capability

Many production systems begin with an infant level of manufacturing capability. For example, a company forms to sell a new product or take advantage of a market niche. It is strongly oriented toward product design or marketing. Manufacturing is a necessary, low-tech activity. Manufacturing employees are unskilled and unsophisticated. Products are produced in a general purpose factory on a poorly managed production system using as many purchased parts as possible. When these companies gain experience, they notice that competitors manufacture in a way that results in lower cost, higher quality, and better delivery, performance, flexibility, and innovativeness. The compa-

Infant 1.0	Average 2.0	Adult 3.0	World Class 4.0
Production system barely contributes to the company's success.	Production system keeps up with competitors and maintains the status quo.	Production system provides market qualifying and order winning outputs at target levels (Chapter 6).	Production system tries to be the best in the industry in each activity in each production subsystem (lever).
Manufacturing is low-tech and unskilled.	Manufacturing consists of standard, routine activities.	Manufacturing decisions are consistent with manufacturing strategy.	Production system is an important source of competitive advantage.

Figure 5-6 Overall Level of Manufacturing Capability

nies make changes to improve production systems. This raises the level of manufacturing capability and the levels of the manufacturing outputs.

Industry Average Overall Level of Manufacturing Capability

In a production system with an industry average level of manufacturing capability, the production system operates like production systems at competitors. Most companies in the industry have similar facilities, employ similar process technologies, use the same suppliers, follow industry-wide employment practices, and so on. Economies of scale are pursued. New techniques and technologies are adopted only when most companies in the industry use them.

An industry average level of manufacturing capability is adequate when the market is growing and an established group of competitors exists. It is not adequate when the market stops growing and there is excess capacity in the industry or when new competitors appear. Sometimes, offshore competitors enter the market and gain market share by providing higher levels of the manufacturing outputs. They can do this because they have higher manufacturing capabilities or use different production systems. Then, companies with industry average levels of capability make improvements in their production systems and increase their capabilities.

Adult Overall Level of Manufacturing Capability

When manufacturing capability is at an adult level, the analysis and planning principles outlined in this book are applied. Focused factories are organized, each with a production system capable of providing the required manufacturing outputs at the required levels (Chapter 6). Management takes a long-term view.

Achieving an adult level of manufacturing capability is quite an accomplishment. However, an even higher level of capability is possible.

World Class Overall Level of Manufacturing Capability

A production system with a world class level of manufacturing capability provides more than just one manufacturing output at the highest possible level. For example, the production system can be the highest quality, lowest cost producer in the industry. Providing two outputs at the highest possible levels gives a company a major competitive advantage over competitors; especially those who, because of low manufacturing capability, struggle to provide even one output at a high level (Chapter 6).

Production systems with world class capabilities develop much of their own process technology because their requirements and expertise exceed the capabilities of equipment suppliers. They acquire expertise in new technologies before the technologies are proven. They make equal investments in structure, such as equipment, facilities, and suppliers; and in infrastructure, such as information systems, operating practices, planning procedures, and training.

Level of Capability of a Manufacturing Lever

A production system's overall capability is the sum of the capabilities of each subsystem or lever: The higher the manufacturing capability of each lever, the higher the overall capability of the production system.

The manufacturing capability of a lever is also measured on a scale from 1.0 to 4.0. A value of 1.0 indicates an infant level of capability; 2.0 is industry average; 3.0 is adult; and 4.0 is world class. Exactly what constitutes each level of each lever varies from industry to industry. Companies use benchmarking (Chapter 14) to make these determinations. The scale in Figure 5-7 is a useful starting point for measuring the level of capability for a lever. It is modified as benchmarking data are collected.

The level of capability is not necessarily the same for each lever. For example, a production system may have an adult level of capability in human resources, an infant level of capability in production planning and control, and industry average levels of capability in process technology and facilities. Levers with lower levels of capability diminish the overall level of capability of the production system. Manufacturing strategy identifies these levers and the adjustments needed to raise the low levels of capability. The goal is to have a production system where all levers have the same high level of capability.

Industry Average Level of Capability for a Lever

A production system with an industry average level of manufacturing capability tends to have a relatively unskilled and closely supervised workforce that has little employment security and involvement in decision making or problem solving. The organization structure is hierarchical, decision making is centralized, and staff groups are influential.

Performance measurement systems are based on cost accounting measures. Production planning and control systems are centralized and include complex procedures for tracking the uses of materials and other resources.

A large network of suppliers is used, and multiple sources are maintained for each purchased item. Suppliers are kept at arm's length. Short-term contracts are awarded on the basis of lowest cost. Process technology is mature. The production system's view of technology is that it is developed by equipment suppliers and is used to reduce costs. Equipment and facilities are general purpose. Changes occur infrequently and are large when they do. The pace of change is controlled by a rigid capital appropriation request procedure (Chapter 17).

World Class Level of Capability for a Lever

A production system with a world class level of manufacturing capability is very different. Human resources are treated as an investment, an asset to be improved through training. Human resource policies include employment security and employee participation in problem solving. Decision making is pushed to the "lowest level of competence," which is the lowest level in the production system where employees have competence to make good decisions. Training raises competence in all levels of the production system.

Organization structure is flat, line groups are more influential, and performance measures are tied to providing high levels of the manufacturing outputs. Frequent, incremental improvements raise the level of manufacturing capability so that higher levels of the outputs are provided. Production planning and control systems are decentralized and simple. Just-in-time techniques, such as pull systems and setup time reduction, are used.

Manufacturing Levers	Level of Manufacturing Capability Infant 1.0	Average 2.0	Adult 3.0	World Class 4.0
Human resources		• Employees are an expense • Unskilled • Human robots		• Employees are an investment • Multiskilled • Problem identification and solving
Organization structure and controls		• Hierarchical, centralized • Cost accounting driven performance measures • Staff is very important		• Flat, decentralized • Competitive performance measures • Line is very important
Production planning and control		• Centralized, complex • Detailed monitoring of resource usage		• Decentralized, simple • Aggregate monitoring of resource usage
Sourcing		• Large number of suppliers • Short-term contracts • Lowest cost		• Small number of suppliers • Partnership, full responsibility • Critical capabilities
Process technology		• Mature technology • Developed externally • Reduce cost		• Modern soft and hard technologies • Developed internally • Provide manufacturing outputs
Facilities		• General purpose • Large, infrequent changes • Capital appropriation driven		• Focused • Frequent, incremental changes • Improve capabilities

Figure 5-7 Level of Manufacturing Capability for Each Manufacturing Lever

Shop floor procedures for monitoring and controlling activities are limited to aggregate control of resources released to production and monitoring products produced.

Partnerships are developed with a small number of suppliers possessing critical capabilities. Long-term contracts are the norm. Suppliers are given responsibility for improving quality, reducing cost, and improving product design. Process technology is often developed internally. Technology is seen as a means of providing higher levels of the manufacturing outputs. Soft and hard technologies are equally important (Chapter 15). Facilities and equipment are more specialized.

The following questions help determine whether a production system has a world class level of manufacturing capability:

How Is New Process Technology Developed?

A production system with a world class level of capability is actively involved (alone or in partnership with others) in developing new process technology. The production system is interested in acquiring expertise in new technology even before the technology is proven. The production system cannot simply purchase technology from equipment suppliers because its capabilities and requirements exceed what suppliers provide.

How Are Employees Compensated?

The compensation systems used in production systems with world class levels of capability have the following characteristics. Incentives (such as gain sharing and profit sharing) are an important part of the compensation package and are used to encourage teamwork. Compensation is linked to mastery of skills. All employee groups sacrifice equally during economic downturns.

In contrast, compensation used in production systems with low levels of capability are characterized by incentives based on individual output, pay scales based on job classifications, and proportionately more layoffs of hourly employees, compared to staff and management employees, during economic downturns.

Another Manufacturing Capability Tool

Figure 5-8 shows another tool that helps assess manufacturing capability. This tool summarizes current policies and practices in each manufacturing lever and assesses strengths and weaknesses.

Manufacturing Capability and Competitive Advantage

Figure 5-9 shows the relationship between the production system, the manufacturing outputs, the manufacturing levers, and the level of manufacturing capability. Situation 5.2 gives an example.

Managers who do not look outside their own companies tend to overrate their manufacturing capability. Accurately assessing the level of manufacturing capability requires information about practices and processes in the company, at other companies in the same industry, and at companies in other industries. *Benchmarking* is the tool used to gather this information (Chapter 14). Benchmarking also discovers better practices that can raise the level of capability.

Strategy is a way to match internal capabilities with external opportunities. Failing to achieve a match, by over- or under-estimating manufacturing capability, can have dire consequences. Situation 5.3 gives an example of what can go wrong. Rolls-Royce's aircraft engine division overestimated its manufacturing capability so badly in the late 1960s that it went bankrupt in 1971.

Summary

A production system consists of six subsystems:

- Human resources
- Organization structure and controls
- Sourcing
- Production planning and control
- Process technology
- Facilities

The subsystems are called manufacturing levers. The positions of the six levers determine whether the production system is a job shop, batch flow, operator-paced line flow, equipment-paced line flow, continuous flow, just-in-time, or FMS.

Adjustments to manufacturing levers should not be made haphazardly. Each adjustment should be appropriate for the existing production system and should help the production system provide the manufacturing outputs at required levels. Small adjustments can be made to one or more levers to improve an existing production system. Extensive

Manufacturing Unit *Wire and Cable Business Unit at Packard Bell*

Manufacturing Lever	Description of Past Policy	Strengths	Weaknesses
Human resources	Strong quality of work life programs	Employees participate in decisions Good communication	Compensation system does not consider quality
Organization structure and controls	Control systems have short-term, tactical orientation Respond to key customer in principal lines	Good control orientation Low risk	Shortsighted system Reactive rather than anticipatory, focus concept ignored
Sourcing	Significant backward integration—all the way to wire rod	Good control over cost and quality	Less focus, transfer pricing complications
Production planning and control	Use overtime, third shift, and inventory to respond to cyclical demand	Flexibility	Costly layoffs and overtime
Process technology	Cable and copper in automated continuous process Printed circuits in job shop Heavy use of statistical process control and cost of quality tools	State-of-the-art in cable and copper Integrated approach, top management support	Automation in printed circuits could reduce costs Quality lags relative to Japanese competition
Facilities	Process focus	Economies of scale	Long physical supply distances

Adapted from Fine, C., and Hax, A., "Manufacturing Strategy: A Methodology and an Illustration," *Interfaces*, Vol. 15, No. 6, pp. 28–46, 1985.

Figure 5-8 Assessing Policies in Manufacturing Levers

adjustments to all six levers are required when the existing production system is changed to a different production system.

The levels at which the manufacturing outputs are provided depend on the production system used and the level of manufacturing capability of the production system. A production system's level of capability is the sum of the levels of capability of each production subsystem or lever.

Manufacturing capability is measured on a continuous scale from 1.0 to 4.0: 1.0 is an infant level of capability; 2.0 is an industry average level; 3.0 is an adult level; and 4.0 is a world class level. Manufacturing capability is the foundation on which changes and improvements are built. The higher the level of manufacturing capability, the easier it is to make changes and improvements. Companies with a world class level of capability

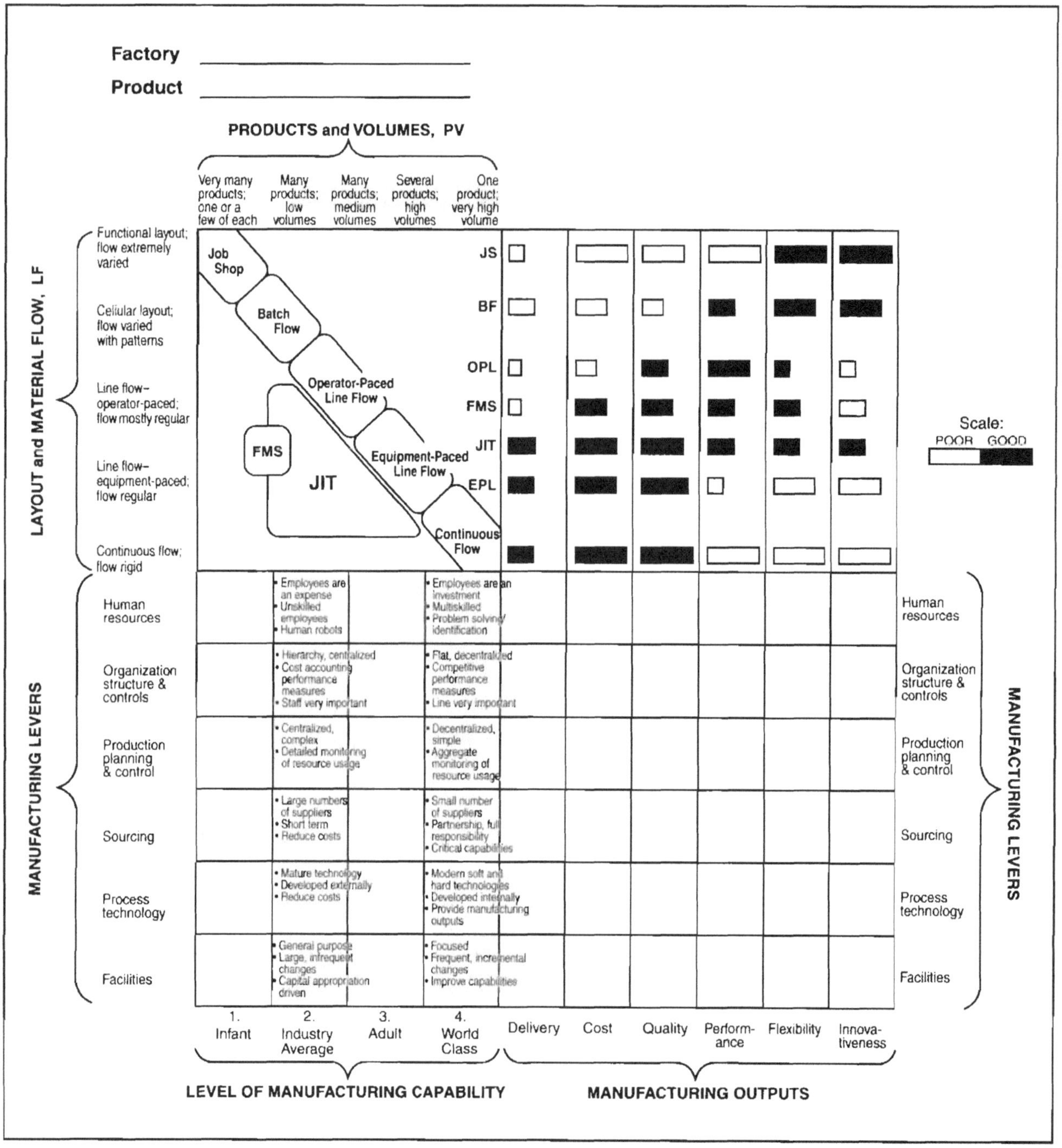

Figure 5-9 Adding Level of Manufacturing Capability to the Worksheet

can provide more than one manufacturing output at the highest possible level. This gives them a major competitive advantage over competitors; especially those who, because of low manufacturing capability, struggle to provide even one output at a high level.

SITUATION 5.2

DEC Raises Level of Manufacturing Capability[4]

IN THE 1970S AND 80S, Digital Equipment Corporation (DEC) enjoyed great success with its technologically innovative products. This success was in spite of manufacturing capabilities at the infant level. Success started to decrease in 1983. Shipments were missed, quality dropped, market share decreased, and stock price fell.

DEC responded with a sustained effort to raise its manufacturing capabilities and transform its factories into sources of competitive advantage. Ten years later and after much hard work, the company had an adult level of manufacturing capability. Figure 5-10 shows results from one factory. The following were some of DEC's accomplishments along the way:

INFANT LEVEL OF CAPABILITY

In 1983, DEC's infant level of capability prevented it from providing manufacturing outputs at the levels required by its customers.

STEP 1: "CLASS A" MRP II

DEC wanted its factories to perform all manufacturing activities competently, so it set a goal to achieve "Class A" MRP II certification. The goal focused improvement efforts on consistency in production, and inventory and bill of material accuracy. By 1986, 25 factories were certified, and the level of manufacturing capability was nearing industry average.

STEP 2: QUALITY AND JUST-IN-TIME

Improvement efforts continued with the introduction of a quality management program to improve quality, and just-in-time techniques to improve cost and delivery. These efforts raised the level of manufacturing capability to industry average. DEC factories provided manufacturing outputs at the levels required by customers.

STEP 3: ADULT LEVEL OF CAPABILITY

By 1989, DEC used benchmarking, continuous improvement, and employee involvement. The level of manufacturing capability was close to the adult level. DEC provided some manufacturing outputs at levels that exceeded customer expectations.

Performance Measures	1985	1986	1987	1988	1989
Manufacturing cycle time	10 weeks	2 weeks	5 days	3 days	2.5 days
Master schedule performance	75%	85%	97%	97%	99%
WIP inventory turns	less than 20	less than 20	23	49	65

Figure 5-10 Some Results from One DEC Factory

SITUATION 5.3

Rolls-Royce Overestimates Its Level of Manufacturing Capability[5]

ROLLS-ROYCE WAS ONCE the most famous engineering company in the world. Although known to the general public as a producer of luxury automobiles, its major product was aircraft engines. For decades, Rolls-Royce performed magnificently in this field. Among other accomplishments, it produced the Merlin piston engine, which powered the Spitfires and Hurricane fighters of World War II, and the first jet engine used in commercial aircraft.

In the mid-1960s, Rolls-Royce found itself in a predicament. Its major aircraft engines were in the maturity, saturation, and decline stages of their product life cycles (Chapter 16), and the company lacked new products to replace them. Several new engine programs had been initiated, but these were for small market segments. Another engine manufacturer had been acquired, but that company's capabilities and order book did not solve many problems for the core Rolls-Royce operation.

In this gloomy situation, the U.S. civil aviation market looked like a saving opportunity. The new wide-body Douglas and Lockheed aircraft were in early development, and Rolls-Royce was determined to enter the market with a new engine. The bidding was intense. Customers were more cost- and delivery-conscious than Rolls-Royce's traditional military and government customers. Rolls-Royce competed against established companies such as Pratt and Whitney and General Electric. In 1968, Rolls-Royce won a major order from Lockheed but at a low, fixed price with significant late delivery penalties.

The happiness over the order faded in the next few months when Rolls-Royce began to realize that it lacked the design and manufacturing capabilities required for the project. Major difficulties emerged in product and process technology, organization structure and controls, and production planning and control.

Product and Process Technology

The new engine incorporated new, unproven technologies. This was difficult for Rolls-Royce because the company was a technology follower, not a leader. Unanticipated problems and delays occurred when internal and supplier capabilities overloaded. Development costs, originally estimated at £65 million, doubled to £135 million by early 1970 and nearly doubled again to £220 million in 1971.

Organization Structure and Controls

Rolls-Royce was a company dominated by engineers. Financial issues often subordinated to technical issues. The company was financially unsophisticated. This, combined with the urgency of the project, enabled serious financial errors to slip by unnoticed.

Production Planning and Control

While Rolls-Royce was well equipped to handle complex, ongoing production activities, it was not equipped to handle complex development projects like this one.

In 1971, Rolls-Royce fell into bankruptcy, mostly from severely overestimating its capabilities.

Endnotes

1. Many articles tell the story of Harley-Davidson's transformation. See, for example, Gelb, T., "Harley-Davidson: A Company That's Taking a Different Route," *Target*, Vol. 1, pp. 4–5, October 1985; and Saathoff, J., "Maintaining Excellence Through Change," *Target*, Vol. 5, No. 1, pp. 13–20, 1989.
2. Adesso, G., "Competitive Manufacturing in the Eighties," *Proceedings of the 1985 Annual Conference of the Association for Manufacturing Excellence*, J. Dilworth (ed.), Cincinnati, Ohio (Sept. 12–13, 1985), 1986.
3. Levels of manufacturing capability are similar to the stages of manufacturing effectiveness in Wheelwright, S., and Hayes, R., "Competing Through Manufacturing," *Harvard Business Review*, pp. 99–109, January–February. 1985.
4. Moody, P., "Digital Equipment Corporation: Journeying to Manufacturing Excellence," pp. 175–186 in *Strategic Manufacturing*, P. Moody (ed.), Homewood, IL: Dow-Jones Irwin, 1990.
5. *The Financial Times*, London, England, p. 16, August 3, 1973.

CHAPTER 6

COMPETITIVE ANALYSIS: SELECTING THE BEST PRODUCTION SYSTEM

A company manufactured five kinds of products for three different markets. The first market demanded high quality. In the second, low cost was critical. In the third, rapid introduction of new products was essential. In spite of these different requirements, top management centralized all manufacturing activities in one factory to achieve economies of scale. The result was a failure to achieve high quality, low cost, or the ability to quickly introduce new products. Manufacturing satisfied none of its customers, serious marketing problems occurred, and the company struggled.[1] The company should have organized focused factories, each with a different production system capable of providing the outputs desired by customers.

A company decides which production systems are most suitable through the competitive analysis element of manufacturing strategy. Customer requirements are determined and translated into specific manufacturing outputs, target levels are set for each output, and the production system best able to hit the targets is identified. Several attempts or iterations are usually required to successfully complete this element. A company performs a competitive analysis by completing the following steps:

Step 1: Define Attributes for Each Manufacturing Output. Collect Data.

Frequently used attributes for each manufacturing output were listed in Figure 4-3 (Chapter 4). Benchmarking (Chapter 14) is used to collect numerical data for each attribute of each output for:

- The company's product
- A typical (or average) product in the marketplace
- A strong competitor's product

Step 2: Classify Manufacturing Outputs. Set Targets.

Determine customer needs and expectations, and translate them into manufacturing attributes and outputs. Then, classify each manufacturing output as:

- Market qualifying
- Order winning
- Unimportant

Set 12-month targets for all attributes of the market qualifying and order winning outputs.

Step 3: Select the Best Production System.

Select the production system that best hits the targets in Step 2. If necessary, return to Step 2.

A manufacturing output (cost, quality, performance, delivery, flexibility, innovativeness) can be unimportant, market qualifying, or order winning, depending on whether it will be provided at a medium, high, or very high level.

Market Qualifying and Order Winning Outputs

Market qualifying outputs are what customers expect to receive. A product needs these outputs to compete in the marketplace, and a company is at a competitive disadvantage if it cannot provide them. Providing a market qualifying output means providing each attribute of that output at a high level, called the *market qualifying level.*

An order winning output is provided at a higher level than the market qualifying level. It is provided at the *order winning level*—the highest level possible in the industry. Order winning outputs are not common in the marketplace. They differentiate companies from one another and are the reasons customers buy from particular companies. If the level of an order winning output is raised, orders increase. Providing an output at an order winning level makes a company an industry leader for that product and output.

Market qualifying outputs in a production system are like satisfier features in a product (Chapter 4). Customers expect a production system to provide market qualifying outputs, and when it does, customers are satisfied. Order winning outputs in a production system are like exciter-delighter features in a product: a pleasant surprise that excites and delights customers.

Figure 4-4 (Chapter 4) gave examples of products for which one manufacturing output was more important than others. These are the order winning outputs. For example, performance was the order winning output for Tide detergent. Customers buy Tide because of its exceptionally high level of performance. Competitors' products cannot clean clothes as well as Tide. Cost and quality are also important manufacturing outputs, and Procter & Gamble, the manufacturer of Tide, provides these outputs at high, market qualifying levels. However, since performance is the order winning output, it is provided at a higher level than the market qualifying level. It is provided at the highest possible level in the industry, a level that few competitors can match.

The ability of a production system to provide market qualifying and order winning manufacturing outputs depends on two characteristics of the production system:

- The type of production system (Chapter 4)
- The level of manufacturing capability of the production system (Chapter 5)

The first task of a production system is to provide market qualifying outputs at market qualifying levels. When this is done, a production system does its best to provide one or perhaps two order winning outputs at order winning levels.

A production system with a less than industry average level of manufacturing capability cannot provide any manufacturing outputs at order winning levels; a production system with an industry average to adult level of manufacturing capability can provide one manufacturing output at an order winning level; and a production system with a world class level of manufacturing capability can provide two manufacturing outputs at order winning levels.

Toyota can provide two manufacturing outputs at order winning levels. Toyota has two marketing slogans: "There's quality and there's Toyota quality," and "Toyota, I love what you do for me." These suggest that Toyota tries to provide quality and performance at order winning levels. Toyota's JIT production system makes this possible.

- A JIT production system provides high levels of quality and performance. (Check the black bars for these outputs in Figure 6-1.)
- Toyota's JIT production system has a world class level of manufacturing capability. A production system with this level of capability can provide two manufacturing outputs at order winning levels.

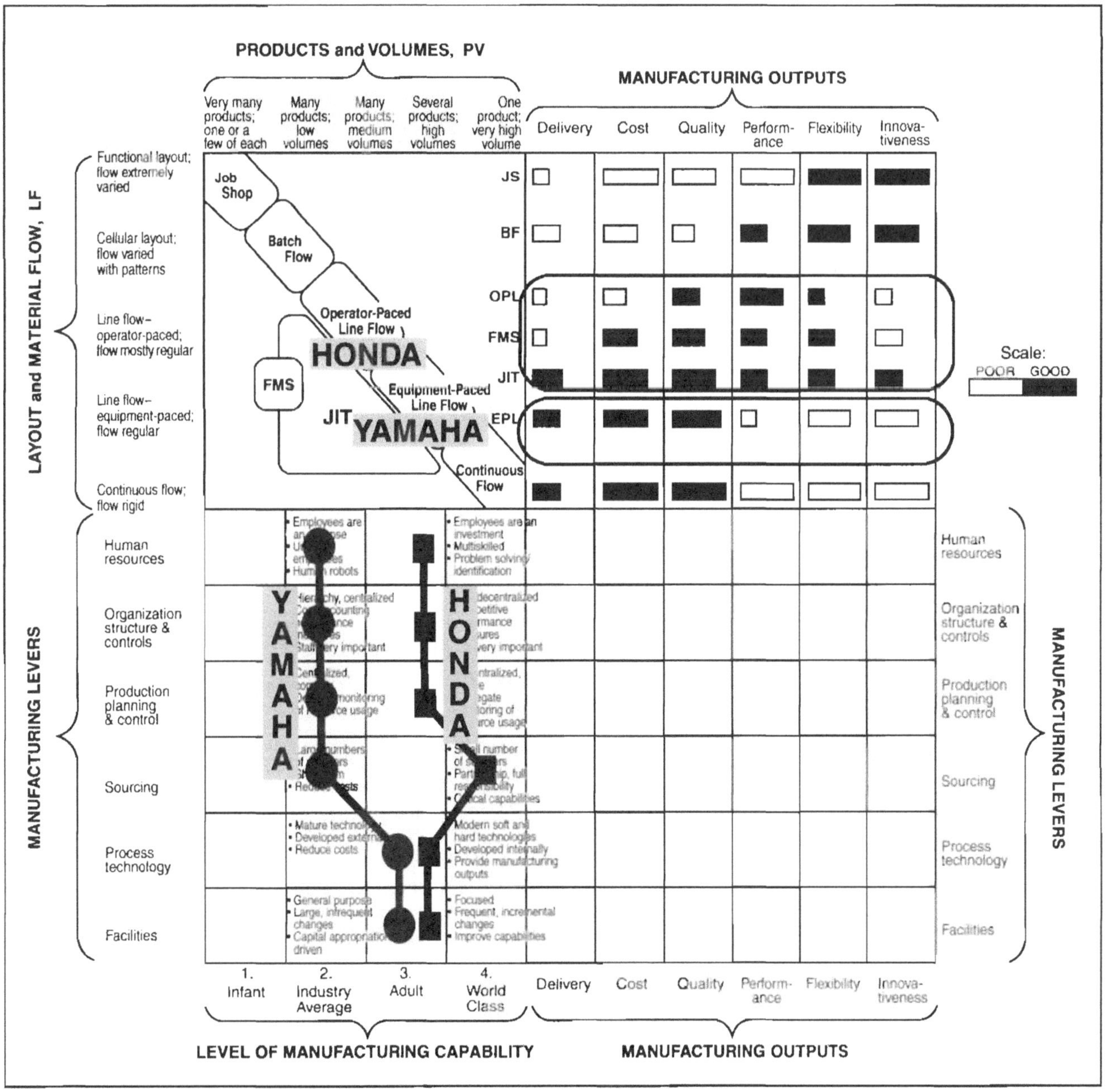

Figure 6-1 Production Systems, Manufacturing Outputs, Level of Manufacturing Capability in the Honda-Yamaha War

SITUATION 6.1

The Honda-Yamaha War[2]

THE HONDA-YAMAHA WAR started in 1981 when Yamaha announced the opening of a new motorcycle factory. That factory made Yamaha the world's largest motorcycle manufacturer, a prestigious position previously held by Honda. Honda had been concentrating on its automobile business, but now, faced with Yamaha's challenge to its motorcycle business, it counterattacked. (Chapter 2 discusses strategic challenges and defensive responses.)

In the war that followed, Honda provided customers with increasingly higher levels of its manufacturing outputs. It raised the levels of its market qualifying outputs, cost and delivery, by cutting prices and flooding distribution channels. It raised the levels of its order winning outputs, innovativeness and performance, by introducing new products and raising the technological sophistication of current products. At the start of the war, Honda and Yamaha each had 60 models of motorcycles. Over the next 18 months, Honda introduced or replaced 113 models, while Yamaha could only manage 37 changes. Honda also introduced four-valve engines, composite materials, direct drive, and other features.

Since Yamaha could not provide these manufacturing outputs at the new market qualifying levels, let alone at order winning levels, demand for Yamaha products disappeared. At one point, Yamaha had more than 12 months of inventory in its dealer showrooms.

Finally, Yamaha surrendered. In a public statement, Yamaha's president announced, "We want to end the Honda-Yamaha war. It is our fault. Of course, there will be competition in the future, but it will be based on a mutual recognition of our competitive positions."

ANALYSIS

Honda raised the level of its market qualifying outputs, cost and delivery, and its order winning outputs, performance and innovativeness, so much that it almost forced its competitor, Yamaha, out of the industry. Figure 6-1 shows the two reasons why Honda was able to do this.

Honda's production systems were more suitable for providing the order winning outputs than Yamaha's. Honda used operator-paced line flow and JIT production systems, while Yamaha used equipment-paced line flow production systems. Operator-paced line flow and JIT production systems can provide higher levels of performance and innovativeness (order winning outputs) than equipment-paced line flow production systems. (Check the black and white bars for these outputs in Figure 6-1.)

The other reason that Honda was able to raise the levels of its market qualifying and order winning outputs was its higher level of manufacturing capability. Yamaha had just completed a period of expansion, during which it built new facilities, hired new employees, started new processes, and launched new systems. The expansion spread Yamaha's existing manufacturing capability over a larger number of sites and operations. This dilution of expertise reduced Yamaha's overall level of manufacturing capability.

Figure 6-1 shows manufacturing capability profiles for Honda and Yamaha at the time of the Honda-Yamaha war. The level of manufacturing capability for each of the first three levers was 3.5 for Honda and 2.5 for Yamaha. The lower figures for Yamaha were due to its expansion. The level of manufacturing capability for sourcing was 4.0 at Honda because Honda's suppliers were the industry's best. The level of manufacturing capability for process technology and facilities was high for Yamaha because many of its processes and facilities were new. The level of manufacturing capability for process technology and facilities was also high for Honda. Although Honda's processes and facilities were older, the company's established improvement programs had made numerous improvements over the years.

Honda's manufacturing capability profile was better than Yamaha's. In addition, those levers that most affected the performance and innovativeness outputs—organization structure and controls, production planning and control, and sourcing—had higher levels of capability at Honda than at Yamaha.

In summary, Honda won the Honda-Yamaha war because Honda's production systems could better provide the outputs customers wanted, and it had higher levels of manufacturing capability.

Competitive Analysis at ABC Company

This section gives a detailed example to show how companies follow the three steps to complete a competitive analysis described at the beginning of this chapter.

ABC was a Fortune 500 company. One of its factories manufactured four product families. Three product families were built to customer order and required significant amounts of custom engineering. The other product family consisted of standard products. All product families were manufactured in a modern factory using a batch flow production system. The factory had been unprofitable for much of the last ten years. Top management decided to make one last attempt to turn the factory around. They assigned a dynamic manager to the factory and told him to make the factory profitable within four years or it would close.

The manager organized a new management team. The team quickly realized that improvements in the production of one product family, QH4500, would have to provide most of the profits for the factory. QH4500 had recently been redesigned, so it was up to date. It had a sizable market share and accounted for almost 50 percent of the factory's sales. Before making any changes in the factory, the team did the following competitive analysis:

Step 1: Define Attributes. Collect Data.

The management team asked the marketing department, located 100 miles away at company headquarters, for information about customer needs and the cost, quality, performance, and delivery of competitors' products. The marketing department was unable and unwilling to provide these data, so the factory gathered it on its own. Customers told the factory:

- "Delivery is a problem in the marketplace. If ABC could deliver the product in 16 weeks, it would own the market."
- "When you buy QH4500, you buy quality."
- "QH4500 is the Cadillac product in the marketplace."

The factory decided that delivery, cost, quality, and performance were the important manufacturing outputs for QH4500.

Figure 6-2 shows other key data collected. Each important output is separated into attributes in the first row. Current values of the attributes are shown in the second row. Delivery consisted of delivery time and delivery time reliability. Delivery time was the number of weeks between accepting an order and delivering it to the customer (currently 22 weeks), and delivery time reliability was the percentage of all customer orders delivered on time (currently 60 percent). Cost was the factory cost of producing one QH4500 unit (currently $40,000). Three important quality attributes were: average factory rework cost per unit (currently $2,000), average defects per unit detected in the final test department (currently 3 defects), and warranty costs as a percentage of sales (currently 4 percent). Performance consisted of the number of standard features (currently 5) and the number of advanced features (currently 3).

The next two rows in Figure 6-2 show current values of the attributes for competitors' products. Values for an "average product" in the market are shown first. Then, values are shown for the strongest competitor's product. For example, delivery time was 25 weeks for an average product and 20 weeks for the strongest competitor. Data could not be obtained for every attribute.

Step 2: Select Market Qualifying and Order Winning Outputs. Set Targets.

The team decided that delivery, cost, quality, and performance were market qualifying outputs and set the following 12-month targets for the market qualifying levels:

- Cost must decrease to $37,000 per unit for QH4500 to remain competitive in the marketplace.
- Quality improvements were needed. The target for rework cost was $1,000 per unit. The target for defects per unit in the final test department was 1.5. No target was set for warranty cost, which was expected to drop when factory improvements were made.
- To provide performance at a market qualifying level, one additional advanced feature was needed.
- The target market qualifying level for delivery time was 20 weeks, and the target for delivery time reliability was 70 percent.

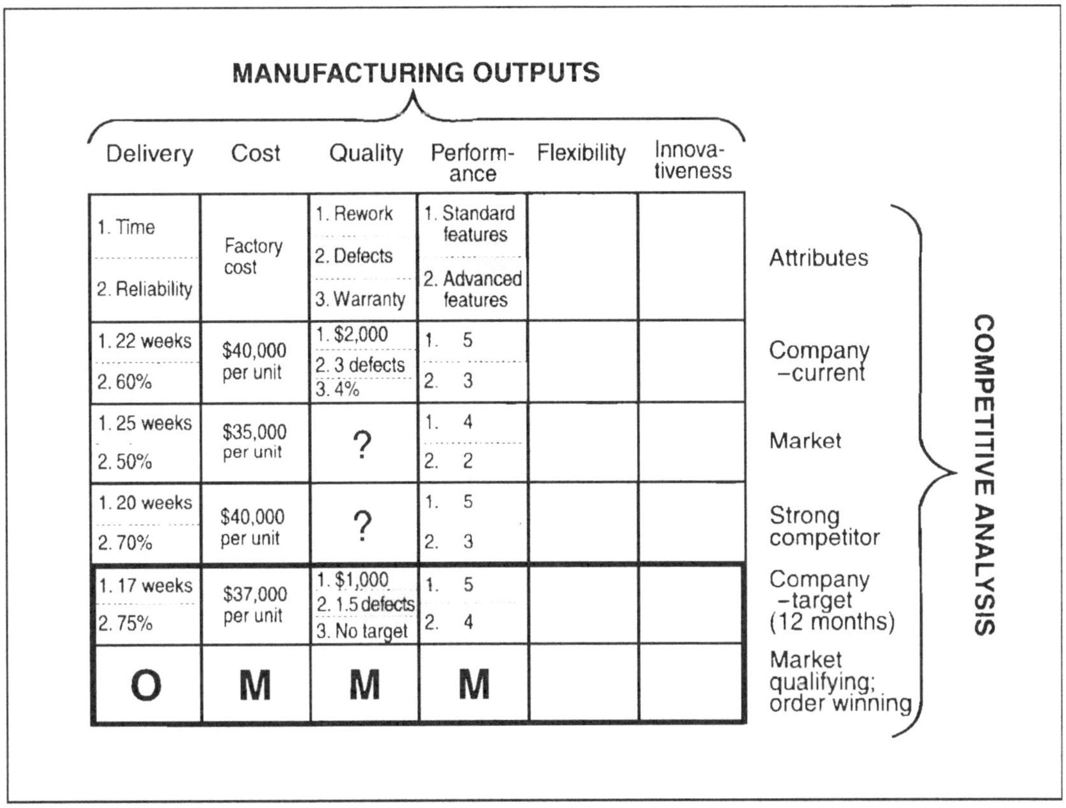

Figure 6-2 Competitive Analysis for Product Family QH4500 at ABC Company

Next, the management team discussed which market qualifying output should become the order winning output. Their deliberations went as follows:

- Cost could not be the order winning output because the factory was located in a part of North America, where the cost of doing business was high. Furthermore, the volume of QH4500 was too low for the batch flow production system to change to an equipment-paced line flow production system, which was necessary to become the industry's low cost producer.
- Quality could also not be the order winning output because the factory lacked the necessary resources to make enough quality improvements to become the industry's quality leader.
- Performance seemed like a good choice for the order winning output because QH4500 already had a reputation for excellent performance. There were two reasons, however, why this output was not selected. First, one new advanced feature was needed in the next 12 months to maintain performance at the market qualifying level. The new feature included a component made from a new material, which required new process technology that the company's engineering department was struggling to sort out. Second, there were problems with communications and cooperation between the factory and the product design group, located 100 miles away at company headquarters.
- Delivery was the unanimous choice for order winning output. Market research indicated

that a delivery time near 17 weeks, and high delivery time reliability would increase orders. The factory was located near its North American customers, giving it a natural advantage over its strong offshore competitors. The management team felt that it had control over almost everything that affected delivery. So the team set 12-month targets for the order winning output. Delivery time was 17 weeks, and delivery time reliability was 75 percent (Figure 6-2).

The team was satisfied with its choice of market qualifying and order winning outputs. These were the outputs that customers wanted. In 12 months, they would be provided at much higher levels than the current levels. One of the outputs would be provided at the highest level in the industry. The team's next task was to determine how the factory would provide these outputs. (We will discuss this later in the chapter.)

Another Competitive Analysis Tool

Simpler frameworks than Figure 6-2 are available. Figure 6-3 shows a competitive analysis framework at Packard Electric. The framework assesses the importance and current level of four manufacturing outputs—cost, quality, delivery, and flexibility—for three product families.

Consider the cable product family. Quality is the most important output (value is 40), then cost (value is 30), and so on. The current level of quality is weak, the current level of cost is very strong, and so on. This suggests that quality is the order winning output, cost and delivery are market qualifying outputs, and the production system producing this product family must improve or change to raise the level of quality.

Selecting the Best Production System

Figure 6-4 adds the competitive analysis element to the other elements of the manufacturing strategy framework for a factory. Multifunctional teams, with members from manufacturing, marketing, human resources, finance, and so on, use this worksheet to determine the market qualifying and order winning outputs, the best production system, and the required adjustments to the manufacturing levers.

A focused factory should use the production system most capable of providing market qualifying and order winning outputs at required levels. Required levels mean the levels customers require today and the levels they will require in the future.

Product Family	Cost		Quality		Delivery		Flexibility	
	Importance	Current Level	Importance	Current Level	Importance	Current Level	Importance	Current Level
Cable	30	Very strong	40	Weak	20	Even	10	Weak
Printed circuits	20	Very weak	50	Even	20	Strong	10	Strong
Copper rod	20	Strong	40	Strong	30	Very Strong	10	Weak

Adapted from Fine, C., and Hax, A., "Manufacturing Strategy: A Methodology and an Illustration," *Interfaces*, Vol. 15, No. 6, pp. 28–46, 1985.

Figure 6-3 Simple Competitive Analysis Tool

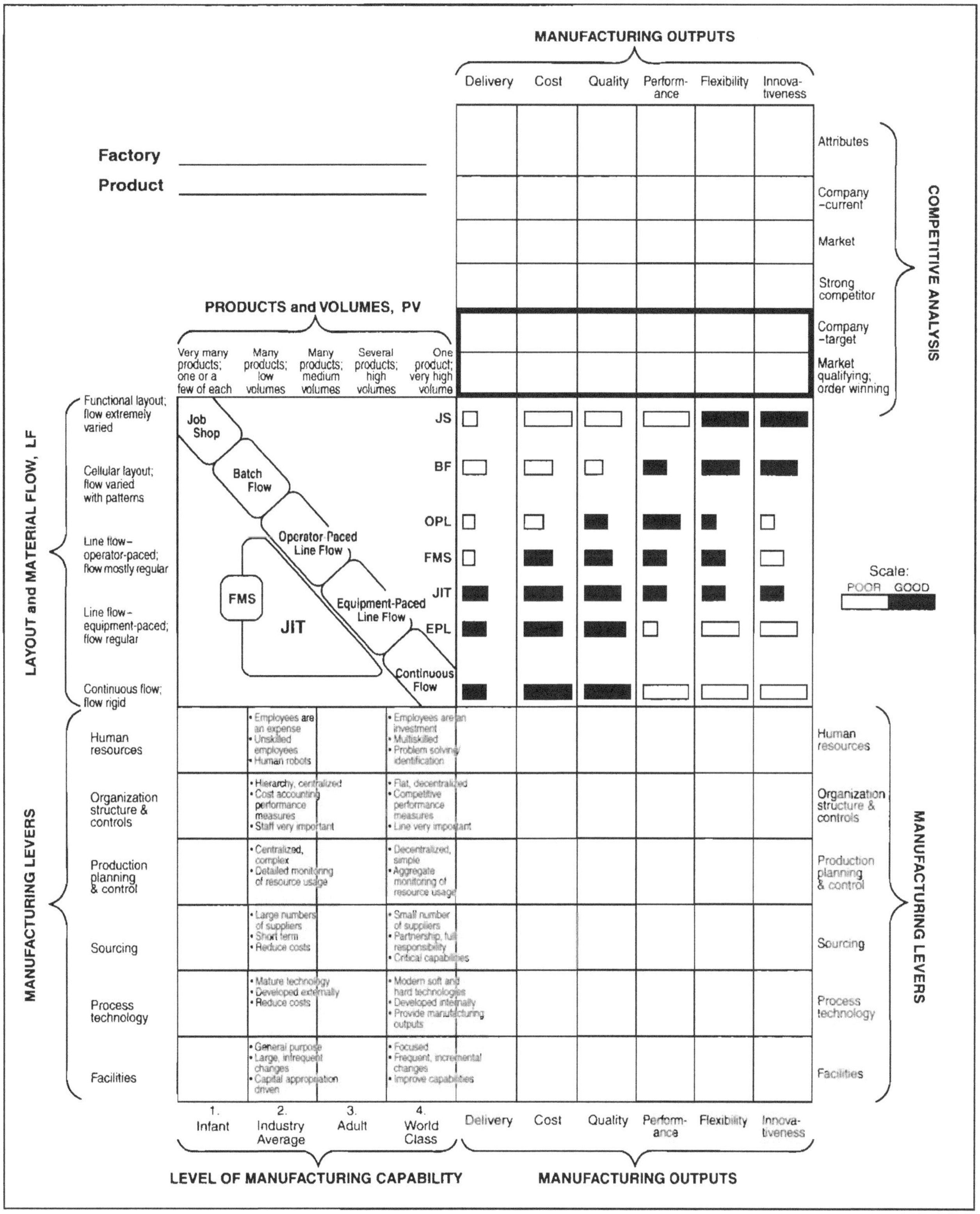

Figure 6-4 Adding Competitive Analysis to the Worksheet

Required levels of market qualifying and order winning outputs increase each year. There are two reasons for this. Every year, customers expect lower cost, higher quality, better performance, better delivery, and more flexibility and innovativeness. Every year, competitors improve their production systems and provide customers with higher levels of market qualifying and order winning outputs.

Sometimes, the current production system is the production system that can best provide market qualifying and order winning outputs at required levels. Sometimes, a different production system is needed. Altogether, there are five possibilities:

- The current production system is the required production system.
- A new production system is required. It is feasible and can be put into service.
- A new production system is required. It is feasible but cannot be put into service.
- A new production system is required, but it is not feasible.
- No production system is capable of providing the required outputs.

A production system is *feasible* for a particular focused factory if it can produce the factory's mix of products and production volumes. For example, a continuous flow production system is not feasible for a focused factory that produces several different products in medium volumes because this production system can only produce one product in a very high volume.

A new production system can be *put into service* when the factory's level of manufacturing capability is high enough to make whatever adjustments are needed to the manufacturing levers (Chapter 5).

The Current Production System Is the Required Production System.

In this situation, the current production system can provide the required market qualifying and order winning outputs at the target levels as long as it is well managed and has a sufficiently high level of manufacturing capability. Well managed means each manufacturing lever is set in the appropriate position for the production system.

A New Production System Is Required. It Is Feasible and Can Be Put Into Service.

In this situation, the current production system cannot provide the required market qualifying or order winning outputs at the target levels. A new production system is identified that can provide the required outputs at the target levels. The new production system is feasible because it can produce the factory's mix of products and production volumes. It can be put into service because the factory has sufficient manufacturing capability to change the current production system to the new one.

A New Production System Is Required. It Is Feasible but Cannot Be Put Into Service.

In this situation, the current production system cannot provide the required market qualifying or order winning outputs at the target levels. A new production system is identified that can provide the required outputs at the target levels. The new production system is feasible because it can produce the factory's mix of products and production volumes. However, it cannot be put into service because the factory lacks the manufacturing capability to change the current production system to the new one. When this happens, management has three options:

- Find a different production system that can provide the required outputs, is feasible, and can be put into service.
- Raise the factory's level of manufacturing capability (Chapters 5 and 14).
- Return to Step 2 of the competitive analysis, and select a different set of market qualifying and order winning outputs.

A New Production System Is Required, but it Is Not Feasible.

In this situation, the current production system cannot provide the required market qualifying or order winning outputs at the target levels. A new production system is identified that can provide the required outputs at the target levels. However, the new production system is not feasible because it cannot produce the factory's mix of products and production volumes. For example, a factory with a job shop production system may wish to change to an equipment-paced line flow production system to lower cost and improve delivery. However, the current production volume is too low to fully utilize the dedicated lines in this production system, and the production volume cannot increase to any great extent. So the equipment-paced line flow production system is not feasible. When this happens, management has two options:

- Find a different production system that can provide the required outputs, is feasible, and can be put into service.
- Return to Step 2 of the competitive analysis, and select a different set of market qualifying and order winning outputs.

No Production System Is Capable of Providing the Required Outputs.

In this situation, none of the seven production systems can provide the required market qualifying and order winning outputs at the target levels. This happens when management wants to provide too many order winning outputs or sets unrealistic targets. Management must return to Step 2 of the competitive analysis, and select a different set of market qualifying and order winning outputs.

Competitive Analysis at ABC Company (*Continued*)

Step 3: Select the Best Production System.

The competitive analysis in Figure 6-3 is shown again on the worksheet in Figure 6-5. It is clear that ABC's batch flow production system cannot provide the market qualifying and order winning outputs. A line flow production system—operator-paced, equipment-paced, JIT, or FMS—is required to provide these outputs. The well-known and easy-to-implement operator-paced and equipment-paced line flow systems are the most attractive. JIT and FMS are less attractive because JIT is difficult to implement and FMS is expensive.

Operator-paced and equipment-paced line flow production systems are feasible when a small number of standard products are produced in medium to high volumes. However, QH4500 was a family of custom-engineered products, and each product was produced in low volumes. To make these production systems feasible, three changes were necessary:

- The ABC design group needed to standardize QH4500. The number of options had to be reduced, and QH4500 had to be redesigned to be easily produced on a line flow production system.
- The ABC marketing group needed to market a standard product with a limited number of options.
- The production volume of QH4500 needed to increase to fully utilize a dedicated production line.

Unfortunately, none of these changes could be made. The design group, located 100 miles away at company headquarters, would not participate in any standardization program beyond an existing program to reduce part numbers to improve the group's CAD system. The marketing group, also located at company headquarters, opposed anything that reduced the options available to customers. As for obtaining extra volume, the factory was told it would not receive new QH4500 volume until it demonstrated it could consistently generate profits.

The inability to standardize QH4500 and obtain higher volumes meant that the operator-paced and equipment-paced line flow production systems were not feasible. The management team

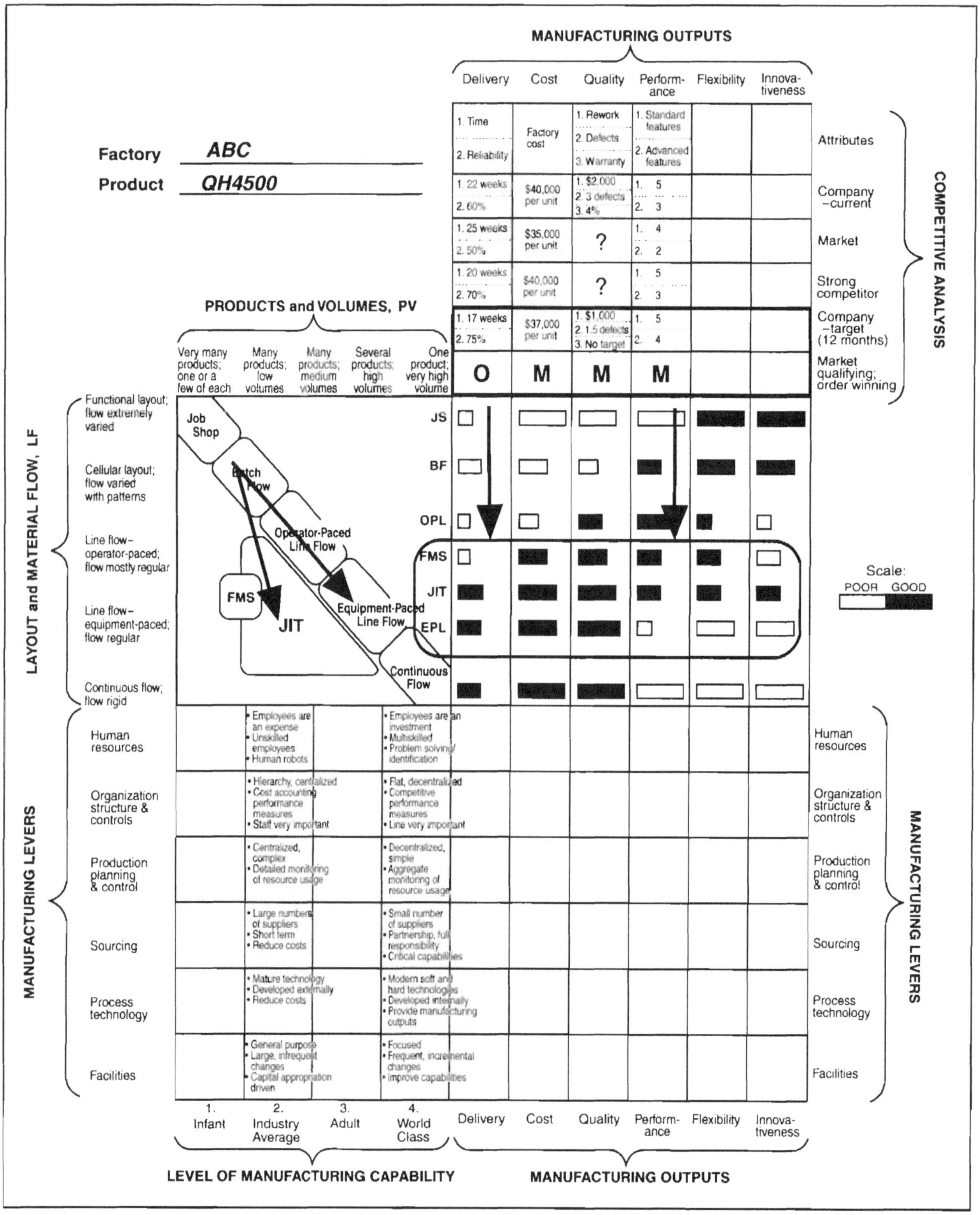

Figure 6-5 Selecting the Best Production System for Product QH4500

ruled out the FMS production system because the factory could not afford the expensive equipment required. The team decided that the required production system for QH4500 would be the difficult-to-implement JIT production system (Figure 6-5).

Next, the management team focused on how the factory would change the current batch flow production system to a new JIT production system. (This is discussed later in the chapter.)

Adjusting Levers and Changing the Production System

When the current production system is the best production system for the focused factory, each manufacturing lever should already be in the right position. All that may be needed are small adjustments to fine-tune the production system. First, each manufacturing lever (human resources, organization structure and controls, sourcing, and so on) is checked and adjusted to ensure it is in the right position for the production system. Then, each lever is adjusted again to help the production system provide the market qualifying and order winning outputs at the target levels.

When the current production system is changed to a new production system, extensive adjustments must be made to the manufacturing levers. Each lever changes from its current position appropriate for the current production system to a new position appropriate for the new production system. More adjustments follow to enable the new production system to provide the market qualifying and order winning outputs at the target levels.

Making extensive adjustments to the manufacturing levers is difficult. An implementation plan is needed to organize the adjustments into a practical plan (Chapter 7). A plan consists of:

- The adjustments to make
- The sequence in which adjustments will be made
- The timetable for making adjustments
- The resources to use

Competitive Analysis at ABC Company (*Continued*)

Figure 6-6 shows some adjustments made to the manufacturing levers when the ABC factory changed its batch flow production system to JIT.

Since the workforce in a JIT production system differs from the workforce in a batch flow production system, numerous adjustments were made to the human resources lever. Training programs taught employees new skills to perform jobs in the JIT production system, and employees learned a range of jobs. The factory and union negotiated a reduction in the number of job classifications and a new pay scheme. The new pay scheme paid employees for the number of jobs they were qualified to do rather than the specific job they did.

The circled number 1 in the row corresponding to the human resources lever in Figure 6-6 represents these adjustments. The position of the circled number is significant for two reasons:

- *Row Position:* The circled number is placed in the row corresponding to the human resources lever because it represents an adjustment that changes this manufacturing lever from one appropriate for the old batch flow production system to one appropriate for the new JIT production system.
- *Column Position:* The circled number is placed in the columns corresponding to the delivery, cost, and quality manufacturing outputs to signify that, of all the adjustments that can be made to this lever, these adjustments are made because they help the new production system provide the required market qualifying and order winning outputs at the target levels.

Chapter 22 examines each of the six levers in a JIT production system.

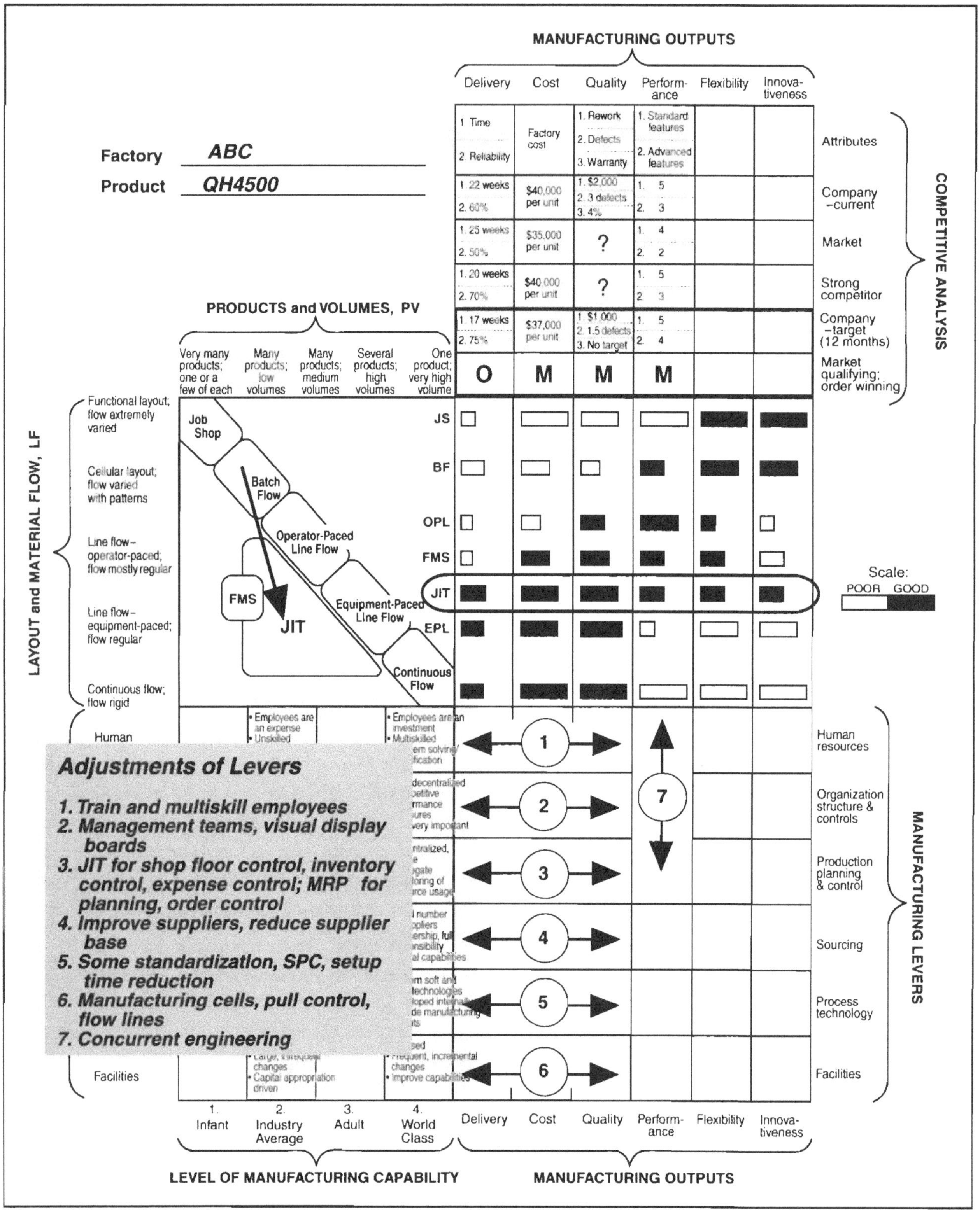

Figure 6-6 Adjusting Levers in the New Production System

Summary

A factory provides six outputs—cost, quality, performance, delivery, flexibility, and innovativeness—to its customers. The levels at which the outputs are provided depend on the production system used and its level of manufacturing capability. No production system can provide all outputs at the highest levels. The outputs that a factory chooses to provide must be those that its customers require.

Competitive analysis is the element of manufacturing strategy that determines what manufacturing outputs customers require and what target levels should be set. A simple and effective way to perform a competitive analysis is outlined in this chapter. It requires data on the factory's products, competitors' products, customer requirements, and the current production system.

Outcomes from the competitive analysis are:

- The market qualifying and order winning manufacturing outputs, with their target levels, for each product or product family
- A production system that can provide the outputs at target levels and can be put into practice by the factory

Several attempts or iterations are usually required to complete the competitive analysis and find a suitable set of outputs and production system.

Endnotes

1. This example is taken from Skinner, W., "Manufacturing Strategy—Missing Link In Corporate Strategy," *Harvard Business Review*, pp. 136–145, May–June 1969.
2. The Honda-Yamaha war is described in Stalk, G., "Time—The Next Source of Competitive Advantage," *Harvard Business Review*, pp. 41–51, July–August 1988.

CHAPTER 7

FRAMEWORK FOR MANUFACTURING STRATEGY IN A FACTORY

A complete framework is now available for developing a factory's manufacturing strategy (Figure 7-1). The framework is used in many ways:

- Analyze a factory.
- Generate and evaluate alternate strategies.
- Analyze competitors' strategies.
- Develop a manufacturing strategy for a factory.
- Help develop a manufacturing strategy for each factory in a manufacturing network.

This chapter examines how the framework develops a manufacturing strategy and implementation plan for a factory. Part III of the book, which begins in the next chapter, uses the framework to help develop a manufacturing strategy for each factory in a manufacturing network.

The procedure for developing a manufacturing strategy for a factory has three steps:

STEP 1: WHERE AM I?

- Determine the factory's current location on the PV-LF matrix and the *production system* in use.
- Assess the current level of capability for each manufacturing lever using the *manufacturing capability* section of the worksheet.

STEP 2: WHERE DO I WANT TO BE?

- Complete a *competitive analysis* to determine the market qualifying and order winning outputs that the production system must provide. Set 12-month targets for each.
- Find the row of outputs on the *manufacturing deliverables* section of the worksheet that best matches the required market qualifying and order winning outputs.
- Determine the *production system* on the PV-LF matrix that best provides these manufacturing outputs.

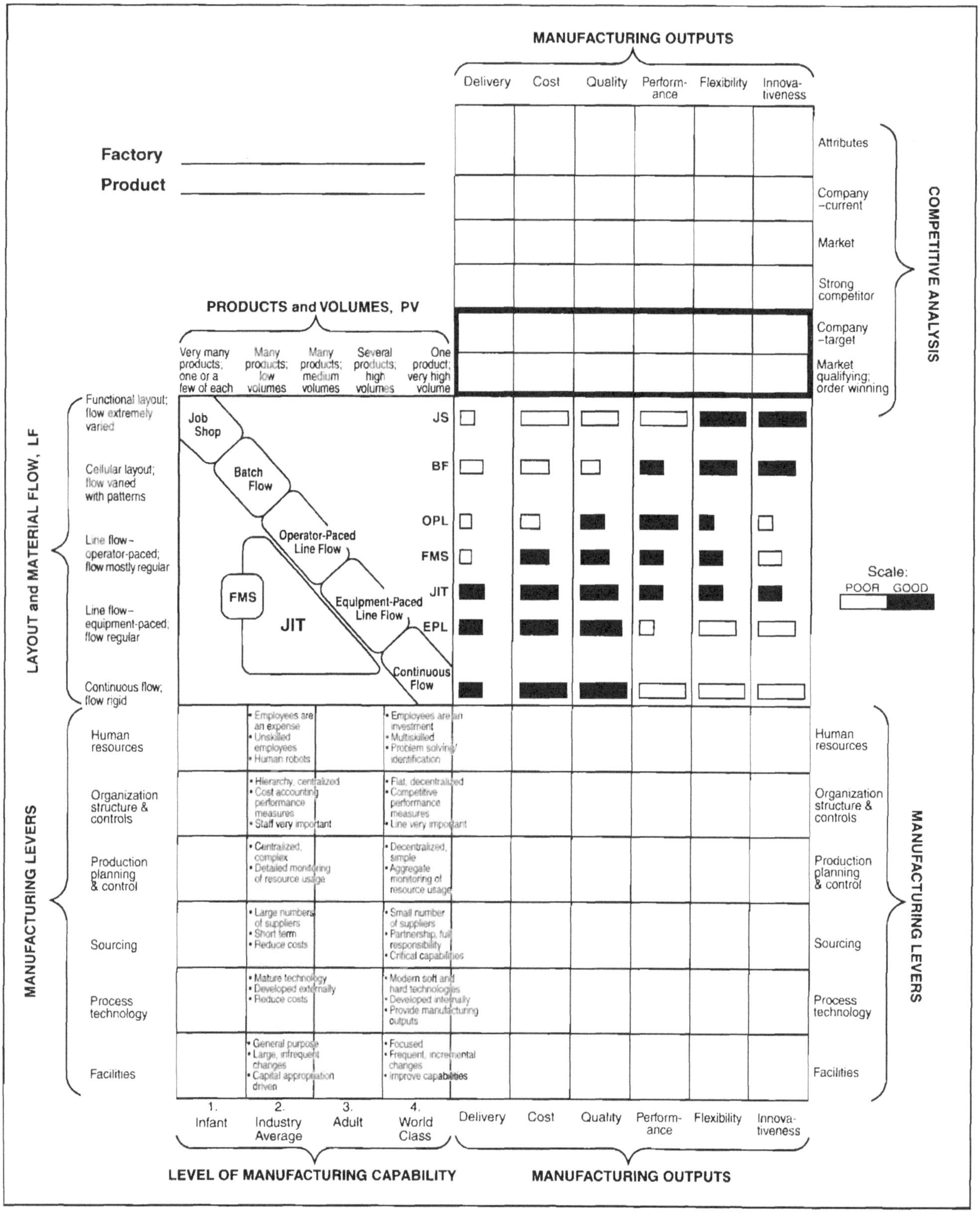

Figure 7-1 Manufacturing Strategy Worksheet for a Factory

Step 3: How Will I Get From Where I Am to Where I Want to Be?

- If the production systems determined in Steps 1 and 2 are the same, adjust the *manufacturing levers* on the levers section of the worksheet so that the production system can better provide the market qualifying and order winning outputs at the target levels. Make sure that these adjustments are possible with the current level of manufacturing capability.
- If the production systems determined in Steps 1 and 2 are not the same, make adjustments to the *manufacturing levers* on the levers section of the worksheet, so:
  - The current production system changes to the desired production system.
  - The required market qualifying and order winning outputs are provided at the target levels.
  - The adjustments can be made with the current level of manufacturing capability.

  If this cannot be done, return to Step 2, select different market qualifying and order winning outputs, and repeat Step 3.

To demonstrate how this procedure works, we show its use at the ABC Company factory from Chapter 6.

Using the Complete Framework at ABC Company

The ABC Company factory's difficulty was an existing batch flow production system that could not provide the new market qualifying and order winning outputs at target levels.

Step 1: Where Is the ABC Factory?

The current production system at the ABC factory was a batch flow system (Figure 7-2). It provided high levels of flexibility and innovativeness—exactly what was required in the past when four families of custom-engineered products were produced by one production system. The current level of manufacturing capability for each lever in the production system is also shown in Figure 7-2. Four levers (organization structure and controls, production planning and control, sourcing, and process technology) had industry average levels of capability. The human resources lever was slightly higher because employees lived in a rural area where people had good work habits. The facilities lever had an adult level of capability because facilities were new and equipment was modern.

The overall level of manufacturing capability for the ABC factory was 2.2, slightly better than industry average. An important consequence of this modest level of capability was that the factory could only implement a small number of changes at any one time.

In summary, the results after Step 1 were:

- Current production system—Batch flow
- Current manufacturing capability—Slightly better than industry average

Step 2: Where Does the ABC Factory Want To Be?

The competitive analysis for product family QH4500 was discussed in Chapter 6. The market qualifying outputs were cost, quality, and performance, and delivery was the order winning output. Twelve-month target levels for these outputs were determined and are shown again in Figure 7-3. The area of the manufacturing deliverables section where these outputs are most easily provided is shown in the figure. The area corresponds to the FMS, JIT, and equipment-paced line flow production systems. Any of these would provide the required outputs for QH4500.

Overlooking product and volume considerations for the moment, the best choice is the equipment-paced line flow production system. This is a well-known production system and is relatively easy to design, install, operate, and manage. JIT and FMS are not as attractive. JIT is a

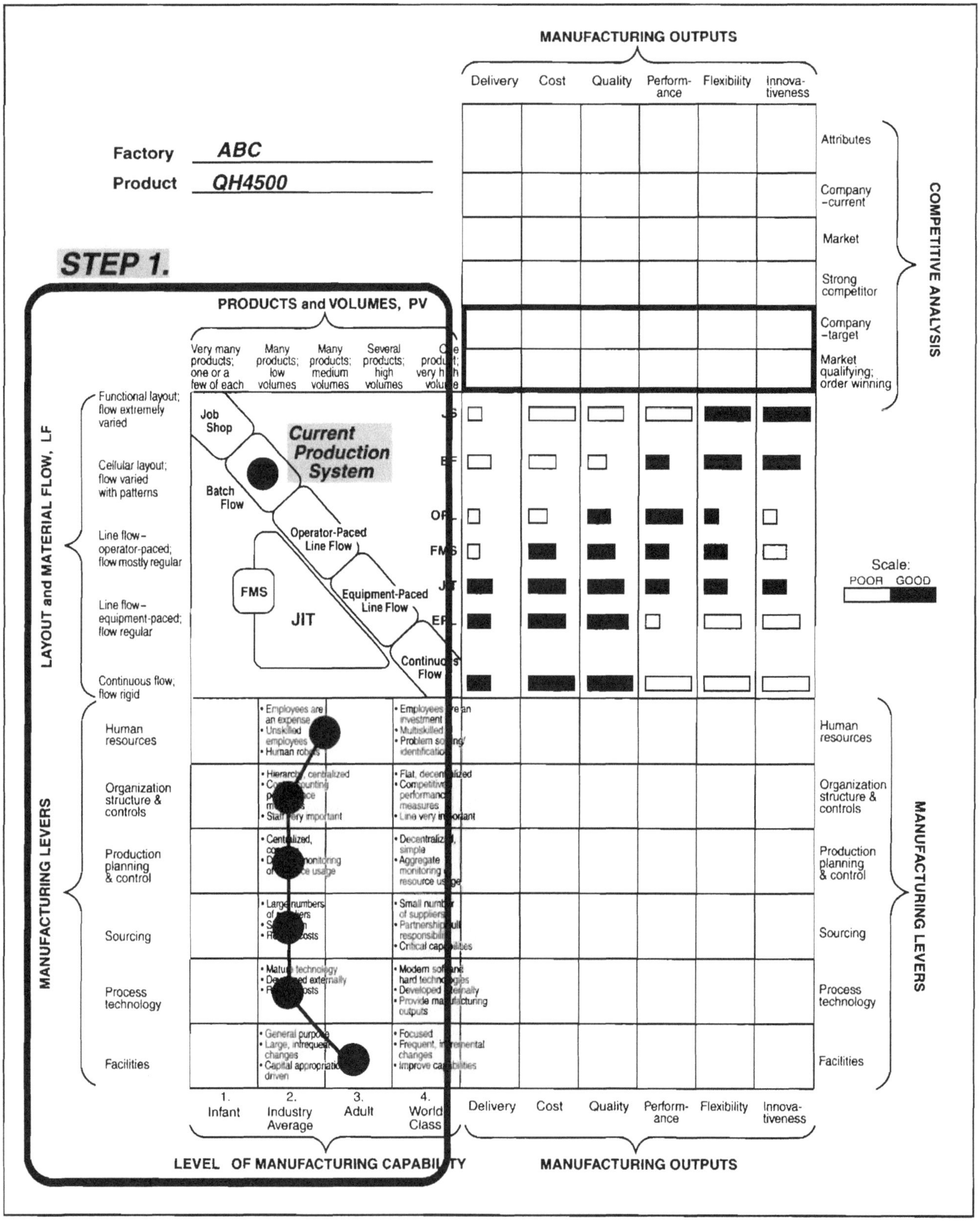

Figure 7-2 Step 1: Where is the ABC Factory?

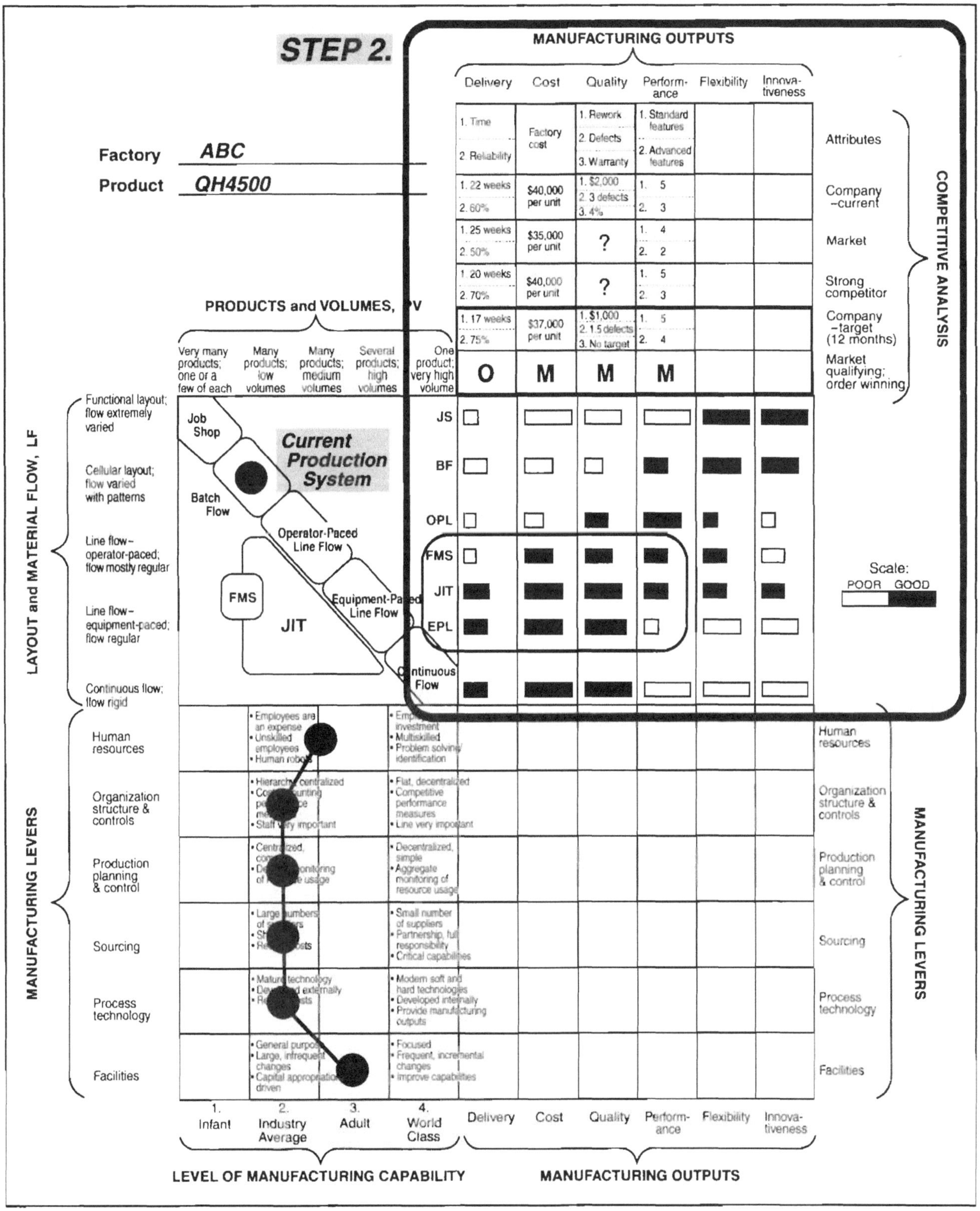

	Delivery	Cost	Quality	Performance	Flexibility	Innovativeness
Attributes	1. Time 2. Reliability	Factory cost	1. Rework 2. Defects 3. Warranty	1. Standard features 2. Advanced features		
Company -current	1. 22 weeks 2. 60%	$40,000 per unit	1. $2,000 2. 3 defects 3. 4%	1. 5 2. 3		
Market	1. 25 weeks 2. 50%	$35,000 per unit	?	1. 4 2. 2		
Strong competitor	1. 20 weeks 2. 70%	$40,000 per unit	?	1. 5 2. 3		
Company -target (12 months)	1. 17 weeks 2. 75%	$37,000 per unit	1. $1,000 2. 1.5 defects 3. No target	1. 5 2. 4		
Market qualifying; order winning	O	M	M	M		

Manufacturing levers	2. Industry Average	4. World Class
Human resources	• Employees are an expense • Unskilled employees • Human robots	• Employees are an investment • Multiskilled • Problem solving/identification
Organization structure & controls	• Hierarchy, centralized • Cost accounting performance measures • Staff very important	• Flat, decentralized • Competitive performance measures • Line very important
Production planning & control	• Centralized, complex • Detailed monitoring of resource usage	• Decentralized, simple • Aggregate monitoring of resource usage
Sourcing	• Large numbers of suppliers • Short term • Reduce costs	• Small number of suppliers • Partnership, full responsibility • Critical capabilities
Process technology	• Mature technology • Developed externally • Reduce costs	• Modern soft and hard technologies • Developed internally • Provide manufacturing outputs
Facilities	• General purpose • Large, infrequent changes • Capital appropriation driven	• Focused • Frequent, incremental changes • Improve capabilities

Figure 7-3 Step 2: Where Does the ABC Factory Want to Be?

very difficult production system to design, operate, and manage (Chapter 22), and FMS requires a large capital investment and highly skilled support personnel (Chapter 20).

Since the QH4500 product family consisted of many custom-engineered products produced in low volumes, it could not be produced on an equipment-paced line flow production system. (See the PV-LF matrix in Figure 7-3.) The ABC factory tried to change the number of products and production volumes for QH4500 so it could be produced on an equipment-paced line flow system.

- The factory asked the product design group to standardize and modularize QH4500. These changes would reduce the number of different products that had to be produced. The design group refused, further straining an already poor relationship between design and manufacturing.
- The factory asked the marketing group to reduce the number of options offered to customers and market a more standard product. The market group refused.
- The factory asked company leaders to give it a larger share of the international market to increase production volume. The leaders refused because of the factory's history of losing money. They said that the factory would not receive more volume until it demonstrated it could consistently earn profits.

The message to the factory seemed to be, "Before a factory can ask other parts of the company to change, it has to make its own changes and achieve significant improvements. When it does this, it earns the right to ask other parts of the company to change."

Because the ABC factory needed to produce many products in low to medium volumes, it had to use an FMS or a JIT line flow production system. FMS was ruled out because the factory could not afford the expensive equipment required. Therefore, it had to use the difficult-to-implement JIT production system. The factory considered changing the market qualifying and order winning outputs to emphasize flexibility and innovativeness but rejected this strategy because market research and the competitive analysis indicated that this was not what customers wanted. Besides, the factory had never been profitable in the past when it had provided high levels of flexibility and innovativeness.

In summary, the results after Step 2 were:

- Market qualifying outputs—Cost, quality, performance
- Order winning output—Delivery
- Required production system—JIT

Step 3: What Must the ABC Factory Do to Get From Where It Is To Where It Wants To Be?

ABC had to change its batch flow production system to a JIT production system. This meant that each manufacturing lever had to move from its current position appropriate for the batch flow production system to a new position appropriate for the JIT production system. Figure 7-4 shows some of the adjustments that were made.

Human Resources

Adjustments to this lever included implementing an employment security policy, new training programs to give employees the needed skills to participate in the change process and to do new jobs in the JIT production system, negotiating a pay-for-knowledge scheme with the union so employees would be paid for the number of jobs they were qualified to do, organizing problem-solving teams, starting a new suggestion program, and improving communications by holding regular meetings and publishing a newsletter. Specialized skills were acquired by hiring a new process engineer and some new managers.

These adjustments are represented in Figure 7-4 by the circle with the number 1 inside and arrows in the manufacturing levers section of the

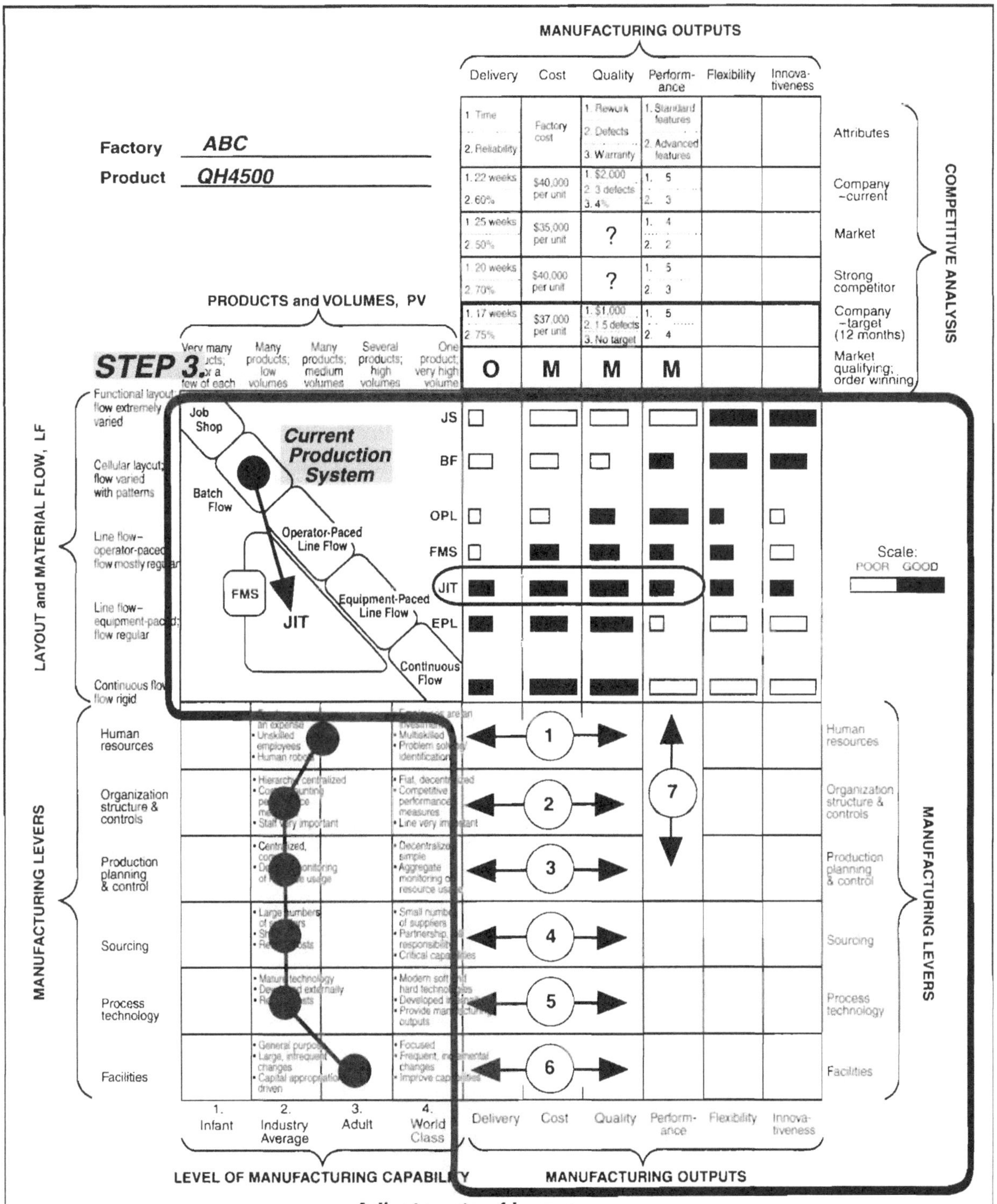

Adjustments of Levers

1. *Train and multiskill employees.*
2. *Management teams, visual display boards.*
3. *JIT for shop floor control, inventory control, expense control; MRP for planning, order control.*
4. *Improve suppliers, reduce supplier base.*
5. *Some standardization, SPC, setup time reduction.*
6. *Manufacturing cells, flow lines, pull control.*
7. *Concurrent engineering.*

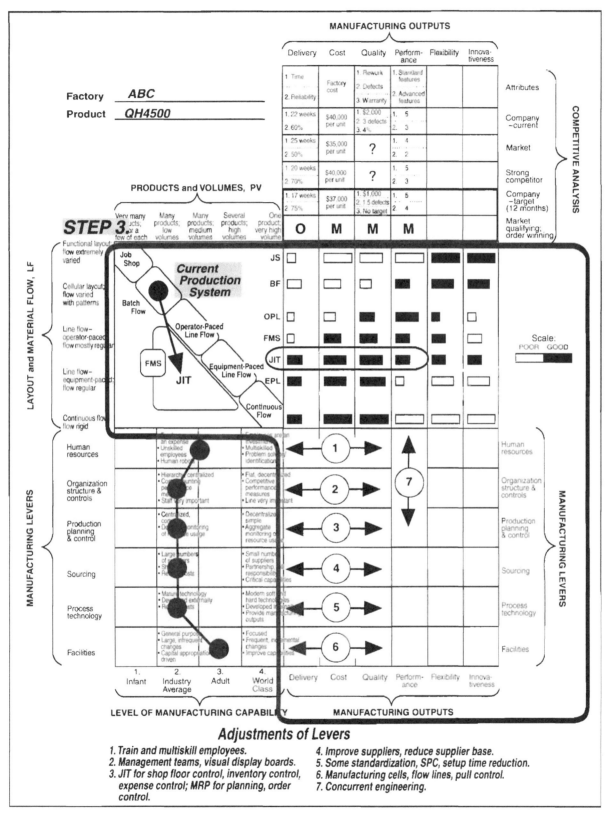

Figure 7-4 Step 3: Lever Adjustments Required to Change the Production System

worksheet. The row on which the circle-and-arrows symbol is located indicates an adjustment to the human resources lever. The columns in which the symbol is located signify that this adjustment helps the production system provide higher levels of the delivery, cost, and quality outputs.

Organization Structure and Controls

Some departments were realigned, and many supervisors were reassigned. Responsibility and decision making were pushed to the lowest possible levels in the factory. Teamwork was stressed, and bonuses were awarded on the basis of team performance. Large display boards were erected around the factory on which important information was displayed. Initiatives were started to develop closer ties with the marketing group and the product design group.

Production Planning and Control

A JIT control system and many JIT techniques were implemented. For example, inventory moved from the stockroom to the factory floor, a two-bin pull system was implemented to control production activities, and lot sizes were reduced. Some standardization and modularization of components was completed. The existing computerized production planning system and cost accounting system were modified to provide better support for the JIT production system.

Sourcing

The number of suppliers decreased. Partnerships were formed with the remaining suppliers, emphasizing quality and fast, reliable deliveries.

Process Technology

Equipment was moved, layout was changed, some manufacturing cells were organized, setup times were reduced, some equipment was improved, and some special tooling was built.

Facilities

The factory was reorganized to accommodate a JIT line flow for product family QH4500. Most of the stockroom was eliminated, and some simple, inexpensive equipment was purchased.

After the necessary changes were determined and summarized on the strategy worksheet, they were reviewed to determine whether they could be implemented. This required checking the capability of each manufacturing lever and checking the overall manufacturing capability.

Check Manufacturing Capability at Each Lever

The following question was asked for each manufacturing lever (Figure 7-5). Given the current level of manufacturing capability for this lever, can the company effectively implement the changes suggested for the lever?

To illustrate, consider the human resources lever. The level of capability was slightly above industry average. ABC identified four major changes for this lever: training and multiskilling, pay-for-knowledge wage scheme, team approaches, and improved communications. Most companies with this level of manufacturing capability would find it difficult to simultaneously implement these four changes. However, the ABC factory did not have a choice; if it did not improve quickly, it would be closed. The situation was the same for the production planning and control lever. It would be difficult to implement the many changes needed (move inventory from the stockroom to the factory floor, implement a two-bin pull system, reduce lot sizes, modify existing computer systems, and so on) when the lever has only an industry average level of capability.

The solution to making many changes to manufacturing levers with only average capabilities was to organize all changes into a careful implementation plan.

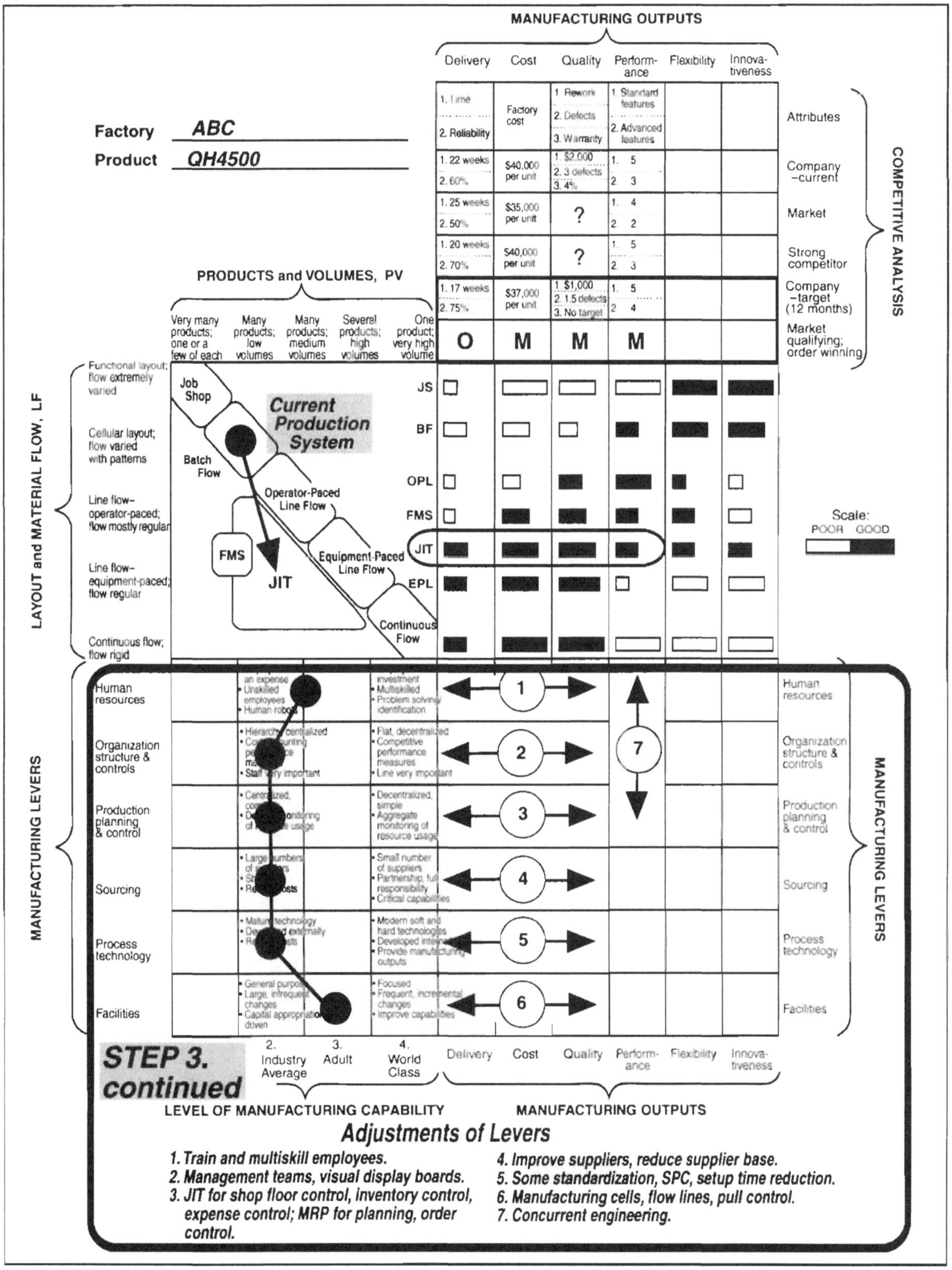

Figure 7-5 Step 3 (continued): Are the Adjustments to the Levers Doable?

Check Overall Manufacturing Capability

After each lever was checked individually, an overall assessment was made.

The ABC factory's overall level of manufacturing capability was slightly better than industry average. This was the foundation on which the factory would make all the changes. This capability was also the major source of resources for implementing the changes. Clearly, it would be difficult for the factory to implement all the changes (Figure 7-5). The factory needed a careful implementation plan. Anything less and the manufacturing strategy would fail, and the factory would be closed.

Implementation Plan

The *implementation plan* is the means by which manufacturing strategy is put into practice. It contains information about what must be done, why it must be done, how it will be done, when it will be done, and who will do it.

What and Why

The *whats* are the adjustments or changes to the manufacturing levers. These adjustments were summarized on the strategy worksheet (in the manufacturing levers section in the columns corresponding to the market qualifying and order winning outputs most affected by the adjustment).

The *whys* are the market qualifying and order winning outputs provided to the customers.

How, When, and Who

Adjustments are converted into projects, and projects are organized into a detailed implementation plan using the worksheet in Figure 7-6. The plan specifies:

- *How:* Each adjustment to a lever is converted into one or more projects.
- *When:* Projects are prioritized and organized into a sequence for implementation. The pace at which projects will be done is specified.
- *Who:* Resources required for the projects are indicated.

Three pieces of information from the manufacturing strategy worksheet are displayed across the top of the implementation plan worksheet (Figure 7-6): product family, production system, and current and target levels of the market qualifying and order winning outputs.

The main part of the worksheet is divided into rows, one for each manufacturing lever. The adjustments or changes to each lever are taken from the strategy worksheet and converted into one or more projects. The projects are organized into a sequence displayed across the rows of the worksheet. The row for each lever can be subdivided into smaller sections if required. For example, the row for the human resources lever can be divided into sections for operators, support personnel, and staff.

Targets and deliverables for each project are shown at the bottom of the worksheet, along with each project's start and finish times.

In addition to being organized according to the manufacturing lever, projects are also organized into three groups based on the times when they will be undertaken. The groups are: *set course* projects, *shoot and aim* projects, and *main* projects.

Set Course Projects

A few simple projects are scheduled at the start so the implementation begins smoothly. A smooth start creates a positive environment for the implementation, builds momentum, and helps employees gain experience. These simple projects set a course for the rest of the implementation.

Shoot and Aim Projects

At this early stage of the implementation, it is more important to get a small number of essential and visible projects started rather than spend a lot of time planning. These projects are called *shoot and aim* because excessive aiming is not necessary. It should be obvious that the projects need completion. The purpose of these projects is to create early

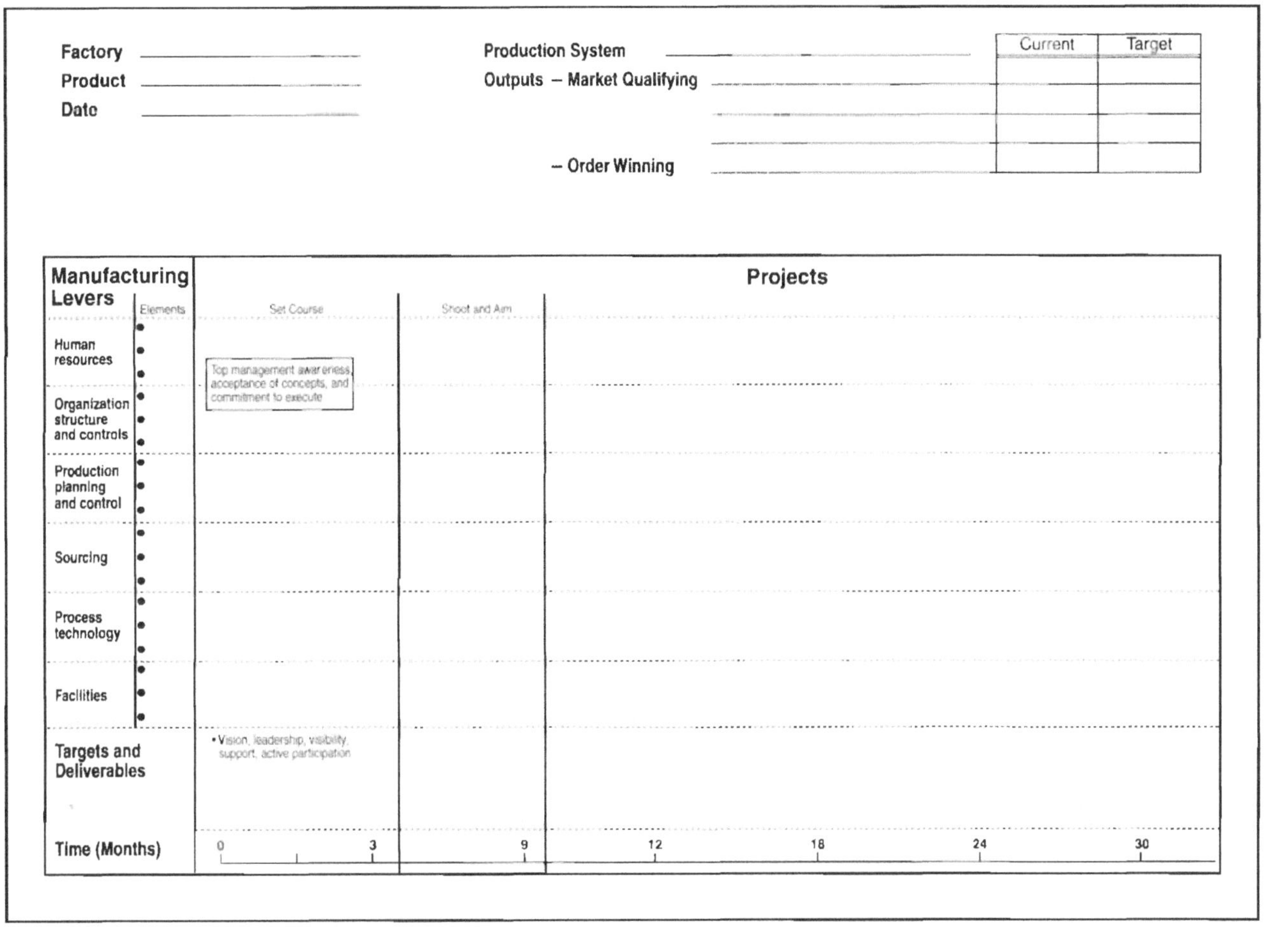
Factory
Product
Date
Production System
Outputs – Market Qualifying
– Order Winning
Current
Target
Manufacturing Levers
Elements
Projects
Set Course
Shoot and Aim
Human resources
Organization structure and controls
Production planning and control
Sourcing
Process technology
Facilities
Top management awareness, acceptance of concepts, and commitment to execute
Targets and Deliverables
• Vision, leadership, visibility, support, active participation
Time (Months)
0
3
9
12
18
24
30

Figure 7-6 Implementation Plan Worksheet

visible successes that, in turn, create momentum for the rest of the implementation, prepare a foundation for the more difficult projects that follow, and prevent "paralysis by analysis" from stalling the implementation.

Main Projects

The bulk of the projects constitute the main part of the implementation plan and are undertaken after the shoot and aim projects. The pace of the implementation—the rate at which projects are started and the time allowed for their completion—depends on three factors: the need for improvement, the amount of resources available for the projects, and the level of manufacturing capability.

Situation 7.1 and 7.2 demonstrate these ideas. In each situation, the need for improvement was urgent, so the implementation was done quickly. About six months was needed to develop a manufacturing strategy and implementation plan. Then, two months were taken to complete the set course projects. Another 18 months were needed to complete the remaining projects.

Projects Frequently Used in Implementation Plans

The implementation plans at ABC and ES contain many of the same projects. A small group of projects is found in most implementation plans that seek to

SITUATION 7.1

Implementation Plan at ABC Company

FIGURE 7-7 SHOWS THE implementation plan for the ABC Company factory. It follows the manufacturing strategy worksheet in Figure 7-5. QH4500 is the product family, and JIT is the production system. Cost, quality, and performance are market qualifying outputs, and delivery is the order winning output. The current and target levels for these outputs are displayed on the top of the implementation plan worksheet.

SET COURSE PROJECTS

The first project in the implementation plan sought to create top management awareness and commitment. The factory knew its improvement efforts would not succeed unless it had the support and active participation of company leaders. They would ensure the cooperation of other parts of the company (especially product design, marketing, human resources, and information systems) was forthcoming when needed. They would also ensure resources were available when needed.

SHOOT AND AIM PROJECTS

Four projects started right away to build momentum and gain confidence:

- Communications were improved.
- Final details of the manufacturing strategy and implementation plan were completed.
- Simple quality improvement activities started.
- Some improvements to equipment were made.

The first two projects focused on infrastructural levers (human resources and organization structure). The other two focused on structural levers (sourcing, process technology, and facilities).

Nine months after the implementation started, the set course and shoot and aim projects were completed, and the following achievements were realized:

- Top management support and participation were obtained. A detailed manufacturing strategy and implementation plan were prepared, which gave everyone a clear sense of the direction in which the factory was headed.
- Early success in the quality improvement and equipment improvement projects created confidence and enthusiasm.
- Champions were found for future projects.

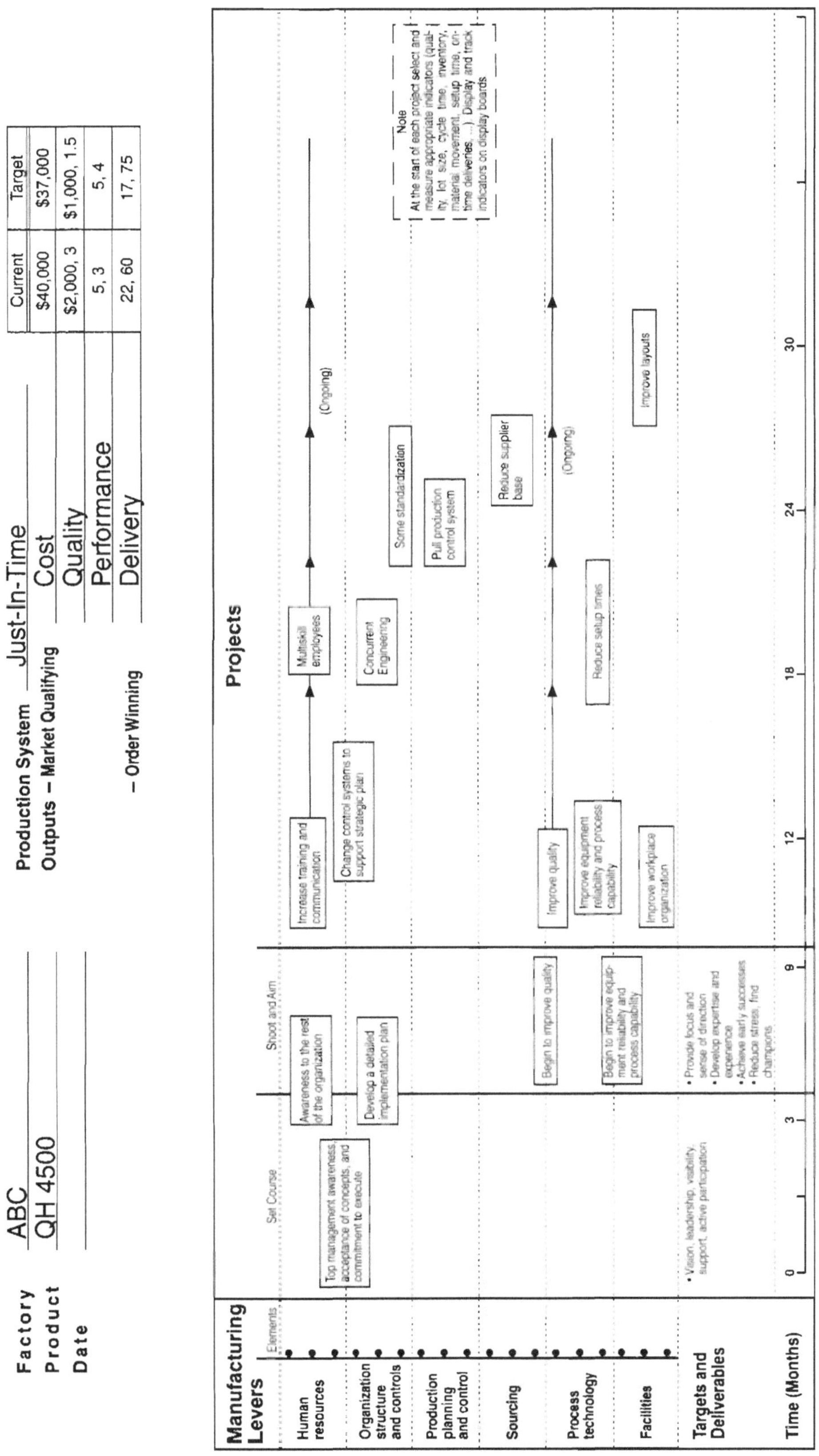

Figure 7-7 Implementation Plan for ABC Factory

SITUATION 7.1

Continued

MAIN PROJECTS

More targeted projects followed. Projects confined to the factory alone were completed by the twentieth month. By that time, the factory had achieved significant improvements in cost, quality, and delivery, and it felt it had earned the right to ask other parts of the company to cooperate on future projects. For example, the concurrent engineering and standardization projects required that product design and marketing cooperate to redesign QH4500 to reduce the number of options offered to customers and make QH4500 easier to manufacture. The project to reduce the supplier base required the cooperation of the corporate purchasing department.

One measure of the factory's performance during the implementation is shown in Figure 7-8. In the first seven months, shipments from the factory remained well below the factory's $16 million per month breakeven point, while the factory struggled with the new JIT production system. In the fourth month (April of year 1), those opposed to the manufacturing strategy pressed top management to stop the implementation. However, top management believed in the strategy, and their commitment kept the implementation going. A few months later, the situation improved. As the level of manufacturing capability rose, shipments increased and other measures of factory performance improved. The factory has been profitable ever since.

SITUATION 7.2

An Implementation Plan at Cincinnati Milacron

THE IMPLEMENTATION PLAN shown in Figure 7-9 was developed from an article[1] and a visit to Cincinnati Milacron's Electronic Systems (ES) Division factory. In the 1980s, ES realized its competitors had significant cost, quality, and delivery advantages. ES needed to improve the levels at which it provided these outputs if it was to survive in the world marketplace. After careful analysis and planning, management decided to organize the ES factory into three focused factories, which it called subplants. A new manufacturing strategy was crafted and implemented through the sequence of projects shown in the figure.

Subplant 1 fabricated printed circuit boards, Subplant 2 assembled boards, and Subplant 3 assembled final products.

Situation 7.2 continued on page 119

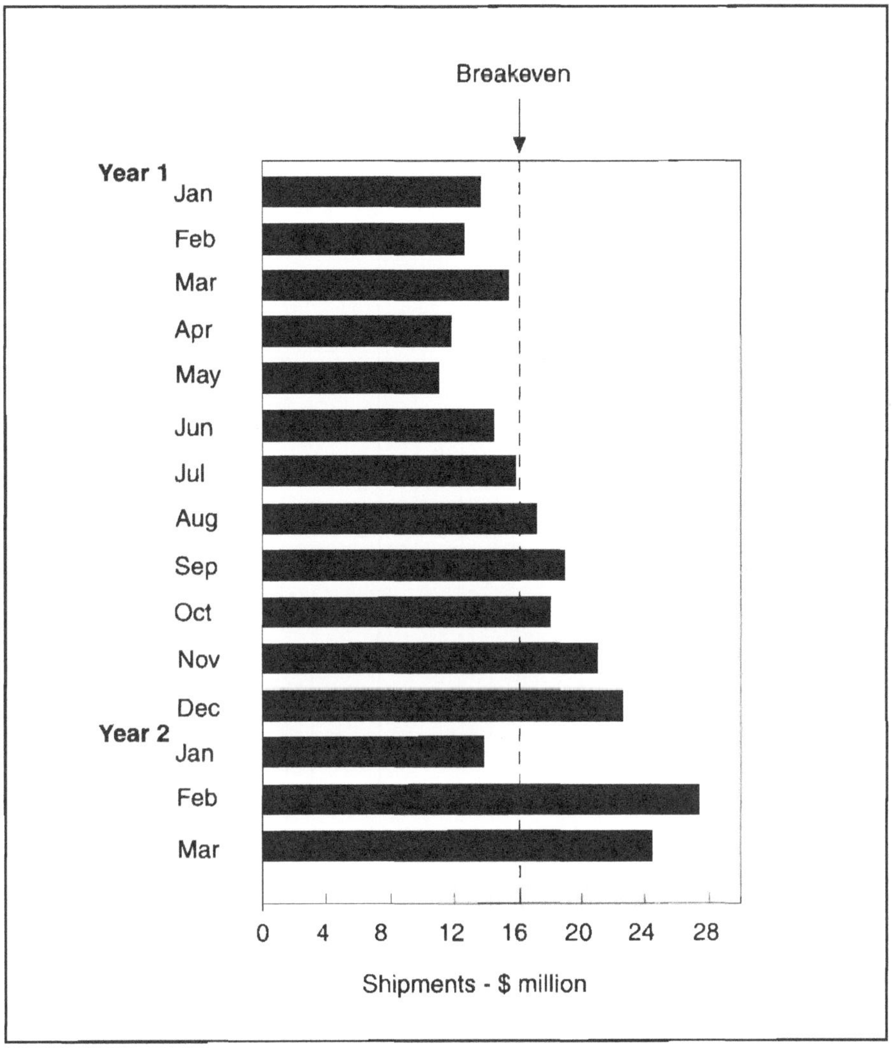

Figure 7-8 Shipments From the ABC Factory During the Implementation

make major improvements in manufacturing capability. These are:

- Top management commitment and participation
- Improvements in quality, equipment, and communications
- Upgrading skills
- Change control systems to support strategy

Top Management Commitment and Participation

Even if not initiated by top management, major changes in manufacturing must be supported actively by this group for success to occur. Major changes create stress in a company and require more cooperation between functional areas. Top management leadership, vision, support, and active participation are required to reduce stress, ensure that cooperation takes place, and shape manufacturing along the lines of the strategy.

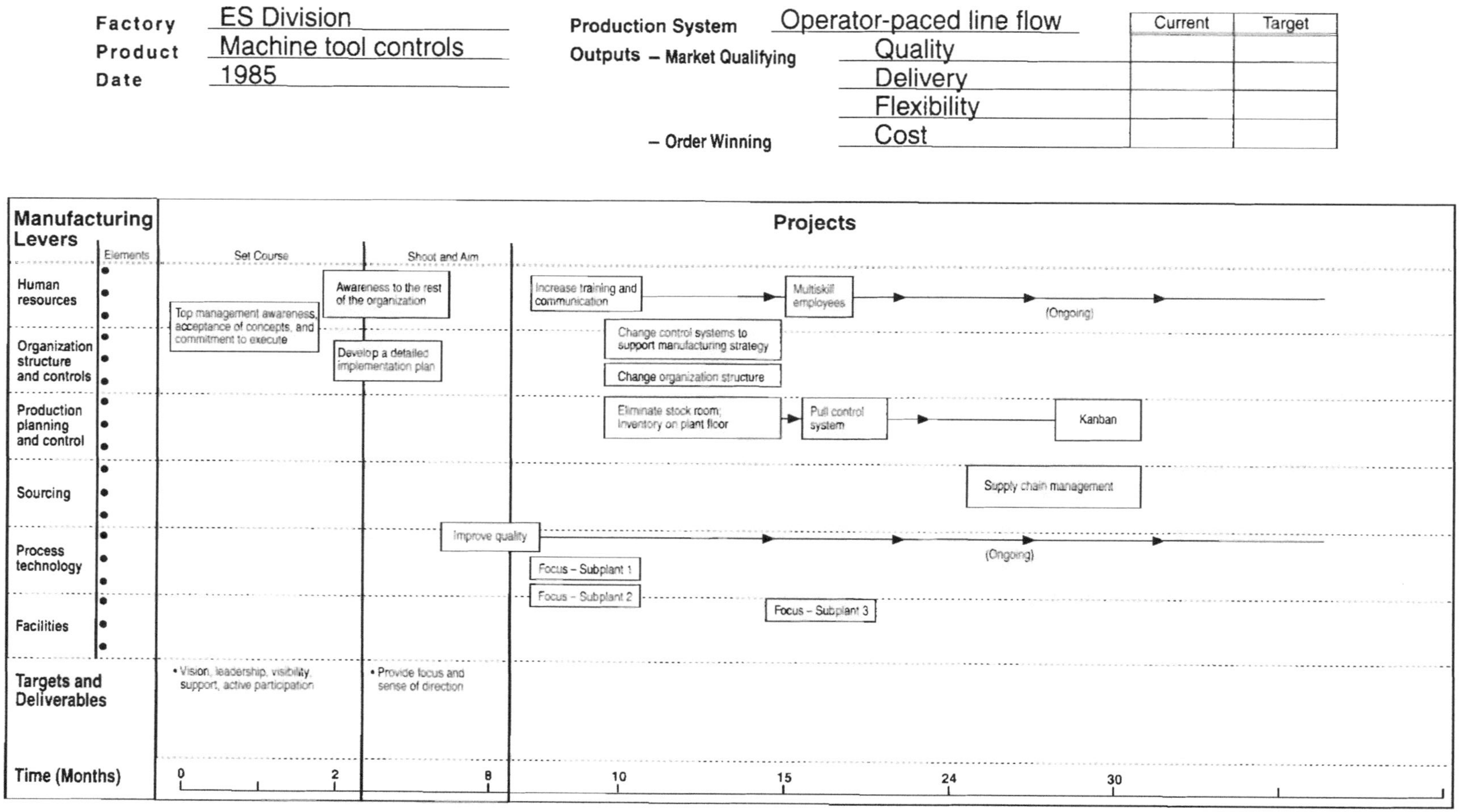

Figure 7-9 Implementation Plan for Cincinnati Milacron ES Division

SITUATION 7.2

Continued

Each subplant used manufacturing cells, flow production lines, and numerous JIT techniques. Inventory was moved from the stockroom to the factory floor, a pull control system was implemented, quality control was expanded, and some workers were multiskilled. The ES Division called its manufacturing strategy a JIT strategy. This was slightly misleading because the production system was an operator-paced line flow production system that extensively used JIT techniques (Chapters 21 and 22).

Other projects included a training program, changes to organization structure, and changes to control systems.

- The training program gave each employee an average of 60 hours of training over two years in quality control and manufacturing, engineering, and management skills.
- Organization structure was changed from seven reporting levels to five, and the number of job classifications was reduced from 70 to 40. Over 80 staff were reassigned, and 2,000 square feet of office space was eliminated by moving staff from production control, industrial engineering, test engineering, and process engineering to the factory floor.
- Extensive changes were made to the MRP production planning and control system, and lot sizes were reduced.

By the thirtieth month, ES had an operator-paced line flow production system with manufacturing capability approaching the adult level. ES was able to provide its market qualifying outputs (quality, delivery, and flexibility) and order winning output (cost) at their target levels.

Improve Quality

Quality tools are used throughout a company to improve quality in all activities (Chapter 14). Employees are trained to use quality tools to monitor and, when appropriate, improve the quality of their work.

In most companies, the cost of purchased materials exceeds 50 percent of the cost of goods sold, so improving the quality of purchased materials is an important part of this project. Buyers, materials personnel, and production planning personnel are trained to use quality tools. Supplier certification programs are started.

Improve Equipment

Once quality improvement activities from the previous project are under way, improving production equipment capability begins. Teams of employees from production, process engineering, maintenance, materials, and tooling study the operations required to produce each product. The process capability of each operation is determined (Chapter 15). Appropriate actions are taken whenever the team finds problems with equipment, tooling, maintenance, operator training, and so on.

A setup time reduction project starts if it is appropriate for the production system. The benefits of short setup times include the ability to produce in small lots, reduced setup and inventory costs, the flexibility to produce new products quickly, and better workplace organization.

Improve Communications

Communication informs employees of planned changes and explains why changes are necessary. The goals of communications are to gain employee support and involve them in the change process. Three types of communications can be used: display boards, newsletters, and meetings.

Large, attractively designed, clearly visible display boards, each with a specific purpose, are located throughout the factory. Some boards display information about efforts to improve quality (SPC charts, repair costs, warranty costs). Others display production information (orders currently being manufactured, new orders, promised delivery dates, inventory levels, manufacturing cycle times). Some boards display information about equipment capability, standard operations, equipment downtime, and repair times.

A newsletter may be used. Topics covered include the company's business plan, financial conditions, new orders, planned changes, information on training programs, and activities in other factories and companies.

Upgrade Skills

Employees need skills to participate in the change process and skills to do new jobs after changes are made. Training in quality tools, industrial engineering, setup time reduction, maintenance, and equipment repair is provided.

Training in quality techniques is given to all employees to improve quality in all activities. Some employees are trained in advanced techniques so that additional improvements can be made.

Many employees need training in industrial engineering concepts such as factory layout, material flow, standard operation time, and maintenance procedures. This training provides a common language and set of tools for those involved in the change process.

Production equipment should consistently produce good products and run for long time periods without breakdowns. This requires responsive maintenance and tooling departments and production operators involved with setups, routine maintenance, and small repairs.

Change Control Systems to Support Strategy

A company's control systems are examined and adjusted so that they support and encourage achievement of the manufacturing strategy. Control systems include the accounting system, the capital appropriation system (Chapter 17), the procedure for selecting suppliers, systems for evaluating employee and department performance, the procedure for bidding on new orders, compensation systems, and so on.

In many cases, control systems were developed at different times for different manufacturing strategies. Some may be inconsistent, which means one system encourages one behavior while another encourages a different behavior. For example, quality may be the order winning output, but the capital appropriation system emphasizes cost reduction. The performance evaluation system encourages departments to improve quality, but the employee compensation system pays employees to produce as many products as possible as quickly as possible.

Special Programs

Many companies organize small sets of complementary projects into programs. Several ways to classify programs include infrastructural or structural, depending on which manufacturing levers are most affected, according to the manufacturing outputs they provide, according to the production systems they are most appropriate for, and so on. Figure 7-10 lists and classifies some popular programs. Programs are also called tactics and can be part of a strategic thrust (Chapter 13).

Program	Type	Manufacturing Lever	Manufacturing Outputs
Job enrichment Total productive maintenance Training Worker safety	Infrastructural	Human resources	Flexibility Cost, quality All outputs Cost
Cost reduction Change labor management relations Information technology Reorganization	Infrastructural	Organization structure and controls	Cost All outputs Delivery, flexibility All outputs
Cycle time reduction MRP Pull production	Infrastructural	Production planning and control	Delivery Delivery, flexibility Cost, quality, delivery
Develop suppliers	Structural	Sourcing	Cost, quality, delivery
Automation Product and process redesign Quality techniques Reduce setup or changeover time	Structural	Process technology	Cost, quality, delivery All outputs Quality Cost, delivery
Close factories Relocate factories	Structural	Facilities	Cost Cost

Figure 7-10 Some Important Manufacturing Programs

The scope of a program can range from narrow to broad. Programs with a broad scope are sometimes called *improvement approaches* (Chapter 14), and programs with a narrow scope are sometimes called *soft* and *hard technologies* (Chapter 15).

Monitoring Projects During the Implementation Plan

It is useful to track the progress of each project on a display board visible to all employees. At the start of a project, appropriate indicators, such as cycle time, inventory level, on-time delivery, open customer orders, setup time, lot size, travel distance, repair cost, and important quality variables, are selected and measured. The values of the indicators should improve as the project progresses. Improvements, however small, are posted on a display board so that they do not go unnoticed. This sustains enthusiasm, builds momentum, and keeps the project on course.

Gaining the support and participation of employees is necessary for successful manufacturing change. Support and participation may be difficult to gain, as many factories must first overcome a long-standing adversarial worker–manager relationship. Three actions help gain this support:

- Improvements achieved in early projects demonstrate the importance of the manufacturing strategy and implementation plan.

- Information is communicated quickly to all employees to avoid surprises or misunderstandings.
- The issue of job security is resolved. Employees do not feel that their livelihood will be affected adversely by their participation in the implementation plan.

The implementation plan worksheet in Figure 7-7 organizes projects according to the manufacturing levers they affect. It is sometimes useful to organize projects according to the manufacturing outputs they affect. Figure 7-11 does this by listing four projects at ABC factory that improve quality. The projects are prioritized, the financial and labor resources required to complete them are described, completion dates are set, and project managers are assigned.

Implementation Instructions

The following instructions are frequently mentioned as ways to increase chances for success and reduce stress levels when implementing major changes in manufacturing:

- High visibility and leadership are required from top management.
- Carefully chosen champions are needed. Initial expectations may be too high. Implementations often move more slowly than planned. Expect unforeseen problems.
- Some groups have difficulty developing plans and will proceed hastily and make mistakes.
- Know the production system. Take time to carefully study the production system so everyone works with reality.

Factory ABC Company

Product QH4500

Manufacturing Output Quality

Project	Priority	Cost	Labor Requirements (employee–years)	Scheduled Completion	Responsibility
Improve quality training	Top priority	$150,000	2	August, year 1	Human resource manager
Determine process capabilities and develop process controls	Very desirable	$80,000	1	End of year 2	Engineering manager
Improve tooling and fixtures	Desirable	$125,000	1 1/2	End of year 1	Engineering manager
Fit quality into incentive wage scheme	Desirable	$60,000	1/2	End of year 1	Plant manager

Figure 7-11 Organizing Projects by Manufacturing Output

- Pay attention to details.
- Be certain that those who contribute to the plan are those who will live with the changes after implementation.
- Groups who lose influence will feel threatened, and groups who gain influence will support change.
- Different functional areas may need encouragement to cooperate with each other.
- Engineering departments will be unhappy when they have to set aside high-tech projects and get out on the factory floor to implement low-tech solutions.
- Top management will worry about profits, middle managers will worry about loss of control, and workers will worry about training and job security.
- Reward and performance measurement systems must change or employees will revert to old habits.
- Old work habits are so ingrained in some managers and workers that change is impossible. These employees should be transferred to other parts of the company.
- It is difficult to overestimate the amount of training needed.

SUMMARY

The elements of manufacturing strategy presented in Chapters 4 to 6 constitute a framework that is used to analyze a factory and develop a strategy and plan for improvement. This chapter describes a three-step procedure for using the framework.

- Step 1: Where am I?
- Step 2: Where do I want to be?
- Step 3: How will I get from where I am to where I want to be?

An example was presented to demonstrate the procedure. The procedure is used also in Part III of the book to help develop a strategy for each factory in a manufacturing network.

The last step in the procedure determines adjustments needed at each manufacturing lever. Adjustments are converted into projects, which are prioritized and organized into a detailed implementation plan using the implementation plan worksheet. The worksheet includes the following information:

- Product family
- Production system
- Current and target levels of market qualifying and order winning outputs
- Set course projects: These simple projects give the implementation a good start.
- Shoot and aim projects: These obvious projects produce early visible successes and prepare a foundation for the main projects.
- Main projects: These projects make most of the changes and generate most of the improvements.

Projects frequently found in implementation plans are discussed. The pace of an implementation depends on three factors: the need for improvement, the amount of resources available for the projects, and the level of manufacturing capability.

APPENDIX: ANOTHER FRAMEWORK FOR DEVELOPING MANUFACTURING STRATEGY

Other frameworks for developing manufacturing strategy are in use. Chapter 15 describes a framework at IBM. Here, we describe briefly a framework at Hewlett-Packard (HP).[2] Both frameworks are similar to the framework in this book.

STEP 1: BUSINESS STRATEGY

Manufacturing participates in the development of a business strategy that specifies the goals of the business, products to manufacture, markets to serve, and basis of competition for the business.

Five product/market characteristics are used in the business strategy:

- Product variety
- Market volume
- Product standardization
- Market growth
- Rate of product change

Values of high, medium, or low are assigned to each characteristic for each product family (Figure 7-12).

Step 2: Manufacturing Success Factors

Product/market characteristics are translated into four critical success factors for manufacturing:

- *Cost:* Ability to produce a product at the lowest possible cost
- *Quality:* Conformance to, or betterment of, customer requirements for a product
- *Availability:* Ability to deliver a product when and where desired, as well as the ability to respond to changes in market demand and opportunities
- *Features:* Manufacturing system allows unique attributes in product design to be included

Values of high, medium, or low are assigned to each critical success factor for each product family (Figure 7-12).

Step 3: Strategic Decisions

Strategic decisions are made in six manufacturing subsystems to provide the critical success factors:

- Capacity/facilities
- Workforce/organization
- Information management/systems
- Vertical integration/sourcing
- Process technology
- Quality

The strategic decisions are summarized on a strategic decision matrix (Figure 7-12).

Step 4: Tactics

Five tactics across the manufacturing subsystems are used to provide the critical success factors:

- Cost reduction
- Quality management
- Short cycle time
- Linking product design with process design
- Hard automation

Values of high, medium, or low are assigned to each tactic for each product family (Figure 7-12).

This framework is a condensed version of the framework outlined in Part II. Steps 1 and 2 are part of Chapters 6 and 13, and Steps 3 and 4 are part of Chapters 4 and 5. The six manufacturing subsystems are similar to the six manufacturing levers. *Tactics* are sets of adjustments to manufacturing levers and are examined in this chapter and in Chapters 14 and 15.

Endnotes

1. Powell, C., "Cincinnati Milacron—Electronic Systems Division: Implementing JIT for Survival in the Machine Tool Market," *Target*, Vol. 3, No. 2, pp. 28–32, Summer 1987.
2. Beckman, S., Boller W., Hamilton, S., and Monroe, J., "Using Manufacturing as a Competitive Weapon: The Development of a Manufacturing Strategy," pp. 53–75, *Strategic Manufacturing*, P. Moody (ed.), Homewood, IL: Dow-Jones Irwin, 1990.

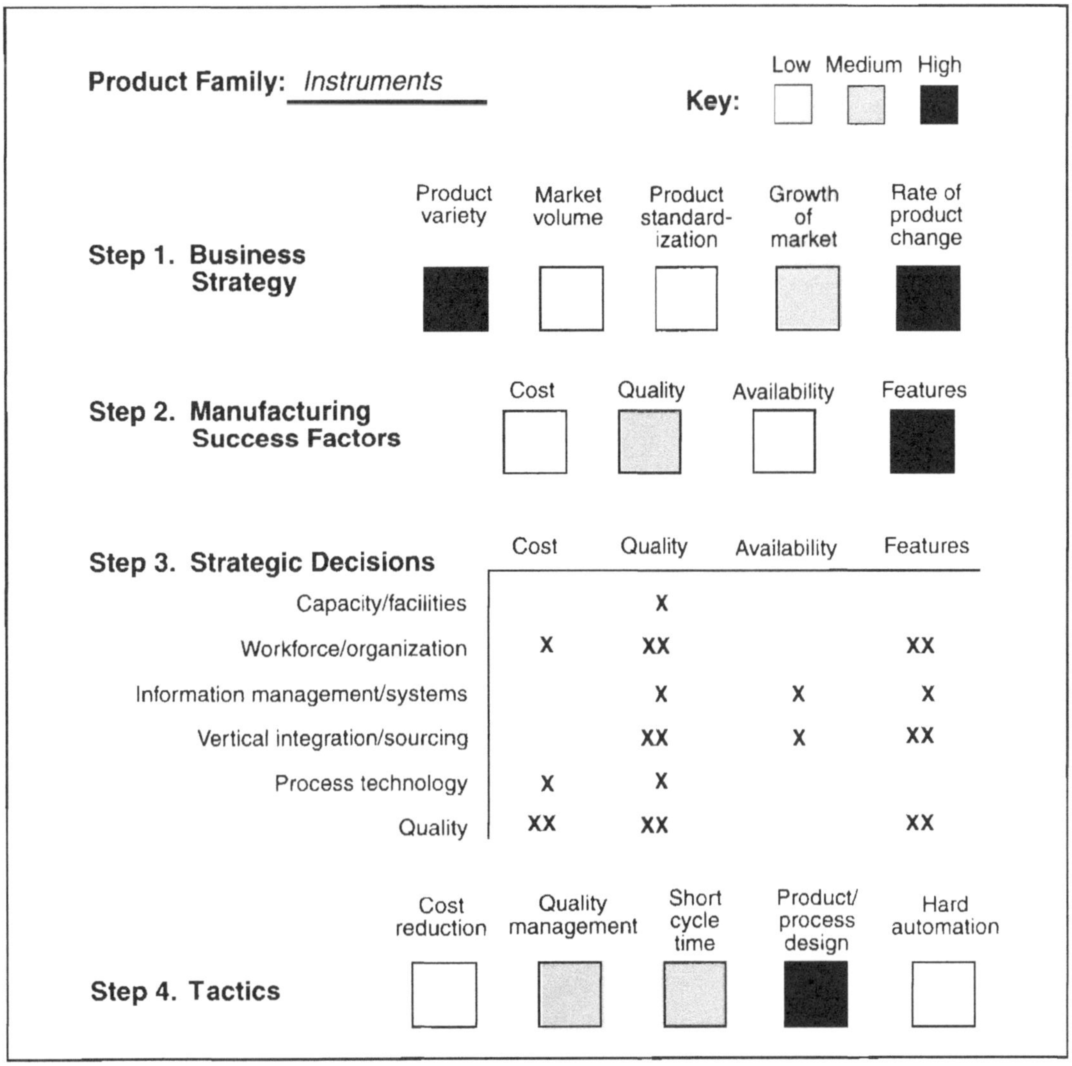

Product Family: *Instruments*

Key: Low Medium High
            ☐   ▨   ■

Step 1. Business Strategy

Product variety	Market volume	Product standard-ization	Growth of market	Rate of product change
■	☐	☐	▨	■

Step 2. Manufacturing Success Factors

Cost	Quality	Availability	Features
☐	▨	☐	■

Step 3. Strategic Decisions

	Cost	Quality	Availability	Features
Capacity/facilities		X		
Workforce/organization	X	XX		XX
Information management/systems		X	X	X
Vertical integration/sourcing		XX	X	XX
Process technology	X	X		
Quality	XX	XX		XX

Step 4. Tactics

Cost reduction	Quality management	Short cycle time	Product/process design	Hard automation
☐	▨	▨	■	☐

Figure 7-12 Four-Step Strategic Planning Process at Hewlett-Packard

Part III

MANUFACTURING STRATEGY IN AN INTERNATIONAL NETWORK OF FACTORIES

CHAPTER 8

PRINCIPLES OF INTERNATIONAL COMPETITIVE STRATEGY

The world economy is globalizing rapidly. Countries once closed to foreign companies are opening their markets. The Internet is shrinking distance. Growth-minded companies are racing to stake out competitive positions in every country where a demand for their products exists. Strong companies in every industry think in terms of global markets.[1]

A domestic company begins transforming into an international company when it enters its first foreign market. Usually, the company has a competitive advantage (Chapter 2), such as a preferred product design, a higher level of product quality, a cost advantage, or a new marketing concept, that can be transferred to a foreign market. After success in its first foreign market, the company expands into others. It uses its increased sales to upgrade its competitive advantages. For example, it achieves economies of scale and the benefits of experience (Chapter 16). Finally, the company establishes facilities in several regions of the world and becomes a vigorous global competitor.

Domestic companies become international companies for many reasons[2]:

- A company with competitive advantage in its domestic market wants to export this advantage to foreign markets. For example, Nokia used its capabilities in mobile phones in Finland to become a global leader in wireless telecommunications.
- A company must sell in more than one country because the domestic market's sales volume is too small to fully capture economies of scale and benefits of experience necessary to improve the company's cost competitiveness. For example, the small size of European country markets led Michelin and Nestle to sell products across Europe, then North America.
- In some industries, companies must operate internationally because raw material supplies are located in foreign countries. For example, Saputo is Canada's largest dairy processor with 45 factories and distribution centers in Canada and the United States.[3] In 2003, it acquired Argentina's third largest dairy processor to gain access to cheaper milk, which it processes into cheese for worldwide export.
- A company seeks new customers in new countries to increase revenues and profits.

This is especially attractive when a company's domestic market is mature. For example, several years ago, Whirlpool analyzed its markets and found that the U.S. market no longer provided enough business for company growth and prosperity. Growth had to come from new markets in Central and Eastern Europe, Mexico, and Asia. Whirlpool created a joint venture with Philips to win the European market and other joint ventures in Mexico and India.

- A company spreads its business risk by operating in more than one country. If the economies of countries in one region temporarily turn down, the company may be sustained by stronger economies in another region.

Patterns of International Competition: Industries

The pattern of international competition varies among countries, industries, and industry segments. A range of patterns exists, starting with multidomestic (the simplest) and ending with global (the most complex). Multidomestic and global patterns are examined in this chapter; other patterns are examined in Chapter 10.

Industries With Multidomestic Competition

The simplest pattern of international competition is *multidomestic*.[4] An industry is present in many countries, but competition in each country (or small group of countries) is independent. The international industry is a collection of domestic industries, hence the name multidomestic. For example, sheet metal fabrication industries in Brazil, China, and Germany have different market conditions and customer expectations. The leading sheet metal fabricators in Brazil differ from those in China and Germany. The competitive battle between Brazil's leading competitors is unrelated to Chinese or German rivalries. Other industries with multidomestic international competition are apparel, beer, construction materials, consumer banking, health services, and many food products.

Most companies in a multidomestic industry are locally owned. When there is foreign ownership, domestic subsidiaries are autonomous, and international trade is small or nonexistent.

Industries With Global Competition

The most complex pattern of international competition is *global competition*.[5] Industries are global when a company's competitive position in one country significantly affects (and is affected by) its position in others. Companies draw on competitive advantages grown from their network of worldwide activities. They combine home base advantages with those from a presence in many countries, such as economies of scale, the ability to serve multinational customers, and a respected brand name. Zeiss, a manufacturer of highly regarded optical instruments, uses large worldwide sales to support R&D activities at its German home base. These activities enable Zeiss to upgrade its design and manufacturing advantages. Examples of industries with global competition are aircraft, agricultural equipment, automobiles, computers, and consumer electronics.

Companies in global industries must compete internationally to create and sustain competitive advantage. For example, Japanese consumer electronics companies initially competed as low cost producers of simple televisions. Their success in foreign markets produced economies of scale and benefits of experience, further reducing cost. As their fortune rose, so did the Japanese yen value, which threatened to end their low cost advantage. They needed to expand their sources of competitive advantage. So they used their worldwide sales to fund large R&D investments to develop proprietary technology for new products and processes and improve their marketing. This created many new sources of competitive advantage.

Industry segments can differ in the pattern of international competition. In lubricants, for example, automotive motor oil tends toward multidomestic competition.[6] Countries have different regulations, driving standards, and weather conditions. Motor oil production blends various base oils and additives. These activities are not subject to economies of scale. Transportation costs are high, and distribution channels vary by country. Domestic companies, such as Quaker State and Pennzoil in the United States, or multinationals with autonomous country subsidiaries, such as Castrol of Great Britain, are leaders in most countries. In contrast, marine engine lubricants is a global industry. Ships move freely around the world and require that the same oil be available everywhere they stop. Brand reputations are global. Successful marine engine lubricant competitors, such as Exxon Mobil, BP Amoco, and Shell, are global.

Vertical stages of an industry can also differ in the pattern of international competition. For example, in aluminum production, the upstream stages (alumina and ingots) are global industries. Alumina and ingots are commodities, so customer needs are identical worldwide. The downstream stages (castings and extrusions) are multidomestic industries. Customer needs for castings and extrusions vary by country, transportation costs are high, and extensive customer service is required.

Patterns of International Competition: Companies

There are important differences between companies that operate domestically, companies that only operate in a few foreign countries, and companies that operate in all of the countries where demand for their products exists (Chapter 10). Companies in the first group are *domestic companies*, companies in the second are *international* or *multinational companies*, and companies in the third group are *global companies*. Regardless of which group a company belongs to, the principles of competitive strategy apply (Chapter 2).

Global companies have more sources of competitive advantage than domestic. A global company locates activities in different countries to achieve its strategic objectives and create sources of competitive advantage. Then the dispersed activities are coordinated to increase advantages. The synergistic combination of home country advantages, benefits from locating activities in different countries, and advantages grown from a coordinated worldwide network create powerful competitive advantages.

Location

Country differences in exchange rates, inflation, wage rates, productivity, energy costs, taxes, and government regulations can create sizably different manufacturing costs.[7] Countries with favorable factors are preferred locations for building factories. For example, Brazil, China, Korea, Malaysia, Mexico, Taiwan, and Vietnam have low wage rates and are favorite locations for manufacturing products with high labor content.

The quality of a country's business environment can be a location advantage. Many countries, such as Ireland, do their best to create favorable business environments. In addition to low tax rates, the government responds to business needs and aggressively recruits companies. The biggest foreign investment in Ireland's history is Intel's largest non-U.S. chip manufacturing plant, a $2.5 billion facility, employing over 4,000 people.

Some countries give preferred treatment to domestic companies, such as subsidies, low interest loans, and government contracts, especially when domestic companies are threatened by a foreign company.

Some countries are unfriendly to foreign companies. They set local content requirements on products made inside their borders, impose tariffs or quotas on imports, restrict exports to ensure adequate local supplies, regulate the prices of imported and locally produced products, and limit withdrawing funds from the country. Foreign companies may face difficult regulations for product certification and require prior government approval for capital spending projects.

Configuring Activities

When a company configures its worldwide activities, it decides where to perform each activity in the value system. Some activities are located at the company's home base; others are located in foreign countries to take advantage of low costs, gain access specialized local skills, or develop relationships with important customers. For example, the Swedish company, SKF, a world leader in ball bearings, has major production and R&D facilities in Germany in close proximity to leading machinery companies and automotive companies, all important ball bearing users.

When a company configures its worldwide activities, it also decides in how many countries to perform each activity in the value system. Two possibilities exist: Concentrate activities in a small number of countries (usually one or two), or disperse activites to many countries.

Concentrated Activities

Activities are concentrated in a small number of countries when countries performing activities have low cost.[8] For example, China and Korea manufacture much of the world's athletic footwear because their wage rates are low.

Activities are also concentrated in locations with superior resources. For example, Samsung established a major R&D facility in Silicon Valley and transferred the know-how gained there back to its South Korean home base. PC motherboards are manufactured in Taiwan because of a highly skilled workforce and low wage rates.[9]

Activities with significant economies of scale or a steep experience curve are concentrated. Since both effects are present in parts fabrication and the final assembly of consumer electronics products, manufacturers of these products gain a cost advantage by operating very large factories. To be global low cost producers, these manufacturers must produce the largest possible volumes in their large factories. For example, Japanese companies manufacture 100 percent of the videocassette recorders sold in the United States. Less than 40 percent of these products carry a Japanese brand name; the rest carry non-Japanese brand names but are sourced from the same manufacturers. In microwave ovens, Japanese brands have less than a 50 percent share of the U.S. market, but the manufacturing share of Japanese companies is over 85 percent.

Manufacturing activities are usually concentrated. Examples of industries that concentrate activities are aircraft, machine tools, and industrial equipment. Concentrated global strategies are more common in China and Korea and less common in the United States and Europe.

Dispersed Activities

While manufacturing activities are usually concentrated, customer-related activities like advertising, technical support, sales, distribution, and after-sale service are usually dispersed.[10] In many industries, these activities must be performed close to customers. For example, companies that make industrial products, such as fans, pumps, valves, and heat exchangers, disperse customer-related activities to many countries to satisfy customer requirements for technical support and after-sale service.

Global companies that effectively disperse customer-related activities can gain a service-based competitive advantage over competitors with more concentrated, customer-related activities. For example, the Big Four public accounting firms have numerous international offices to serve the foreign operations of their multinational corporate customers. This is why the Big Four have been so successful relative to second tier accounting firms.

Dispersed activities are favored when one or more of the following conditions hold:

- High transportation and storage costs make it inefficient to operate from one location.

- Exchange rate risks, political risks, and risks of supply interruption make performing an activity in only one location risky.
- Dispersed activities enhance local marketing in a foreign country by signaling commitment to local customers.
- Customer needs vary by country, so products are customized for country markets. Washing machines and refrigerators are two examples. Customers in France prefer top loading washing machines, while customers in most European countries prefer front loading machines. Northern Europeans buy large refrigerators because they tend to shop once a week; Southern Europeans prefer small refrigerators because they shop daily. Asian customers prefer 4-feet-high refrigerators because they have small homes and use the space above the refrigerator for storage. Customizing products for country markets reduces the economies of scale and experience benefits that stem from producing standard products in one large factory.
- Dispersing an activity to many countries enables a company to accumulate expertise in the activity if locations share information.
- Dispersing some activities may allow the benefits of concentrating others to be gained. For example, performing final assembly in several countries may allow freer import of components produced in one large factory at home base.
- Government is a powerful force in some industries for dispersing activities through tariffs, nontariff barriers, and nationalistic purchasing.

Coordinating Activities

Global companies also gain competitive advantage by coordinating activities located in different countries. For example, a company can use an enterprise resource planning system (ERP) to share information (Chapter 15); it can use the same suppliers and production systems in each country; or it can use the same brand name and sales approach.

Coordination involves sharing information, allocating responsibility, and aligning efforts. It produces several benefits[11]:

- Knowledge and expertise about product and process technology, customer needs, and marketing techniques accumulated in different countries is shared. For example, information about improvements made in a German factory is shared with U.S. and Japanese factories so that appropriate improvements can be made.
- Coordinating dispersed activities enables a company to respond to changing exchange rates, material costs, or labor costs. For example, incrementally increasing production volume at a location currently enjoying favorable exchange rates can lower overall costs. Japanese companies used this practice in the late 1980s when the Japanese yen value was high.
- Coordination achieves economies of scale if activities are placed in locations that can specialize. For example, SKF produces a range of bearings in each of its foreign factories. Then, it transships products between factories to give each country marketing subsidiary a full product line.
- Coordination enhances a company's differentiation with internationally mobile or multinational customers. Consistency in product positioning and its approach to business on a worldwide basis reinforces a company's brand reputation.
- Coordination gives a company flexibility to respond to competitors. A global company can choose where and how to challenge a competitor (Chapter 3). For example, it may challenge a competitor in the country from which the competitor has its greatest cash flow, reducing the competitor's resources for

competing in other countries. IBM and Caterpillar used this approach in Japan against their Japanese competitors.

Achieving coordination among activities, facilities, and countries is challenging because of complexity, language problems, cultural differences, the need to share information, and the difficulty of aligning managers' interests with the company's. It is not unusual for one factory manager to withhold information from others in order to outperform them in a company's internal performance review. This is especially common when factories are located in different countries.

Achieving Competitive Advantage by Competing Globally

A company has four important ways to gain competitive advantage when it expands outside its home market:

- The company disperses activities like R&D, purchased materials, parts manufacturing, assembly, distribution, marketing, sales, and service to different countries in a manner that lowers costs or creates differentiation.
- The company coordinates activities located in different countries. Coordination involves sharing information about products, processes, and customers, allocating responsibility, and aligning efforts. Coordination gives the company flexibility to respond to changes in customer needs, exchange rates, and production factor costs, and to challenge and respond to competitors.
- Sharing resources and capabilities with many locations helps develop broader and deeper capabilities. Ideally, it helps a company achieve dominating depth in some competitively valuable activity. A domestic company usually cannot achieve dominating depth because its one country customer base is too small for such a resource buildup. For example, a Canadian company with seven factories in North America and Europe is the world's largest supplier of exhaust manifolds to the North American automobile industry. This was still insufficient to provide dominating depth in iron casting and machining, so the company acquired a U.S. manufacturer of suspension and brake components with strong capabilities in these important production processes.
- A company enhances its brand reputation by using the same differentiating features in all products worldwide. For example, Honda's reputation for quality, established in motorcycles, then in automobiles, created an immediate competitive advantage when it introduced lawn mowers and power generators.

Generic Global Strategies

A company can follow several generic strategies when it decides to expand outside its domestic market and compete internationally[12]:

- One country production base exporting to foreign markets
- Multicountry strategy
- Global strategy
- Focused and broad-line strategies
- License foreign companies to use company technology or produce and distribute company products
- Strategic alliances with foreign companies

The first four strategies establish the scope of a company's international manufacturing activities. The last two determine how a company partners with foreign companies.

One Country Production Base Exporting to Foreign Markets

The simplest strategy is an export strategy. A company uses its domestic factories as a production base for exporting to foreign markets.[13] A company further limits its foreign country involvement by contracting with foreign companies experienced in importing, distribution, and marketing. Many Chinese, Italian, and Korean companies follow this strategy. If it is advantageous to control distribution and marketing activities, a company can establish its own distribution and marketing organizations in some foreign countries.

Since an export strategy minimizes capital requirements, it is a smart initial strategy for pursuing international sales. Long-term success depends on manufacturing costs in the home country and transportation costs. A company gains economies of scale and experience benefits from centralizing production in factories in its home country. However, its manufacturing and transportation costs must be lower than similar costs in foreign countries where competitors have factories.

Multicountry Strategy

A multicountry strategy is used when there are significant differences in customer needs or in competitive, cultural, economic, or political conditions in country markets.[14] While a company with a multicountry strategy may use the same general competitive advantage, it makes country specific variations to satisfy customer needs and position itself against competitors. A company may aim at broad market segments in some countries and focus on market niches in others. A company coordinates activities by transferring ideas and capabilities successful in one country market to others. Nestle follows a multicountry strategy for coffee (Situation 8.1).

Multicountry strategies have some disadvantages. It is difficult to transfer capabilities and resources across country borders and to coordinate activities in different countries.

Situation 8.1

Multicountry Strategy for Coffee[15]

NESTLE IS THE WORLD'S largest food company, with over $50 billion in sales, market share in all regions of the world, and factories in over 70 countries. Coffee is an important product for Nestle, accounting for over $5 billion in sales. The company produces 200 blends of "Nescafe instant coffee," from lighter blends for the United States to dark expressos for Latin America. Nestle has four coffee research laboratories responsible for matching the coffee blends marketed in each country with the tastes of coffee drinkers in that country. They are also responsible for adjusting coffee blends to suit changing tastes and for developing new blends for new market segments.

In addition to adapting its products to each country market, Nestle also adapts its marketing activities. In Britain, the number of instant coffee drinkers was small, so Nestle advertised extensively to increase this number. In Japan, instant coffee was a luxury item, so Nescafe was packaged in fancy containers suitable for gift giving. In 1993, in China, customers had never heard of instant coffee, so Nescafe coffee and Coffee-Mate creamer were marketed as new products.

Global Strategy

A global strategy is one where a company's approach is similar in all countries. Minor country-to-country differences in strategy exist to accommodate local competitive conditions, but the company's fundamental competitive strategy is identical worldwide. A company that follows a global strategy sells in most if not all countries where there is significant demand for its products. It also integrates and coordinates activities worldwide to create a competitive advantage over competitors.

If country-to-country differences are small enough for accommodation within the framework of a global strategy, then global strategy is preferred to multicountry strategy. Global strategy creates competitive advantages that are very difficult for competitors to beat. Figure 8-1 compares multicountry and global strategies.

Focused and Broad-Line Strategies

Each of the previous generic strategies can be focused or broad-line depending on whether a company chooses to serve a narrow or a broad market segment. A global focused strategy and a global broad-line strategy are both possible. BMW has a global focused strategy, focusing on the high performance, luxury automobile worldwide market segment. Ford has a global broad-line strategy, producing automobiles for all worldwide market segments.

A focused strategy can be the first step toward a broad-line strategy. A company begins to compete in a segment of the industry poorly served by broad-line competitors. For example, Japanese automobile companies established themselves in North America by focusing on the neglected, compact automobile market segment. Later, they introduced larger automobiles, small trucks, and luxury vehicles and became broad-line competitors.

License Foreign Companies to Use Technology or Produce and Distribute Products

Licensing is a good strategy for a company with valuable technology or a unique patented product but without the capability or resources to enter a foreign market.[16] By licensing technology or production rights to foreign based companies, the company generates revenue but does not bear the costs or risks of entering foreign markets.

One disadvantage is the danger of providing valuable technological know-how to foreign companies, as some will become competitors. Another disadvantage is the difficulty of ensuring that foreign companies carefully follow the license agreement. They may, for example, modify product designs or cut corners on quality and delivery.

Strategic Alliances With Foreign Companies

Strategic alliances (Chapter 3) with foreign companies range from simple to complex.[17] A company forms a simple alliance with a foreign company to distribute products or perform marketing activities in a new region of the world. A company forms routine alliances with foreign companies to manufacture components, participate in joint research, and share production facilities. A company forms a complex alliance with a foreign company to mass produce a complicated product. For example, when Ford formed an alliance with Mazda, Mazda produced cars for Ford, and Ford sold the cars through its European and U.S. dealerships.

Export-minded companies in industrialized countries have always sought alliances with companies in less-developed countries to gain access to new country markets. Governments in less-developed countries may even require these arrangements. More recently, companies from different parts of the world have formed alliances to serve entire continents or trading regions (Chapter 9).[18]

- Airbus Industrie comprises an alliance of aerospace companies from Britain, France, Germany, and Spain that competes against Boeing in designing and manufacturing large commercial aircraft for worldwide markets.
- Renault of France formed an alliance with Nissan of Japan to create a global partnership

	Multicountry Strategy	Global Strategy
Geographic area	Selected countries and trading regions	Most countries where demand for company products exists Most companies have facilities in North America, Europe, Asian Pacific, and South America
Strategy	Custom strategies to fit conditions in each country Little or no strategy coordination across countries	Same basic strategy worldwide; minor country-to-country variations when necessary
Products	Adapted to culture and local customer needs	Mostly standardized products sold worldwide; moderate customization where and when necessary
Production	Factories in many countries, each manufactures products suitable for local customers	Factories located on the basis of maximum competitive advantage (low cost countries, close to markets, minimize transportation costs, or large scale factories to maximize economies of scale and experience benefits)
Sourcing	Suppliers in local country preferred Some local sourcing may be required by government	Best suppliers from anywhere in world
Marketing and distribution	Adapted to practices and culture of each country	Worldwide, tightly coordinated systems Minor adaptation to local country conditions when necessary
Sharing ideas and resources	Transfer successful ideas, technologies, and capabilities in one country to others whenever transfer appears advantageous	Use the same technologies and capabilities in all country markets Ideas and capabilities successful in one country transfered to others
Company organization	Form subsidiary companies to perform activities in each country Each subsidiary operates autonomously	All major strategic decisions are closely coordinated by home base Global organization structure used to standardize activities in each country

Adapted from Thompson and Strickland, *Strategic Management*, McGraw-Hill Irwin, p. 208, 2001. Used with permission of The McGraw-Hill Companies.

Figure 8-1 Differences Between Multicountry and Global Strategies

capable of competing against Daimler Chrysler, Ford, General Motors, and Toyota.

- General Electric and SNECMA, a French maker of jet engines, formed a partnership to manufacture jet engines for aircraft made by Boeing and Airbus. The alliance is called CFM International. Its market share in the 100+ passenger aircraft market segment increased from about 35 percent in the 1980s to 50 percent in 1995.
- Japanese and U.S. companies form alliances with European companies to compete in the European Union and to enter new markets in Eastern Europe.
- European and U.S. companies form alliances with Asian companies to enter new markets in China, India, and other Asian countries.

Small- and medium-sized companies, not just large companies, compete globally. Small- and medium-sized companies account for a substantial portion of international trade in European countries such as Denmark, Germany, and Italy. They compete in small industries or focus on narrow market segments. Because of their small size and limited resources, they face challenges in gaining access to foreign markets, understanding customer needs, and providing after-sale support. Forming alliances with importers, distributors, and trading companies, overcomes these challenges.

Alliances produce many benefits. Economies of scale are captured in production and marketing, and gaps in technology and knowledge of markets are filled. New distribution channels strengthen access to customers. Partners direct their competitive energies toward mutual competitors and away from each other.

To gain these benefits, a company must select a partner who shares the company's view of the alliance's purpose. A company should avoid a partner where a potential for competition exists because of overlapping product lines or other conflicting interests.

Alliances that aim at technology sharing or providing market access are usually short lived. After a few years, the benefits have occurred, and companies are ready to go their own ways. In these alliances, it is important for a company to quickly learn its partner's technology and practices and transfer that knowledge to its own facilities. Alliances with suppliers and distributors, where each company's contribution involves activities in different parts of the value system, last longer.

Alliances are not easy. They require countless meetings among numerous people who work together in good faith over months and years. They also require people from one company to share information and perform activities for people in another. When these activities are executed poorly, tensions build, working relationships sour, and the potential benefits never materialize.

Company cultures and egos can clash. Key people, on whom success depends, may have little personal chemistry and be unable to work together or come to a consensus. For example, an alliance between Northwest Airlines and KLM Airlines to link airport hubs in Detroit and Amsterdam resulted in a bitter feud among top management of both companies. The dispute stemmed from a clash of business philosophies (the American way versus the European way), cultural differences, and an executive power struggle.

An alliance is a tool for extending competitive advantage, not a means for sustaining it. Sustaining competitive advantage ultimately requires companies, especially industry leaders, to develop internal sources of competitive advantage. Companies must not let alliances distract them from this important task.

SUSTAINING GLOBAL COMPETITIVE ADVANTAGE

A company's competitive advantage results from particular activities within its value system. These activities are the sources of competitive advantage (Chapter 2). Sources differ in their ability to sustain competitive advantage. Lower order sources are easy for competitors to copy, so competitive advantage based on lower order sources is not sustainable. Examples of lower order sources include low cost factors of production (equipment, labor, and material), one-time design ideas, simple activities involving readily available technology, and common distribution channels. Higher order sources are more difficult to copy. For this reason, competitive advantage based on higher order sources is sustainable. Examples include proprietary process technology, superior product designs, established brand names resulting from years of marketing effort, and loyal distribution channels.

Differentiation competitive advantage involving high quality, advanced features, proprietary technology, high levels of service, and a stream of new and improved products is usually more sustainable than low cost competitive advantage, even when low cost competitive advantage is based on economies of scale or large initial capital investments. Determined competitors, sometimes with the support of accommodating governments, can easily copy cost-based competitive advantage by building large factories and buying the newest equipment.

For example, Chinese companies have lower order sources of competitive advantage. They purchase readily available materials, use standard process technology, and have low labor costs. Their low cost competitive advantage nullifies when foreign companies purchase from the same suppliers, buy the same equipment, and locate in nearby countries with low labor cost.

In the long run, all competitive advantages can be copied. Chinese companies have matched the ability of other Asian companies to mass produce standard products. Brazilian companies have leather footwear designs and technology comparable to Italian companies.

Some companies survive for a long time on the strength early competitive advantages such as established customer relationships, economies of scale in existing technologies, and the loyalty of distribution channels. But sooner or later, competitors overcome these advantages by finding better or cheaper ways to do things. For example, British and then American companies lost century-old positions in machine tools when foreign competitors took advantage of new computer technology. German companies lost leadership in cameras for similar reasons.

Competitive advantage is sustained by improvement. It is management's job to make sure a company improves. Improvement is a continual search for better ways to organize, manage, and perform activities in the value system. It is manifested in new product designs, better production systems, a fresh approach to marketing, a superior organization structure, a faster distribution system, and so on.

Improvement does not come naturally. Companies would rather stay the same. Particularly in a successful company, powerful forces work against change. Successful companies institutionalize practices, build specialized facilities, train personnel in one mode of behavior, and screen out information that challenges current approaches. Strong pressures are required to counteract these forces and allow change or improvement to occur. These pressures rarely come exclusively from inside a company. For the most part, they come from customers and competitors outside a company. A global company is exposed to these pressures and naturally responds by making improvements that sustain its competitive advantage.

Role of the Home Base

The natural tendency in successful companies is to preserve the practices, technology, and facilities that caused success. Management must work hard to overcome this complacency so that improvements can be made. This is difficult in a global company whose activities are dispersed worldwide. The home country (or home base) is the critical factor in determining whether improvement can succeed in a global company. It succeeds when the home base supports and pushes it.

Competitive advantage originates and is sustained from the home base. The presence of demanding customers, advanced suppliers, and world class competitors in the home base helps improve the entire company.[19]

- The home base should find the most sophisticated and demanding customers. These customers stimulate the fastest improvement because they are knowledgeable, expect the best performance, and have the most difficult needs. For example, some have difficult operating requirements (e.g., temperature, humidity, hours of use, vibration), face cost disadvantages in their businesses that create unusual pressures for performance, have tough competitors, follow strategies that put heavy demands on the company's products (e.g., low cost, high quality, or fast delivery), or operate in countries with tough product standards and environmental regulations. These needs challenge the home base, and subsequently, the entire company to upgrade performance and extend features and services.
- The home base should purchase from the most advanced international suppliers. Suppliers who possess competitive advantage, as well as insight from international activities, challenge the company to improve and assist the company as it improves.
- The home base should identify outstanding competitors who closely match or exceed the company's competitive advantages and set them as a standard for comparison. They become a source of learning, a focal point to motivate change for the entire company, and a common rival to surpass. For example, at one time, Komatsu saw Caterpillar as an outstanding competitor to surpass. The goal of beating Caterpillar energized remarkable improvements in Komatsu's products and processes.

Perceiving Industry Change

After pressure to improve, another important aid to sustain competitive advantage is early insight into new customer needs and environmental changes.[20] Sometimes, this comes from being in the right country at the right time. Often, it comes from looking for the right things. For example, Toyota knew the importance of good quality, low-priced, fuel-efficient, small cars from its experiences in the 1950s and 60s in Japan. The company began exporting to the United States in 1958 but stopped in 1960 when it became evident that its products were unsuitable for the U.S. market. It resumed exports in 1964 with better products, and by 1967, exports to the United States were up to 39,000 cars. When the worldwide oil shock of 1973 hit, Toyota was ready with the fuel-efficient, small cars that U.S. customers wanted. U.S. car companies were slow to recognize changing customer needs and slow to improve their products and processes. In 1979, the second oil crisis hit, and U.S. sales of Toyota cars skyrocketed.[21]

Some customers will encounter new problems or have new needs before others because of their demographics, location, industry, or strategy. Superior companies seek out these customers, wherever they are in the world. For example, Scandinavian and German companies often face labor shortages and so have the greatest need for the best automation equipment. University teaching hospitals experience the most difficult medical cases and usually are the first to experiment with new procedures and equipment. Some regions of the world, like California, have the highest concerns for social problems such as safety and the environment. Instead of avoiding these customers or regions, as some companies do, superior companies seek them out and set internal goals to meet or exceed these customer needs and concerns.

Companies should identify the places in the world where the best new knowledge is created and establish and maintain relationships with these research centers and sources of talented people.

SUMMARY

A domestic company competes internationally when it enters its first foreign market. Usually, the company has a competitive advantage that can be transferred to the foreign market. The company expands into other foreign markets and uses its increased sales to sustain and increase its competitive advantages.

The pattern of international competition varies among countries, industries, and industry segments. A range of patterns start with multidomestic competition and end with global competition. Industries are global when a company's competitive position in one country significantly affects (and is affected by) its position in other countries. Global companies combine home base competitive advantages with those that stem from their network of worldwide activities.

When a company configures its worldwide activities, it decides where to perform each activity in the value system. Some activities are located at the home base; others, in foreign countries, take advantage of low costs, gain access to specialized skills, and develop relationships with important customers. Activities may be concentrated in a small number of countries or dispersed to many countries. Activities must be carefully coordinated to create competitive advantage.

Three generic strategies for international manufacturing are: one country production base exporting to foreign markets, multicountry strategy, and global strategy. These strategies can be focused or broad-line. Whenever possible, a global strategy is preferred to a multicountry strategy because global strategy coordinates a company's worldwide activities to create competitive advantages difficult for competitors to copy. Two generic strategies for partnering with foreign companies are: license foreign companies to use company technology or produce and distribute company products, and strategic alliances.

In the long run, all competitive advantages can be copied. A company sustains competitive advantage by developing new, higher order sources of competitive advantage and by improving. Improvement is a continual search for better ways to organize, manage, and perform activities in the value system. Improvement is difficult in a global company because activities are dispersed worldwide. The home base (or home country) is the critical factor in determining whether improvement can succeed in a global company. It succeeds when the home base supports and pushes it. The presence of demanding customers, advanced suppliers, and aggressive competitors in the home base helps the home base improve the entire company. Another aid to sustain competitive advantage is early insight into new customer needs and environmental changes.

ENDNOTES

1. A substantial portion of this chapter draws on material from:
   - Porter, M., *The Competitive Advantage of Nations*, The Free Press: New York, Chapters 2, 11, 1990.
   - Thompson, A., and Strickland, A., *Strategic Management: Concepts and Cases*, McGraw-Hill Irwin: Boston, Chapter 6, 2001.
2. Thompson and Strickland, *Strategic Management*, p. 200.
3. *Financial Post (Canada)*, p. FP1, October 3, 2003.
4. Porter, *The Competitive Advantage of Nations*, pp. 53–54; Thompson and Strickland, *Strategic Management*, p. 203.
5. Porter, *The Competitive Advantage of Nations*, pp. 54–55, 61–63; Thompson and Strickland, *Strategic Management*, p. 204.
6. Ibid, p. 204.
7. Ibid, pp. 202–203.
8. Porter, *The Competitive Advantage of Nations*, pp. 55–56; Thompson and Strickland, *Strategic Management*, p. 210.
9. Ibid, pp. 210–211.
10. Porter, *The Competitive Advantage of Nations*, pp. 56–57; Thompson and Strickland, *Strategic Management*, p. 211.

11. Porter, *The Competitive Advantage of Nations*, pp. 58–59; Thompson and Strickland, *Strategic Management*, p. 212.

12. Ibid, p. 205.

13. Ibid, pp. 205–206; Hodgetts, R., and Luthans, F., *International Management: Culture, Strategy, and Behavior*, Irwin McGraw-Hill: Boston, p. 269, 2003.

14. Thompson and Strickland, *Strategic Management*, p. 206.

15. Tully, S., "Nestle Shows How to Gobble Markets," *Fortune*, pp. 74–78, January 16, 1989; "Nestle: A Giant in a Hurry," *Business Week*, pp. 50–54, March 22, 1993.

16. Hodgetts and Luthans, *International Management*, p. 268; Porter, *The Competitive Advantage of Nations*, pp. 191–193.

17. Porter, *The Competitive Advantage of Nations*, pp. 65–67; Thompson and Strickland, *Strategic Management*, pp. 213–217.

18. Doz, Y., and Hamel, G., *Alliance Advantage: The Art of Creating Value Through Partnering*, Harvard Business School Press: Boston, 1988.

19. Porter, *The Competitive Advantage of Nations*, pp. 577, 585–587, 606–607.

20. Ibid, pp. 587–589.

21. McCraw, T., *Creating Modern Capitalism*, Harvard University Press: Cambridge, MA, Chapter 11, 1997.

CHAPTER 9

MANUFACTURING IN THE WORLD'S MAJOR TRADING REGIONS

Economic Developments

Numerous companies purchase, produce, and sell in international markets.[1] International trade volume increases every year. Several economic developments played a large part in bringing this about[2]:

- The North American Free Trade Agreement (NAFTA) between the United States, Canada, and Mexico removed barriers to trade between these countries and created a huge North American market. This market may expand to include Latin American countries and South American countries, such as Argentina, Brazil, and Chile, and as a result, create a giant North/South American market.
- The European Union (EU) between 15 countries (Austria, Belgium, Denmark, Finland, France, Germany, Great Britain, Greece, Ireland, Italy, Luxembourg, the Netherlands, Portugal, Spain, and Sweden) removed barriers to trade between these countries and created a common currency called the Euro. The EU will expand to include the Czech Republic, Hungary, Poland, and other Eastern European countries, and as a result, create a giant East/West European market.
- Economic activities in Southeast Asia continue to increase. Despite problems in the 1990s, Japan remains the primary economic force in the region followed by China. The Four Tigers (Hong Kong, Singapore, South Korea, and Taiwan) have become developed economies. The Baby Tigers (Indonesia, Malaysia, and Thailand) are positioned to become major export-driven economies. An economic bloc called the Association of Southeast Asian Nations (ASEAN) between nine countries (Brunei, Cambodia, Indonesia, Malaysia, Myanmar, the Philippines, Singapore, Thailand, and Vietnam) helps these countries expand their international activities.
- Central and Eastern Europe, Russia, and other republics of the former Soviet Union are transitioning to market economies. Although the Czech Republic, Hungary, Poland, and Slovenia have completed the process, other countries lag behind. All are possible locations for international companies interested in expansion in the region.

- Economic activity in South America continues to increase. Mercosur is a trade agreement between Argentina, Brazil, Paraguay, and Uruguay that creates a common market between these countries. The Andean Common Market is a similar agreement between Bolivia, Colombia, Ecuador, Peru, and Venezuela.
- The World Trade Organization (WTO) is an organization dedicated to increasing international trade, and 126 countries, accounting for about 90 percent of world trade, are members. The WTO monitors trade policies and has considerable power to enforce rulings in trade disputes.
- Many governments in less-developed countries are redefining their relationships with foreign companies. India is an example. For years, it's had a love/hate relationship with international companies. Government policy recently changed, and many foreign companies are now attracted to India. The change occurred with the realization that many foreign companies choose between India and China, and investments not made in India may be forever lost to China.

Trade and Foreign Investment

North America, the European Union, and Southeast Asia are the world's major trading blocs.[3] The relative volume of trade from these blocs remains fairly constant over the years. Between 1983 and 1996, their share of world exports rose from 56.5 percent to 59.2 percent, and their share of world imports rose from 59.4 percent to 59.8 percent.

The United States is the largest player in the North American bloc and the world. During the same period, U.S. exports rose from slightly over $200 billion to $580 billion, and imports rose from $269 billion to $770 billion. The EU countries, mainly because of within-EU trading, had more activity. During the same period, exports rose from almost $600 billion to $1,911 billion, and imports rose from just over $625 billion to $1,902 billion. Japan is the largest player in the Southeast Asian bloc. During the same period, Japanese exports rose from $147 billion to $443 billion, and imports rose from $126 billion to $336 billion.

As trade barriers continue to fall, the volume of trade continues to rise. Most developed countries now export a growing share of their production output. The nature of trade flows is changing. Many international companies now look more at emerging markets outside the major trading blocs.

Foreign direct investment (FDI) has increased substantially. FDI measures the amount that companies from one or more foreign countries invest in another country. In 1998, FDI in the United States was over $600 billion. The largest investors were Great Britain, Japan, the Netherlands, Germany, and Canada. FDI by U.S. companies was almost $800 billion. The largest investments were in the EU, Canada, and Japan. Much of Japan's FDI goes to the EU because of the projected growth for the EU in the coming years and entry barriers into EU markets that make it more profitable to have facilities inside the EU. U.S. and Canadian companies invest in the EU for the same reasons.

Trade and foreign investment do not depend exclusively on companies exporting or building facilities in foreign countries. In many cases, it is better for a foreign company to buy a local company. For example, beer companies know that customers prefer local beer. Rather than export beer to a foreign country, a beer company will acquire or form an alliance with a local brewery. The name of the local company stays the same, and customers are unaware of the change in ownership. There are other examples. Gillette, a U.S. company, owns Braun, a "German" manufacturer of household appliances. Grand Metropolitan PLC, a British company, owns Green Giant, a well-known "American" company.

Economic Issues in the World's Major Trading Regions

North America

North American Free Trade Agreement

In 1989, the United States and Canada signed a free trade agreement, and Mexico joined in 1994, creating the North American Free Trade Agreement[4] (NAFTA). The agreement seeks to eliminate tariffs as well as import and export quotas, open government procurement markets, increase opportunities to make investments in other countries, ease travel between countries, and remove restrictions on agricultural products, auto parts, and energy goods.

United States

U.S. companies compete worldwide.[5] U.S. companies are a major force in the computer industry in Europe and Southeast Asia. U.S. telecommunications companies are formidable competitors in international markets. Ford and General Motors are leaders in the North American automobile industry. They have strong market positions in Europe and are making inroads in Japan and Asia. Procter & Gamble and other U.S. consumer goods companies are expanding into foreign countries. Coca-Cola has a soft drink plant and distribution center in Moscow and is expanding into Eastern Europe.

Many European companies have a presence in the United States. BMW has a facility in South Carolina, and Mercedes has one in Alabama. In 1998, Alcatel, France's giant telecom equipment manufacturer, purchased Texas-based DSC Communications for $4.4 billion. That same year, Daimler-Benz purchased Chrysler for $39.5 billion. Hoechst AG, of Germany, paid over $7 billion for Marion Merrell Dow, a subsidiary of Dow Chemical.

Currently, Japanese companies are more interested in Asia than the United States. In the United States, their subsidiaries work with U.S. companies who have strong capabilities and can help them improve quality and cost. There are many examples: Isuzu, Suzuki, and Toyota buy antilock brake systems from General Motors; Mitsubishi Electric buys computers from IBM; and Ricoh buys customized controllers from Motorola.

Canada

Canada[6] is the United States' largest trading partner. The United States has large FDI in Canada, more than any other country except Great Britain. Ford, General Motors, IBM, Kodak, Procter & Gamble, and Xerox have factories in Canada. Canada's culture, language, legal and business environment, and geography are similar to the United States, therefore, trade between the two countries is easy.

Canadian companies invest heavily in the United States. For example, Canadian Pacific owns the Delaware & Hudson Railway, and Bombardier owns Learjet. Canadian companies do business in many other countries, including Germany, Great Britain, Japan, and Mexico. Canada has vast natural resources such as gold, lumber, natural gas, nickel, and oil.

Canada is a favorable target for FDI by European and Asian companies anxious to access its natural resources and take advantage of the opportunities provided under NAFTA to access U.S. and Mexican markets.

Mexico

In 1994, Mexico[7] became part of NAFTA and was close to becoming a major economic power in Central and South America. Unfortunately, Mexico struggled through a few years of economic problems. Since that time, the Mexican economy has succeeded.

Even before NAFTA, Mexico had a strong maquiladora assembly industry. Maquiladora zones employ over 1.2 million highly skilled people. Productivity is good, quality is high, and wage rates are significantly lower than in the

United States. Under NAFTA, parts and materials originating in one of the three NAFTA countries enter the maquiladora zones duty free. Anything originating outside the three countries is subject to tariffs up to 25 percent, though exceptions exist. In some cases, imported items from the EU enter duty free because Mexico signed a free trade agreement with the EU in 1999.

Most large international companies have a presence in Mexico. Daimler-Benz, General Motors, Nissan, Philips, and Siemens have large factories there. Ford's factory in Hermisillo is one of the company's best. Volkswagen manufactures the Beetle in Mexico for export to the United States.

Many Mexican companies now produce products for U.S. companies, which were previously purchased from Asia. The Mexican companies' competitive advantages are low labor costs and proximity to the U.S. market. For example, Hewlett-Packard increased its imports of copier products by 25 percent from Mexican companies. IBM is pushing its Asian suppliers to establish joint ventures in Mexico, so its own costs and inventories decrease.

South America

The 1980s and early 90s were difficult economic times for many South American countries.[8] Argentina, Brazil, Chile, and Venezuela accumulated large foreign debts, and along with other countries in the region, were devastated by severe inflation. In the following period, most countries underwent needed economic reforms. By 1998, the gross domestic product (GDP) in Argentina increased 8 percent per year, industrial production rose 7 percent per year, and inflation was low. In Brazil, inflation dropped to 5 percent in 1998 from as high as 50 percent three years earlier. Foreign companies invested in Argentina and Brazil. Compaq Computer opened a factory to produce 400,000 PCs per year. Anheuser-Busch spent $105 million on a brewery. General Electric constructed $9 billion worth of coal-fired electricity plants. Brazil is now doing well, but Argentina is struggling again.

Chile is the economic success story of South America. Its economy is growing at a fast rate. Export volume is more than double that of Brazil, Venezuela, or Mexico, and FDI is increasing. Some foreign companies are interested in Chile because they believe it might enter NAFTA.

Trade between South American countries is growing due to efforts by Mercosur and the Andean Common Market. Ninety percent of trade between Mercosur countries is duty free. Countries in the Andean Common Market have common external tariffs and almost no duties between member countries. Negotiations are in progress to merge Mercosur and the Andean Common Market into a South American Free Trade Association.

Europe

Three major economic developments have occurred in Europe in the last ten years[9]:

- The EU became an effective economic union.
- Many traditionally nationalized industries were privatized, such as telecommunications and transportation in France and Great Britain.
- Economic linkages formed between the EU and newly emerging countries in Central and Eastern Europe.

European Union (EU)

The EU eliminated trade barriers between member countries, created a common currency and central bank, and established common duties and economic policies regarding non-EU countries.[10] Companies based in EU countries can manufacture and sell products anywhere in the EU duty free and without quotas or exchange rate fluctuations. Many companies from other regions of the world have set up facilities and joint ventures in EU countries to reap these benefits.

Some companies are surprised that it remains necessary to adapt products and processes to local country needs. Many EU-based companies "plan globally, but act locally." There are many examples. The Renault 11 is an economy car in Great Britain and a luxury item in Spain. Appliance makers add a self-cleaning option to ovens for the French market but leave it out of units for the German market, where food is generally cooked at lower temperatures.

Many EU-based companies are organized into multicountry networks of companies and facilities. For example, Philips and Siemens have an alliance to develop computer chips. Philips assembles televisions in Belgium using picture tubes from Germany, transistors from France, plastics from Italy, and electronic components from the Netherlands.

The EU's biggest challenge is determining how to include its eastern neighbors, the former communist bloc countries, in the union. Its success will create the largest economic market in the world. Foreign companies are positioning themselves in the EU and the Eastern European countries to prepare for these advantages.

Central and Eastern Europe

In December of 1989, the Berlin Wall came down, and two years later, on December 8, 1991, the Soviet Union ceased to exist.[11] Each of the individual republics that comprised the Soviet Union declared independence. Russia has the most people, territory, and influence, but others, such as the Ukraine, are also important. The Russian economy is less strong than the economies of its once-dominated neighbors, the Czech Republic, Hungary, and Poland. It will be years before it matches the economies of neighboring countries in Western Europe.

Russia is removing many government administered prices and subsidies and letting free market forces work. However, this approach causes inflation when demand exceeds supply, and inflation causes hardship for many people. Other problems in Russia are crime and political uncertainty. The country is privatizing many state enterprises, handing some over to managers and workers who set up boards of directors and control enterprise operations. Enterprises issue stock, and employees and outside investors purchase shares and become owners.

The future potential is so high in Russia that many international companies want to establish an early presence there. For example, IBM is providing 40,000 computers for Russian schools. DaimlerChrysler is constructing a $140 million factory to build buses. Alcatel, the giant French telecommunications company, has a $2.8 billion contract to supply advanced digital telephone switches.

The Czech Republic, Hungary, and Poland are the next most visible former communist countries. All have made significant economic progress and have attracted foreign investment. Foreign companies are interested in the large markets for their products and the availability of skilled workers and professionals to hire for wages much lower than in EU countries.

- Asea Brown Boveri, the giant Swiss conglomerate, purchased Zamech, a turbine manufacturer in Poland.[12]
- Britain's Telfos Holdings paid $19 million for 51 percent of Ganz, a Hungarian locomotive and rolling stock manufacturer.
- Ford constructed an $80 million components factory in Hungary.
- General Electric purchased Tungsram, a giant electric company.
- Italy's Ilwa purchased Salgotarjay Iron Works for $25 million.
- Japan's Fravalex purchased Sklo-Union Teplice, a glass manufacturer, for $1 billion.
- Linde of Germany invested $106 million in Technoplyn, a natural gas company.
- Siemens of Germany invested $35 million in Electromagnetica, a medical equipment company, and $15 million in Telsa Karin, a telecommunications firm.
- Suzuki invested $110 million in a joint venture with Autokonzern to produce cars.

- Swedish furniture maker IKEA invested $60 million in a furniture plant in Trnava.
- Volkswagen purchased a $6.6 billion share of the Skoda Auto Works.

Many other former communist countries are still struggling and are less attractive to foreign companies.

Southeast Asia

Despite a lingering economic downturn that started in 1997, Southeast Asia is still a major force in the world economy. Southeast Asian countries are popular locations for manufacturing high quality, low cost products. They are also very competitive in services. For example, the national airlines of Malaysia, Singapore, and Thailand regularly top the service quality rankings in polls of international business travelers. Singapore's Changi International Airport has been ranked number one in the world, as have Asian hotel groups like the Shangri-La and Mandarin Oriental.

Japan

Japan's economic success has no precedent.[13] The country has a large positive trade balance, the yen is strong, and Japanese companies are world leaders in manufacturing and numerous consumer products. Some of the Japanese economy's early success is attributed to the Ministry of International Trade and Industry (MITI), a government agency that identifies and nurtures industrial interests for the country.

Japan's success also results from the influence of keiretsus (Chapter 10). A *keiretsus* is an organizational arrangement that binds a large group of vertically integrated companies together by cross-ownership, interlocking boards of directors, and social ties. Drawing on the resources of other parts of the keiretsus helps a Japanese company solve problems and exploit opportunities faster and more profitably than competitors.

Japanese companies have invested billions of dollars abroad. The pace slowed in the 1990s when their economy fell into a long recession. Japan, in turn, has been the target of considerable foreign investment. For example, General Motors now sells its Saturn line of cars in Japan through a network of dedicated dealerships.

China

China enjoyed spectacular growth in the 1980s and 90s.[14] This recently slowed due to fierce competition in the production of low cost products from neighboring Southeast Asian countries. Exports are still high, particularly to the United States, where China has a huge trade surplus. Foreign companies establish facilities in China because of the country's low wages. As wages begin to rise, China is trying to increase productivity and improve technology to sustain growth.

Thanks to Hong Kong, Southeast China has become an industrial powerhouse. Its economy is already bigger than the economy of France; and some observers predict that this area of China will soon have a GDP that is larger than that of every other country except Japan and the United States.

China is not an easy place for foreign companies to do business. The government requires foreign companies to have local partners. Product piracy is common, contractual agreements are difficult to enforce, and labor practices are often wretched. The government can be heavy handed. However, with 1.2 billion people, China is a major world market, and international companies know they must have a presence there.

Some foreign companies underestimate the capabilities of local Chinese companies. One company entered China hoping to sell high-tech equipment and was surprised to find local companies producing similar products with better quality and lower cost. Chinese companies now outperform foreign companies in PCs, CAT scanners, radiation therapy machines, and power generation equipment below 600 megawatts. Even Chinese car makers are improving. Sales of the Alto have grown faster than those of any other car in China. The car was designed by Suzuki

SITUATION 9.1

Levi Strauss in China

LEVI STRAUSS is a strong company with a reputation for good quality. Business magazines describe it as "most admired." Part of Levi Strauss' mission is "responsible commercial success," meaning the company will be ethical and profitable.

In 1992, Levi Strauss established guidelines for its worldwide suppliers in the areas of employee working conditions and environmental impact. These guidelines were the first adopted by any global company. Levi Strauss regularly checked its suppliers for compliance. As a result of these checks, the company terminated business with 30 suppliers and demanded changes at 120 others. In 1993, the company terminated business with all Chinese suppliers ($50 million per year).

The decision to withdraw all business from China was not made lightly. Levi Strauss knew it had serious implications for future business with China. Competitors would have a head start in the local market, and the Chinese government could make it difficult for the company to re-enter. Six years later, conditions in China improved, and Levi Strauss made plans to do just that.

and is manufactured by Norinco, an all-Chinese company.

Many foreign companies are doing well in China. Motorola invested $120 million in facilities to produce semiconductors and mobile phones. General Motors invested $100 million in a truck assembly plant and built a new $1.5 billion car assembly plant in Shanghai. Procter & Gamble invested $10 million in a joint venture factory to produce laundry and personal care products.

The Four Tigers

Hong Kong, Singapore, South Korea, and Taiwan have arrived as major economic powers.[15] Numerous foreign companies, including Hewlett-Packard, IBM, Matsushita, Motorola, Nestle, Nissan, Philips, Sharp, and Volkswagen, have facilities in one or more of these countries.

Hong Kong, which became part of China in 1997, and Singapore are headquarters for some of the world's most successful trading companies. Most observers place Hong Kong and Singapore at the top of the list of most competitive economies in the world. Hong Kong is Southeast China's trading and financial center and is where Southeast China and the world meet to do business. Singapore is the trading and financial center for the rest of Southeast Asia.

In South Korea, the major conglomerates (called chaebols) include such internationally known companies as Samsung, Daewoo, Hyundai, and the LG Group. Chaebols are large, family-held conglomerates with considerable economic and political power (Chapter 10). Many key managers were educated in the West, where, in addition to their academic training, they learned Western culture and language. This knowledge now crafts formidable international strategies for their companies.

Taiwan is moving from a labor-intensive economy to one dominated by technologically sophisticated industries, such as banking, computers, petroleum refining, and power generation.

Other Southeast Asian Countries

Indonesia, Malaysia, Thailand, sometimes called the Baby Tigers, and Vietnam are developing along the lines of the Four Tigers.[16] Each has a large population, inexpensive labor, natural resources, and social stability. Many international companies from Japan, the Four Tigers, North America, and the EU have a presence in these countries.

A growing number of international companies began conducting business in Vietnam in 1994, after the United States ended its trade embargo. For example, AT&T began providing long-distance telephone service; Caterpillar supplied equipment for a $2 billion highway project; Coca-Cola began bottling operations; and Mobil teamed with three Japanese partners for offshore drilling.

Less-Developed Countries

Countries are considered "less developed" if they have several of the following characteristics[17]:

- Low GDP
- Slow GDP growth per capita
- High unemployment
- High international debt
- Large population
- Unskilled or semiskilled work force
- Considerable government intervention in economic affairs

Examples are India and many Asian and African countries.

India

India's population is about one billion people.[18] While some are well educated and speak English, 60 percent are illiterate. Despite a large middle- and upper-class market for goods and services, the per capita GDP is low.

In the past, the government barely encouraged foreign companies to invest in the country. For example, Gillette (United States) once waited eight years for acceptance of its application to enter the country. For a long time, government regulations restricted foreign ownership to a maximum of 40 percent of any business.

The government is now relaxing its rules. Coca-Cola received permission in eight weeks to build a 100-percent-owned facility, and Motorola received permission in two days to build a new production line. The government realizes that many foreign companies make a choice between investing in India or China, and that any investment not made in India could be forever lost to China.

The relaxation of rules brings investment from many foreign companies, such as Daimler-Chrysler, Procter & Gamble, and Whirlpool. Foreign companies are attracted by the large market for their products and by the skilled workers, engineers, and computer scientists for hire at much lower wages and salaries than developed countries.

Africa

Despite considerable natural resources, most African countries are poor and undeveloped.[19] International trade is not a major source of income. One obstacle for international companies interested in doing business in Africa is the population's overwhelming diversity. Africa's 700 million people come from 3,000 tribes and speak 1,000 languages and dialects. Political instability in many countries makes direct foreign investment risky.

Cultural Differences

An international company performs activities in many different countries. Some of these countries have cultures different from the culture in the company's home country. An international company must understand the cultures in different parts of the world because culture affects behavior—both from employees and customers.[20]

Culture is acquired knowledge people use to interpret experience and compose social behavior. Culture is acquired by learning and experience. It is shared between people who are members of a group, organization, or society. Culture is cumulative; it is passed down from one generation to the next. It is adaptive because it changes as conditions in the environment change.

Values are a part of culture. *Values* are basic convictions people have regarding right and wrong, good and bad, important and unimportant. They are learned from the culture in which a person is reared, and they help direct a person's behavior.

Understanding the impact of culture on behavior is important for companies that perform activities in different countries. To illustrate, Situation 9.2 reviews some business behaviors that rely on a country's culture.[21]

Culture can be organized into dimensions. Seven dimensions are useful for understanding how business people from one country and culture should behave when they do business with people from a country with a different culture. The dimensions are[22]:

- Universalism versus particularism
- Individualism versus collectivism
- Neutral versus emotional
- Specific versus diffuse
- Achievement versus ascription
- Sequential- or synchronous-time; past-, present-, or future-orientation
- Control outcomes versus letting things take their course

These dimensions also allow us to identify groups of countries with similar business cultures.

Universalism Versus Particularism

Universalism is the belief that ideas and practices can be applied everywhere without modification.

Particularism is the belief that circumstances dictate how ideas and practices should apply.

In cultures with high universalism, the focus is more on formal rules than on relationships. Business contracts are followed closely. In cultures with high particularism, the focus is more on relationships and trust than on formal rules. Figure 9-1(A) shows the degree of universalism and particularism in different countries. The United States and Germany have high universalism, while China and Russia have high particularism.

When people from cultures with high particularism do business with people from cultures with high universalism, they can expect rational, professional arguments, and a "let's get down to business" attitude. When people from cultures with high universalism do business with people from cultures with high particularism, they should be prepared for personal meandering and irrelevancies that seem to lack direction. They should not regard personal, get-to-know-you attitudes as mere small talk. Situation 9.3 gives an example of the problems that can occur when a company from a universalistic culture (Corning, United States) forms an alliance with a company from a particularistic culture (Vitro, Mexico), but does not realize that it needs to adjust its business behaviors.

Individualism Versus Collectivism

Individualism refers to people regarding themselves as individuals, while *collectivism* refers to people regarding themselves as part of a group. Figure 9-1(B) shows the degree of individualism and collectivism in different countries. The United States has high individualism and Japan has high collectivism. Russia has high individualism. Many people assume that a former communist country like Russia would be collectivistic. Perhaps it was at one time, but culture changes. This illustrates the danger of making uninformed generalizations about cultures.

In cultures with high individualism, people achieve things independently, negotiations are typically made on the spot by a representative, and individuals assume a great deal of personal responsibility. In cultures with high collectivism, people achieve things in groups, groups make decisions, and people assume responsibility together.

When people from cultures with high individualism do business with people from cultures with

Situation 9.2

Business Behavior and Country Culture

Centralized versus decentralized decision making

In some cultures, top managers make all-important decisions. In other cultures, middle and lower level managers participate in, and make, important decisions.

Safety versus risk taking

In some cultures, decision makers are risk averse, whereas others accept risk taking.

Individual versus group rewards

In some cultures, individual rewards are most common. Employees with above average performance receive individual rewards such as bonuses, commissions, and promotions, but in other cultures, group rewards are most common.

Formal versus informal procedures

In some cultures, formal, carefully established, rigidly followed procedures are favored. In others, informal procedures are more common.

High versus low organizational loyalty

In some cultures, people identify strongly with their organization or company. In other cultures people identify more with their profession (accountant, machinist) or interests (community, family).

Cooperation versus competition

Some cultures encourage cooperation between individuals or groups; others encourage competition.

Short-term versus long-term horizons

Some cultures have short-term horizons, such as short-term goals for profit and efficiency. Other cultures prefer long-term goals, such as market share and technological development.

Stability versus innovation

Some cultures encourage stability and resist change; others place a high value on innovation and change.

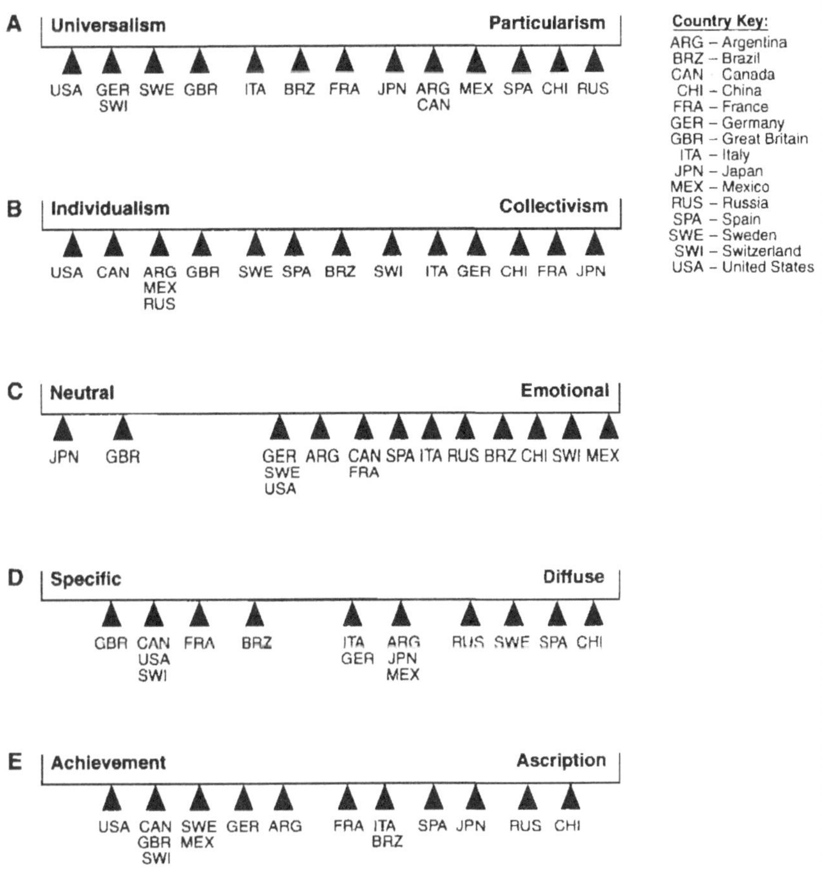

Adapted from Hodgetts and Luthans, *International Management*, Irwin McGraw-Hill, p. 126, 2003.
Used with permission of The McGraw-Hill Companies.

Figure 9-1 Country Orientations on Selected Dimensions of Culture

high collectivism, they should have patience, allow time for consultation, and try to build lasting relationships. When people from cultures with high collectivism do business with people from cultures with high individualism, they should be prepared to make faster decisions and commit their company to these decisions. Also, a collectivistic person dealing with an individualistic person should realize that they are dealing with one person (as opposed to a group) because this person is respected by his or her company and has the authority to make commitments.

Neutral Versus Emotional

A *neutral culture* is one in which emotions are held in check. Japan and Great Britain are neutral cultures (Figure 9-1 [C]). People in these countries try not to show their feelings. They act stoically and maintain their composure.

An *emotional culture* is one in which emotions are openly and naturally expressed. People in emotional cultures often smile a great deal, talk loudly when excited, and greet each other with a great deal of enthusiasm.

SITUATION 9.3

Joint Venture Between Corning and Vitro[23]

CORNING IS A U.S. COMPANY best known for its oven-ready glassware. Over the years, Corning has formed about 50 alliances and joint ventures. A very early success was an alliance in the 1920s, with St. Gobain, a French glassmaker, to produce Pyrex cookware in Europe. Only nine of Corning's 50 alliances have failed. This is an excellent record considering that commonly half of all alliances fail. In a recent five-year period, sales from Corning's alliances exceeded $3 billion.

Corning establishes joint ventures for two reasons. One, it gains access to markets it cannot penetrate quickly enough on its own. The Corning-Samsung alliance, in which Corning wanted to win market share in the Asian television tube market, is an example. Two, it brings Corning technology to market. The Corning-Mitsubishi alliance, in which Corning produced ceramic materials for automotive catalytic converters, is an example.

Vitro, a glass manufacturer located in Monterey, Mexico, specializes in the production of drinkware, but it also produces many other products from automobile windshields to washing machines. The company has a long history of successful joint ventures.

In 1992, Corning signed a joint venture with Vitro. Corning expected that Mexico would join NAFTA (1994) and wanted to prepare early to bring its products to the large Mexican market.

Cultural clashes broke out immediately. The Americans felt that their Mexican partners:

- Wasted time being too polite
- Moved too slowly
- Would not acknowledge problems
- Took a passive sales approach

The Mexicans felt that their American partners:

- Were too forward
- Moved too quickly

Corning was:

- Lean
- Decisions were made by groups of middle managers

Vitro was:

- Bureaucratic and hierarchical
- Loyalty was to family members and company patrons
- Decisions were made by top executives

The joint venture was unable to overcome the differences between Corning's universalistic culture and Vitro's particularistic one. Twenty-five months after signing the agreement, Corning and Vitro dissolved the joint venture. In its place, they agreed to simply distribute each other's products.

When people from emotional cultures do business with people from neutral cultures, they should write down as much as possible for the other side and should realize that lack of emotion does not mean disinterest. When people from neutral cultures do business with people from emotional cultures, they should not be put off stride when the other side creates scenes or grows animated and boisterous; instead they should try to respond warmly to the other side's emotional affections.

Specific Versus Diffuse

A *specific culture* is one in which individuals have a large "public space" they readily let others enter and share, and a small "private space" they guard closely and share with only close friends and associates.

A *diffuse culture* is one in which public space and private space are similar in size and overlap significantly. Work and private life overlap. Individuals guard their public space because entry into public space affords entry into private space.

Great Britain and the United States are specific cultures, while Spain and China are diffuse cultures (Figure 9-1 [D]). When people from specific cultures do business with people from diffuse cultures (for example, a U.S. company does business in China), they should respect a person's title, age, and background and not lose patience when a person is indirect. When people from diffuse cultures do business with people from specific cultures, they should try to be efficient and to the point, use agendas to structure meetings, and not use their titles or acknowledge achievements irrelevant to the issues being discussed.

Achievement Versus Ascription

An *achievement culture* is one in which people are given status based on how well they perform their jobs. For example, the product manager who launches a successful new product, the designer who wins an award, the salesperson with the highest sales, and the crew that sets a production record, all have high status.

An *ascription culture* is one in which status is attributed based on who or what a person is. Status is based on age, years of service, or social connections. For example, a person who has worked with a company for 40 years is respected because of his or her age and longevity with the company. A person with friends in high places is afforded status because of who he or she knows.

The United States and Switzerland are achievement cultures, while China and Japan are ascription cultures (Figure 9-1 [E]).

When people from achievement cultures do business with people from ascription cultures, they should include older, senior, formal position-holders in their group to impress the other side and should respect the status and influence of their counterparts. When people from ascription cultures do business with people from achievement cultures, they should make sure that their group has technical advisers and knowledgeable people to prove that their group is competent and should respect the knowledge and information of the other group's counterparts.

Sequential- or Synchronous-Time; Past-, Present-, or Future-Orientation

In cultures with a *sequential approach* to time, people tend to perform one activity at a time, strictly keep appointments, and follow plans as laid out.

In cultures with a *synchronous approach* to time, people tend to perform more than one activity at a time, appointments are approximate and can change at a moment's notice, and schedules are subordinate to relationships. People often stop what they are doing to greet individuals entering their office. People in sequential-time cultures are less likely to do this.

In the United States, people have a sequential-time attitude and set a schedule and stick to it. In France, people have a synchronous-time attitude and tend to be more flexible and build slack into their schedules to allow for interruptions.

Another time-related dimension is the degree to which cultures are *past-*, *present-*, or *future-oriented.*

In the United States and Germany, the future is most important. In Indonesia and Spain, the present is most important. In France, the time periods are equally important. When doing business with future-oriented cultures, individuals should emphasize the opportunities that an agreement will create and agree to specific deadlines for getting things done. When doing business with present- or past-oriented cultures, individuals should emphasize the reasons for the agreement, the events that led to it, and agree to future meetings. They should not fix deadlines.

Control Outcomes Versus Let Things Take Their Course

People have different views of their relationship with the world. At one extreme, people believe they must have control over what happens. "What happens to me is my own doing." The United States, Switzerland, and Australia feel strongly that they are masters of their own fate. People adopt an aggressive, take-charge approach in business activities and become irritated when things do not turn out the way they want.

At the other extreme, people believe that things must take their own course. Asian cultures, such as China, Japan, and Singapore, have this view. They believe that events move naturally, and one must "go with the flow." A flexible attitude, characterized by a willingness to compromise and be in harmony with the environment, is important.

When doing business with people from cultures that believe in dominating the environment, it is important to negotiate aggressively, test your opponent, win some objectives, and lose from time to time. When doing business with people from cultures that believe in letting things take their natural course, it is important to be polite and persistent, maintain good relationships, and try to win together.

Countries With Similar Cultures

Countries can be grouped into five clusters based on similarities in the cultural dimensions discussed in the previous section.[24] The clusters are: Anglo, Asian, Latin American, Latin European, and Germanic (Figure 9-2).

Countries in the same cluster have similar business cultures. For example, the United States, Great Britain, Canada, and Australia are in the Anglo cluster. None of these countries have identical cultural dimensions. Figure 9-2 shows two differences between the United States and Canada. The United States is universalistic, while Canada is particularistic; and the United States is at the midpoint of the neutral/emotional dimension, while Canada is more emotional. The one difference between the United States and Great Britain is that Great Britain is much closer to neutral.

Countries in different clusters have significantly different cultures. For example, the culture in the United States differs from France (Latin European cluster) in four of the five cultural dimensions.

The Asian cluster of countries, Japan, China, Indonesia, Hong Kong, and Singapore, have practically identical cultures. This culture is the opposite of the U.S. culture. Notice all five cultural dimensions differ between the United States and all countries in this cluster.

Three of the four countries in the Latin American cluster, Argentina, Mexico, and Venezuela, have similar cultures. Brazil's culture is sufficiently different that some people label it unique. The same is true for Spain in the Latin European cluster. France, Belgium, and Italy have similar cultures, but Spain's culture is somewhat unique.

Figure 9-2 is a simple tool to help international companies recognize cultural differences and adjust their practices when doing business with people from different countries. It is also important to remember that cultures change over time, and that within each culture people vary greatly.

Dimensions of Culture	Anglo Cluster				Latin American Cluster				Latin European Cluster			
	United States	Great Britain	Canada	Australia	Argentina	Mexico	Venezuela	Brazil	France	Belgium	Italy	Spain
Universalism (U) versus Particularism (P)	U	U	P	P	P	P	P	U/P	U/P	U	U	P
Individualism (I) versus Collectivism (C)	I	I	I	I	I	I	C	I/C	C	C	C	I/C
Neutral (N) versus Emotional (E)	N/E	N	E	N/E	N/E	E	E	E	E	N/E	E	E
Specific (S) versus Diffuse (D)	S	S	S	S	D	D	D	S	S	S	D	D
Achievement (Ac) versus Ascription (As)	Ac	Ac	Ac	Ac	Ac	Ac	As	Ac/As	Ac/As	Ac/As	Ac/As	As

Dimensions of Culture	Germanic Cluster				Asian Cluster				
	Austria	Germany	Switzer-land	Czecho-slovakia	Japan	China	Indonesia	Hong Kong	Singa-pore
Universalism (U) versus Particularism(P)	U	U	U	U	P	P	P	P	P
Individualism (I) versus Collectivism (C)	I	C	C	C	C	C	C	C	C
Neutral (N) versus Emotional (E)	N	N/E	E	E	N	E	N	N	N
Specific (S) versus Diffuse (D)	S	D	S	S	D	D	D	D	D
Achievement (Ac) versus Ascription (As)	Ac	Ac	Ac	As	As	As	As	Ac/As	As

Adapted from Hodgetts and Luthans, *International Management*, Irwin McGraw-Hill, p. 132, 2003. Used with permission of The McGraw-Hill Companies.

Figure 9-2 Clusters of Countries with Similar Cultures

Managing Across Cultures

For companies with activities in many countries, an important problem is whether these activities are performed abroad the same way as at home or whether they will be adapted for local culture and needs.[25]

At one time, companies believed that one worldwide approach to business was the key to effectiveness and efficiency. They also believed:

- Good management is universal.
- A good manager from the home country will be a good manager in any other country. State-of-the-art processes and technology will adequately handle the challenges of doing business in any country.

Today, this view is considered a parochial view of old-fashioned managers from companies in advanced countries. This view started to change in the 1970s, when many companies expanded their international activities. They discovered that it was impossible to do business the same way in every country. They discovered that only a small number of home country best practices could be implemented abroad without too much modification (Situations 9.4 and 9.5).

Superior companies recognize that strategies and practices must reflect the culture of each country in which they operate. They also recognize that culture is not the only difference they encounter when they operate in different countries.

Local customers may prefer local suppliers or need customized products. Televisions are an example. Different regions of the world have different technical standards for televisions, and customers in these regions prefer different types of television sets. Companies may need to produce locally to meet local standards and customer needs. Thomson SA, a French consumer electronics company, produces televisions in France, Germany, Great Britain, Spain, and Mexico. Each factory focuses on a particular type of television set for a particular market. For example, the German factory makes large, upscale sets for European markets; the Spanish factory makes low cost, small sets for European markets; and the Mexican factory makes sets (under the RCA and GE brand names) for the U.S. market.

In some industry segments, customer needs are identical worldwide, and a standard product can be produced. Some high and low end products are examples. High end products, such as Heineken beer, Hennessey brandy, and Porsche cars, appeal to fairly homogenous market niches, regardless of

Situation 9.4

Employee Stock Plan at Gillette[26]

In the mid-1990s, Gillette considered offering a stock plan to its 33,000 employees worldwide.

The plan was well liked in the United States where employee stock plans are popular. However, foreign exchange controls in some countries (Brazil) prohibited out-of-country stock investment. Labor unions in some countries (Great Britain) opposed stock plans. Government permission was required in some countries (Eastern Europe). Fluctuating exchange rates made stock plans less attractive (Japan). Labor laws (Mexico) could make a one-time stock grant an annual requirement. Employees would have to pay a hefty tax when stock options were issued (the Netherlands).

Because of these problems, Gillette did not offer the plan.

SITUATION 9.5

Performance Evaluation at Shell[27]

SHELL OIL'S HEAD OFFICE required its subsidiaries in the Netherlands, France, Germany, and Great Britain to use the following five criteria for performance evaluation of managers:

- *Analysis:* Ability to logically and completely evaluate situations
- *Imagination:* Ability to be creative
- *Leadership:* Ability to inspire personnel
- *Extensiveness:* Ability to take a broad view
- *Reality:* Ability to realistically use information

The head office allowed each country subsidiary to prioritize the five criteria as it saw fit. The results were:

- *Netherlands:* Reality, analysis, extensiveness, leadership, imagination
- *France:* Imagination, analysis, leadership, extensiveness, reality
- *Germany:* Leadership, analysis, reality, imagination, extensiveness
- *Great Britain:* Extensiveness, imagination, reality, analysis, leadership

Notice that none of the country subsidiaries had the same criterion at the top of their list. The criterion at the top of the list for the Netherlands was at the bottom of the list for France. The German list was in the reverse order of Great Britain's.

As a result, managers were evaluated differently in each country subsidiary.

geographic location. The same is true for some low end products, such as fast foods and blue jeans. However, even when standard products are appropriate, factory practices and marketing approaches should adjust for local culture.

Adapting strategies and practices for local culture presents several challenges for international companies:

- All country markets are not the same. Management must stay up to date on local conditions.
- Management must know the strengths and weaknesses of country subsidiaries.
- Management must give country subsidiaries resources to meet local needs and autonomy to respond to changes in needs.

This is examined in the next chapter.

SUMMARY

Internationalization became popular in the 1970s and grew because of developments such as:

- International trade agreements (EU, NAFTA, ASEAN, Mercosur, Andean Common Market)
- Economic activity in different regions of the world

- Political developments (WTO, fall of the former Soviet Union, market openings in Central and Eastern Europe and India)

Companies are attracted to foreign countries because of the presence of skilled, low cost workers and professionals who can produce their products, and large populations who will buy their products.

International companies cannot manage their dispersed facilities with "one-size-fits-all" practices. Cultures and customer needs might differ in each country. Companies must understand the impact of culture on behavior to adapt their strategies and practices for each country market. Seven dimensions of culture are useful for understanding how culture affects business behavior. Countries are grouped into clusters based on similarities in culture: Anglo, Asian, Latin American, Latin European, and Germanic. Countries in the same cluster have similar cultures.

ENDNOTES

1. The first half of this chapter examines economic developments in the world's major trading regions. This material is from:
   - Hodgetts, R., and Luthans, F., *International Management: Culture, Strategy, and Behavior*, Irwin McGraw-Hill: Boston, chapters 1, 2, 4, 2003.
2. Hodgetts and Luthans, *International Management*, pp. 6–8.
3. Ibid, pp. 8–11.
4. Ibid, p. 12.
5. Ibid, p. 12.
6. Ibid, p. 13.
7. Ibid, pp. 13, 165.
8. Ibid, p. 14.
9. Ibid, p. 15.
10. Ibid, pp. 15–16, 78–81.
11. Ibid, pp. 16–19, 157–158.
12. Acquisitions are reported in ibid, pp. 18–19.
13. Ibid, pp. 19–21, 76–78.
14. Ibid, pp. 21, 81–85, 154–157.
15. Ibid, pp. 21–23, 155.
16. Ibid, p. 23.
17. Ibid, p. 23.
18. Ibid, pp. 23, 158, 159.
19. Ibid, p. 24.
20. The second half of this chapter examines cultural differences in the world's major trading regions. This material is from:
    - Hodgetts, R. and Luthans, F., *International Management: Culture, Strategy, and Behavior*, Irwin McGraw-Hill: Boston, chapters 5–8, 2003.

    Much of Hodgetts and Luthans' material on cultural differences is from:
    - Hampden-Turner, C., and Trompenaars, F., "A World Turned Upside Down: Doing Business in Asia," pp. 275–305, *Managing Across Cultures: Issues and Perspectives*, Joynt, P., and Warner, M. (eds.), International Thomson Business Press: London, 1996.
    - Trompenaars, F., *Riding the Waves of Culture*, Irwin: New York, 1994.
21. Hodgetts and Luthans, *International Management*, pp. 110–111.
22. Dimensions are examined in ibid, pp. 124–133
23. Ibid, pp. 370–371.
24. Ibid, pp. 131–133.
25. Ibid, pp. 149–153.
26. Ibid, p. 152.
27. Ibid, p. 153.

CHAPTER 10

INTERNATIONAL MANUFACTURING NETWORKS

An international manufacturing network of factories, distribution centers, offices, and so on can be organized in many ways. As seen in the following situations, the best organization is the one that satisfies customer needs and achieves the company's strategic goals.[1]

SITUATION 10.1

Global Product Manufacturing Network at Procter & Gamble[2]

IN THE MID-1990S, Procter & Gamble set a goal to double sales over the next ten years. The company reorganized to help achieve its goal. Its old organization structure was based on geographic regions; the new structure was based on global products. There were seven global business units, each focused on a product group: baby care products, beauty care products, home care products, and so on.

Aside from helping the company achieve its growth goal, the new structure was designed to meet the needs of Procter & Gamble's important international chain-store customers: Wal-Mart (United States), Carrefour (France), and others. These customers had three key needs: high quality products, recognizable brand names, and global supply. The old structure could not satisfy the last need. Global supply meant consistent global prices and standardized worldwide distribution. Under Procter & Gamble's old structure, customers negotiated prices and distribution on a country or regional basis. An international chain store paid different prices for products in the United States, Europe, and Latin America, but this was no longer acceptable. International chain-store customers needed consistent global prices and distribution.

SITUATION 10.2

Global Mixed Manufacturing Network at Motorola[3]

MOTOROLA SET A GOAL to increase its share of the worldwide cellular telephone market. To achieve its goal, Motorola needed to reduce costs and increase its presence in Asia and Europe. The company modified its international manufacturing network. Motorola expanded operations in Korea, the Philippines, and Taiwan, and built a $750 million plant in China and a $150 million plant in Germany. Motorola also merged six business units into two divisions. One was organized by product. This division produced consumer products, such as cellular telephones and pagers. The other was organized by manufacturing activity. It produced infrastructure products for communication networks.

SITUATION 10.3

Multidomestic Electronic Manufacturing Network at Li & Fung[4]

LI & FUNG IS A HONG KONG based company. In the 1970s, it was a sourcing agent for international companies interested in buying products from Southeast Asia. Li & Fung used its contacts with regional manufacturing companies and its knowledge of the region's government regulations to help customers find and purchase products. Over time, Li & Fung's capabilities increased, and services expanded. By the late 1980s, the company offered customers an entire value system of activities from product concept to prototype to low cost production to delivery of goods. Regional companies owned all activities, and Li & Fung contracted work with them. Li & Fung's international manufacturing network operated as follows.

A European retailer might place an order with Li & Fung for a large number of fashionable dresses. Li & Fung decided where to buy yarn in the world market. Then, Li & Fung selected the best companies to weave and dye cloth, produce items such as buttons and zippers, cut and sew dresses, and package and ship finished products to the retailer. Almost all transactions between Li & Fung and its contractors were done by telephone, fax, and computer. This approach to manufacturing is called *electronic manufacturing*. Its flexibility enabled Li & Fung to design the best value chain for each customer order.

SEVEN STRATEGIES FOR INTERNATIONAL MANUFACTURING

The best way an international company can organize manufacturing activities depends on its strategy for international manufacturing. There are seven different strategies. Each is a response to two important pressures international companies face: pressure for globalization and pressure for local responsiveness.

Pressure for Globalization

Pressure for globalization is the need for companies to design, manufacture, and market products on a worldwide basis. Pressure for globalization comes from a company's domestic and foreign competitors who challenge the company in every market segment where it operates. When this pressure is low, a company only needs to operate in its home country. When pressure is medium, a company needs to export to foreign countries. When pressure is high, a company needs to acquire or build facilities in foreign countries and create an international manufacturing network. (Chapters 2, 3, and 9 discuss level of competition in an industry, competitive challenges, and defensive responses.)

Pressure for Local Responsiveness

Pressure for local responsiveness is the need for companies to respond to differing requirements from customers, employees, and governments. Customer requirements may be different in various markets where a company competes; employee requirements may be different in various regions where a company works; and government regulations may be different in various countries where a company operates.

When pressure for local responsiveness is low, companies can produce and market a standard product and employ standard practices in their facilities. Standard products may even be regulated by international standards. Examples are chemicals, electronic components, and foods. When pressure for local responsiveness is high, companies must disperse activities and give facilities autonomy to respond to local needs.

Figure 10-1 shows the two pressures on a matrix. Pressure for globalization is on the vertical axis. Movement up the axis represents increasing pressure for globalization. Pressure for local responsiveness is on the horizontal axis. Movement to the right represents decreasing pressure for local responsiveness. The figure shows the relationship between seven strategies for international manufacturing and the two pressures. For example, companies use a domestic export strategy when pressure for globalization is low to medium and pressure for local responsiveness is low.

Figure 10-2 describes some characteristics of each strategy. For example, companies use a global strategy when pressure for globalization ranges from high to very high, and pressure for local responsiveness is low. Manufacturing activities are dispersed to facilities around the world, and products are sold in global markets. Facilities are organized into one of three global manufacturing networks: global product, global function, and global mixed. Companies in the computer industry use a global product network; companies in the mining industry use a global function network; and companies in the consumer electronics industry use a global mixed network. In Situation 10.1, Procter & Gamble used a global product network; in Situation 10.2, Motorola used a global mixed network.

Before examining the different manufacturing networks, the seven strategies for international manufacturing are reviewed.

Domestic Strategy

Domestic strategy is the simplest strategy. Pressure for globalization is low, so companies compete in local domestic markets where they manufacture. Pressure for local responsiveness can be low or high.

Many companies in the construction industry follow a domestic strategy. Pressure for local responsiveness is low in some industry segments (construction materials such as cement, aggregates, lumber) and high in others (construction projects such as offices, shopping malls, hospitals).

Consider a company that produces cement. The cost to transport cement is high, so factory capacity should not exceed demand in the local market (i.e., within a 10-hour drive of the factory). This limits the economies of scale that can be achieved, so pressure for globalization is low. Customer needs are on-time delivery of high quality cement at a low price. Quality means conformance to an international standard for the chemical composition of cement.

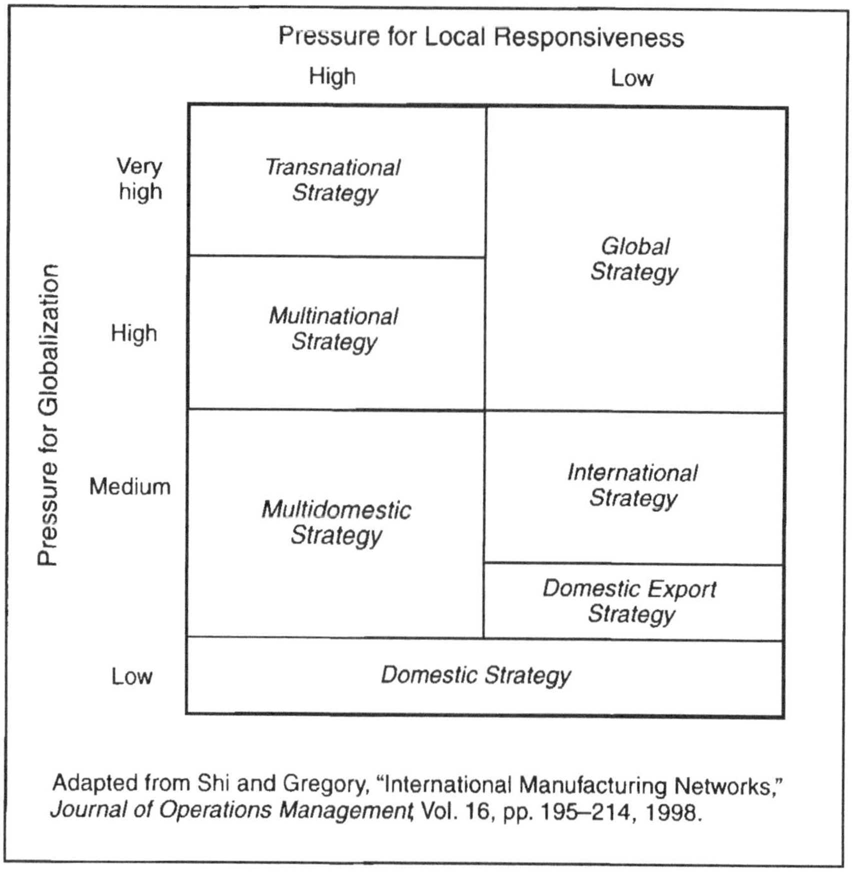

Figure 10-1 Seven Strategies for International Manufacturing

These needs are identical in most regions of the world, so pressure for local responsiveness is low. Low pressure for globalization and low pressure for local responsiveness enable a company to follow a domestic strategy (Figure 10-1).

Multidomestic Strategy

Multidomestic strategy is used when pressure for globalization is medium and pressure for local responsiveness is high. Companies that follow this strategy establish manufacturing facilities in different regions of the world to produce unique products that satisfy customer needs in local markets. Economies of scale cannot be achieved because products are unique. Companies that manufacture apparel, packaged goods, and steel follow this strategy. In Situation 10.3, Li & Fung followed a multidomestic strategy.

International Strategy and Domestic Export Strategy

International strategy is used when pressure for globalization is medium and pressure for local responsiveness is low. Customer needs are the same in all country markets, so standard products are produced. This leads to price competition. Companies must achieve economies of scale to be competitive, so large factories are established in different regions of the world or mergers and acquisitions are used to increase production volume. Pharmaceutical companies follow this strategy, as does Airbus Industrie, the European aircraft-manufacturing consortium.

Strategy	Pressure for Globali-zation	Pressure for Local Responsive-ness	Geographic Dispersion of Manufacturing Activities	Markets Served	Manufacturing Network	Examples of Industries and Companies
Domestic	Low	Low	National	Domestic	Domestic	Cement, building materials
	Low	High	National	Domestic	Domestic	Construction, metal fabrication
Domestic Export	Low to medium	Low	National	Domestic and export	Domestic export	Shipbuilding, Boeing
International	Medium	Low	Regional	International	International	Pharmaceuticals, Airbus
Multidomestic	Medium	High	Regional	Multiple domestic	Multidomestic	Clothing, packaged goods, steel, Li & Fung
Multinational	High	High	Multinational	All major national markets	Multinational	Pumps, mechanical equipment, food processing equipment
Global	High	Low	Worldwide	Global market	Global product	Computers, Procter & Gamble
					Global function	Mining, oil and gas
	Very high	Low	Worldwide	Global market	Global mixed	Consumer electronics, cameras, Motorola
Transnational	Very high	High	Worldwide	All national markets	Transnational	Telecom-munications, Honda, John Deere, Whirlpool

Figure 10-2 Characteristics of Strategies for International Manufacturing

When pressure for globalization is less, companies follow a special international strategy called domestic export strategy, in which they produce a standard product in a large domestic factory and export it to countries worldwide. Companies in the ship building industry and Boeing, the U.S. aircraft manufacturer, follow this strategy.

Global Strategy

Global strategy is used when pressure for globalization is high to very high and pressure for local responsiveness is low. Consider, for example, products such as consumer electronics, cameras, automobiles, computers, and minerals such as copper and nickel. Most customers in the world's largest trading regions (North America, the European Union, and Southeast Asia) purchase the same standardized products. Price competition is intense, and quality requirements are very high. Companies relentlessly pursue economies of scale in production, marketing, and distribution. Economies of scale and benefits of experience (Chapter 16) are realized when companies produce and sell larger and larger volumes of standard products and services to global markets. A regional or multinational manufacturing network cannot provide the volumes needed, so a tightly controlled, optimized, global manufacturing network is used. Activities are dispersed to the best locations around the world, and are carefully coordinated and tightly controlled. Procter & Gamble (Situation 10.1) and Motorola (Situation 10.2) are companies that follow a global strategy.

Multinational Strategy and Transnational Strategy

Multinational strategy is used when both pressures for globalization and local responsiveness are high. Companies establish factories in most countries worldwide where significant demands for their products exist. Factories have autonomy to adapt products to meet customer needs in local markets. Acquisitions and joint ventures are used to gain access to new country markets.

When pressure for globalization is very high, companies follow a special multinational strategy called transnational strategy. The very high pressure for globalization increases price competition, which forces companies to optimize their manufacturing networks. Companies call this "localize with a global focus" or "act locally and think globally." Many of the best manufacturing companies

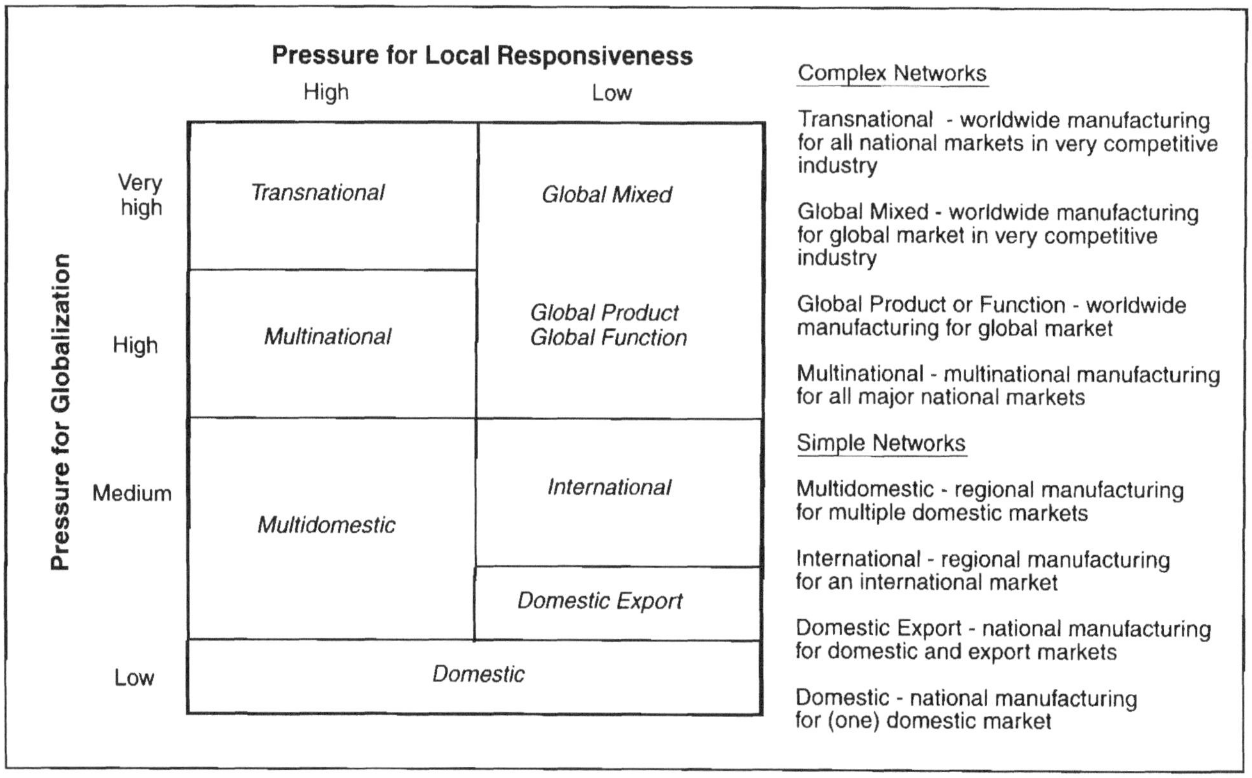

Figure 10-3 Nine International Manufacturing Networks

in the world, such as Honda, John Deere, and Philips, follow a transnational strategy.

NINE MANUFACTURING NETWORKS

International companies organize their manufacturing activities into networks. There are nine well-known manufacturing networks (Figure 10-3):

- Domestic
- Domestic export
- International
- Multidomestic
- Multinational
- Global product
- Global function
- Global mixed
- Transnational

The best network for a company depends on its strategy (Figure 10-1). One network is appropriate for each strategy, except global strategy (Figure 10-2), where three networks are appropriate. In addition to being appropriate for different strategies, manufacturing networks also differ with respect to size and focus of facilities, markets served, and geographic dispersion of manufacturing activities.

There are four geographic dispersions: national, regional, multinational, and worldwide. Networks that disperse activities to national and regional locations are *simple networks*. The simple networks are domestic, domestic export, international, and multidomestic and are appropriate for strategies at the bottom of Figure 10-1, where pressure for globalization is low to medium.

Networks that disperse activities to multinational and worldwide locations are *complex networks*. The complex networks are multinational, global product, global function, global mixed, and transnational. They are appropriate for strategies at the top of Figure 10-1, where pressure for globalization is high to very high.

In addition to the four simple and five complex networks, other manufacturing networks are possible. Most of the other networks are the result of mergers, acquisitions, and joint ventures. They combine one or more simple or complex networks with unique elements that address special circumstances.

SIMPLE NETWORKS

DOMESTIC: National Manufacturing for Domestic Market

This network is used when a company follows a domestic strategy. Pressure for globalization is low, and pressure for local responsiveness is high or low. A company operates one or more facilities in its home country and sells all products there.

The company produces a standard product when all customers have identical needs. Otherwise, the company adapts products to satisfy customer needs in different market segments. Figure 10-4 (A) shows a typical organization chart. It is a simple organization structure for a company using a simple network to achieve a simple strategy.

DOMESTIC EXPORT: National Manufacturing for Domestic and Export Markets

This network is used when a company follows a domestic export strategy. Pressure for globalization is low to medium, and pressure for local responsiveness is low. A company operates one or more facilities in its home country where a standard product is produced. Some units are sold in the home country; the rest are exported. The number of units exported is not high. Often, products are technologically advanced and have little competition, permitting a company to charge premium prices. Rolls-Royce automobiles and Boeing aircraft are examples.

Exports are the responsibility of an export manager. When export sales are very low, the export manager reports to the head of marketing.

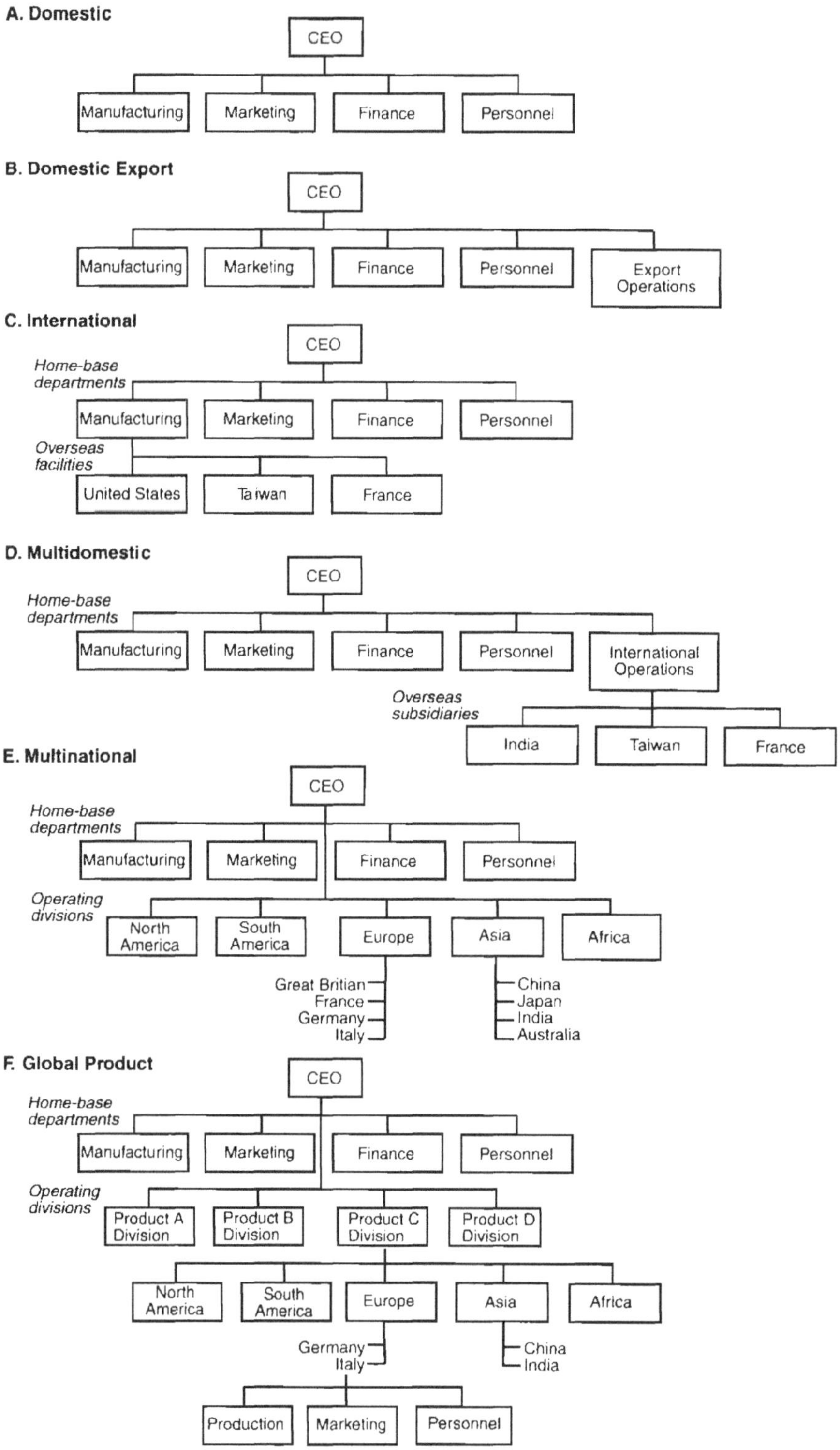

Adapted from Hodgetts and Luthan, *International Management*, Irwin McGraw-Hill: Boston, pp. 311-317, 2003

Figure 10-4 Organization Charts for Manufacturing Networks

G. Global Function

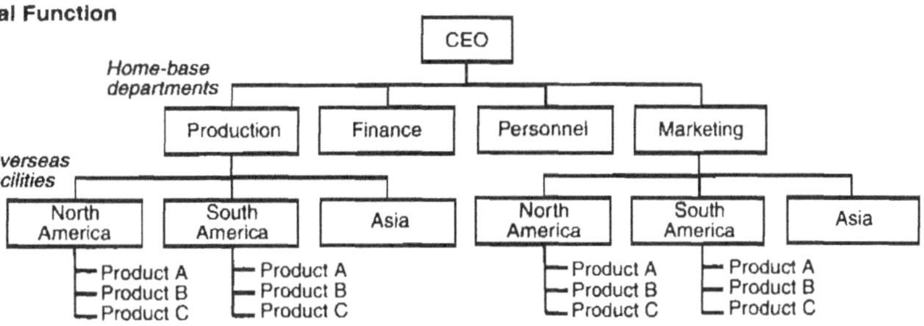

H. Global Mixed

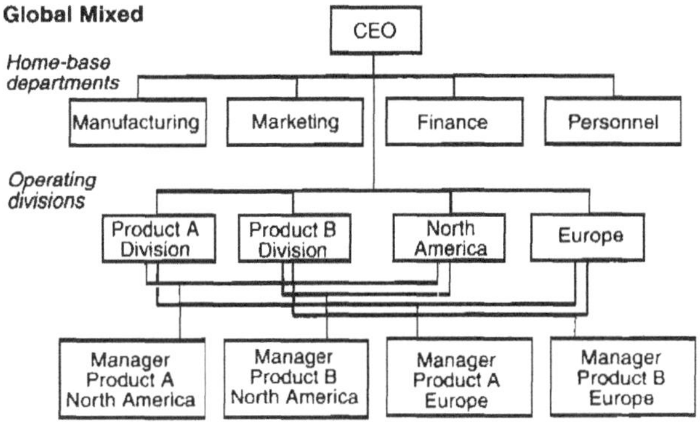

I. Transnational

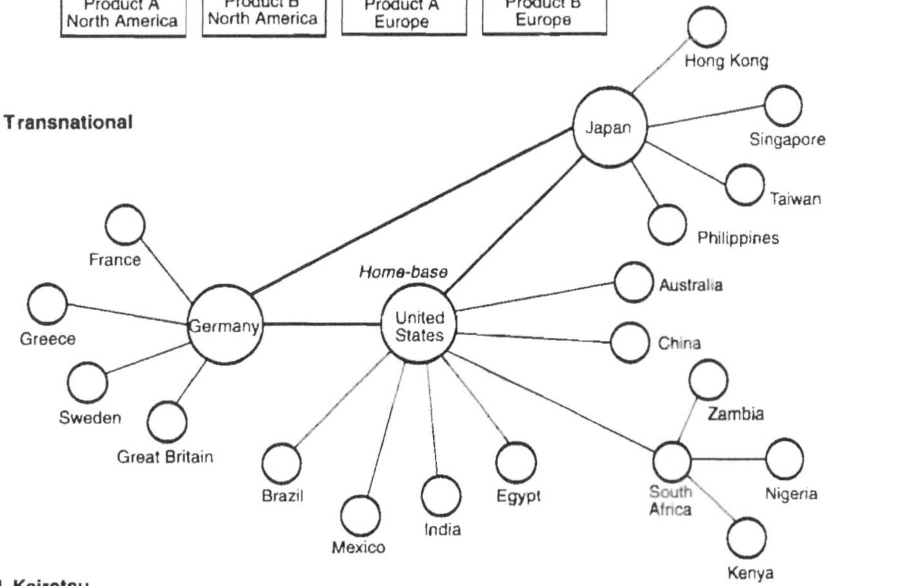

J. Keiretsu

Note: Mitsubishi Keiretsu in 1990. Percentages refer to share of each company held by other members of keiretsu.

Figure 10-4 *(continued)*

The marketing department handles logistics and provides sales support. When export sales are higher, the export manager heads a separate department and reports directly to the president (Figure 10-4 [B]). This network works well if competition is mild and if the number of units exported is not high.

INTERNATIONAL: Regional Manufacturing for an International Market

This network is used when a company follows an international strategy. Pressure for globalization is medium, and pressure for local responsiveness is low. A company operates a home base facility in its home country and foreign facilities in various regions of the world. All facilities produce standard products and seek economies of scale. Foreign facilities may be joint ventures or acquisitions and are established in response to competitor threats or pressure from foreign governments. They are also established to reduce transportation cost, which reduces product cost.

Figure 10-4 (C) shows a typical organization chart. The head of each overseas facility reports to the senior executive responsible for all manufacturing operations. All activities in the network are closely coordinated and tightly controlled. Many pharmaceutical companies use international networks.

MULTIDOMESTIC: Regional Manufacturing for Multiple Domestic Markets

This network is used when a company follows a multidomestic strategy. Pressure for globalization is medium, and pressure for local responsiveness is high. The company operates a home base facility in its home country and foreign facilities in countries where a significant demand for its products exists. Foreign subsidiaries produce unique products to meet the unique needs of customers in their country markets. Foreign subsidiaries have broad autonomy for activities in their geographic areas.

Figure 10-4 (D) shows a typical organization chart. Each subsidiary reports to a senior executive who heads the company's international division. The executive coordinates international activities and reports to the chief executive. Grouping international activities under one senior executive produces a unified approach to international affairs and ensures that international matters receive top management attention. It also helps the company develop a group of internationally experienced managers, and it relieves the chief executive of the work of monitoring numerous small international operations.

This is a simple network and a simple organization structure for international manufacturing. It is useful for companies in the developmental stages of international business, and for companies with small international sales, limited geographic dispersion, and few executives with international experience. One shortcoming of the network is that it separates domestic and international managers. The two groups of managers may not share information or may pull the company in different directions. Another shortcoming appears when international activities grow. The home country may be unable to think and act strategically. For example, R&D activities may be domestically oriented, ideas for new products or processes in international markets may be given low priority, and resources may not be allocated on a global basis. The more complex manufacturing networks try to overcome these shortcomings.

COMPLEX NETWORKS

Strong competition from formidable competitors forces companies to compete internationally using more sophisticated manufacturing networks. In other words, when pressure for globalization ranges from high to very high, companies must use one of the following complex networks.

MULTINATIONAL: Multinational Manufacturing for all Major National Markets

This network is used when a company follows a multinational strategy. Pressures for both globalization and local responsiveness are high. A company operates facilities in its home country and in almost all foreign countries with a significant demand for its products. Facilities have a great deal of autonomy to deal with the following local conditions:

- Customer needs differ in each country, so each facility produces unique products to satisfy local needs. For example, a food company produces dark, bitter coffee for customers in Italy, Portugal, Spain, and Turkey and a milder, sweeter blend for customers in Australia, Canada, Great Britain, and the United States; a company produces heavily spiced foods for customers in the Middle East and Asia and plain foods for customers in Europe and the United States; and an appliance manufacturer produces top-loading washing machines for customers in France and front-loading washing machines for customers in Great Britain.
- The intensity and nature of competition differs in each country, so each facility competes differently.
- Employee needs differ in each country, so each facility adapts its practices for local employee needs.

Figure 10-4 (E) shows a typical organization chart. The structure is called a "geographic area division structure." All activities in a geographic area are grouped into a division. Foreign divisions are on the same level as home country divisions. This means foreign activities are equally as important as home country activities. Facilities are located in many countries to provide access to local markets and important production factors such as labor, raw materials, and suppliers. The chief executive, along with a top management team, ensures that divisions work together in harmony and carefully allocate resources to divisions to achieve company strategy. International companies that produce automobiles, beverages, cosmetics, food, and mechanical equipment use this network. British Petroleum adopted it when it acquired U.S.-based Standard Oil.

High pressure for globalization means intense competition from competitors. Divisions seek economies of scale in purchasing, production, distribution, and marketing. They reduce distribution cost by manufacturing locally instead of importing products.

A multinational network has three weaknesses: inconsistent product image, duplication of effort, and short-term focus.

- When a product is sold worldwide, a number of divisions manufacture and market it. Product quality, price, marketing, and distribution can vary considerably around the world. In Situation 10.1, this was a problem for Procter & Gamble and its large chain-store customers.
- Duplication of effort between divisions exists in activities such as purchasing, manufacturing, marketing, distribution, and R&D.
- Divisions may favor a short-term focus on established processes and proven products. They may neglect the important work of developing new products based on the latest technology; something needed to keep the company successful in the long term.

GLOBAL NETWORKS: Worldwide Manufacturing for a Global Market

A company facing high pressure for globalization and low pressure for local responsiveness can use a global product network or a global function network. When pressure for globalization is even higher, a company can use a global mixed network.

All three networks consist of domestic and foreign facilities located in parts of the world that most benefit the company. These are locations with low cost labor or raw material, or locations close to customers, suppliers, or sources of new technology. It is necessary (because competition is fierce) and possible (because the company produces standard products) to tightly control and closely coordinate all facilities in the network.

Global Product

When pressure for globalization is high and pressure for local responsiveness is low, standard products are produced and sold worldwide. Consumer electronics products and personal care products are examples. This combination produces intense competition between large, strong companies. Developing, distributing, manufacturing, and marketing products are not easy activities in this environment. Another difficulty is that products may be in different stages of their life cycle (Chapter 16) in different regions of the world. A global product network is a good manufacturing network for this environment.

Figure 10-4 (F) shows a typical organization chart. The structure is called a "global product division structure." All worldwide activities related to a product family are grouped into a division. Divisions are usually headquartered in the home country and operate as profit centers. Divisions have considerable authority and autonomy. All activities related to a product family, whatever the function (finance, human resources, manufacturing, marketing, R&D) and whatever the location (home base, foreign countries), report to a division general manager. All activities are tightly controlled and carefully coordinated. Division general managers make most of the important decisions. The chief executive, along with a top management team, approves budgets and capital expenditures, monitors profits, and ensures that divisions work together to achieve company strategy.

The global product network creates direct lines of communication between customers and those in the company who develop, produce, distribute, and market products. This enables the division to meet the needs of customers wherever they are in the world. Procter & Gamble adopted this network in Situation 10.1.

A global product network has three weaknesses:

- Duplication of effort between divisions exists in activities such as purchasing, manufacturing, marketing, distribution, and R&D.
- Division managers may be short sighted. They may focus on currently attractive country markets and neglect other markets with long-term potential.
- Division managers who come up through the ranks of domestic operations may focus on the domestic market and neglect foreign markets because the domestic market is convenient and they are more experienced in domestic operations.

Global Function

When pressure for globalization is high and pressure for local responsiveness is low, standard products are produced and sold worldwide. This combination produces intense competition between large, strong companies. Mining companies and companies in the oil and gas industry are examples. A global function network is a good network for these companies.

Figure 10-4 (G) shows a typical organization chart. All worldwide activities are grouped first by function (usually production), then by geographic area (or product). The global function network emphasizes functional expertise. It enables a company to tightly control and closely coordinate activities within each function with a relatively small staff of highly qualified employees. It is favored by companies that need tight, centralized control of complex integrated production processes to achieve very high quality and very low cost. Examples are mining companies, steel companies, and transportation companies.

A weakness of the global function network is its difficulty coordinating activities between functions, especially production and marketing. Another weakness is that the chief executive is the only person accountable for profits.

Global Mixed

When pressure for globalization is very high and pressure for local responsiveness is low, standard products are produced and sold worldwide. This combination produces fierce competition between formidable competitors. The global mixed network is the best network for this environment.

Figure 10-4 (H) shows a typical organization chart. This structure combines product structure and geographic structure. A global mixed network can combine any two of the three basic organization structures: function, geographic area, and product. One basic structure is called the primary structure, and another structure, called the secondary structure, is added to it. Organizational relationships are created to link the primary and secondary structures. The result is a mixed or matrix structure. In Figure 10-4 (H), the primary structure is product divisions A and B. The secondary structure is the North America and Europe geographic divisions. The figure shows that different managers are responsible for each product in each geographic area.

The advantage of the global mixed network is that a company can create a structure that best meets it needs. A disadvantage is that the structure is complex. This makes it harder to coordinate activities. It is also difficult for all personnel to work toward common goals.

TRANSNATIONAL: Worldwide Manufacturing for All National Markets in a Very Competitive Industry

This network is used when a company follows a transnational strategy. Pressure for globalization is very high, and pressure for local responsiveness is high. The network is designed to help a company achieve global economies of scale and experience benefits, while staying very responsive to local customer needs. A transnational network is characterized by:

- A mixture of the three basic organization structures (function, geographic area, product)
- Facilities dispersed around the world

It is difficult to draw an organization chart of a transnational network. It is somewhat easier to draw a network diagram (Figure 10-4 [I]). A diagram should include three important elements: dispersed units, specialized activities, and linkages. (Figure 10-4 [I] only shows dispersed units.)

- Dispersed units are facilities located in parts of the world that most benefit the company. Some facilities access important markets, some exploit low factor costs (labor and raw materials), some are close to suppliers, and some provide access to new technologies or information on new customer needs.
- Specialized activities are important activities carried out by dispersed units. Examples are a production system producing a product family, an R&D lab working on new products, and a sales group supporting a key customer.
- Linkages are processes for sharing information and resources between dispersed units and specialized activities.

Figure 10-4 (I) is adapted from a diagram of Philips' transnational network. Philips produces a wide range of products. It has eight product divisions and dispersed units in more than 60 countries engaging in numerous specialized activities. Some dispersed units are autonomous; others are tightly controlled by home base.

OTHER NETWORKS

MERGERS AND ACQUISITIONS

Other manufacturing networks are possible. Many result from mergers, acquisitions, and joint ventures. In these situations, manufacturing networks from two companies join to form a new network. Sometimes, all that is needed is an interface between the two networks. Other times, the two networks are fully integrated. The new network combines one or more of the networks discussed earlier in this chapter, with additional, unique elements that address special circumstances at the two companies. There are many examples.

Ford owns 75 percent of Aston Martin Lagonda (Great Britain), 49 percent of Autolatina

(Brazil), and 34 percent of Mazda (Japan). Ford has special structures that connect its manufacturing network with the manufacturing networks of these partners. Samsung has joint ventures with AT&T, Motorola, NEC, Toshiba, and others. Samsung and each of its partners built interfaces between their networks to make interaction, coordination, and cooperation easier.

When Procter & Gamble acquired Richardson-Vicks, it got the Richardson-Vicks distribution network in India. This gave Procter & Gamble the desired quick access to the large Indian market. The company also got the Richardson-Vicks manufacturing network, which included production capacity in North America that was not needed. The company integrated the Procter & Gamble network and the Richardson-Vicks network. Many Procter & Gamble facilities and Richardson-Vicks facilities closed, not because they were ineffective or inefficient, they simply weren't needed any more. When Daimler-Benz acquired Chrysler Corporation, it had to integrate two manufacturing networks. Its objectives for the reorganized network were to create synergy and encourage local initiative.

Keiretsu

A Japanese keiretsu includes a manufacturing network.[5] A keiretsu is a large, vertically integrated group of companies that work together closely. Members of the keiretsu are bound together by cross-ownership, long-term business dealings, interlocking boards of directors, and social ties. Figure 10-4 (J) shows the Mitsubishi keiretsu. Three flagship companies, 25 core companies, and hundreds of small companies make up the keiretsu. The flagship companies are Mitsubishi Corporation, a trading company, Mitsubishi Bank, which finances the keiretsu's activities, and Mitsubishi Heavy Industries, a leading international manufacturer.

Keiretsus are found outside Japan. In South Korea, they are called chaebols (Chapter 9). Many large companies build organization structures that resemble keiretsus. Most begin by integrating backward (Chapter 3) to acquire suppliers and forward to acquire distribution companies and financial services companies. For example, Ford created a giant keiretsu that includes parts production, vehicle assembly, R&D, financial services, and marketing. In parts production, Ford has ownership interests in Cummins (engines), Excel Industries (windows), and Decoma International (body parts, wheels). These companies are major suppliers to Ford. In vehicle assembly, Ford has ownership interests in companies in Europe, South America, and Asia and uses these arrangements to manufacture and sell automobiles in these regions. In R&D, Ford belongs to eight research consortia that conduct research in areas such as advanced materials, electronics, and new production techniques. In financial services, Ford has ownership interests in seven companies that provide a range of services from consumer credit to commercial lending.

Electronic Manufacturing Network

An electronic manufacturing network is another type of manufacturing network. A company with an electronic network subcontracts almost all activities in the value system to external contractors. Almost all transactions between the company and the external contractors are electronic. The fashion accessories company, Topsy Tail, is an example.[6] Topsy Tail has revenues of $80 million and only three employees. Employees use design agencies to create products and packaging. They contract with foreign manufacturers to produce products, and distribute and sell through a network of independent distributors and sales representatives. At the beginning of this chapter, we saw that Li & Fung used a multidomestic electronic manufacturing network.

Xilinx Company of California is another company that uses an electronic manufacturing network.[7] Xilinx is one of the world's largest suppliers of programmable logic semiconductors. The company was founded in 1984. In 1997, annual revenue was $611 million. Manufacturing operations are divided into two steps: wafer fabrication and customization. Xilinx contracts wafer fabrication to one group of external contractors. These contractors produce unfinished products called dies, which they hold in inventory. When Xilinx receives customer orders, it authorizes release of the dies to another group of external contractors. These contractors customize the dies into finished products and ship products to customers. Xilinx also subcontracts logistics, sales, and distribution. The company performs research, circuit design, marketing, manufacturing engineering, customer service, demand management, and supply chain management in house.

SUMMARY

There are seven different strategies for designing and operating international manufacturing networks. Each strategy is appropriate for a different trade-off between pressure for globalization and pressure for local responsiveness. Each strategy disperses manufacturing activities in a different way and uses a different manufacturing network.

There are nine well-known manufacturing networks. Domestic, domestic export, international, and multidomestic are simple networks, appropriate when pressure for globalization is low to medium. They disperse activities to national and regional facilities.

Multinational, global product, global function, global mixed, and transnational are complex networks, appropriate when pressure for globalization is high to very high. They disperse activities to multinational and worldwide facilities.

ENDNOTES

1. The material in this chapter is adapted from:
   - DuBois, F., Toyne, B., and Oliff, M., "International Manufacturing Strategies of U.S. Multinationals: A Conceptual Framework Based on a Four-Industry Study," *Journal of International Business Studies*, pp. 307–333, Second Quarter, 1993.
   - Hodgetts, R., and Luthans, F., *International Management: Culture, Strategy, and Behavior*, Irwin McGraw-Hill: Boston, Chapter 11, 2003.
   - Shi, Y., and Gregory, M., "International Manufacturing Networks—To Develop Global Competitive Capabilities," *Journal of Operations Management*, Vol. 16, pp. 195–214, 1998.
2. *Business Week*, pp. 95–96, October 5, 1998.
3. Rhoads, C., "A Contrarian Motorola Picks Germany," *Wall Street Journal*, p. A18, October 10, 1997; Hardy, Q., "Motorola Readies Major Restructuring," *Wall Street Journal*, pp. A3, 14, March 31, 1998; and Smith, C., "Motorola Expands Operations in China," *Wall Street Journal*, p. A9, June 12, 1998.
4. Magretta, J., "Fast, Global, and Entrepreneurial: Supply Chain Management, Hong Kong Style. An Interview with Victor Fung," *Harvard Business Review*, September–October, 1998.
5. Hodgetts and Luthans, *International Management*, pp. 320–321.
6. Ibid, p. 322.
7. Brown, A., Lee, H., and Petrakian, R., "Xilinx Improves its Semiconductor Supply Chain Using Product and Process Postponement," *Interfaces*, Vol. 30, No. 4, pp. 65–80, 2000.

CHAPTER 11

NETWORK OUTPUTS, LEVERS, AND CAPABILITIES

NETWORK MANUFACTURING OUTPUTS[1]

Chapter 4 examined the six strategic outputs provided by a production system in a factory. They are cost, quality, performance, delivery, flexibility, and innovativeness; and they are called the factory manufacturing outputs. The level at which each output is provided depends on the type of production system and the level of capability of the production system (Figure 1-1). Each focused factory in a manufacturing network provides factory manufacturing outputs.

A manufacturing network provides four additional strategic outputs. They are accessibility, thriftiness, mobility, and learning (Figure 11-1 [A]); and they are called the network manufacturing outputs.[2] The level at which each network manufacturing output is provided depends on the type of network (Chapter 10) and the level of capability of the network.

Figure 11-1 (B) shows that two elements, geographic dispersion of facilities and degree of coordination between facilities, are important for understanding the relationship between the type of network and the level at which network manufacturing outputs are provided. Networks with worldwide dispersion of facilities (transnational and global mixed) provide the highest possible levels of accessibility to production factors and mobility. Networks with multinational dispersion of facilities (multinational, global product, global function) provide the highest possible levels of accessibility to markets and learning about cultures and needs. Networks with a high degree of coordination (global mixed, global product, global function, international, domestic export) provide the highest possible levels of thriftiness and learning about technology. Networks with national dispersion of facilities (domestic, domestic export) provide low levels of accessibility, mobility, and learning about cultures and needs.

ACCESSIBILITY

Geographic dispersion of facilities and amount of autonomy given to dispersed facilities determine how close a company gets to the people and organizations that are important to it.[3] When facilities and activities are widely dispersed, a company is in close proximity to customers, factors of production, and governments in most parts of the world (Figure

Accessibility	Ease of access a company has to present and future market segments, factors of production, and government agencies.
Thriftiness	Ability of a company to achieve economies of scale and avoid duplication of activities.
Mobility	Ease with which a company can transfer products, processes, and personnel between facilities, move facilities to new locations, and change production volumes.
Learning	Ability of a company to learn about cultures and needs of customers, workforces, and governments, as well as process technology, product technology, and management systems; and the ease with which this knowledge can be shared.

A. Network Manufacturing Outputs

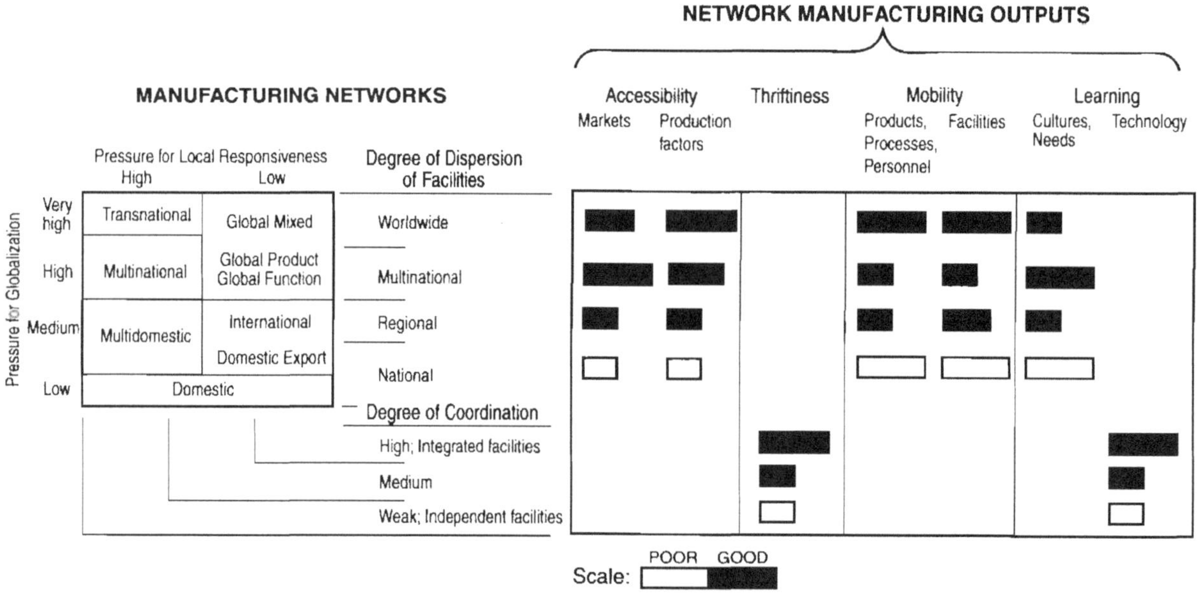

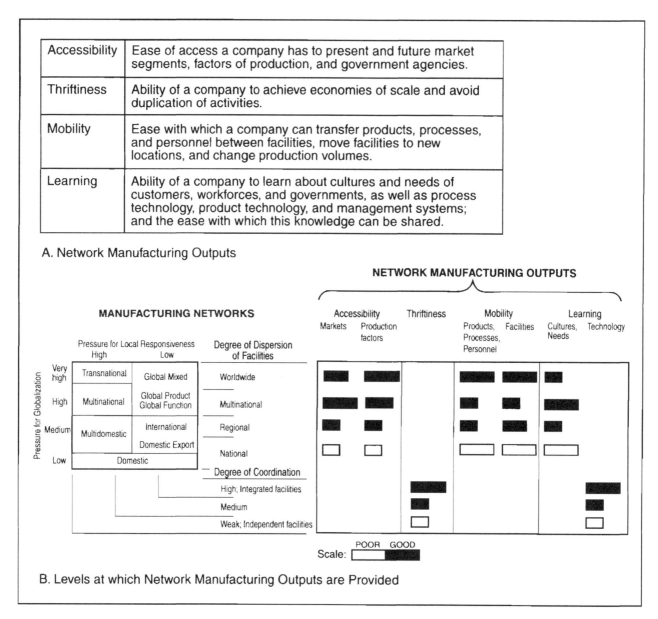

B. Levels at which Network Manufacturing Outputs are Provided

Figure 11-1 Network Manufacturing Outputs

11-1 [B]). If these facilities and activities have a high degree of autonomy, the company can develop close relationships with customers, employees, suppliers, and governments (Situation 11.1). While accessibility is important for all international companies, it is critical when pressure for local responsiveness is high. It is also important in rapidly changing industries.

THRIFTINESS

The more tightly coordinated a manufacturing network, the more thrifty it becomes (Figure 11-1 [B]).[4] A high degree of coordination is required to standardize products, manufacturing processes, and management systems and prevent duplication of activities. A high degree of coordination helps a company achieve economies of scale and

SITUATION 11.1

Industrial Boiler Manufacturer Builds Manufacturing Network[5]

IN THE 1970S, a North American manufacturer of industrial boilers followed a domestic export strategy from its North American home base. Unable to generate the growth it desired, the company chose, in the mid-1980s, to establish a manufacturing presence in a few developing countries. The company would be in a better position to bid on projects in these countries, and the low cost labor would help reduce costs. The company set up joint venture factories in Indonesia in 1984 and in China in 1986. Costs quickly improved due to lower labor, material, and transportation costs. Delivery time and service to local customers also improved. Within a short time, the company had 30 percent of the Chinese market and made inroads in nearby country markets.

Encouraged by its success, the company established manufacturing facilities in other countries where it sought access to local markets: India in 1988, Turkey in 1989, and Egypt in 1994. By the mid-1990s, the company had a multidomestic manufacturing network of widely dispersed, highly autonomous facilities. The key network manufacturing output was accessibility.

realize the benefits of experience (Situation 11.1 continued).

MOBILITY

Geographic dispersion of facilities and amount of specialization determine the level at which the mobility output is provided.[6] Worldwide and regional dispersion of facilities give the highest level (Figure 11-1 [B]). Opportunities for mobility exist when facilities are dispersed worldwide or in some or all of the world's major trading regions. In these situations, facilities are less tied to individual countries compared to multinational or national dispersion of facilities, so moves are easier to make. In addition, the more specialized the facility, process, or personnel, the more difficult it is to move.

Companies move products, processes, personnel, and facilities in response to changes in customer needs, production factors, competitors' actions, government regulations, and company strategy. Mobility is important for all international companies, but it is critical when pressure for globalization is high to very high. It is also important in rapidly changing industries. The apparel industry and the computer industry are examples.

In the apparel industry[7] and other low technology industries, barriers to entry are low. Thriftiness is the most important network output. Mobility is second because shortened lead times enable companies to respond faster to demand, fashion, or season changes. Apparel companies produce three product types:

- *Simple garments:* Simple garments, such as T-shirts, undergarments, work clothes, and jeans, are made in foreign factories with low labor costs.
- *Intermediate quality fashion garments:* Companies produce these garments in medium cost factories located close to major customers. These factories can change production volume

SITUATION 11.1

Continued

As THE COMPANY'S multidomestic manufacturing network grew in the 1980s and 90s, so did the amount and cost of duplication. In the mid-1990s, the company changed its manufacturing strategy to emphasize cost reduction (thriftiness). It had the required level of accessibility, and management felt the time was right to make the manufacturing network thrifty.

The number of duplicated activities was reduced. Facilities in different countries specialized their product lines. For example, the facility in China specialized in the design and manufacture of large, high-pressure boilers. Key manufacturing processes were centralized, and facilities were tightly coordinated. The multidomestic network was transformed into a global product network.

Figure 11-2 draws the company's international experiences on a network worksheet. The company started as a domestic company (number 1 on the worksheet). Its first international business venture was as a domestic exporter (number 2), and the key network output was thriftiness. Next, it expanded its network to multidomestic to gain access to foreign markets (number 3). Accessibility was the key network output. Finally, it upgraded to a global product network to improve thriftiness and learning about product and process technology (number 4).

volume quickly in response to demand, fashion, or season changes. Apparel factories in the Caribbean and Mexico that produce garments for U.S. markets are examples.

- *High quality, high price, fashion garments:* Highly skilled workers in relatively high cost foreign locations, such as Hong Kong, make these garments. These garments have a high value-to-weight ratio, so it is economical to transport them to market by airplane.

Apparel companies that produce all three product types use networks of regionally dispersed facilities with high levels of thriftiness and mobility. Then, companies can quickly and easily move products and processes to respond to changes in customer needs, costs, or competitors' actions.

Companies in the computer industry also use manufacturing networks that have high levels of mobility.[8] They manufacture the newest generation of printed circuit boards, communication devices, screens, and printers at home base facilities. This enables manufacturing and R&D to work through the numerous engineering changes that are part of all new product launches. Once the design is stable and production and quality problems are solved, production moves to low labor cost, foreign facilities. This frees capacity the at home base for the next generation of new products. This mobility pattern is common in industries with rapid change, advanced technology, and sophisticated customer needs (Situation 11.2).

LEARNING

There are two types of learning (Figure 11-1 [B]).[9] The first is learning about cultures, customer needs, employee needs, and government regulations. This learning is easiest when geographic

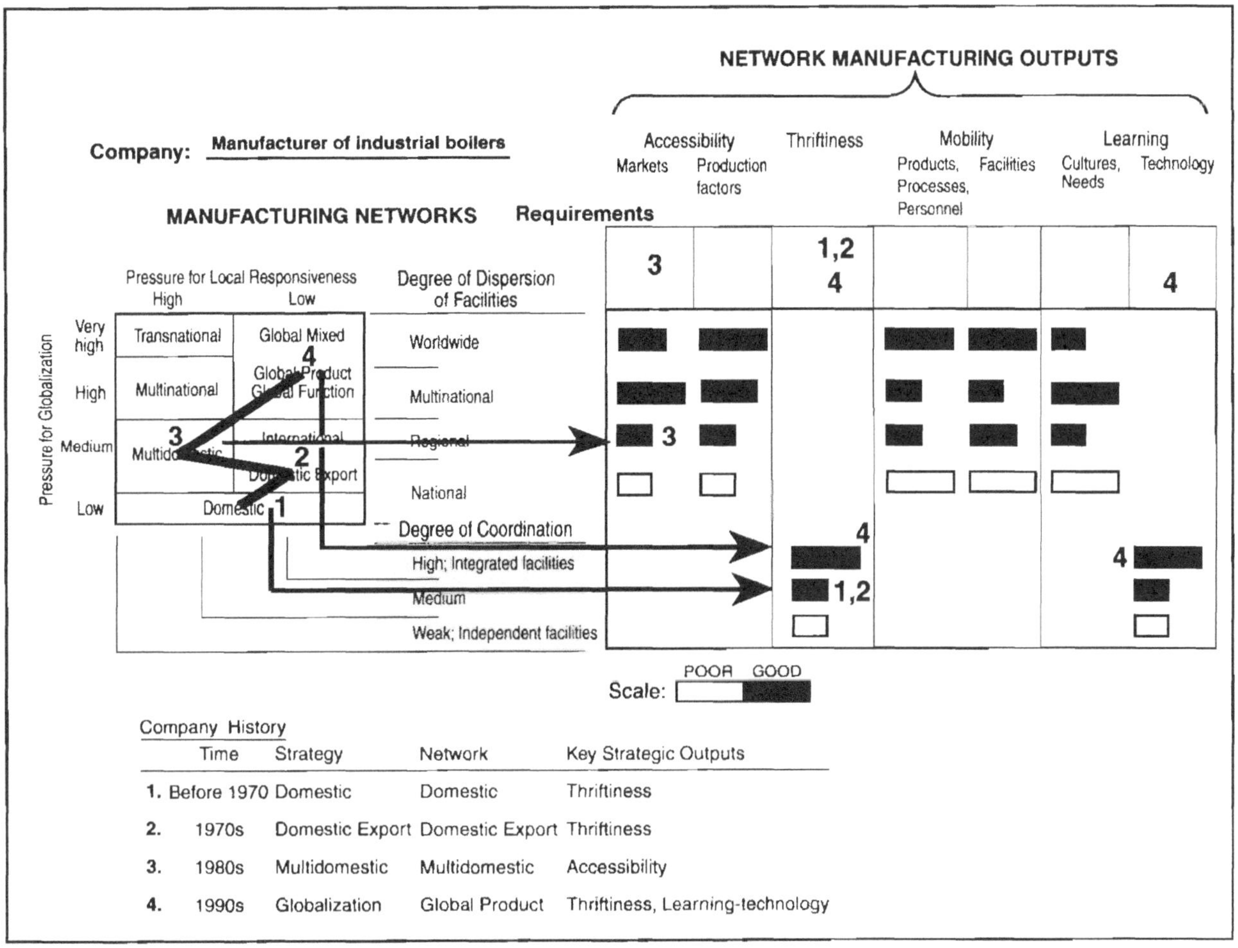

Figure 11-2 Industrial Boiler Manufacturer's International Activities

SITUATION 11.2

Importance of Mobility at Li & Fung

LI & FUNG, the Hong Kong company discussed in Situation 10.3 in Chapter 10, relies on a multidomestic electronic manufacturing network for a high level of mobility. A product at Li & Fung is a customer order. When an order is placed, Li & Fung creates a manufacturing process for the order and assigns each step in the process to the best facility in its network. The company tightly coordinates and carefully controls all activities related to the order at each facility. Li & Fung moves effortlessly between facilities as customer orders, currency rates, and facility workloads change.

dispersion of facilities is high and level of autonomy in facilities is high. The second is learning about product technology, process technology, and managerial systems. This is easiest when degree of coordination between facilities is high. Situations 11.3 and 11.4 examine both learning types.

SITUATION 11.3

Company A Uses Multinational Network to Learn Customer Needs

COMPANY A MANUFACTURES electronic components for industrial customers. The company uses a multinational network of facilities so it is always in close physical proximity to its customers. Customers are concerned about quality and delivery reliability because problems with these can negatively effect customer production processes.

Customers purchase from a small number of companies with broad product lines. In return for this business, customers expect companies to learn and even anticipate their needs. To help this happen, Company A's multinational network has facilities in every country where it has a customer. Managers joke that the company is "dragged around the world by its customers."[10]

Figure 11-3 (top) shows Company A's strategy on a manufacturing network worksheet. Accessibility to markets (customers) and learning about customer needs are the most important network outputs. Mobility of products, processes, and personnel is also important. The multinational network can best provide these outputs.

SITUATION 11.4

Company B uses Global Mixed Network to be Thrifty and Learn Technology

COMPANY B IS A MAJOR competitor in the hand tool industry.[11] Pressure for local responsiveness is low. For example, with minor exceptions, tools sold in Brazil are the same as tools sold in Germany. Product quality and cost are important.

Company B uses a global mixed network. The company is vertically integrated all the way back to the production of specialty steel—the raw material for hand tools. The company produces high-quality specialty steel in a large scale, cost efficient factory in its home country. Casting, forging, heat treatment, and machining operations are performed in a tightly coordinated network of specialized factories in and around the home country. Final assembly is done in foreign factories close to foreign markets.

Specialization and tight control of all activities in the value system keep the company at the forefront of product and process technology. Doing final assembly in foreign countries rather than in the home country helps the company learn about cultures and customer needs.

Figure 11-3 (bottom) shows Company B's strategy on a manufacturing network worksheet. Thriftiness and learning about product and process technology are the most important network outputs. Learning about culture and customer needs is also important. The global mixed network can best provide these outputs.

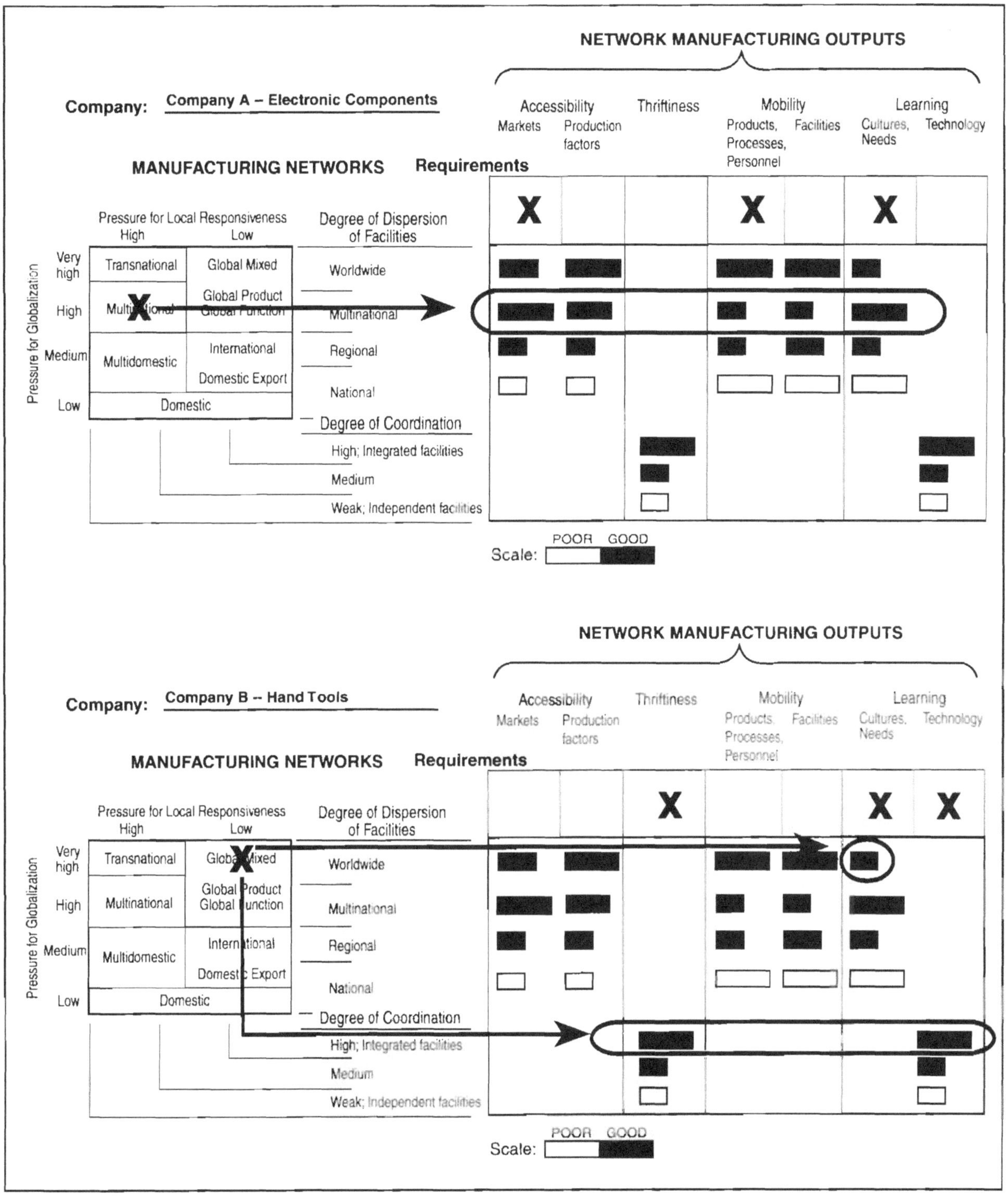

Figure 11-3 Manufacturing Network Worksheets for Company A and Company B

Manufacturing Network Levers

A manufacturing network consists of eight elements[12] (Figure 11-4):

- Facility characteristics
- Geographic dispersion
- Vertical integration
- Organization structure
- Coordination mechanisms
- Knowledge transfer mechanisms
- Response mechanisms
- Capability building mechanisms

The first four elements are called structural elements. The last four elements are called infrastructural elements. Structural elements are physical parts of the network: facilities, locations of facilities, production processes within factories, and so on. Infrastructural elements are managerial systems that coordinate the structural elements and make the network work.

Elements are called *levers* to reflect that each element can be adjusted. Adjustments vary in size. Small adjustments are made to one or more levers to improve an existing network. Large adjustments are made to all eight levers to greatly improve an existing network or to change an existing manufacturing network to a different network.

Structural levers	
Facility characteristics	Types of facilities in a network and their characteristics such as size, focus, and capabilities.
Geographic dispersion	Where value system activities are dispersed around the world.
Vertical integration	Extent to which a network contains facilities engaged in upstream activities involving sources of supply and downstream activities involving customers.
Organization structure	How facilities, departments, and personnel are organized in a network.
Infrastructural levers	
Coordination mechanisms	Managerial systems and computer systems used to organize data, make information available, and plan, monitor, and control activities.
Knowledge transfer mechanisms	How product knowledge and process knowledge are transferred between facilities and departments in a network.
Response mechanisms	Systems and procedures for recognizing, analyzing, and acting on threats and opportunities that arise anywhere in a network.
Capability building mechanisms	Systems and procedures for creating, sustaining, and improving capabilities in areas such as design, production, and service.

Figure 11-4 Manufacturing Network Levers: Eight Elements that Make Up a Manufacturing Network

The current position of a lever is the result of management decisions over a long time period. The current positions of the eight levers completely determine:

- The type of manufacturing network
- How well the manufacturing network works
- The levels at which network manufacturing outputs are provided

Figure 11-5 adds the levers to the manufacturing network worksheet.

Facility Characteristics

Factories, offices, research centers, and warehouses are some of the many facilities in a manufacturing network. Companies set facility characteristics, such as size, focus, and capabilities, for the particular manufacturing network in use. For example,

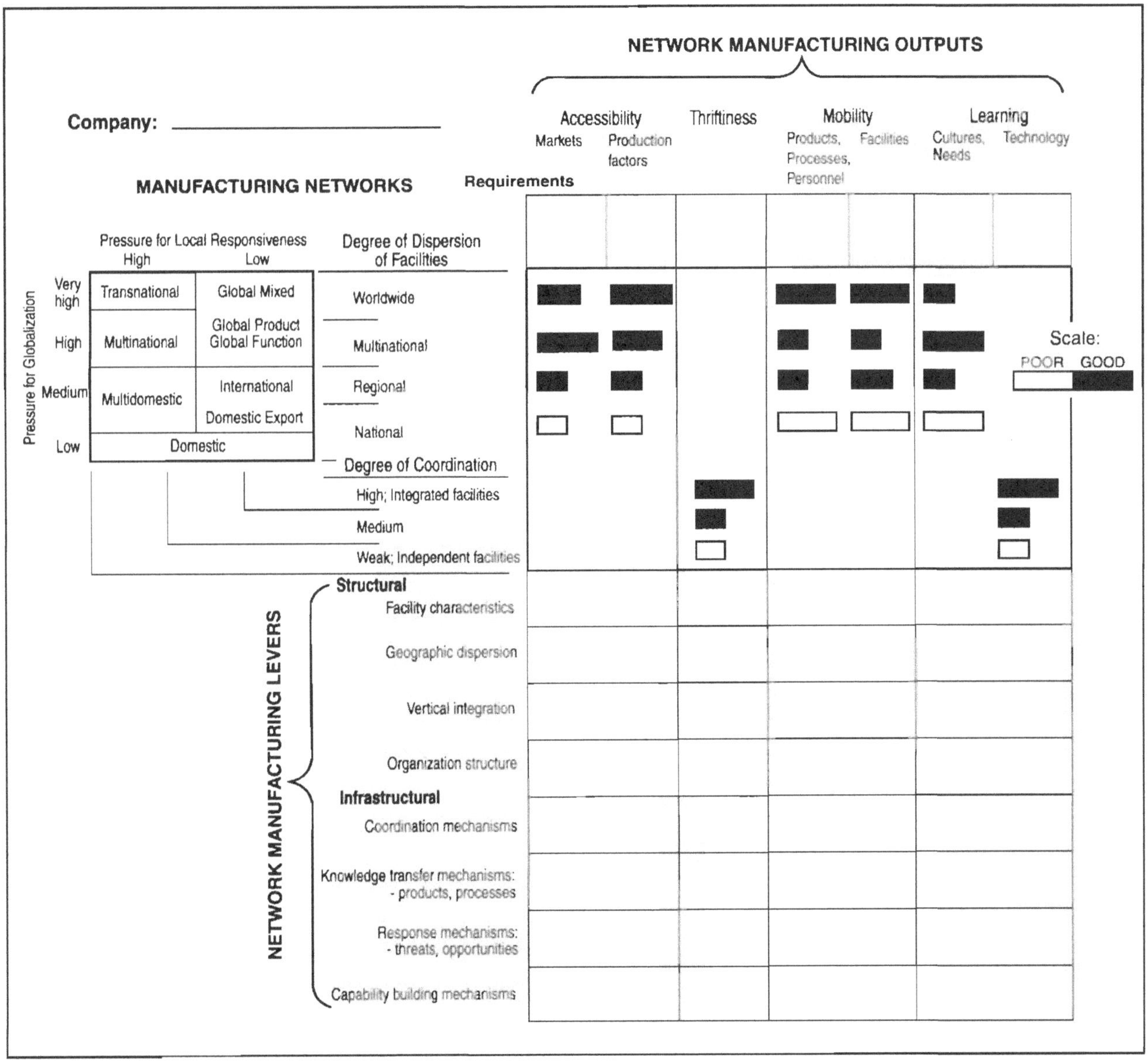

Figure 11-5 Levers or Elements in a Manufacturing Network

factories in a multidomestic network are large, general purpose factories. They employ a variety of processes to produce unique products for local markets. Factories in a global network are highly specialized and focused. They perform a small number of operations to produce standard products for worldwide markets.

Geographic Dispersion

Several ways to disperse value system activities exist. A domestic export network concentrates activities in the home country. Multidomestic and international networks locate activities in each of the world's major trading regions (Chapter 9). The levels at which network outputs must be provided, especially accessibility and mobility, determine how to disperse activities.

Vertical Integration

Vertical integration is the extent to which a network contains facilities engaged in upstream activities involving sources of supply, and downstream activities, such as distribution and sales, involving users of final products. Greater vertical integration of upstream activities provides higher levels of the thriftiness and learning outputs. Greater vertical integration of downstream activities provides a higher level of the accessibility output.

Organization Structure

Chapter 10 showed that each manufacturing network uses a particular organization structure (Figure 10-4). Small differences in structure are possible within each network. A company designs an organization structure appropriate for its network, consistent with its capabilities, and best able to provide the required levels of the network outputs.

Coordination Mechanisms

Manufacturing networks would be impossible without modern computer and communication technologies. Most networks require enterprise resource planning (ERP) systems to organize data and make information available to all parts of the network (Chapter 15). Mechanisms are also needed to set plans for activities in the network and to monitor and control execution of plans.

Knowledge Transfer Mechanisms

How product knowledge and process knowledge are transferred between facilities and departments in a manufacturing network affects the levels at which network outputs are provided, especially thriftiness and learning. Different networks use different knowledge transfer mechanisms. For example, Erickson's global mixed network uses "technology groups," and Dofasco's multidomestic network uses "centers of excellence." These mechanisms link specialists at different facilities and make it easy for specialists to share knowledge about product and process technology.

A measure of the effectiveness of a company's knowledge transfer mechanisms is the ease with which it makes product and process changes as products move through their life cycles (Chapter 16).

Response Mechanisms

Threats and opportunities can arise anywhere in a network. They must be recognized, analyzed, and when appropriate, acted upon. The systems and procedures for doing this depend on the network in use and the levels at which network outputs are provided.

For example, a domestic export network providing a high level of thriftiness monitors prices and competitors' actions in each of its export markets. When threats arise, it responds quickly by dropping prices or offering incentives so customers do not switch. A transnational network providing high levels of accessibility and mobility monitors challenges from competitors, changes in government regulations, currency fluctuations, and country market openings. It responds when threats or opportunities arise by quickly moving activities from one country to another.

Capability Building Mechanisms

Competitive advantage is built and sustained by improving and upgrading sources of competitive advantage. In the long run, all sources of competitive advantage can be copied, so a company also needs mechanisms to build new sources (Chapter 8). For example, a multinational network providing a high level of accessibility uses quality management and lean manufacturing (Chapter 14) to upgrade its capabilities. A global product network providing a high level of thriftiness uses cost reduction, value engineering, and six sigma (Chapter 15).

Adjustments to network levers should not be made haphazardly. Each adjustment should be appropriate for the network in use and should help the network provide the required outputs at the required levels (Situation 11.4 continued).

Manufacturing Network Capability

Consider two companies operating the same type of manufacturing network. The first company's network is new and has moderate capabilities. The second company's network is older and has outstanding capabilities because the company's established improvement programs made numerous improvements to the network over the years. The second company's network will provide higher levels of the network manufacturing outputs: accessibility, thriftiness, mobility, and learning. The levels at which network outputs are provided depend on:

- The type of manufacturing network
- The capabilities of the network

Capabilities develop over time. Capabilities are the result of experience but do not develop unless management takes actions such as the following:

- Select and design the right manufacturing network.
- Start a program to make incremental improvements. Examples are cost reduction, quality manufacturing, and kaizen (Chapter 14).
- Establish a program to make large improvements. Examples are six sigma (Chapter 15) and reengineering.
- Build new capabilities by constructing new facilities and purchasing new equipment.
- Acquire new capabilities through joint ventures and acquisitions.

Situation 11.4

Continued

FIGURE 11-6 DISPLAYS the positions of network levers at Company B. Two adjustments are shown for the organization structure lever. All facilities are cost centers, and the company has a formal procedure to keep it close to key customers.

The positions of adjustments on the worksheet are important. The first adjustment to the organization structure lever is in the column corresponding to the thriftiness output. This indicates that this adjustment helps the network provide the thriftiness output. The second adjustment is in the column for learning about cultures and needs. This indicates that this adjustment helps the network provide the learning about cultures and needs output.

The manufacturing network in use is a global mixed network. The adjustments on the worksheet are appropriate for this network.

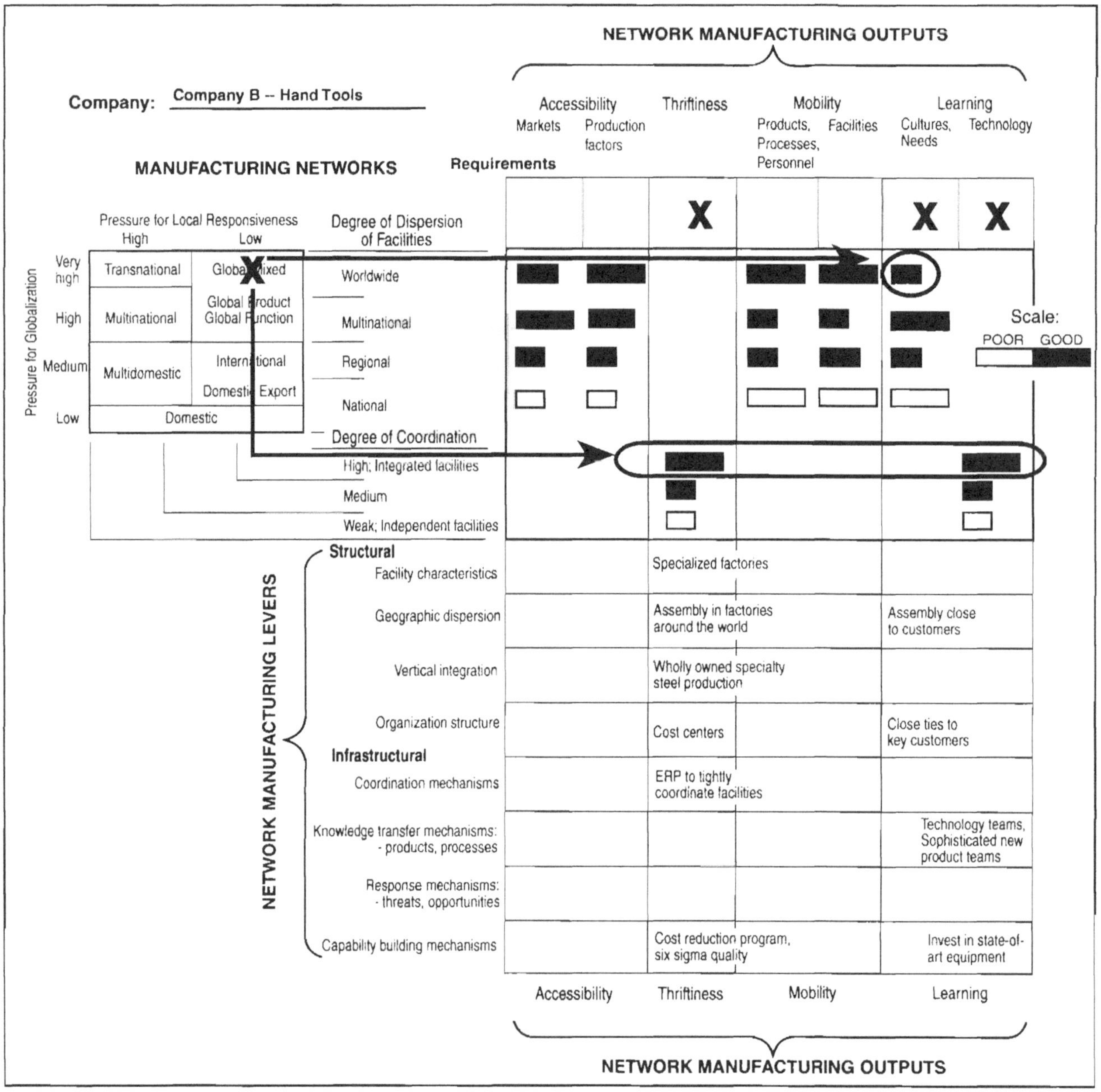

Figure 11-6 Setting Network Levers at Company B

The level of capability of a network depends on the level of capability of each lever in the network. A company assesses the level of capability of its network and each lever in the network by benchmarking against networks and levers at other companies. Level of capability is measured on a continuous scale from 1.0 to 4.0. A value of 1.0 is the lowest possible value. It is called an "infant" level of capability. It is the level of capability of a new manufacturing network. A value of 2.0 is an "industry average" level of capability. It is the result of five to ten years of experience and improvement activities. Since it is an average level, about half of the networks in the industry have less capability and half have more. A value of 3.0 is an "adult" level of capability. It is achieved by a company's determined effort to improve and become an industry leader. A value of 4.0 is a "world class" level of capability. A network with this level of capability is among the world's best. It provides network manufacturing outputs at the highest possible levels. Figure 11-7 adds level of capability to the manufacturing network worksheet.

The level of capability is not necessarily the same for each lever. For example, a company may have an infant level of capability in facility characteristics, an adult level of capability in geographic dispersion, and industry average levels of capability in vertical integration and organization structure. Levers with lower levels diminish the overall level of capability of the manufacturing network. Manufacturing strategy identifies these levers and the adjustments needed to raise the low levels of capability. The goal is to have a manufacturing network where all levers have the same high level of capability.

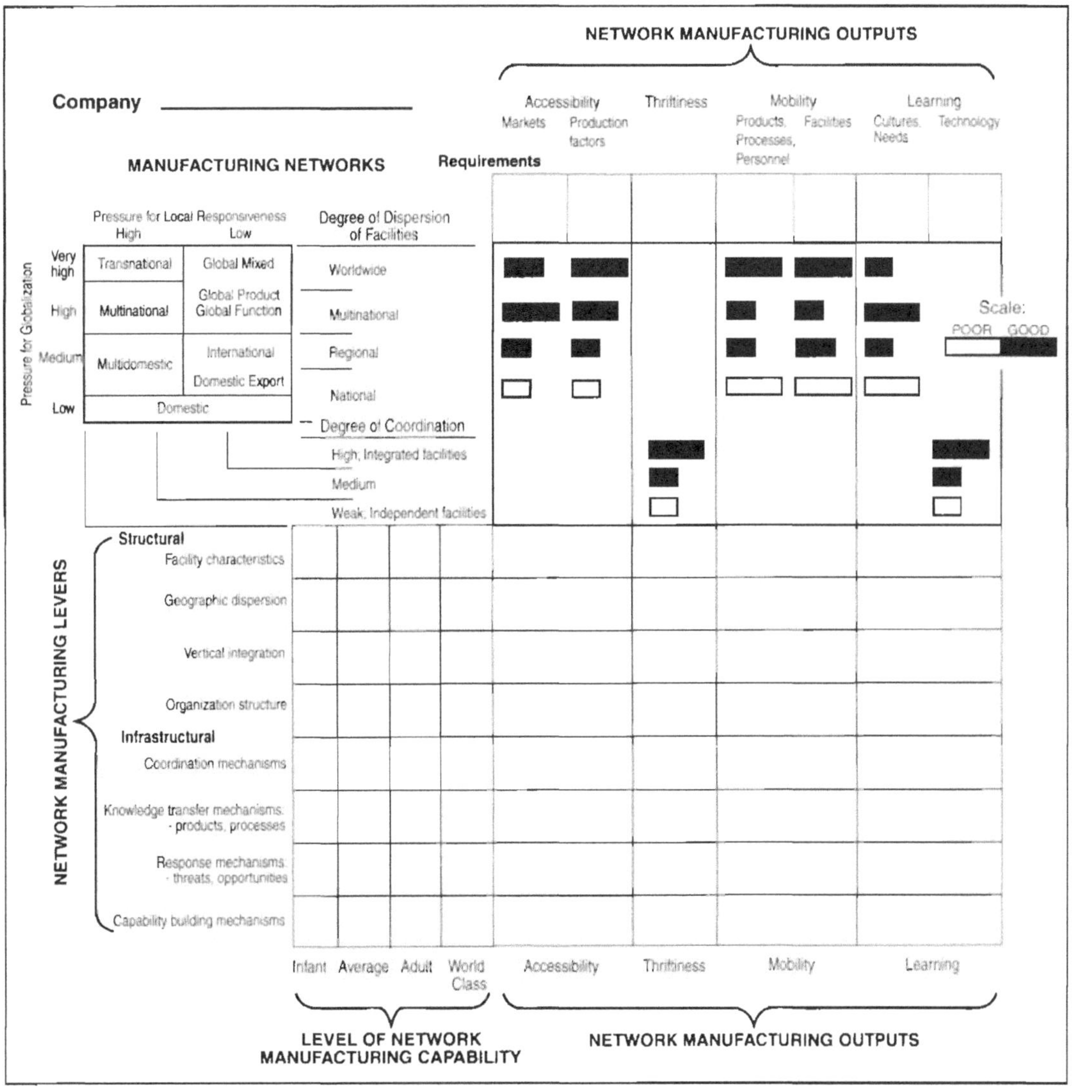

Figure 11-7 Adding Capability to the Manufacturing Network Worksheet

SITUATION 11.4

Continued

FIGURE 11-8 SHOWS the levels of capability at Company B. Two levers have an adult level of capability: facility characteristics and knowledge transfer mechanisms. Five levers have industry average capabilities. The response mechanisms lever has infant capability.

No adjustments to the response mechanisms lever are shown on the worksheet. This is a weakness in Company B's network. The company must make adjustments to this lever to increase its capability to average or higher.

After this is done, the company should adjust every lever with an average level of capability to increase its capability to the adult level. Then, Company B's manufacturing network will have an adult level of capability. Not only does a higher level of capability produce higher levels of outputs, it also makes it easier for a network to build new capabilities, take advantage of new opportunities, and respond to challenges from competitors. New capabilities are built on a foundation of existing capabilities. The larger this foundation, the easier it is to build on (Chapters 5 and 14).

OTHER CONSIDERATIONS

Other factors can influence the design, operation, and improvement of manufacturing networks. In this section, we examine three factors: product technology, industrial versus consumer products, and logistics.

PRODUCT TECHNOLOGY

Product technology is another factor that affects international manufacturing networks. Technology intensive products are produced in facilities located close to a company's design group. Several reasons for this are:

- Technology changes quickly, so technology intensive products have short product life cycles. Customer needs are sophisticated and also change quickly. This produces a continuous stream of engineering changes from the design group to production. To implement these changes effectively, design and production must be in close proximity.
- Technology intensive products are difficult to manufacture. They present a large number of production problems, especially quality problems, during the early stages of their product life cycles (Chapter 16). Correcting these problems quickly requires close collaboration between production and design.

Technology intensive products are produced at the home base factory or at a lead factory (Chapter 12) during the early stages of their product life cycles. When the design stabilizes and production methods are perfected, production transfers to another factory to take advantage of low cost production, proximity to key customers or suppliers, and so on. This releases capacity at the home base or lead factory for the next technology intensive product.

INDUSTRIAL OR CONSUMER PRODUCTS

Typical customer needs for industrial products are high quality, just-in-time delivery, secure supply, technical support, and design assistance. So pres-

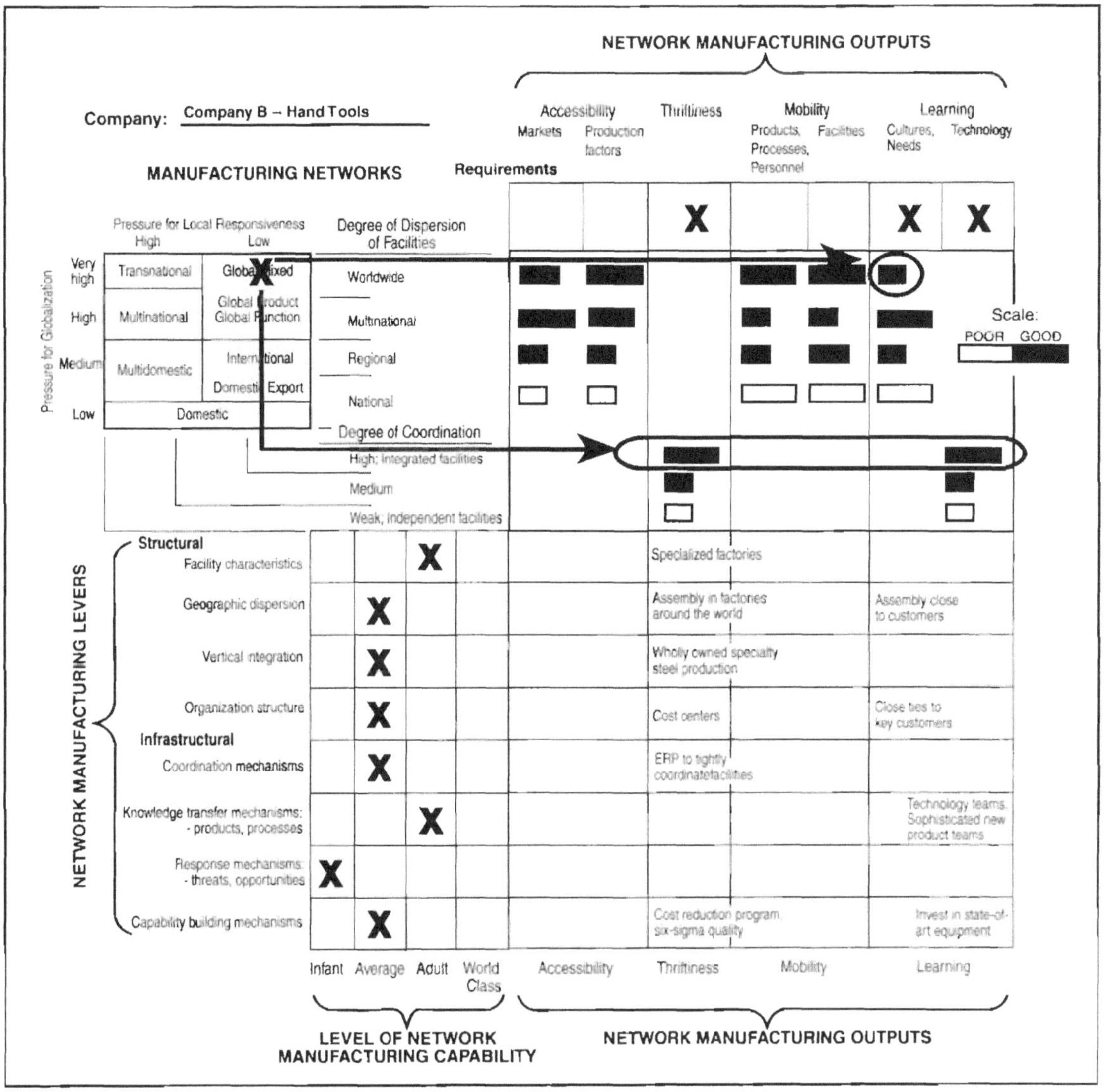

Figure 11-8 Manufacturing Network Worksheet at Company B

sure for local responsiveness is high for industrial products, and manufacturing networks on the left side of the manufacturing networks matrix (Figure 11-7) are best. Company A in Situation 11.3 is an example.

Typical customer needs for consumer products are low price and high quality. So pressure for local responsiveness is low, and manufacturing networks on the right side of the manufacturing networks matrix are best. Company B in Situation 11.4 is an example.

Logistics

Products with high weight or volume are expensive to transport, which is especially troublesome when the price of the product is low. Examples are construction materials, such as brick, concrete, and gravel, and grocery products, such as bread and milk. These products have low value-to-weight or value-to-volume ratios and so are produced in factories located close to customers. Companies producing these products use multidomestic and multinational networks. For example, bread is produced in large bakeries located close to major cities.

On the other hand, products with low weight and volume are inexpensive to transport. If product price is high, transportation cost is even more affordable. Examples are electronic components, expensive garments, and jewelry. These products have high value-to-weight and value-to-volume ratios and so are produced in remote facilities, far away from customers, to take advantage of low cost production, highly skilled workers, and so on. Companies producing these products use domestic export, international, global, and transnational networks. For example, expensive fashion garments are produced in Hong Kong to take advantage of highly skilled, low cost workers. These garments are light and can be shipped inexpensively by air to customers in North America and Europe. Watches manufactured in Switzerland are another example.

SUMMARY

Manufacturing networks provide four strategic outputs: accessibility, thriftiness, mobility, and learning. They are called network manufacturing outputs. The level at which each output is provided depends on the type of manufacturing network used and the level of capability of the network.

A manufacturing network consists of eight elements: facility characteristics, geographic dispersion, vertical integration, organization structure, coordination mechanisms, knowledge transfer mechanisms, response mechanisms, and capability building mechanisms. Elements are called levers to reflect the notion that each element can be adjusted.

The level of capability of a network depends on the level of capability of each lever in the network. Level of capability is measured on a continuous scale from 1.0 to 4.0. A value of 1.0 is an "infant" level of capability. A value of 2.0 is an "industry average" level of capability. A value of 3.0 is an "adult" level of capability. A value of 4.0 is a "world class" level of capability. Higher levels of capability produce higher levels of the network outputs. They also make it easier for a network to build new capabilities, take advantage of new opportunities, and respond to challenges from competitors.

ENDNOTES

1. The material in this chapter is adapted from:
    - DuBois, F., Toyne, B., and Oliff, M., "International Manufacturing Strategies of U.S. Multinationals: A Conceptual Framework Based on a Four-Industry Study," *Journal of International Business Studies*, pp. 307–333, Second Quarter, 1993.
    - Hodgetts, R., and Luthans, F., *International Management: Culture, Strategy, and Behavior*, Irwin McGraw-Hill: Boston, Chapter 11, 2003.
    - Shi, Y., and Gregory, M., "International Manufacturing Networks—To Develop Global Competitive Capabilities," *Journal of Operations Management*, Vol. 16, pp. 195–214, 1998.
2. Shi and Gregory, "International Manufacturing Networks," p. 202.
3. Ibid, pp. 202, 209.
4. Ibid, pp. 202, 209.
5. Adapted from ibid, Case 1 on pp. 205–205.
6. Ibid, pp. 202, 209.
7. DuBois, Toyne, and Oliff, "International Manufacturing Strategies," pp. 317–324.
8. Ibid, pp. 317–324.
9. Shi and Gregory, "International Manufacturing Networks," p. 209.
10. Adapted from DuBois, Toyne, and Oliff, "International Manufacturing Strategies," p. 323.
11. Based on Valley Tools in ibid, pp. 316–328.
12. Shi and Gregory, "International Manufacturing Networks," p. 201.

CHAPTER 12

FACTORY-TYPES IN INTERNATIONAL MANUFACTURING NETWORKS

There are many types of facilities in a manufacturing network[1]: factories, offices, R&D centers, warehouses, and so on. This chapter examines one type of facility, factories. Factories can be categorized in many ways:

- Chapter 4 examined macro factories and micro, or focused, factories.
- Factories can be home base, domestic, or foreign, depending on location. Home base facilities are located at company headquarters in the company's home country; domestic facilities are located in the home country away from company headquarters; and foreign facilities are located outside the home country.
- Factories can be server, outpost, offshore, contributor, lead, or source, depending on their role in a company's manufacturing network. These categories are called factory-types. Some types are more common for foreign factories than for home base or domestic factories.

This chapter examines the last two categorizations. The next section addresses foreign factories and factory-types are examined later.

Foreign Factories

Companies establish foreign factories to gain access to:

- Low cost factors of production such as cheap labor and inexpensive raw materials
- Foreign country markets
- Advanced suppliers
- Sources of technology

When the purpose is to gain access to low cost factors of production, companies usually organize foreign factories as cost centers and manage them as cash cows. These factories have low levels of capability. They are common in simple manufacturing networks (multidomestic, international). They are less common in complex manufacturing networks (multinational, global, transnational), because, as seen later in this chapter, complex networks require factories with high levels of capability.

Foreign factories with low levels of capability provide low levels of factory manufacturing outputs: cost, quality, performance, delivery, flexibility, and innovativeness (Chapter 4). In addition, the simple networks they comprise provide low levels of network manufacturing outputs: accessibility, thriftiness, mobility, and learning (Chapter 11). When higher levels of factory or network outputs are required, foreign factories must upgrade to raise their level of capability.

There are many impediments to transforming a foreign factory with a low level of capability to one with a high level of capability[2]:

- Foreign factories, organized as cost centers and managed as cash cows, do not have the necessary resources to improve.
- Some companies cut costs at foreign factories or shift production between foreign factories each time a change in the competitive environment occurs. The instability these actions cause makes it difficult for foreign factories to improve. Examples of changes in the competitive environment that cause instability at foreign factories include challenges by competitors (Chapter 3) and changes in exchange rate, labor cost, material cost, customer needs, and government regulations.
- In exchange for government incentives, some companies place foreign factories in locations far from key customers, advanced suppliers, and technology centers. This makes it difficult for foreign factories to improve (Chapter 8).
- Some managers place limits on how far foreign factories can develop because they fear dependency on foreign factories for critical skills. They insist on locating all critical skills in home base or domestic factories.
- Some managers are inexperienced in international activities and uncomfortable in foreign countries. They prefer to keep foreign activities as simple as possible. This attitude makes it difficult for foreign factories to improve.

Transforming a low-capability foreign factory to a high-capability foreign factory requires years of sustained commitment, effort, and resources. Transforming a simple network with low-capability foreign factories to a complex network with high-capability foreign factories is many times more difficult. However, this is exactly what superior companies do. High-capability foreign factories in complex manufacturing networks provide high levels of factory and network manufacturing outputs. Low cost production, access to new groups of capable suppliers, superior customer support, sophisticated logistics, customized products for country markets, and modified processes for foreign cultures are sources of competitive advantage found in complex networks of high-capability foreign factories.

Many low-capability foreign factories are anxious to improve themselves because they realize that the long-term prospects for low-capability foreign factories are not as good as they are for high-capability foreign factories.[3]

- Tariffs have declined worldwide from an average of 40 percent in 1940, to 7 percent in 1990. This is partially due to trade agreements, such as the EU, NAFTA, and Mercosur (Chapter 9). This reduces the need for foreign factories whose only purpose is to overcome trade barriers.
- Superior companies keep R&D and production close together because these functions must share ideas and information and work together effectively. Sometimes, R&D and production are placed in the same facility. This reduces the need for foreign factories whose only job is to produce products designed and developed elsewhere.
- The increasing sophistication of R&D and production and the growing importance of advanced suppliers force companies to consider more than just low wages when they choose locations for foreign factories. For example, 3M chose Bangalore as its manufacturing location in India. Land is more expensive and wages are higher than other locations in India; but Bangalore has skilled labor and capable suppliers. Xerox chose to

produce copiers and toner in Shanghai, and Motorola located a pager manufacturing factory in Tianjin. Although Shanghai and Tianjin are two of China's higher cost cities, they have advanced infrastructure, skilled labor, and capable suppliers.

FACTORY-TYPES

Factories in a manufacturing network can be divided into six factory-types depending on the scope of activities in the factory and the strategic reason for the factory. Scope of activities can be narrow or broad. Strategic reasons for a factory can be access to low wages or other factors important for low cost production, proximity to country or regional markets, or access to knowledge or skills.

The six factory-types are[4]:

- Server
- Outpost
- Offshore
- Contributor
- Lead
- Source

Figure 12-1 shows the six factory-types in the upper left area of the manufacturing network worksheet.

The first three factory-types (server, outpost, offshore) have a narrow scope of activities and a low level of manufacturing capability. A low level of capability is any level from infant to industry average (Chapter 5). These factory-types are commonly used in simple manufacturing networks (multidomestic, international). The last three factory-types (contributor, lead, source) have a broad scope of activities and a high level of manufacturing capability. A high level of capability is any level from adult to world class (Chapter 5). These factory-types are commonly used in complex networks (multinational, global, transnational). The lead factory has the broadest scope of activities and a world class level of manufacturing capability.

Superior companies have a larger portion of their factories in the high-capability categories (contributor, lead, source) than average companies. Highly skilled employees prefer to work in these factories.

OFFSHORE FACTORY

Many foreign factories begin as offshore factories.[5] An offshore factory is established to gain access to low wages, cheap raw materials, or other factors important to low cost production, and it is managed as a cost center. It has a narrow scope of activities, which are limited to low cost production of products exported for further processing or for sale. Investments in equipment and infrastructure are kept to a minimum. Factory managers do not choose key suppliers or negotiate prices. An offshore factory follows the instructions and plans received from other facilities in the network. It relies on others for expertise in new processes, products, and technologies.

An offshore factory has an infant or industry average level of manufacturing capability. Innovation is not expected. If an offshore factory makes enough improvements to raise its level of capability to the adult level, it can become a source factory (Figure 12-2).

SOURCE FACTORY

A source factory[6] provides more than just low cost production. A source factory has a broad scope of activities and is responsible for all activities related to developing and producing one or more products for a company's worldwide markets. It is the company's source of expertise for these products. Investments in equipment and infrastructure are high. Factory managers have authority over suppliers, product customization, product development, production planning, process improvements, and logistics. In the industrial boiler manufacturer in Situation 11.1 from Chapter 11, the company used a global product manufacturing network. The factory in China was the company's source factory for large, high pressure boilers.

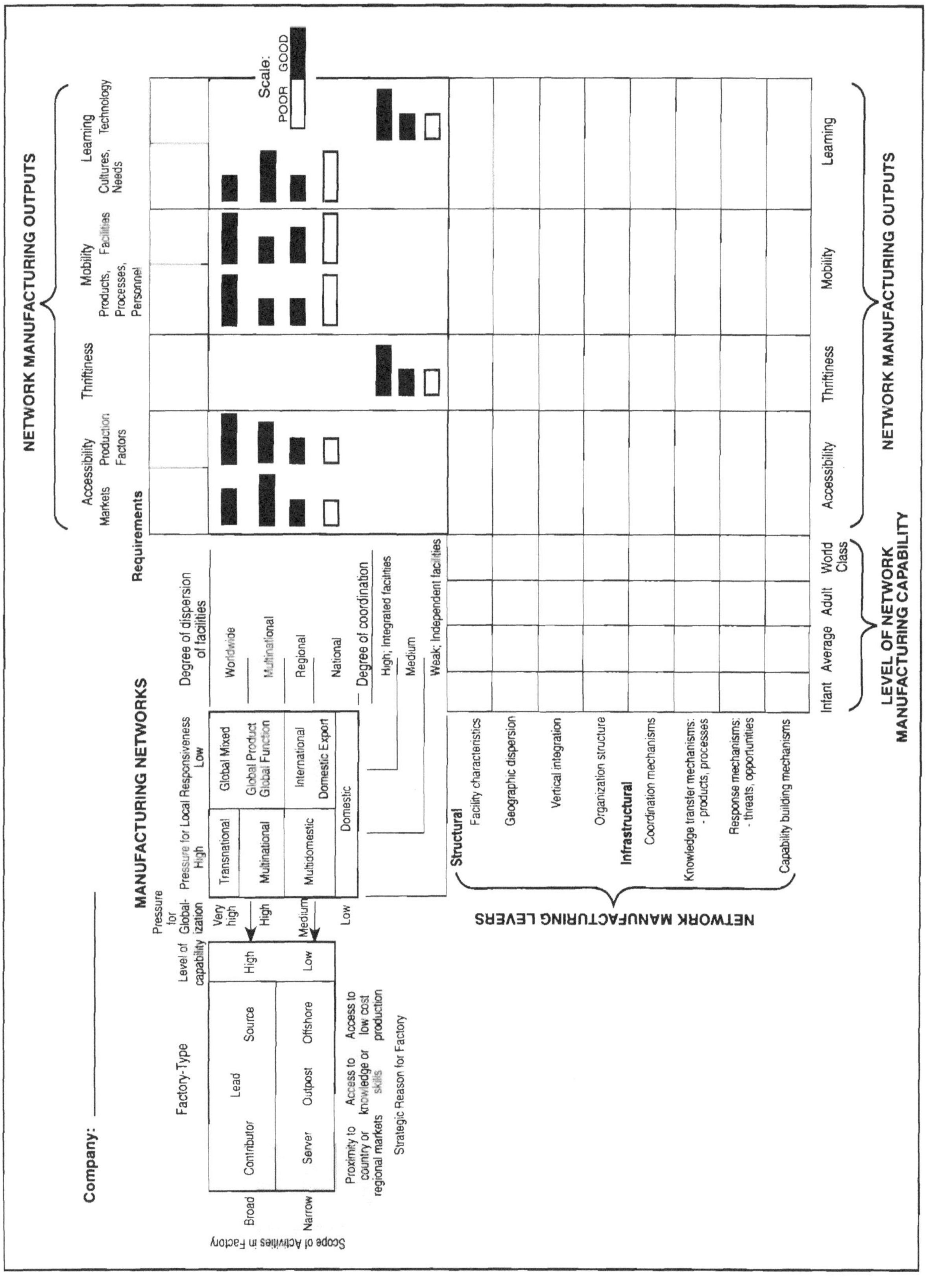

Figure 12-1 Adding Factory-Types to the Manufacturing Network Worksheet

Source factories are located in places where production costs are low, infrastructure is developed, and a skilled workforce is available. A source factory has an adult level of manufacturing capability and can become a lead factory if it makes enough improvements to raise its level of capability to world class (Figure 12-2).

SERVER FACTORY

Many foreign factories begin as server factories.[7] A server factory serves a specific country or regional market. It is established to gain access to customers, overcome trade barriers, reduce taxes and logistics costs, or reduce exposure to exchange rate fluctuations. A server factory has a narrow scope of activities, and it has some autonomy to modify products and processes to fit local conditions.

A server factory has an infant or industry average level of manufacturing capability. Innovation is not expected. If a server factory improves enough to raise its level of capability to the adult level, it can become a contributor factory (Figure 12-2).

In Company A in Situation 11.3 from Chapter 11, the company used a multinational manufacturing

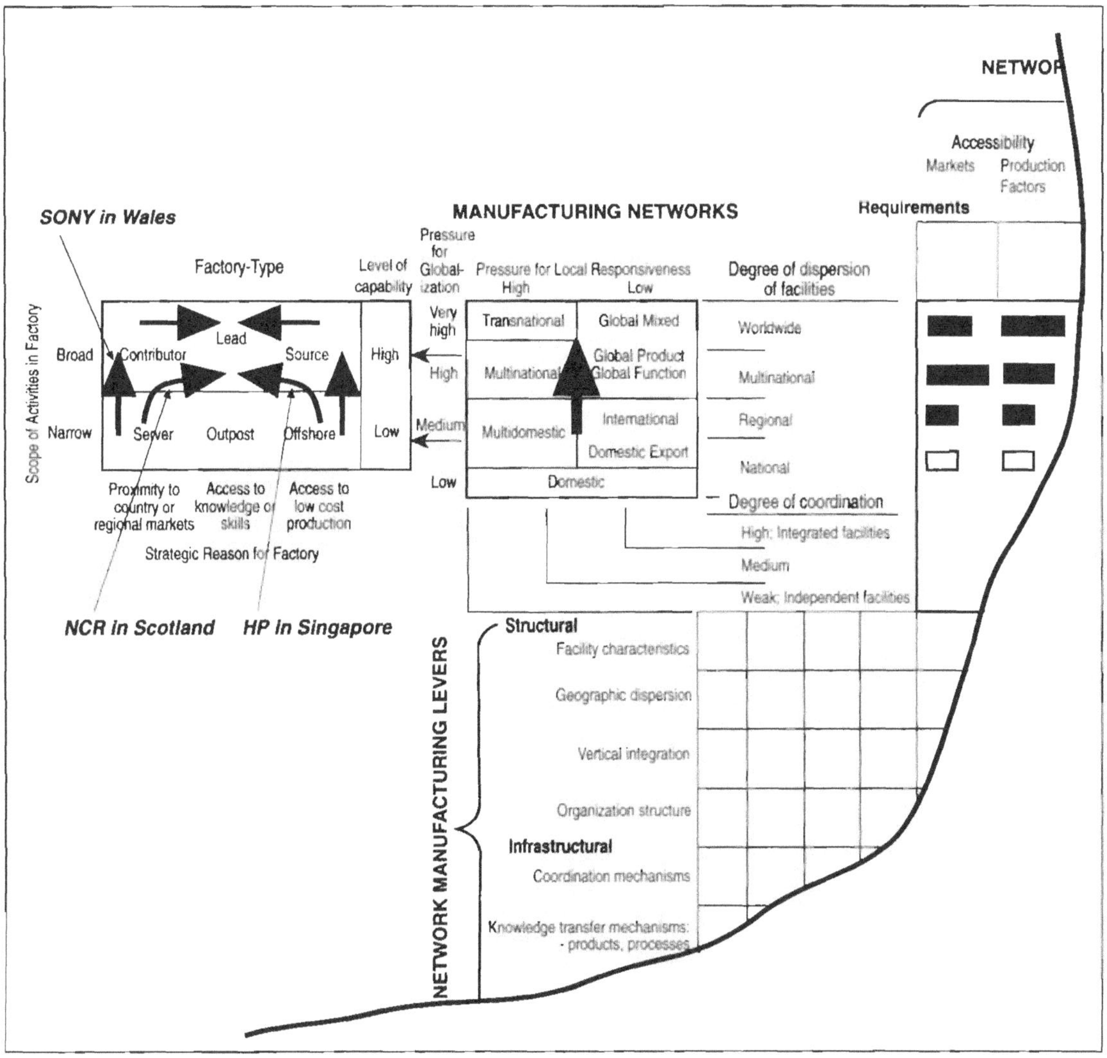

Figure 12-2 Changing Factory-Types

network to stay close to its customers. Most of Company A's foreign factories were server factories.

Contributor Factory

A contributor factory[8] also serves a specific country or regional market. A contributor factory has a broad scope of activities, which include those performed by a server factory, plus selection and development of suppliers and product and process engineering. Factory managers have authority over suppliers, product customization, product development, and process improvements.

A contributor factory has its own development and engineering staff and competes against other factories in the network for new products and new process technologies. A contributor factory has an adult level of manufacturing capability and can become a lead factory if it improves enough to raise its level of capability to world class (Figure 12-2).

Outpost Factory

An outpost factory[9] is established to gain access to knowledge or skills that a company needs. It is located near key customers, advanced suppliers, research laboratories, and strong competitors. It usually has a secondary role as an offshore factory, to manufacture some products, or as a server factory, to serve some markets. An outpost factory has a narrow scope of activities and an infant or industry average level of manufacturing capability.

Lead Factory

A lead factory[10] has knowledge and resources to create new products, processes, and technologies, and improve existing products, processes, and technologies. Employees work closely with key customers, equipment manufacturers, research laboratories, and other knowledge centers. It combines external knowledge with its own resources and expertise to create useful products and processes. A company's lead factories are its global centers of product and process knowledge. A lead factory has a world class level of manufacturing capability and provides manufacturing outputs at the highest possible level.

Company B in Situation 11.4 from Chapter 11 used a global mixed manufacturing network. The company produced hand tools and was vertically integrated all the way back to the production of specialty steel. Its steel-making factory was a lead factory. It had a world class level of manufacturing capability and was the company's source of knowledge for steel. It created new specialty steels, which the company used to develop new products and improve existing products.

Changing a Factory-Type

Periodically, a company strategically reviews the factories in its manufacturing network. The company assesses the current capability and factory-type of each factory. Then, based on its business strategy (Chapter 13), the company decides what future role each factory should play. Comparing the current assessment with the future role identifies gaps that may exist between actual and desired capabilities and factory-types. For example, one company's business strategy included expansion into a new regional market. The company's review of its factories revealed that the factory supplying the planned expansion had insufficient capability and was the wrong factory-type. So the company slowed the expansion and gave the factory time and resources to improve its capabilities and upgrade its factory-type.

Other internal events can trigger changes to capabilities and factory-types. A merger may add new factories to a network, or other factories in the network may expand or contract. External events also trigger changes. Increasing wage rates, declining tariffs, and growing local markets may require factories to change capabilities or factory-types. For example, as the details of the 1992 European Union were unfolding in the late 1980s, companies with factories in many European countries questioned why they needed so many factories; those with factories in only a few countries questioned how they were going to supply new markets or cope with new competitors in their current markets.[11] Companies in North America faced the same issues in the late-1980s and early-1990s, when the North American Free Trade Agreement was created.

Almost every factory begins as a factory-type with a low level of capability (server, outpost, offshore). Long-term prospects are insufficient for a factory that remains at a low level of capability for too long. Good managers at factory-types with low levels of capability try to increase capabilities and upgrade factory-types. Managers have several reasons for doing this:

- A factory-type with a low level of capability is easier to close or relocate than a high one.
- Managers in a factory-type with a low level of capability are less visible to company leaders than managers in factory-types with high levels of capability. In addition, the scope of activities in factory-types with low levels of capability is too narrow to expose managers to all the important activities in a company. For these reasons, managers in factory-types with low levels of capability are less likely to advance to senior positions in the company.
- A factory-type with a low level of capability is treated as a cost center and cash cow and lacks resources for improvement and innovation.
- The possibility of being closed, the limited scope of activities, and the lack of resources make it difficult to recruit and retain good employees.

Figure 12-2 shows four ways in which a factory improves capabilities or changes factory-type[12]:

1. The factory is a factory-type in the bottom of the factory-type matrix (server, outpost, offshore). There is no need to change factory-type. However there is pressure to reduce cost. The factory makes improvements that reduce cost, which also increase capability (Chapter 14).
2. The factory is a factory-type in the bottom of the factory-type matrix (server, outpost, offshore). There is no need to change factory-type. The company increases slightly the scope of activities at the factory.
3. The factory is a server or offshore factory-type in the bottom of the factory-type matrix. The factory makes large improvements and moves vertically up to a contributor or source factory-type in the top of the factory-type matrix.
4. The factory is a contributor or source factory-type in the top of the factory-type matrix. The factory makes large improvements and moves horizontally across the factory-type matrix to a lead factory.

The first way is the easiest. The factory is a factory-type with a low level of capability (server, outpost, offshore) with no need to change factory-type but faces pressure from the company to improve cost performance. These factory-types are usually treated as cost centers, so their cost accounting and performance measurement systems are geared to forcing cost reductions. The factory makes improvements that reduce cost, which also increase capability. Coca-Cola Company is an example.[13] Because of high transportation costs, Coca-Cola needs hundreds of bottling plants worldwide. Most plants are server factories, and each serves a small geographic market. Coca-Cola expects each plant to improve cost performance.

Cost reduction is not limited to server, outpost, and offshore factory-types. Almost all companies try to improve cost performance. All factory-types are expected to make improvements that reduce cost, and in so doing, increase capability.

The second way in which capabilities improve occurs when the factory is a factory-type in the bottom of the factory-type matrix (server, outpost, offshore); there is no need to change factory-type; and a company slightly increases the scope of activities at the factory. For example, a European pharmaceutical company decided to increase the scope of activities at its factory in Turkey.[14] The factory was a server, producing and supplying products to a regional market. In the early 1990s, the company asked the factory to produce some products for export to other European countries. The factory received extra resources so that it could perform the additional activities. The company installed new equipment to meet the packaging and labeling requirements of different European countries. The existing outbound logistics system was redesigned, and cost accounting methods were improved. The factory's foreign language skills were expanded, and new channels of communication with sales offices in other countries were opened.

The third way in which capabilities improve, or factory-type changes, occurs when the factory is a server factory-type in the bottom of the factory-type matrix and becomes a contributor in the top of the matrix (Situation 12.1) or when the factory is an offshore factory-type in the bottom of the factory-type matrix and becomes a source in the top of the matrix (Figure 12-2). In both cases, the factory makes large improvements to increase its scope of activities and raise its level of capability from infant or average to adult. Moving from the bottom of the factory-type matrix to the top makes the factory more important in the company's manufacturing network. The challenges of making these large improvements are substantial. They require years of effort and a large investment of resources.

The final way in which capabilities improve and factory-type changes occurs when a factory moves horizontally across the top of the factory-type matrix from contributor to lead factory or from source to lead factory (Figure 12-2). The lead factory has the highest level of capability (world class) of all factory-types. It takes years of effort and another large investment of resources to create a lead factory.

Superior manufacturers have a larger portion of their factories in the high-capability categories (contributor, lead, source) than average manufaturers. Complex manufacturing networks (transnational, global, multinational) rely on high-capability factories to provide high levels of factory and network manufacturing outputs (Figure 12-1). Superior manufacturers using high-capability factories in complex manufacturing networks disperse their technical resources worldwide. Average manufacturers using low-capability factories in simple networks keep most of their technical resources at home base.

Figure 12-2 shows three factories that changed factory-type:

- A Sony server factory in Wales became a contributor factory (Situation 12.1).
- An NCR server factory in Scotland became a lead factory (Situation 12.2).
- An HP offshore factory in Singapore became a lead factory (Situation 12.3).

For all three factories, a company decision to change an existing simple manufacturing network to a new complex manufacturing network triggered the change.

A factory's long journey from a low-capability server or offshore factory to a world class lead factory moves through three stages.[15] First, the factory improves existing capabilities. It improves physical layout, machinery, work design, and quality. It trains employees and implements improvement programs such as quality management and cycle time reduction (Chapter 14). Second, the factory acquires new capabilities and develops its own base of suppliers. It acquires product and process R&D capabilities. It develops logistics skills in international shipments. It develops multilanguage customer support skills and acquires sophisticated computer communication technology. Third, the factory develops the ability to generate new knowledge for the company's future activities.

This journey from a low-capability server or offshore factory to a world class lead factory can only occur when a factory is growing. Growth means increasing sales and production volumes. When a factory grows, it designs new products and processes and redesigns and improves old ones. It

SITUATION 12.1

Sony Changes a Server Factory to a Contributor Factory[16]

IN THE 1960s AND 70s, pressure for globalization and pressure for local responsiveness were both medium in the consumer electronics industry. Sony's international manufacturing network was ideal for this environment. In 1973, Sony added a new factory to its network. It built a new server factory in Bridgend, Wales to manufacture televisions for the European market. Bridgend was built to overcome trade barriers. It assembled finished products from parts imported from Sony Japan.

From the beginning, Bridgend management wanted the factory be more than just a server factory. In the early 1980s, pressure for globalization increased in the consumer electronics industry. Sony responded by upgrading its manufacturing network to a global product network. The combination of local management ambition and the new company strategy gave Bridgend an opportunity to improve its capabilities and upgrade its factory-type.

The factory's first action was to improve production processes. It started a quality improvement program, raised process capabilities, and implemented just-in-time manufacturing. Next, it reduced its dependence on Sony Japan by producing more parts itself and purchasing more from European suppliers. In 1986, it extended its quality program to suppliers. By 1989, European-made parts comprised nearly 90 percent of its product's content.

The next action improved product design capabilities. In 1984, Sony established an engineering and development department at Bridgend. By 1987, all full-time staff in the department were local employees. Since 1988, Bridgend has designed and developed most of the products it produces.

In the early 1990s, Bridgend's capabilities reached the level of a contributor factory (Figure 12-2). Bridgend was a server factory for ten years. It took another ten years for Bridgend to become a contributor factory.

expands its pool of skilled employees by hiring engineers, technicians, computer experts, logistics managers, and quality managers. It buys new equipment, develops new suppliers, and works with new customers. The atmosphere inside the factory is dynamic, engaging, and challenging. All of this facilitates change and improvement.

The capital cost of a high-capability foreign factory is larger than for a low-capability foreign factory. This is not an obstacle for superior companies. German companies have a reputation for making large investments in their foreign factories. For example, when BMW entered the Japanese market in 1981, its initial investment was several times larger than that required for its small operation. The extra investment enables a foreign factory to do its own research and become an expert in production, quality, technology, and service.

SITUATION 12.2

NCR Changes a Server Factory to a Lead Factory[17]

SERVER TO CONTRIBUTOR

In the 1960s, pressure for local responsiveness was high in the banking equipment industry. NCR used a multidomestic manufacturing network of independent facilities to serve the needs of diverse country markets. NCR's facility in Dundee, Scotland served customers in Western Europe. Six server factories with 6,000 employees comprised the Dundee facility.

In the early 1980s, NCR restructured into business units and changed its manufacturing network to a global product network. Company leaders challenged facilities in the network to either become world class manufacturers or face closure. At Dundee, one server factory with 700 employees met the challenge—first, it transforms itself into a contributor factory, then it transformed again into a lead factory. The other five Dundee factories could not meet the challenge and were closed.

The successful Dundee factory started by setting two priorities: improve production processes and speed up product development. To improve production processes, the factory launched quality management, just-in-time production and purchasing, cellular manufacturing, and a continuous improvement program. It also strengthened its relationship with local suppliers. To improve product development, the factory built a strong R&D department with special competencies in quickly developing and launching new products.

By 1985, the successful Dundee factory was transformed into a contributor factory. It was one of only two factories in NCR's global network that developed and produced ATMs (automated teller machines) for worldwide markets.

CONTRIBUTOR TO LEAD

The Dundee factory continued to improve its production processes and product development capabilities.

- It developed even closer relationships with key customers and suppliers. Employees visited customers, and customers visited the factory. It sourced 80 percent of purchased material from local suppliers.
- It strengthened its relationship with research laboratories at the University of Dundee and funded a new department of mechatronics there.

By 1990, the Dundee factory had transformed itself into NCR's lead factory for ATMs.

SITUATION 12.3

HP Changes an Offshore Factory to a Lead Factory[18]

IN THE 1960S AND 70S, pressure for globalization was medium and pressure for local responsiveness was low in the electronic instruments industry. HP's international manufacturing network of regional factories was ideal for this environment. The network had many offshore factories whose duties were limited to low cost production of components and finished products.

When HP needed a location for a new offshore factory, it chose Singapore over other Asian locations because labor costs were low, the local workforce was well educated and spoke English, and HP felt it could attract and keep good employees. HP negotiated special deals on taxes and tariffs. Infrastructure in the country was good, and the government was stable.

OFFSHORE FACTORY

The Singapore factory was built in 1970. Its manufacturing task was to produce simple labor-intensive products, such as integrated circuits, keyboards, and handheld calculators, at low cost for export to other HP facilities. HP designed and developed these products at its U.S. home base. During the introduction, growth, and shakeout stages of their product life cycles (Chapter 16), the products were produced in the United States. When the products entered the maturity and saturation stages of their life cycles (and the basis of competition changed to price), HP transferred production to low cost, offshore factories like Singapore to reduce production costs.

Each transfer required the Singapore factory to set up a production process for a new product, ramp up production, and improve the process to reduce cost and increase quality. Doing this successfully time after time raised the factory's level of capability.

The need to reduce cost and increase quality forced local managers to notice product design and discover new designs that made products easier to produce. An example was the HP 41C, a premium handheld calculator. When HP transferred production of this product to Singapore, factory managers set a goal to reduce cost by 50 percent. This ambitious goal could only be achieved by redesigning the product. The redesign required reducing the number of integrated circuit boards from two to one. However, the factory lacked the required expertise in integrated circuit design. The factory convinced HP that

SITUATION 12.3

Continued

developing this expertise would aid the factory's cost reduction efforts for the 41C and for many other products. HP allowed 20 factory engineers to go to the United States for one year to learn how to design integrated circuits. When they returned, the factory achieved the 50 percent cost reduction for the 41C and also used its new expertise to reduce the cost of several other products.

The need to reduce cost and increase quality led the Singapore factory to develop a pool of capable Asian suppliers. They delivered low cost parts just in time, participated in product development, and worked with the factory to increase quality.

Offshore to Source

Singapore managers were not content to let the factory remain an offshore factory depending solely on low cost production. Around the same time, pressure for globalization increased in the electronic instruments industry. HP responded by upgrading its manufacturing network to a global mixed network. The combination of local management ambition and new company strategy gave the Singapore factory an opportunity to improve its capabilities and upgrade its factory-type.

The factory's top priority was to continue upgrading its product development capability. HP agreed and began sending some product development work to the factory. To lead this work, they transferred a senior U.S. manager with extensive experience in R&D and manufacturing to Singapore. He started a small R&D group with three engineers. The group, which grew in size over the years, developed several areas of expertise.

In 1984, HP transferred the job of producing an important inkjet printer to Singapore, just four months after the printer had been introduced in the United States. Reducing the printer's production cost was critical to its commercial success. Within a few months, the factory reduced the printer's cost by 30 percent. One-third of the reduction resulted from efficient production, one-third resulted from improving the product's design, and one-third resulted from using Asian suppliers.

By the mid-1980s, the Singapore factory's capabilities had reached the level of a source factory. In addition to low wages, efficient production, and high quality, the factory could redesign products, do joint development work with suppliers, and distribute products worldwide.

Source to Lead

Local managers initiated new projects, and HP assigned more global responsibilities to the factory. In the late 1980s, HP gave the factory the job of modifying for the Japanese market a new printer just introduced in the United States. This was the first time the factory had full responsibility for a business venture. The factory was responsible for design, production, distribution, and marketing of a new product in a new market. The product was launched in Japan in 1991, but it did not succeed.

The factory learned from its mistakes and quickly followed with another new product, which was successful. The factory continued to develop new small inkjet printers for Japanese and other markets. In the process, it developed considerable expertise in producing small printers. It is now HP's lead factory for the design, development, and manufacture of portable printers for worldwide markets. It is also HP's lead factory for keyboards.

When problems occur, the factory solves them quickly with in-house employees. Companies that make large investments in foreign factories leave expatriate managers in their positions for long periods of time so they become familiar with the local culture and market and can better respond to customer needs. These practices have been successful for many small- and medium-sized German companies such as Booder (fish processing machines), Gehring (honing machines), Stihl (chainsaws), and Wetbasto (automobile sunroofs). Some of these companies have world market shares in the 70 to 90 percent range.

Maintaining a critical mass of technical resources at each high-capability factory in a manufacturing network while avoiding duplication of activities is difficult. The solution lies in specialization. Whenever possible, each factory should develop a specialization. Company leaders manage this by setting a direction for each factory, providing resources, and monitoring progress.

The best manager for a factory depends in part on the factory-type[19]:

- The best manager for a low-capability factory (server, outpost, offshore) is a specialist from home base with expertise and experience in the factory's standardized processes.
- When a low-capability factory upgrades and the focus broadens to include suppliers, customers, and others outside the factory, a manager with broad management experience and knowledge of local conditions is best.
- A contributor factory requires a manager with superior local knowledge including proficiency in the local language.
- A source factory needs a manager with technical expertise to optimize factory performance.
- A lead factory requires a manager with deep technical knowledge, familiarity with local conditions, and strong knowledge of the company.

Changing a Manufacturing Network

Complex manufacturing networks (transnational, global, multinational) provide high levels of the network manufacturing outputs because a large portion of their factories are in the high-capability categories (contributor, lead, source). This large number makes a network robust. A robust network can cope with changes in the competitive environment without resorting to extreme measures such as major shifts of production from one country to another, acquiring new factories, or closing existing factories.

For example, when exchange rates fluctuate, a company with a simple network of low-capability factories shifts production to keep costs down. Low cost production is the only advantage these factories provide, so currency fluctuations greatly impact what a company receives from its network. In contrast, a company with a robust network of high-capability factories does not shift production because the benefits are too small. Low cost production is one of many advantages these factories provide (others are access to market segments, advanced suppliers, and sources of new technology, as well as product development capability, customer support, and sophisticated logistics), so currency fluctuations have a smaller impact on what a company receives from its network.

The decision to increase a factory's capability is not made lightly. It is not easy to increase capabilities, but if it can be done, considerable benefits are gained. The factory's future is more secure, and a high-capability factory provides the company with high levels of manufacturing and network outputs (Situations 12.1 to 12.3). When a company upgrades a simple network to a complex network, it must increase capabilities at several factories at the same time. Some companies underestimate how difficult this is to do and try to upgrade too much, too quickly. When they fail, the companies weaken and are vulnerable to attack from competitors (Chapter 3).

Situation 12.4

Upgrading Networks in a Company with Three Business Units[20]

A COMPANY HAS three business units: household and toiletry products, over-the-counter pharmaceutical products, and food products. In the early 1990s, after many years of mergers, acquisitions, and direct investment, the company had factories in 120 countries. Most were low-capability server factories. Pressure for local responsiveness was high in all three businesses, so the company organized its factories into a loosely coordinated, multidomestic manufacturing network.

The company's strategy brought considerable success and made it an industry leader. At the same time, a considerable duplication of activities in the network was present. In 1995, the company decided to rationalize its manufacturing network by upgrading to a global mixed network. The company started in its most important business unit, household and toiletry products.

Most Important Business Unit

The company's rationalization plan followed six steps:

1. The company divided the world into seven regions based on geographic and cultural characteristics.

2. The company centralized manufacturing activities in each region in a small number of large factories. Each factory supported an entire regional market and was able to achieve economies of scale.
3. The company standardized many manufacturing and managerial processes. Whenever possible, factories in each region followed the same standard processes.
4. Factories performed product development activities to transform country products into regional products, and where possible, regional products into global products.
5. The company reorganized its home base staff and directed staff to tightly coordinate new product activities and manufacturing processes at all factories.
6. Factory managers launched continuous improvement programs in their factories.

The rationalization raised the levels of capability of the server factories from infant to average, and in some cases, adult levels. A few factories were transformed into contributor and source factories.

Other Business Units

In 1996, the company started to rationalize manufacturing activities for pharmaceutical products in its European region. Sixteen European server factories were transformed into two source factories and one contributor factory. Plans were drawn to reduce the number of factories in other regions of the world. A goal was set to have a total of ten high capability factories serving seven regions of the world.

Results

Early results showed that the network was easier to manage after reducing the number of factories. Fewer factories with higher capability and standardized processes simplified knowledge sharing, problem solving, and improvement activities.

Some difficulties appeared. The first was outsourcing. The previous multidomestic network employed a large number of small suppliers, but the new, tightly coordinated, global network required a small number of large, highly capable suppliers. Since not enough of these suppliers existed, the company had to develop them.

SITUATION 12.4

Continued

Another difficulty was how to handle customers whose needs could not be satisfied with regional or global products. The company's reputation and success resulted from its previous multidomestic strategy of producing customized products for country markets. Many in the company were nervous about abandoning this strategy, in favor of a global strategy where the company produced high volumes of regional and global products on standardized processes in upgraded factories. Whether knowingly or not, the decision to rationalize manufacturing networks was changing the company's strategy from its previous market-driven multidomestic strategy, emphasizing local responsiveness and proximity to country markets to a new, unproven global strategy that emphasized efficiency, specialization, and coordination.

Figure 12-3 summarizes the company's rationalization plan for its household and toiletry products business unit. The plan begins in the upper right corner of the worksheet where company leaders specify the required network outputs: accessibility to markets, accessibility to low cost production factors, thriftiness, and learning about product and process technology. Each is shown with a large X in the requirements area of the worksheet. Next, company leaders identified the current manufacturing network (multidomestic). The current network could not provide the required network outputs, so company leaders selected a new network (global mixed).

The decision to change the current multidomestic network to a new global mixed network is shown with a large arrow in the manufacturing networks box on the worksheet. The arrows in the factory-type box to the left indicate that this change requires the company to upgrade server factories (current network) to contributor and source factories (new network).

Some adjustments to the network levers are shown in the lower right of the worksheet. Consider, for example, the facility characteristics lever. This lever is set for the current multidomestic network and must be adjusted for the new global mixed network. One adjustment is establishing contributor and source factories to provide the thriftiness output. Another is factory specialization, which helps provide the learning about product and process technology output.

Two special adjustments relate to the previously discussed difficulty regarding customer needs that cannot be satisfied with

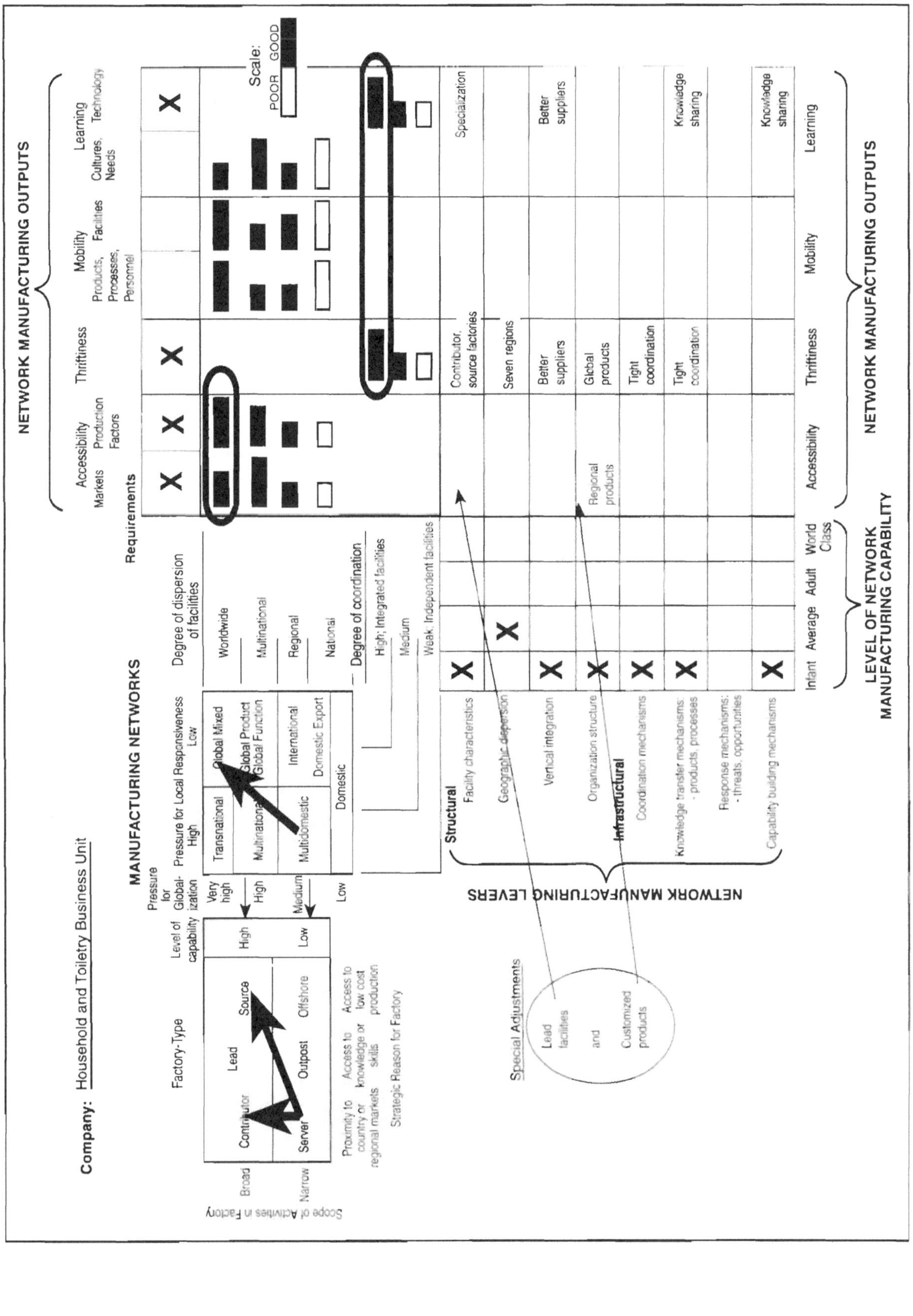

Figure 12-3 Multidomestic to Global Mixed Network (Situation 12.4)

SITUATION 12.4

Continued

regional or global products. The company must upgrade some factories to lead factories. Lead factories have a world class level of capability, so they can support a few focused factories (Chapters 4 and 15) to design and produce customized products for these customers.

The level of capability of the global mixed network is assessed in the lower left of the worksheet. Almost all network levers have the lowest possible level of capability. All levers were set for the current multidomestic network. It will take years of effort to make the numerous adjustments needed to change this network to a global mixed network and even more to raise the capabilities of the new network to average and adult.

The plan outlined in Figure 12-3 is unwise because the company has underestimated how difficult it is to upgrade a manufacturing network and is trying to do too much, too quickly. The plan is likely to fail and leave the company weakened and vulnerable to attack from competitors. The mistakes in the plan are visible when the following requirements are checked:

- Can the manufacturing network provide the required network outputs?
- Does the company have enough manufacturing capability to make the required changes to the network manufacturing levers?

The second requirement is usually the most difficult. As the worksheet (Figure 12-3) shows, a multidomestic network and a global mixed network are as far apart as any two networks can be. A multidomestic network is a simple network of low-capability, independent, server and outpost factories dispersed to country markets, in an industry where local responsiveness is very important. A global mixed network is a complex network of high-capability, tightly coordinated, source and lead factories dispersed to the best locations in the world. It is impossible to move from one network to the other in one step.

A better strategy is to move from a multidomestic network to a multinational network by upgrading a few server facilities to contributor and source facilities. Next, the company upgrades a few of these to lead facilities. This strategy builds factory and network capabilities and strengthens global expertise. After this is done, the company can move to a transnational or global mixed network. Situation 12.5 is an example of a company that followed a correct approach.

SUMMARY

Factories in a manufacturing network can be home base, domestic, or foreign. Companies establish foreign factories to gain access to low cost factors of production, foreign country markets, advanced suppliers, or sources of technology. When the only purpose is to gain access to low cost factors of production, foreign factories are organized as cost centers and managed as cash cows. This makes it difficult for foreign factories to improve capabilities.

Factories in a manufacturing network are organized into six factory-types: server, outpost, offshore, contributor, lead, and source. The first three have infant to average levels of capability and are commonly used in simple manufacturing networks (multidomestic, international). The last

Situation 12.5

Upgrading a Small Multidomestic Network[21]

A SUCCESSFUL MANUFACTURER of food processing equipment had a multidomestic network of five server factories located in Australia, Great Britain, and the United States. Pressure for local responsiveness was high. Food processing equipment was highly engineered and custom designed. The company's sales catalog had more than 500 products. Products were large, heavy, and expensive to transport. The multidomestic manufacturing network was ideal for the company.

One server factory in Australia served markets in the South Pacific; two server factories in Great Britain served Europe; and two server factories in the United States served North and South America. Each factory performed similar activities. In 1993, company leaders decided to reduce the amount of duplication in the factories. To achieve this, they launched three initiatives:

- *Develop global products:* The company assigned engineers from the three countries where it had factories to develop the company's first global product. The new product had a modular design, so it could be configured to meet customer requirements worldwide.
- *Improve factories through specialization:* The company upgraded its factory in Australia to a lead factory and upgraded one factory in Great Britain and one factory in the United States to source factories. The other factories remained as server factories.
- *Upgrade the multidomestic network to a global product network:* The lead factory developed standard manufacturing processes that other factories followed. All new products were developed in the lead factory. The company also developed a plan to build a new server factory in China.

three have adult to world class levels of capability and are commonly used in complex networks (multinational, global, transnational). The lead factory has the highest level of capability. Superior companies have a larger portion of their factories in the high capability categories (contributor, lead, source) than average companies.

It is not easy to transform a factory with a low level of capability to one with a high level of capability. It requires years of work and a considerable investment of resources (Chapters 5 and 14). Transforming a simple network with many low-capability factories to a complex network with high-capability factories is many times more difficult. Some companies underestimate the difficulty and try to upgrade too much, too quickly. When they fail, the companies weaken and are vulnerable to attack from competitors.

A factory's journey from a low-capability factory to a high-capability factory moves through three stages, and can only happen when a factory is growing. First, a factory improves existing capabilities (e.g., it improves production processes and product design processes). Second, a factory acquires new capabilities (e.g., it develops its own base of suppliers). Third, a factory develops the ability to generate new knowledge for the company's future activities.

ENDNOTES

1. A substantial portion of this chapter draws material from Ferdows, K., "Making the Most of Foreign Factories," *Harvard Business Review*, pp. 73–88, March–April, 1997. Used with permission of *Harvard Business Review*. Copyright © 1997 by the Harvard Business School Publishing Corporation; all rights reserved.
2. Ibid, pp. 87–88.
3. Ibid, pp. 74–75.
4. Ibid, pp. 76–77.
5. Ibid, pp. 76–77.
6. Ibid, pp. 76–77.
7. Ibid, pp. 76–77.
8. Ibid, pp. 76–77.
9. Ibid, pp. 76–77.
10. Ibid, pp. 76–77.
11. Ibid, p. 77.
12. Ibid, p. 79.
13. Ibid, p. 78.
14. Ibid, p. 79.
15. Ibid, pp. 83–85.
16. Ibid, p. 84.
17. Ibid, p. 83.
18. Ibid, pp. 80–81; Harvard Business School Cases—Hewlett-Packard: Singapore A, B, C, D (694035/6/7, 694053).
19. Ferdows, "Making the Most of Foreign Factories," p. 87.
20. Adapted from Case 2, pp. 205–206 in Shi, Y., and Gregory M., "International Manufacturing Networks—To Develop Global Competitive Capabilities," *Journal of Operations Management*, Vol. 16, pp. 195–214, 1998.
21. Adapted from ibid, Case 4, pp. 207–208.

PART IV

MANUFACTURING STRATEGY AND BUSINESS STRATEGY

CHAPTER 13

INTEGRATING MANUFACTURING STRATEGY WITH BUSINESS STRATEGY

Manufacturing is one of several functional areas in a company that formulates and implements strategic plans. Marketing, finance, distribution, and R&D are other functional areas that do the same. This chapter examines the relationship between a company's business strategy, manufacturing strategy, and the strategies of other functional areas.

A company's *business strategy* is the plan used to establish a market position, conduct operations, attract and satisfy customers, compete successfully, and achieve its goals.[1] Business strategy says, "Among all the plans and actions we can choose, we have decided to move in this direction, focus on these markets and customer needs, compete in this fashion, allocate our resources and energies in these ways, and rely on these approaches to doing business."

Competitive strategy is a subset of business strategy. While business strategy deals with all strategic issues a company faces, competitive strategy deals only with how a company competes against its competitors. Winning competitive strategies are grounded in sustainable *competitive advantage* (Chapters 2 and 8). A company has competitive advantage when it has an edge over competitors in attracting customers and in defending itself against challenges (Chapter 3). Many routes to competitive advantage exist, but the most basic provides customers with superior value, namely, a good product at a low price, a superior product worth paying more for, or a best value product—an attractive combination of price, features, and services.[2]

Formulating and executing strategic plans are important managerial jobs. Superior business performance almost always results from skilled managers who execute sound strategic plans. It rarely results from lucky breaks, gut feel, or freewheeling improvisation. Other benefits of first rate strategic plans are:

- Everyone knows what the company is attempting. The company is unified.
- Managers are more alert to opportunities and threats and are proactive.
- Managers understand the rationale for resource allocation (Chapter 17).

Elements of Business Strategy

Business strategy is organized into three elements: goals, product-market domain, and competitive advantage.[3]

Goals

Companies pursue a mix of hard and soft goals (Figure 13-1). Hard goals are based on traditional measures of financial performance, whereas soft goals relate to what a company, as a social entity, wishes to achieve (Situation 13.1). The particular goals sought in a business strategy depend on a company's internal capabilities and the opportunities and threats in its external environment.

Goals can be short term or long term. Short-term goals force managers to make changes today that produce immediate performance improvements, and long-term goals force managers to make changes today for the company to succeed in the future.

Goals must be consistent. Suppose a domestic company uses an equipment-paced line flow production system to manufacture products in the maturity stage of their product life cycles (Chapter 16). Cost is the company's order winning output. The company's business strategy goals are to double sales, increase profit margins, and maintain an entrepreneurial climate in the company. These goals are not consistent with each other or with the production system used. There are three inconsistencies. It is very difficult to increase sales of mature products. It is very difficult to increase profit margins for mature products that compete on the basis of cost. It is very difficult for an equipment-paced line flow production system to be entrepreneurial.

Hard Goals	**Measures**
Profitability	• Return on sales, return on assets, return on equity • Economic value added, market value added, earnings per share
Market position	• Market share • Rank in industry, position in international markets • Diversity of product line
Growth	• Increase in sales, assets, earnings • Increase in earnings per share
Risk	• Liquidity • Ratio of debt to equity • Fixed charge coverage
Soft Goals	**Measures**
Management	• Autonomy • Status
Employees	• Economic security • Opportunities to advance • Working conditions, quality of working life
Community	• Control of externalities • Contribution to welfare, cultural life
Society	• General benefits through innovation and efficiency • Preservation of environment • Responsible political involvement

Figure 13-1 Business Strategy Goals

SITUATION 13.1

Examples of Business Strategy Goals[4]

ALCAN

Hard Goals: To be the lowest cost producer of aluminum and outperform the average return on equity of the Standard & Poor Industrial Stock Index.

3M

Hard Goals: To achieve annual growth in earnings per share of 10 percent or better, on average; a return on stockholders' equity of 20 to 25 percent; a return on capital employed of 27 percent or better; and have at least 30 percent of sales come from products introduced in the past four years.

FORD

Hard and Soft Goals: To satisfy our customers by providing quality cars and trucks, developing new products, reducing the time it takes to bring new vehicles to market, improving the efficiency of all our plants and processes, and building teamwork with employees, unions, dealers, and suppliers.

HEWLETT-PACKARD

Hard Goals

- *Profit:* To achieve sufficient profit to finance our company growth and to provide necessary resources to achieve our other company objectives.
- *Growth:* To let our growth be limited only by our profits and our ability to develop and produce technical products that satisfy real customer needs.
- *Customers:* To provide products and services of the greatest possible value to our customers, thereby gaining and holding their respect and loyalty.
- *Fields of interest:* To enter new fields only when our ideas, together with our technical, manufacturing, and marketing skills, ensure that a needed and profitable contribution to the field can be made.

Soft Goals

- *Our people:* To help Hewlett-Packard people share in the company's success, which they make possible, to provide job security based on performance, to recognize their individual achievements, and to ensure the personal satisfaction resulting from a sense of accomplishment in their work.
- *Management:* To foster initiative and creativity by allowing the individual freedom of action in attaining well-defined objectives.
- *Citizenship:* To honor our obligations to society by being an economic, intellectual, and social asset to each nation and community in which we operate.

Product-Market Domain

This element of business strategy defines, on a product-market matrix (Figure 13-2), the environment in which a company competes. Products are grouped into product lines on the basis of factors such as product characteristics, production processes, and marketing features. Markets are divided into market segments on the basis of factors such as customers, distribution channels, and competitors. Products and markets form two sides of the product-market matrix. Cells in the matrix contain information such as annual sales, market share, profitability, assets employed, and other information useful for strategic analysis (Situation 13.2).

Competitive Advantage

Strategy guides the way a company organizes and performs activities in its value system. Activities and linkages between activities are potential sources of competitive advantage. Competitive advantage comes from organizing and performing activities and managing linkages between activities in better ways than competitors (Chapter 2).

All functional areas include sources of competitive advantage. For example, R&D provides

		Market Segment				
Product Line	**Produced in Factories**	**Agricultural** Major customers are contractors	**Industrial** Major customers are supply dealers	**Municipal** Direct selling	**Overall**	**Major Competitors**
4-inch pipe • Continuous flow production system • Mature product, commodity • High volumes	A, B C, E	$210 M* 12%*	$90 M 15%	none none	$300 M 13%	Small producers of plastic and clay pipes
6- to 14-inch pipe • Batch flow production system • Medium volumes • Special dies required	A, B, D	$60 M 24%	$10 M 30%	$20 M 25%	$90 M 25%	
14-inch and larger pipe • Operator-paced line flow production system • Produced on special equipment • Low to medium volume	D, E	none none	$10 M 40%	$60 M 65%	$70 M 61%	Producers of galvanized steel pipes
Overall		$270 M 15%	$110 M 19%	$80 M 55%	$460 M 23%	

*Annual sales (millions) and market share

Figure 13-2 Product-Market Matrix for a Pipe Manufacturer

SITUATION 13.2

Product-Market Matrix for a Pipe Manufacturer

A COMPANY PRODUCES plastic pipe in a range of sizes for use in large drainage applications.[5] Products are manufactured in five factories that comprise a small international manufacturing network. The product-market matrix in Figure 13-2 describes the environment in which the company competes.

Products are grouped into product lines on the basis of product size and production system. For example, one product line is a medium-size pipe (6- to 14-inch) produced on batch flow production systems in factories A, B, and D.

Markets are divided into three market segments on the basis of customer-type. Market segments are agricultural, industrial, and municipal customer-types.

Cells in the product-market matrix contain information on annual sales and market share. For example, the largest annual sales are for 4-inch pipes in the agricultural market segment ($210 million). The largest market share is for 14-inch and larger pipe in the municipal market segment (65 percent). The matrix also gives information on competitors.

innovative new products. Manufacturing provides high levels of network outputs (accessibility, thriftiness, mobility, learning) and market qualifying and order winning levels of factory outputs (cost, quality, performance, delivery, flexibility, innovativeness). Marketing, finance, and other functional areas provide high levels of pre-purchase assistance, post-purchase service, packaging, distribution, financing, and warranties. These combined advantages from several functional areas create a company's competitive advantage. Strategy determines the way functional areas cooperate to provide a particular combination of advantages.

The basic types of competitive advantage are low cost and differentiation. Low cost requires that products be manufactured at the lowest possible cost, and differentiation means providing products that differ from competitors'. An attractive combination of low cost and differentiation is called best value. Best value means providing a product that attractively combines cost, features, and services (Situation 13.3).

One mistake companies sometimes make is viewing differentiation too narrowly. Inexperienced managers underestimate the number of ways a company can differentiate. For example, four factory outputs (performance, flexibility, innovativeness, and delivery), three network outputs (accessibility, mobility, and learning), and numerous outputs from other functional areas, either alone or combined, create a large number of ways to differentiate.

HIERARCHY OF STRATEGIES

Whether in a small domestic company with one factory, a medium-sized international company with several regional facilities, or a large global corporation with a complex network of facilities, those who formulate strategy are often overwhelmed by the amount of information to gather and analyze and the number of possibilities to explore. To manage this, a hierarchy of strategies is established[6] (Figure 13-3). Functional areas such as manufacturing, marketing, finance, distribution, and R&D are at the bottom of the hierarchy.

SITUATION 13.3

Directive to Create Competitive Advantage

TOP MANAGEMENT directed the general managers of each business unit in the company to create a low cost, differentiation, or best value competitive advantage. Here is an excerpt from a memo sent by top management[7]:

"The businesses within the company are expected to achieve and maintain a leadership position in attractive industries. A true leadership position means having a significant and well-defined advantage over all competitors. This can be achieved through continuous, single-minded determination to achieve one or both of the following positions within an industry:

LOWEST DELIVERED COST

A business with the lowest delivered cost has greater economies of scale than other competitors. Economies of scale are available in the manufacturing, distribution, and installation steps where large amounts of costs are incurred . . .

DIFFERENTIATED PRODUCTS

Differentiated products are those that offer the customer some important and unique benefit. Typically, patents, trademarks, brand names, or specialized skills prevent competitors from copying such products. If a product is truly differentiated, the customer is selectively insensitive to price. Increasing customer price sensitivity is a sign that a product is losing its differentiation advantage."

Functional areas make up a strategic business unit or company, business units make up a corporation, and corporations make up an industry. Strategic plans are formulated at each level in the hierarchy, starting at the top, and are fed downward. Plans made at higher levels set boundaries within which plans at lower levels are made. Lower level plans are are fed back up the hierarchy. This guarantees consistent strategic plans at all levels.

The hierarchy makes it easier to formulate and implement strategic plans and helps a corporation manage its business units. After a corporation approves the strategies of its business units, it can allow the business units to operate autonomously while it monitors each business unit's progress toward the goals, product-market domain, and competitive advantage in its business unit strategy.

INDUSTRY STRATEGY

Strategy at this level focuses on issues such as financial markets, government policies, import and export practices, incentives for investment, international trade agreements, and infrastructure such as communications, education, health care, and transportation.

CORPORATE STRATEGY

Managers set corporate strategy first. Corporate strategy answers the questions: "What businesses

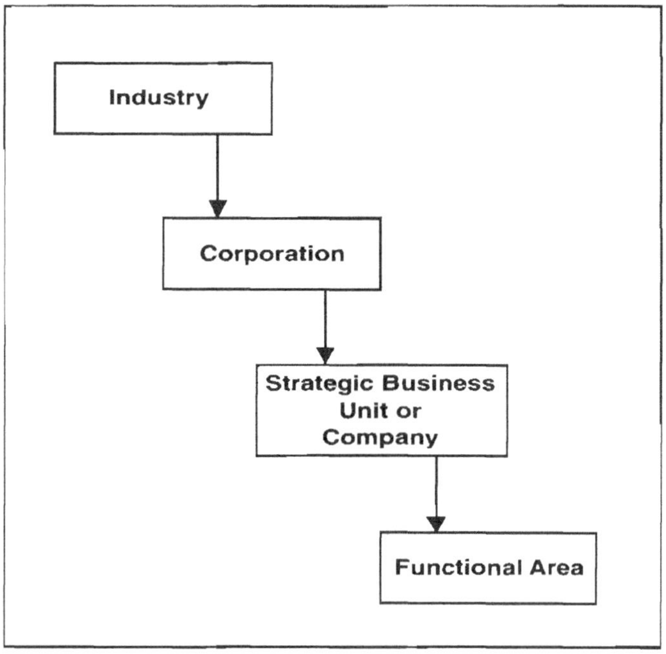

Figure 13-3 Hierarchy of Strategies

are we in? How will we compete?" Corporate strategy begins with a mission statement and a strategic vision. Goals, product-market domain, and competitive advantage follow.

The mission statement describes where the corporation presently stands, while the strategic vision describes where the corporation wants to be in the future. The mission statement states "who we are and what we do." It outlines the corporation's present capabilities, customer focus, and business makeup. The strategic vision describes the corporation's long-term direction. It outlines future customer focus, technology and capabilities to develop, and geographic and product markets to pursue. It describes the kind of company that management is trying to create.

The mission statement and strategic vision are start and finish lines for the race the corporation runs against its competitors. They are the basis for a strategy to get the corporation from where it is to where it wants to be. Figure 13-4 gives examples of mission statements and strategic visions.

After the mission statement and strategic vision are set, goals are developed, product-market domain is defined, and basis of competitive advantage is decided. Goals are long term and aggregate, and are described using measures such as return on sales, return on equity, rank in industry, and growth. Product-market domain defines the portfolio of businesses that comprise the corporation. The relative importance of each business may be described, and the corporate resources committed to each business may be outlined. Basis of competitive advantage is described in general terms.

Strategic Business Unit or Company Strategy

A strategic business unit is what this book has been calling a company. It may be part of a corporation, and it has most of the following characteristics:

- It has external customers.
- It has external competitors.

Corporation	Mission Statement	Strategic Vision
3Com	3Com's mission is to connect more people and organizations to information in more innovative, simple, and reliable ways than any other networking company in the world.	Our vision of pervasive networking is a world where connections are simpler, more powerful, more affordable, more global, and more available to all.
Bristol-Meyers Squibb	The mission of Bristol-Myers Squibb is to expand and enhance human life by providing the highest quality health and personal care products.	We intend to be the preeminent global diversified health and personal care company.
Otis Elevator	Our mission (and vision) is to provide any customer with a means of moving people and things up, down, and sideways over short distances with higher reliability than any similar enterprise in the world.	

Adapted from Thompson and Strickland, *Strategic Management: Concepts and Cases*, McGraw-Hill Irwin: Boston, p. 8, 2001.

Figure 13-4 Examples of Mission Statements and Strategic Visions

- It is relatively autonomous. It decides what products to produce, what processes to use, how it will vertically integrate, what suppliers and distributors to use, how to market products, and so on.
- It is a profit center.

The business unit or company strategy is more short term in outlook than the corporate strategy. It contains a more detailed statement of goals, product-market domain, and basis of competitive advantage. Business unit strategy must support corporate strategy. The most important question for business unit strategy is: "How are we going to compete?" What are the important network manufacturing outputs and market qualifying and order winning factory manufacturing outputs, and what are the important nonmanufacturing outputs?

Functional Strategy

Each functional area (manufacturing, marketing, finance, distribution, R&D, human resources, and so on) develops a functional strategy to support the business unit strategy. All functional strategies must be consistent.

Functional strategies emphasize the actions that will be taken to achieve the goals in the business unit strategy. Some actions are deliberate and purposeful, whereas others are reactions to unanticipated developments, changing market conditions, and challenges from competitors. Some actions are new, and others are holdover actions from functional strategies in previous years.

The framework outlined in Parts II and III of this book is used to develop the manufacturing strategy. First, the network manufacturing worksheet (Figure 1-2) is used to develop a strategy for the manufacturing network. Then, the factory manufacturing worksheet (Figure 1-1) is used to develop a strategy for each factory in the network. The outputs element of the network worksheet and the competitive analysis element of the factory worksheet are also elements of the business unit strategy because the desired network outputs and the market qualifying and order winning outputs are sources of competitive advantage for the business unit.

Integrating Strategies

The corporation's CEO leads the tasks of developing and executing strategy.[8] Other company leaders, such as vice presidents for manufacturing, marketing, finance, distribution, R&D, and human resources, also have important responsibilities. Tasks may be delegated to subordinates in business units, staff groups, factories, and R&D laboratories. Tasks and personnel are divided into four groups:

- The CEO and other corporate-level executives make important strategic decisions that affect all business units.
- Managers who have profit-and-loss responsibility for business units develop and execute business unit strategies.
- Functional managers in business units develop and execute functional strategies.
- Managers of major operating units, such as factories, sales offices, distribution centers, and R&D laboratories, develop and execute their piece of a functional or business unit strategy.

International corporations with diversified business units and geographically dispersed facilities use all four groups to develop and execute strategy. This is the only way a large corporation can gather and analyze information from activities in its many operating units and country markets. Single business unit corporations use two groups: the CEO and executives group and the functional managers group. Partnerships and owner-managed companies use one group: the CEO and executives group.

Companies use a six-step process to integrate corporate, business unit, and functional area strategies (Figure 13-5):

Step 1: Formulate corporate strategy.

Step 2: Formulate business unit strategies.

The corporate strategy is sent to each business unit. Each business unit develops a strategy that supports the corporate strategy.

Step 3: Formulate functional strategies.

Business unit strategies are sent to each functional area: manufacturing, marketing, finance, distribution, R&D, human resources, and so on. Each

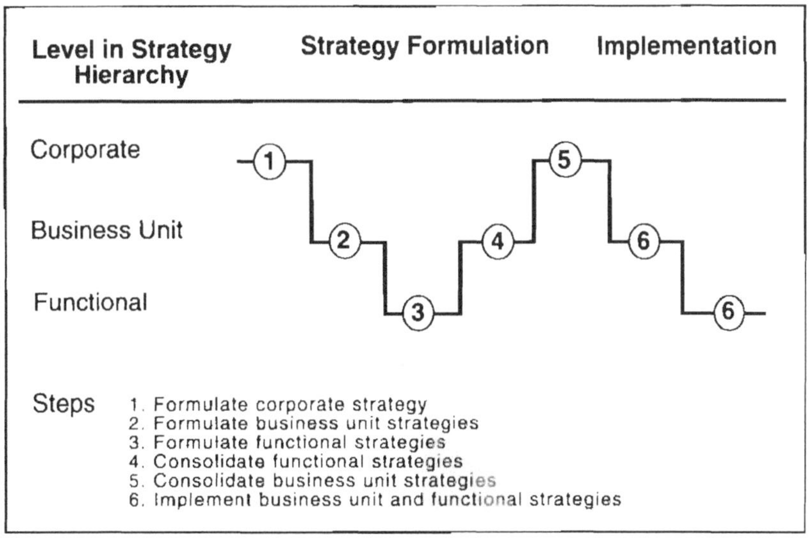

Figure 13-5 A Process for Integrating Business Strategy

area develops a functional strategy (and implementation plan) that supports the business unit strategy.

Step 4: Consolidate functional strategies.

Each business unit reviews the functional strategies from its functional areas. If required, functional strategies are sent back to the functional areas for revision. This continues until the functional strategies are consistent with each other and support the business unit strategy.

Step 5: Consolidate business unit strategies.

The corporation reviews the business unit strategies. If required, business unit strategies are sent back to the business units for revision. This continues until business unit strategies are consistent with each other and support the corporate strategy.

Step 6: Implement strategic plans.

After all strategies are finalized, implementation begins. Implementation plans specify when and how to achieve corporate, business unit, and functional strategies.

SITUATION 13.4

Integrating Strategy at IBM[9]

IN THE MID-1980s, IBM changed its process to formulate and implement strategy. The new process was similar to the six-step process described above. Around the same time, IBM also changed its corporate strategy and set a soft goal to become the world's best in manufacturing. IBM launched a strategic thrust called "high-volume, low cost manufacturing" to achieve this soft goal.

Two important elements of high-volume, low cost manufacturing were:

- Change all production systems to line flow production systems to provide the best possible levels of cost and quality.
- Raise the levels of manufacturing capability of all production systems in all factories to world class levels.

The new process and new strategy produced significant changes at IBM's RTP facility (Figure 13-6).

Before the changes, manufacturing at RTP was described as follows:

- More than 250 products consisting of more than 60,000 parts were developed, programmed, and manufactured.
- Products had many options.
- Many products were difficult to produce.
- Production was make-to-order.
- Schedule changes were frequent.
- Variability in production volumes was high.
- More than 250 machine types were used.
- Manufacturing processes were complex.
- Production planning and control systems were complex.

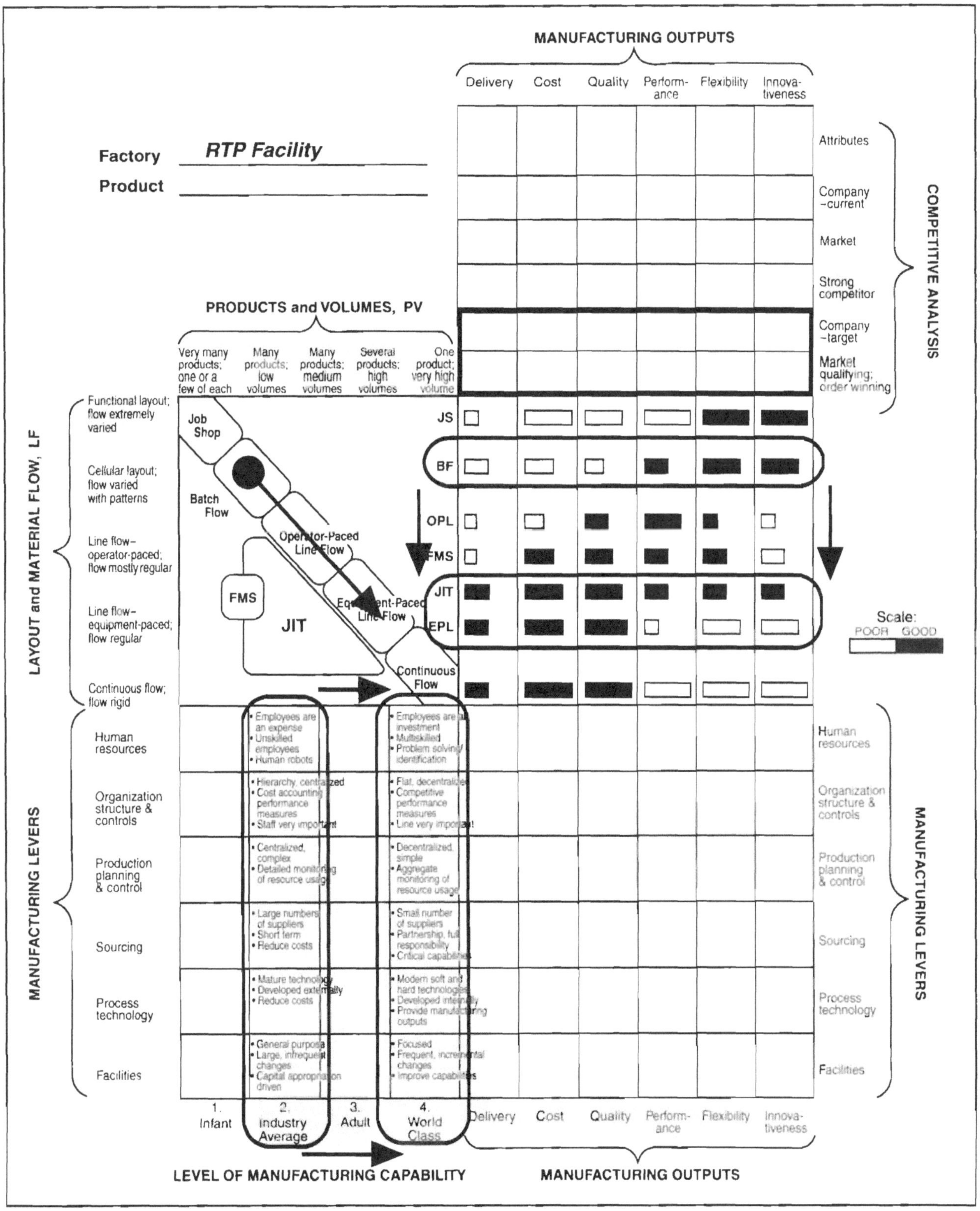

Figure 13-6 Manufacturing Strategy at IBM's RTP Factory

SITUATION 13.4

Continued

IBM's new process for formulating and implementing strategy proceeded as follows at the RTP facility.

STEP 1: CORPORATE STRATEGY

IBM set a corporate strategy goal to become the world's best in manufacturing and launched a strategic thrust called "high-volume, low cost manufacturing" to achieve this goal.

STEP 2: BUSINESS UNIT STRATEGY

The RTP facility reorganized into business units. Each formulated a business unit strategy. The strategies included goals for profitability, sales growth, cost, quality, delivery, and flexibility. Market qualifying and order winning outputs for product families were selected.

STEP 3: FUNCTIONAL STRATEGIES

Manufacturing, design, marketing, distribution, finance, and other functional areas developed functional strategies and implementation plans to support business unit strategies.

STEP 4: CONSOLIDATE FUNCTIONAL STRATEGIES

IBM called this step "strategic sizing." Functional strategies were summarized and compared to identify inconsistencies between them. Inconsistencies were communicated to the functional areas who made appropriate revisions to their strategies and implementation plans. This iterative process stopped when all functional strategies were consistent with each other and with the business unit strategies.

The following highlights are taken from some of the functional strategies:

Manufacturing

Only production systems located in the lower part of the PV-LF matrix (Figure 13-6) were used because these systems provided the best levels of cost and quality. The number of products decreased and volumes increased, so production systems were fully utilized.

Focused factories called factories-within-a-factory were organized so that products could be manufactured on dedicated production systems. Robotics-based automation was installed, products were standardized, production was make-to-stock, schedules were stabilized, and finished goods inventory was maintained at a distribution center so orders could be delivered to customers within one week.

Design

Design strategy focused on standardizing products and designing products easy to manufacture.

Marketing

Marketing strategy focused on marketing standard products with competitive prices, high quality, and a one-week delivery. Marketing also focused on increasing sales volumes because higher volumes were required to fully utilize the new production systems.

Distribution

Distribution strategy focused on maintaining finished goods inventory and delivering products to customers within one week of receipt of a customer order.

Finance

Finance strategy focused on making funds available to implement the manufacturing, design, marketing, and distribution changes. New costing methods were developed for the focused factories to more accurately calculate cost data.

Strategic Thrusts and Special Programs

Corporations regularly identify important issues to address over the medium term (three to five years) to maintain or improve their competitive positions. Examples include developing new products, improving quality, upgrading manufacturing networks, and reducing cycle times. When this happens, a corporation includes a "strategic thrust" or direction in its strategy that it wants all business units to follow. For example, in the late 1990s, some corporations launched "supply chain management" strategic thrusts to reduce the cost and improve the quality of purchased material, and improve delivery times (Chapter 15).

Strategic thrusts have different consequences for different business units and their functional areas. "Special programs" are ways functional areas try to achieve strategic thrusts. One strategic thrust may require manufacturing to initiate one or more special programs. For example, a supply chain management strategic thrust may require manufacturing to initiate special programs in supplier development, enterprise resource planning (ERP) systems, and product redesign (Situation 13.5). Some popular special programs were listed in Figure 7-10.

Summarizing Manufacturing Strategy in a Business Unit

A corporation may have many business units, each business unit may have a manufacturing network with many factories, and each factory may have several production systems. Special tools are used to summarize and compare production systems, factories, and business units. The Manufacturing Strategy Summary, Attractiveness-Strength-Contribution Graph, and Requirements-Capability Profile are three tools that summarize, in a way that is convenient for study and analysis, the strategic roles of production systems in a business unit. The first two tools are also used to summarize the strategic roles of business units in a corporation.

Manufacturing Strategy Summary

The Manufacturing Strategy Summary[10] (Figure 13-7) is usually used to summarize the strategic roles of production systems in a business unit. The summary is divided into five columns: business unit goals, product-market domain, competitive advantage (how products qualify and win orders), production systems, and manufacturing levers. The CEO and executives group enter the information in the first column, and marketing managers enter the information in the second column. Marketing managers and manufacturing managers both enter information in the third column, then manufacturing managers enter information in the last two columns. The summary checks the manufacturing strategy for each production system. It also checks that manufacturing strategy is consistent with marketing strategy. Finally, it checks that manufacturing strategy and marketing strategy are consistent with business unit strategy. Situation 13.2 (continued) is an example.

Attractiveness-Strength-Contribution Graph

The Attractiveness-Strength-Contribution Graph[12] is a flexible tool that summarizes the strategic roles of production systems in a business unit so management can analyze and compare production sys-

Situation 13.5

Strategic Thrusts at 3M[11]

3M's VISION IS "to be the most innovative enterprise in the world and the preferred supplier in all served markets." To help reach this vision, 3M launched two strategic thrusts called "3M Acceleration" and "Six Sigma."

- The goal of 3M Acceleration was to increase innovation. In 2003, the target was to double the number of new product ideas and triple the value of new products successful in the marketplace.
- The goal of Six Sigma was to improve quality and reduce cost. One of several special programs in the strategic thrust was called "Six Sigma with Our Customers." In this special program, 3M employees worked with key customers in customer factories, warehouses, and offices to solve the customers' most important problems.

Business Unit Goals	Product-Market Domain
1. Profit as a percent of sales exceeds industry average.	Product Lines: 4-inch 6- to 14-inch 14-inch and larger
2. Increase sales of 4-inch pipe by becoming the industry's low cost producer.	Market Segments: Agricultural Industrial Municipal
3. Increase sales of 14-inch and larger pipe by reducing delivery time 25 percent.	Customers: 5 chain stores 62 independent stores 450 contractors and major customers Sales Department: 40 representatives Technical support, promotional activities, order entry and processing Competitors: 4-inch Many small producers 14-inch and larger 3 strong producers

Competitive Advantage: How Products Qualify and Win Orders | Production Systems | Manufacturing Levers

Product line market segment	Market qualifying	Order winning	Production system	Manufacturing levers
4-inch Agricultural Industrial	Quality, delivery Cost, delivery	Cost Quality	} Continuous flow	Raise level of manufacturing capability to adult or higher.
6- to 14-inch Agricultural Industrial Municipal	Quality, delivery } Performance, quality	Cost Cost Quality	} Batch flow	Increase run size. Expand quality activities.
14-inch & larger Industrial Municipal	} Quality, cost, delivery	Performance	Operator-paced line flow	Reduce delivery time. Raise level of manufacturing capability to adult or higher

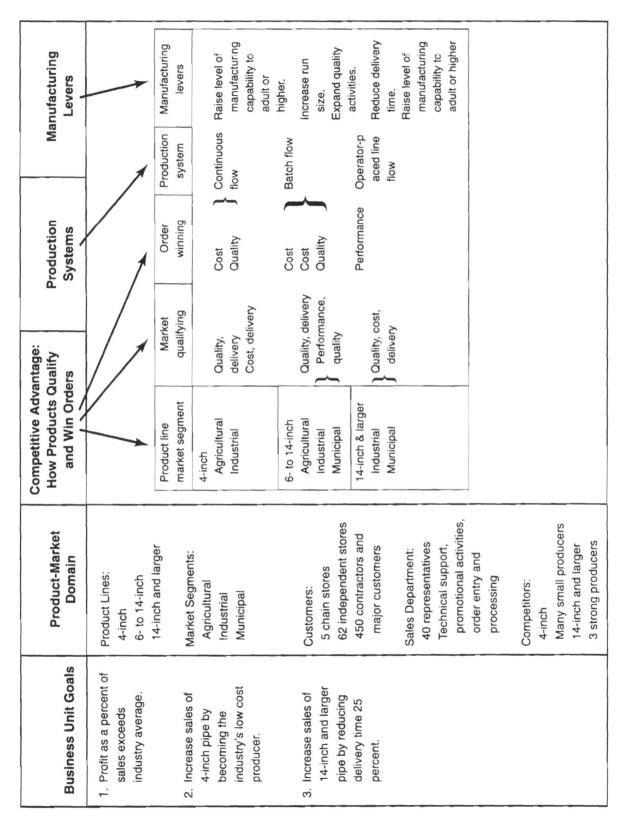

Figure 13-7 Manufacturing Strategy Summary for Pipe Manufacturer in Situation 13.2

SITUATION 13.2

Continued

FIGURE 13-7 SHOWS the Manufacturing Strategy Summary for the pipe manufacturer.

BUSINESS UNIT GOALS

There are three business unit goals: raise profit (as a percent of sales) to above industry average, increase sales of 4-inch pipe by becoming a low cost producer, and increase sales of 14-inch and larger pipe by reducing delivery time.

PRODUCT-MARKET DOMAIN

Marketing divides products into three product lines: 4-inch pipe, 6- to 14-inch pipe, and 14-inch and larger pipe (Figure 13-2). It also divides customers into three market segments: agricultural, industrial, and municipal.

Forty sales representatives handle sales to five chain stores, 62 independent stores, and 450 contractors and major customers. Sales representatives visit customers, give technical assistance, distribute technical and sales material, manage order taking and order processing, and gather information on competitors. The sales department prepares technical and sales literature and advertises in industry journals.

Two of the three product lines face serious competition. Competition in 4-inch pipe comes from many small producers with low to average levels of manufacturing capability. Competition in 14-inch and larger pipe comes from three large producers with high levels of capability.

COMPETITIVE ADVANTAGE: HOW PRODUCTS QUALIFY AND WIN ORDERS

Market qualifying and order winning outputs for each product line-market segment combination are shown in the next column of the summary. For example, the market qualifying outputs for 4-inch pipe sold to agricultural customers are quality and delivery. The order winning output is cost.

PRODUCTION SYSTEMS AND MANUFACTURING LEVERS

Production systems and manufacturing levers are shown in the last two columns. For example, 4-inch pipe sold to agricultural customers is produced in a continuous flow production system.

Information in all columns is consistent and supportive. For example, the second goal (first column) is to increase 4-inch pipe sales by becoming a low cost producer. This is achieved by using a continuous flow production system (second last column) and by raising the level of capability of the continuous flow production system to adult or higher (last column).

tems (Figure 13-8). It also summarizes the strategic roles of factories in a business unit or business units in a corporation.

The Attractiveness-Strength-Contribution Graph for production systems in a business unit has the following dimensions:

- Attractiveness of the market in which products from the production system is sold
- Strength of the production system
- Contribution of the production system to the business unit

Market growth rate for products produced by the production system usually measures the attractiveness of the market. This measure is placed on the vertical axis of the graph.

Relative market share usually measures the strength of the production system. Relative market share is the market share held by the products produced by the production system expressed as a percentage of the strongest competitor's market share. This measure is placed on the horizontal axis of the graph.

A measure, such as sales, profits, or return on assets, is used for the contribution of the production system to the business unit. This measure is shown as a circle of varying diameter on the graph.

Each production system is represented by a circle on the graph. The circle's position depends

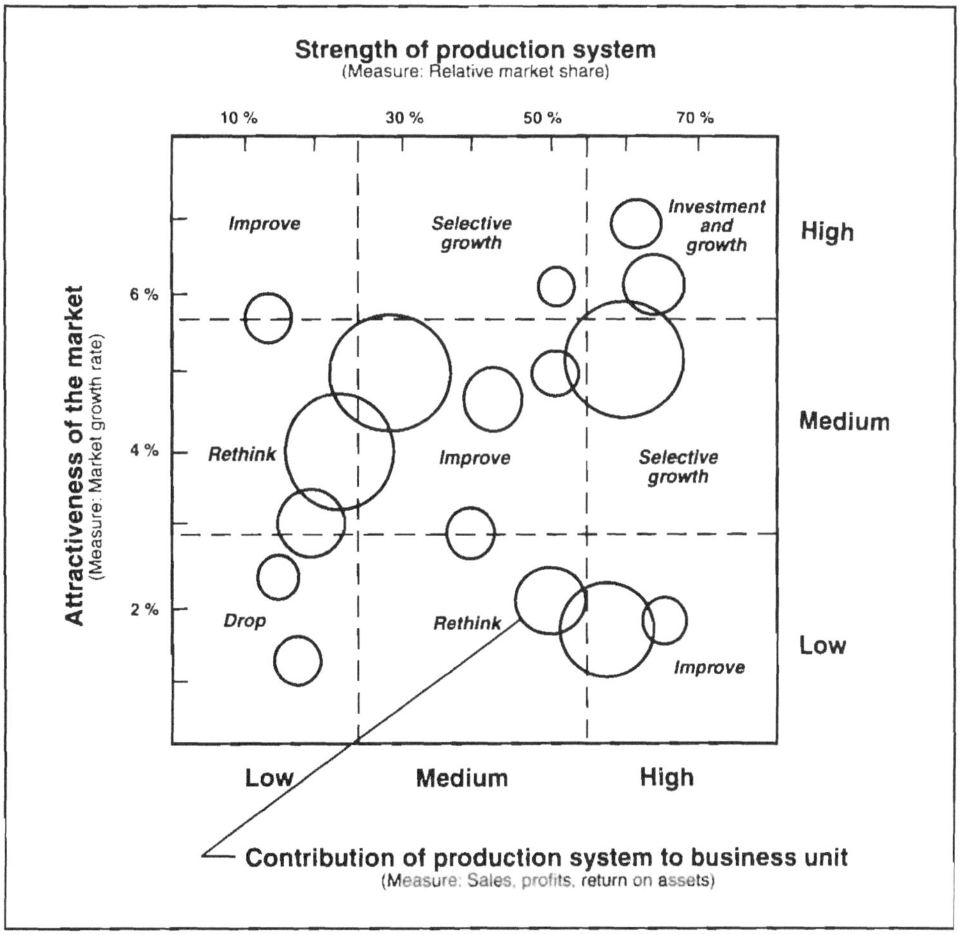

Figure 13-8 The Attractiveness-Strength-Contribution Graph

on the values of the first two dimensions. The size of the circle depends on the value of the third dimension.

The graph is divided into regions. Each region suggests a strategic direction for the production systems located there. For example, when measures of market attractiveness, strength of the production system, and contribution of the production system to the business unit are high (large circles in the upper right corner of the graph), the natural strategy is to invest in the production system so it will grow and generate more sales and profit. On the other hand, when measures of all three dimensions have low values that cannot be improved (small circles in the lower left corner), the natural strategy is to discontinue the production system. When measures of attractiveness, strength, and contribution have intermediate values, the business unit must carefully consider what resources it allocates to the production system and what instructions it gives to production system managers.

SITUATION 4.1

Continued

SITUATION 4.1 IN Chapter 4 described six focused factories at a manufacturing facility. The Attractiveness-Strength-Contribution Graph shown in Figure 13-9 was prepared for the facility. Since data was difficult to collect, simple measures of attractiveness, strength, and contribution were used (Figure 13-10). Market share was the measure for attractiveness of the market, level of manufacturing capability was the measure for strength of the production system, and productivity was the measure for contribution of the production system to the business unit.

Figure 13-9 shows that the production systems in the discs and sweeps focused factories are the best production systems. Both are large circles in an "improve" region of the graph, which means factory managers should try to improve them. This will move the production systems into the upper right area of the graph where they qualify for additional investment from the business unit to help them grow. The other four production systems are in bad shape. All are small circles in "rethink" regions of the graph, which means business unit managers must think carefully about whether or not the production systems should continue.

Business unit managers responded to Figure 13-9 by launching two special programs: a continuous improvement program to improve quality and a program to rationalize suppliers and increase outsourcing. They hoped these special programs would increase market share, raise the level of manufacturing capability, and increase contributions of the production systems to the business unit. That is, they hoped the two programs would increase the size of the circles and move them toward the upper right corner.

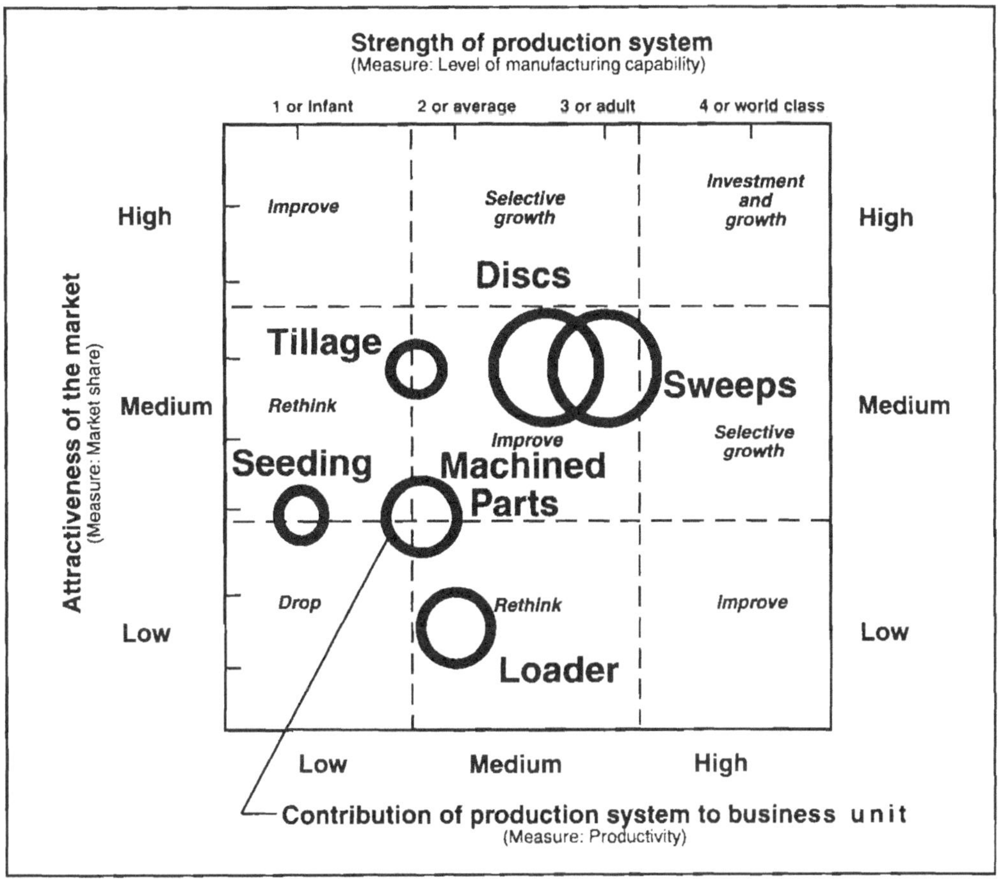

Figure 13-9 Attractiveness-Strength-Contribution Graph in Situation 4.1

Macro Factory	Focused Factory	Production System	Market Share	Manufacturing Capability (1 to 4)	Productivity (percent)
North Plant	Disks	Equipment-paced line	Medium	2.5	78
	Sweeps	Batch flow	Medium	3	78
South Plant	Machined parts	Batch flow	Low to Medium	1.8	69
	Seeding	Operator-paced line	Low to Medium	1	64
	Loader	Operator-paced line	Low	2	71
	Tillage	Operator-paced line	Medium	1.8	63

Note: Market share, manufacturing capability, and productivity are the measures of attractiveness, strength, and contribution respectively.

Figure 13-10 Values of Attractiveness, Strength, and Contribution Measures in Situation 4.1

More complex measures can be used for each dimension. For example, the attractiveness of the market can be measured by analyzing factors such as market size, market growth rate, competitive structure, barriers to entry, industry profitability, technology, government regulations, labor availability, and environmental issues. The strength of the production system can be measured by analyzing factors such as market share, level of manufacturing capability, levels of market qualifying and order winning outputs, improvement activities, customer service, international activities, and financial resources.

Requirements-Capability Profile

The Manufacturing Strategy Summary and the Attractiveness-Strength-Contribution Graph help a business unit understand how well its production systems support business unit requirements. The Requirements-Capability Profile[13] is another tool for doing this. It is formed by reorganizing the factory manufacturing worksheet (Figure 1-1) to emphasize the fit between customer requirements and production system capabilities.

Figure 13-11 shows a Requirements-Capability Profile worksheet. Theoretical requirements and capabilities are given for each production system. The requirements area of the profile comes from two elements in the factory manufacturing worksheet: competitive analysis and manufacturing outputs. The capabilities area of the profile comes from two other elements of the worksheet: manufacturing levers and level of manufacturing capability. A company draws a profile of its current or future requirements and capabilities on this worksheet. The profile shows how well the company's production systems support the company's current and future requirements.

Situation 13.6

New Production System Changes Manufacturing Performance

About ten years ago, a telecommunications company installed a standard operator-paced line flow production system in all 14 server factories in its transnational manufacturing network.

At a recent annual factory performance review, business unit managers were disappointed again with the performance of five server factories. Year after year, these factories turned in the worst performance, even after additional investments were made, training was increased, and factory managers were changed. After many years of trying, business unit managers wondered whether it was time to close some of the factories.

Before making a decision, a careful analysis was undertaken. The analysis revealed two important issues:

- The number of products and production volumes in the under-performing factories were different from those in the other factories. The under-performing factories produced almost twice as many products in substantially lower volumes compared to the other factories.
- The standard operator-paced line flow production system that all server factories were required to use was the right production system for the high-performing factories, but

		Production System					
		Job Shop	Batch Flow	JIT	OP Line	EP Line	Continuous
Requirements							
Products and volumes	Number of products	High					Low
	Order size	Small					Large
	Customize products	Yes					No
	New products	High					Low
	Schedule changes	High					Low
Manufacturing outputs (1 to 10)	Delivery	2	1	6	4	8	10
	Cost	1	3	7	4	8	10
	Quality	1	3	7	5	8	10
	Performance	1	6	6	10	4	1
	Flexibility	10	8	7	6	2	1
	Innovativeness	10	8	7	4	2	1
Capabilities							
Human resources	Personnel	Highly skilled					Unskilled
	Management task	Meet due dates					Reduce cost
Organization structure & controls	Orientation	Customer					Company
	Culture	Entrepreneurial					Bureaucratic
	Major cost	Labor					Equipment
Production planning & control	Production volume	Low					High
	Product changes	Easy					Hard
	Schedule changes	Easy					Hard
	Make-to-?	Order					Stock
Sourcing	Control on supplier	Low					High
	RM inventory	Low					High
Process technology	Equipment	General purpose					Specialized
	Flexibility	Flexible					Inflexible
	Setups	Easy					Hard
Facilities	Capital investment	Low					High
	Size	Small					Large

Figure 13-11 Requirements-Capability Rate Profile

SITUATION 13.6

Continued

it was the wrong production system for the under-performing factories. The under-performing factories should use a batch flow production system.

These issues are clear when the Requirements-Capability Profile is used (Figure 13-12). Three profiles are shown:

1. The company's standard operator-paced line flow production system
2. Situation in a high-performing factory
3. Situation in an under-performing factory

The operator-paced line flow production system (1) fits perfectly the situation in a high-performing factory (2). High-performing factories have a low number of products, large order size, medium rate of product customization and new product launches, and low frequency of schedule changes. The factories provide medium levels of cost and quality and a high level of performance. The factories need a production system with unskilled personnel because production is simple and cost reduction is a priority. Organization structure is bureaucratic, production volume is high, and equipment is specialized.

The operator-paced line flow production system (1) does not fit the situation in an under-performing factory (3). Under-performing factories have different requirements: a high number of products, small order sizes, high rate of new product launches, and high frequency of schedule changes. The factories provide medium levels of cost, quality, and performance, and a high level of flexibility. The factories need a production system with skilled personnel focused on meeting due dates and satisfying customers. Organization structure is entrepreneurial, production volumes are low, equipment must be general purpose and flexible, and setups must be easy.

When business unit managers studied the Requirements-Capability Profile, they concluded that the company needed a standard batch flow production system. A standard batch flow production system was developed and installed in the five under-performing factories. Performance improved immediately. Before long, the under-performing factories were top performers. Follow-up analysis showed that the batch flow production systems in the five factories had adult levels of manufacturing capability. The ten years these factories spent trying to make the wrong production system work had actually raised their manufacturing capabilities above the company's other factories.

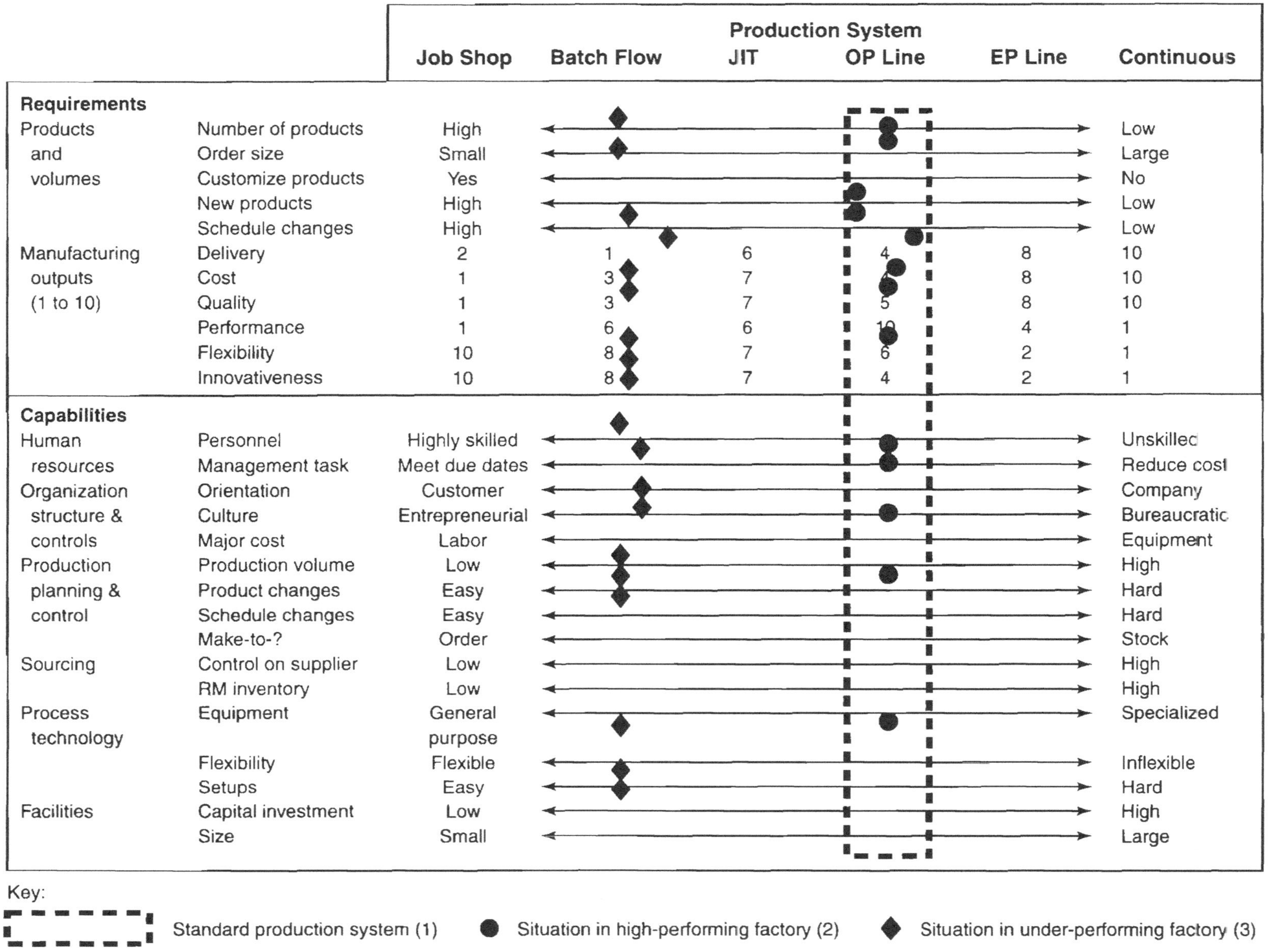

Figure 13-12 Requirements-Capability Profile for Situation 13.6

Situation 13.7

New Marketing Requirements Change Production System

A FACTORY PRODUCED a line of standard products on an equipment-paced line flow production system, which created low cost, high quality, and steady profits.

The factory had unused capacity, so business unit management pressed the factory to increase production. The factory, in partnership with the marketing department, agreed on a strategy to broaden the product line. New products were added, orders for customized products were accepted, minimum order quantities were decreased, requests for fast delivery were accepted, and changes to order quantities and promise dates were allowed.

Several years later, production and sales were up, but profits were down, and the factory was struggling. The Requirements-Capability Profile in Figure 13-13 shows the problem. Three profiles are shown:

1. Company's original equipment-paced line flow production system
2. Situation before the product line was broadened
3. Situation after the product line was broadened

The equipment-paced line flow production system (1) fits perfectly the situation before the product line was broadened (2). However, the equipment-paced line flow production system (1) does not fit the situation after the product line was broadened (3).

The poor fit means the factory must change production systems. Most likely, it should organize two focused factories: one with an operator- or equipment-paced line flow production system and the other with a just-in-time production system.

The Requirements-Capability Profile shows the fit between current or future requirements and the capabilities of existing or proposed production systems. The fit is not always perfect. It is perfect when a new production system is implemented because the production system is designed to meet current customer requirements. Requirements change over time, sometimes quickly, but production systems change more slowly. It takes a long time to purchase and install new equipment and processes, hire and train new employees, find and develop new suppliers, and so on. Allowing the fit between customer requirements and production system capabilities to deteriorate for a time can suffice as long as a company makes this choice knowingly.

Common Business Unit Strategies

Different business unit strategies were common in the 1970s, 1980s, and 1990s. In the 1970s, two generic strategies, flexibility and efficiency, were popular.[14] These strategies depended on the product life cycle (Chapter 16). In the early stages of the

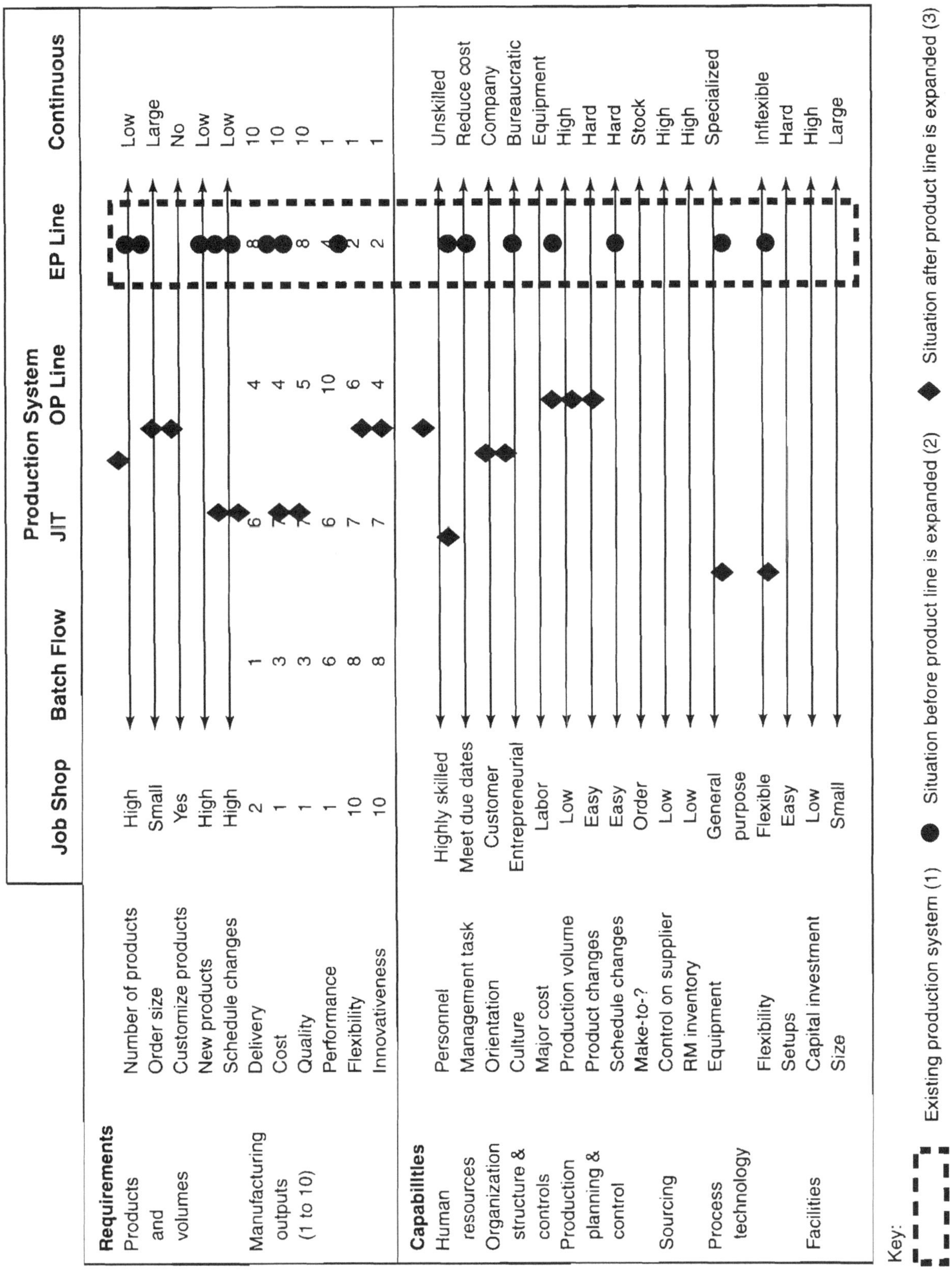

Figure 13-13 Requirements-Capability Profile for Situation 13.7

product life cycle, strategy emphasized flexibility. After the early stages, strategy emphasized efficiency. In the early 1980s, Porter's three generic strategies were popular: low cost, differentiation, and best value (Chapter 3). In the late 1980s and early 1990s, three generic strategies were popular: technology-based strategy, market-based strategy, and cost-based strategy.[15]

Technology-Based Strategy

A company with a technology-based strategy emphasizes R&D activities to develop new, advanced products. The product is the most important competitive advantage; manufacturing capability, for example, is relatively unimportant. Priorities include developing and launching new products, making design changes and adding new features to existing products, and developing new technologies (Figure 13-14). R&D expenses are high, and profit margins are high. The company exits from the market when products enter the maturity and saturation stages of the product life cycle and the basis of competition switches to low cost. Performance and innovativeness are the most important factory manufacturing outputs. Sometimes, this strategy is called product strategy.

Market-Based Strategy

A company with a market-based strategy concentrates on fast delivery, broad product line, broad distribution, and the ability to respond rapidly to demand changes. Priorities include flexibility to change production volume and adapt product design to meet customer requirements and the ability to produce in low volumes. Quality is also important. Cost is less important and has a relatively small effect on profit margins and sales (Figure 13-14). Sometimes, this strategy is called service strategy.

			Generic Strategies		
			Technology-Based Strategy	Market-Based Strategy	Cost-Based Strategy
Factory Manufacturing Outputs	Cost				✓
	Quality				✓
	Delivery			✓	✓
	Performance		✓		
	Flexibility			✓	
	Innovativeness		✓	✓	
Network Manufacturing Outputs	Accessibility	Markets		✓	
		Production factors			✓
	Thriftiness				✓
	Mobility	Products, processes, personnel	✓	✓	
		Facilities			✓
	Learning	Cultures, needs		✓	
		Technology	✓		

Figure 13-14 Important Factory and Network Outputs for Generic Strategies

Cost-Based Strategy

A company with a cost-based strategy concentrates on producing standard products with the lowest cost, best quality, and fastest delivery (Figure 13-14). Economies of scale are sought through large factories located in countries with low wage rates. Profit margins are small.

Summary

This chapter examined the relationships between a company's business strategy, manufacturing strategy, and the strategies of other functional areas such as marketing, R&D, and finance. A company's business strategy is the plan used to establish a market position, conduct operations, attract and satisfy customers, compete successfully, and achieve its goals.

Business strategy is organized into three elements: goals, product-market domain, and competitive advantage. Goals can be hard or soft. Product-market domain describes the environment in which a company competes. Competitive advantage comes from network manufacturing outputs (accessibility, thriftiness, mobility, and learning), market qualifying and order winning levels of factory manufacturing outputs (cost, quality, performance, delivery, flexibility, and innovativeness), and nonmanufacturing outputs from other functional areas (pre-purchase assistance, post-purchase service, packaging, distribution, financing, warranty, and so on).

The corporation's CEO leads the tasks of developing and executing strategy. Other company leaders and managers have important responsibilities. Companies use a six-step process to integrate corporate, business unit, and functional strategies:

- **Step 1:** Formulate corporate strategy.
- **Step 2:** Formulate business unit strategies.
- **Step 3:** Formulate functional strategies.
- **Step 4:** Consolidate functional strategies.
- **Step 5:** Consolidate business unit strategies.
- **Step 6:** Implement strategic plans.

A corporation may have many business units, each business unit may have a manufacturing network with many factories, and each factory may have several production systems. Special tools summarize and compare production systems, factories, and business units. The Manufacturing Strategy Summary, Attractiveness-Strength-Contribution Graph, and Requirements-Capability Profile are three tools that summarize, in a way that is convenient for study and analysis, the strategic plans of production systems in a business unit.

Endnotes

1. Thompson, A., and Strickland, A., *Strategic Management: Concepts and Cases*, McGraw-Hill Irwin: Boston, 2001, p. 1.
2. Ibid, p. 3.
3. The material in this section is based on Fry, J., and Killing, J., *Strategic Analysis and Action*, Prentice-Hall: Toronto, Chapter 1, 1986.
4. Thompson and Strickland, *Strategic Management*, p. 11.
5. Adapted from Fry and Killing, *Strategic Analysis and Action*, p. 13.
6. Ibid, pp. 19–24.
7. Adapted from Hax, A., and Majluf, N., "The Corporate Strategic Planning Process," *Interfaces*, Vol. 14, No.1, pp. 47–60, 1984.
8. Thompson and Strickland, *Strategic Management*, pp. 21–28.
9. Adesso, G. A., "Competitive Manufacturing in the Eighties," *Proceedings of the 1985 Annual Conference of the Association for Manufacturing Excellence*, J. B. Dilworth (ed.), Cincinnati, Ohio, 1986.
10. Adapted from the Manufacturing Strategy Framework on page 32 in Hill, T., *Manufacturing Strategy*, Irwin McGraw-Hill, Boston, Third Edition, 2000.
11. From information on the 3M Company website and Lockamy, A., Beal, R., and Smith, W., "Supply-Chain Excellence for Accelerated Improvement," *Interfaces*, Vol. 30, No. 4, pp. 22–31, 2000.

12. Adapted from Hax, A., and Majluf, N., "Use of the Industry Attractiveness-Business Strength Matrix in Strategic Planning," *Interfaces*, Vol. 13, No. 2, pp. 54–71, 1983.

13. Adapted from Product Profiling in Chapter 6 of Hill, T., *Manufacturing Strategy*, Irwin McGraw-Hill, Boston, Third Edition, 2000.

14. Utterback, J. and Abernathy, W., "A Dynamic Model of Process and Product Innovation," *Omega: International Journal of Management Science*, Vol. 3, No. 6, pp. 639–656, 1975.

15. Stobaugh, R., and Telesio, P., "Match Manufacturing Strategy Policies and Product Strategy," *Harvard Business Review*, Vol. 61, No. 2, pp. 113–120, March–April 1983. Miller, J., and Roth, A., "A Taxonomy of Manufacturing Strategies," *Management Science*, Vol. 40, pp. 285–304, 1994.

PART V

PROGRAMS USED FREQUENTLY IN MANUFACTURING STRATEGY

CHAPTER 14

IMPROVEMENT PROGRAMS IN MANUFACTURING

The objective of a manufacturing improvement program is to:

> *Raise the capabilities of the levers in a production system or a manufacturing network in order to raise the levels of the factory or network outputs.*

All improvement programs follow two steps. First, they identify activities that contain significant amounts of "waste." Second, they make improvements that eliminate these wastes.

Cost cutting is the most common improvement program. In the first step, cost cutting assumes that high cost activities also have significant amounts of waste. A company's accounting system easily identifies all high cost activities. In the second step, improvements are made in these activities. Wastes in the activities are eliminated, and costs decrease.

Quality management is the second most common improvement program. In the first step, quality management assumes that activities that have poor quality also have significant amounts of waste. In the second step, improvements are made to reduce or eliminate the waste in these activities. This raises the level of quality and also reduces cost and delivery time. One reason for the popularity of quality management is historical. In the 1970s, the quality of Japanese products exceeded that of North American products in several industries, so companies in these industries focused their improvement efforts on raising the level of quality. A second reason for the popularity of quality management is the availability of well-known techniques for identifying and solving the problems that cause poor quality. A third reason is that, in addition to raising the level of quality, the quality management techniques also reduce cost and improve delivery.

Cost cutting, quality management, cycle time reduction, and agile manufacturing are popular improvement programs. They use cost, quality, time, and flexibility, respectively, in the first step to select activities where improvements will be made. Cost cutting selects activities where costs are high. Quality management selects activities where quality is poor. Cycle time reduction, also called time-based competition, selects activities that require long times to perform. Agile manufacturing selects inflexible activities. All programs are effective. The best improvement program for a company is the program that a company finds easiest to implement.

One way in which improvement programs differ is how they perform the first step (identify activities where improvements will be made). Improvement programs differ in other ways. The frequency and size of improvements varies. There are three possibilities. A program such as kaizen produces a steady stream of small or incremental improvements. A program such as six sigma (Chapter 15) produces large improvements at somewhat regular intervals (e.g., every six months). A program such as reengineering produces very large or breakthrough improvements. Programs also differ in the scope of activities where improvements are made. A narrow improvement program concentrates on activities in a small number of processes or production systems, whereas a broad program makes improvements in a large number of activities (e.g., activities in all functional areas of a business unit).

Improvement programs also make improvements or adjustments to factory and network levers to bring levers into the correct position for the production system or manufacturing network used. After this is done, improvement programs make fine adjustments to the levers to raise the level of manufacturing capability.

Improvement programs use a technique called benchmarking to gather information on what improvements are possible. In the remainder of this chapter, we examine how manufacturing strategy uses benchmarking, quality management, cycle time reduction, agile manufacturing, kaizen, and reengineering. Theoretical foundations for making improvements are the experience curve and the product life cycle. They are examined in Chapter 16.

BENCHMARKING

It is not easy to convince employees that changes are necessary. Information such as the following helps:

- How effective are we compared to our competitors and to companies in other industries?
- How do product cost and quality, delivery time, equipment utilization, maintenance and repair time, minimum order size, the number of new products introduced each year, and so on, compare to competitors in the same region, to the best competitors in the industry, and to the best companies in other industries?
- How much better are we today than we were last year?
- Are we good enough?

Benchmarking is used to gather this information. Benchmarking information is obtained at professional meetings, from trade journals and books, and from conversations with professionals, suppliers, sales representatives, and employees at other companies. Obtaining information from companies in the same industry is difficult because of the natural reluctance of companies to share information with their competitors. Obtaining information from companies in other industries is easier. Professionals working in noncompeting companies often gladly exchange information and ideas. Small companies supplying products to larger companies can obtain information from these companies.

Benchmarking is not easy. Collecting information is expensive and time consuming. After information is collected, it must be carefully interpreted because it comes from companies that produce different products using somewhat different processes, and follow different manufacturing strategies for different competitive environments.

There are two types of benchmarking information: performance benchmarking information and best practices benchmarking information.

Performance benchmarking information consists of performance measures used at other companies and the values of the performance measures. Examples include defect rate, delivery time, new products introduced per year, unit labor cost, unit material cost, employee participation rate, and so on. Xerox benchmarks more than 200 performance measures. They collect three values for each measure: industry average benchmark (the mean

SITUATION 14.1

Benchmarking at Xerox[1]

WHEN XEROX STARTED BENCHMARKING in 1979, management's objective was to analyze performance measures, such as unit costs, defect rates, and cycle times, in its manufacturing operations. By the mid-1980s, the benchmarking focus changed to analyzing best practices, the practices used by other companies to achieve superior performance.

Xerox started a benchmarking study in 1981 to help improve its warehousing and distribution operations. After studying the trade literature and talking to professionals in the field, Xerox discovered the L.L. Bean Company. L.L. Bean was a sporting goods retailer and mail-order house. L.L. Bean and Xerox both had a warehousing and distribution system that handled a wide variety of products.

When the Xerox benchmarking team visited L.L. Bean in 1982, they found many differences in performance measures and practices. L.L. Bean was three times more efficient than Xerox on two important measures: the number of customer orders completed per day per employee and the total number of items on these orders. The benchmarking team documented the practices L.L. Bean used to achieve this superior performance. The team also visited a drug wholesale company, an electrical components manufacturer, and a catalog service bureau.

Xerox used the performance benchmarking information to set new performance targets and the best practices benchmarking information to design new practices for its warehouse and distribution operations. The new practices helped these departments achieve the new performance targets.

performance of companies in the industry), competitive benchmark (the best performance in the industry), and world class benchmark (the best performance in any industry).

Figure 14-1 shows a worksheet for performance benchmarking information. It is an expanded version of the competitive analysis element in the factory strategy worksheet (Figure 1-1) and the outputs element in the network strategy worksheet (Figure 1-2). Measures for each factory and network output are selected. Values for each measure are collected from companies in the same industry and from companies in other industries. These external values are compared to values in the company. Market qualifying and order winning outputs are determined, and 12-month and 24-month targets are set.

Best practices benchmarking information is the second type of benchmarking information. It is information on practices and processes used at other companies to achieve superior performance. Figure 14-2 shows a worksheet for best practices benchmarking information. It is an expanded version of the levers elements in the factory strategy worksheet (Figure 1-1) and the network strategy worksheet (Figure 1-2). Information on best practices are

Factory and Network Outputs		Company		Competitors from Same Industry								Competitors in Other Industries				Market Qualifying, Order Winning, or Not Important		
				Company A		Company B		Industry Average Competitor		Best Competitor		Company C		Company D		M, O	Targets	
	Measures	Current year	Last year	This year	Last year	This year	Last year	This year	Last year	This year	Last year	This year	Last year	This year	Last year		12 months	24 months
Factory Outputs																		
Cost	Unit cost																	
	Labor productivity																	
	Machine utilization																	
	Yield																	
Quality	Percent defective																	
	Rework costs																	
	Mean time between failures																	
Performance	Number of standard features																	
	Number of advanced features																	
	Product resale price																	
Delivery	Quoted delivery time																	
	Percentage on-time shipments																	
	Order entry cycle time																	
	Average lateness																	
	Number of expeditors																	
Flexibility	Number of products in product line																	
	Number of options allowed																	
	Minimum order size																	
	Length of frozen schedule																	
	Average lot size																	
Innovativeness	Lead time to design new products																	
	Lead time to prepare customer drawings																	
	Number of engineering change orders per year																	
	Number of new products introduced each year																	
Network Outputs																		
Accessibility	Network type																	
	Number of countries with a foreign factory																	
	Market share in each trading region																	
	Number of important foreign suppliers and distributors																	
	Number of foreign joint ventures																	
Thriftiness	Degree of coordination																	
	Use of ERP																	
	Number of contributor, source and lead factories																	
Mobility	New products per year per foreign factory																	
	Degree of dispersion of facilities																	
Learning	Relationship with key customers and suppliers																	
	Number of technology centers																	
	Relationship with foreign research centers																	

Figure 14-1 Worksheet for Benchmarking Factory and Network Performance Measures

Factory and Network Levers		Best Practices Used at Same/Other Companies in Same/Other Industries									
		Factory Outputs Affected:						Network Outputs Affected:			
	Elements	Cost	Quality	Performance	Delivery	Flexibility	Innovativeness	Accessibility	Thriftiness	Mobility	Learning
Factory Levers											
Human resources	Line operators Supervisors Maintenance Material handling Compensation Training, promotion										
Organization structure and controls	Performance measurement Capital budgeting Culture, departments Communication between departments										
Production planning and control	Order taking MRP system Shop floor control Inventories, lot sizes										
Sourcing	Short delivery time On-time shipments Make versus buy Supplier relations Purchasing										
Process technology	Fabrication Assembly Waste treatment Mechanical technology Electronic technology New technology										
Facilitles	Size, focus, age Static, developing Location Shared resources										
Network Levers											
Facility characteristics	Types Capabilities										
Geographic dispersion	Activities dispersed in national regional, multinational, worldwide locations Activities in particular countries										
Vertical integration	Ownership of upstream and downstream activities Partnerships with suppliers Partnerships with distributors										
Organization structure	Network type Centralized, decentralized										
Coordination mechanisms	Managerial systems ERP and computer systems Organization structure										
Knowledge transfer mechanisms	Managerial systems Computer systems Organization structure										
Response mechanisms	Procedures for recognizing and acting on threats and opportunities										
Capability building mechanisms	Managerial systems Budget process Organization structure										

Figure 14-2 Worksheet for Benchmarking Factory and Network Best Practices

collected from companies in the same industry and from companies in other industries. Practices that help a company provide market qualifying and order winning outputs at target levels are identified. These practices are adjustments that can be made to manufacturing levers in the company's factories and network.

A benchmarking study consists of the following steps:

1. Determine what performance measures and best practices to benchmark.
2. Form a benchmarking team.
3. Identify sources of benchmark information.
4. Collect information.
5. Analyze information.
6. Use information to make improvements.

Quality Management

Quality management defines quality in broad terms. For example, the definition at Procter & Gamble is, "Quality is the unyielding and continually improving effort by everyone to understand, meet, and exceed the expectations of customers."[2] Sometimes, this definition causes confusion because it is so broad and it differs from the definition of quality used in manufacturing strategy (Chapter 4). However, we will see that the quality management definition and the manufacturing strategy definition are consistent.

Understanding quality management starts with understanding two important words in quality management: customer and process. A *customer* is anyone who receives a product. This means a customer can be external or internal to a company. A *process* is a sequence of one or more activities that produces a product for a customer. Products are goods or services. Consumers who purchase finished products from a company are external customers. Employees are internal customers when they receive products from processes in the company. They must inform processes of their quality needs. Employees are parts of a process when they produce products. They must understand the quality needs of their customers. Quality needs include market qualifying and order winning levels of factory manufacturing outputs, high levels of important network manufacturing outputs, and high levels of important nonmanufacturing outputs. The quality output in manufacturing strategy is one of these quality needs. Consequently, the (narrow) manufacturing strategy definition of quality falls within the (broad) quality management definition of quality.

In quality management, meeting and exceeding customer expectations is achieved by means of features and zero defects. Features relate to products, and zero defects relates to processes. Features are characteristics of the product. Processes learn what features customers need, then meet and exceed these without fail. When processes perform activities correctly each time, they have zero defects.

A quality management improvement program assumes that activities with poor quality also have significant amounts of waste. Improvements are made to reduce or eliminate the waste in these activities. This raises the level of quality and also reduces cost and delivery time.

Quality management uses many tools to identify poor quality and waste and solve the problems that cause poor quality and waste. Examples include cost of quality (Situation 14.3), plan-do-check-act improvement cycle (Situation 14.4), statistical process control, house of quality, design of experiments, process capability and six sigma (Chapter 15), and charts and diagrams such as the checklist, histogram, run chart, Pareto chart, cause-and-effect diagram, and scatter diagram.

Implementing quality management is not easy. Quality management affects many people and processes and requires a considerable amount of information. Templates or models of effective quality management systems are available to help companies develop and improve their quality systems. Two such models are ISO 9000 and the Malcolm Baldrige National Quality Award.

SITUATION 14.2

Quality Management at Florida Power and Light[3]

IN THE LATE 1970S, Florida Power and Light (FPL) experienced problems similar to those faced by many manufacturers. Fuel costs were rising, large capital expenditures seemed unavoidable, customers demanded more reliable service at lower cost, and new competitors were entering the industry.

After several trips to Japan to study quality practices there, FPL developed and launched its Quality Improvement Program. The program consisted of three elements.

The first element was quality improvement teams, which started in 1982. By 1988, 70 percent of employees were participating in quality improvement teams.

The second element was policy deployment, which started in 1984. Policy deployment was how FPL translated quality goals in the company's strategic plan (Chapter 13) into special programs for functional areas.

The third element was quality in daily work, which started in 1986. This element was the most difficult. It was the application of quality management to each employee's job. Three tasks comprised quality in daily work. First, each employee's work process was stabilized so a predictable and consistent level of quality was produced. Next, improvements were made at each process. Then, standards were updated to capture the improvements.

In 1987, FPL created a crisis to inspire itself to raise quality to the highest possible level in its industry. FPL announced it would try to win the Deming Prize, the world's highest award for quality management. Peer pressure to excel spread quickly through the company. No department wanted to be the culprit that prevented FPL from winning the prize.

The crisis stimulated employees to give the extra effort needed to change FPL from a company that employed quality practices to a company where quality was a way of life. In November 1989, FPL became the first company outside Japan to win the Deming Prize.

SITUATION 14.3

Cost of Quality[4]

QUALITY EXPERTS ESTIMATE that companies spend between 5 and 25 percent of total sales revenue on quality-related activities. Companies with good quality management systems spend close to 5 percent, while companies with poor systems spend close to 25 percent. The cost of quality report (Figure 14-3) is a tool to help management manage these activities and reduce their costs.

SITUATION 14.3

Continued

The report is prepared as follows. First, the cost of each quality-related activity is estimated. Then, quality-related activities are organized into four categories: prevention, appraisal, internal failure, and external failure. Prevention costs are incurred for activities that prevent defects from occurring. Appraisal costs are incurred for activities that assess the level of quality in products. Failure costs are incurred when a defective product is produced. Failure costs are external when the defect is discovered after a customer receives the product and are internal when the defect is discovered during production of the product.

The report is used as follows. Activities with high costs, especially high failure costs, are targets for improvement. Other activities where improvements are needed are identified from an analysis of the distribution of costs among the four categories.

The cost of quality report in Figure 14-3 is for a manufacturer with annual sales of $55 million. The data in this report is analyzed as follows:

- The total cost of quality-related activities is $6,335,000/ $55,000,000 = 0.115, or 11.5 percent of revenue. Because companies spend in the range of 5 to 25 percent of sales revenue on quality-related activities, this figure is not high, especially if the company is in the early stages of quality management. Suppose that top management sets a goal to reduce this figure to 10 percent over 12 months.
- Three activities are obvious targets for improvement: rework; downtime; and returns, replacements, and allowances. Each has a high cost and is a failure activity, which means it affects internal and external customers.
- External failure activities account for 915,000/6,335,000 = 0.14, or 14 percent of total quality costs. Internal failure activities account for 64 percent, appraisal is 13 percent, and prevention is 9 percent. This is a poor distribution of costs because too much cost is incurred for activities to correct failures (14 + 64 = 78 percent of total quality costs). A common distribution for companies in the early stages of quality management is 50 percent for failure activities, 50 percent for prevention and appraisal activities, and a total cost of quality of about 10 percent of revenue. For companies with mature quality management systems, the targets are 20 percent for failure activities, 80 percent for prevention and appraisal, and a total cost of quality of 2 to 5 percent of revenue.
- A 12-month plan that follows from this analysis is given in the last column in Figure 14-3. Reduce the total cost of

Activities	Current Cost (in $1,000)	12-Month Plan
External Failure		
Complaint investigation and adjustment	43	
Returns, replacements, and allowances	610*	
Warranty expenses	24	
Liability and related legal costs	38	
Goodwill losses	200	
	915 (14%)	770 (14%)
Internal Failure		
Disposition	105	
Scrap	290	
Rework	2,150*	
Retest	120	
Yield losses	65	
Downtime	910*	
Defect-generated overtime	390	
	4,030 (64%)	1,980 (36%)
Appraisal		
Incoming material inspection	60	
In-process testing	630	
Maintenance of test equipment	120	
	810 (13%)	1,375 (25%)
Prevention		
Quality planning	135	
Product design review teams	90	
Process design review teams	100	
Quality-related training	75	
Statistical process control	15	
Data collection, analysis, and reporting	95	
Quality improvement programs	70	
	580 (9%)	1,375 (25%)
Total Cost of Quality-Related Activities	6,335	5,500

*Activities targeted for improvement over next 12 months

Figure 14-3 Cost of Quality Report for Situation 14.3

quality to 10 percent of revenue ($5.5 million) by increasing prevention and appraisal activities that focus on reducing the wastes and costs of the three activities identified previously: rework; downtime; and returns, replacements, and allowances.

SITUATION 14.4

Plan-Do-Check-Act Improvement Process

MAKING IMPROVEMENTS REQUIRES identifying and solving problems. Simple problems are easily solved. Quality management calls this "picking the low-hanging fruit." Chronic problems are more difficult. Often, the stated problem is a symptom of other, unknown problems. Data collection and analysis are needed to identify these problems, find their root causes, and develop possible solutions. This requires the expertise of a team operating under a formal improvement process.

There are many improvement processes. Most consist of six to ten sequential steps. Each step must be completed and approved before the next step can start. Specific data analysis tools are used at each step. Most improvement processes are extensions of Deming's Plan-Do-Check-Act process:

- **Plan:** Study the current situation by gathering data from the process. Identify problems, find causes, and develop solutions.
- **Do:** Implement the proposed solution on a trial basis. Collect data to evaluate the solution.
- **Check:** Study the trial to determine if other problems exist. Modify the solution, and if necessary, return to the previous step.
- **Act:** Implement the solution, and change standards so that the new practice becomes the standard. Continue to the first step to follow up on other ideas.

ISO 9000 Quality Management System

In 1986, the International Organization for Standardization (ISO) published the first edition of the document "Guidelines for Third Party Assessment and Registration of a Supplier's Quality System." A year later, it released the ISO 9000 series of standards. Great Britain released British Standards Institute BS5750, and the United States released the Q90 quality standard. Except for small terminology differences, the three standards were identical. Revisions to ISO 9000 followed in 1994 and 2000. The most recent standard is called ISO 9000:2000.

ISO 9000 was a response to three developments that began in the 1980s:

- The expansion of free trade in Europe, North America, and other parts of the world (Chapter 9) created a need for an international quality standard that assured countries that the quality of products produced outside their borders was high enough to be imported without inspection.
- Many companies developed international manufacturing networks (Chapter 10). A common quality standard was needed to ensure that material and components produced or purchased in different parts of the world met the same high-quality standards.
- Suppliers expended considerable resources adjusting their quality systems to satisfy dif-

ferent requirements of different customers. A common quality standard administered by an independent third party that satisfied the quality requirements of all customers would reduce or eliminate this.

ISO 9000 is a series of standards in which a third party assesses and registers a company's quality management system. In most industries, ISO 9000 represents a minimum or market qualifying level of quality.

The ISO 9000:1994 standard divided a quality management system into 20 elements:

- Management responsibility
- Quality system
- Contract review
- Design control
- Document and data control
- Purchasing
- Control of customer-supplied product
- Production identification and traceability
- Process control
- Inspection and testing
- Control of inspection, measuring, and test equipment
- Inspection and test status
- Control of nonconforming product
- Corrective and preventive action
- Handling, storage, packaging, preservation, and delivery
- Control of quality records
- Internal quality audits
- Training
- Servicing
- Statistical techniques

These 20 elements comprise a quality management system called the 9001 standard. Two other standards, 9002 and 9003, were available for quality systems with fewer elements.

ISO 9000:2000 replaces 9001, 9002, and 9003 with a single standard called ISO 9001. It also replaces the 20 elements with a more modern, process-based model of a quality management system (Figure 14-4). Elements of a quality management system are organized into four areas:

1. Management responsibility
2. Resource management
3. Product realization
4. Measurement, analysis, and improvement

Areas form a cycle and are linked to customers. The cycle starts at management responsibility, which leads to resource management. Product realization follows. This area includes elements such as design, production, and distribution. Measurement, analysis, and improvement are next. This area ensures that customer requirements are satisfied and management objectives are realized. Results from measurement, analysis, and improvement are an input to management responsibility. At this point, the cycle repeats, thus facilitating continual improvement. Compared to the 1994 standard, the 2000 standard increases the emphasis on satisfying customer requirements, the role of top management, and the importance of continual improvement.

There are four key documents in ISO 9000: 2000:

1. 9000: Fundamentals and vocabulary
2. 9001: Requirements for a quality management system
3. 9004: Guidance for improving a quality management system
4. 19011: Guidelines on quality and environmental auditing

The process of obtaining ISO 9001:2000 certification works as follows:

- **Step 1.** The company prepares a quality manual that documents its practices in each of the four areas.

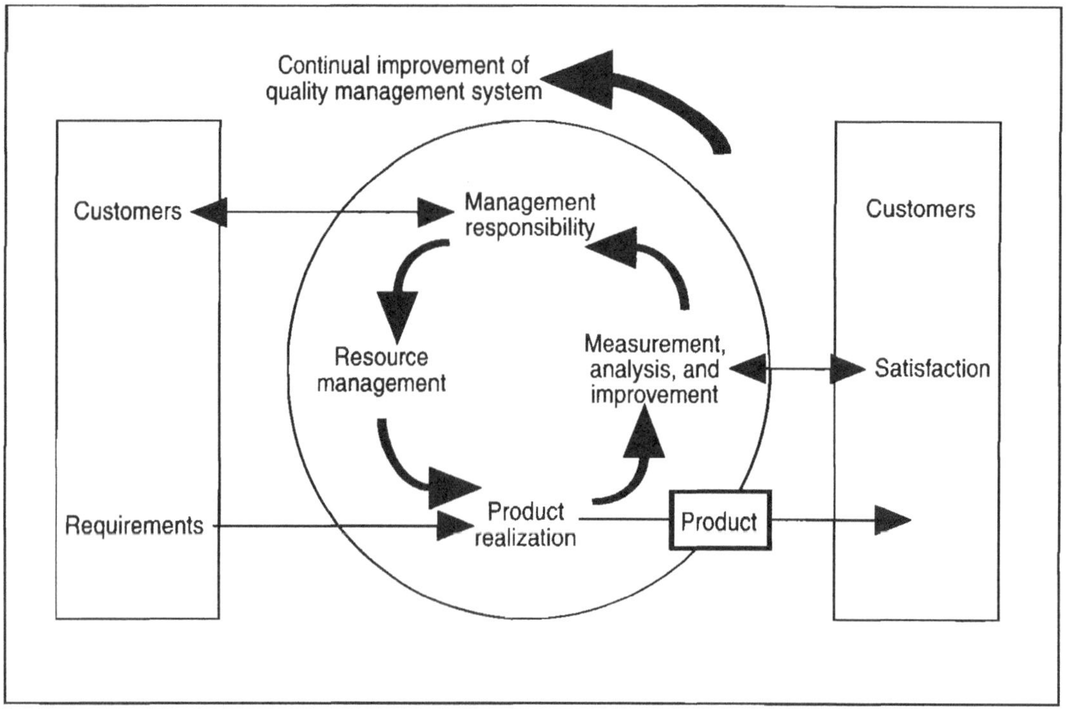

Figure 14-4 ISO 9000:2000 Model of a Quality Management System

- **Step 2.** A third party auditor, called a registrar, audits the quality manual.
- **Step 3.** The registrar visits the company to audit actual practices in the four areas.
- **Step 4.** If the audit is successful, the company receives a certificate from the registrar saying it is registered to ISO 9001, and the company is entered into the registrar's registry of certified companies. If the audit is unsuccessful, the company receives a list of deficiencies to correct before it can be considered again for registration.
- **Step 5.** Every six months, the registrar completes an inspection. Every three years, the company is reregistered.

Some companies are frustrated with the emphasis on documentation and record keeping. This is more likely to occur at companies with low levels of manufacturing capability. Companies with adult and higher levels of capability already have efficient record-keeping systems and up-to-date documentation.

The major benefit of seeking ISO 9001 certification is not the certification itself, but the improvements a company makes when its quality management system is brought into alignment with the 9001 standard.

Malcolm Baldrige National Quality Award

In 1987, the U.S. government established the Malcolm Baldrige National Quality Award (MBNQA). The objectives were:

- Stimulate U.S. companies to improve quality.
- Recognize the achievements of companies that make significant improvements in the quality of their goods and services.
- Provide role models for other companies to imitate.

- Establish a quality management system framework and criteria for judging business performance that companies can use to design and improve their quality management systems.

The award was named after President Reagan's Secretary of Commerce, who was instrumental in developing the award, but died in an accident before the award was established. The award is administered by the U.S. National Institute of Standards and Technology. The website, www.quality.nist.gov, gives information about the award, award winners, the quality management system framework, and the performance criteria.

The MBNQA framework for a quality management system consists of seven categories (Figure 14-5):

- Leadership
- Strategic planning
- Customer and market focus
- Information and analysis
- Human resource focus
- Process management
- Business results

Leadership, strategic planning, and customer and market focus are called the leadership triad. This part of the quality management system consists of the processes company leaders use to set business strategy and run a company in a way that focuses on customer and market needs. The human resource focus and process management categories are the engine that produces goods and services in a way that achieves the goals from the leadership triad. Business results track outcomes in all key areas: customer satisfaction, financial and marketplace performance, product and service performance, human resource results, and operational performance. Results are tracked in absolute terms and relative to competitors. The information and

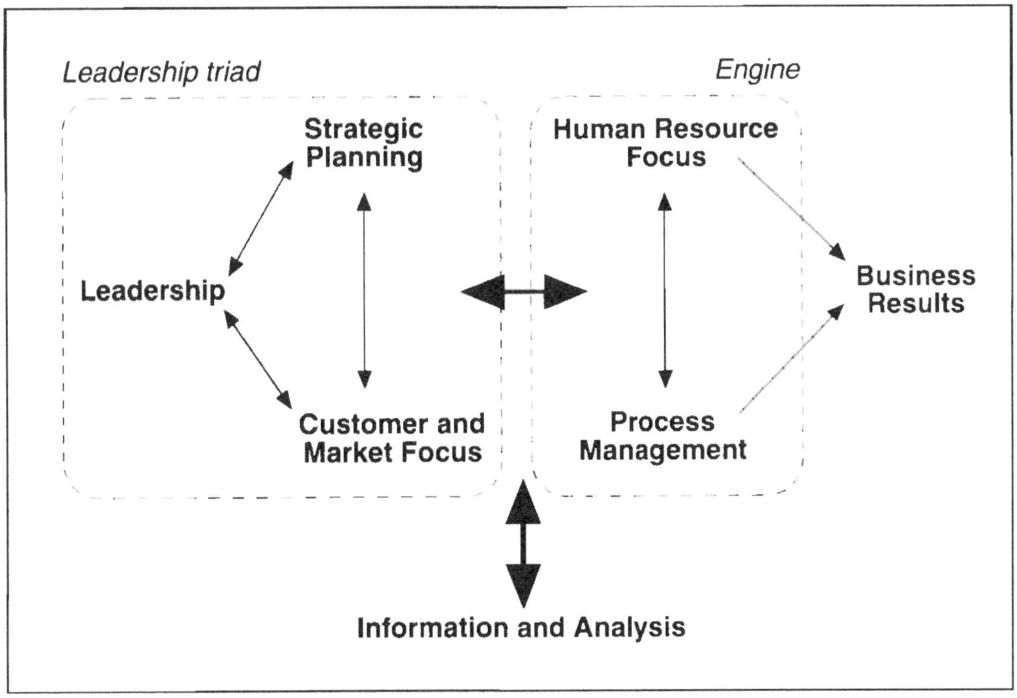

Figure 14-5 MBNQA Model of a Quality Management System

analysis category is the infrastructure that supports activities in the other categories.

Categories are broken down into items, and items are further broken down into areas to address. A total of 1,000 points are allocated across the items in the categories. A company scores points in each item depending on its:

- *Approach:* Methods used to satisfy the requirements in the item
- *Deployment:* Extent to which the approaches are used by all appropriate processes in the company
- *Results:* Performance achieved relative to appropriate comparisons and benchmarks

This quality management system framework and these criteria for judging performance are a popular template for designing and improving a quality management system.

Cycle Time Reduction

The term cycle time in cycle time reduction is equivalent to the term delivery time in manufacturing strategy. Cycle time begins when a customer order is received and ends when a customer accepts

Situation 14.5

MBNQA at TI's Defense Systems and Electronics Group

TEXAS INSTRUMENTS' Defense Systems and Electronics Group (DSEG), now part of Raytheon Systems Company, was a $2 billion Dallas-based maker of precision-guided weapons and other advanced defense technology. DSEG employed 15,000 people and operated 11 manufacturing, testing, research, and distribution facilities.

In 1989, Texas Instruments asked each of its business units to prepare a mock MBNQA application as a way to assess the business unit's quality management system. The self-assessment revealed that the DSEG quality management system had far to go to reach the level of a MBNQA winner.

DSEG decided to use the framework as a guide for improving its entire business. It selected one category, customer and market focus, to be a common emphasis for how it would improve activities in all its functional areas. It used the slogan, "Focusing on customers to make the business more competitive," to help push improvements in every activity, including activities in nonmanufacturing areas such as staff and support functions, which had been unreachable in the past.

The results impressed the Malcolm Baldrige National Quality Award examiners. DSEG topped its competitors in 11 customer satisfaction categories ranging from cost-effective pricing to product support. Costs decreased 20 to 30 percent, and in-process defects decreased 90 percent. Cycle times dropped from 4 weeks to 1 week, and customer complaints fell 62 percent. In 1992, DSEG won the Malcolm Baldrige National Quality Award.

delivery of a product. It is made up of five cycles: order processing, product design, purchasing, production, and distribution (Figure 14-6 [A]). Numerous activities are performed during each cycle (Figure 14-6 [B]), sequentially or concurrently, depending on the production system in use. For example, in a job shop production system, most products are custom designed, so order processing and product design are done concurrently.

In a cycle time reduction improvement program, management selects cycles and activities where it wants to make improvements. Cycle time reduction reduces the amount of time available to perform these activities. This exposes wastes in the activities. Improvements are made to eliminate the wastes. This enables activities to be performed in the time allowed. It also reduces cost and improves quality. Sometimes activities can be eliminated outright, sometimes activities are improved, and sometimes improvements to other activities are made. For example, suppose management reduces the time available for inspection and rework activities and charges a team to make the necessary improvements. Suppose the team finds that these activities are necessary because of poor quality in some purchased materials, and breakdowns and scrap production at some machines. Then, reducing cycle time in inspection and rework activities forces improvements to be made in the quality of purchased materials and the reliability and process capability of machines.

Agile Manufacturing

Agile manufacturing is the application of affordable, flexible automation to a production system

Situation 14.6

Air Conditioner Manufacturer Implements Cycle Time Reduction[5]

NORTH AMERICA'S SECOND LARGEST manufacturer of home and commercial air conditioners had factories in Illinois, Ontario, and Tennessee. Faced with excess capacity in 1991, the company had to choose between closing the Illinois factory or the Ontario factory.

The Ontario factory had some disadvantages: Wages and benefits were 30 percent higher than the Illinois factory, local taxes were 400 percent higher, and freight costs to major customers in the hot, southern U.S. states were 20 percent higher. The factory also had some advantages. Five years earlier, it started a cycle time reduction program, and by the summer of 1991, the factory had reduced cycle time, the time from receipt of a customer order to delivery of a finished air conditioner, from 22 days to 5 days. Work-in-process inventory was reduced from $21 million to $3 million, and the factory's capacity had doubled without increasing the size of the factory or the number of employees. Because of cycle time reduction, the factory could provide market qualifying and order winning levels of delivery, cost, quality, and flexibility.

In late 1991, the company decided to close the Illinois factory and focus the Ontario and Tennessee factories. All commercial products would be produced in the Ontario factory, and all residential products would be produced in the Tennessee factory.

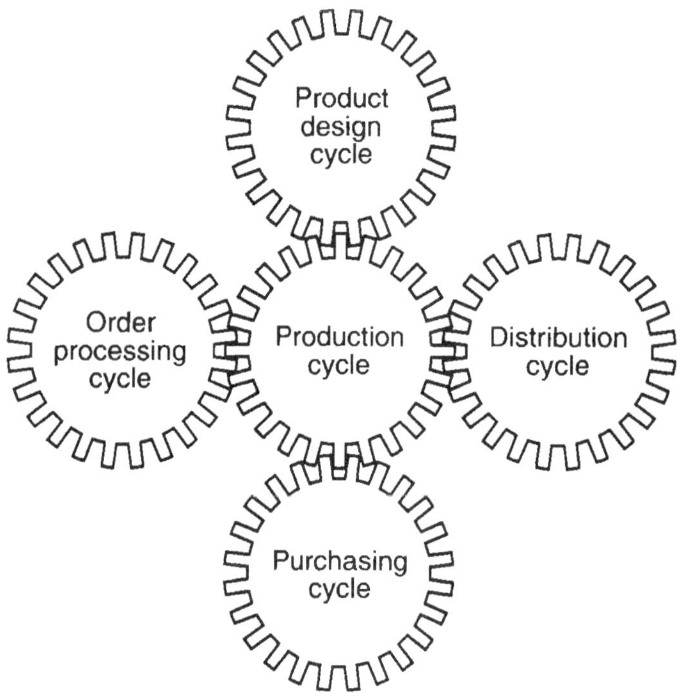

A. Five Cycles in Manufacturing Cycle Time

Order processing cycle
- Respond to customer inquiries
- Create order
- Determine price
- Book production time in factory
- Check customer credit
- Detemine promised delivery date

Purchasing cycle
- Make versus buy decision
- Identify, evaluate, and develop suppliers
- Negotiate terms
- Release orders for materials and components
- Release orders for tooling
- Set delivery dates

Production cycle
- Production planning and control
- Materials management
- Setups, processing
- Rework
- Maintenance

Design cycle
- Modify standard design to meet customer requirements
- Obtain customer approved drawings
- Design new products
- Conduct market research
- Analyze product technology
- Develop prototype
- Process planning

Distribution cycle
- Ship products to distribution centers
- Receive, count, inspect material
- Generate pick lists
- Pick material for customer orders
- Ship material to customers

B. Some Activities in Each Cycle

Figure 14-6 Cycles in Manufacturing Cycle Time

SITUATION 14.7

Toyota Slashes Cycle Time[6]

PRIOR TO 1982, Toyota's Japanese operations were divided into two separate companies: Toyota Motor Manufacturing and Toyota Motor Sales. The production cycle at Toyota Manufacturing was less than two days, however, the order processing cycle and the distribution cycle at Toyota Sales took between 15 and 26 days. Toyota Manufacturing took less than two days to manufacture a car, and Toyota Sales took between 15 and 26 days to take a customer order, transmit the order to the factory, schedule the order, and deliver the car to the customer. In addition to using more time, Toyota Sales also incurred more cost. Cost at Toyota Sales was more than the cost of manufacturing the car at Toyota Manufacturing. The order processing and distribution cycles at Toyota Sales were good candidates for cycle time reduction.

In 1982, Toyota Sales and Toyota Manufacturing merged. All Toyota Motor Sales directors retired, and executives from Toyota Motor Manufacturing filled their jobs. Cycle time reduction and other improvement programs were launched. Within five years, the time to perform order processing and distribution activities decreased to six days, and costs decreased significantly.

SITUATION 14.8

Cycle Time at Ford's Rouge River Factory[7]

HENRY FORD WAS ONE of the first people to understand the importance of cycle time. The following observations are from Chapter 10, "The Meaning of Time," in his book, *Today and Tomorrow* (written in 1926). They describe improvements at his Rouge River factory and illustrate principles just as important today as they were then.

Ordinarily, money put into raw materials or into finished stock is thought of as live money. It is money in the business, it is true, but having a stock of raw material or finished goods in excess of requirements is waste—which, like every other waste, turns up in high prices and low wages...

The time element in manufacturing stretches from the moment the raw material is separated from the earth to the moment when the finished product is delivered to the ultimate consumer...

If we were operating today [i.e. 1926] under the methods of 1921, we should have on hand raw materials to the value of about $120 million, and we should have unnecessarily in transit finished products to the value of about $50 million. That is, we should have an investment in raw material and finished goods of not far from

SITUATION 14.8

Continued

$200 million. Instead of that, we have an average investment of only $50 million, or, to put it another way, our inventory, raw and finished, is less than it was when our production was only half as great.

The extension of our business since 1921 has been very great, yet, in a way, all this great expansion has been paid for out of money which, under our old methods, would have lain idle in piles of iron, steel, coal, or in finished automobiles stored in warehouses. We do not own or use a single warehouse!...

Our production cycle is about 81 hours from the mine to the finished machine in the freight car, or 3 days and 9 hours instead of the 14 days, which we used to think was record breaking.

for the purpose of increasing flexibility. Agile manufacturing enables any production system to produce a wider range of products in lower volumes than was possible in the past. For example, an agile equipment-paced line flow production system can produce what in the past could only be produced on an operator-paced line flow production system (Situation 14.9).

Agile manufacturing is a shift to the left of the production systems in the PV-LF matrix (Figure 14-7). Implementing agile manufacturing is not easy. Flexible automation, concurrent engineering, and information technology are three foundations on which agile manufacturing is built. Agile manufacturing requires significant increases in the level of capability of the organization structure and

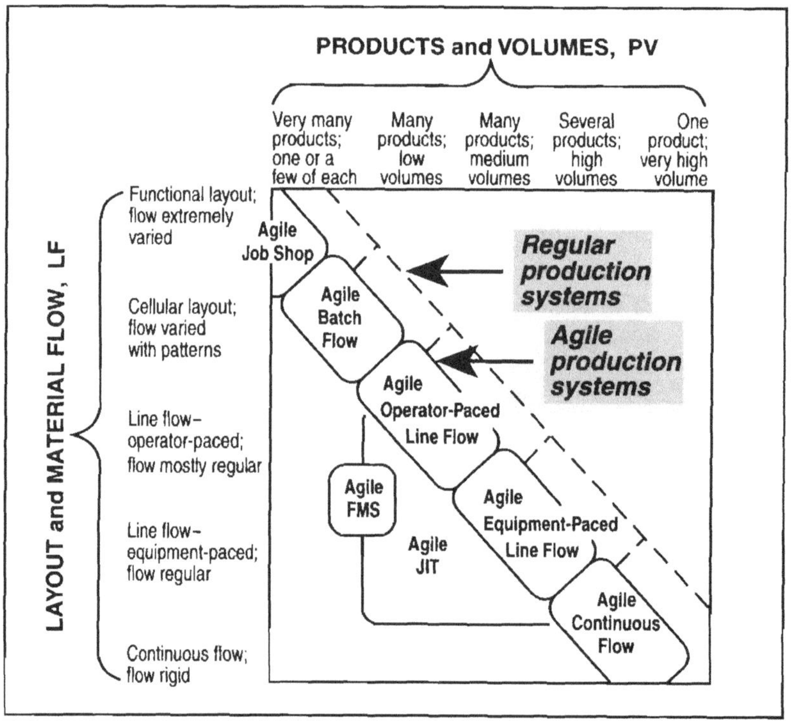

Figure 14-7 Agile Production Systems

SITUATION 14.9

Motorola's Agile Equipment-Paced Line Flow Production System

IN 1987, AFTER 18 MONTHS of design work, Motorola started a state-of-the-art, equipment-paced line flow production system to manufacture its Bravo pager. The production system produced a small family of pagers, each using the same printed circuit board and working on a single frequency band. The production system produced market qualifying and order winning levels of the cost, quality, and delivery manufacturing outputs.

In the years that followed, improvements were made, and flexible automation was added. By 1989, more than one board could be processed at the same time. In 1990, products with different frequency bands could be produced, and in 1991, different colors could be produced. In 1993, a new agile equipment-paced line flow production system was organized to manufacture products with different boards and different bands in single-unit lots. Concurrent with the development of the agile production system was a complete redesign of the product.

Agility was achieved through flexible automation, carefully designed products, and the many improvements made to the previous production system. Before the availability of agile manufacturing, Motorola would have needed an operator-paced line flow production system to produce this mix and volume of products.

SITUATION 14.10

Agile Manufacturing at a Bicycle Manufacturer[8]

NBI WAS ONE OF JAPAN'S largest bicycle manufacturers. In the late 1980s, it used three different production systems to supply about 9 percent of the Japanese market of eight million bicycles per year.

Standard design bicycles, which sold for about $350, were mass-produced on equipment-paced line flow production systems.

Custom bicycles were produced in a job shop production system. They were built by skilled craftspeople to a customer's individual body measurements, riding style, and preference for components and finishing. Custom bicycles took two months to deliver and sold for about $3,000.

In 1987, NBI began producing "personalized semi-custom bicycles" on an agile operator-paced line flow production system. It took eight to ten days to produce a bicycle, and 50 to 60 bicycles were produced every day. Each semi-custom bicycle, which sold for about $1,300, was treated as a package of

SITUATION 14.10

Continued

options. Options included 18 models, 15 frame sizes, 18 handlebar styles, 6 pedals, 4 tires, and more than 200 finishes. While this number of bicycles was large, it was a small fraction of the number of custom bicycles.

The agile operator-paced line flow production system worked as follows. Customer orders were taken at bicycle shops all over Japan. A customer's body measurements and preferences were entered on a detailed order form, which was sent electronically to the NBI factory. A computer in the factory generated a CAD/CAM drawing of the bicycle, assigned a bar code number for components, and released a production order. Each order was assigned to a skilled craftsperson responsible for overseeing production of the personalized bicycle. Almost all fabrication operations, such as cutting, brazing, gluing, checking dimensions, cleaning, and painting, were done by robots. Finer, more detailed operations, such as fitting, assembly, and finishing, were done by the craftsperson. Once complete, the bicycle was packaged and shipped to the bicycle shop where the customer order originated. The shop completed the assembly and presented the bicycle to the customer.

control lever, and the process technology lever. It also requires modest increases in the level of capability of the other levers. Because the level of capability of a production system increases under agile manufacturing and a higher level of capability produces higher levels of manufacturing outputs, agile manufacturing produces higher levels of the manufacturing outputs.

Three factors account for much of the popularity of agile manufacturing:

- Agile manufacturing offers an alternative to the difficult JIT and expensive FMS production systems. Agile operator- and equipment-paced line flow production systems produce the same mix and volume of products as JIT and FMS and provide similar levels of manufacturing outputs but are much easier to design and operate.
- Some companies want to develop expertise with the hardware and software that make up flexible automation in agile manufacturing. This manufacturing expertise is a source of competitive advantage for these companies.
- Manufacturing engineers enjoy the work associated with implementing agile manufacturing: purchasing new equipment, working with suppliers to develop flexible automation, installing and debugging new technology, and so on.

KAIZEN[9]

Kaizen is a hands-on, do-it-now improvement program that emphasizes action over planning. It produces a steady stream of small or incremental improvements. The following are typical steps in a kaizen program:

Step 1. Organize kaizen sessions, kaizen points, and kaizen teams
Every three or four months, management organizes a "kaizen session," which lasts 2½ or 3½ days. Management selects the areas where improvements will be made, called "kaizen points," and sets goals for each kaizen point. Three to six "kaizen teams" of eight to ten members each are formed. Team members come from all parts of the company, and new teams are formed for each session. Teams are charged with making improvements at the kaizen points. There are almost no restrictions on the improvements teams can make. Teams can change layouts, eliminate operators, modify tooling, move equipment, reduce inventories, and revise procedures. During a kaizen session, support personnel, such as engineering, material handling, tooling, and trades, are on "kaizen alert" to provide immediate assistance to the teams.

Step 2. Learn
The session leader starts the kaizen session with a half day of learning and action planning. The leader guards against prolonged planning because it leads to "pencil kaizening" or "paralysis through analysis."

Step 3. Hit the floor running
After the half day of learning, teams are dispatched to the factory floor. Team members, attired in bright shirts and caps, are visible all over the factory. Accurate observations and data collection are mandatory. Data is analyzed, and improvements are made. Layouts are changed, tooling is modified, equipment is moved, procedures are revised, and documentation is prepared. Every two or three hours, teams reassemble to review progress with the session leader. Then, they return to the factory floor to make more improvements.

Step 4. Boast
Each kaizen session ends with team presentations. Pride in accomplishment and admiration within and across teams produces good-natured discussion and boasting. After the last presentation, the session leader recaps the accomplishments, praises the teams, recounts the principles of kaizen, and gives each participant a small reward.

REENGINEERING[10]

Reengineering is a response to two business problems that occurred in the late 1980s. First, many companies found that improvement approaches, such as cost cutting, quality management, cycle time reduction, and kaizen, were not generating the huge improvements their companies needed to survive. They needed more radical changes; entire business processes needed to be rebuilt. Second, many companies could not make their huge investments in information technology pay off. Reengineering solved these two problems. In reengineering, existing business processes and the underlying rules and assumptions are discarded in favor of new processes that make extensive use of information technology.

Reengineering is a useful improvement approach when companies change manufacturing networks or production systems. After reengineering a business process, network, or production system, the other improvement approaches discussed in this chapter are used to make additional improvements.

Process redesign is well known in manufacturing. What is different about process redesign in reengineering is the application of process redesign to business processes, the linking of process redesign with information technology, and the goal of achieving major improvements in business results.

Only business processes with broad and deep scopes are suitable for reengineering. These processes require significant time and resources to reengineer.[11] A team of skilled employees, committed full-time and almost always aided by external consultants, can take one year to envision, design, prototype, and test a new business process. Then, another year or two is needed to build the new process and implement it throughout the company.

The following are typical steps in a reengineering project:

Step 1. **Develop objectives.**

Step 2. **Identify the business process, manufacturing network, or production system to reengineer.**

Business processes have three important characteristics: They have customers, they cross organization boundaries, and have a major effect on the company's bottom line. Each of the five cycles that make up manufacturing cycle time (Figure 14-7) is a business process. Almost any business process can benefit from a redesign. However, the work involved creates practical limitations. Most companies know which business processes are critical to their success and are most in need of change. Few companies can support more than one reengineered process per year.

Step 3. **Understand and measure the existing process.**

It is important to understand and measure a process before trying to redesign it. Problems must be understood so they are not repeated. Measurements must be taken to track improvements.

Step 4. **Identify process enablers, especially information technology.**

Visioning is used to question existing assumptions and generate ideas for new processes. Benchmarking is used to find process enablers, such as information technology, that other companies use to make their processes work better.

Step 5. **Design and build a prototype of the reengineered process.**

Step 6. **Implement the reengineered process.**

STANDARDS

A company should revise its standards each time it makes an improvement. This prevents employees from slipping back into old ways of performing activities. Standards are how improvements become the accepted way of performing activities. Standards prevent a company from losing the benefits gained through improvements and are the foundation on which the next improvements are made.

Henry Ford was a strong believer in standards. In 1926, he wrote the following:[12]

> *To standardize a method is to choose, out of the many methods, the best one, and use it . . . What is the best way to do a thing? It is the sum of all the good ways we have discovered up to the present. It therefore becomes the standard . . . Today's standardization, instead of being a barricade against improvement, is the necessary foundation on which tomorrow's improvement will be based. . . If you think of standardization as the best that you know today, but which is to be improved tomorrow—you get somewhere. But if you think of standards as confining, then progress stops.*

SUMMARY

Improvement programs identify and eliminate wastes in a production system or manufacturing network for the purpose of raising the levels of factory and network outputs. Cost cutting, quality management, cycle time reduction, and agile manufacturing are four common improvement programs that use cost, quality, time, and flexibility, respectively, to select activities where improvements will be made. Kaizen and reengineering are two other common improvement programs.

The size, frequency, and scope of improvements partially depend on the improvement program. Cost cutting, quality management, cycle time reduction, and agile manufacturing all produce incremental improvements. Kaizen also produces incremental improvements. Six sigma, examined in the next chapter, produces larger improvements. Reengineering produces very large, breakthrough improvements. The best improvement program for a company is the one that is easiest for the company to implement.

Benchmarking gathers information on performance and best practices at superior companies. This information motivates and guides improvement efforts. It is important to guard against losing improvements after they are made. Standards capture improvements and provide starting points for other improvements.

ENDNOTES

1. Tucker, F., Zivan, S., and Camp, R., "How to Measure Yourself Against the Best," *Harvard Business Review*, January–February, 1987.
2. Evans, J., and Lindsay, W., *Management and Control of Quality*, St. Paul: West Publishing, p. 16, 1993.
3. "Building a Quality Improvement Program at Florida Power and Light," *Target*, Vol. 4, No. 3, pp. 4–12, Fall 1988.
4. Juran, J., and Godfrey, A., *Juran's Quality Handbook*, New York: McGraw-Hill, Chapter 8, 1999.
5. *The Toronto Star*, p. B8, November 1, 1991.
6. Stalk, G., "Time: The Next Source of Competitive Advantage," *Harvard Business Review*, pp. 41–51, July–August, 1988.
7. Ford, H., and Crowther, S., *Today and Tomorrow*, reprinted by Productivity Press, Portland, Oregon, Chapter 10, 1988.
8. Bell, T., "Bicycles on a Personalized Basis," *IEEE Spectrum*, pp. 32–35, September 1993.
9. Imai, M., *Kaizen*, New York: Random House, 1986.
10. Hammer, M., and Champy, J., *Reengineering the Corporation*, New York: Harper Collins, 1993.
11. Hall, G., Rosenthal, J., and Wake, J., "How to Make Reengineering Really Work," *Harvard Business Review*, pp. 119–131, November–December, 1993.
12. Ford and Crowther, *Today and Tomorrow*, p. 82.

CHAPTER 15

FOCUS, SOFT TECHNOLOGIES, HARD TECHNOLOGIES

Regardless of the improvement approach used (Chapter 14), there is always a sequence in which improvements should be made. First, manufacturing is focused, then soft technologies are used to improve the focused operations, and finally, hard technologies are added. Many attempts to improve manufacturing fail because one of these steps (focus, soft technologies, hard technologies) is missed or steps are done in the wrong order.

Focus

Many companies try to perform too many activities in the same factory, resulting in a large factory that does not perform any activity particularly well. This is tolerable when competitors behave in the same way. However, when competitors focus their factories, companies with large unfocused factories become uncompetitive.

Companies focus the factories in their manufacturing network by giving each factory a specialization (Chapter 12) and by dividing each factory into small factories-within-a-factory (FWFs). FWFs may be separated by partitions and use different entrances, rest areas, and so on (Figure 15-1). Each FWF focuses on a limited number of products, activities, and customers, and uses the best production system. The best production system is the system most able to provide the market qualifying and order winning outputs (Chapter 6).

The benefits of focus include the ability to use the best manufacturing network and production systems, higher levels of network and factory outputs, closer ties to customers, effective cooperation between functional departments, improved reaction to problems, and more opportunities to improve.

Focus does not occur naturally. In fact, strong forces in finance, marketing, and even manufacturing work against it. The finance department's emphasis on cost cutting and short-term profits make it difficult to get funds to cover the cost of organizing factories into FWFs. The marketing department's emphasis on responding to customer needs (no matter how small or unprofitable) forces manufacturing to add new, low volume products to existing factories. This pushes manufacturing away from focus (Situation 15.5). The manufacturing department also inhibits focus when it restricts itself to past practices or is driven solely by pursuit of economies of scale.

It is usually not possible to focus all parts of a network and all parts of each factory. Parts of a

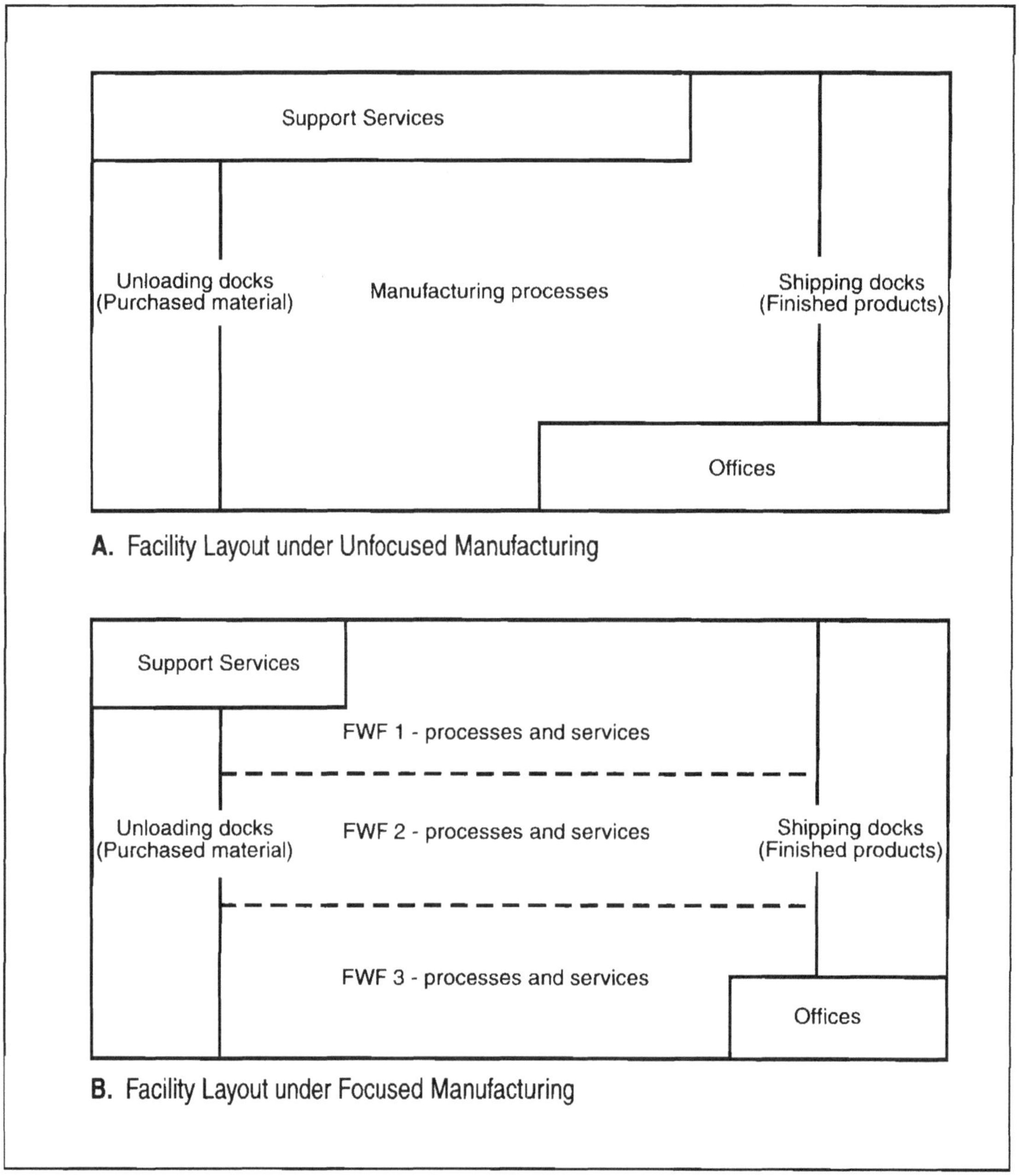

Figure 15-1 Factories-Within-A-Factory (FWFs) Under Focused Manufacturing

network or factory that produce seasonal products, or products in the decline stage of their product life cycle (Chapter 16), and parts of a network or factory where the cost of additional equipment is excessive are not focused. In addition, it is not always easy to focus those parts of a network or factory that can be focused. When starting to focus, a company should proceed slowly and focus one part of a network or factory at a time. This produces benefits within the focused parts and simplifies the parts that remain unfocused.

Superior companies hold the view that focusing manufacturing does not require financial or strategic justification. Instead, justification is required for not focusing. Focus is so widespread that the onus is on those opposed to focus to show why it is inappropriate.

SITUATION 15.1

Furniture Company Focuses Manufacturing[1]

FOR 12 YEARS AFTER Fernand Fontaine founded the company, Dutailer made rocking chairs and living room and bedroom furniture. Then in 1988, the Canadian company dropped its living room and bedroom furniture to focus solely on rocking chairs. It was a turning point for Dutailer. The company was no longer a small furniture manufacturer "trying to be all things to all people."

In the early 1990s, Dutailer produced 35 models of its glider rocker in 12 finishes from plain varnished pine to the season's most fashionably colored lacquers. Customers chose from 60 chair coverings from printed fabrics to stylish Italian leathers. Finishes and fabrics were changed twice a year in response to changes in customer demand.

Focus worked for Dutailer. In 1991, 550 people were employed in four factories, up from fewer than 200 in 1988. Seventy-five percent of production was exported to Europe and the United States.

SITUATION 15.2

Focusing Manufacturing at AT&T

THE AT&T DALLAS WORKS factory in Mesquite, Texas, was the largest manufacturer of power systems in the world. In 1989, the factory was completely rearranged and modernized. Four focused factories were organized: board mounted power, off-line switchers, energy systems, and converters and mature products. The cost of the multimillion-dollar project was recovered in less than a year. Delivery time was reduced by as much as 60 percent, material costs were reduced, and quality was improved.

Even more focus was achieved by moving product management and marketing personnel from the AT&T Bell Lab in New Jersey to the factory in Mesquite. This made each focused factory the center of all activity for its product family, from design to manufacturing to marketing.

SITUATION 15.3

Automotive Parts Producer Focuses Manufacturing

AN AUTOMOTIVE PARTS FACTORY grew rapidly during the 1980s by increasing the number of products it manufactured. The new products were products its automotive customers had decided to outsource. While sales and profits increased, the large number of products made it difficult to plan and control manufacturing activities, even after numerous improvements were made to the company's computerized planning and control systems.

In the 1990s, global competition arrived, and customer requirements for cost, quality, delivery, performance, flexibility, and innovativeness increased at an alarming rate. The factory considered three possible solutions:

- Become a computer-integrated factory in which sophisticated computer programs direct and control all activities from order entry, through fabrication and assembly, to shipping.
- Build smaller, independent factories with 100 to 200 employees.
- Organize FWFs, each with about 50 employees, to produce similar products and perform similar activities.

The first alternative was rejected because of the earlier disappointment with computerized information systems, and the second because of the high cost of building new factories. The third was selected, and FWFs were organized.

Each FWF was run by a small team responsible for cost, quality, scheduling, and employee attendance. Each FWF developed budgets, forecasts, and long-range plans, and had direct contact with customers.

Competition among FWFs was keen, but top management checked that the self-interests of the FWFs supported, rather than conflicted with, the company's overall goals.

SITUATION 15.4

Yacht Manufacturer Organizes Factories-Within-a-Factory[2]

PROBLEM

GRE Yachts was a prestigious builder of custom design sailing yachts. To capitalize on its reputation for excellent design and workmanship and secure a piece of the growing market for standard design yachts, GRE designed and launched a standard yacht. The yacht was aimed at the high end of the standard yacht market and had many of the features found on the company's custom design yachts. However, even this end of the market was more price sensitive and less conscious of performance than GRE's custom design customers.

All of the company's yachts were manufactured in the same factory and shared the same equipment and skilled labor force. Custom design yachts were given priority in production because of their higher profit margins. During the past year, as sales of the standard yacht increased, costs and deliveries of all yachts began to slide. Many yachts were strewn around the yard in various stages of completion.

Solution

Recall from Chapter 7 the three-step procedure for developing manufacturing strategy in a factory.

- **Step 1:** Where is the factory?
- **Step 2:** Where does the factory want to be?
- **Step 3:** How will the factory get from where it is to where it wants to be?

Step 1: Where is GRE?

GRE manufactured many products (different custom design yachts and the standard yacht) in volumes ranging from "one of" to "low volumes." The factory layout was a combination of functional and cellular, and the material flow was varied with patterns. The production system was batch flow (Figures 15-2 and 15-3), and its level of manufacturing capability was industry average for all manufacturing levers except production planning and control, which was lower due to the current scheduling problems and high level of work-in-process inventory.

Step 2: Where does GRE want to be?

Custom design yachts: In its custom design yacht business, GRE provided high levels of performance (fast, attractive, comfortable yachts), quality (excellent workmanship), and innovativeness and flexibility (the ability to produce a yacht that satisfied each customer's requirements). Performance, quality, and flexibility were the market qualifying outputs, and innovativeness was the order winning output (Figure 15-2). Innovativeness required designers, suppliers, and manufacturing work together closely to complete designs and manufacture them easily and quickly. The unique designs did not always include the newest,

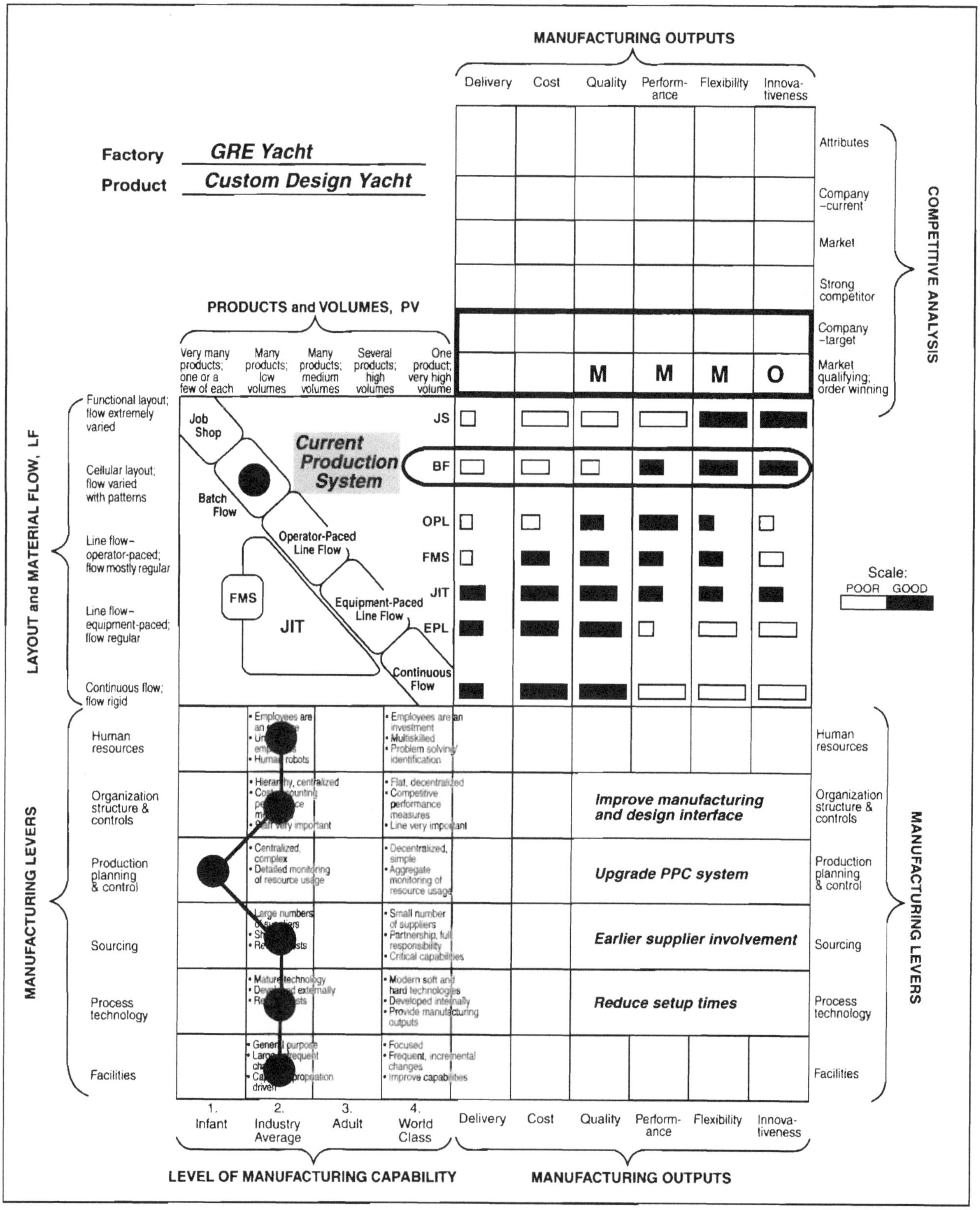

Figure 15-2 Manufacturing Strategy Worksheet for the Custom Design Yacht

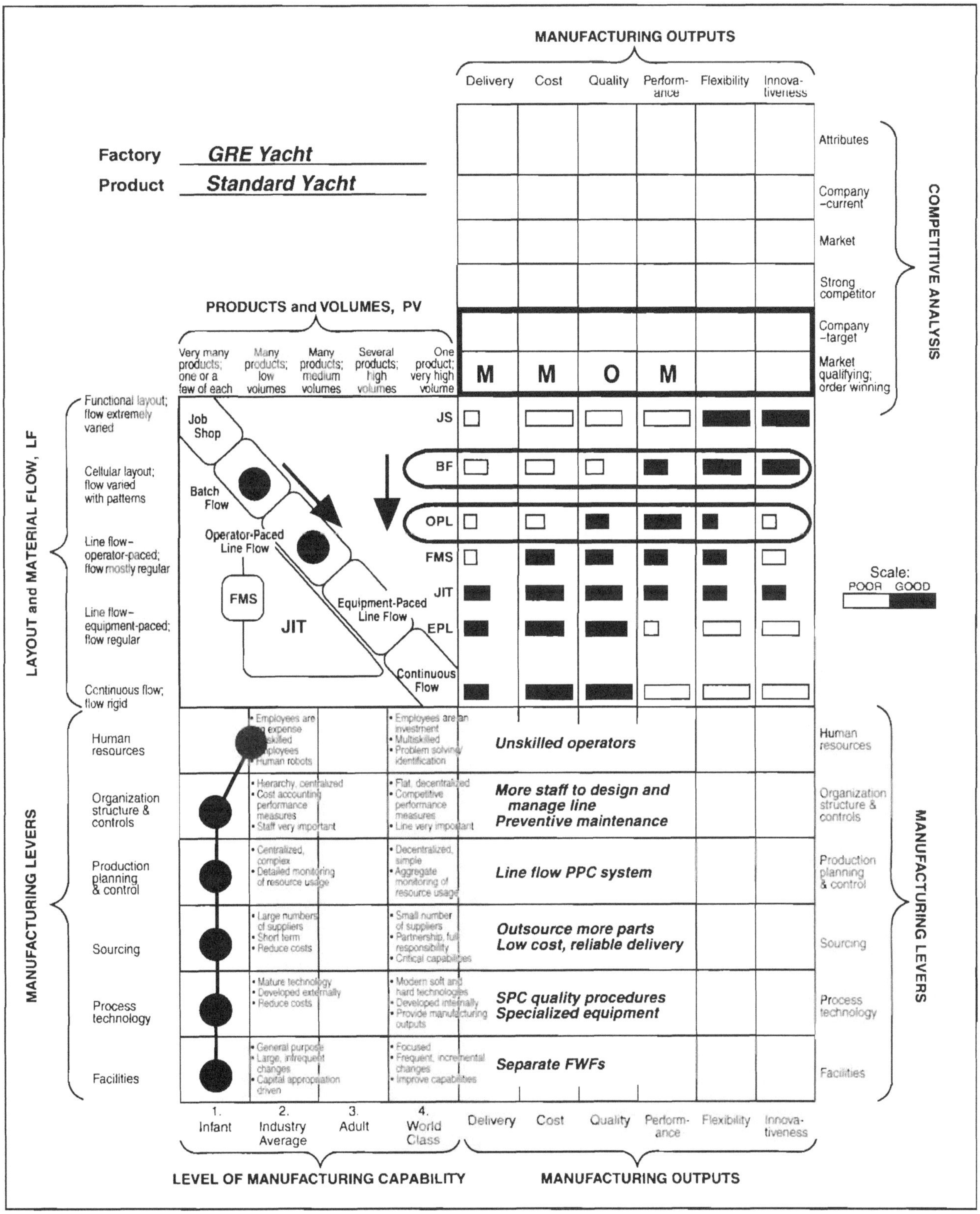

Figure 15-3 Manufacturing Strategy Worksheet for the Standard Design Yacht

SITUATION 15.4

Continued

most advanced features in the industry, which would be necessary if performance was the order winning output.

Standard design yachts: The standard design yacht is a single product produced in medium to high volumes (relative to the production volume of the custom design yacht). The market qualifying outputs were cost, delivery, and performance, and quality was the order winning output (Figure 15-3). This took advantage of GRE's reputation for quality in the custom design yacht business. Flexibility and innovativeness were not as important in the standard yacht business. The existing batch flow production system is not appropriate for this product mix and volume or for the market qualifying and order winning outputs. An operator- or equipment-paced line flow production systems is more appropriate.

Step 3: How will GRE get from where it is to where it wants to be?

Custom design yachts: Figure 15-2 shows that the existing batch flow production system can provide the market qualifying and order winning outputs if all the manufacturing levers are set in the proper positions and the level of manufacturing capability is near adult. Several adjustments to the levers are required, such as raising the level of capability of the production planning and control lever to the same level as the other levers. Implementing an MRP system for make-to-order manufacturing will do this. The relationship between design and manufacturing can be strengthened (because innovativeness is the order winning output) by emphasizing concurrent engineering and design for manufacturing programs. Starting a setup time reduction program will raise the capability of the process technology lever, and adopting the kaizen improvement program will raise the capability of the entire production system.

Standard design yachts: An operator- or equipment-paced line flow production system is required for the standard design yacht (Figure 15-3). Since this production system differs from the existing batch flow system, a separate FWF must be created. Each manufacturing lever must be adjusted to put it in the correct position for the new production system. Adjustments include:

- Use employees with fewer skills, and pay them less.
- Assign engineering staff to design, organize, and support the line, prepare quality control procedures, and so on.

- Develop close ties with suppliers who will supply larger volumes of standard parts. Suppliers will be selected on the basis of cost, quality, and delivery, and more components will be outsourced.
- Implement a line flow scheduling system and a standard MRP system for controlling materials and activities.
- Use specialized machines and tooling.

Adopting the quality management improvement program can raise the level of capability of this production system.

GRE's level of manufacturing capability for an operator-paced line flow production system is at the infant level, making it very difficult to make such a large number of adjustments. GRE should set up a small operator-paced line flow production system in a separate FWF and should begin by producing a small number of the standard design yacht. As experience with the new production system is gained, the volume can be increased.

Situation 15.5

Focused Manufacturing at Cummins[3]

THE CUMMINS ENGINE COMPANY is a well-known manufacturer of engines. For years, its NT diesel engine family was an industry leader with the company's market share at more than 50 percent. This changed in the 1970s, when the U.S. government introduced emissions regulations and competition with Komatsu and Caterpillar increased. Customers' expectations increased for lower prices, faster deliveries, and more flexibility. Cummins responded by rolling out seven generations of the NT family, launching three new engine families, and cutting prices on new products by 20 to 40 percent.

By 1986, the Cummins catalog contained more than 100,000 parts. Even though design engineers were sensitive to the difficulties of manufacturing so many parts, the number of parts kept increasing. For example, one new engine family had 86 different flywheels, 49 flywheel housing options, and 17 starter motors with 12 possible mountings, all of which could be assembled in 1,200 ways.

Between 1980 and 1985, most of the company's factories, frustrated by high costs, long delivery times, and high work-in-process inventory, made the transition to focused manufacturing, which Cummins called cellular manufacturing. However, traditional cellular manufacturing could not meet the challenge of Cummins' greatly proliferated product line. Setup time was the problem because cells organized to produce seven parts in

SITUATION 15.5

Continued

batches of 5,000 were now expected to produce 14 parts in batches of 500. With so many parts (many with low volumes), it became impossible to change tools and fixtures quickly enough. Low volume parts were choking the cells.

In 1987, the company commissioned a team to develop insights into the problem of reorganizing factories for the proliferated product line. After careful study and analysis, the team announced two results: Aggressive setup time reduction was required, and factories needed to be focused on the basis of product *and* volume. The team identified four classes of products and five classes of volume.

- Product classes were skeletal parts (such as blocks, heads, and connecting rods), engine subsystem parts (such as water pumps and lubricating pumps), application parts (such as exhaust manifolds and flywheel housings), and performance parts (such as turbochargers and compression brakes).
- Volume classes were defined by three parameters: volume (high, medium, or low), predictability of demand (predictable or unpredictable), and stability of design (stable or evolving).

Parts with the same product class and volume class were grouped into a family, and all parts in a family were produced by the same production system. The only exception was when a part had vastly different setup requirements. Such a part could be produced on a different production system. Cummins used four production systems: job shop, batch flow, FMS, and equipment-paced line flow.

Figure 15-4 describes how these results were implemented at one factory, which produced blocks, water pumps, manifolds, flywheel housings, and other products.

BLOCKS

Blocks A and B in Figure 15-4 are in the same product class. Both are in the same volume class because either the volume is high (block A) or the volume is medium and the setup time is short (block B), demand is predictable, and design is stable. Consequently, both parts are produced on the same equipment-paced line flow production system.

WATER PUMPS

Water pumps A, B, and C share the same product class but are in two volume classes. The volume of pump A is high, but it

Part	Product Class	Annual Production Volume	Delivery Frequency	Design Stability	Setup Times	Production System
Block A	Skeletal	75,000	Daily	Stable	Changeover from A to B takes 30 minutes.	EP line flow
Block B		5,000	Monthly	Stable		Same EP line flow
Water pump A	Engine subsystem	75,000	Daily	Two-year design life	A and B have common features.	FMS
Water pump B		2,000	Unpredictable	Stable	Changeover from A to B takes 8 hours.	Same FMS
Water pump C		5.000	Daily	Stable	C is a very different pump. Changeover from A to C takes 2 days.	Batch flow
Manifold A	Application	75,000	Daily	Stable	Changeover from A to B takes 8 hours on a boring machine.	EP line flow
Manifold B		5.000	Monthly	Stable		Same EP line flow
Manifold C		20	Unpredictable	Stable	Changeover from A to C takes 2 days.	Job shop

Figure 15-4 Assigning Part Families to FWFs at Cummins

cannot be produced by an equipment-paced line flow production system. Such a system would require an investment in specialized equipment, which could not be recouped because the pump has a design life of only two years. In this factory, high volume parts with rapidly evolving designs are manufactured in FMSs (along with prototypes and new products).

Pump B, which shares many design features with pump A, has a low, unpredictable demand. The setup time for pump B is eight hours on traditional equipment but only one hour on FMS. Consequently, it is assigned to the same FMS as pump A.

The flexibility of an FMS is wasted on pump C. This product has medium volume, predictable demand, and a stable design. The most economical way to produce it is to use conventional equipment in a batch flow production system.

SITUATION 15.5

Continued

Manifolds

Manifolds A, B, and C are in the same product class but in different volume classes. Manifold A is produced on an equipment-paced line flow production system because of its high volume, predictable demand, and stable design.

It would be difficult to manufacture manifold B on the same line because it takes eight hours to set up a boring machine. The setup time on a CNC boring machine would be minimal. A practical solution is to use a CNC boring machine rather than a conventional machine in the line producing manifold A. The CNC machine will slow the line speed, but it would permit manifolds A and B to be produced on the same line.

Manifold C, with its low volume, unpredictable demand, and lengthy setup time, is too disruptive to produce on the line producing manifolds A and B. Consequently, it is assigned to a job shop production system (machine shop).

Flywheel Housings

Another product class was flywheel housings (not shown in Figure 15-4). A total of 160 flywheel parts were divided into a high volume family (11 parts representing 85 percent of total volume) and a low volume family (149 parts). The high volume family was produced in a dedicated equipment-paced line flow production system. The low volume family was produced in a newly acquired FMS. Figure 15-5 shows the significant improvements in cost, quality, and delivery that were achieved.

Performance Measure	Before Focusing	After Focusing
Labor efficiency	42%	96%
Hours of output per operator	3.6	7.7
Number of operators	43	18
Number of salaried employees	6	2
Throughput time	1.8 days	40 minutes
Internal distance traveled	650 feet	256 feet
Inventory reduction		
• Raw material	6 days	1 day
• Work-in-process	1.4 days	1 hour
• Finished goods	4 days	1 day
On-time delivery	30%	100%
Product cost	—	43% reduction
Scrap	—	99% reduction
Full-time rework employees	3	0
Full-time inspectors	3	Audit only

Figure 15-5 Results of Focused Manufacturing for Flywheel Housings

SOFT TECHNOLOGIES

Many techniques, tools, and technologies developed over the last 25 years can be divided into two groups: soft technologies and hard technologies. Soft technologies improve manufacturing infrastructure. They are systems- and people-oriented, inexpensive to acquire, and difficult to implement (Figure 15-6).

Certain soft technologies work better with certain production systems. For example, total productive maintenance, an approach where operators perform routine maintenance tasks on their equipment, is effective in job shop, equipment-paced line flow, and some other production systems. However, it does not work well in FMS or continuous flow production systems because equipment is too complex and operators are too unskilled. Of

Concurrent Engineering
Program where design engineering and process engineering work together from the start of product design through pilot production until the product is being produced on a routine basis. The objective is to optimize product design and process design.

Problem-Solving Techniques
Techniques for identifying and prioritizing problems, finding root causes, and determining and implementing solutions.

Process Capability
Measure of the amount of variation in a process relative to the customer's specification for the product being produced.

Pull Production Control System
System where production at an upstream operation is triggered by consumption of a product at a downstream operation.

Setup Time Reduction
Program to reduce the amount of time required to set up or change over a manufacturing operation so that production of a new product may begin.

Small Lot Production
Program to facilitate economic production of small batches of products.

Standardization
Program to reduce the amount of variety in products and processes.

Statistical Process Control
Use of statistical techniques to monitor and control variation in a process.

Supply Chain Management
Program that synchronizes a company's order processing, design, production, and distribution activities with those of its suppliers, distributors, and customers.

Team Approaches
Approach wherein groups of employees work together to achieve common goals.

The 5S's
Program for organizing the work area and keeping it tidy. The 5S's are: Seiri-proper arrangement, Seiton-orderliness, Seiso-cleanliness, Seiketsu-clean up, and Shitsuke-discipline.

Total Productive Maintenance
Program wherein production operators participate in the maintenance of their equipment.

Figure 15-6 Some Soft Technologies

the soft technologies appropriate for a particular production system, soft technologies that help the production system provide higher levels of market qualifying and order winning outputs are best.

We examine three popular soft technologies to illustrate their nature: process capability and six sigma quality, concurrent engineering, and supply chain management.

Process Capability and Six Sigma Quality

This section begins with an example that illustrates the principles of process capability and six sigma quality.

NML produced inexpensive but important parts at a U.S. factory for a customer in Japan. The NML factory never had any problems with cost, quality, or delivery. The customer recently sent a team to the factory to collect information to help it decide whether to renew its supply contract with NML. The team needed to determine the process capability of the manufacturing processes that produced the parts.

The team collected data to calculate process capability indices (C_p and C_{pk}). The critical quality characteristic for one part was the width of a slot. The customer's specification was 400 ± 10. Widths smaller than 400 – 10 = 390 caused problems on the customer's assembly line. Widths larger than 400 + 10 = 410 could cause the customer's finished product to fail after a period of use by the end consumer.

Two hundred parts were examined in one week (Figure 15-7). No slot had a width of more than 406 or less than 393, so there were no defective parts (parts with slot widths outside the specifications). The average or mean width was 401.38 and the standard deviation was 2.17. Standard deviation, also called sigma, σ, is a measure of the variability in the manufacturing process.

The process capability index, C_p, is defined as:

$$C_p = \frac{\text{specification width}}{6\sigma}$$

The specification width is 10 + 10 = 20, so $C_p = 20/(6 \times 2.17) = 1.54$.

Another process capability index, C_{pk}, considers the difference between the specification target and the process average.

$$C_{pk} = C_p \times \left(1 - \frac{k}{(\text{specification width}) / 2}\right)$$

where $k = |\text{target} - \text{average}|$. The specification

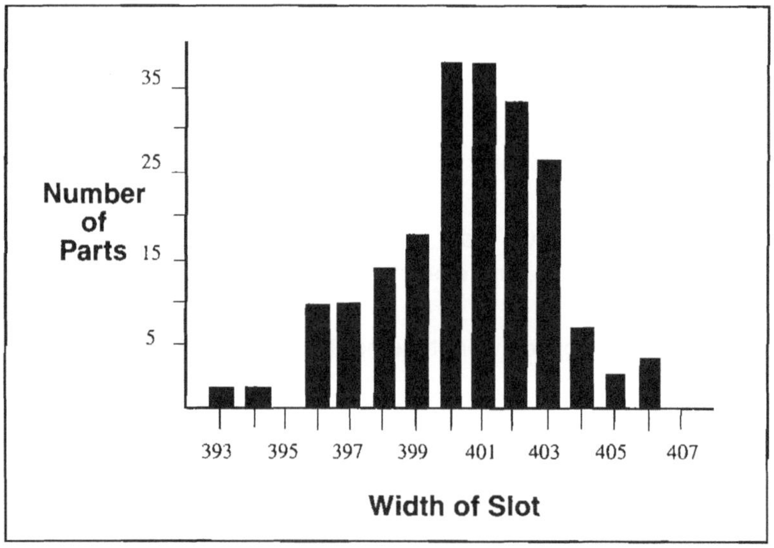

Figure 15-7 Values of Quality Characteristic

target is 400 and the process average is 401.38.
So $k = |400 - 401.38| = 1.38$ and
$C_{pk} = 1.54 \times (1 - 1.38/(20/2)) = 1.33$.

The Japanese customer explained to NML that while process capability values of at least 1.33 were required in the 1980s (Figure 15-8), values of at least 2.0 were now required for important quality characteristics. Therefore, NML would have to improve the capability of its production process. NML would have to bring the process average closer to the specification target and reduce the process standard deviation σ.

Notice that the variable in the numerator of C_p comes from the product design and the variable in the denominator comes from the manufacturing process. Consequently, C_p is a measure of the fit between design and manufacturing. The higher the value of C_p the easier it is for manufacturing to produce the design.

Usually, variation in a manufacturing process follows a normal distribution. Then, the number of defects that occur when $C_p = 1.0$ is 2,700 ppm (parts per million). When $C_p = 2.0$, the number of defects drops to 0.002 ppm (Figure 15-8).

Another important reason for pursuing high process capabilities is that in some manufacturing processes, such as those that run unattended, the process average may drift, perhaps as much as 2σ from the specification target. For example, in the early days of quality management, Motorola found that its processes drifted by 1.5σ. Process control charts detect this drift after a short time lag. However, until detection, a drifted process may produce defective parts.

The effect of a drift of 1.5σ on a process with $C_p = 1.0$ is an extreme drop in quality. To see this, notice that $C_p = 1.0$ means:

$1.0 = (\text{specification width})/(6\sigma)$,

or $(\text{specification width})/2 = 3\sigma$.

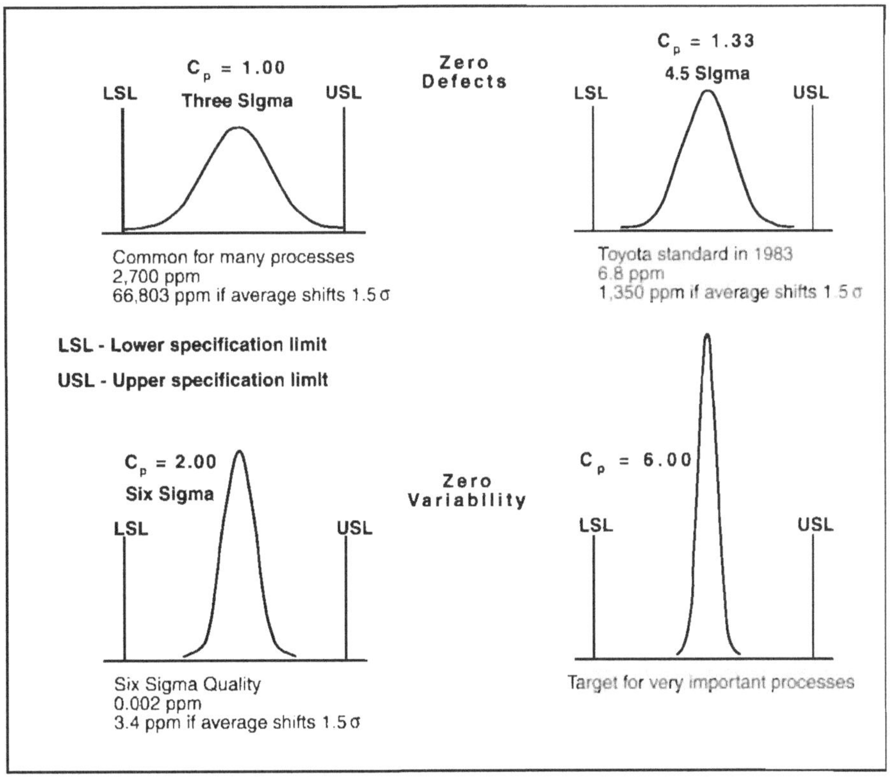

Figure 15-8 Values of the Process Capability Index

A drift of 1.5σ means $k = 1.5\sigma$. Then $C_{pk} = 1.0 \times (1 - 1.5\sigma/3\sigma) = 0.5$ and the number of defects jumps to 66,810 ppm. However, when $C_p = 2.0$, (specification width)/2 = 6σ, the same drift gives $C_{pk} = 2.0 \times (1 - 1.5\sigma/6\sigma) = 1.5$. The number of defects is 3.4 ppm (Figure 15-8). Therefore, a high C_p guarantees a high level of quality even when the process average drifts or some other process problem occurs.

Six sigma at General Electric, Motorola, Ford, and other superior manufacturers is roughly equivalent to $C_p = 2.0$. This is because the term six sigma comes from a requirement that the variation in the process should be sufficiently small, that the upper specification limit is at least six standard deviations (6σ) above the process average, and the lower specification limit is at least 6σ below the process average. So

$$C_p = \frac{\text{specification width}}{6\sigma} = \frac{6\sigma + 6\sigma}{6\sigma} = 2.$$

$C_p = 2.0$ gives a level of quality of .002 ppm when there is no drift and 3.4 ppm when the process average drifts 1.5σ.

Today, six sigma quality means a quality level of 3.4 ppm for each quality characteristic important to the customer. For most processes, this means $C_p = 2.0$ with a drift of 1.5σ. A lower C_p is acceptable if a manufacturing process guarantees little or no drift. For example, when the maximum drift is 0.5σ, a process capability of $C_p = 1.67$ gives 3.4 ppm or six sigma quality.

Six sigma started as a way of measuring process capability and evolved into a general improvement program. The philosophy underlying the six sigma improvement program is based on three ideas:

- Train highly qualified improvement experts (called "green belts," "black belts," and "master black belts") who will apply statistical tools, lead improvement teams, and train employees.
- Set stretch goals for improvement projects. Set a quality target of 3.4 ppm for each important quality characteristic.
- Focus improvement projects on customer needs and strategic goals. Improve quality in nonmanufacturing areas such as administration, design, and marketing. Measure quality in units of defects per million opportunities (dpmo) in these areas, rather than the defective parts per million (ppm) used in manufacturing areas.

Concurrent Engineering

A rule of thumb in manufacturing called the 40/30/30 rule states that about 40 percent of all quality problems result from poor product design, 30 percent result from errors made during manufacturing, and 30 percent result from defective materials purchased from suppliers. Concurrent engineering is a soft technology that focuses primarily on problems in the first category. It recognizes that improvements are easiest to make when the design of the product is still on paper. Concurrent engineering organizes multifunctional teams with members from marketing, product design, production, finance, suppliers, and so on, and charges them to 1) design a product that is easy to manufacture, 2) use the best manufacturing processes to produce the product, and 3) reduce the time required to launch the product (Situations 15.6 and 15.7).

Supply Chain Management

Value chain activities can be organized into five processes: sales, design, purchasing, production, and distribution. Sales takes customer orders and promises delivery dates. Purchasing decides which suppliers to use, negotiates contracts, monitors supplier performance, and manages raw material inventory. Production develops schedules, produces products, and manages work-in-process inventory. Distribution manages the transportation and storage of finished products from production to warehouses to customers. These processes usually operate somewhat independently (Figure 15-9 [A]).

SITUATION 15.6

Concurrent Engineering at Motorola[4]

AT SOME COMPANIES, the "product development cycle" is the time from conception of the product until the product is released to manufacturing. At superior companies like Motorola, it is the time from conception of the product until the product is manufactured at the quality level required by customers.

To improve its product development cycle, Motorola uses a five-step process and a contract book. The five steps are:

1. Determine physical and functional characteristics of the product required to satisfy customers.
2. Identify key characteristics of the design that control the requirements in Step 1.
3. Identify the process controlling each key characteristic in Step 2.
4. Determine the capability index C_{pk} of the process used for each key characteristic in Step 3.
5. When C_{pk} is less than 2.0, seek design or process alternatives.

The contract book sets specific, unchangeable deliverables for documentation, completion time, quality, reliability, and cost, and defines relationships between design, manufacturing, and marketing.

SITUATION 15.7

Northrop Implements Concurrent Engineering

MANAGEMENT AT NORTHROP INDUSTRIES wanted to improve its chances of winning a multibillion-dollar contract for a 1990s fighter airplane. The company competed by providing order winning levels of performance and innovativeness and market qualifying levels of cost, quality, and delivery. However, it became increasingly difficult to provide the required levels of cost and delivery because of the rising number of engineering change orders the company had to handle.

To solve this problem, the company launched a concurrent engineering program called parallel release that reduced the number of change orders and made it easier to handle the remaining change orders. Desks and people were moved so that designers and process engineers were side by side and could work in parallel. Designers accounted for process capabilities in their designs. Process engineers understood designers' problems and made needed process improvements. Benefits came quickly. Change orders decreased by 70 percent, and cost and delivery improved.

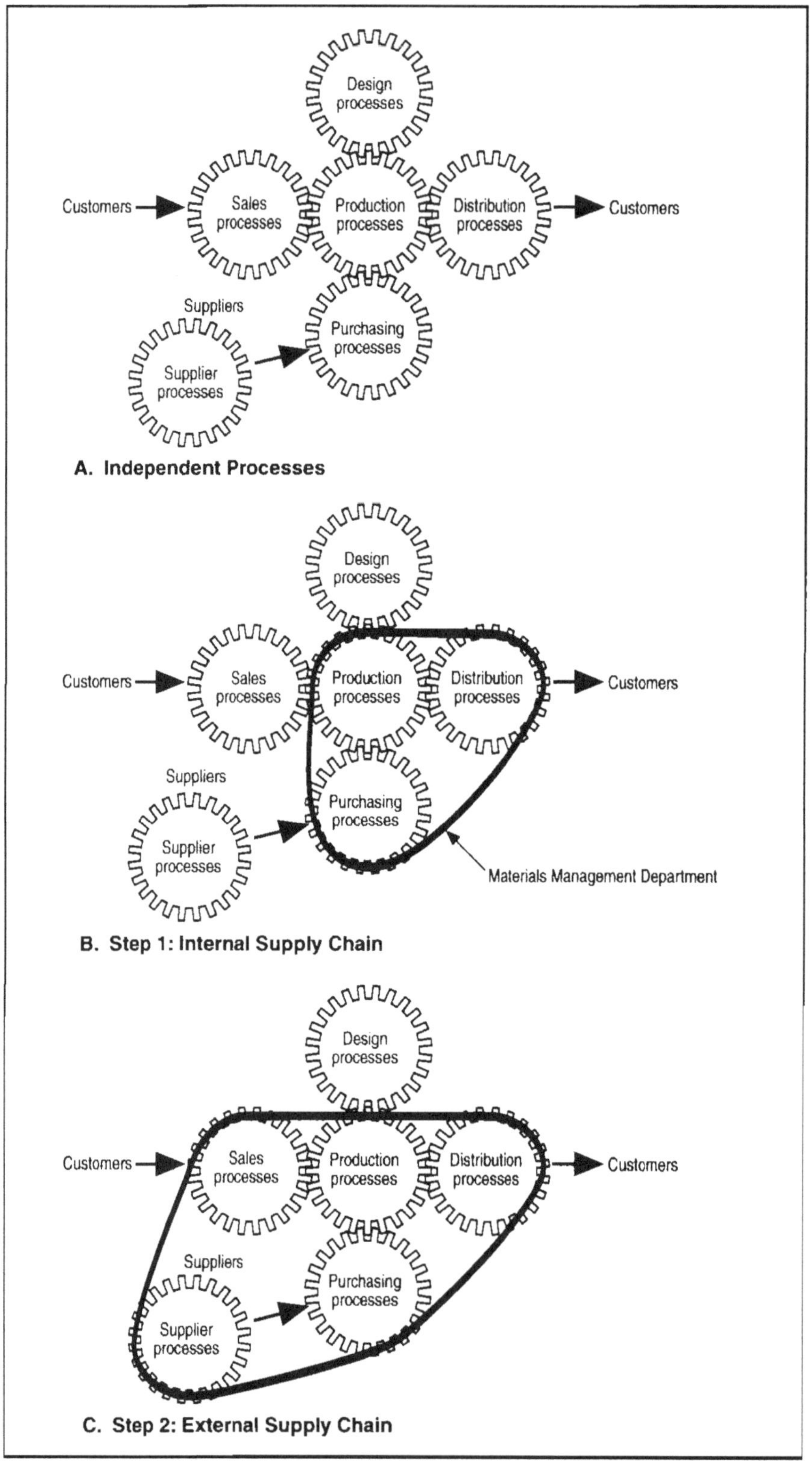

Figure 15-9 Supply Chain Management

Supply chain management increases cooperation and synchronization between processes. This is not easy to do. Independent processes are wary about becoming synchronized elements of a supply chain. Three arguments are used to encourage change:

- After a process successfully improves itself, the next opportunity for improvement involves coordination with other processes, customers, and suppliers.
- Actions taken by one process have significant effects on other processes. For example, late deliveries from suppliers can force production to work overtime and delay shipment of customer orders. Cooperation and synchronization improves this.
- Timely exchange of information between processes reduces the amount of inventory that is needed. Inexpensive information replaces expensive inventory.

The goal of supply chain management is to synchronize a company's activities with those of its suppliers and customers to match the flow of materials, services, and information with customer demands.

Supply chain management is implemented in two steps called internal supply chain and external supply chain. The first step is to develop an internal supply chain. A company combines purchasing, production, and distribution into a single department called materials management (Figure 15-9 [B]), which is responsible for purchased materials and services, inventories, production, staffing, schedules, distribution, and so on. The materials management department uses a comprehensive information system to coordinate activities. Customers and suppliers are still treated as independent processes outside the supply chain. Relations with them are formal, and little information is shared.

A successful internal supply chain is the foundation on which an external supply chain is built. A company begins the second step by learning as much as it can about customer and supplier processes. The company uses this knowledge to extend its internal supply chain to include the external customer and supplier processes (Figure 15-9 [C]).

An important element in developing the external supply chain is the interface between the internal supply chain, and customers and suppliers. Many companies use the Internet to smooth this interface. Business-to-customer (B2C) systems are Internet systems that manage the interface between a company and its customers. The Dell customer website is an example (Situation 15.8). Another example is Cisco Systems' customer website. Cisco receives over 80 percent of its sales orders ($10 billion in 2000) on its customer website.[5] Customers use website software to configure each customized product on each sales order. Business-to-business (B2B) systems are Internet systems that manage the interface between a company and its suppliers. Dell's supplier website is an example (Situation 15.8). Customer and supplier interfaces are linked to a company's comprehensive information system—usually an enterprise resource planning (ERP) system. ERP systems are examined later in this chapter.

Design and operating decisions in supply chain management are divided into two categories: structural decisions and coordination decisions. Structural decisions include where to locate facilities, such as factories and warehouses, what capacities facilities should have, what products should be produced in each factory, and what modes of transportation should be used between suppliers, factories, and warehouses. Coordination decisions include how customer orders are processed, how much raw material, work-in-process, and finished goods inventory should be held, where inventory should be located, and how inventory should be replenished.

To illustrate, consider the decision about where to locate finished goods inventory. One approach, called forward placement, places inventory close to customers at a warehouse, distribution center, wholesaler, or retailer. The advantage of forward placement is fast delivery. The extreme application

SITUATION 15.8

Supply Chain Management at Dell[6]

THE DELL COMPUTER COMPANY is a mass customizer of personal computers. In 1996, Dell sold laptops, desktops, and servers at the rate of $1 million a day. By 1999, sales had grown to $30 million a day, and Dell was an industry leader.

Dell produces to order, and its competitive advantage is speed. It provides market qualifying levels of cost, quality, and flexibility, but delivery time is the order winning output. Dell begins production when it receives a customer order on its website. The finished customized computer is on a delivery truck within 36 hours. This fast delivery enables Dell to keep low inventories (16 days of sales) and low prices (10 to 15 percent below competitors).

Cooperation and synchronization between Dell and its suppliers is an important part of this capability. Dell's top 33 suppliers supply 90 percent of all components. They manage their own inventories in Dell warehouses, located within 15 minutes of Dell's Austin (Texas), Limerick (Ireland), and Penang (Malaysia) factories. Dell pays for components at the time it pulls them from a warehouse to assemble a computer for a customer order. Dell's supplier website gives suppliers accurate, timely information on inventory, production, and customer orders so that suppliers know when to replenish stock at warehouses.

Dell uses service providers such as UPS to speed delivery and reduce cost. For example, Dell can send an electronic message to UPS requesting that a computer monitor be sent to a customer as part of a purchased computer system. UPS pulls a monitor from the monitor supplier's inventory and schedules it to arrive at the same time as the computer.

Careful synchronization of materials and services from suppliers with Dell's production and customer processes enables Dell to operate more efficiently than its competitors. Other companies perform similar activities, but Dell's high level of capability enables better performance.

of forward placement is vendor-managed inventory, where inventory is located at customers' facilities. Dell's warehouses for purchased components are an example (Situation 15.8). The opposite approach is inventory pooling, in which a company keeps finished goods inventory in a central location (often its factory) and ships directly to customers. This reduces the amount of inventory needed compared to forward placement. (When inventory is stored in one location rather than several, the location serves more customers. There is a greater opportunity for higher-than-expected demand from one customer to offset lower-than-expected demand from another customer. This reduces the amount of inventory needed to provide a desired level of customer service.) The disadvantages of inventory pooling are longer delivery time and the high cost of shipping smaller, uneconomical quantities long distances to customers.

In the same way that products are designed to be easy to manufacture (concurrent engineering), products are also designed for easy supply chain management. Postponement is a product design idea for supply chain management. It means customization of a product is delayed until the last possible moment. This enables production to focus on producing standard components. The last possible moment can occur in the distribution channel. For example, a distributor can perform the final, customized assembly of a product before delivering the product to a customer. The last possible moment can also occur at a customer's facility. For example, Cisco arranges for FedEx to collect up to 100 different boxes from factories worldwide and deliver them to a particular customer within hours of each other for final assembly.

Supply chain management and the Internet change the way companies deal with suppliers. Invoices, purchase orders, transportation documents, and payment documents are exchanged electronically. Buyers use electronic catalogs to browse for items they wish to purchase. Buyers and suppliers use electronic marketplaces to come together to do business. Electronic marketplaces are used for spot purchases, where buyers make an immediate purchase of a commodity item, such as oil, steel, or energy, at the lowest possible price. An auction is an electronic marketplace where buyers place competitive bids to buy a variety of products and services. For example, companies like refineries or steel mills with excess capacity can offer their capacity for sale to the highest bidder. A reverse auction is an electronic marketplace where suppliers bid for contracts.

Supply chains are designed to be efficient or responsive. An efficient supply chain coordinates material flows to minimize inventories and maximize production efficiency. Efficient supply chains are used in environments where demand is predictable, new product introductions are infrequent, product variety is small, cost is the order winning output, and thriftiness is the important network output. Responsive supply chains position inventory and capacity around the supply chain to respond quickly to changes at customers, suppliers, and competitors. Responsive supply chains are used when demand varies, product variety is high, and competitive priorities are flexibility, speed, accessibility, and mobility. Poor supply chain performance often results from using the wrong supply chain design. A common mistake is to use an efficient supply chain in an environment that requires a responsive supply chain.

An efficient supply chain builds tight linkages between companies. In this situation, an adverse effect, called the bullwhip effect, can occur if information is inaccurate or information flow is slow. In the bullwhip effect, a small action at a downstream company causes a large reaction or bullwhip effect at an upstream company. Figure 15-10 gives an example. Part A shows a supply chain segment involving three companies. Material flow is from C to B to A, and information flow is from A to B to C. Part B of the figure shows a small change in demand at company A that produces a large change in demand at company C. This happens when B mistakenly thinks that the increasing requirement from A is long term. B orders a large quantity from C, but later, B realizes its mistake (now B's inventory is too high), so B reduces or cancels its next order to C. This causes big swings in demand at C. When the bullwhip effect is present in a supply chain, upstream companies such as C need to be responsive even when the supply chain is designed to be efficient.

Supply chain software is needed to manage modern supply chains. Supply chain software is usually part of an ERP system, but it can also be purchased separately. Typical modules in supply chain software include order commitment, configuration, demand management, master planning, material planning, replenishment planning, scheduling,

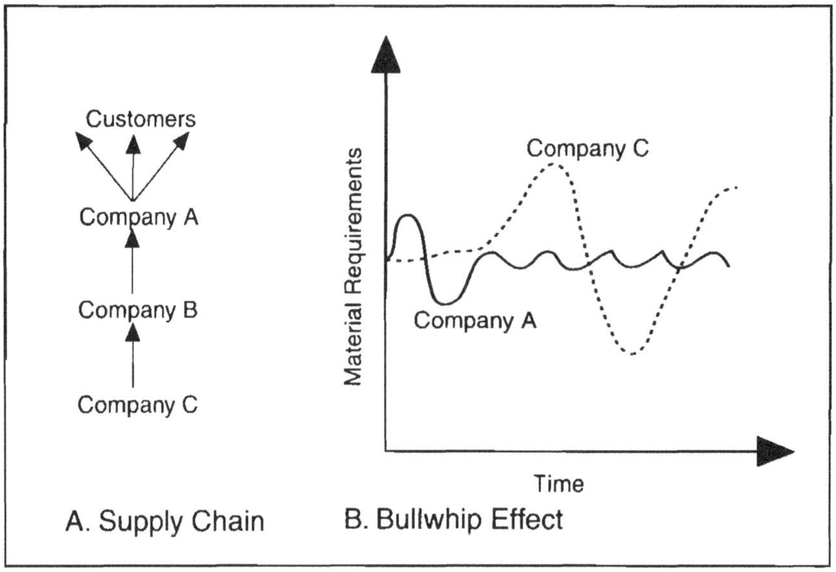

Figure 15-10 Bull Whip Effect in Supply Chain Management

purchasing management, vendor-managed inventory, and transportation management.

Hard Technologies

The development of new materials and fast computing produced most of the equipment and processes that we call hard technologies (Figure 15-11). Hard technologies are expensive. Compared to soft technologies, they are easy to implement. Engineering purchases them and installs them on the factory floor. The vendor helps with startup. After startup, engineering hands them over to production. Many companies have been disappointed with the benefits that many hard technologies finally provide.

Hard technologies must be appropriate for the manufacturing network and production system in use. They should be selected because they provide important network manufacturing outputs and market qualifying and order winning factory manufacturing outputs. They should not be implemented

Situation 15.9

Zepf Succeeds With Hard Technology

ZEPF TECHNOLOGIES is a world leader in the design and manufacture of feedscrews. Feedscrews are used to orient and shunt high volumes of fast-moving products in continuous flow and linked batch flow production systems (Chapter 19). For example, a single row of bottles moving at high speed may enter a parallel set of rotating feedscrews, each about 20 cm in diameter and 150 cm in length, and emerge as an evenly spaced, double row of bottles ready to go into shipping containers. The geometry of modern feedscrews could not be designed or produced prior to the mid-1980s because the necessary hard technologies were not available.

NC (numerical control) Machine
Machine with a control system that enables a program to produce a part.

CNC (computer numerical control) Machine
NC machine controlled by its own computer, which permits faster development, handling, and execution of NC programs, and provides more control over the machine.

Machining Center
Machine with the functionality of several different CNC machines.

DNC (direct numerical control)
Several CNC machines and other equipment controlled by the same supervisory computer.

Robot
Programmable manipulator used to grasp and move parts while performing activities such as painting, welding, loading and unloading, and assembling.

AGV (automated guided vehicle)
Programmable device for moving materials around a factory.

CAD (computer aided design)
Design of a part and production of a part drawing on a computer.

CAE (computer aided engineering)
Design and engineering of a part, and production of a part drawing on a computer.

CAD/CAM (computer aided design/computer aided manufacturing)
Production of an NC program to manufacture a part (developed by CAD) on NC and CNC machines.

MRP (manufacturing resources planning or material requirements planning)
Computer and software to generate production plans (for material, labor, and equipment), and monitor and control execution of plans.

CIM (computer-integrated manufacturing)
Computer and software to integrate all manufacturing activities, including order entry, product design, production planning, performing manufacturing operations, inspection, shipping, and billing.

ERP (enterprise resource planning)
Computers, integrated information systems database, and application programs to support all company-wide processes such as sales, order processing, production, distribution, accounting, and quality.

Figure 15-11 Some Hard Technologies

Zepf Technologies was a pioneer in the use and development of hard technology in this industry. In 1980, when it had just passed $1 million in sales, Zepf spent $750,000 on CNC machines. No financial justification report was necessary. The company needed this equipment to provide market qualifying outputs. Without the equipment, it would go out of business.

The CNC machines worked quickly, causing long idle periods when machines waited for the NC programs needed to run them. In those days, it took a long time to design a feedscrew, calculate cutting paths for machining operations, and prepare

SITUATION 15.9

Continued

NC programs. In 1981, Zepf started to automate this process. The goal was to present the designer with a series of prompts for screw specifications. A computer program would take the specifications, calculate cutting paths, and prepare NC programs. This is called computer aided engineering, CAE (Figure 15-11).

In 1986, when sales were $2.7 million, a new $200,000 computer was purchased. Soon programming and design activities occupied the time of 20 percent of the company's employees.

In 1992, Zepf was on its fourth generation of CAE software. It built its own CNC machines. Engineering, design, quality, process planning, DNC, and CNC were fully integrated. Remarkable improvements in productivity were achieved. The time to design and program a simple feedscrew decreased from 32 hours in 1981 to 0.5 hours in 1991, and the time to machine the same feedscrew decreased from five hours in 1981 to 0.5 hours in 1991. For a complex feedscrew, the time for design and programming decreased from 100 hours to one hour in the same time period, and the time for machining decreased from ten hours to two hours.

until manufacturing has been focused and appropriate soft technologies have been implemented.

Enterprise Resource Planning

Enterprise Resource Planning (ERP) systems are enablers of modern manufacturing networks, especially international networks. ERP is an integrated information system that supports a company's data storage and business process information needs. ERP is based on a three-tier, client-server architecture. The three tiers are:

- Large database to store master data and transactions data
- Software application modules to support business functions such as accounting, asset management, cash management, controlling, distribution, logistics, maintenance, material management, production, purchasing, quality, sales, and strategic planning
- Consistent graphical user interface in application modules

Although application modules are organized into traditional business functions, all follow a process-oriented view of business activities. Business processes are supported in a seamless way across functions, so users do not realize which application modules they are using. ERP supports multicountry activities. It handles multiple currencies and has country-specific documents for quotes, delivery notes, invoices, payroll forms, accounts, and so on.

ERP solves a major problem in large companies—fragmentation of information. A large company gathers, stores, and analyzes vast amounts of data in many locations, business functions, and computer systems. Maintaining different systems, updating programs, and creating ways to transfer data from one location to another are expensive, time consuming, and error-prone activities. Even more troublesome are hidden costs. For example, if sales personnel cannot get fast, accurate information from production, they make delivery promises that production cannot keep, leading directly to dissatisfied customers. By replacing incompatible, inconsis-

SITUATION 15.10

ERP in Action[7]

A U.S. COMPANY'S Berlin-based salesman enters information about a customer's needs into his laptop computer. The company's ERP system quickly generates a quote in German, giving product specifications, delivery date, and price. After the customer accepts the quote, ERP verifies the customer's credit limit, generates a contract, and records the order.

A logistics application then schedules shipment using the best available routing. Backing up from the delivery date, a production application reserves the necessary materials from inventory and determines when to release production orders to factories and purchase orders to suppliers.

Another application updates sales and production forecasts, while still another credits the salesman's payroll account with the appropriate commission in German marks. One accounting application calculates the standard product cost and profitability in U.S. dollars and enters the transaction in the accounts payable and accounts receivable ledgers. Another application accumulates actual cost as the order moves through the production process. Divisional and corporate balance sheets are updated, as are cash levels.

In this way, ERP supports all business processes activated as a result of the sale.

tent information systems with one fast accurate system, ERP reduces cost and improves service.

The main benefits to a company come from ERP's ability to process transactions efficiently and provide effective record-keeping structures for master and transactional data. Some benefits come from ERP's planning capabilities, however, these benefits are small because decision support intelligence in ERP is still limited.

The big suppliers of ERP systems are SAP (www.sap.com), Oracle (www.oracle.com), PeopleSoft (www.peoplesoft.com), J. D. Edwards (www.jdedwards.com), and Baan (www.baan.com). Figure 15-12 shows a menu of application modules in SAP.

ERP is not for every company. The cost of an off-the-shelf system is high—$2 million for software and $10 million for implementation. The cost for a very large company can skyrocket to $50 to $500 million. A full implementation can take four or five years. Implementing the accounting and financial applications can take two months, whereas implementing the production application can take two years. Many companies must reengineer some business processes (Chapter 14) before implementing ERP.

Small ERP systems are available for midsize companies (less than $1 billion in sales). ERP is less useful for small companies ($25 to $50 million in sales). The problem of fragmented information is smaller in these companies, so ERP's benefits are smaller. At the same time, the cost to purchase and implement ERP is too high for small companies.

Not all ERP implementations succeed. Fox Meyer points to ERP as a major cause of its bankruptcy. Mobile Europe's expenditure of millions of dollars was wasted when its merger partner did not want ERP. Hershey lost $140 million in sales when its ordering and distribution applications failed to

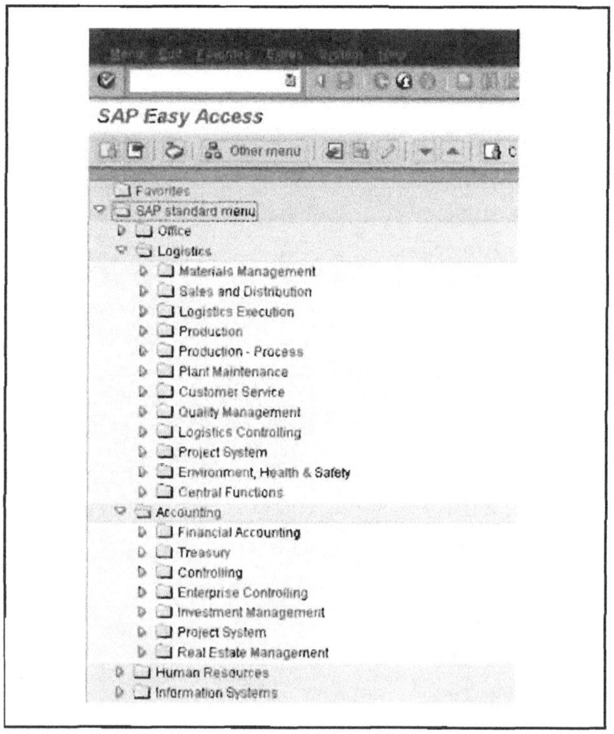

Figure 15-12 Menu of Applications in SAP

deliver products to major distributors in time for Halloween. Problems in Whirlpool's ERP system caused shipping delays, which drove Home Depot to switch to Maytag and General Electric.[8]

Summary

There is a sequence in which types of improvements should be made. First, manufacturing is focused. Then, soft technologies are used to improve focused operations. Only then are appropriate, and by this time, obvious, hard technologies added. Unsuccessful attempts to improve manufacturing fail because one of these steps is missed or steps are done in the wrong order.

Focus is the most important step. Companies focus factories in their manufacturing network by giving each factory a specialization and by organizing each factory into small factories-within-a-factory (FWFs). An FWF focuses on a limited number of products, activities, and customers, and uses the best production system. Superior companies feel that focusing manufacturing does not require financial or strategic justification. Instead, justification is required for not focusing.

Soft technologies are systems- and people-oriented, inexpensive to acquire, and difficult to implement. Three popular soft technologies are examined: process capability and six sigma quality, concurrent engineering, and supply chain management. Hard technologies are usually the application of sophisticated new materials and fast, cheap computing to traditional manufacturing equipment and processes. Hard technologies are expensive. Compared to soft technologies, they are easy to implement.

Certain soft and hard technologies work better with certain networks and production systems. Of the soft and hard technologies appropriate for a network and production system, the best ones are those that help provide high levels of important network manufacturing outputs and factory manufacturing outputs.

Endnotes

1. Wickens, B., "Lessons in How to Survive," *Mcleans Magazine*, Vol. 104, No. 32, p. 32, August 12. 1991.
2. Adapted from a problem on page 754 in R. Schmenner, *Production and Operations Management*, 4th edition, New York: Macmillan, 1987.
3. Adapted from R. Venkatesan, "Cummins Engine Flexes Its Factory," *Harvard Business Review*, March/April 1990. Used by permission of *Harvard Business Review*. Copyright © 1990 by the Harvard Business School Publishing Corporation; all rights reserved.
4. Smith, B., "Six sigma Design," *IEEE Spectrum*, pp. 44–45, September 1993.
5. "Meet Mr. Internet," *Business Week*, pp. 129–140, September 13, 1999.
6. McWilliams, G., "Whirlwind on the Web," *Business Week*, pp. 132–136, April 17, 1997; and p. 229 in Simchi-Levi, D., Kaminsky, P., and Simchi-Levi, E., *Designing and Managing the Supply Chain*, New York: McGraw-Hill Irwin, 2003.
7. From p. 205 in Krajewski, L., and Ritzman, L., *Operations Management*, New Jersey: Prentice Hall, 2002.
8. Ibid, p. 209.

CHAPTER 16

BENEFITS OF EXPERIENCE AND THE PRODUCT LIFE CYCLE

A product doesn't last forever: It is developed and introduced to a market, and if it succeeds, demand grows rapidly. Eventually, growth stops, and a stable, mature stage begins. This stage ends when customer preferences change or new products appear that render the product obsolete. These stages constitute a product life cycle. The requirements for design, production, and network and factory outputs change as a product moves through the stages of its life cycle. Different manufacturing networks and production systems are best at different stages.

More and more units are produced as a product moves through its life cycle. This gives a company experience, which enables it to learn and improve product design, manufacturing network and production systems, and raise the levels of network and factory manufacturing outputs. Before examining the benefits of experience and the product life cycle, we examine a situation where experience and the product life cycle helped a company become an industry leader in an important consumer product.

SITUATION 16.1

Experience and the Product Life Cycle at Samsung[1]

IN 1976, AFTER ONE YEAR of work, Samsung's first prototype microwave oven was ready for testing. The chief engineer pushed the on button, and in front of his eyes, large plastic sections of the oven began to melt. Many weeks of hard work followed before the second prototype was ready, which produced the same result; when the oven was turned on—parts melted. It was a discouraging time. Japanese and American companies were selling 4 million microwave ovens a year, and Samsung Company of Korea failed to get a single prototype to work.

In June 1978, another prototype was ready, and this time, nothing melted. The product was simple and rough, but at least it worked. Samsung organized a job shop production system to

SITUATION 16.1

Continued

build between one and five ovens each day. Production costs were high because of the low volume. Samsung's strategy for winning orders was to customize the microwave oven to meet the special needs of foreign customers. Samsung provided high levels of flexibility and innovativeness, which other manufacturers did not. A year later, Samsung won an order from a Panama retailer for 240 ovens. Within weeks, Samsung redesigned the product to meet the retailer's needs, manufactured the ovens, and shipped the order. The successful order gave Samsung confidence to apply for Underwriters' Laboratory (UL) approval, which would allow the company to export to the United States. Late in 1979, Samsung received UL approval.

In 1980, J.C. Penney, one of the U.S. largest retailers, asked Samsung if it could produce a microwave oven to sell for $299. At the time, microwave ovens sold for $350 to $400. J.C. Penney had been looking for an oven it could sell for less but hadn't found one with U.S. or Japanese manufacturers. Samsung accepted an order for a few thousand units. A team of factory and product design personnel was formed for the important order. A new J.C. Penney microwave oven and a new batch flow production system were concurrently designed. Between 10 and 15 ovens were produced by day, and at night, improvements were made to the production system. Improvements were also made at suppliers. Before long, production increased to 60 ovens a day, enough to meet the order. J.C. Penney liked the ovens and increased the order to 200, and then 250, ovens per day. When the volume increased and the design stabilized, Samsung changed the production system to an operator-paced line flow system.

In 1982, Samsung produced 200,000 microwave ovens, and the big manufacturers in Japan and the United States, who produced over 5 million ovens annually, took notice and lowered their prices. Samsung recognized that to keep growing, it also had to lower its price. Managers scrutinized the cost structure and found two ways to lower the cost of the microwave oven:

- Increase vertical integration backward to the production of expensive components.
- Increase volume so that the production system could be changed to an equipment-paced line flow.

Increase Vertical Integration

The most expensive item in Samsung's oven was the magnetron tube (the device that generated microwaves). Samsung bought the magnetron tube from a Japanese supplier. It was the most complex device in the oven, and Samsung lacked the expertise to manufacture it. Samsung approached a number of Japanese manufacturers to form a joint venture to produce the tubes but was turned down each time. Then, Samsung learned that Amperex, the only U.S. manufacturer of magnetron tubes, was exiting the magnetron tube business because it could not compete against Japanese manufacturers. Samsung quickly bought Amperex's magnetron tube production process. The Amperex equipment arrived in Korea in early 1983, and before long, Samsung manufactured its own magnetron tubes.

Implement an Equipment-Paced Line Flow Production System

In 1983, General Electric (GE) decided to source small- and mid-sized microwave ovens from Asia and manufacture only full-sized models in the United States. The biggest orders went to Japan, but Samsung won a small order for 15,000 ovens. At first, Samsung's ovens did not meet GE standards, but with the help of GE's quality engineers, they improved. GE was impressed, and more orders followed. To produce the higher volume, Samsung changed its production system to an equipment-paced line flow system.

Samsung continued to gain experience and improve its manufacturing capability. By 1984, it had four equipment-paced assembly lines producing microwave ovens for its domestic market and export markets in France, Germany, Scandinavia, and the United States.

In 1985, GE stopped U.S. production of microwave ovens because its level of manufacturing capability had fallen far behind companies like Samsung, and it had no choice but to exit. GE continued to do sales and service, but Samsung did all manufacturing.

Experience

Experience was an important factor in Samsung's success with the microwave oven.

- Experience led to learning. Samsung learned about the product and the production process when it developed prototypes, and it learned from its customers in Panama, at

J.C. Penney, and at General Electric, from its suppliers, and from equipment vendors like Amperex.

- Learning led to improvements in products and production systems. As Samsung gained experience, it improved product design, changed production systems, and increased vertical integration.
- Improvements raised the level of manufacturing capability, which raised the levels of the manufacturing outputs. As Samsung became a more capable producer of microwave ovens, it was able to meet and then exceed customer expectations for cost, quality, performance, delivery, flexibility, and innovativeness.
- The benefits of experience were not automatic. Samsung developed formal systems to ensure that learning occurred and the benefits of experience were realized. The company organized teams of product design and factory personnel to develop new product models. Personnel were sent to other countries to learn from customers and other manufacturers. They were encouraged to try new ideas. Samsung invested in new processes and equipment.

The benefits of experience accumulate as production volume increases. The benefits of experience are shown on a graph called the experience curve (Figure 16-1). The cost to manufacture a product is plotted against total production volume at different points in time. When cost is difficult to estimate, price is used as a substitute. The graph shows that product cost decreases over time as the production volume increases. The rate of decrease is called the slope of the experience curve.

Figure 16-1 (A) shows the experience curve for color photographic paper produced by Japanese companies. In 1967, after 10 million square meters had been produced, the price was 3.4 yen per square meter. By 1982, 900 million square meters had been produced and the price was about 0.6 yen per square meter. When cost or price and total production are plotted on logarithmic scales, the experience curve appears as a straight line. The slope of the experience curve in Figure 16-1 (A) is $S = 77$ percent. S is interpreted as follows: Each time the cumulative production doubles, the price drops by $100 - S$ percent. For example, $S = 77$ means the price of color paper drops by $100 - 77 = 23$ percent each time cumulative production doubles.

Figure 16-1 (B) shows how the price of the Model T automobile fell when Henry Ford made his legendary improvements at the Rouge River plant (Situation 14.8). The slope of this experience curve is 85 percent. Another example of the benefits of experience is shown in Part C of the figure. The slope of the experience curve for limestone was 80 percent over the period from 1929 to 1971. The price was \$1.70 per ton in the mid-1940s, when the cumulative production was 3 billion tons. When the total production doubled to 6 billion tons, the price dropped to \$1.70 × 80 percent = \$1.36. A target for the price when the cumulative production doubles again to 12 billion tons is \$1.36 × 80 percent = \$1.09 per ton. This price reduction will not happen automatically; it only happens when companies make improvements. Companies use improvement programs like quality management, cycle time reduction, agile manufacturing, kaizen, and reengineering (Chapter 14) to generate improvements. They also focus processes, hire personnel, and purchase new equipment (Chapter 15).

Dramatic examples of experience come from the electronics industry. Prices of calculators, computers, radios, televisions, and watches dropped dramatically in the years following their introduction. Figure 16-1 (D) shows data for the RAM chip. The price is in thousandths of a cent per bit of memory. In 1978, the 1 trillionth bit was manufactured at a price of .075 cents per bit. Within three years, 10 trillion bits had been manufactured at a price of .015 cents per bit. The slope of the experience curve is a remarkable 62 percent.

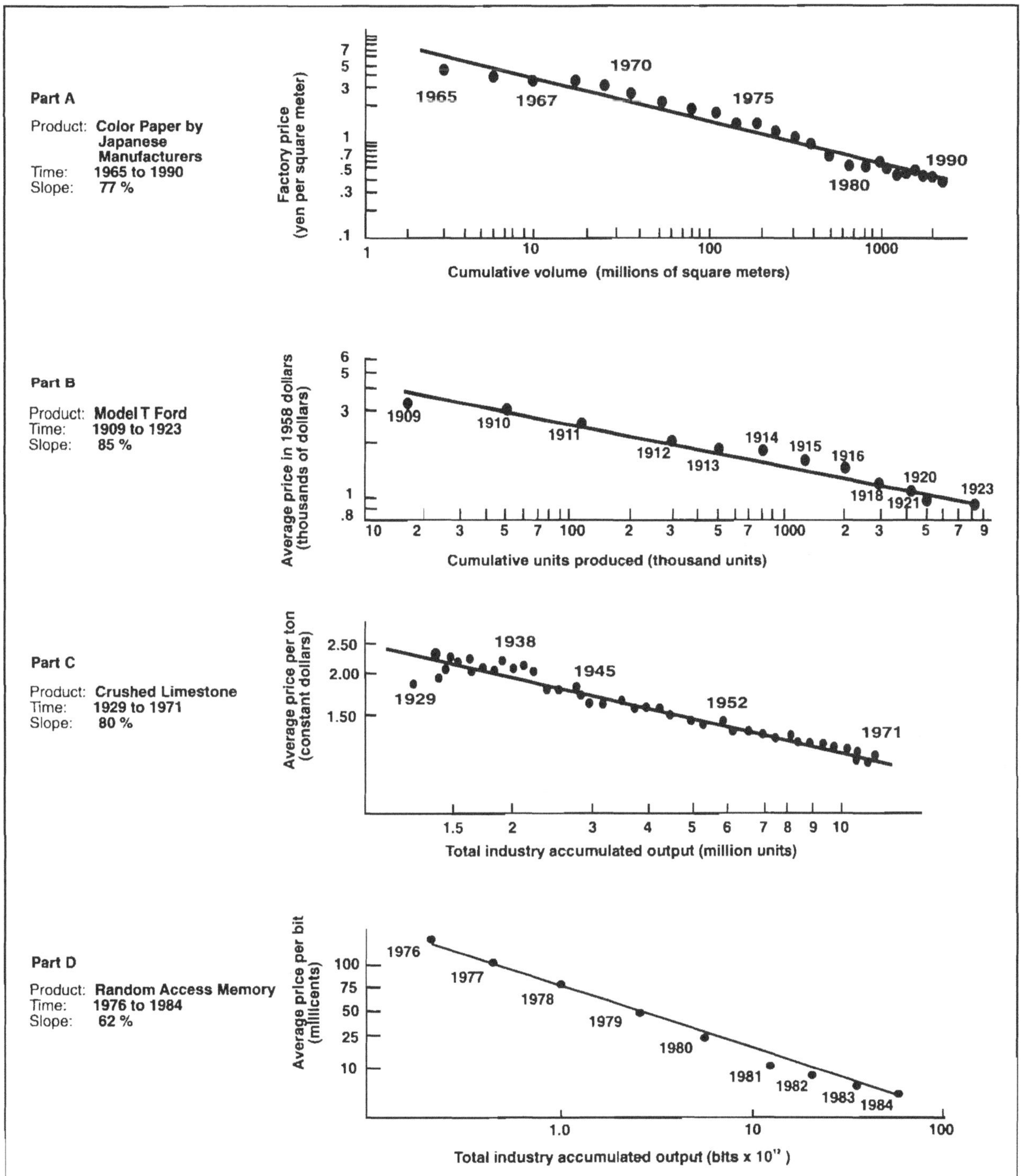

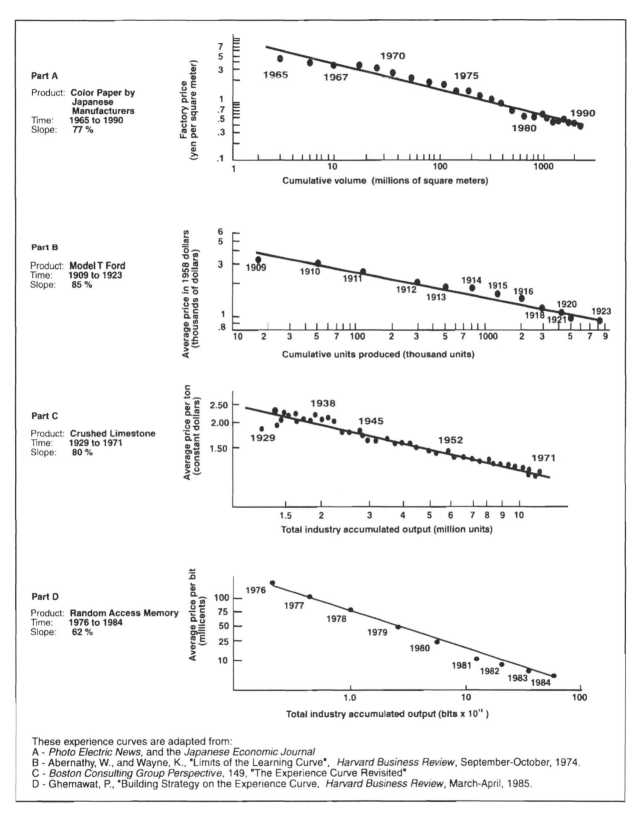

These experience curves are adapted from:
A - *Photo Electric News*, and the *Japanese Economic Journal*
B - Abernathy, W., and Wayne, K., "Limits of the Learning Curve", *Harvard Business Review*, September-October, 1974.
C - *Boston Consulting Group Perspective*, 149, "The Experience Curve Revisited"
D - Ghemawat, P., "Building Strategy on the Experience Curve, *Harvard Business Review*, March-April, 1985.

Figure 16-1 Well-Known Experience Curves

SITUATION 16.2

Using Experience Curves to Track Improvements

A FOOD PRODUCTS COMPANY has two factories that produce cheese. Factory 1 is a small, U.S. factory, and Factory 2 is a large, European factory. Figure 16-2 shows the benefits of experience on direct cost and overhead cost in each factory over ten years.

- Direct cost decreased significantly in both factories as the amount of cheese produced increased. The slopes of the experience curves for the factories are similar, suggesting that both factories were making similar improvements.
- Overhead cost over the ten years decreased slightly in Factory 1 and barely in Factory 2. This suggests that little improvement occurred in overhead activities, especially in Factory 2.

The company should launch an improvement program, such as six sigma (Chapter 15), to stimulate improvements in overhead activities.

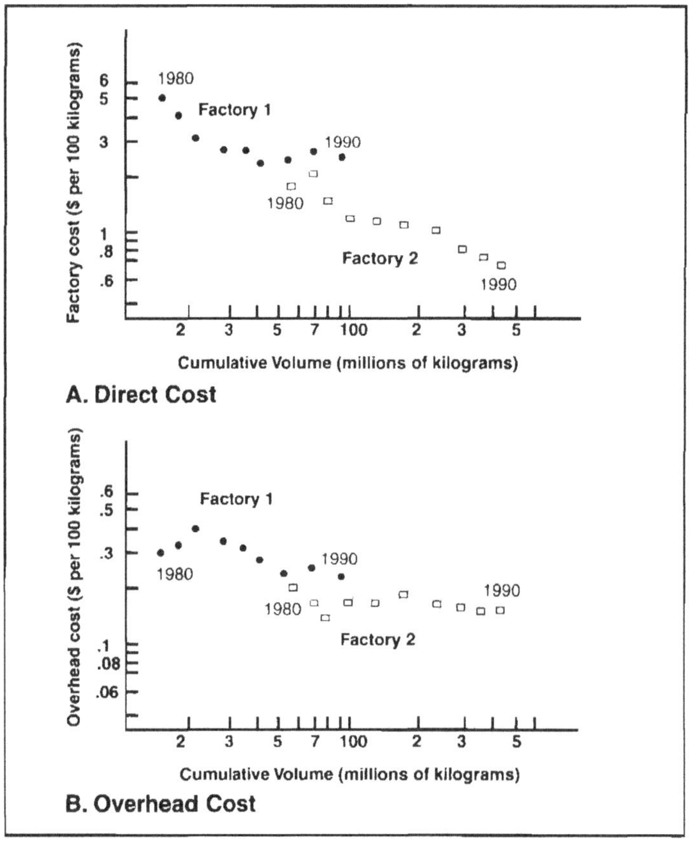

Figure 16-2 Using Experience Curves to Track Improvements

Experience Curve Calculations

The slope of the experience curve is S percent, $0 < S \leq 100$. The cost per unit decreases by $100 - S$ percent when the number of units produced doubles. Mathematically, this means:

$$C_n = C_1(n^b)$$

where $b = \log(S/100)/\log 2$

C_1 = cost to manufacture the first unit

C_n = cost to manufacture the nth unit

Situation 16.3 gives an example.

Experience is associated with individual products and their cumulative production volumes. Production volumes vary as products move through the stages of their product life cycles. So experience and its benefits change as products move through the stages of their product life cycles.

Product Life Cycle

A product's sales follow a pattern over the time the product is in production. The pattern is called the product life cycle, and it consists of six stages: development, growth, shakeout, maturity, saturation, and decline (Figure 16-3).

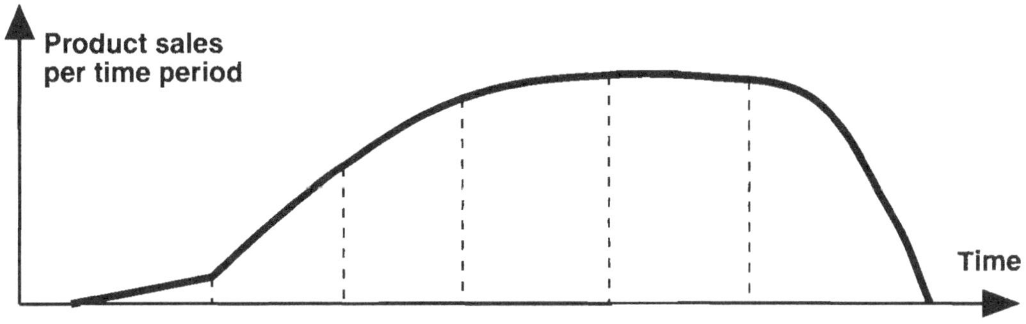

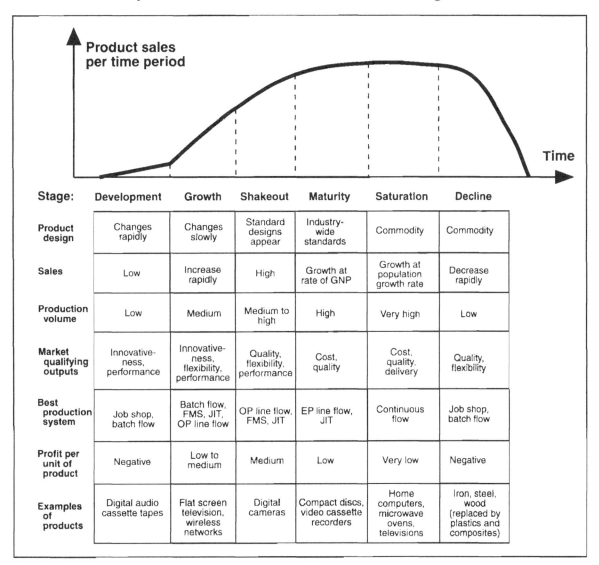

Stage:	Development	Growth	Shakeout	Maturity	Saturation	Decline
Product design	Changes rapidly	Changes slowly	Standard designs appear	Industry-wide standards	Commodity	Commodity
Sales	Low	Increase rapidly	High	Growth at rate of GNP	Growth at population growth rate	Decrease rapidly
Production volume	Low	Medium	Medium to high	High	Very high	Low
Market qualifying outputs	Innovativeness, performance	Innovativeness, flexibility, performance	Quality, flexibility, performance	Cost, quality	Cost, quality, delivery	Quality, flexibility
Best production system	Job shop, batch flow	Batch flow, FMS, JIT, OP line flow	OP line flow, FMS, JIT	EP line flow, JIT	Continuous flow	Job shop, batch flow
Profit per unit of product	Negative	Low to medium	Medium	Low	Very low	Negative
Examples of products	Digital audio cassette tapes	Flat screen television, wireless networks	Digital cameras	Compact discs, video cassette recorders	Home computers, microwave ovens, televisions	Iron, steel, wood (replaced by plastics and composites)

Figure 16-3 Stages in the Product Life Cycle

Situation 16.3

Using the Experience Curve to Set Improvement Targets

Problem 1

The price of a RAM chip (Figure 16-1 [D]) in 1978, when the 1 trillionth bit was manufactured, was 0.075 cents per bit. By 1984, 80 trillion bits had been manufactured. What should the price be in 1984 if the slope of the experience curve is 62 percent? What if it is 50 percent?

Let C_1 = \$0.075 be the price for the 1 trillionth bit.

Let C_{80} be the price for the 80 trillionth bit.

If S = 62 percent:

$$b = \log(62/100)/\log 2 = -.69$$

$$C_{80} = C_1(n^b) = .075(80^{-.69}) = \$0.004$$

If S = 50 percent:

$$b = \log(50/100)/\log 2 = -1.0$$

$$C_{80} = C_1(n^b) = .075(80^{-1.0}) = \$0.0009$$

The price per bit is \$0.004 if the slope of the experience curve is 62 percent, and four times less, \$0.0009, if the slope of the experience curve is 50 percent.

Problem 2

The experience curve for color photographic paper is shown in Figure 16-1 (A). In 1990, a new competitor decides to enter the industry, but it will take until 1995 to develop products and a production system. What target should the competitor set for its cost to manufacture color photographic paper in 1995?

The cumulative industry volume in 1995 can be forecasted from the actual volumes in 1980 through 1990. An estimate of 2,900 million square meters in 1995 is obtained from a simple forecasting model. Figure 16-1 (A) shows the cumulative volume and actual price in 1990: 2,100 million square meters and 0.4 yen.

Let $C_{2.1}$ = 0.4 be the actual price when the 2.1 billionth unit was manufactured in 1990.

Let $C_{2.9}$ be an estimate of the price when the 2.9 billionth unit is manufactured in 1995.

S = 77 percent. Therefore:

$$b = \log(77/100)/\log 2 = -.377$$

$$C_{2.1} = 0.4 = C_1\,(2.1^{-.377}) \text{ or } C_1 = 0.529 \text{ yen}$$

$$C_{2.9} = C_1(n^b) = .529(2.9^{-.377}) = 0.354 \text{ yen}$$

The new competitor's target cost in 1995 should be less than the estimated price of 0.354 yen.

Development Stage

A new product is designed, prototypes are developed and tested, and small volumes of the product are produced by skilled workers on general purpose equipment in a job shop production system. Design and production costs are high. Marketing tries to gain acceptance for the product from distributors and customers.

Growth Stage

Orders are won. Product design is modified to satisfy the requirements for different orders, and adjustments are made to the production process for new designs to be manufactured. As more orders are won, the job shop production system struggles to produce higher volumes of customized products, so production is moved to a batch flow production system.

Shakeout Stage

Markets become more competitive, and standard designs and features emerge. Customer expectations for quality, performance, and flexibility rise, and companies that fail to meet and exceed expectations drop out. Production systems improve to provide the required levels of the manufacturing outputs. Some competitors find market niches and begin to specialize. An operator-paced line flow production system is used.

Maturity Stage

Industry-wide, standard designs emerge. Customer expectations for cost and quality are high, as are sales, which grow at about the same rate as the economy. Production volume is high, so production is moved to an equipment-paced line flow production system.

Saturation Stage

The product becomes a commodity, competes on the basis of cost, quality, and delivery, and is produced by a small number of competitors. Production volume is very high and grows slowly. Continuous flow production is used.

Decline Stage

Customer preferences change. New products appear, and orders for the old product rapidly drop. Sales are too low to adequately utilize a dedicated production system, so production is moved back to a batch flow or job shop production system.

Examples of products at different stages in their product life cycle are given in the bottom row of Figure 16-3. The length of a stage, the sales at a stage, and the overall length of the life cycle vary among products and depend on factors such as customer preferences, the amount of competition, and the rate of technological change in products and processes. For example, a wafer fabrication factory at Intel is obsolete in four years because of technological change, while an engine plant at General Motors is still productive after twenty years. In general, product life cycles are shorter today than in the past. Newer, better products are designed and launched at a faster rate.

The best production system for a product changes as the product moves through its life cycle. Figure 16-4 shows the relationship between the product life cycle and the type of production system. A job shop is used during most of the development stage. Near the end of this stage, the production system changes to a batch flow system, which is also used in the growth stage. During the growth stage, the production system changes to an operator-paced line flow system. This system is also used during the shakeout stage. When the product is about to begin the maturity stage, the production system changes to an equipment-paced line flow system. A continuous flow production system is used during the saturation stage, when the product is a commodity.

The JIT and FMS production systems can begin earlier and be used for more stages of the life cycle than traditional line flow systems. The FMS production system starts during the latter part of the development stage and is used during the growth and shakeout stages. The JIT production system starts during the growth stage and is used during the shakeout and maturity stages.

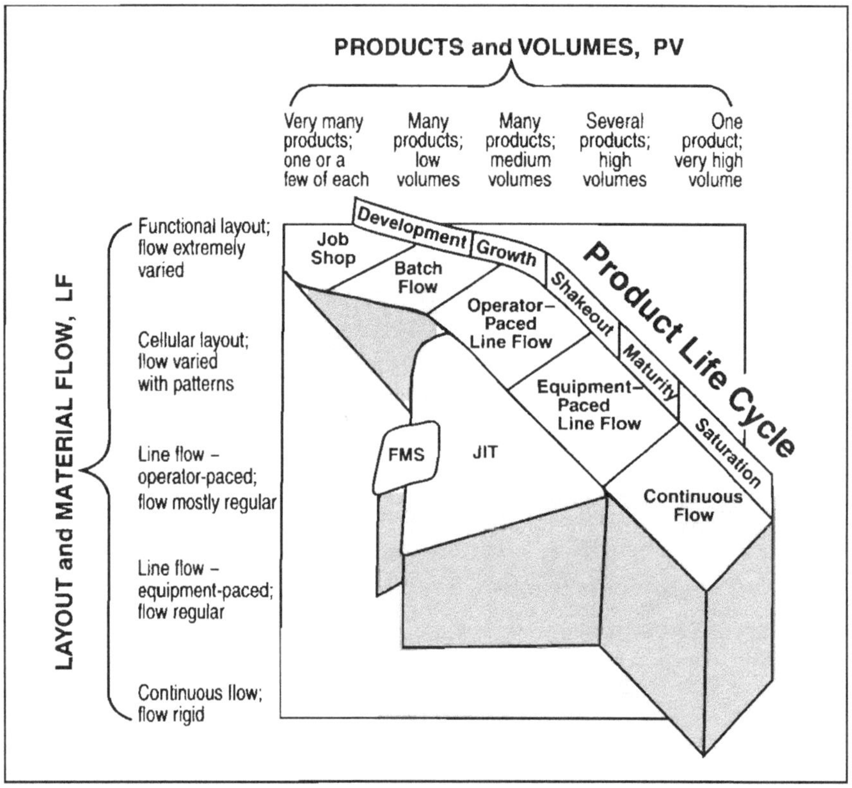

Figure 16-4 Product Life Cycle and the Production System

SITUATION 16.1

Continued

FIGURE 16-5 SHOWS the product life cycle for the Samsung microwave oven. Notice how frequently and quickly Samsung changed production systems. Samsung always used traditional production systems, never the difficult JIT and FMS systems.

SITUATION 16.4

Product Life Cycle at LKO Packaging Company

LKO PACKAGING manufactures customized packaging. Customers and LKO engineers design a color, material, print, shape, and size of packaging for customers' products. Figure 16-6 gives some data for a sample of LKO products.

The first product, Small Rosebud, is named after the customer's product for which the packaging is made. The current demand is 770,000 units per year, whereas last year, the volume was 230,000 units. The product is one year old and still in the development stage of its life cycle. Performance is the order winning output. The selling price is $0.022 per unit and the

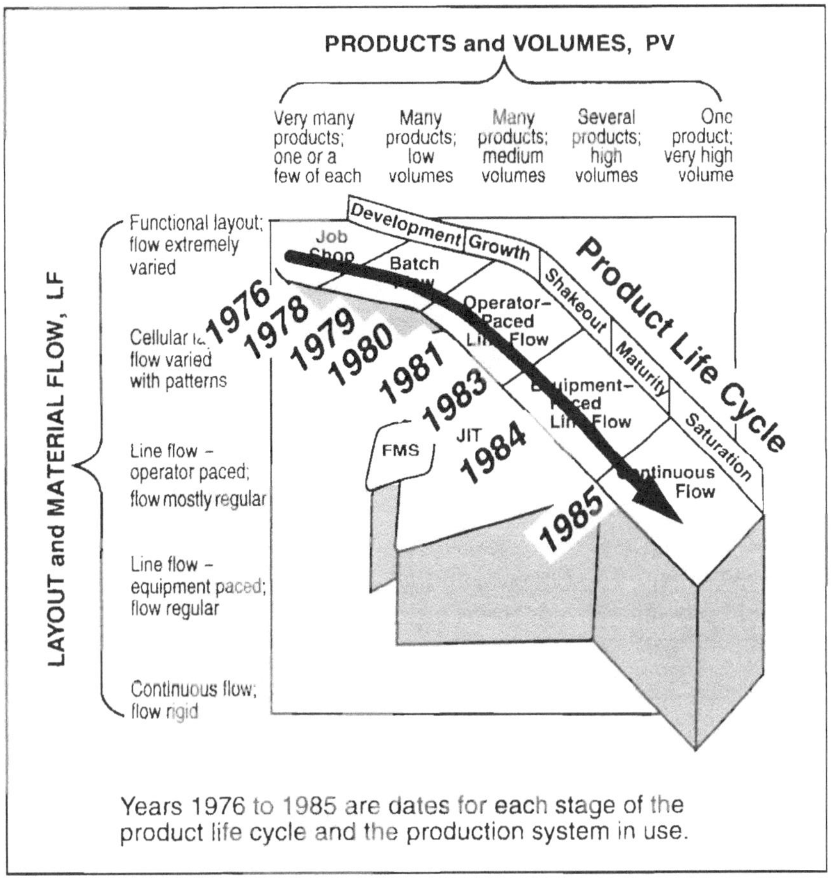

Figure 16-5 Product Life Cycle for the Samsung Microwave Oven

contribution to overhead and profit is -$0.010 per unit. Total sales are 770,000 × 0.022 = $16,940, and total contribution is 770,000 × -0.01 = -$7,700. Small Rosebud packaging is produced in a batch flow production system.

Four observations follow from the data in the Figure 16-6:

- During the development stage of the product life cycle, volume is low, price is high, and contribution is negative. The product is new, so design changes are frequent. LKO is losing money. A batch flow production system is used.
- During the growth stage of the life cycle, volume is low, and price and contribution are high. Design changes are less frequent. A batch flow production system is still used.
- During the shakeout stage of the life cycle, volume increases, and price and contribution decrease. Design

Product	Annual Sales (000s units) Current Year	Current year minus 1	2	3	Product Life Cycle Stage	Years Since Introduction	Order Winning Output
Small Rosebud	770	230	0	0	Development	1	Performance
Medium Rosebud	830	760	420	0	Growth	2	Performance
Family Tree	660	480	430	400	Shakeout	4	Quality
Step Repellant	2,980	2,210	1,800	1,250	Shakeout	5	Quality
Medium Bath	4,240	3,910	4,650	4,200	Maturity	6	Cost
Large Frystan	8,800	8,460	9,620	9,540	Maturity	6	Cost
Medium Multiscan	10,900	11,800	12,400	11,400	Saturation	7	Cost
Small Photo	480	540	720	990	Decline	10	Flexibility
Power Saver	220	330	840	1,610	Decline	11	Flexibility

Product	Selling Price ($)	Contribution per Unit ($)	Production System	Total Sales ($)	Total Contribution ($)
Small Rosebud	0.022	-0.010	Batch	16,940	-7,700
Medium Rosebud	0.022	0.014	Batch	18,260	11,620
Family Tree	0.011	0.004	Operator-paced line	7,260	2,640
Step Repellant	0.009	0.003	Operator-paced line	26,820	8,940
Medium Bath	0.004	0.002	Equipment-paced line	16,960	8,480
Large Frystan	0.005	0.002	Equipment-paced line	44,000	17,600
Medium Multiscan	0.004	0.002	Equipment-paced line	43,600	21,800
Small Photo	0.003	0.001	Batch	1,440	480
Power Saver	0.003	0.001	Batch	660	220

Figure 16-6 Sample of LKO Packaging Products

SITUATION 16.4

Continued

changes decrease. An operator-paced line flow production system is used.

- During the maturity and saturation stages, volume is high, and price and contribution are low. However, total contribution is high because the volume is high, and an efficient equipment-paced line flow production system is used.
- During the decline stage, volume, price, and contribution all drop. Products are at least ten years old, and LKO uses its batch flow production system.

This pattern is common in many companies.

SITUATION 16.5

Product Life Cycles at Texas Instruments and Hewlett-Packard[2]

TEXAS INSTRUMENTS (TI) and Hewlett-Packard (HP) are companies whose manufacturing strategies in the early 1980s depended on the product life cycle.

TI was most comfortable when its market qualifying outputs were cost, quality, and delivery. As soon as TI developed a new product, it quickly moved toward line flow and continuous flow production systems where it was easy to provide high levels of these outputs (Figure 16-7 [A]). Cost was the order winning output, so TI made improvements and sought the benefits of experience. Cost reductions led to more orders and higher volume, which was needed to fully utilize the line flow and continuous flow production systems.

HP was most comfortable when its market qualifying outputs were performance, flexibility, and innovativeness. Consequently, HP liked to develop new products and keep them until they reached the maturity stage of their product life cycles (Figure 16-7 [B]). HP sought niche markets where customers wanted specialized products, but exited when its products matured and the basis of competition changed to cost. Experience effects at HP were less than TI because volumes at HP never reached the high levels reached at TI (Figure 16-8).

HP manufacturing managers were pioneers in the United States with the JIT production system. Two reasons for this were:

- HP produced many products in low to medium volumes, and JIT was a good production system for this mix.
- Whereas HP corporate strategy emphasized performance, flexibility, and innovativeness, manufacturing managers were evaluated on the basis of cost, quality, and delivery. The JIT production system was the only production system that could provide high levels of all these outputs.

TI, on the other hand, was less interested in the JIT production system. It used traditional line flow and continuous flow production systems, which provided the highest possible levels of the outputs important to TI: cost, quality, and delivery.

Figures 16-7 and 16-8 describe HP's strategy in the early 1980s. The strategy changed in the early 1990s. HP changed its international manufacturing network to a global mixed network (Situation 12.2 in Chapter 12). This enabled HP to use offshore and source factories to manufacture products during the maturity, saturation, and decline stages of the product life cycle.

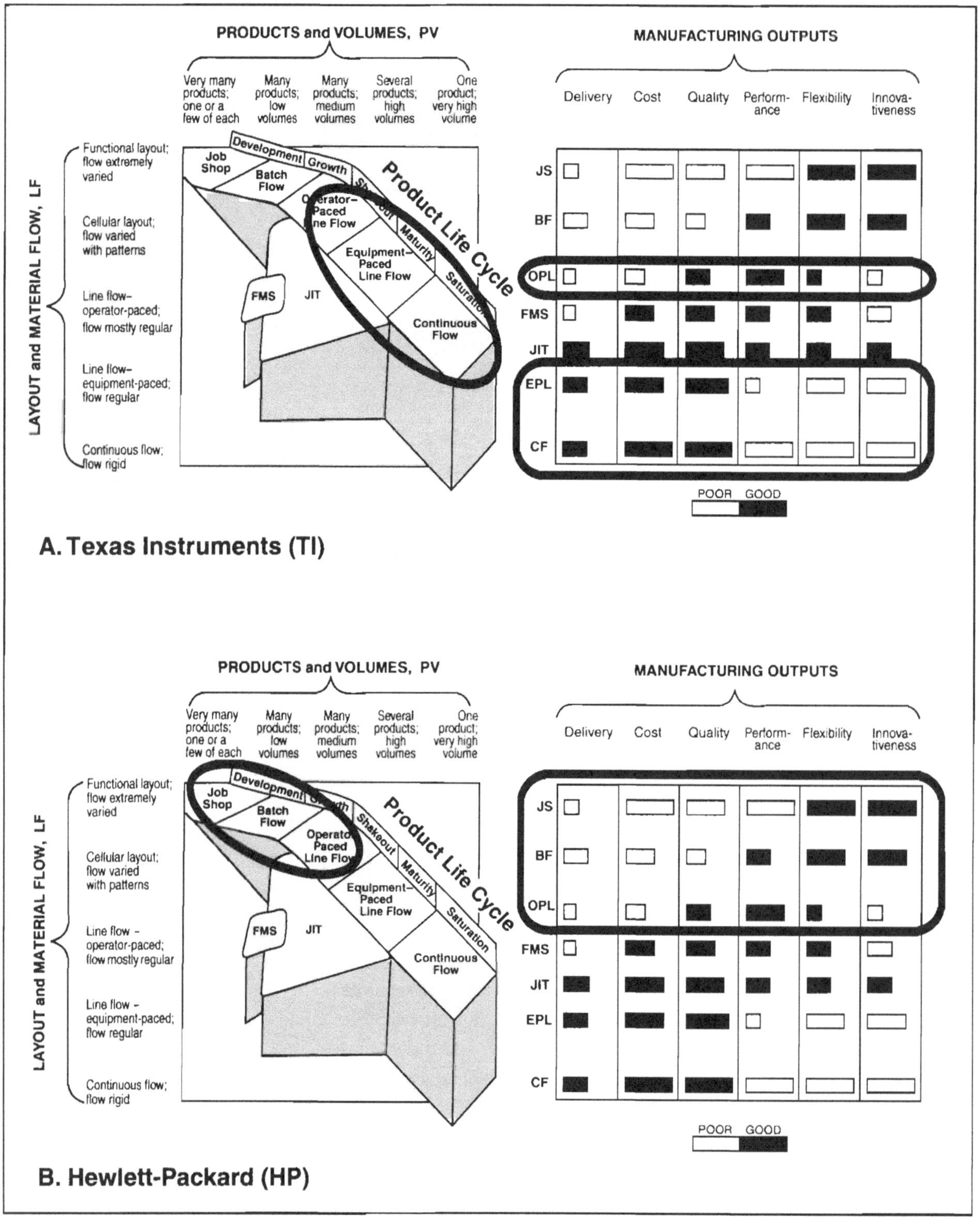

Figure 16-7 Product Life Cycle and Manufacturing Strategy at TI and HP

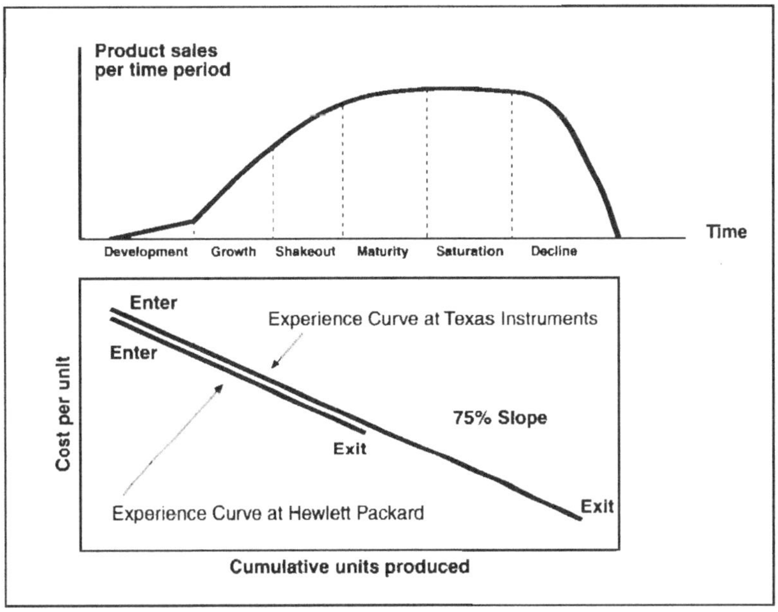

Figure 16-8 Benefits of Experience at TI and HP

International Manufacturing Networks

Companies with international manufacturing networks (Chapter 10) produce products in different domestic and foreign factories during different stages of the product life cycle.

Changing product design, changing production volumes, and increasing manufacturing capability characterize the first three stages of the product life cycle for many products. During the development stage, product design rapidly changes in response to evolving customer needs. In the growth stage, demand rapidly increases as a product wins new customers. Product features desired by customers become known and design stabilizes. During the shakeout stage, markets become more competitive, and standard designs and features emerge.

During the first three stages of the product life cycle, the most important network manufacturing output is learning (about customer needs and about product and process technology). When a company uses a simple manufacturing network (domestic, domestic export, international, multidomestic), production is at the home base facility (Chapter 12) for these three stages of the life cycle because the production group and the design group must work together to solve the numerous production and design problems common for new products.

When a company uses a complex manufacturing network (global, multinational, transnational), production is at a lead facility (Chapter 12) for the first three stages of the life cycle. A lead facility is a special facility with high levels of capability in production and design, and can take new products through these stages of the life cycle.

The maturity stage begins with the emergence of a standard design for the product. Demand is high and steady during the maturity stage and the saturation stage. Competition increases, and the basis of competition shifts from product features (performance) and flexibility to price. Cost and quality are the most important outputs for the production system and thriftiness and mobility are the most important outputs for the manufacturing network. When a company uses a domestic or domestic export network, automation and cost reduction programs are used to reduce product cost. When a company uses one of the other manufacturing networks, production is transferred to a low cost foreign factory (Chapter 12).

During the decline stage of the product life cycle, demand for the product rapidly decreases. Production volume too low to utilize the production system used during the maturity stage is transferred to a flexible, low volume production system. Mobility is the most important manufacturing network output.

Some companies develop new products and manufacture them only in the development, growth, and shakeout stages. HP in the early 1980s is an example (Situation 16.5). These companies drop out when products reach the maturity stage and the basis of competition switches to price. Simple manufacturing networks are satisfactory for these companies. Other companies produce a product during all stages of the life cycle. TI in Situation 16.5 is an example. These companies need complex networks so they can transfer production between domestic and foreign factories and between high capability and low capability factories during different stages of the life cycle. HP in the 1990s is another example (Situation 12.3).

Summary

Experience is the theoretical foundation for continuous improvement. A company gains experience when it produces more and more units of a product. Experience leads to learning. Learning leads to improvements in products, manufacturing networks, and production systems. Improvements raise the levels of network and factory capabilities, which raise the levels of network and factory manufacturing outputs. Higher levels of outputs increase customer satisfaction. These are the benefits of experience.

The benefits of experience do not come automatically. A company uses formal systems to realize the benefits of experience. It seeks improvements by focusing manufacturing, using improvement programs, and investing in people and processes.

The benefits of experience are shown on a graph called the experience curve. The cost to manufacture a product is plotted against total production volume at different points in time. When cost is difficult to estimate, price is substituted. The graph shows that product cost decreases over time as the production volume increases. The rate of decrease is called the slope of the experience curve.

Experience and the benefits of experience change as products move through their product life cycle stages. The product life cycle has six stages: development, growth, shakeout, maturity, saturation, and decline. The length of a stage, the sales at a stage, and the overall length of the life cycle, vary among products and depend on factors such as customer preferences, the amount of competition, and the rate of technological change in products and processes. The best production system for a product differs at different stages of the product life cycle.

A company with an international manufacturing network produces products in different home base, domestic, and foreign factories during different stages of the product life cycle.

Endnotes

1. Adapted from Magaziner, I., and Patinkin, M., "Fast Heat: How Korea Won the Microwave War," *Harvard Business Review*, January–February, 1989.
2. Adapted from Wheelwright, S., "Strategy, Management, and Strategic Planning Approaches," *Interfaces*, Vol. 14, No. 1, pp. 19–33, 1984.

CHAPTER 17

EVALUATION OF INVESTMENTS IN MANUFACTURING

The capital appropriation process can frustrate manufacturing managers and financial managers. Manufacturing managers cannot convince financial managers that their proposals for investments in manufacturing are financially sound, and financial managers cannot convince manufacturing managers that rejection of their proposals is in the best long-term interests of the company. Situation 17.1 is typical of the frustration that can surround this process.

This chapter reviews the criteria used to assess proposed investments in manufacturing. There are six interrelated criteria, three strategic and three economic. Figure 17-1 shows the criteria and the sequence in which they are checked.

Assessing Strategic and Economic Criteria

Strategic criteria assess whether the proposed investment is consistent with the business strategy and the manufacturing strategy. Three strategic criteria check elements of these strategies. Some criteria check the fit between the proposed investment and elements on the factory and network manufacturing strategy worksheets (Figures 1-1 and 1-2).

Situation 17.1

Redirecting Investment from Inventory to Process Equipment

A MANUFACTURING MANAGER at a Fortune 500 company had the following complaint.

"I can take $750,000 out of this region's inventory and maintain customer service levels by spending $500,000 to upgrade a production process with new equipment. Common sense tells me this is a good investment. The company saves $250,000 and gets a better production process. All this can be done in one year. But the financial people will not give me any money. They say the project has a four-year payback."

Is the manufacturing manager right? This question is answered at the end of the chapter.

Criterion Type	Sequence	Criterion Description

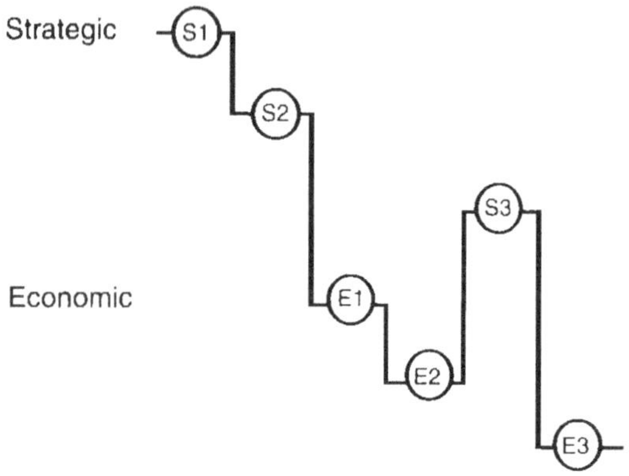

S1 – Is the investment appropriate for the business strategy?
Is the investment appropriate for the international manufacturing strategy?
Is the investment appropriate for the production system?

S2 – How will the investment affect the market qualifying and order winning outputs and the network outputs?

S3 – What effect will the investment have on each manufacturing lever? Is there sufficient manufacturing capability to make the required adjustments to each lever?

E1 – How safe is the investment?

E2 – How profitable is the investment?

E3 – How robust is the investment?

Outcome	Action
A criterion is not satisfied.	Reject the proposed investment. If appropriate change the proposal and restart the process.
All criteria are satisfied.	Undertake the proposed investment.

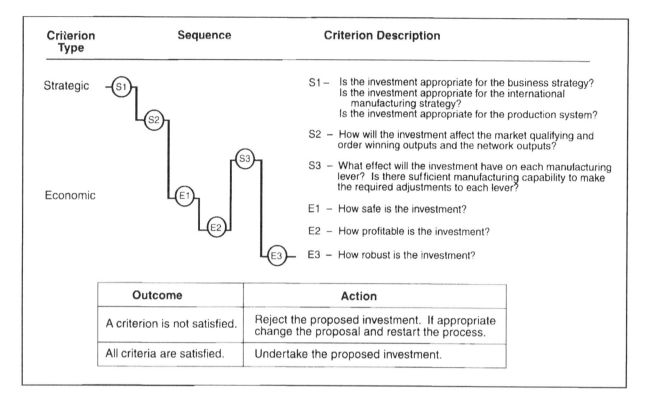

Figure 17-1 Assessment Process for Evaluating Investments in Manufacturing

Three economic criteria assess the financial benefits of the proposed investment. They account for benefits that are realized in the future, and so are not known with certainty.

The assessment process stops when a proposed investment fails to satisfy a criterion. In this case, the proposed investment is rejected. If all six criteria are satisfied, the proposal is accepted. When a proposal is rejected, insights developed during the assessment process can be used to develop a new and better proposal.

Step 1: Strategic Criterion 1

The first criterion is an assessment of a proposed investment's fit with a company's business strategy, international manufacturing strategy, and factory manufacturing strategy. The criterion is assessed by asking three questions.

Is the Investment Appropriate for the Business Strategy?

A company's business strategy (Chapter 13) is the plan used to establish a market position, conduct operations, attract and satisfy customers, compete successfully, and achieve its goals. How successfully a company executes this plan determines the company's profitability. Proposed investments in manufacturing must fit with, and contribute to, a company's business strategy. Proposed investments should help a company execute business strategy.

The elements of business strategy are goals, product-market domain, and basis of competitive advantage. Proposed investments in manufacturing should help a company achieve its goals. For example, market share, volume growth, and long-term profits are important goals in many German and Japanese companies. These companies assess proposed investments in manufacturing for their ability to increase market share and volume and generate long-term profits.

A company has competitive advantage when it has an edge over competitors in attracting customers and defending itself against challenges. There are many sources of competitive advantage. A company's business strategy specifies which sources the company will emphasize. Proposed investments in manufacturing should help a company develop and sustain its sources of competitive advantage.

Each investment in manufacturing is related to every other investment in manufacturing because all investments in manufacturing fit within a company's business strategy. Therefore, proposed investments in manufacturing should not be treated as unrelated, stand-alone investments. Situation 17.2 gives an example of what can happen when they are treated this way.

Is the Investment Appropriate for the International Manufacturing Strategy?

A company with international operations follows a particular international manufacturing strategy, uses a particular manufacturing network, and assigns roles called factory-types to its factories (Chapters 10, 11, 12). Proposed investments in manufacturing must be consistent with this international

End of Year	Cash Out-flows Capital Costs	Cash In-flows Government Incentives	Contribution from New Sales	Operating Cost Savings	Total	Cumulative
Small Factory						
0	$10,000,000	—	—	—	—	—
1	—	$3,000,000	$2,000,000	$50,000	$5,050,000	$5,050,000
2	—	1,000,000	2,000,000	50,000	3,050,000	8,100,000
3	—	1,000,000	2,000,000	—	3,000,000	11,100,000
4	—	—	2,000,000	—	2,000,000	13,100,000
...	—	—	2,000,000	—	2,000,000	15,100,000
Large Factory						
0	$38,000,000	—	—	—	—	—
1	—	$5,000,000	$2,000,000	$50,000	7,050,000	7,050,000
2	—	$2,000,000	4,000,000	100,000	6,100,000	13,150,000
3	—	1,000,000	6,000,000	100,000	7,100,000	20,250,000
4	—	—	8,000,000	100,000	8,100,000	28,350,000
5	—	—	10,000,000	100,000	10,100,000	38,450,000
6	—	—	10,000,000	50,000	10,050,000	48,500,000
7	—	—	10,000,000	—	10,000,000	58,500,000
...	—	—	10,000,000	—	10,000,000	68,500,000

Note:
To keep this example simple, we do not consider the effect of taxes on cash flows. When taxes are considered, cash flows become after-tax cash flows. Situation 17.7 (Figure 17-3) considers taxes and therefore is a more exact analysis.

Figure 17-2 Costs and Savings in Situation 17.2

SITUATION 17.2

Adding Capacity in a Piecemeal Way

A COMPANY COMPETING on the basis of low cost and fast delivery needed to increase production capacity to meet a projected increase in sales in each of the next five years. Two proposed investments in manufacturing capacity were under consideration. The first was to build a small factory with enough capacity to satisfy requirements for one year. The second was to build a large factory with enough capacity to satisfy requirements for five years. Figure 17-2 gives cash in-flows and out-flows for the two proposals.

The small factory has a cost of $10 million. Government incentives in years 1, 2, and 3 total $5 million. Contribution from new sales is $2 million per year. Operating cost savings is $50,000 per year in years 1 and 2. The total cash in-flow in year 1 is $5,050,000. The cumulative cash in-flow in years 1 and 2 is $8,100,000. Then, the payback period is 2½ years. This is the time when the total cash in-flow equals the total cash out-flow. In other words, the company will recover its $10 million investment in 2½ years. Figure 17-2 shows that the proposal to build a large factory has a payback of 5 years. The company chose to build the small factory because the shorter payback period was very attractive to the comptroller and the company's banker.

One year later, the company needed to increase capacity again. Since, the cash flows were similar to the previous year, the company chose to build another small factory. One year later, the company built its third small factory, and before long the company had five small factories.

Shortly afterward, the company realized there was excessive duplication of activities in the five factories. In addition, the cost to handle and transport material between factories was high, and scheduling and control were difficult. In hindsight, the company wished it had built one large factory.

The company's mistake was failing to realize that investments in manufacturing are related to each other and to the business strategy. A small factory is an attractive investment when it is treated as a stand-alone investment and unattractive when treated as one investment in a sequence of many. Small stand-alone factories were not consistent with the company's business strategy. One large factory, organized into focused factories-within-a-factory, was consistent. The company should have rejected the initial proposal to build a small factory because it did not satisfy strategic criterion 1; the investment was inappropriate for the business strategy.

manufacturing strategy and must not pull the company, network, or factories in unintended directions (Situation 17.3).

Domestic and foreign governments sometimes offer land, tax breaks, assistance in hiring and training employees, and other handouts to persuade international companies to take over ailing businesses or locate factories in distressed areas. Companies that do not have clear business strategies or assess proposals using only economic criteria sometimes make poor business decisions by accepting these offers.

Is the Investment Appropriate for the Production System?

Manufacturers have access to many soft and hard technologies. None should be considered until after manufacturing has been focused (Chapter 15). Then, those appropriate for the production system in use are considered.

The amount of new technology should also be assessed. This assessment considers whether a company is a technology leader or a technology follower. Companies with capability at or above the adult level can be technology leaders, whereas companies with capability near the industry average level are technology followers. Technology followers should not adopt new technologies until others have adopted them, and the benefits are well known.

Some proposed investments are for equipment to produce new products. These proposals often mistakenly do not consider all stages of the product life cycle: development, growth, shakeout, maturity, saturation, and decline (Chapter 16). Some only consider high volume production during the maturity and saturation stages. By overlooking the investment needed during other stages, proposals can force a factory to use inflexible, high-volume equipment when flexible, low-volume equipment is needed. This makes it difficult to

SITUATION 17.3

Investment to Change a Server Factory

AN INTERNATIONAL COMPANY was reviewing a proposal from an overseas factory. The overseas factory manufactured a wide range of electrical cables. The factory purchased connectors, plastic, wire, and raw materials from other company factories and from external suppliers. The factory sold its products to other company factories and to external customers.

The proposal was for the factory to increase vertical integration by integrating backward into production of wire. The factory requested money to purchase wire drawing equipment so that it could produce its own wire. This would reduce cost and delivery time and improve manufacturing capability. It would also increase profits and position the factory to make a larger strategic contribution to the company. The payback period for the proposal was three years.

However, the factory was a server factory in the company's multinational manufacturing network. The company already had a lead factory for wire drawing and cable manufacturing. The company decided that its international manufacturing strategy was best served by having the overseas factory remain a server factory. The proposal was rejected.

provide market qualifying and order winning outputs at each stage of the product life cycle.

Step 2: Strategic Criterion 2

How Will the Investment Affect the Market Qualifying and Order Winning Outputs and the Network Outputs?

The proposed investment is assessed for its ability to close the gap between current and target levels of factory manufacturing outputs (cost, quality, performance, delivery, flexibility, and innovativeness) and network manufacturing outputs (accessibility, thriftiness, mobility, and learning). The proposed investment can be accepted if it helps manufacturing meet its targets. It should not be accepted if it provides unneeded outputs.

Step 3: Economic Criterion 1

How Safe Is the Investment?

This step is the first economic check.[1] It assesses the effect of uncertainties external to the proposed investment. For example, what if new opportunities appear in the future that are more attractive than the proposed investment, or what if problems develop that change a currently attractive investment into an unattractive investment? It is customary to assume that the longer it takes for an investment in manufacturing to start generating a profit, the greater the risk posed by external uncertainties.

The payback period is a measure of this risk. It is the time required for an investment to return earnings equal to the cost of the investment. The shorter the payback period, the sooner the company

SITUATION 17.4

Welding Machine Producer Considers Two Improvement Projects

A WELDING MACHINE MANUFACTURER produced many different products in medium volumes on an operator-paced line flow production system. Cost was the market qualifying output and quality was the order winning output.

The company was considering two proposals, only one of which could be accepted.

- The engineering department wanted to upgrade an old CAD system to a modern CAD/CAM system. The new system would reduce the time to prepare drawings and CNC programs and help the department standardize designs and reduce the number of part numbers. The investment would shorten delivery time and reduce cost.
- The production department wanted to replace an old, manual punch press with a new CNC machine with automated material handling. The investment would reduce cost and increase quality.

The company rejected the first proposal because it did not satisfy strategic criterion 2. The investment would improve delivery time, but delivery was not a market qualifying or order winning output.

The second proposal satisfied strategic criterion 2. The CNC press with automated material handling would help the company provide market qualifying and order winning levels of cost and quality.

A FACTORY THAT PRODUCED plastic packaging materials wanted to upgrade the equipment in its operator-paced line flow production system. A proposed investment for new equipment requested $16 million and had a payback of 5½ years. The factory produced many make-to-order products in medium volumes. Delivery was the market qualifying output, and performance was the order winning output.

The international company that owned the factory required a payback of less than four years for all investments in manufacturing equipment. The company calculated that the factory needed to increase production volume by 50 percent to get its payback close to the four year target. The factory agreed to increase volume, and the $16 million proposal was approved.

Numerous changes were made to win new orders. The factory standardized many products, cut prices, and produced standard products for stock. While this generated more orders, it also generated problems. Delivery time slipped due to difficulties in scheduling standard, high volume products with nonstandard, medium volume products. Profit margins shrank because the low prices on standard products barely covered their cost of production. More changes were planned to correct these problems.

The result of all the changes was a change in production system and manufacturing strategy. The operator-paced line flow production system changed to an equipment-paced line flow production system, and the order winning output changed from performance to cost. This happened without the factory ever making an explicit decision to change its manufacturing strategy.

The investment proposal should not have been approved. It did not satisfy strategic criterion 2 because it produced unneeded manufacturing outputs.

SITUATION 17.5

Factory Accidentally Changes Production System and Strategy

ABC WAS A SMALL MANUFACTURER of machine controls for the dairy industry. The ABC factory fabricated components in a batch flow production system and assembled finished products in an operator-paced line flow production system. ABC had just rejected a $2 million proposal from its materials department to upgrade the company's aging MRP system.

ABC's products were changing from electromechanical devices to predominately electronic devices. In the past, ABC produced in-house about 80 percent of the components used in

SITUATION 17.6

Manufacturer Misses Chance to Improve Outputs

SITUATION 17.6

Continued

its electromechanical products. Now, it purchased about 80 percent of the components used in its electronic products. Each electronic product used components from several suppliers, and if any component was unavailable, production of the product was delayed. When a late component finally arrived, ABC worked overtime to catch up and meet delivery promises. A recent study showed that 40 percent of products were delayed because purchased components arrived late.

ABC needed to reorganize its supplier processes because of the change in products from electromechanical devices to predominantly electronic devices and the accompanying increase in importance of purchased components. Although ABC did not realize it, a modern MRP system was necessary to properly manage supplier processes. ABC's old MRP system was good at controlling complex internal fabrication and assembly operations, and managing work-in-process inventory. However, it was not good at introducing new products, scheduling and monitoring suppliers, and managing purchased components inventory.

ABC should have accepted the proposal to upgrade the old MRP system. Changing the MRP system would force ABC to scrutinize and improve its supplier processes. This is the only way ABC can provide its market qualifying and order winning outputs.

will recover its money. The shorter the payback period, the sooner the company can invest its money in other projects.

Most companies require that the payback period for an investment be less than a specified maximum period. The maximum period depends on the type of investment, the scarcity of funds, and the rate of change of products and processes in the industry. For example, in the early 1980s, most companies in the semiconductor industry required paybacks of less than two years for investments in manufacturing equipment. Companies were growing rapidly, investment funds were in short supply, and the rate of change of products and processes was high. In the late 1970s, many companies in the automotive industry accepted paybacks of up to five years on investments in energy conservation projects. This lengthy payback period reflected the feeling that energy prices would remain high, so these projects would remain attractive regardless of external uncertainties.

STEP 4: ECONOMIC CRITERION 2

How Profitable Is the Investment?

The second economic criterion assesses the ability of the proposed investment to generate profits. An investment is profitable when the net cash flows it generates exceed the cost of the investment. Three measures of profitability are return on investment, internal rate of return, and net present value.

Return on investment (ROI) is calculated from:

$$\text{ROI} = \frac{\text{Average annual net cash flow}}{\text{Initial investment}}$$

A shortcoming of ROI is that it does not consider timing of cash flows. Obviously, the sooner positive cash flows are received, the better. Internal rate of return and net present value remedy this shortcoming.

Internal rate of return (IRR) is the discount rate that equates the present value of the stream of cash flows with the initial investment. Net present value (NPV) is a current dollar amount equivalent to the stream of cash flows. NPV discounts the value of future cash flows to reflect the time value of money. NPV uses a discount rate that has three properties:

- It is the rate of return required for an investment with a particular amount of risk.
- It is the rate of return a company could expect to receive elsewhere for an investment of comparable risk.
- It exceeds the company cost of investment funds.

Regardless of which measure of profitability is used, companies require that the profitability of a proposed investment exceeds a minimum value. The minimum value depends on the profitability of other investments that are available to the company.

SITUATION 17.7

Stamping Plant Assesses Investment in New Equipment

A STAMPING PLANT uses a batch flow production system to produce metal stampings for its automotive customers. The plant wanted to replace an old press with a modern high speed press. An attractive feature of the new press was its ability to do fast setups, which was important because the plant produced many different products in low volumes. The new press cost $450,000 and had an economic life of ten years. It was expected to reduce operating cost by $80,000 per year and increase contribution to overhead and profit by $40,000 per year.

The press would be depreciated over five years. The plant had a tax rate of 40 percent. The discount rate was 12 percent, which comprised an 8 percent risk-free rate and a 4 percent adjustment to reflect the risk for this type of investment.

The proposed investment satisfied strategic criteria 1 and 2. The next step was to check economic criterion 1.

ECONOMIC CRITERION 1: HOW SAFE IS THE INVESTMENT?

Figure 17-3 shows the after-tax cash flow for the proposed investment. The sum of the after-tax cash flows is $432,000 for the first four years and $540,000 for the first five years. The cost of the investment is $450,000. This is between $432,000 and $450,000. The payback period calculates at 4.2 years. If this payback exceeds the maximum payback period, the proposal is rejected, and the assessment process stops. Otherwise, the investment is assessed to be safe, and the assessment process continues to the next step.

SITUATION 17.7

Continued

ECONOMIC CRITERION 2: HOW PROFITABLE IS THE INVESTMENT?

Return on investment is:
ROI = 90,000 / 450,000 = 20 percent

Internal rate of return is calculated from:

$$450{,}000 = 108{,}000/(1 + IRR) + 108{,}000/(1 + IRR)^2 + \ldots + 108{,}000/(1 + IRR)^5 + 72{,}000/(1 + IRR)^6 + 72{,}000/(1 + IRR)^7 + \ldots + 72{,}000/(1 + IRR)^{10}$$

This gives IRR = 17 percent.

Net present value with a 12 percent discount rate is:

$$NPV = -450{,}000 + 108{,}000/(1 + 0.12) + 108{,}000/(1 + 0.12)^2 + \ldots + 108{,}000/(1 + 0.12)^5 + 72{,}000/(1 + 0.12)^6 + 72{,}000/(1 + 0.12)^7 + \ldots + 72{,}000/(1 + 0.12)^{10}$$

NPV = $86,588

These profitability values (ROI = 20 percent, IRR = 17 percent, and NPV = $86,588) are average and should satisfy this company's minimum requirement for profitability.

End of Year	Capital Cost	Depreciation[1]	Operating Cost Savings[2]	Contribution to Overhead and Profit[3]	After-Tax Cash Flow[4]
0	$450,000	—	—	—	—
1	—	$90,000	$80,000	$40,000	$108,000
2	—	90,000	80,000	40,000	108,000
3	—	90,000	80,000	40,000	108,000
4	—	90,000	80,000	40,000	108,000
5	—	90,000	80,000	40,000	108,000
6	—	—	80,000	40,000	72,000
7	—	—	80,000	40,000	72,000
8	—	—	80,000	40,000	72,000
9	—	—	80,000	40,000	72,000
10	—	—	80,000	40,000	72,000
					Average = $90,000

Notes:

1. In each of the first five years, there is $90,000 of depreciation. This reduces taxes by $90,000 × 40% = $36,000.
2. In each of the ten years, there is a savings in operating cost of $80,000. Forty percent of this savings will be paid in taxes, leaving an after-tax cash flow of $80,000 ×(1.0 – .4) = $48,000.
3. In each of the ten years, there is an additional contribution to overhead and profit of $40,000 because of reduced scrap, increased production due to lower setup times, and so on. 40 percent of this contribution will be paid in taxes, leaving an after-tax cash flow of $40,000 ×(1.0 – .4) = $24,000.
4. The after-tax cash flow is the sum of the after-tax saving due to depreciation, the after-tax operating cost saving, and the after-tax contribution to overhead and profit. In year 1, this is $36,000 + $48,000 + $24,000 = $108,000.

Figure 17-3 After-Tax Cash Flows in Situation 17.7

STEP 5: STRATEGIC CRITERION 3

What Effect Will the Investment Have on Each Manufacturing Lever? Is There Sufficient Manufacturing Capability to Make the Required Adjustments to Each Lever?

This step examines the adjustments to manufacturing levers (in the production system and in the manufacturing network) needed to implement the proposed investment. This step also assesses the company's ability to make these adjustments. A company with a high level of manufacturing capability can better make difficult adjustments for difficult investments than a company with a low level of capability.

This step also assesses the proposed investment in light of a company's track record for implementing investments in manufacturing. One measure in this track record is the fraction of potential benefits a company has realized from past investments in manufacturing. To document the track record, a company must have a process for completing post-audits of accepted proposals for investments in manufacturing. Investment proposals outline tasks to be done and benefits that will be gained. Post-audits check the important tasks and benefits in these proposals after the investments are completed to determine what tasks have been completed and what benefits have been realized.

Post-audits establish track records that verify the reliability of proposal writers and provide useful information for assessing future proposals. When post-audits are not done, proposal writers are tempted to exaggerate benefits and downplay costs to help their proposals get accepted.

STEP 6: ECONOMIC CRITERION 3

How Robust Is the Investment?

The final step in the assessment process is a sensitivity analysis to determine how sensitive the profitability of the proposed investment is to uncertainty in the important variables. Examples of important variables are costs, the life of the investment, and the size and timing of cash flows. Uncertainty that, when resolved, produces lower costs and larger, earlier cash flows is not a problem. A problem is uncertainty that may result in an investment that is not safe (economic criterion 1) or profitable (economic criterion 2).

Three values—optimistic, most likely, and pessimistic—are estimated for each important variable. The probability that each value will occur is also estimated. Then, a measure of profitability, such as NPV, is calculated for these data, and results are displayed on a graph. This is a straightforward task when modern spreadsheet software is used.

SITUATION 17.7

Continued

THE PROPOSED INVESTMENT passed the first five steps. Now step 6 is undertaken. Management realizes that the estimated operating cost savings and the contribution to overhead and profit are uncertain. A sensitivity analysis will determine how changes in the values of these variables affect the proposed investment's profitability.

Figure 17-4 (A) shows estimates for optimistic, most likely, and pessimistic values of the operating cost savings and the contribution to overhead and profit. An NPV is calculated for each combination of savings and contribution. Since nine combinations exist, part B of the figure shows nine NPVs. Each NPV has a particular probability of occurrence. For example, if the optimistic annual savings of $90,000 occurs and the most likely annual contribution of

SITUATION 17.7

Continued

$40,000 occurs, the NPV is $120,489. The probability that this will occur is 0.2 × 0.5 = 0.1.

Figure 17-4 (C) shows the distribution of NPV values and probabilities. This graph quantifies the investment's robustness. The largest possible loss is $82,919. The probability that the investment will produce a loss is the probability that the NPV is less than zero, which is 0.2. The probability that NPV will meet or exceed $86,588, the value calculated earlier under economic criterion 2, is 1 – .32 = .68. The probability of high profitability, such as NPV greater than $100,000, is 1 – .66 = .34. The largest possible profit is $137,440.

Management uses this graph to assess how sensitive profitability is to changes in the values of the important variables. The proposed investment is judged to be robust because there is only a small probability of a loss and a high probability of a profit above $86,588, the NPV from economic criterion 2. The proposed investment is accepted.

SITUATION 17.1

Continued

SITUATION 17.1, at the beginning of this chapter, described a manufacturing manager who proposed to improve a production process using funds freed up by inventory reduction. Figure 17-5 shows the cash flow for the proposed investment.

The new equipment has a capital cost of $500,000 and an economic life of eight years. The equipment is depreciated at the rate of $100,000 per year for five years. The company has a 40 percent tax rate, producing a tax savings of $100,000 × 0.4 = $40,000 per year for five years.

The company's cost of carrying inventory is 20 percent per year. This is the cost of capital, insurance, obsolescence, and other expenses incurred as a result of carrying inventory. Reducing inventories by $750,000 produces a cash saving of $750,000 × 0.2 = $150,000 per year. The after-tax cash flow is $150,000 × (1 – 0.4) = $90,000 per year.

In addition, $20,000 per year is required for two years to train maintenance personnel and purchase spare parts. The after-tax cash flow is -$20,000 × (1 – 0.4) = -$12,000 per year for two years.

STEP 1: IS THE INVESTMENT APPROPRIATE FOR THE BUSINESS STRATEGY?

The company produces low-cost consumer products and keeps large inventories because it must provide high service levels. Large inventories also allow products to ship in full truckloads, which reduces transportation cost. The marketing manager and the distribution

Variable		Optimistic	Most Likely	Pessimistic
Operating cost savings	Value Probability	$90,000 .2	$80,000 .6	$40,000 .2
Contribution to overhead and profit	Value Probability	$45,000 .3	$40,000 .5	$30,000 .2

A. Estimates for the Important Uncertain Variables

Combination		1	2	3	4	5	6	7	8	9
Operating cost savings	Value[1] Probability	$90 .2	90 .2	90 .2	80 .6	80 .6	80 .6	40 .2	40 .2	40 .2
Contribution to overhead and profit	Value Probability	$45 .3	40 .5	30 .2	45 .3	40 .5	30 .2	45 .3	40 .5	30 .2
Net present value,[2] (NPV)	Value Probability	$137 .06	120 .10	87 .04	104 .18	87 .30	53 .12	-32 .06	-49 .10	-83 .04

1. Values are in thousands of dollars.
2. Discount rate is 12 percent.

B. All Possible Values of Net Present Value

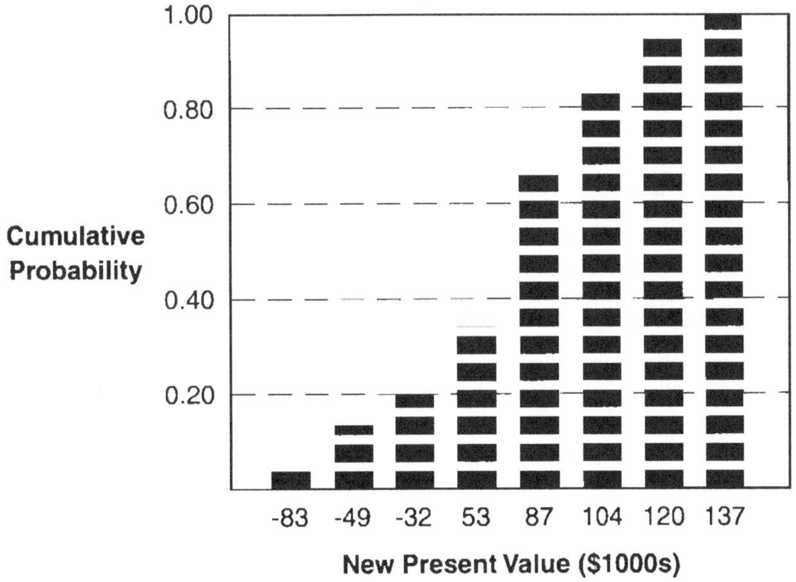

C. Net Present Values and Probabilities of Occurrence

Figure 17-4 Sensitivity Analysis to Assess Economic Criterion 3 in Situation 17.7

End of Year	Capital Cost	Depreciation	Inventory Cost Savings	Training and Spare Parts	After-Tax Cash Flow[1]
0	$500,000	—	—	—	—
1	—	$100,000	$150,000	−$20,000	$118,000
2	—	100,000	150,000	−20,000	118,000
3	—	100,000	150,000		130,000
4	—	100,000	150,000		130,000
5	—	100,000	150,000		130,000
6	—	—	150,000		90,000
7	—	—	150,000		90,000
8	—	—	150,000		90,000
					Average = $112,000

Note:
The after-tax cash flow is the sum of the after-tax saving due to depreciation and the after-tax inventory cost saving, less the after-tax cost of training and spare parts. In year 1, this is 100,000 × .4 + 150,000 × (1 − .4) − 20,000 × (1 − .4) = $118,000.

Figure 17-5 After-Tax Cash Flows for Situation 17.1

SITUATION 17.1

Continued

manager want to increase, not decrease, inventory. The marketing manager thinks customer service will slip if inventory is reduced. The distribution manager worries that he will have to ship less than full truckloads if inventory is reduced.

Reducing inventory does not support this business strategy, so the proposed investment should be rejected. Although the assessment process would stop here, we will examine the other steps to see if we can learn more about this proposed investment.

Is the investment appropriate for the international manufacturing strategy?

The international manufacturing strategy is unaffected by the proposed investment.

Is the investment appropriate for the production system?

The production system is an equipment-paced line flow system. The equipment that will be purchased is appropriate for this production system.

STEP 2: HOW WILL THE INVESTMENT AFFECT THE MARKET QUALIFYING AND ORDER WINNING OUTPUTS?

Cost and quality are market qualifying outputs. Delivery is the order winning output. A large inventory is required to provide delivery at an order winning level. Taking $750,000 out of inventory could affect delivery time and delivery time reliability. It could also affect the company's ability to ship full truckloads, which would increase cost. The proposed investment could adversely affect the market qualifying and order winning outputs, so the proposal should be rejected.

STEP 3: HOW SAFE IS THE INVESTMENT?

The sum of the after-tax cash flows is $496,000 for the first four years (Figure 17-5). The cost of the investment is $500,000. The payback period calculates at 4.03 years. Since this is close to the company's maximum payback period, four years, the proposed investment is judged to be safe.

STEP 4: HOW PROFITABLE IS THE INVESTMENT?

The average cash flow is $112,000, and so ROI = 112,000/500,000 = 22 percent. IRR is calculated from:

$$500{,}000 = 118{,}000/(1 + IRR) + 118{,}000/(1 + IRR)^2 + \ldots + 130{,}000/(1 + IRR)^5 + 90{,}000/(1 + IRR)^6 + 90{,}000/(1 + IRR)^7 + 90{,}000/(1 + IRR)^8$$

This gives IRR = 16 percent. NPV is calculated from:

$$NPV = -500{,}000 + 118{,}000/(1 + 0.12) + 118{,}000/(1 + 0.12)^2 + \ldots + 130{,}000/(1 + 0.12)^5 + 90{,}000/(1 + 0.12)^6 + 90{,}000/(1 + 0.12)^7 + 90{,}000/(1 + 0.12)^8 = \$70{,}998$$

A discount rate of 12 percent is used in the NPV calculation.

ROI is good, IRR and NPV are average, and so the proposed investment is judged have average profitability.

STEP 5: WHAT EFFECT WILL THE INVESTMENT HAVE ON EACH MANUFACTURING LEVER? IS THERE SUFFICIENT MANUFACTURING CAPABILITY TO MAKE THE REQUIRED ADJUSTMENTS TO EACH LEVER?

New equipment is an adjustment to the process technology lever (Figure 1-1). Training is needed for operators and maintenance personnel, which is an adjustment to the human resources lever. An adjustment to the production planning and control lever is needed in the areas of scheduling and production lot sizes to ensure that delivery time and delivery reliability do not slip when inventory is reduced. Adjustments may also be needed to the sourcing lever.

These adjustments are not difficult, and the company has a high level of manufacturing capability. The company also has a good track record at implementing new technologies, so the proposed investment satisfies this criterion.

SITUATION 17.1

Continued

STEP 6: HOW ROBUST IS THE INVESTMENT?

The manager may be optimistic in his estimate of the amount of inventory that can be eliminated without affecting customer service. Suppose there is a 70 percent chance that inventory can be reduced by $750,000, and there is a 30 percent chance that inventory can be reduced by only $500,000. The resulting NPVs are: a 70 percent chance of $70,998 and a 30 percent chance of -$78,031. Therefore, there is a significant chance that the proposed investment will produce a large loss. The proposed investment is not robust, so the proposal should be rejected.

In summary, the proposed investment failed in Steps 1, 2, and 6. The investment is not appropriate for the business strategy. It does not support the market qualifying and order winning outputs. It is not robust. The proposed investment passed Steps 3, 4, and 5. The investment is safe. It has average profitability. The company has sufficient manufacturing capability to put the proposed investment into operation.

SUMMARY

Confusion and frustration often surround the process of evaluating investments in manufacturing. A systematic approach that takes account of strategic and economic concerns should be used. The approach presented in this chapter consists of a sequence of six checks or criteria: three strategic and three economic. The strategic criteria assess whether the proposed investment is consistent with business strategy and manufacturing strategy. The economic criteria assess the safety, profitability, and robustness of the proposed investment.

Safety, profitability, and robustness are well-known concerns in financial management. Measures exist for each, but no single measure combines all three. Many companies use payback period to measure safety, internal rate of return to measure profitability, and net present value to measure robustness.

ENDNOTES

1. Economic criteria 1 and 2 are adapted from Hayes, R., and Wheelwright, S., *Restoring Our Competitive Advantage: Competing Through Manufacturing,* New York: John Wiley & Sons, pp. 138–163, 1984.

Part VI

SEVEN PRODUCTION SYSTEMS FOR FOCUSED FACTORIES

CHAPTER 18

JOB SHOP PRODUCTION SYSTEM

Products and Volumes

Most companies have one or more focused factories organized as job shop production systems. These general-purpose facilities produce low volumes of a wide variety of different products (Figure 18-1). Once produced, the same product may not be produced again for a long time period, or it may never be produced again. Consequently, investment in specialized machines and tools is not justified.

Layout and Material Flow

In a job shop production system, departments and equipment are arranged in a functional layout (Chapter 4). That is, equipment and processes of the same type are located in the same department. Employees work in one department only and are highly skilled on its equipment. Because many different products are produced in low volumes, there is no possibility to specialize equipment and tooling, so equipment and tooling are general purpose. Most often, the material flow through the job shop differs for each job. Work-in-process inventory is high, and delivery times are long because material handling is always needed to move jobs considerable distances from department to department. Delivery times are also long because jobs sit idle in work-in-process inventory for long periods waiting for busy equipment and operators to become available.

Competitive Advantage

Machine shops, welding shops, specialty clothing manufacturers, specialty electronics manufacturing, upscale restaurants, custom bakeries, and small hospitals are well-known examples of job shop production systems. Each provides great product variety and caters to each customer's unique needs. A job shop production system is designed to provide high levels of flexibility and innovativeness, which it needs to satisfy customer demands for a wide variety of existing and new products.

A job shop production system provides relatively low levels of the other manufacturing outputs: cost, quality, performance, and delivery (Figure 18-1). This is not a disadvantage when competitors also use a job shop, but it is a disadvantage when a competitor can manufacture the

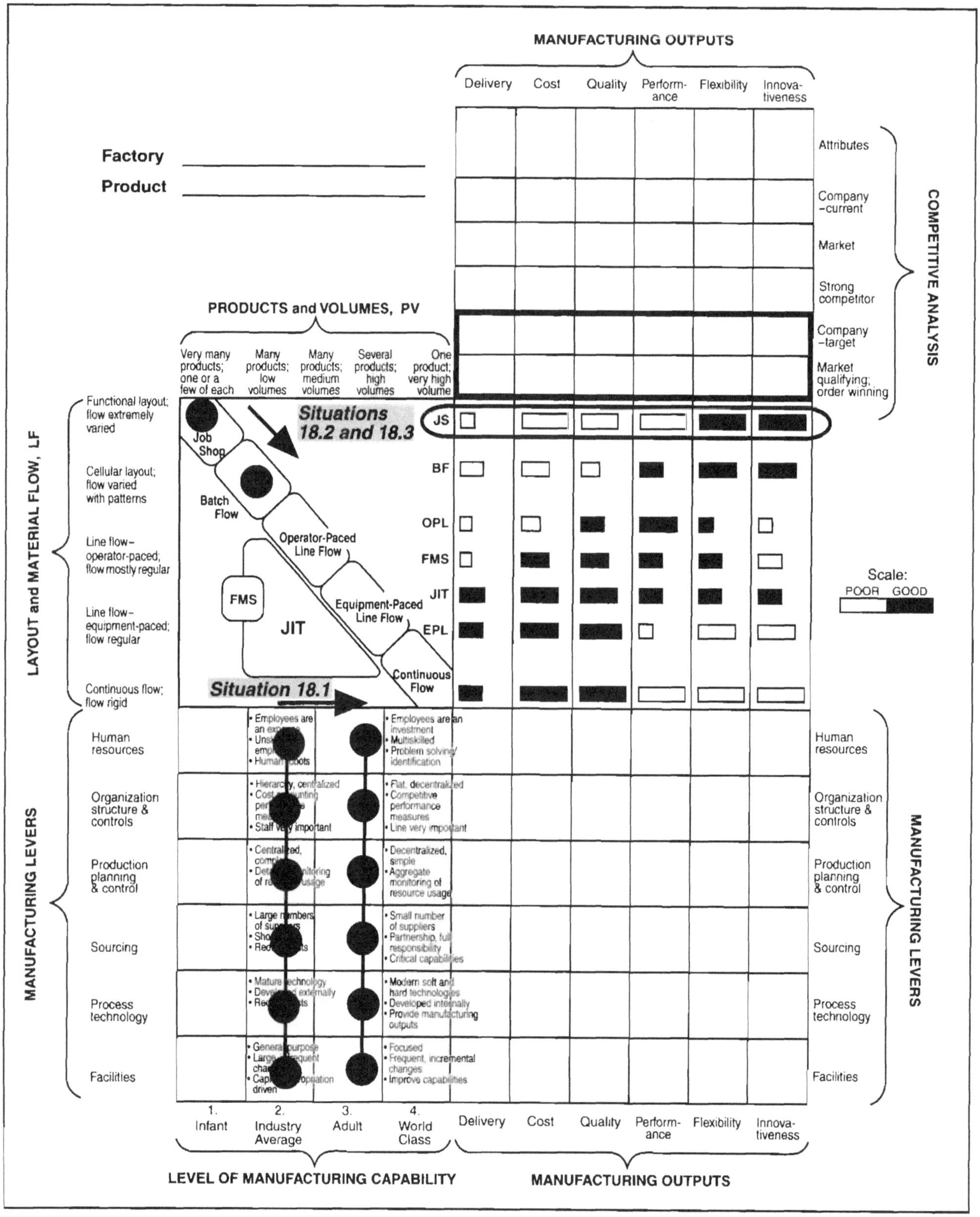

Figure 18-1 Job Shop Production System

same products on a line flow production system. In this situation, the levels of cost, quality, performance, and delivery provided by a job shop will be too low. The conventional wisdom is to use a job shop production system only in situations where volumes are too low and differences between products are too great to use batch flow or line flow systems.

Companies with job shop production systems that need to raise the levels of cost, quality, and delivery have two options:

- Raise the level of manufacturing capability of the job shop production system, which raises the level of all manufacturing outputs (Situations 18.1 and 18.2).
- Change the job shop production system to a batch flow, FMS, JIT, or operator-paced line flow production system (Situations 18.3 and 18.4).

MANUFACTURING LEVERS

HUMAN RESOURCES

Highly skilled employees operating general purpose machines are the most important resource in a job shop production system. The amount of in-house training is small because employees learn their skills in apprenticeship programs outside the company. Once trained, employees rarely need to improve their skills. Because it is difficult to find and keep highly skilled employees, wages are high relative to other production systems, and incentive pay schemes are used.

Staffs are small. They concentrate on bidding for new work, working with customers to finalize the designs of new products, and expediting orders through the factory.

ORGANIZATION STRUCTURE AND CONTROLS

Companies with job shop production systems have flat organization structures, organized by function. Staff departments are small and less important than line departments. Operations are decentralized and entrepreneurial for quick response to customers' unique needs.

Fixed costs such as buildings and equipment are low, and variable costs such as material and labor are high. Material and labor are tightly controlled. Equipment is often idle, but labor is used efficiently.

Line departments prefer to have a backlog of orders to remain busy. This improves labor and equipment utilization but increases work-in-process inventory and delivery time.

Quality is the responsibility of equipment operators and their immediate supervisors.

SITUATION 18.1

Quality Management Raises Level of Capability

IN JANUARY 1990, the Standard Aero Company of Winnipeg started an aggressive implementation of quality management (Chapter 14) to raise the industry average level of manufacturing capability in its job shop production system. Fifteen months later, the job shop's manufacturing capability improved so much that the company was on the short list for a $10 million contract to overhaul aircraft engine gearboxes for the U.S. military. The company's cost and delivery so exceeded its competitors that the Pentagon dispatched 13 officers to visit the company and investigate the bid. They were impressed with Standard Aero's capabilities, and the company was awarded the contract.

Sourcing

There is little vertical integration. Some purchased materials are stocked, but most are purchased for each customer order. Purchase orders are small and irregular, and many different suppliers are used. This makes the job shop a relatively unimportant customer of its suppliers. Consequently, a job shop production system has little control over suppliers.

Production Planning and Control

Orders are received through a competitive bidding process. Production is make-to-order. Raw material inventory and finished goods inventory are small, and work-in-process inventory is large.

Significant differences can exist between products, and products can be complex. A routing is developed for each product. The routing and a product drawing accompany each order or job through the factory.

Shop floor control consists of:

- Issuing dispatch lists to work centers listing the jobs to produce with the deadlines
- Using input-output control to monitor the flow of jobs and use of resources

Shop floor control is difficult. Expediting is used extensively to push important jobs through the factory. Scheduling employees is easy, but scheduling jobs is difficult. Overtime is used when extra capacity is needed.

Maintenance is relatively easy. Breakdowns are not as disruptive as in other production systems because each type of machine has multiple units. When one machine breaks down, production is moved to another machine. General purpose machines in the job shop are easier to maintain and repair than specialized, highly automated machines used by some other production systems. Maintenance departments develop considerable expertise in maintaining the multiple units of each type of machine.

Process Technology

There are no economies of scale in a job shop production system. Job shops are labor intensive and use flexible, general purpose machines. Machines tend to be older because technological change is slow. The job shop is a technology follower, not a technology leader. Setups are long because so many different products are produced. Run times are longer than they would be if specialized machines were used.

Frequent capacity imbalances exist between departments because the product mix on the factory floor changes frequently. This causes bottlenecks and results in backup of jobs at various machines. The pace of production is slow because of the many delays, long setups, and slow machines. Machine operators are responsible for the quality of their work. There is also a large final inspection and test area where products are checked and tested before being shipped to customers.

Facilities

Facilities are small, general purpose, and often old. For example, many job shop production systems are located in old multistory buildings where departments are located on different floors. Storage areas for raw materials, purchased components, and finished goods are small. Work-in-process inventory is stored on the factory floor, which makes the job shop look crowded and somewhat disorganized.

Manufacturing Outputs

Cost and Quality

Although the quality of the products produced in a job shop production system is satisfactory (otherwise, customers would not accept the products), it is difficult for a job shop to meet very tight specifications. This is because equipment is general purpose, tooling is low volume, and production volumes are too low to gain the benefits of experience (Chapter 16). Similarly, although cost is satisfactory (otherwise customers would not buy the products), it is very difficult for a job shop to match the cost of a competitor that produces the same product in much higher volumes using specialized equipment in a line flow production system.

Performance

A job shop production system often produces products with high levels of performance. However, compared to other production systems, it cannot provide the highest possible level of performance year after year. The production volume of any particular product is so low that the company cannot afford the design engineering time needed to design new, advanced features into the product, and the process engineering time needed to design new processes to produce the products.

Delivery

A job shop production system can provide on-time deliveries for its customers by expediting jobs when necessary. However, expediting cannot always be done. The functional layout increases the distance a job travels and the amount of material handling required. The variety and number of jobs in the factory make scheduling difficult and create delays at bottleneck machines. It takes more time to do setups and perform the required operations on general-purpose machines than it does on specialized machines. All these factors increase the time required to complete a job.

Flexibility and Innovativeness

A job shop production system is designed to produce a wide variety of products in very low volumes. Job shops specialize in producing customized products. Equipment and tooling are general purpose and employees are highly skilled. Consequently, it is relatively easy to change product mix and volumes, make design changes, and introduce new products. A job shop production system provides the highest possible levels of flexibility and innovativeness.

The following situations describe companies with job shop production systems that must raise the levels of their manufacturing outputs. In Situation 18.2, a company makes improvements to each manufacturing lever in the production system. This raises the level of manufacturing capability, which produces higher levels of the manufacturing outputs. In Situations 18.3 and 18.4, companies implement group technology principles to change their job shop production systems to batch flow systems (Chapter 19), raising the levels of the cost, quality, and delivery outputs.

Situation 18.2

Improving CWM's Job Shop Production System

CWM WAS A MULTINATIONAL producer and marketer of low volume, heavy-duty mechanical products for use in agricultural, construction, and forest harvesting equipment. CWM's products were designed to customer specifications and produced in small lots. Prices ranged from $300 to over $10,000. CWM had two problems:

- The number of late deliveries of products to customers was growing.
- The level of work-in-process inventory in its factories was at an all-time high.

CWM had four factories in North America and Europe. General purpose machine shops organized as job shop production

SITUATION 18.2

Continued

systems occupied two-thirds of the floor space in each factory. Assembly and testing areas occupied the remaining one-third. For example, the machine shop in the largest factory had 320 machines.

A typical job was routed through 10 to 15 machines in a machine shop. When a job reached a machine, it waited in a queue until the machine became available. A machine operator set up the machine to produce the job according to instructions on the production order that accompanied the job. Completed jobs moved to the assembly area. A typical product was assembled from about 200 parts. The lot size was determined by the production control department and was usually set equal to the number of units in a customer order.

CWM was sure that a job shop production system was best for its machine shops. However, after visiting other factories with the same production system, CWM realized that its job shops had only an industry average level of manufacturing capability. CWM needed to raise the level of capability to adult (Figure 18-1) to solve its delivery and inventory problems. So CWM made the following improvements to the manufacturing levers:

- *Production planning and control:* Manage the release of new orders to avoid overloading the factory. Use input-output control at important machines to ensure that schedules are met. Increase the number of common components, produce these to a forecast, and store them in inventory.
- *Sourcing:* Work with important suppliers to improve delivery time and delivery time reliability. Reserve capacity at suppliers' factories and release orders against this capacity at the latest possible moment.
- *Process technology:* When possible, standardize machines and eliminate unnecessary machines. Reduce setup times on the busiest machines. Schedule and control these machines carefully.
- *Human resources:* Begin a limited program of training employees to operate more than one machine.

SITUATION 18.3

Manufacturer Changes Job Shop to Batch Flow

STRUCTURAL PARTS for medium- and heavy-duty trucks were manufactured in a job shop production system. Figure 18-2 (A) shows the job shop's functional layout. One of the

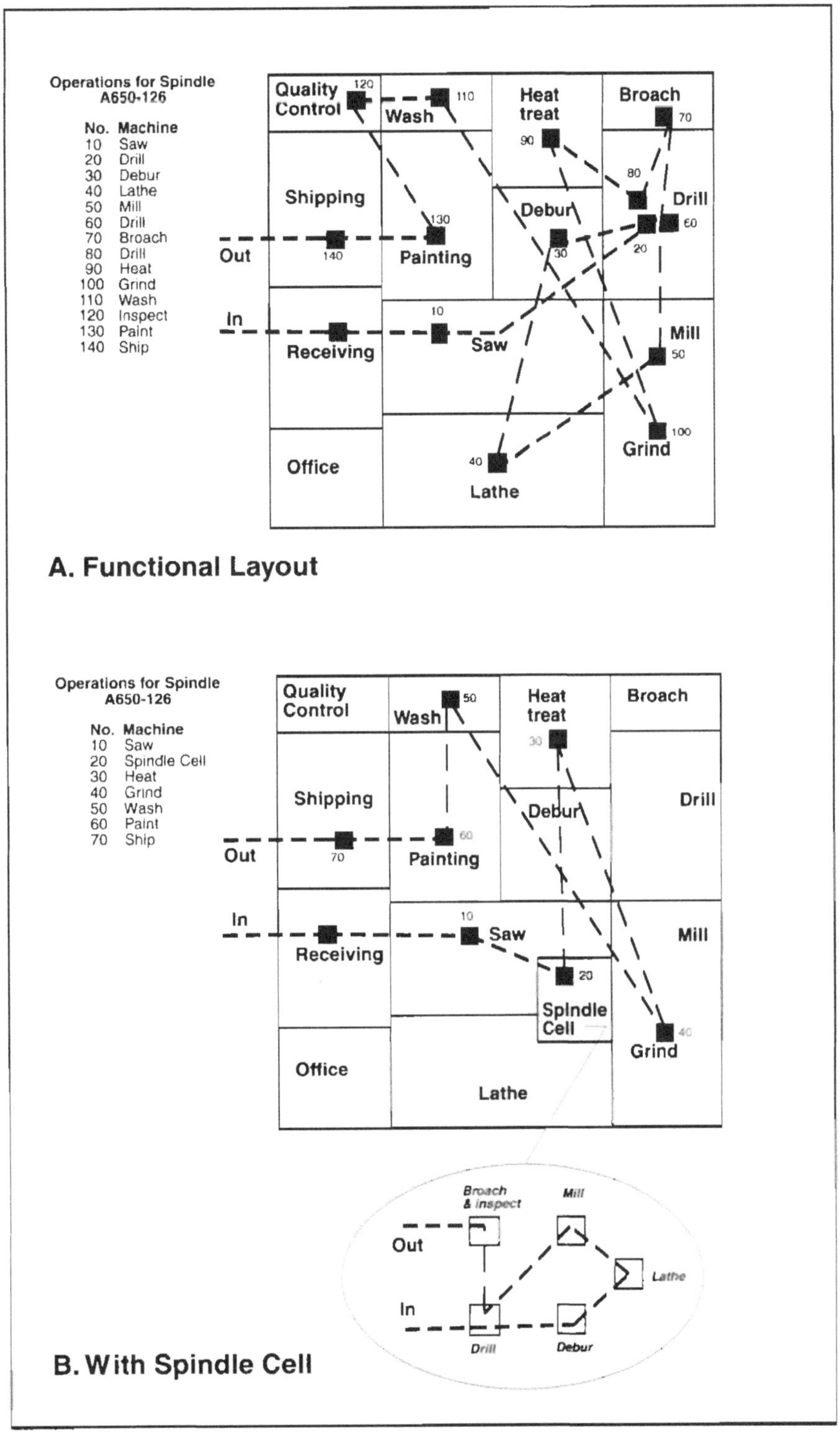

Figure 18-2 Moving from Job Shop to Batch Flow in Situation 18.3

SITUATION 18.3

Continued

many parts produced by the job shop was a spindle. The material flow for one spindle part is shown in the figure. The factory produced 15 different spindles.

The factory needed to reduce the cost of all its parts and also improve quality and delivery. The factory analyzed its job shop production system using group technology concepts and found that a family consisting of spindles and five similar parts had a combined volume high enough to utilize a dedicated manufacturing cell.

The factory moved drill, debur, lathe, mill, and broach machines, and test equipment into a new spindle cell (Figure 18-2 [B]). The spindle cell parts were sufficiently different in terms of setups, tooling, and operations, that the best way to produce them was in batches. Space was left around each machine where containers of parts waiting to be processed could be placed. The result was a small batch flow production system. The new production system provided better levels of cost, quality, and delivery for the spindle cell parts than the old job shop production system.

SITUATION 18.4

Applying Group Technology at John Deere

IN THE MID-1880S, John Deere analyzed its many job shop production systems using group technology concepts, which it called cellular manufacturing principles. The goal was to convert job shop production systems whenever possible to batch flow and line flow systems, thereby raising the levels of the manufacturing outputs. Factories moved machines and parts into manufacturing cells and lines and modified machines and tooling for the parts they would produce.

The initiative was successful. One factory reduced its total number of machines by 25 percent and the number of departments handling an average part by 70 percent. All factories reduced setup times and material handling costs.

These and other improvements raised John Deere's manufacturing capability, which enabled it to provide higher levels of manufacturing outputs than its competitors. This helped John Deere withstand a prolonged slump in the farm implements market in the late 1980s and early 1990s.

CHAPTER 19

BATCH FLOW PRODUCTION SYSTEM

Products and Volumes

A batch flow production system produces many different products in low volumes (Figure 19-1). Products are produced in batches. A batch is usually a customer order and can also be a group of customer orders for the same or similar products. There are two kinds of orders:

- Customers place one-time orders for small quantities.
- Customers place small repeat orders from time to time.

Production of products is usually make-to-order. Common parts, when they exist, can be make-to-stock.

Layout and Material Flow

A batch flow production system uses functional and cellular layouts (Chapter 4). In a functional layout, equipment of the same type is located in the same department. In a cellular layout, different types of equipment are located in the same department or cell so that all operations required to produce any product within a product family are performed in the cell. Group technology principles determine product families and equipment cells.

Material flow in a batch flow production system is varied, but patterns of flow are present especially when products are produced in cells. When a functional layout is used, material flow is irregular and considerable material handling is needed to move batches from department to department. Once moved, batches endure long delays waiting for equipment and operators to become available. When a cellular layout is used, material flow is less varied. Some material handling is needed to move small batches between machines in a cell, and short delays occur.

A special batch flow system called a *linked batch flow production system* occurs when the number of equipment types is small, usually two or three. In this situation, equipment can be arranged in a line layout. This production system is examined at the end of the chapter.

Competitive Advantage

A batch flow production system produces many different products in low volumes. It is easy to make design changes to existing products, introduce

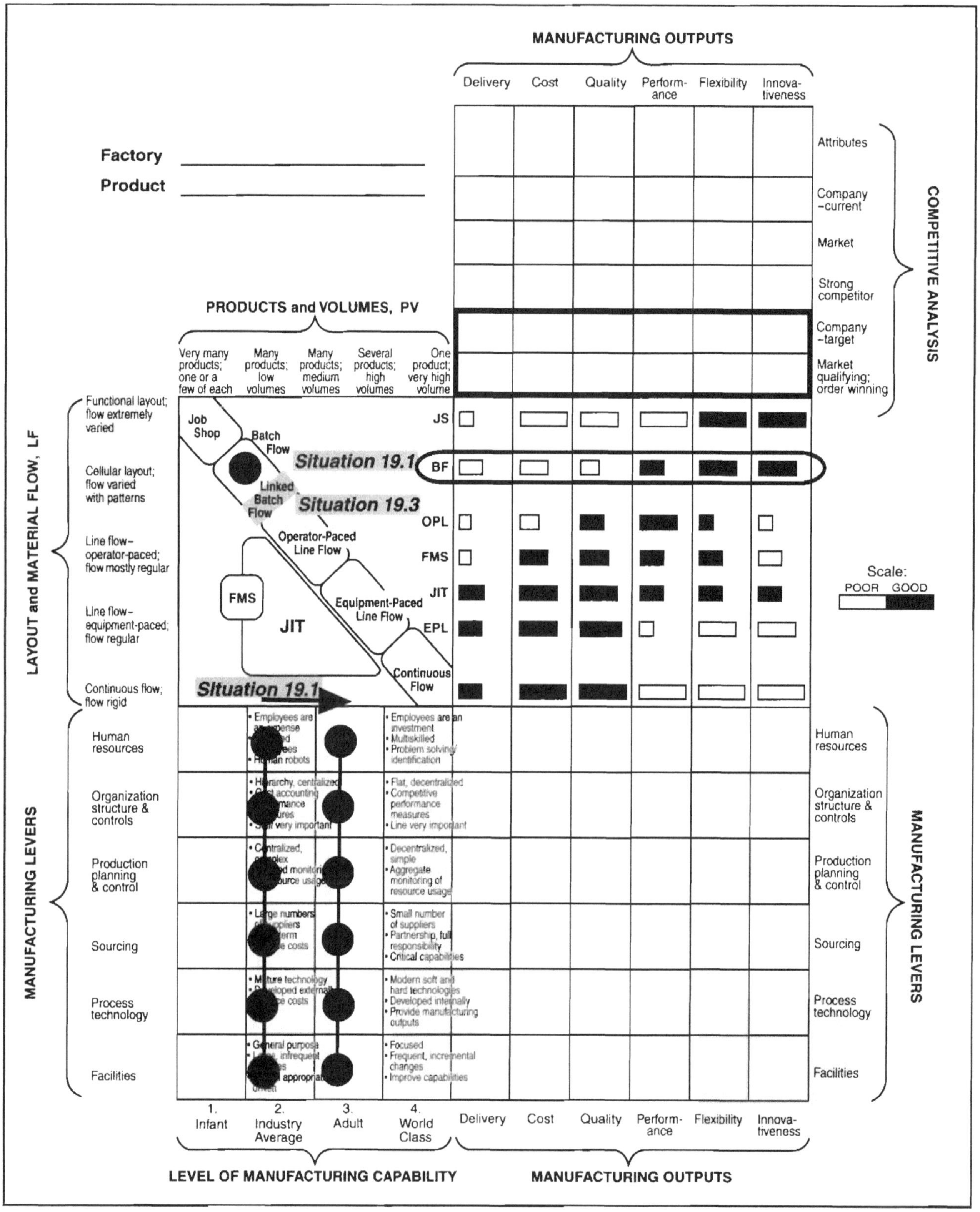

Figure 19-1 Batch Flow Production System

new products, and change production volumes. The production system is designed to provide high levels of flexibility and innovativeness, which it needs to satisfy customer demands for a wide variety of products.

The volume of a product in a batch flow system is higher than in a job shop production system, so fixed costs, such as order processing and setup, are spread over more units. Higher volume enables the benefits of experience to be gained (Chapter 16), so improvements are made. The results are better levels of cost and quality than in a job shop production system. However, the levels are not as good as line flow production systems.

A batch flow production system provides a higher level of performance than a job shop production system. Because the volume of a product is higher, a company can assign more engineering resources to improve product features and make manufacturing improvements. The volume is lower than line flow production systems, so a batch flow system cannot afford as many resources as these systems. The conventional wisdom is to use a batch flow production system in situations where many products are produced in volumes too low for line flow production systems.

A company has two options when it is not satisfied with the levels of manufacturing outputs provided by a batch flow production system:

- Make improvements to raise the level of capability of the batch flow production system (Situation 19.1), which raises the level of all manufacturing outputs.
- Change the batch flow production system to an operator-paced line flow production system (Situation 5.2 in Chapter 5) or a just-in-time production system (Chapter 22).

The second option can be difficult in young companies. Many new companies are formed to produce new products. The companies use job shop and batch flow production systems to produce new products during the introduction, growth, and shakeout stages of the product life cycles (Chapter 16). The companies are often managed by entrepreneurs who founded the companies or have been with the companies from the beginning. The tenacity and energy that helped these entrepreneurial managers build their companies can become obstacles to change when companies need to change production systems. Line flow production systems require more systematic and less hands-on management processes than these managers are used to.

Manufacturing Levers

Human Resources

Employees are assigned to one department or manufacturing cell and trained to operate all equipment there. Incentive pay schemes are used. Staffs are small and concentrate on bidding for new work, working with customers to finalize designs of new products, and managing orders through the factory.

Organization Structure and Controls

Like a job shop production system, operations are decentralized and entrepreneurial for quick response to changes in customer needs. Organization structure is flat. Staff departments are small and less important than line departments. Quality is the responsibility of equipment operators and their supervisors.

Sourcing

There is little vertical integration. Some purchased materials are stocked, but most are purchased for each customer order. Purchase orders are small and irregular, and many suppliers are used. This makes the batch flow production system a relatively unimportant customer of its suppliers. Consequently, it has little control over suppliers and must work very hard to obtain purchased materials with the cost, quality, and delivery it needs.

Production Planning and Control

Traditional MRP systems are used to plan and control production activities. Orders are received through a process of competitive bidding. Production of products is usually make-to-order, and production of common components is make-to-stock. Raw material inventory and finished goods inventory are small and work-in-process inventory is large.

Equipment utilization is more important in a batch flow production system than in a job shop system. To increase utilization, orders for similar products are batched and manufactured together, which reduces setup cost and generates efficiency.

Time to complete an order can be long and unreliable. Four elements comprise this time: time to receive material from suppliers, material handling time, waiting time, and processing time. Material handling time is the time to move batches from department to department. Waiting time is the delay batches endure waiting for equipment and operators to become available. When these times threaten to make an order late, staff intervenes to expedite the order through the factory.

Process Technology

Equipment and tooling are mostly general purpose with some specialization when volumes of similar parts permit formation of manufacturing cells. Setup times are long because of the general purpose equipment and tooling. The number of setups is high because of the large number of different products produced.

Batch flow production systems are labor intensive. Machines tend to be older, and the rate of technological change is slow. Like a job shop production system, a batch flow system is a technology follower, not a technology leader.

Facilities

Facilities in a batch flow production system tend to be larger than in a job shop system. Linkages between departments are loose. When one department completes its operations on a batch, the batch is moved to the next department. Frequent capacity imbalances exist between departments because of the changing product mix in the facility. The results are bottlenecks and buildups of work-in-process inventory in different departments at different times.

Manufacturng Outputs

Cost and Quality

Cost is more important in a batch flow production system than a job shop system because:

- The volume of each product is larger, so even a small reduction in the cost to produce a product can generate a large total saving.
- Some customer orders are repeated from time to time. Cost can be an important factor in these customers' decisions about where to place their orders.

Because a small volume of each product is produced, fixed costs, such as the cost of setups, are spread over more units. In addition, experience benefits can be realized if learning occurs and improvements are made. All of this results in better levels of cost and quality compared to a job shop production system. Nevertheless, it is difficult for a company with a batch flow system to match the cost and quality of a competitor who produces the same product in higher volume on special-purpose equipment in a line flow production system (Figure 19-1).

Performance

A batch flow production system provides a higher level of performance than a job shop system because the volume of any particular product or product family is higher. Higher volume permits a company to assign modest engineering resources to work with customers to design new features into products and better processes for manufacturing products. The volume is not nearly as high as it is for line flow production systems, so some of these systems provide a higher level of performance.

Delivery

Time to complete orders can be long and unreliable. A large number of orders are produced simultaneously, so orders must wait for equipment and operators to become available. The pace of production is slow because of the buildup of work-in-process inventory, slow general purpose machines, long setup times, and material handling. Delivery times for purchased materials from suppliers can be long. Scheduling is difficult because of the large number of orders and machines.

When these difficulties threaten to delay an order, staff intervenes to expedite the order through the factory. However, expediting cannot always be done.

Flexibility and Innovativeness

A batch flow production system relies on skilled employees and general purpose equipment to provide high levels of flexibility and innovativeness. It is easy to change product mix and volumes, make design changes, and introduce new products.

Situation 19.1

Forest Harvesting Equipment Manufacturer Improves Batch Flow System

THE CJC FACTORY produced four lines of forest harvesting equipment. Annual sales exceeded $500 million. The factory employed 1,200 people and was organized into seven functional departments: forge, heat treatment, machine shop, weld shop, paint shop, subassembly, and final assembly. The factory purchased 12,000 parts, fabricated 6,000 parts, and produced 280 finished products ranging in price from $2,000 to $40,000.

All fabricated parts had low volumes and were produced in batches. The first operation usually occurred in the forge department, where steel plates and bars were sheared, heated, and formed into intricate shapes. The second operation was usually in heat treatment. Next, parts moved to the machine shop for machining, drilling, and grinding. Then, some parts moved to the weld shop for welding operations. All parts moved to the paint shop for cleaning and painting. From there, parts went to the subassembly department and were assembled with other parts. Finally, parts moved to one of the final assembly lines where finished products were assembled from purchased and fabricated parts. After final assembly, products were tested, packaged, and loaded for shipment to customers.

A small number of fabricated parts had similar processing requirements. When the combined volume of these parts was high, the parts were grouped into a family and produced in a specialized manufacturing cell.

Job shop and batch flow production systems were used in five of the seven departments: forge, heat treatment, machine shop, weld shop, and paint shop. Projects were underway to change the job shop production systems to batch flow systems

SITUATION 19.1

Continued

and to improve the batch flow systems. The objective was to raise the levels of the manufacturing outputs, especially cost, quality, and delivery (Figure 19-1). The projects were not easy. One of the difficulties was the large size of the departments. The forge department had 100 workstations, the machine shop had 130 machines, and the weld shop had 40 workstations.

Operator-paced line flow production systems were used in the other two departments: subassembly and final assembly. An MRP system was used to plan and control production activities in the seven departments.

In the following discussion, the manufacturing levers in the batch flow production systems in the forge department, machine shop, and weld shop are examined.

Human Resources

The factory was unionized, and jobs were assigned on the basis of seniority. There were 120 job classifications. Production operators were trained to operate one or two pieces of equipment in their department. Material handlers moved parts between workstations. Maintenance personnel maintained and repaired equipment. Production operators were responsible for the quality of the parts they produced. No statistical quality procedures were used. A small engineering department provided technical support for processes and products.

Work-in-process and finished goods inventories were used to smooth production. Demand for some products was seasonal, so overtime and layoffs were also used to bring production into line with demand.

The factory used an incentive wage scheme based on individual labor standards to determine compensation for production operators. A labor standard was the time an operator was allowed to complete a setup or operation for a part on a machine. The forge department, machine shop, and weld shop produced 6,000 parts, and each part required an average of four operations. So there were $6{,}000 \times 4 = 24{,}000$ possible labor standards. Operator efficiencies of 125 percent were common. This meant operators produced and earned 25 percent more than that calculated from the standards.

It was difficult to keep labor standards up to date. Each time an improvement was made, many standards needed revision. As the pace of making improvements increased, the backlog of standards needing revision increased.

The incentive wage scheme did not work well in the manufacturing cells. Machines were more specialized, and operators ran more than one machine at the same time. This could earn some operators more than one incentive at the same time. When this happened, cooperation and teamwork in the cells deteriorated.

CJC needed to make several adjustments to the human resources lever, such as reducing the number of job classifications and changing the incentive wage scheme. CJC was discussing these and other changes with the union.

Organization Structure and Controls

Departments were cost centers. Departments were evaluated on their ability to keep actual costs below budgeted costs, so they tried to keep machine utilizations and labor efficiencies high. Departments were also evaluated on their ability to complete orders on time. Supervisors and expediters spent a great deal of time rushing parts through workstations so orders were completed on time and workstations were not forced down because of a shortage of parts.

Staff groups were small. One staff group managed production planning and control. Another group managed information flows between suppliers and the factory, and the factory and the sales group. These were difficult activities because of the large number of machines, parts, and products.

Sourcing

Many years ago, CJC had a high degree of vertical integration. This changed when the company decided to increase the number of parts it outsourced. Some parts were outsourced to existing suppliers. In many cases, existing suppliers did not have the required manufacturing capability, so new suppliers were found.

CJC did not have close ties or much control over suppliers because the amount of business it had with any one supplier was low. Suppliers were selected on the basis of low cost from those who had the capability to produce the parts. Many orders were delayed because purchased materials did not arrive on time. CJC needed to improve its processes for managing suppliers.

SITUATION 19.1

Continued

PRODUCTION PLANNING AND CONTROL

The sales group developed a 12-month forecast for final products. The forecast was updated monthly to account for changes in the market. Capacity planning decisions concerning number of employees, levels of inventories, and amount of overtime were made on the basis of the forecast.

An MRP system released manufacturing orders to the factory and purchase orders to suppliers at the beginning of each week. Seasonal demand for some products created a great deal of variation in the timing and quantity of manufacturing and purchase orders. Manufacturing orders for final products usually represented customer orders. Sometimes, orders for final products were for inventory, for example, when it was necessary to anticipate seasonal demands. Common parts were produced for inventory, which reduced the lead time for final products and smoothed workloads in the factory.

Each manufacturing order was released a length of time equal to its lead time before it was needed. Lead times were difficult to predict because they depended on many factors: number of units to produce, setup and run times at the workstations where the part would be produced, workload at the workstations, equipment and tooling problems, material handling resources, and operator availability.

There were more than 2,000 manufacturing orders on the factory floor at any one time. This made it difficult to monitor and control material flows. A great deal of expediting was needed to speed orders through the factory to meet delivery dates and keep key workstations busy. Depending on which parts were produced, different workstations became bottlenecks, and overtime was necessary to create capacity.

In the forge, machine shop, and weld shop, each part was produced in a batch size equal to one month of requirements. Smaller batch sizes were desirable to reduce work-in-process inventory and lead times. However, setup times at most workstations were too long to permit smaller batch sizes to be produced economically. Moderate inventories of raw materials and purchased parts were maintained. Work-in-process inventory was large. Finished goods inventory was small unless products were produced early to meet seasonal demands.

The incentive wage scheme created a problem for production planning and control since an operator could earn more by producing high volumes of a few products at one machine, compared to producing low volumes of many products at several machines. This made it difficult for supervisors to move operators to different machines to meet production planning schedules.

CJC implemented a computerized shop floor control system to solve this problem. Each employee received an identification card with a bar code of his or her employee number. Each manufacturing order released to the factory had an order document with bar codes of the order number, order quantity, due date, operations, workstations, and so on. Reader stations were set up throughout the factory. When an operation was completed, the operator scanned and entered required information at a reader station: employee number, manufacturing order, operation number, number of units completed, number of units scrapped, and so on. The data was transmitted to a central computer, which updated the status of the order, the level and location of work-in-process inventory, and calculated payroll information for the employee, labor efficiency, and equipment utilization. Operators were only paid for producing required quantities of parts on due dates specified on manufacturing orders. This stopped operators from overproducing or producing too early. It also forced operators to move to different machines according to the production schedule.

Process Technology

CJC used many process technologies. The forge department had saws and shears for cutting steel bars, tubes, and sheets. The department also had drop hammers, presses, wheelabraters, and heat treating and stress relieving equipment. The machine shop had many different drills, lathes, mills, and grinders. The weld shop had many varieties of mig, arc, manual, and robotic welders. There were various metal cleaning and painting facilities. Technologies, though large in number, were traditional. Machines and tooling were general purpose, designed to produce many different parts. Setup times were long.

All these process technologies were needed to complete numerous operations on many parts. No single technology was most important. A small engineering group was charged with staying up to date on developments in process technologies. This was difficult because the group was small and the number

SITUATION 19.1

Continued

of technologies was large. When new process equipment was acquired, it was difficult to realize all the potential benefits. The engineering group did not have the time or resources to make changes to upstream and downstream processes, which were needed to exploit the capabilities of the new process technology.

There was a proliferation of parts, machines, and tooling. Many machines were used only a few times a year when particular products were produced. Communications between the factory and the product design group, which was located hundreds of miles away, needed improvement. The factory had just started standardization and design for manufacturability programs.

There was no quality control program. Sometimes this resulted in batches of parts having to be reworked to correct a defect that was not detected in time. There was incoming inspection for parts received from suppliers, but there was no supplier certification program to ensure that suppliers could deliver high-quality parts on time.

FACILITIES

The many different parts and processes made the factory complex. CJC tried to reduce complexity by decreasing vertical integration (purchasing more parts from suppliers) and by standardizing wherever possible.

The factory and the departments were medium-sized, too small to achieve economies of scale. Links between departments were loose; when operations in one department were completed, parts were sent to the next department.

SITUATION 19.2

Analysis of a Batch Flow Production System at a Furniture Manufacturer[1]

THE BRACEBRIDGE FURNITURE Company was best known for its high-quality kitchen and dining room furniture in oak, cherry, and hickory. Designs were Colonial and early American. Products were solid wood or had a solid wood look.

Bracebridge Furniture was a small manufacturer. Quality was the order winning output, and performance and cost were market qualifying outputs. Customers valued durability and wear (quality) in a style that would not go out of date (performance) and were prepared to pay a price (cost) in the lower part of the upper price range.

Bracebridge Furniture wanted to increase sales growth to 10 percent per year and raise profitability to industry average levels. Last year, sales grew by 5.3 percent, and profits were 4.2 percent of sales, compared to 8 percent for the industry average (Figure 19-2 [A]). Return on assets was 6.5 percent, compared to 9 percent for the industry average. To increase sales and profitability, Bracebridge recently started expanding its product line to become a full-product-line manufacturer. It now manufactured bedroom furniture in its own factories and upholstered living room furniture in a nearby factory it acquired five years ago.

Bracebridge Furniture organized its products into four lines: case, table, chair, and upholstered. Case products included cabinets, dressers, headboards, pedestals, and foundations. Table products included kitchen and dining room tables, coffee tables, end tables, and side tables. Chair products included kitchen, dining room, and side chairs. Upholstered products included living room sofas and upholstered chairs.

Figure 19-2 (B) shows operating data for the four product lines. The average selling price for a case product was $950, of which $190 was contribution to overhead and profits, and 950 − 190 = $760 was the direct cost to manufacture an average product. Last year, 53,081 case units were sold. They were produced at the rate of 20 units per hour. The quality level was 38,000 defects per million units, which is about 3.3-sigma quality (Chapter 15).

Figure 19-2 (C) gives an analysis of the operating data. Total sales of case products were $950/unit × 53,081 units = $50.4 million, which is 32 percent of total sales. Total contribution was $190/unit × 53,081 units = $10.1 million, which is 21 percent of total contribution. Contribution was generated at the rate of $190/unit × 20 units/hour = $3,800 per production hour in the case final assembly area. Total production hours in this area were 53,081 units ÷ 20 units/hour = 2,654 hours. Bracebridge worked 40 hours/week on one shift or 80 hours/week on two shifts, and 48 weeks per year. Total production hours for case products utilized 2,654 / (80 × 48) = 0.69 or 69 percent of two-shift capacity.

	Last Year		Previous Year		Industry Averages
Sales	$155,248,845	100%	$147,434,800	100%	100%
Cost of goods sold	$121,094,099	78%	$116,473,492	79%	75%
Net profit before tax	$6,520,451	4.2%	$5,160,218	3.5%	8%
Return on assets	$10,091,175	6.5%	$8,846,088	6%	9%
Growth		5.3%		4.6%	

A. Financial Data

Product Line	Price $/unit	Contribution $/unit	Sales (last year) units	Production Rate[1] units/hour	Quality ppm
Case	950	190	53,081	20	38,000
Table	460	200	38,312	30	21,000
Chair	204	76	357,846	100	1,800
Upholstered	620	150	22,900	25	17,000

1. Production rate in final assembly areas.

B. Operating Data

Product Line	Sales (last year)		Contribution			Required Production Hours[1]	Utilization[2]	
	$	%	$	%	$/hour		1-shift	2-shifts
Case	50,426,874	32%	10,085,375	21%	3,800	2,654	—	69%
Table	17,623,387	11%	7,662,342	16%	6,000	1,277	67%	—
Chair	73,000,584	47%	27,196,296	56%	7,600	3,578	—	93%
Upholstered	14,198,000	9%	3,435,000	7%	3,750	916	48%	—
Totals	155,248,845		48,379,013					

1. Required production hours in final assembly areas.
2. Utilization in final assembly areas. Table and upholstery assembly areas work one shift. Case and chair assembly areas work two shifts.

C. Analysis of Operating Data

Figure 19-2 Selected Financial and Operating Data for Situation 19.2

SITUATION 19.2

Continued

The following observations follow from the data and analysis in parts B and C of the figure:

- The chair product line is the most important product line. It generates 56 percent of total contribution. Producion is fast—100 units/hour. Quality is high—1,800 ppm or about 4.5-sigma quality. Contribution per production hour is high—$7,600/hour. Capacity utilization is high—93 percent over two shifts. Bracebridge Furniture should add production capacity and increase sales of chair products.

- The table product line is another good product line. It represents 11 percent of sales but generates 16 percent of total contribution. Contribution is $200 per unit or $6,000 per production hour. Capacity utilization is 67 percent over one shift, so unused capacity is available for increased sales. Improving quality (21,000 ppm) is a priority because quality is the order winning output, and the company needs to win more orders to meet its growth objective.
- The case product line needs improvement. High sales, 32 percent of total sales, generate only 21 percent of total contribution. Contribution per unit is low—$190 compared to a price of $950. Production is slow—20 units/hour. Quality is poor—38,000 ppm. All of this results in a low contribution per production hour—$3,800. Bracebridge needs to make improvements here.
- Upholstered furniture is a weak product line. Sales are low—9 percent of total sales. Contribution is low—7 percent of total contribution and $3,750 per production hour. Quality is poor—17,000 ppm. There is considerable unused capacity. Bracebridge needs to make improvements here.

Bracebridge needs to adjust the manufacturing levers in the batch flow production systems that produce case products and upholstered products. The adjustments will raise the level of capability of the production systems, which will raise the level of all manufacturing outputs, especially quality (order winning output) and cost (market qualifying output). This will help the company achieve its growth and profitability objectives. Cycle time reduction (Chapter 14) is a good improvement program to use for the case and upholstered product lines because in addition to improving these production systems, Bracebridge needs to speed up production of these products.

Bracebridge Furniture operated four factories: components, chairs, tables and cases, and upholstered furniture. Each factory used a batch flow production system.

SITUATION 19.2

Continued

- The component factory manufactured 900 parts. The factory was organized into three departments: kilns, rough mill, and fine mill. Kilns reduced the moisture content of wood, the rough mill processed wood into blank parts free of defects, and the fine mill processed defect-free wood into final shapes and dimensions using turning, shaping, routing, sawing, bending, boring, and sanding machines.
- The chair factory manufactured 100 products. The factory was organized into four departments: milling, where wood was machined into final shapes, assembly, where components were assembled into products, finishing, where products were cleaned and painted, and packaging, where products were wrapped and shipped to customers or the warehouse.
- The table and case factory manufactured 240 products. The factory was organized into three departments: assembly, finishing, and packaging.
- The upholstery factory manufactured 80 products. The factory was organized into three departments: sewing, assembly, and packaging.

Figure 19-3 (A) gives some inventory data. Bracebridge Furniture organized sku's (stock keeping units) into three volume categories: A, B, and C. Sku's in the A category had annual volumes of 500 or more. B sku's had annual volumes between 200 and 500. C sku's had annual volumes of 200 or less. The average contribution per unit was highest for the low volume C sku's. This was because many low volume sku's were in the early stages of their product life cycles (Chapter 16). They were newly designed products for which Bracebridge charged high prices. Most higher volume A and B sku's were products in the maturity and saturation stages of their life cycles and competed on the basis of cost (and quality) and so were priced lower.

Quality was highest for high volume sku's and lowest for low volume sku's because Bracebridge focused improvement activities on high volume products. As soon as volume was sufficiently high, Bracebridge grouped several machines into a cell, added automation, and scheduled larger batches. This increased production speed, lowered cost, and produced better quality.

ABC Category	Annual Volume Units	Contribution $/Unit	Quality ppm	Lead Time Days	% of Items in Finished Goods Inventory
A	500 or more	90	2,100	29	50
B	Between 200 and 500	130	19,500	21	43
C	200 or less	180	43,000	12	7

A. Summary Data

Sku Number	ABC Code	Product Line	Weekly Demand	Current Inventory	Scheduled Production	Order Point	Order Quantity	Adjustment? Order Point	Adjustment? Order Quantity
4507	A	Case	18	41	110	72	144		yes
1687	A	Chair	14	126	0	56	112		
6193	A	Chair	22	56	0	88	176	yes	
2211	A	Table	16	98	0	64	128		
1771	A	Upholstered	11	77	0	44	88		
625	B	Case	8	111	0	24	128		
2059	B	Chair	5	65	0	15	80		
940	B	Chair	7	19	100	21	110		
1055	B	Table	6	45	50	18	96	yes	
2844	B	Table	5	59	23	15	80		
2448	B	Upholstered	8	30	0	24	128		
1076	C	Case	1	-2	25	0	48		yes
728	C	Case	1	15	0	0	48		
6469	C	Chair	4	1	50	0	192	yes	
609	C	Chair	2	24	0	0	96		
409	C	Table	1	19	0	0	48		
886	C	Table	4	-2	100	0	192		yes
849	C	Upholstered	2	0	100	0	96		
			135	782			1,990		

B. Analysis of Sample Inventory Data

Figure 19-3 Inventory Data for Situation 19.2

Bracebridge Furniture produced to stock. It used two systems to plan production and control inventory. The first system was an order point, order quantity system. Each sku had an order point and an order quantity, which were calculated as follows:

SITUATION 19.2

Continued

ORDER POINTS

A and B sku's: Order point = weekly demand × (lead time + safety time)

C sku's: Order point = 0

Lead time = 3 weeks

Safety time = 1 week (A), 0 weeks (B)

ORDER QUANTITIES

Order quantity = weekly demand × 48 weeks per year × number of production runs per year

Number of production runs per year = 6 (A), 3 (B), 1 (C)

Figure 19-3 (B) analyzes some data on inventories and production orders. Sku 4507 is a case item. The average demand is 18 units per week or 18 × 48 weeks/year = 864 units per year, so 4507 is an A sku. The lead time to manufacture an A sku is three weeks, and the safety time is one week, so the order point is 18 × (3 + 1) = 72 units. An A sku is manufactured six times per year, so the order quantity is 18 × 48 ÷ 6 = 144 units. The order point, order quantity system work as follows: Each time, the inventory level of sku 4507 drops to 72 units or less, a production order is scheduled to produce 144 units. The order must be completed within the three-week lead time. Figure 19-3 (B) shows that the current inventory is 41 units, which is less than the order point, so a production order is scheduled. However, the production order is for 110 units not 144 units; the production planner adjusted the order quantity. There are five other adjustments in Figure 19-3 (B). Consider sku 6193. The current inventory is 56 units, which is less than the order point, 88 units. However, no order is scheduled. This is an adjustment to the order point. Adjustments occurred because of Bracebridge's second planning system.

The second system operated as follows. The marketing department developed a master production schedule every two weeks. The schedule specified final products, quantities, and shipping dates. The schedule was sent electronically to production planners in the four factories. Each planner checked inventory levels, availability of components, and capacity at bottleneck workcenters, and prepared a final production schedule for his or her factory. In the course of preparing final schedules, planners often decreased order quantities so that a larger number of different sku's could be produced. This made marketing happy and reduced inventory levels, which made finance happy. However, it increased the number of setups, and the smaller order quantities reduced quality.

Total actual inventory for the 18 sku's in Figure 19-3 (B) is 782 units or 782 ÷ 135 = 5.8 weeks of inventory. If no adjustments are made to the order point or order quantity, the total inventory is:

Total inventory = ½ (total order quantity) + total safety inventory

Safety inventory = safety time × weekly demand

Only A sku's had safety time, so total safety inventory = 1 × 18 + 1 × 14 + ... + 1 × 11 = 81. Total order quantity = 1,990, so total inventory = ½ × 1990 + 81 = 1,076 units or 1,076 ÷ 135 = 8 weeks. This is 38 percent higher than total actual inventory. Bracebridge is operating its batch flow production systems with insufficient inventory. While finance may be happy with the low inventory level, manufacturing is wasting production time and resources performing extra setups. Smaller order quantities mean manufacturing must produce each product more often than the specified number of production runs.

Linked Batch Flow Production System

A linked batch flow production system is a special batch flow system with the following characteristics:

- The number of processes is small, usually two or three.
- Processes are arranged in a line.
- Processes are either linked together or separated by small decoupling inventories.
- The time to produce a batch is small; usually a few hours to a few days of setup and processing time.
- When a batch is completed, all linked processes stop, and a changeover or setup is completed before the next batch starts.

Figure 19-4 shows the most common configuration for a linked batch flow production system. The decoupling inventory allows process 1 and process 2 to continue for a short time when either

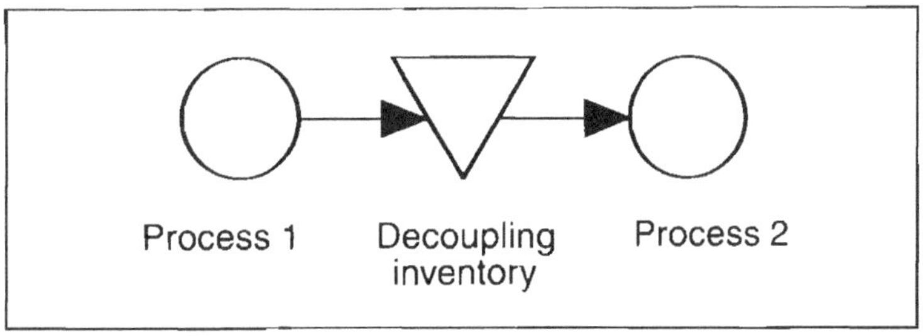

FIGURE 19-4 Linked Batch Flow Production System

process stops. Process 2 is often a packaging operation for a product that can be packaged in many package types, sizes, labels, and so on.

Linked batch flow production systems are common in processing industries such as chemicals, food, and pharmaceuticals. Figure 19-1 shows the linked batch flow system on the factory manufacturing strategy worksheet. It occupies the region of the batch flow production system closest to the operator-paced line flow production system.

SITUATION 19.3

Analysis of a Linked Batch Flow Production System at a Pharmaceutical Company[2]

ADMI PHARMACEUTICALS' Pointe Claire factory manufactured four types of medications: antianxiety, flu, headache, and high blood pressure. Medications were manufactured in solid (capsules and tablets) and liquid forms, in over-the-counter and prescription strengths, with a range of ingredients, and in a range of sizes (12, 24, 50, 100 tablets or capsules, and 50, 150, 250 ml). The factory's annual revenue was $235 million, and it employed 220 people.

The factory was organized into two main departments: bulk processing, and filling and packaging. Bulk processing used a batch flow production system, and filling and packaging used a linked batch flow production system.

The bulk processing department converted powdered and liquid ingredients into bulk tablet, capsule, and liquid forms. Blending, compression, coating, cooling, filtering, heating, and mixing operations were performed in general purpose tanks assisted by pumps, mixers, heat exchangers, and filters. Equipment was dedicated to one operation. Pipes connected equipment, and pumps pushed materials through pipes from one tank to another to complete the necessary operations. The department used three tank sizes: 2,000, 5,000, and 10,000 liters. Batch size corresponded to tank size, so production orders were for 2,000, 5,000, or 10,000 liters.

The filling and packaging department had four production lines. Each line placed tablets, capsules, and liquids into bottles or packets, attached labels, and packed bottles and packets into cases. The typical sequence of operations was:

- Plastic bottles are delivered to the line and fed into a hopper.
- Bottle enters the line and is cleaned.
- Quantity of the product is placed in the bottle.
- Moisture absorbent cube and cotton wool are placed in the bottle (when product is a tablet or capsule).
- Bottle opening is sealed.
- Cap is placed on the bottle.

- Plastic band is heat shrunk around the cap and neck of the bottle.
- Label is placed on the bottle.
- Bottle is placed in a carton.
- Carton is placed in a case.

The batch size in the filling and packaging department corresponds to the batch size in the bulk processing department. For example, suppose the bulk processing department produces 5,000 liters of a medication that will be packaged in 250 ml bottles. Then, the batch size in the filling and packaging department is 5,000 ÷ 0.250 = 20,000 bottles.

At the end of each batch, a crew of three operators clean all equipment, adjust equipment for the next product to be produced, and put the necessary materials in place (powdered ingredients, bottles, caps, labels, cartons, and cases). This takes about four hours during which time the equipment is not producing. Two costs are incurred as a result of changeovers: the cost of doing the changeover, 3 operators × 4 hours = 12 operator-hours, and the cost of lost production, 4 hours × contribution per hour for bulk processing equipment or filling and packaging line.

Figure 19-5 (A) gives operating data for a sample of stock keeping units (sku's). The first sku is T101-24 Tablets. Its annual volume is 160,000 liters (in bulk processing). It is packaged in bottles of 24 tablets. One tablet requires 20 ml = 0.02 liters, so this annual volume corresponds to 160,000 ÷ (24 × 0.02) = 333,333 bottles. T101-24 Tablets is an A sku because its annual production exceeds 150,000 bottles. The bulk processing department produces A sku's in 10,000 liter batches, so there are 160,000 ÷ 10,000 = 16 batches per year. The batch size in the filling and packaging department is 10,000 ÷ (24 × 0.02) = 20,833 bottles. The production rate for bottles of 24 tablets is 1,200 bottles per hour, so the time to complete a batch of T101-24 Tablets in filling and packaging is 20,833 ÷ 1,200 = 17.4 hours.

The time to complete one batch of each of the eight products in Figure 19-5 (A) is 98.2 hours. The total changeover time is 8 batches × 4 hours per changeover = 32 hours. Therefore, 32 ÷ (98.2 + 32) = 0.25 or 25 percent of time in filling and packaging is spent doing changeovers, which is a high value. Time spent doing changeovers is particularly high for B and C sku's. Consider, for example, T101-100 Tablets. It is produced three times each year in batches of 1,000 bottles. The time to produce

Sku	Batch Processing (liters) Annual Production	Batch Size	Batches per Year	Filling and Packaging (bottles) ABC Category[1]	Annual Production	Batch Size	Production Rate (bottles/hour)	Hours per Batch
T101-24 Tablets	160,000	10,000	16	A	333,333	20,833	1,200	17.4
C220-24 Caplets	130,000	10,000	13	A	270,833	20,833	800	26.0
C275-24 Caplets	85,000	10,000	9	A	177,083	20,833	800	26.0
T535-24 Tablets	50,000	5,000	10	B	104,167	10,417	1,200	8.7
T533-24 Tablets	45,000	5,000	9	B	93,750	10,417	1,200	8.7
C324-12 Caplets	8,000	2,000	4	C	33,333	8,333	1,000	8.3
T150-50 Tablets	8,000	2,000	4	C	8,000	2,000	1,200	1.7
T101-100 Tablets	6,000	2,000	3	C	3,000	1,000	700	1.4
Totals			68		1,023,500	94,667		98.2

1. ABC Categories: A sku's (more than 150,000 bottles), B sku's (50,000 to 150,000), C sku's (less than 50,000).

A. Data for a Sample of Sku's

Sku	Production Date	Batch Size (bottles)	Production Rate (bottles/hour)
T101-24 Tablets	Jan. 4	25,566	1,144
T101-24 Tablets	Jan. 24	28,434	1,232
T101-24 Tablets	Feb. 25	28,020	1,156
T101-24 Tablets	Mar. 3	29,014	1,256
T535-24 Tablets	Jan. 11	10,900	1,002
T535-24 Tablets	Feb. 20	10,001	972
T533-24 Tablets	Feb. 3	9,290	951
T150-50 Tablets	Mar. 15	1,913	964
T101-100 Tablets	Mar. 15	1,160	727

B. Batch Sizes and Production Rates

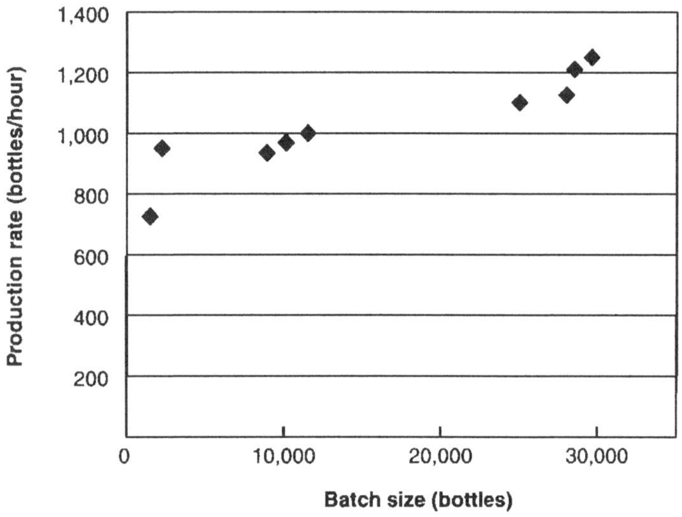

C. Relationship Between Batch Size and Production Rate

Figure 19-5 Analysis of a Linked Batch Flow Production System

SITUATION 19.3

Continued

one batch is 1,000 ÷ 700 = 1.4 hours plus four hours for a changeover. Suppose T101-100 Tablets are produced just once each year. Then:

- Batch size increases from 1,000 to 3,000 bottles.
- Total changeover time decreases from 3 × 4 = 12 to 1 × 4 = 4 hours.
- Inventory increases from ½ × 1,000 = 500 to ½ × 3,000 = 1,500 bottles.

Figure 19-5 (B) gives recent data on actual batch sizes and actual production rates for the Tablet sku's. Consider T101-24 Tablets again. This product is produced four times. On March 3, the production rate is highest—1,256 bottles per hour, when the batch size is largest—29,014 bottles. All batch sizes and production rates are graphed in part C of the figure. The graph shows that the filling and packaging line runs faster when batch sizes are large.

Higher batch sizes have many benefits: lower changeover cost, more time available to produce products, and faster production rate. But higher batch sizes also increase inventory.

ENDNOTES

1. Based on Tyndall Furniture Company Cases (A, B, C), pp. 531–562, in Hill, T., *Manufacturing Strategy: Text and Cases*, Irwin McGraw-Hill: Boston 2000.
2. Based on Rumack Pharmaceuticals Case, pp. 477–484, in Hill, T., *Manufacturing Strategy: Text and Cases*, Irwin McGraw-Hill: Boston 2000.

CHAPTER 20

FLEXIBLE MANUFACTURING SYSTEM

A flexible manufacturing system (FMS) is a group of automated guided vehicles, CNC machines, robots, and other sophisticated, computerized equipment connected to an automated material handling system and controlled by a supervisory computer. An FMS produces many different products in low volumes in any random order and can run unattended for long periods of time. A small FMS has five to ten machines, a similar number of robots, and one to three automated guided vehicles (Figure 20-1).

SITUATION 20.1

FMS Production System at Fanuc

THE FUJITSU FANUC robot factory produces 100 robots, 75 machining centers, and 75 electrodischarge machines each month. The factory's machining department produces many of the parts used in these products.

The machining department uses an FMS production system. Parts are fixed to pallets. Automatic guided vehicles move pallets from machining cell to machining cell and into and out of automated storage and retrieval warehouses. There are 29 machining cells. Each cell has one or more CNC machines, as well as robots and pallet changers that load and unload the CNC machines.

Nineteen operators run the machining department during the day. At night, the cells run unattended while a single operator watches from a control room. Machine availability is close to 100 percent, and machine utilization averages 67 percent over 24 hours.

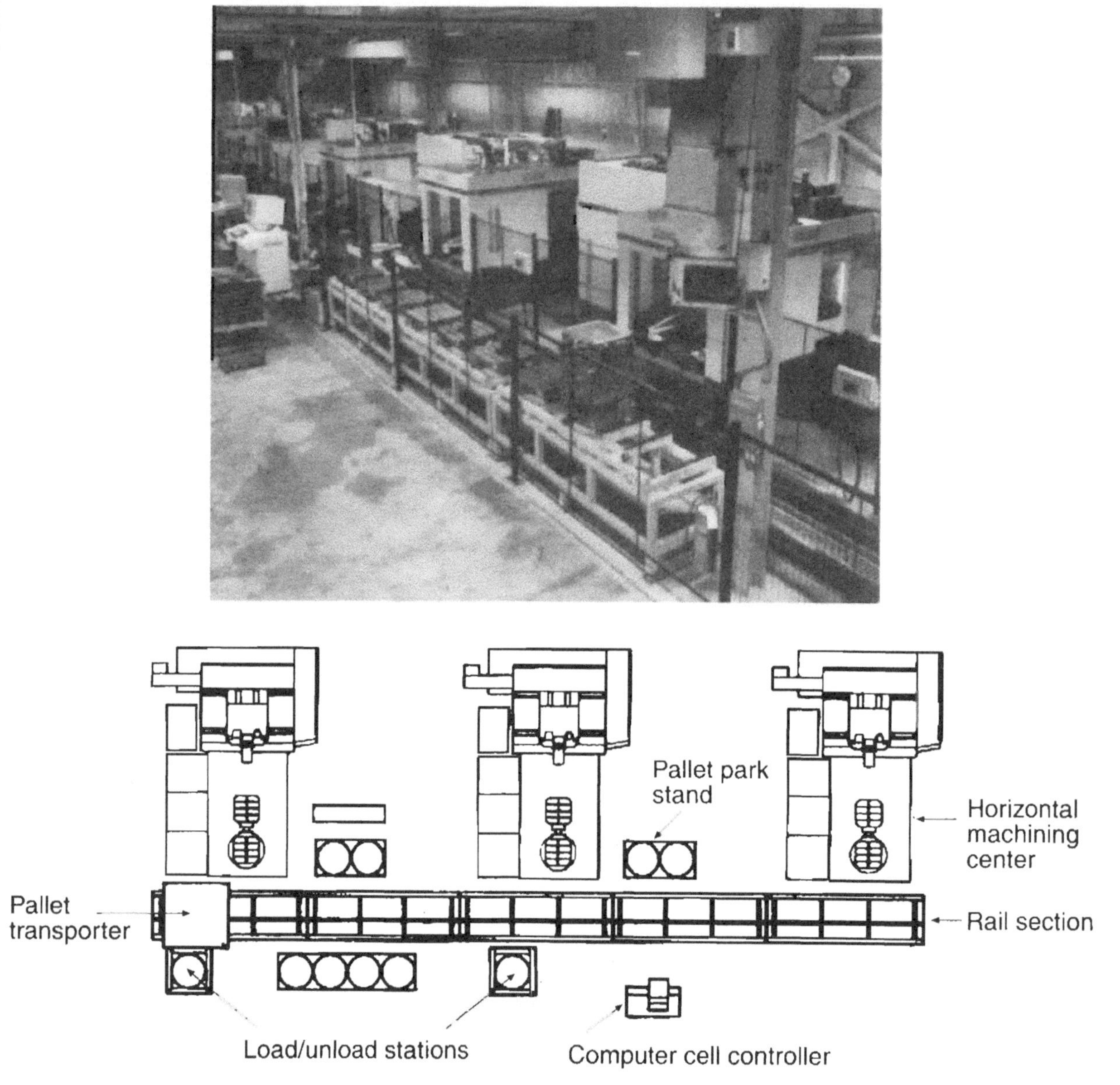

Source: Cincinnati Milacron 1994. With permission.

Figure 20-1 Example of an FMS Production System

Products and Volumes

An FMS production system produces many different products in low volumes (Figure 20-2). Products are produced in batches, in any random order, and the batch size can be as small as one unit. A batch is a customer order, and production is make-to-order.

An FMS can produce the same mix and volume of products as a batch flow production system. However, an FMS can also produce smaller batch sizes.

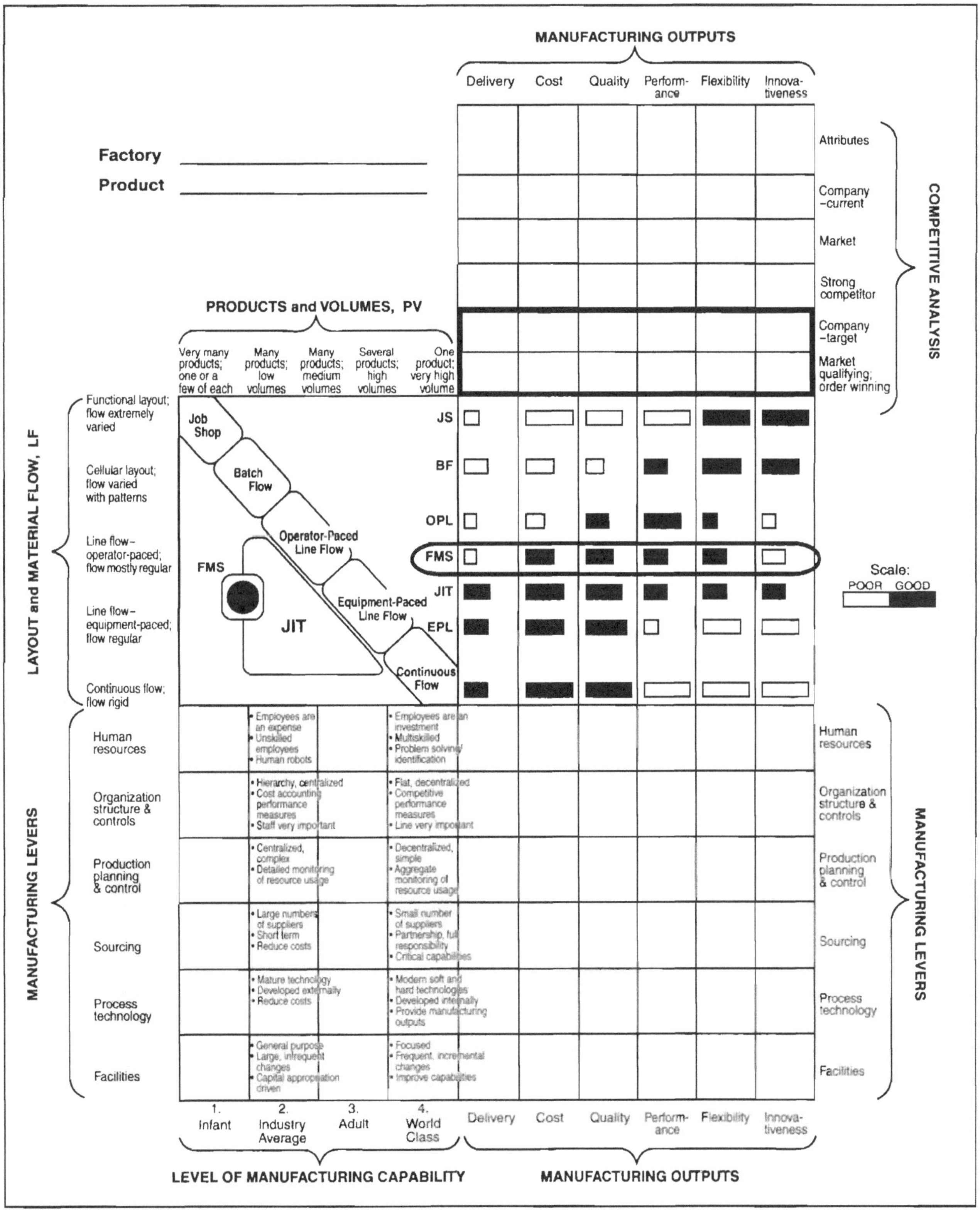

Figure 20-2 FMS Production System

Layout and Material Flow

An FMS is a special line flow production system because while the layout is cellular, the material flow is line.

In a cellular layout, different equipment types are located in the same department or cell so that all operations required to produce any product within a product family are performed in the cell (Chapter 4). Group technology principles determine product families and equipment cells.

Automated material handling equipment moves material through an FMS as if it were a line flow production system. Robots load material into CNC machines. Then automatic tool changers load tools, computers retrieve programs, and the CNC machines quickly and reliably perform operations. All of this enables economical production of a wide variety of low volume products.

Competitive Advantage

There are three important reasons why companies use FMS production systems:

- Better manufacturing outputs
- Fast setup times
- Expertise in new technology

Better Manufacturing Outputs

An FMS production system is an alternative to a batch flow production system, and to a lesser extent, a job shop production system. All produce many different products in low volumes. However, an FMS provides the best levels of the cost and quality outputs. The conventional wisdom is to use an FMS rather than a batch flow production system when the level of quality provided by a batch flow system is too low.

When an FMS is working effectively, product cost is low. Very high equipment utilization is not necessary to provide low cost. For example, the FMSs in Situations 20.1 and 20.3 provide low costs when equipment utilizations are 67 and 80 percent respectively.

The high level of quality in an FMS is the result of sophisticated, flexible equipment that, despite being general purpose, can produce products with very tight specifications. For some products, such as dies, fixtures, and parts in the aerospace industry, the specifications are so tight and the volume is so low that these products can only be produced on the type of computer-controlled equipment used in an FMS (Situation 20.2).

An FMS provides a better level of delivery time and delivery time reliability than a batch flow production system because an FMS is a line flow production system.

An FMS provides a high level of flexibility. However, it provides a lower level of innovativeness than a batch flow production system. An FMS is designed to produce many different products in low volumes, so it is relatively easy to change products and volumes. It is more difficult to introduce new products and make design changes to existing products because new pallets, fixtures, and computer programs are required.

Fast Setups

An FMS is sometimes used when setup times on conventional machines are too high.

Some companies assign too many different products to their batch flow and operator-paced line flow production systems. The differences between products may be small but they often are large enough to require additional setups. This can easily lead to spending a large amount of time on setups. Situation 15.5 in Chapter 15 and Situation 19.3 in Chapter 19 are examples. This is costly and reduces production capacity.

Setup times are very small on the flexible machines in an FMS. Even when many setups are required, the total time spent on setups is still small, so only a small amount of production capacity is lost (Situation 20.4).

Expertise in New Technology

Some companies need to gain technical and managerial expertise with flexible manufacturing systems because this technology is a source of competitive advantage for them. They use this technology in their products and production processes.

Companies like Cincinnati Milacron, Fanuc, and Allen-Bradley produce the machine tools, robots, and computer controllers used in an FMS. These companies use FMS production systems, rather than batch flow or traditional line flow production systems, to learn more about how their products work, which helps them improve their products. It also showcases their products for marketing purposes (Situation 20.6).

Companies like John Deere and General Motors want expertise with the technologies that constitute an FMS. When the technologies' worth becomes evident, these companies will move quickly to use the technologies in their other production systems.

Manufacturing Levers

Human Resources

Automated guided vehicles, CNC machines, robots, and other sophisticated, computerized equipment perform all operations in an FMS production system. A small number of operators perform support tasks such as placing products on pallets, putting parts in automatic material feeders, loading tools into tool carousels, and adding cooling fluids for the cutting tools. Operators are paid an hourly rate; no incentive pay scheme is used.

Maintenance is very important. Equipment in an FMS has a high level of mechanical and electronic complexity, so it is difficult to maintain. Highly skilled and well-trained maintenance personnel are responsible for preventive maintenance, maintaining spare parts, and making repairs during breakdowns.

Organization Structure and Controls

An FMS production system is usually a cost center. Line departments are small because machines do most of the work. Numerous staff departments are required for activities such as designing pallets and fixtures, managing maintenance activities, obtaining new orders, production planning and control, quality, and writing computer programs for CNC machines.

The quality department is responsible for all aspects of quality. This includes statistical process control in the production system, quality of purchased materials, and quality improvement projects.

Sourcing

There is little vertical integration. Some purchased materials are stocked, but most are purchased for specific customer orders. An FMS has little control over its suppliers because it uses many suppliers, and it places small and irregular purchase orders.

The machines, fixtures, and tooling in an FMS are precise. To work properly, they require materials with very tight tolerances. Consequently, the quality of materials received from suppliers must be high. Suppliers are evaluated on their ability to provide a high level of quality, short delivery time, and low cost.

Production Planning and Control

Orders are received from external customers through a competitive bidding process or from internal customers through an allocation process. Production is make-to-order. Raw material and finished goods inventories are small, work-in-process inventory is not large. Products can be complex, and there can be significant differences between products. Process planning, which includes writing computer programs for each operation at each machine, is costly and time-consuming. Situation 15.9 in Chapter 15 is an example.

Computerized information systems enable real-time scheduling and control. Systems are flexible and react immediately to changing conditions such as new order arrivals, due date changes, quality problems, and breakdowns. Bottlenecks are frequent and occur in different places as conditions change. The number of setups is high because of the many different products produced, but individual setup times are short, so total setup time is not excessive.

Process Technology

General purpose, flexible, sophisticated, computer-controlled machines, robots, and material handling equipment are used in an FMS production system. Tooling, such as fixtures and pallets, are also general purpose. Everything is automated and expensive.

An FMS production system is capital intensive, material cost is high, direct labor cost is low, and indirect costs, especially those associated with support activities, such as engineering and maintenance, are high.

Process technology is very important because machines produce most of the "value added" in the products. An FMS production system is usually a technology leader. The engineering department must stay up to date on developments in process technology. Technological change can be incremental or revolutionary.

Facilities

Facilities are usually new and clean. Facilities are medium-sized, with limited economies of scale. Considerable infrastructure is needed in areas such as computer communication networks, and maintenance and repair facilities.

Bottlenecks frequently change because so many different products are produced. The speed of the production system is medium. Equipment utilization is high compared to a batch flow production system, which is important because it spreads the high capital cost of the FMS over a large number of products.

Manufacturing Outputs

Cost and Quality

Three production systems produce many products in low volumes: job shop, batch flow, and FMS. Of these, an FMS provides the best levels of the cost, quality, and delivery outputs. Quality is provided at a high level because sophisticated equipment is used, and operators perform few, if any, operations. Equipment and tooling are general purpose but are so sophisticated that they can produce complex parts with tight specifications.

A high level of manufacturing capability is required to operate an FMS because such advanced technology is used. When an FMS works effectively, equipment utilization is sufficiently high that products are produced at low cost. A small opportunity for learning to occur and improvements to be made occurs because a small volume of each product is produced. An FMS must be well managed to ensure that available learning opportunities are pursued.

An FMS is a line flow production system, so it provides cost and quality outputs at line flow levels. These outputs are provided at the lowest levels of all line flow production systems (Figure 20-2) because other line flow systems manufacture a smaller number of products in higher volumes using more specialized and less expensive equipment.

Performance

An FMS production system provides the performance output at the same high level as the batch flow and just-in-time production systems. There are two reasons for this:

- The volume of each product is enough that the company can commit a small amount of engineering resources to work with customers to design new, advanced features into the product.
- The equipment is so flexible and sophisticated that only a few changes, such as writing new computer programs and building new fixtures, are needed to produce a product with new features.

The level of the performance output is lower than that provided by the operator-paced line flow production system but higher than that provided by the job shop and continuous flow production systems.

Delivery

Because many different products are produced at the same time, products sometimes wait for equipment to become available, which increases the time to produce a product.

Scheduling is difficult because many orders are in the FMS at the same time, so it is difficult to provide delivery time reliability that is as good as other line flow production systems.

Flexibility and Innovativeness

Expensive, sophisticated, general purpose equipment make an FMS flexible. An FMS produces many different products in low volumes, so it is relatively easy to change products and volumes.

The level of innovativeness is lower than the level of flexibility. It is somewhat more difficult to introduce new products and make design changes to existing products because new pallets, fixtures, and computer programs may be needed. Nevertheless, an FMS provides a higher level of innovativeness than traditional line flow production systems.

Machining and Assembly FMSs

There are two classes of FMS: machining and assembly. Machining FMSs are described in Situations 20.1, 20.2, 20.4, and 20.5, and assembly FMSs are described in Situations 20.3 and 20.6. In all these situations, an existing batch flow production system is replaced with an FMS because the batch flow system cannot provide required levels of the market qualifying and order winning outputs. In all these situations, quality is the order winning output, and cost and flexibility are the market qualifying outputs.

Situation 20.2

Aircraft Parts Manufacturer Installs FMS[1]

In 1984, LTV AIRCRAFT PRODUCTS installed an FMS to machine parts for the Rockwell B1-B bomber. The FMS was designed and built by Cincinnati Milacron. By 1988, the system had paid for itself in inventory savings alone. The FMS was so flexible that the company produced each part when it was needed and often in a batch size of one unit. In addition to reductions in inventory cost, labor cost decreased and product quality increased. When the bomber contract ended, the company planned to use the FMS to make parts for other aircraft and for products in other industries.

Situation 20.3

Assembly FMS at an Engine Factory

Problem[2]

In the early 1980s, the Perkins engine plant invested $120 million in new technology, including an FMS for assembling cylinder heads. The FMS assembled 50 different cylinder heads for three-, four-, and six-cylinder engines in volumes averaging 13 units of each product per day.

The FMS consisted of five computers, a conveyor system, parts feeders, eight robots, test equipment, and a washstation. Robots inserted valves, valve springs, retaining caps, cotters,

SITUATION 20.3

Continued

and oil seals. Automation checked quality at each critical operation. Test equipment checked completed cylinder heads for leaky valves. Different cylinder heads were produced in small batch sizes, some as small as one unit.

The FMS produced the following benefits:

- The number of employees decreased from 30 to 18.
- Product quality improved.
- Delivery time improved.
- Inventory decreased.
- Perkins gained valuable experience with new process technologies.

ANALYSIS

Figure 20-3 analyzes the Perkins FMS. The figure shows that the FMS is the best production system for the mix and volume of products, and the market qualifying and order winning outputs.

- Many products are produced in low volumes: 50 products in volumes averaging 13 units of each product per day.
- Engines are in the maturity and saturation stages of their product life cycles (Chapter 16), so they compete on the basis of high quality and low cost. At Perkins, quality is the order winning output, and cost is a market qualifying output.
- Flexibility is a market qualifying output because Perkins produces a large number of different engines.

Prior to implementation of the FMS, Perkins used a batch flow production system. The following adjustments to manufacturing levers are needed to complete the change from the batch flow production system to an FMS.

HUMAN RESOURCES

Training is required for production operators and personnel in maintenance, material handling, and other support departments.

ORGANIZATION STRUCTURE AND CONTROLS

Maintenance and other support departments must adjust their procedures and activities to support the FMS.

PRODUCTION PLANNING AND CONTROL

Since the current planning and control system was designed for a batch flow production system, it must be changed. For example, the system must plan and schedule more frequent production of small batches.

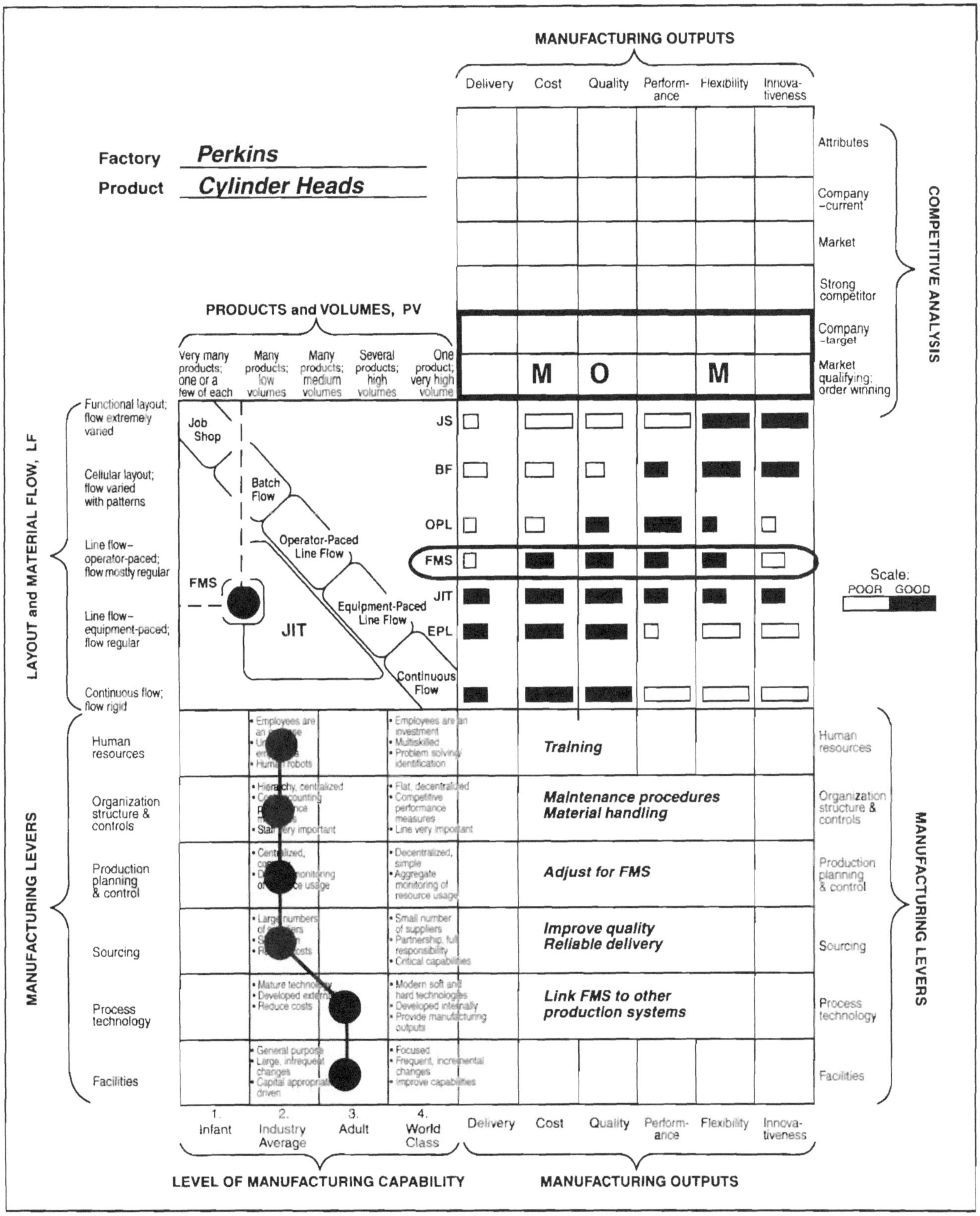

Figure 20-3 FMS Production System at Perkins

SITUATION 20.3

Continued

SOURCING

Products are produced more frequently and in smaller batches, so delivery quantities and schedules for purchased parts must be adjusted. Equipment and tooling in an FMS are so precise that they require high quality materials and parts to work properly, so the quality of purchased materials and parts should improve.

LEVEL OF MANUFACTURING CAPABILITY

Perkins has an adult level of manufacturing capability in facilities and process technology (because of its large investment in new technology) and an industry average level of capability in the other levers. For the Perkins FMS to be as effective as possible, all manufacturing levers should have the same high level of capability. Perkins should implement an improvement program, such as quality management (Chapter 14), to raise the manufacturing capability of all levers to the adult level.

SITUATION 20.4

Machining FMS at Caterpillar[3]

IN 1989, CATERPILLAR, with sales of $11 billion, and Komatsu, with sales of $6 billion, were engaged in a worldwide struggle in the heavy equipment industry. Caterpillar had a solid reputation for quality and service, but its costs were too high, and it knew that cost cutting (Chapter 14) alone would not make it competitive. It decided to invest $2 billion into improving its factories. Caterpillar nicknamed the plan, Plant-with-a-Future, PWAF.

One plant produced 120 types of transmissions. The plant's machining department used two production systems: an old batch flow production system and a new FMS production system. The batch flow production system was located on the left side of the plant's main aisle. Thirty-five old machine tools produced transmission cases. The area around the machines was crowded with bins of cases waiting to be machined. Each machine had its own operator and could produce only one kind of transmission case at a time. When a batch of cases was finished, the operator spent between four hours and two days setting up for the next batch. Once the setup was complete, the operator made additional adjustments on the first few cases to get the machine to run correctly. Sometimes, these adjustments damaged a case, and a $1,000 product became scrap.

Across the aisle from the batch flow production system were four (of an eventual 32) flexible machining systems. These machining systems were part of the FMS production system. The four flexible machining systems did the same work of milling, drilling, boring, tapping, deburring, and reaming. They were programmed to produce any case the plant made, and the setup time was only a few seconds. The flexible machining systems selected the right tools from a rotating belt and inserted them into the machine's spindles. There was almost no scrap because the tool did the job right the first time. Tool wear was checked electronically by monitoring the torque on the spindle. Before a tool broke or cut incorrectly, the spindle stopped, and the worn tool was replaced automatically.

Other departments in the plant (gearmaking, heat treatment, assembly, final testing) were also being converted to FMS production systems. In 1990, the time to build a transmission was down to 15 days (from three months), and costs were down significantly.

Figure 20-4 analyzes the changes at the plant. Delivery, quality, and flexibility were the market qualifying outputs, and cost was the order winning output. Komatsu was such a strong competitor that the current and future levels of the market qualifying and order winning outputs were very high and could not be provided by a batch flow production system or from a production system with an infant or industry average level of manufacturing capability. The Caterpillar plant changed its batch flow production system to an FMS and raised its level of manufacturing capability from industry average (for batch flow) to adult (for FMS).

SITUATION 20.5

FMS Production System at Pratt and Whitney

IN 1980, PRATT AND WHITNEY opened a factory in Halifax, Canada to machine 70 different products in volumes ranging from 30 to 1,000 units per product per year. Pratt and Whitney selected an FMS production system for the factory. The company needed the quality and cost of a line flow system, but the high number of products and the low volumes made it impractical to use an operator- or equipment-paced line flow or JIT production system. Pratt and Whitney also wanted to gain experience with the new technologies in the FMS production system.

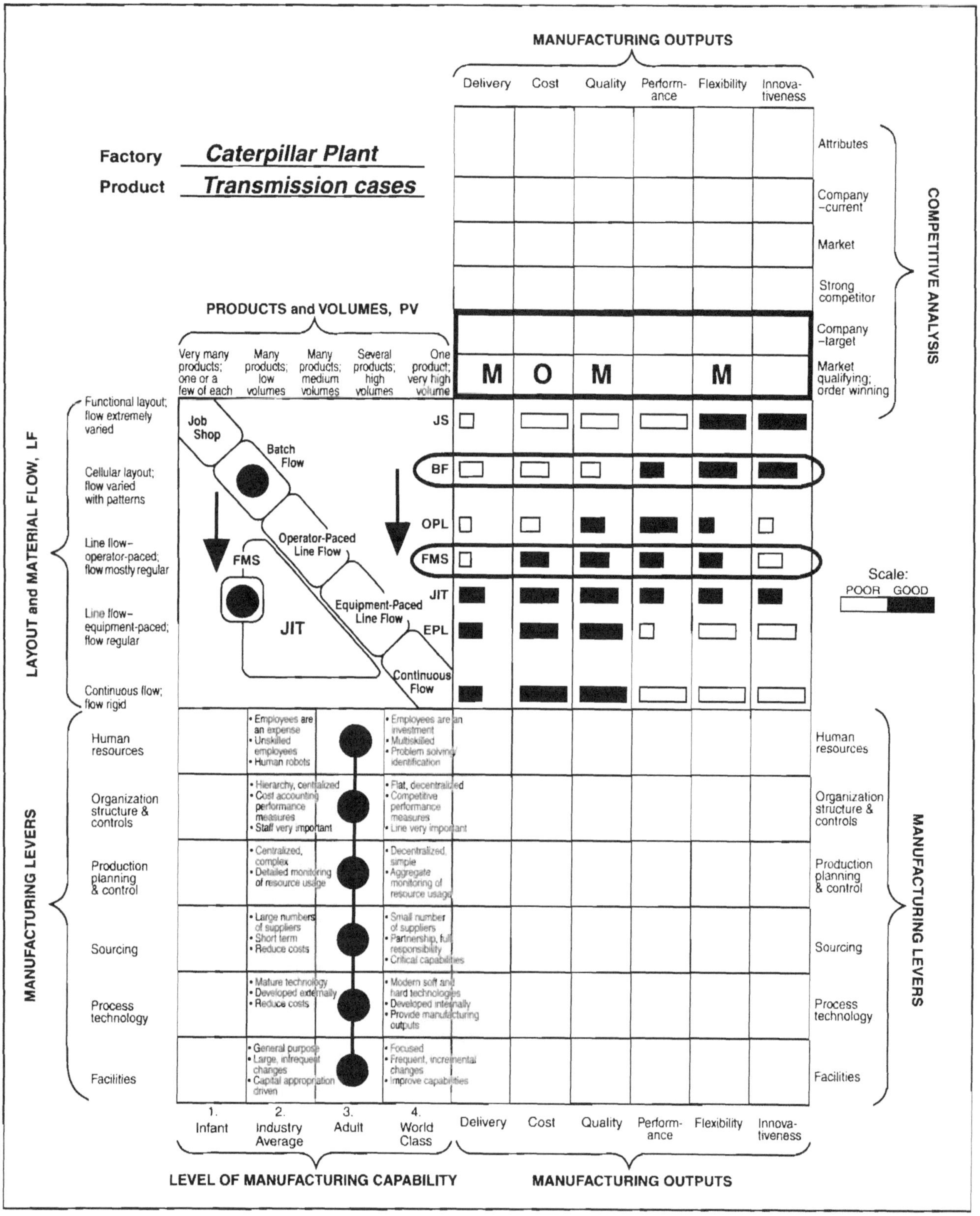

Figure 20-4 FMS Production System at the Caterpillar KK Plant

SITUATION 20.6

Allen-Bradley Showcase FMS[4]

ALLEN-BRADLEY manufactures automation controls, everything from contactors and relays for starting motors to programmable logic controllers for directing the activities of equipment in FMSs. One objective in Allen-Bradley's corporate strategy was to increase sales of components used in factory automation. This objective was difficult to achieve because Allen-Bradley could not convince enough customers to adopt its ideas for FMSs and factory automation.

In the early 1980s, the company decided to build the kind of FMS it tried to sell its customers. The FMS would replace an existing production system that manufactured motor contactors and control relays. That production system was struggling to provide the levels of cost and quality required to be competitive in the world market.

A few years later, the FMS production system was ready. It produced 125 variations of contactors and relays. Ten years (and many improvements) later, the FMS produced 937 variations at a rate of 600 units per hour, in batches as small as one unit, with no direct labor. Setup was automatic and took less than six seconds.

Allen-Bradley believed its FMS production system was the lowest-cost producer of contactors and relays in the world. The flexibility of the FMS enabled the company to respond quickly to customer needs. The FMS had a world class level of manufacturing capability and could provide cost, quality, and flexibility at order winning levels. All these order winning outputs helped Allen-Bradley win orders away from its competitors.

ENDNOTES

1. Brandt, R, and Port, O., "LTV Aircraft Products Group: Only the Beginning," *Industry Week*, pp. 50–54, March 21, 1988.
2. Wylie, P., "Perkins £50m Drive Aims for Diesel Lead," *The Engineer*, p. 36, November 29, 1984.
3. *Fortune*, pp. 59–60, May 21, 1990.
4. "Case Study: Allen-Bradley," *IEEE Spectrum*, pp. 37–39, September 1993.

CHAPTER 21

OPERATOR-PACED LINE FLOW PRODUCTION SYSTEM

Products and Volumes

An operator-paced line flow production system produces a large family of similar products in medium volumes on equipment arranged in a line layout (Figure 21-1). Compared to a batch flow production system, the volume of each product is higher and more regular. Compared to an equipment-paced line flow production system, the volume is lower and more variable. Compared to a JIT production system, an operator-paced line flow system produces fewer products in higher volumes, but the variability in product volumes is about the same.

Layout and Material Flow

An operator-paced line flow production system produces products on equipment arranged in a line layout (Chapter 4). Many production systems use line layouts. To understand these systems, we distinguish between lines where operators set the line speed and lines where equipment sets the line speed. In an operator-paced line flow production system, the line speed or production rate depends on the number of operators assigned to stations on the line, the speed at which operators work, and how well operators work together as a team.

The material flow in an operator-paced line flow production system is regular mostly. There are some variations from product to product and from time to time when requirements for products change. Equipment and tooling are modified for the family of products produced on the line and so are more specialized than a job shop or batch flow production system. However, product families are large, and the amount of specialization is less than in an equipment-paced line flow system.

Competitive Advantage

An operator-paced line flow production system provides good levels of all manufacturing outputs. It is used when the number of products is too high and the production volume is too low or too variable for an equipment-paced line flow production system. An operator-paced line flow production system is more flexible than an equipment-paced line flow production system. For example, an operator-paced line flow production system can run at more speeds than an equipment-paced line flow production system.

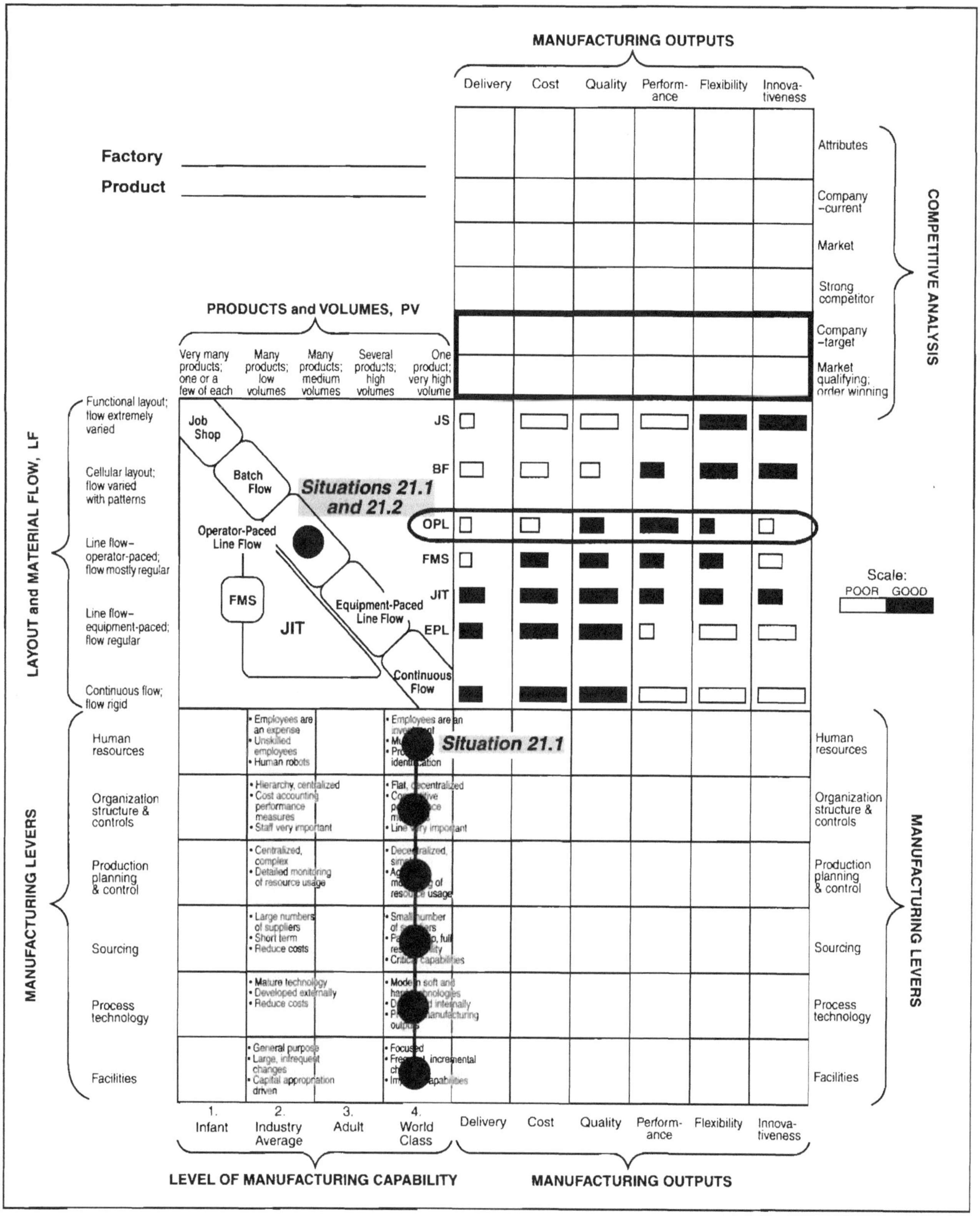

Figure 21-1 Operator-Paced Line Flow Production System

McDonald's restaurants runs one of the best-known operator-paced line flow production systems. A limited variety of different products are produced in volumes that vary during the day. Many products are produced on the same line. Adjusting the number of operators on the line changes the line speed or production rate. Teamwork is important for effective operation of the production system.

Manufacturing Levers

Human Resources

Production operators are less skilled than those in a job shop, batch flow, or JIT production system, and more skilled than those in an FMS, equipment-paced line flow, or continuous flow production system. Procedures and standards for performing production operations are carefully developed and improved. Procedures and standards are necessary to sustain line speed and maintain product quality.

Operators are members of a team. They work in stations on the line performing similar operations on different products produced on the line. Operators are trained to work at more than one station. Sometimes, they do routine maintenance on equipment in their stations. They also participate in problem-solving and improvement activities. Incentive wage schemes are used. One element of these schemes is a reward that depends on team performance.

Many staff groups, such as engineering, materials management, production planning and control, and quality, provide services. Staff groups are small and responsive to the needs of the production line.

Organization Structure and Controls

Job shop, batch flow, and operator-paced line flow production systems are usually profit centers and are relatively autonomous as far as corporate influence is concerned. Organization structure is not as flat as a job shop or batch flow production system, but it is not as hierarchical as an FMS, equipment-paced line flow, or continuous flow production system. The organization structure is similar to that found in the JIT production system.

Two important issues in an operator-paced line flow production system are managing materials and scheduling production. These have a considerable effect on whether:

- The production line runs efficiently.
- The many different products are produced on time.
- Setups and inventories are minimized.
- Other management objectives are achieved.

Sourcing

Influence over suppliers is higher than a job shop or batch flow production system, but it is not as high as an equipment-paced or continuous flow production system. Several factors account for the moderate influence an operator-paced line flow production system has over its suppliers:

- Many different products are produced in medium volumes.
- Customer demand and hence production are irregular.
- Products are redesigned frequently and new product launches are common.

These factors combine to produce small, irregular purchase orders to numerous suppliers. This makes it difficult to control or influence any particular supplier. An operator-paced line flow production system needs high quality and fast, reliable deliveries to keep the line running. It must work hard with its suppliers to achieve these needs.

Production Planning and Control

Raw material inventory is large to ensure that the line does not stop because of shortages of purchased materials. Work-in-process inventory is small because products are produced continuously and quickly on the line. Finished goods inventory is usually small because production is make-to-order.

Sometimes products are produced early and stored in finished goods inventory to smooth workloads in the factory.

An operator-paced line flow production system is flexible. Scheduling is flexible and frozen schedules are short—if they exist at all. Expediting is used sparingly, except when shortages of purchased materials threaten to stop the line.

Process Technology

Equipment, fixtures, and tooling are not general purpose as they are in a job shop, batch flow, or FMS production system, nor are they as specialized as in an equipment-paced or continuous flow production system. Production runs are long for some products and short for others. Because many products are produced on the same line, setups are frequent, and reducing setup times and scheduling to minimize production time lost due to setups are important management issues.

Process engineers and product design engineers work together to launch new features and new products, and make design changes to existing products.

Operator-paced line flow production systems are not as widespread as batch flow and equipment-paced line flow production systems, so they follow technology developments in these production systems and modify them as needed for their own use.

Facilities

Facilities are medium-sized, with limited economies of scale. The average line speed or production rate is medium. The production system is neither labor nor capital intensive. Equipment capacity on the line is balanced. Consequently, bottlenecks are infrequent, and equipment utilization and labor efficiency are high.

Manufacturing Outputs

Cost and Quality

Cost and quality are better than a job shop or batch flow production system for several reasons:

- Equipment and tooling are specialized for the products produced on the line.
- Operators are well trained to perform the small number of tasks assigned to them.
- Products are produced in medium volumes on a somewhat regular basis. This permits learning to occur and improvements to be made.

Performance

An operator-paced line flow production system provides the highest possible level of performance for several reasons:

- The volume of each product and product family is sufficiently high to justify the research and development work needed to design a steady stream of new features.
- The volumes are high enough to justify the engineering work needed to design new processes to produce new products, and to improve existing processes to produce existing products.
- Operators, equipment, and tooling are somewhat specialized but also flexible. This makes it easier to make the necessary changes for the new features and new processes.

Delivery

Delivery is provided at a high level because all operations required to produce a product are performed on equipment arranged along a line. Once production of a product starts, only a short time passes before the product is finished.

Flexibility and Innovativeness

Compared to a job shop or batch flow production system, an operator-paced line flow production system provides lower levels of flexibility and innovativeness. An operator-paced system produces a smaller number of different products on more specialized equipment and tooling, which makes it more difficult to change products and volumes, introduce new products, and make design changes to existing products.

Compared to an equipment-paced or continuous flow production system, an operator-paced line flow production system provides higher levels of flexibility and innovativeness. Equipment-paced and continuous flow production systems use very specialized operators, equipment, and tooling, which makes it more difficult for these production systems to be flexible and innovative.

SITUATION 21.1

Lincoln Electric's Operator-Paced Line Flow Production System[1]

THE LINCOLN ELECTRIC COMPANY of Cleveland is a good example of an operator-paced line flow production system with a world class level of manufacturing capability.

John C. Lincoln founded the company in 1895, as a repair shop for electric motors. Before long, the company was manufacturing its own brand of electric motors. In 1912, it became interested in welding equipment when welding began to gain widespread acceptance as a process for joining metal. From these beginnings, Lincoln Electric became one of the world's largest manufacturers of welding machines and welding electrodes.

Lincoln Electric has a lot of experience with the operator-paced line flow production system. In 1914, James F. Lincoln took over leadership of the company. One of his early actions was to ask employees to elect representatives to a committee that would advise him on company operations. During the advisory board's first year, working hours decreased from 55 to 50 hours per week. In 1915, each employee was given a paid-up life insurance policy. In 1918, an employee bonus plan was attempted, but it did not catch on. It succeeded when it was tried again in 1934. The first annual bonus amounted to about 25 percent of wages, and there has been a bonus every year since then. A suggestion plan was started in 1929. By 1944, employees enjoyed a pension plan, a policy of promotion from within, and continuous employment. Basic wage levels for jobs at Lincoln Electric were determined by a wage survey of similar jobs in the Cleveland area and were adjusted quarterly for changes in the consumer price index. Whenever possible, basic wage levels were translated into piece rates. Practically all production workers and many other employees were paid by piece rate.

Welding machines are manufactured at Lincoln's main factory (Figure 21-2). The operator-paced line flow production system that manufactures these products works as follows. Materials flow from a receiving dock on the north side of the factory through the production lines to a small storage and loading area on the south side of the factory. Materials are stored

SITUATION 21.1

Continued

close to the workstation where they are used. The lines are designed to produce several different welding machines on the same line by adjusting the line speed, changing the assignment of workers to workstations, and using different tooling. Piece rates are paid to teams of workers, rather than individuals, so that workers work together as a team.

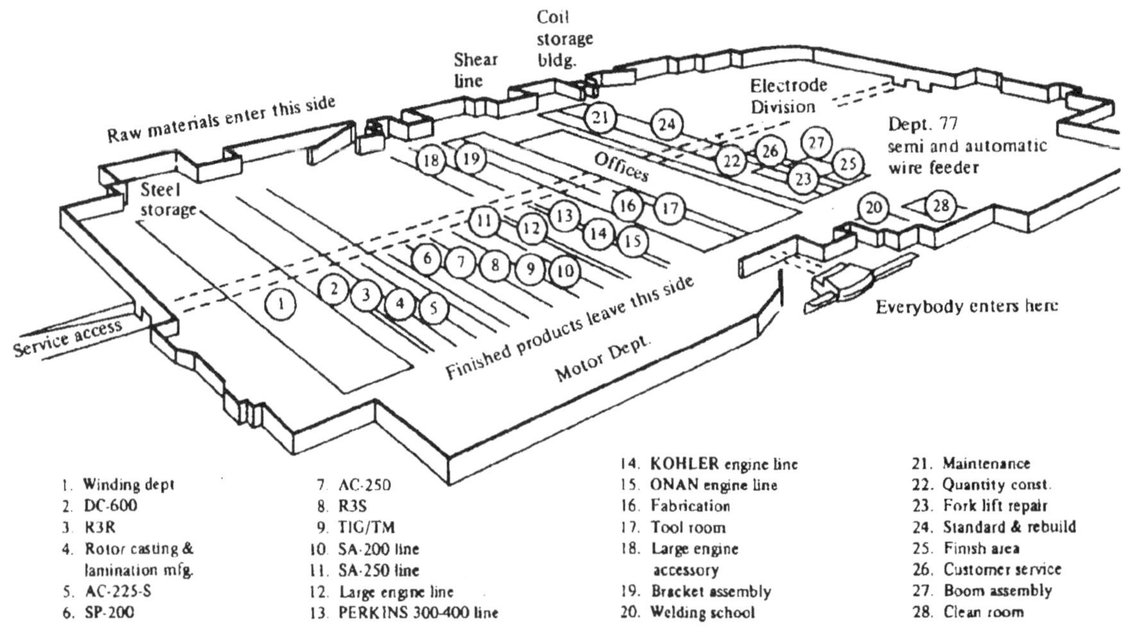

Source: A. Sharplin 1989. With permission.

Figure 21-2 Factory Layout at Lincoln Electric

SITUATION 21.2

European Company Improves Operator-Paced Line Flow Production System

NDL COMPANY, a European manufacturer of transportation equipment costing over $80,000 per unit, wondered whether it should change the way it competed against its two largest competitors. The competitors dominated the market and offered customers standard products with a small number of options. Quality was high and price was low. NDL, on the other hand, produced many models and options with so many combinations that production managers joked that the company never produced the same product twice. Occasionally, a new combination of options created problems on the production line when it was discovered that the particular combination could not be produced because of interferences between parts. Customers were fiercely loyal to NDL. They knew they could get precisely what they needed for their unique applications. NDL used an operator-paced line flow production system.

Human Resources

Workloads on the production line varied because of the many models and options. NDL responded by training employees for a variety of tasks. Production lines were divided into sections, and a team of employees was assigned to each section. Each team was responsible for completing all operations at the stations in their section. Each team had a leader who assigned employees to stations. Depending on team member skills and the production schedule, operations could be shifted to different stations or shared between stations. Sometimes, more than one employee was assigned to the same station, and sometimes, employees at adjacent stations helped each other. The speed of the lines increased or decreased to meet the production schedule by adding or removing employees.

There were few job classifications. Employees transferred back and forth between sections with a minimum of red tape. All production employees received the same hourly wage, regardless of what tasks were assigned. In addition to the hourly wage rate, employees participated in an incentive plan and a profit-sharing plan.

Under the incentive plan, each team member received an equal share of a set price for each product produced without defects. The team was penalized a set cost, equal to approximately ten times the set price, for each defect it produced. The set cost pushed employees to stop the line rather than produce a defect. The incentive plan also awarded each employee an attendance bonus. The employee received x cents an hour if he or she arrived on time, another y cents an hour if he or she arrived on time every day for one week, and another z cents an hour if he or she arrived on time every day for four consecutive weeks.

Under the profit-sharing plan, about 30 percent of NDL's pretax, prebonus profit became a bonus pool. Each employee's share of the pool was determined by a semiannual merit rating that measured the employee's performance. Four factors figured

SITUATION 21.2

Continued

in the merit rating: dependability, quality, output, and ideas and cooperation.

ORGANIZATION STRUCTURE AND CONTROLS

NDL had a flat organization structure. Relatively large staff groups were responsible for product design, process engineering, materials management, maintenance, and so on. Much of the staff groups' time was spent managing the many models and options produced. Every staff group employee and all senior managers spent one day a year working on the production lines and another day working in the sales department. No one in the company had an "it's not my job" mentality.

PRODUCTION PLANNING AND CONTROL

Production of final products was make-to-order, and no finished goods inventory was kept. Many common parts were make-to-stock; that is, they were built to a forecast and inventoried. Large inventories of raw materials and purchased parts were kept. A modern MRP system planned production, managed materials, and controlled and monitored activities in the factory.

SOURCING

NDL purchased many materials and parts in medium volumes from a large number of suppliers. It was difficult to reduce the cost of purchased materials and parts, and improve quality and delivery.

NDL's influence over suppliers was less than desired. To increase its influence, NDL reduced the number of suppliers by eliminating poor suppliers and giving more orders and longer contracts to suppliers with good records of cost, quality, and delivery, and high levels of manufacturing capability. NDL worked with these suppliers to reduce cost and improve quality and delivery. In addition, NDL needed suppliers with product design skills to help NDL provide high levels of performance and innovativeness.

PROCESS TECHNOLOGY

Equipment, tooling, and fixtures were neither general purpose nor specialized. Some equipment and most fixtures were designed and built by NDL to be flexible enough for all the different models and options produced. Like all line flow production systems, there was a substantial amount of automation.

Communication between product design engineers and process engineers was good. Both groups were located at the same site. A formal design for manufacturability program was in place. Process engineers were involved early in the design process, which reduced the time needed to introduce new options and models. It also reduced production cost and improved quality because parts were designed to be easy to manufacture, using existing production processes.

FACILITIES

The NDL factory was large, modern, and clean. Line speeds were slower than in other factories where similar products were produced on equipment-paced line flow production systems. Fabricated parts were produced in other departments using batch flow and job shop production systems.

ENDNOTES

1. Adapted from Arthur Sharplin, "Lincoln Electric: 1989." Used with permission from Arthur Sharplin, Austin, TX.

CHAPTER 22

JUST-IN-TIME PRODUCTION SYSTEM

Just-in-time (JIT) is a manufacturing philosophy in which producing products and making improvements are two equally important objectives. The purposes for making improvements are to reduce cost and improve quality and delivery. The means for making improvements are singling out wastes and forcing the production system to remove them.

Many companies use JIT. In some companies, JIT is a collection of techniques for making improvements in a job shop, batch flow, FMS, operator-paced line flow, equipment-paced line flow, or continuous flow production system. In other companies, JIT is a distinct production system.

COLLECTION OF TECHNIQUES

Beginning in the early 1980s, new techniques were developed and old techniques were rediscovered for improving production systems. These include the improvement approaches in Chapter 14 and the soft and hard technologies in Chapter 15. Often called "JIT techniques," all production systems use them.

DISTINCT PRODUCTION SYSTEM

Over a 20-year period beginning in the early 1950s, the Toyota Motor Company of Japan developed a new production system for producing automobiles. The Toyota production system produced cars and trucks with lower cost, higher quality, and in less time than the traditional batch flow, operator-paced line flow, and equipment-paced line flow production systems used by Toyota's Asian, European, and North American competitors.

When an oil embargo plunged Japan into deep recession in the early 1970s, many Japanese companies, desperate to cut costs, implemented and adapted the new Toyota production system in their own factories. The results exceeded their most optimistic expectations.

In the 1980s, the Toyota production system spread to other parts of the world. It is now used in industries far removed from the automobile industry. It goes by many different names: just-in-time, lean production, stockless production, and zero inventories. While the new production system uses all the JIT techniques, it is considerably more than a collection of techniques. It is a production system that produces products, and at the same time, forces continuous improvement by identifying wastes and compelling the production system to eliminate them.

Most companies use JIT techniques in their production systems. A small number of companies use a JIT production system. It is not easy to change an existing production system to a JIT production system, and few companies willingly undertake the change. Most companies change when JIT is the only production system that can provide cost, quality, delivery, and flexibility at the levels required by their customers. These companies know that without a JIT production system, they will lose customers and go out of business.

Products and Volumes

A JIT production system is a line flow production system like the operator-paced and equipment-paced line flow production systems. A JIT production system produces many products in low to medium volumes (Figure 22-1). Before the JIT production system was developed, this product mix could only be produced on a batch flow production system. Operator-paced or equipment-paced line flow production systems could not be used because the number of products was too high and product volumes were too low.

Layout and Material Flow

The JIT production system was developed so that a particular product mix, many products in low to medium volumes, could be produced on a line flow production system rather than a batch flow production system. The objective was the lower cost and higher quality of line flow production compared to batch flow production.

Toyota began developing JIT in 1950. At that time, Toyota produced small volumes of many models of cars and trucks for numerous domestic and foreign markets. Toyota's batch flow production system struggled to match the levels of cost and quality provided by the line flow production systems of its larger, foreign competitors. Toyota could not use an operator-paced or equipment-paced line flow production system because it produced too many different products in low volumes. So Toyota developed a new line flow production system that could produce many products in low to medium volumes.

Taiichi Ohno, the vice president of Toyota and creator of JIT, gave some of the credit for JIT to Henry Ford for his work in the 1920s at the Ford Rouge River Plant in Detroit. Ohno said, "I think that if the American King of Cars were still alive, he would be headed in the same direction as Toyota."[1]

Figure 22-1 shows that the JIT production system occupies a large region of the PV-LF matrix. Different points in this region correspond to different degrees of implementation of JIT. As we will see, the top part of the region uses a "virtual" line flow, while the bottom part of the region uses a "physical" line flow. Implementing JIT is a journey of many small steps that form a path through the JIT region. The path starts in the top corner of the JIT region and ends in the bottom right corner.

Competitive Advantage

JIT is a line flow production system that produces many products in low to medium volumes. JIT provides cost, quality, and delivery at the same levels as operator-paced and equipment-paced line flow production systems because JIT is a line flow production system. It provides flexibility and innovativeness at the same levels as a batch flow production system because JIT and batch flow production systems both produce many products in low to medium volumes.

All production systems produce a mix and volume of products. JIT differs from other production systems because it forces continuous improvement at the same time as it produces a mix and volume of products. JIT does this by making wastes visible and forcing the production system to remove them.

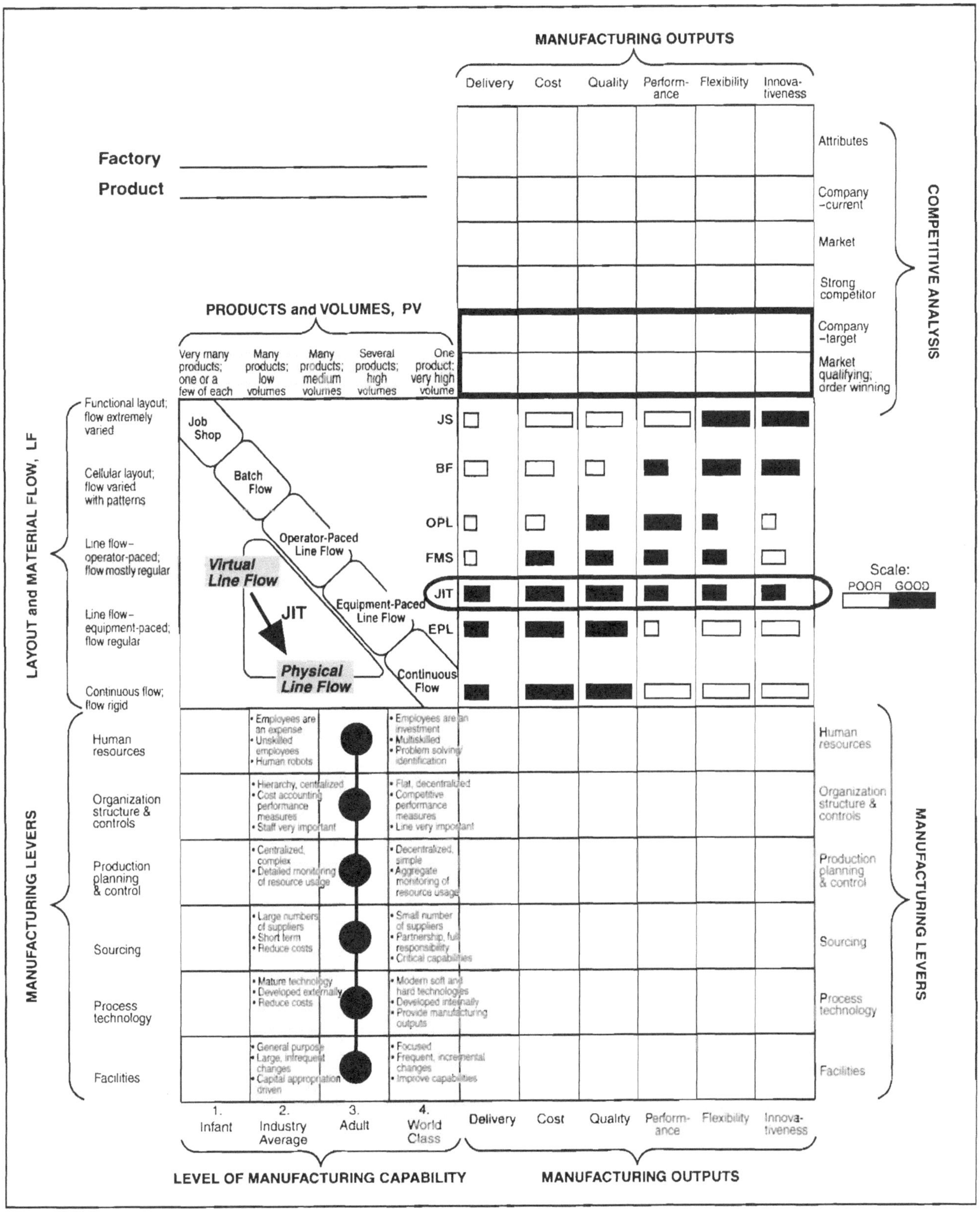

Figure 22-1 Just-In-Time (JIT) Production System

A JIT production system uses the following mechanism to identify and eliminate waste:

1. Inventory is moved from the stockroom to the factory floor to locations where inventory is used and produced. Maximum levels are set for the amount of inventory held at each location.
2. Management lowers maximum inventory levels at the parts of the production system where it wants to make improvements. The production system strains to produce its mix and volume of products without the cushion of a large inventory.
3. Soon, problems develop that prevent parts of the production system from completing their work before inventory runs out. Shortages occur, which causes production stoppages. A production stoppage is a call to action: Personnel are mobilized to seek out the problems or wastes that caused the stoppage. Problems or wastes are studied carefully. Root causes are identified. Permanent solutions are found and implemented so that these problems do not reoccur. Typical solutions are:
   - Employees are trained to do multiple tasks.
   - Greater use is made of quality control techniques to prevent defective products.
   - Product design improves so that products are easier to produce.
   - Scheduling improves.
   - Setup times are reduced to facilitate small lot production.
   - Tooling and materials improve.
   - Work procedures improve.

   As soon as a problem is identified, the inventory level is increased to its original level so that production can continue without further disruptions while personnel find and implement a permanent solution for the problem. When the solution is implemented, inventory is reduced again to expose the next problem.
4. This routine of removing inventory to strain different parts of the production system to force them to identify and eliminate wastes is repeated again and again until all waste is eliminated. The analogy of water flowing over rocks is used to describe this process (Figure 22-2). Water represents inventory and rocks represent problems. Rocks or problems are exposed when the water or inventory level is lowered. The

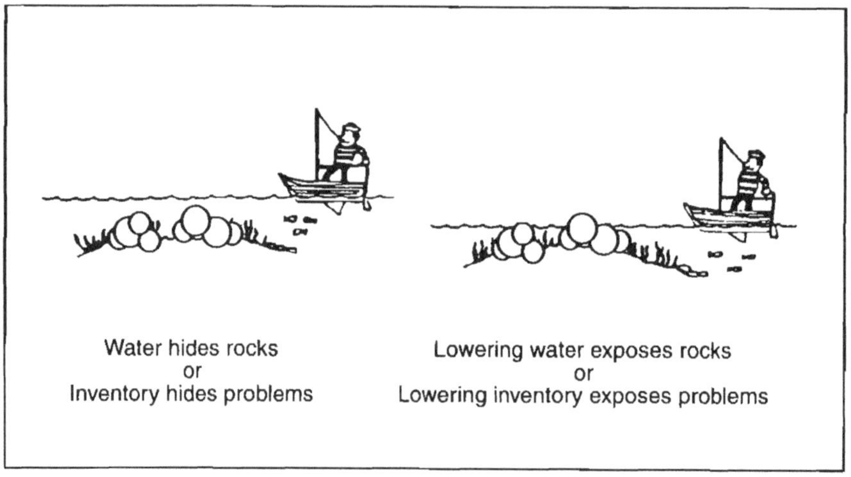
Water hides rocks
or
Inventory hides problems
Lowering water exposes rocks
or
Lowering inventory exposes problems

Figure 22-2 Reducing Inventory to Identify and Eliminate Waste

objective is to remove all rocks, beginning with the largest, at a rate that is appropriate for the company.

Difficult Production System

A JIT production system is the most difficult of all production systems to design, implement, manage, and operate. The primary reason is that, unlike other production systems that only produce a mix and volume of products, JIT also continuously identifies and removes waste from the production system. This requires very high levels of manufacturing capability. Employees, equipment, processes, and suppliers must have very high capabilities. Toyota needed more than 20 years to implement JIT, which is evidence enough of its difficulty.

The conventional wisdom is to use a JIT production system when three conditions hold:

- Many products are produced in low to medium volumes. The current production system is a batch flow system, and an operator-paced or equipment-paced line flow production system cannot be used because too many products are produced in volumes that are too low.
- Higher levels of cost, quality, and delivery are required than what a batch flow production system with a high level of manufacturing capability can provide.
- The level of manufacturing capability is high.

A JIT production system is the best production system for an environment where products are offered in a wide variety of options, products are tailored to meet the needs of small-niche markets, product life cycles are short, and customers demand high levels of cost, quality, performance, and flexibility.

Situations 22.1 and 22.2 describe two companies positive and negative experiences with a JIT production system. There are many reasons why companies like DP (Situation 22.1) can move from a batch flow production system to a physical line flow JIT production system and companies like LG (Situation 22.2) cannot.

- DP had a higher level of manufacturing capability.

Situation 22.1

Instrument Panel Manufacturer Implements JIT

DP COMPANY is located in New Hampshire, about 900 miles from its automotive assembly plant customers in Detroit. Four years ago, DP changed its batch flow production system to a physical line flow JIT production system (Figure 22-3).

The factory layout and material flow changed from a functional layout with production in batches to product-focused lines. The production rate for each line was flexible, and DP changed the rate as required to match customer requirements, thus permitting products to be produced and shipped just-in-time. DP reduced setup times from eight hours to 20 minutes and started programs for improvement teams, returnable containers, level schedules, and statistical process control.

DP was pleased with its JIT production system. Inventory turns increased from 7.5 to 28 turns per year. Product costs decreased, quality improved, and manufacturing cycle time dropped.

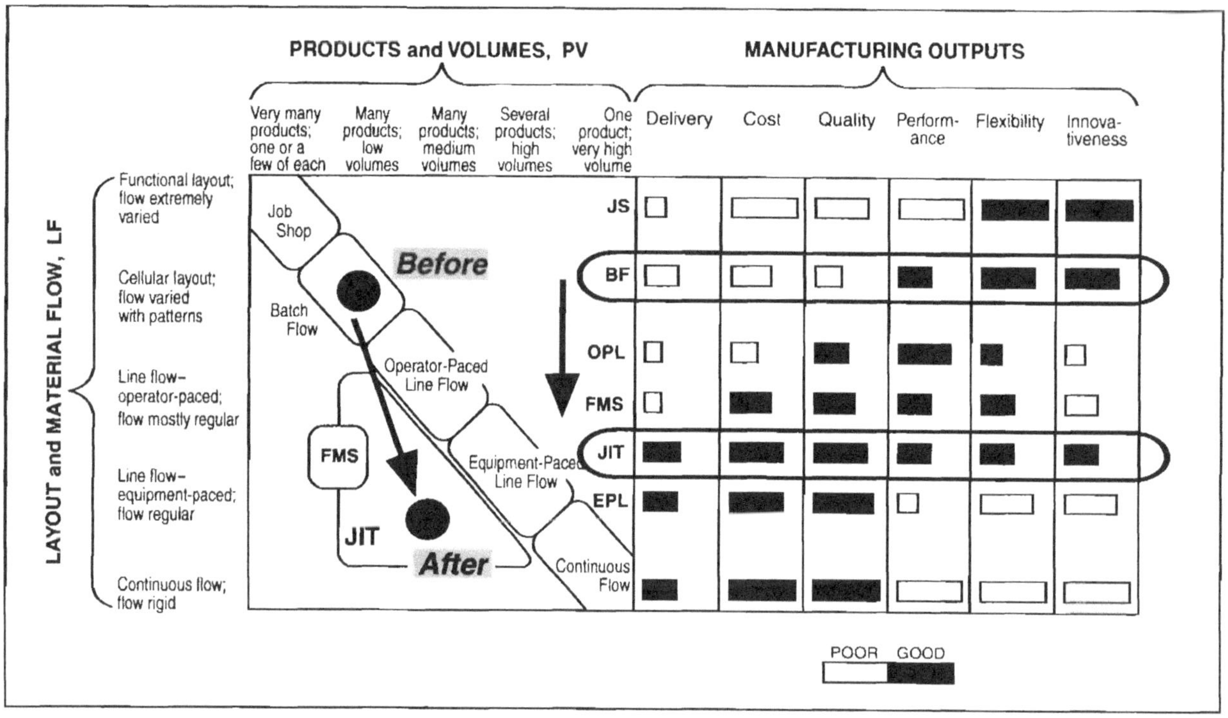

Figure 22-3 JIT Production System at DP Company

SITUATION 22.2

Heat Exchanger Manufacturer is Disappointed with JIT

LG COMPANY manufactured heat exchangers at a factory located near Toronto. After learning about JIT, LG decided to relocate some production equipment from four areas of the factory (Figure 22-4 [A]) into a physical line flow JIT production system. Equipment was arranged into a U-shaped production line (Figure 22-4 [B]). Stations on the line were designed to eliminate unnecessary effort and allow work to be shared. Operators were trained to work at all stations, tools and fixtures were standardized, and buffer inventories between stations were eliminated.

Problems occurred as soon as the new line started. The most common problems were quality problems caused by poor materials and tooling, inadequate operating and maintenance procedures, and material shortages. Problems took a long time to solve, and while being solved, the line was stopped. Deliveries slipped, and costs increased.

After eight months of trying to make JIT work, LG put the JIT project on hold. Stations were spread apart to make room for buffer inventories. Inventories decoupled stations so that problems at one station did not force others to stop. Batch sizes increased to previous levels, and LG reverted to its old batch flow production system.

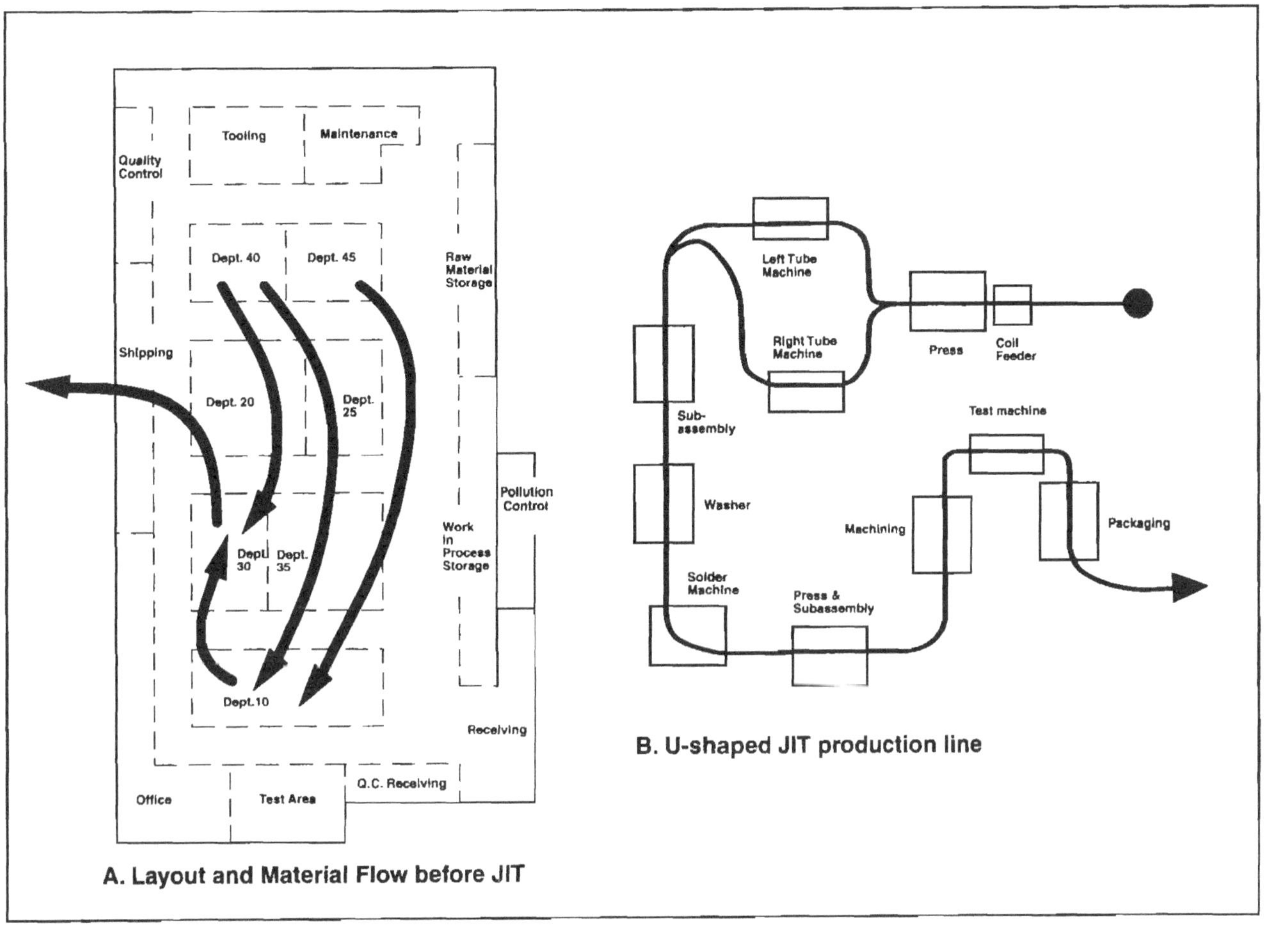

Figure 22-4 Layout and Material Flow at LG Company

- DP had a more effective implementation plan, and its execution was better.
- When problems were exposed at DP, resources were available to find and implement solutions. These resources were not available at LG, so problems were exposed but not solved. A JIT production system exposes problems that a company must solve. If a company cannot solve exposed problems, a JIT production system will fail.
- It took DP four years to achieve the desired results, whereas LG stopped its JIT implementation after less than one year.

Regardless of the level of manufacturing capability, the thoroughness of the implementation plan, and the determination to stay the course, jumping from a batch flow production system to a physical line flow JIT production system is usually a bad idea. The number of adjustments to manufacturing levers and the size of the adjustments are such that, unless the company has a high level of manufacturing capability, the chances of failure are too high.

The conventional wisdom is to implement JIT gradually:

- Move from a batch flow production system to a virtual line flow JIT production system at the top of the JIT region (Figure 22-1).
- Later, move into the middle of the JIT region.
- Finally, move to a physical line flow JIT system at the bottom of the region.

Three-step implementations have worked well in many companies, although some, like DP, require fewer steps. More than three steps are rarely required.

Three-Step Journey for Implementing JIT[2]

This section examines a three-step procedure for implementing JIT. The steps are general, and the details vary somewhat from company to company.

Step 1. Change the current batch flow production system to a *two-bin virtual line flow* JIT production system. Store inventory in bins on the factory floor in the areas where inventory is used. Force improvements by lowering the amount of inventory in the bins.

Step 2. Change the two-bin system to a *kanban virtual line flow* JIT production system. Store inventory in "move" and "production" kanbans in the areas where inventory is used and produced. Force improvements by reducing the number and size of kanbans.

Step 3. Create a *physical line flow* JIT production system by moving the equipment in the kanban JIT system into a physical line flow. Force improvements by lowering inventory toward a target of zero.

These steps have the following features:

- Each step makes a small number of adjustments to the manufacturing levers. The adjustments are simple, require little capital expenditure, and cause no disruption to production activities.
- Each step reduces cost and improves quality and delivery.
- Each step creates a foundation on which the next step builds.
- The JIT journey can stop at any step. Each step produces an effective JIT production system. If a company is satisfied with the achieved improvements or if other priorities arise, the company can pause or stop at that step.

The next sections describe each step in detail. In addition to outlining the mechanics of implementing a JIT production system, the descriptions give an appreciation for what constitutes a JIT production system, how it differs from other production systems, and how it is much more than a collection of JIT techniques. This is important if companies want to avoid the outcome experienced by LG Company in Situation 22.2.

Step 1: Two-Bin Virtual Line Flow

The two-bin JIT production system stores parts and products in two-bin containers (Figure 22-5 [A]) on the factory floor in the areas where each part or product is used. Each container has a clear plastic envelope called a JIT package that contains a JIT card, visual control tag, manufacturing order, and part drawing. The package is placed in the second bin of the two-bin container. Containers and packages are used in a pull production control system that works as follows:

1. Parts are taken from the first bin as needed. When the first bin is empty, parts are taken from the second bin, whereupon the JIT package is taken from the second bin and placed in a nearby pickup area. The JIT package is now an authorization to produce a specified number of parts, the *replenishment quantity*, within a specified number of days, the *lead time*. This information is printed on the JIT card.
2. A material handler collects JIT packages from the pickup areas at regular intervals and delivers them to the manufacturing areas where the parts are produced. In the case of purchased parts, the JIT packages

are delivered to a dispatching area, then go to suppliers.

3. Control boards are located in each manufacturing and dispatching area (Figure 22-5 [B]). A control board is divided into six columns, one for each working day—Monday through Friday—and one overdue column. The columns are separated into weeks. When the material handler delivers a JIT package to a manufacturing or dispatching area, he or she takes the visual control tag from the JIT package and places it on the control board in a position corresponding to the day and week when the replenishment must be completed. For example, if the replenishment is triggered on Monday and the lead time on the JIT card is three days, then the visual control tag is placed in the Wednesday column on the row corresponding to the current week. If the replenishment is not complete on Wednesday afternoon, the tag is moved to the overdue column, and action is taken to complete the replenishment quickly.
4. When the replenishment is complete, the visual control tag is removed from the control board and placed in the JIT package. The material handler delivers the replenishment quantity and the JIT package to the area where the JIT package originated. There, users check that the order is complete, and the quality is good. Users place parts in the two-bin container. The second bin is filled to its specified level, and the remaining parts are placed in the first bin. The number of parts in the second bin is sufficient to meet the usage during the lead time, plus some safety stock. The replenishment quantity is a quantity of parts sufficient to satisfy a management-specified number of weeks of use.

The two-bin JIT system has several attractive features.

- Inventory is stored on the factory floor in the areas where it is used. This eliminates inventory transactions in and out of a stockroom. The stockroom can be reduced and sometimes eliminated, which frees up floor space and reduces cost.

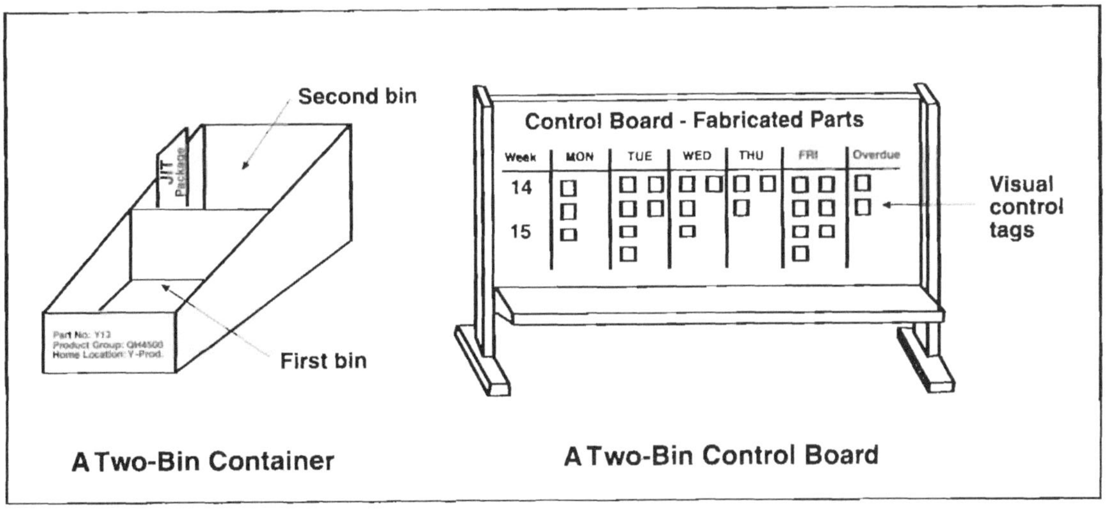

Figure 22-5 Two-Bin JIT Production System

- Inventory is visible, making it easier to manage. Overproduction cannot occur because there is nowhere to put extra inventory.
- Production problems are visible. An examination of the control boards shows which parts are late and which manufacturing areas and suppliers are busy.
- Each part is controlled by the area that uses it. The area triggers the replenishment, checks the quality, and holds the inventory.
- The two-bin system is only effective for parts with a regular usage and a moderate lead time. Parts not satisfying these criteria are controlled using the regular batch flow control system. These parts can be studied to see whether they can be standardized, replaced by other parts, produced in a different way, and so on, so that they can also be controlled by the two-bin JIT system.

After the two-bin system has been working properly for some time, management reduces the amount of inventory by decreasing lead times or replenishment quantities in areas of the factory that they want to improve. Then, replenishments occur more frequently and in smaller quantities. This strains the production system. Soon, shortages and production stoppages occur. Stoppages draw attention to problems and force the production system to find, and implement permanent solutions.

As soon as a problem is identified, lead times and replenishment quantities are increased to original levels so that production can continue without more stoppages, while personnel find and implement a permanent solution for the problem. When the solution is implemented, inventory is reduced again to expose the next problem.

Improvements reduce cost and improve quality and delivery. This process of reducing inventory and making improvements is repeated again and again in all areas of the factory until all wastes are eliminated.

SITUATION 22.3

Two-Bin JIT System for a Product Family

TWO PRODUCTS, m31 and m32, are assembled from 11 subassemblies and fabricated parts: x7, x12, x13, x17, y2, y7, y11, y13, z1, z3, and z5. Figure 22-6 shows the bills of material. Products m31 and m32 have demands of 40 units per day each.

A two-bin virtual line flow JIT production system produces all parts. Figure 22-7 (A) shows the existing factory layout, and Figure 22-7 (B) shows the layout in the two-bin JIT system. The only changes to the existing layout are the relocation of inventory from the stockroom to factory floor areas where parts are used and the addition of two-bin containers and control boards.

Eleven two-bin containers are required. Four containers, for parts x7, x12, x13 and x17, are located at the beginning of the final assembly line because this is the area where they are used. Four containers for y2, y7, y11, and y13 are located at the input area of the x-assembly area where they are used. Three containers for z1, z3, and z5 are located at the y-production area.

These changes are easy to make and require a small capital expenditure.

Product m31			Product m32		
Level	Part Number	Usage	Level	Part Number	Usage
0	m31	1	0	m32	1
..1	..x7	1	..1	..x7	1
....2	....y2	1	2	....y2	1
......3	......z1	3	3	......z1	3
......3	......z3	1	3	......z3	1
....2	....y7	1	2	....y7	1
......3	......z1	1	3	......z1	1
......3	......z3	1	3	......z3	1
......3	......z5	1	3	......z5	1
..1	..x12	1	..1	..x13	1
....2	....y2	1	2	....y7	1
......3	......z1	3	3	......z1	1
......3	......z3	1	3	......z3	1
....2	....y11	1	3	......z5	1
......3	......z1	2	2	....y11	1
......3	......z3	2	3	......z1	2
......3	......z5	1	3	......z3	2
			3	......z5	1
			2	....y13	1
			3	......z3	2
			3	......z5	2
			..1	..x17	1
			2	....y11	1
			3	......z1	2
			3	......z3	2
			3	......z5	1
			2	....y13	1
			3	......z3	2
			3	......z5	2

Figure 22-6 Bills of Material in Situation 22.3

Management specifies the following initial values for replenishment quantities, lead times, and safety stock:

- All replenishment quantities are equal to two weeks (10 days) of average use.
- All lead times are equal to three days. That is, x-assembly area and y- and z-production areas must replenish orders within three days.

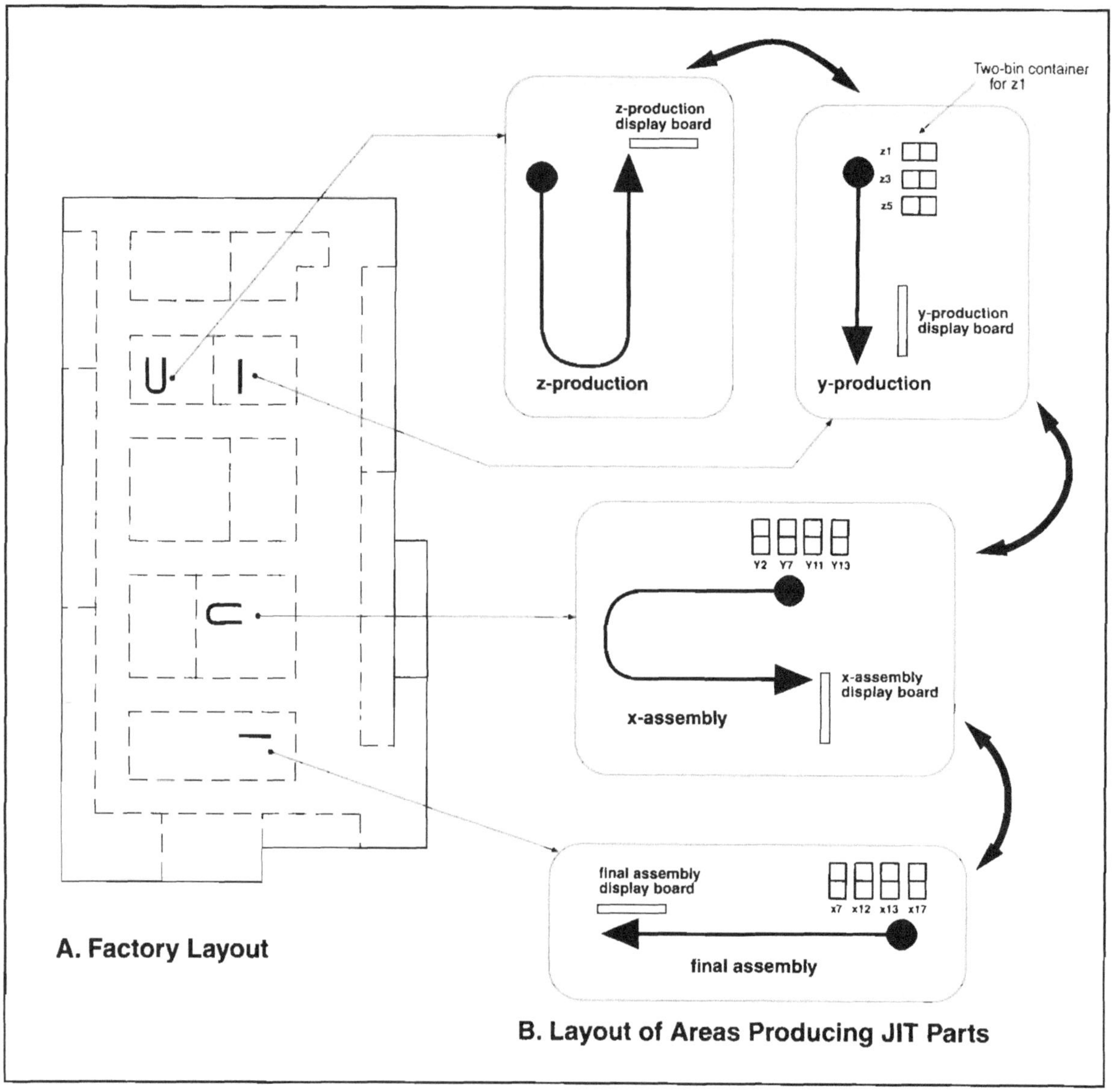

Figure 22-7 Layout for Two-Bin JIT in Situation 22.3

SITUATION 22.3

Continued

- All safety stocks are equal to 50 percent of average use over the lead time.

Figure 22-8 shows the calculations for the inventory quantities. Consider part x7. Since one unit of x7 is required for each unit of product m31 and for each unit of m32, 80 units of x7 are required every day. The replenishment quantity is 80 units per day × 10 days = 800 units. The second bin quantity is (80 units per day × 3 days) + 50 percent safety stock = 240 + 240 × 50 percent = 360 units. So the two-bin container for part x7 must be large enough to hold 360 units in the second bin and approximately 560 units in the first bin (calculated as the 800-unit replenishment quantity minus the expected usage over the lead time, 80 units per day × 3 days = 240 units).

It is also easy to calculate quantities for parts used in both JIT and non-JIT products. For example, x7 is used in m31 and m32, which are JIT products. Suppose x7 is also used in non-JIT products. In this case, the requirements for x7 include the JIT requirements (as calculated in Figure 22-8) and the non-JIT requirements (as calculated by the batch flow production system).

After employees are accustomed to the two-bin system and it has operated properly for some time, management reduces inventory levels in the areas where they wish to make improvements. For example, suppose management is looking for improvements in the departments where y- and z-parts are produced. Management can reduce replenishment quantities to one week's use and lead times to two days for these parts and direct the y- and z-production areas to make improvements to their production processes so smaller quantities can be produced within the shorter lead time. The last two columns of Figure 22-8 show the new inventory quantities. The average inventory levels for y- and z-parts are 46 percent lower. This routine of reducing inventory levels and making improvements continues for one or two years until further improvements are impossible.

Notice that production is intermittent and replenishment quantities are still relatively large. Consider part y7. Under the initial values, one batch of 1,200 units is produced every 10 days. When inventory levels are reduced, one batch of 600 units is produced every five days. Under JIT, the ultimate goal is to produce all parts on a continuous basis, which, in the case of y7, means producing 120 units each day or 15 units each hour (assuming eight hours are worked each day). This goal cannot be achieved with the two-bin system. However, the next step, the kanban JIT system, moves the company closer to this goal. Continuous production has several advantages:

- Each part is produced on a regular basis, making it easy to study and improve the operations required to produce it.
- It is possible to use smaller, less expensive equipment. In the case of part y7, 15 units could be produced each hour on a small machine, compared to infrequent batches of 1,200 units for which a larger machine would likely be required.

Part	Location	Parent Parts	Requirements per Day	Initial Quantities		Later Quantities	
				Replenishment[1]	Second Bin[2]	Replenishment[3]	Second Bin[4]
x7	final assembly	m31 m32	1 x 40 = 40 1 x 40 = 40 80	800	360	same	same
x12	final assembly	m31	1 x 40 = 40	400	180	same	same
x13	final assembly	m32	1 x 40 = 40	400	180	same	same
x17	final assembly	m32	1 x 40 = 40	400	180	same	same
y2	x assembly	x7 x12	1 x 80 = 80 1 x 40 = 40 120	1200	540	600	360
y7	x assembly	x7 x13	1 x 80 = 80 1 x 40 = 40 120	1200	540	600	360
y11	x assembly	x12 x13 x17	1 x 40 = 40 1 x 40 = 40 1 x 40 = 40 120	1200	540	600	360
y13	x assembly	x13 x17	1 x 40 = 40 1 x 40 = 40 80	800	360	400	240
z1	y assembly	y2 y7 y11	3 x 120 = 360 1 x 120 = 120 2 x 40 = 80 720	7200	3240	3600	2160
z3	y assembly	y2 y7 y11 y13	1 x 120 = 120 1 x 120 = 120 2 x 120 = 240 2 x 80 = 160 640	6400	2880	3200	2160
z5	y assembly	y7 y11 y13	1 x 120 = 120 1 x 120 = 120 2 x 80 = 160 400	4000	1800	2000	1200

Notes:

1. Initial replenishment quantity is ten days' usage.
2. Initial second bin quantity is 150 percent of the usage over a three-day lead time.
3. Later replenishment quantity in departments y and z is five days' usage.
4. Later second bin quantity in departments y and z is 150 percent of the usage over a two-day lead time.

Figure 22-8 Two-Bin JIT System Calculations in Situation 22.3

This system is called a *virtual*, rather than a *physical*, line flow production system because it behaves like a line even though it does not look like a line. For example, the layout in Figure 22-7 is not a line layout. However, the two-bin containers, control boards, and pull control system make the production system behave like a line.

When the two-bin JIT system has made all possible improvements, the second step on the JIT journey, the kanban virtual line flow JIT production system, is taken. This step is relatively easy because the two-bin system and the kanban system share many common elements. The kanban system may be viewed as an *m*-bin system, where *m* is a number larger than two.

Step 2: Kanban Virtual Line Flow

A kanban consists of a container and a document. The container is a standard size and contains a fixed number of parts. The document controls use of the container and its contents. The document can be as simple as a card specifying the part, the quantity in the container, and the location for the container (Figure 22-9 [A]), or as detailed as the JIT package used in the two-bin JIT system. The kanban document is placed in a clear plastic sleeve on the side of the kanban container.

There are two types of kanban: move and production. Move kanbans are located at the beginning of the production area where the part is used. When a move kanban container is empty, it moves

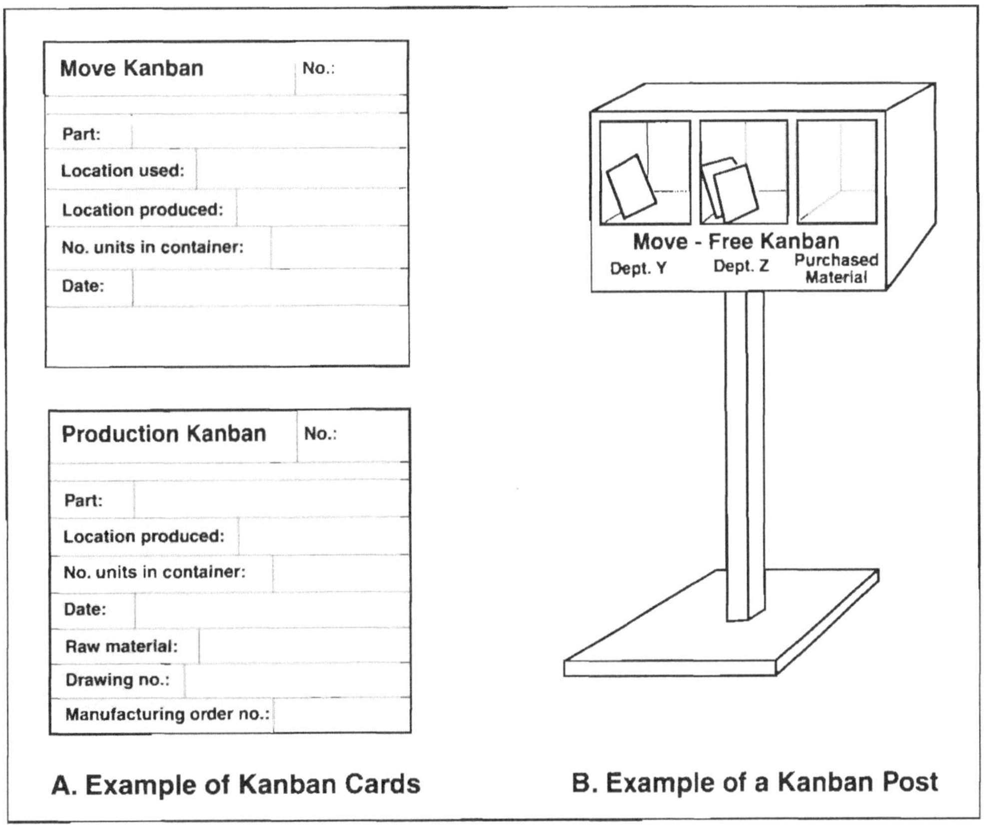

Figure 22-9 Kanban JIT Production System

to the production area where the part is produced. The empty container is replenished there. Production kanbans are located at the end of the production area where the part is produced. Production kanbans do not move away from this area.

Kanbans are used in a pull production control system that works as follows:

1. Initially, all move and production kanban containers are full.
2. The final assembly line takes parts from a move kanban container and uses the parts to produce final assemblies. When the last part from a move kanban container is removed, the kanban document is taken from the container and placed on a kanban post (Figure 22-9 [B]). The kanban is now called a move-free kanban. The final assembly line continues production using parts from the next move kanban container.
3. A material handler visits all kanban posts at regular intervals. He or she collects the move-free kanban containers and documents, and transports them to the production areas where the parts are produced. There, he or she replenishes each move-free kanban by transferring parts from a production kanban container to an empty move kanban container. Then, he or she returns the full move kanban containers to the areas where they originated.
4. If a production kanban container is emptied while the material handler transfers parts from the production kanban to the move kanban, he or she takes the document from the production kanban container and places it on the kanban post. The kanban is now called a production-free kanban and signals the production area to produce enough parts to fill the empty production kanban container.

If there are too few move kanbans, the area where the part is used will use all units in the containers before a replenishment is made. If there are too few production kanbans, empty move kanbans arriving at the production area will not be replenished because more units than are available will be needed. Either of these events causes a stoppage at the area where parts are used.

The required numbers of move and production kanbans are calculated so that there is sufficient inventory to prevent stoppages. Calculations use the following variables:

d_i – Rate of use of part i

s_i^m – Number of units of part i in a move kanban container

s_i^p – Number of units of part i in a production kanban container

t_i^m – Move time for part i move kanban

t_i^p – Production time for part i production kanban

The move time is the sum of three times: the time to transport a move-free kanban from the area where it is used to the area where it is replenished, the time to transfer parts from production kanban containers to the move kanban container, and the time to transport the full move kanban container back to the area where it originated. The production time is the time to produce units to replenish an empty production kanban container.

s_i^m / d_i and s_i^p / d_i are the times that one move kanban and one production kanban will last, usually between one and eight hours. $t_i^m /(s_i^m/d_i)$ is the number of move kanban containers required to guard against shortages during the move time. $t_i^p /(s_i^p/d_i)$ is the number of production kanban containers required to guard against shortages during the time it takes to replenish an empty production kanban. Then, the minimum numbers of move and production kanbans for part i are:

$$k_i^m = \max(2,[t_i^m /(s_i^m/d_i) + 1]^+)$$

$$k_i^p = \max(k_i^m s_i^m / s_i^p,[t_i^p /(s_i^p/d_i) + 1]^+)$$

where $[x]^+$ denotes the smallest integer that is greater than or equal to x.

These numbers of kanbans provide just enough inventory to ensure that move kanban containers will always be replenished. Variations of the pull control system, such as posting a move kanban when the first part (rather than the last part) from a move kanban container is used, produce slightly different equations.

Advantages of the kanban JIT system include those for the two-bin JIT system and some others:

SITUATION 22.4

Kanban JIT System for a Product Family

THE COMPANY WISHES to make further improvements beyond what was achieved with the two-bin JIT production system and decides to implement the kanban JIT system.

Management specifies initial values for kanban sizes, move times, and production times:

Production Area	s_i^m and s_i^p	t_i^m	and t_i^p
x-assembly	10 units	4 hours	8 hours
y-production	20	4	8
z-production	40	4	8

In this situation, each production area uses the same size containers for move and production kanbans, and each production area works eight hours per day.

Figure 22-10 shows the calculations for the minimum number of kanban containers. Consider part x7: 40 units per day ÷ 8 hours per day = 5 units per hour of x7 are required for product m31 and 5 units per hour are required for product m32, so $d = 80 \div 8 = 10$ units per hour. Because each kanban container contains $s = 10$ units, one kanban satisfies $s/d = 1$ hour of requirements. The move time is four hours, so the minimum number of move kanban is $\max(2, [4/1 + 1]^+) = 5$. The production time is eight hours, so the minimum number of production kanban is $\max(5 \times 10/10, [8/1 + 1]^+) = 9$.

Figure 22-11 shows the changes to the two-bin JIT layout (Figure 22-7) that are needed. The changes are small and inexpensive. In the two-bin system, inventory is located in one area—the area where the part was used. Now, inventory is located in two areas: the area where the part is used and the area where it is produced. Although inventory is located in two areas, the total number of units in inventory is smaller than the two-bin JIT system. For example, the maximum inventory for part x7 is (5 + 9) kanban × 10 units per kanban = 140 units. In the two-bin system, the maximum inventory exceeded 800 units (Figure 22-8).

Part	Location	Parent Parts	Requirements per hour	No. of Units in Kanban	Initial No. of Kanban		Later No. of Kanban	
					Move[1]	Production[2]	Move[1]	Production[2]
x7	final assembly	m31 m32	1 x 5 = 5 1 x 5 = 5 10	10	5	9	3	4
x12	final assembly	m31	1 x 5 = 5	10	3	5	2	3
x13	final assembly	m32	1 x 5 = 5	10	3	5	2	3
x17	final assembly	m32	1 x 5 = 5	10	3	5	2	3
y2	x assembly	x7 x12	1 x 10 = 10 1 x 5 = 5 15	20	4	7	3	3
y7	x assembly	x7 x13	1 x 10 = 10 1 x 5 = 5 15	20	4	7	3	3
y11	x assembly	x12 x13 x17	1 x 5 = 5 1 x 5 = 5 1 x 5 = 5 15	20	4	7	3	3
y13	x assembly	x13 x17	1 x 5 = 5 1 x 5 = 5 10	20	3	5	2	2
z1	y assembly	y2 y7 y11	3 x 15 = 45 1 x 15 = 15 2 x 15 = 30 90	40	10	19	6	6
z3	y assembly	y2 y7 y11 y13	1 x 15 = 15 1 x 15 = 15 2 x 15 = 30 2 x 10 = 20 80	40	9	17	5	5
z5	y assembly	y7 y11 y13	1 x 15 = 15 1 x 15 = 15 2 x 10 = 20 50	40	6	11	4	4

Notes:

1. $k_i^m = \max(2,[t_i^m/(s_i^m/d_i) + 1]^+)$. For x7, initial $k^m = \max(4,[4/1 + 1]^+) = 5$.
2. $k_i^p = \max(k_i^m s_i^m/s_i^p,[t_i^p/(s_i^p/d_i) + 1]^+)$. For x7, initial $k^p = \max(5 \times 10/10, [8/(10/10) + 1]^+) = 9$.

Figure 22-10 Kanban JIT System Calculations in Situation 22.4

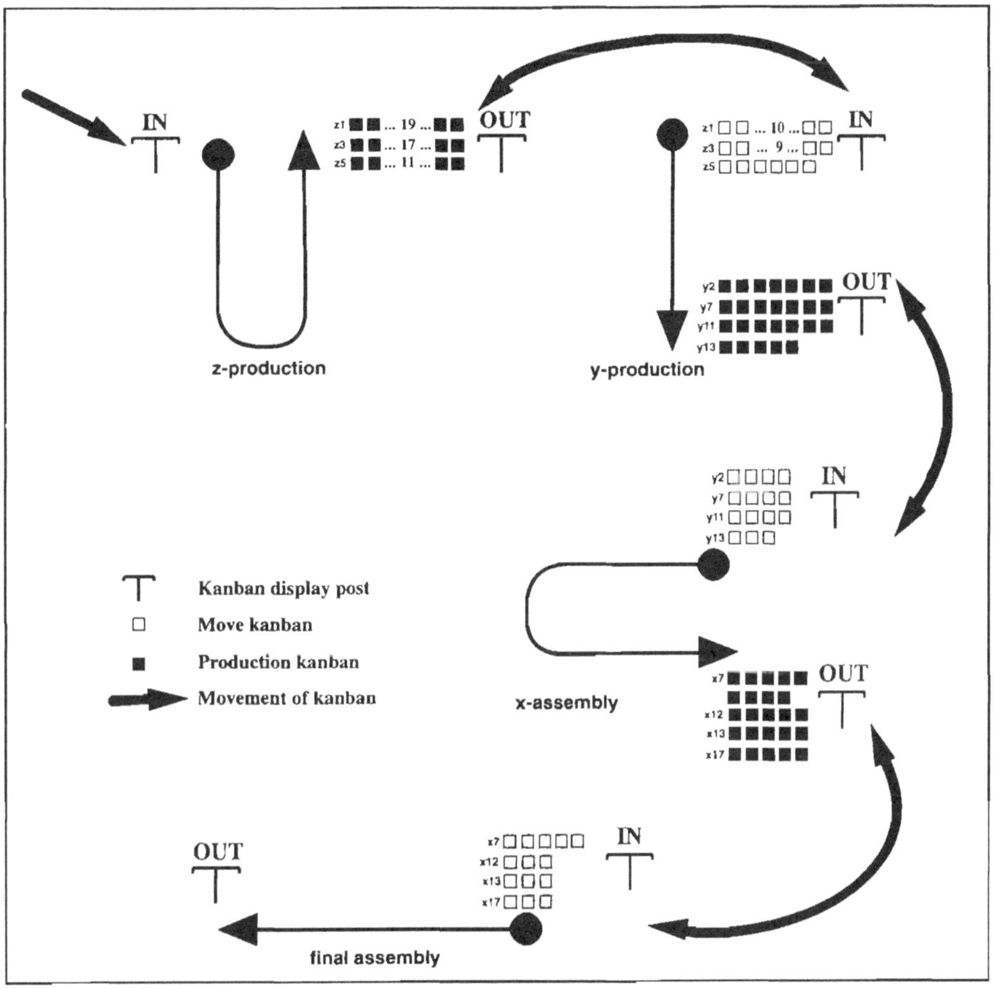

Figure 22-11 Layout for Kanban JIT in Situation 22.4

- Production problems are visible. Large numbers of move-free kanbans indicate problems with scheduling and material flow, and large numbers of production-free kanban indicate bottleneck workstations. Too few move-free or production-free kanbans indicate inventories are too high.
- The area using a part goes to the area producing the part for frequent, small replenishments. This improves communication, which, for example, ensures that quality and other concerns are immediately addressed.
- Each part is produced on a regular basis, making it easy to study and improve the operations required to produce it.
- Smaller, less expensive equipment can be used.

After the kanban JIT system has worked properly for some time, management reduces the amount of inventory by removing some kanbans or by reducing the size of some kanban containers in areas of the factory that they want to improve. Removing kanban or reducing the size of kanban containers reduces inventory. Replenishments then occur more frequently and in smaller quantities, which strains the production system. Soon, shortages and production stoppages occur. Stoppages draw attention to problems and force the production system to find and implement permanent solutions.

As soon as a problem is identified, inventory is increased to its original level by adding kanbans or increasing the size of kanban containers so that production can continue without more stoppages, while personnel find and implement a permanent solution for the problem. When the solution is implemented, inventory is reduced again to expose the next problem.

Improvements reduce cost and improve quality and delivery. This process of reducing inventory by removing kanban or reducing the size of kanban containers and making improvements is repeated again and again in all areas of the factory until all wastes are eliminated.

The kanban JIT system allows management to fine-tune improvement efforts. Management can reduce the number of kanban and the size of kanban containers for certain parts at certain workstations to focus improvement efforts in areas with the greatest need.

This routine of removing kanban, reducing the size of kanban, and making improvements continues for one or two years. When the kanban JIT system has made all possible improvements, it is time to start Step 3 of the JIT journey, the physical line flow JIT production system. This step is not difficult because of the improvements already made by the two-bin and kanban JIT systems.

Step 3: Physical Line Flow

Considerable improvements in cost, quality, and delivery have been achieved with the two-bin system and the kanban system. However, some companies require even lower costs, higher quality, and shorter delivery times. These companies move to the last step on the JIT journey, implementation of a physical line flow JIT production system.

Elements of the production process so carefully improved under the two-bin and kanban systems are now moved from their current locations to a new location and are arranged into a physical line. Disruption to production is not excessive because the same equipment and kanban used in the kanban JIT system are used in the physical line flow system. Capital expenditure is significant because machines and equipment are relocated.

A physical line flow JIT production system has several advantages:

Situation 22.4

Continued

After employees are accustomed to the kanban system, and it has operated properly for some time, management begins the process of reducing inventory to force improvements. For example, management may set new values for move times and production times.

Production Area	t_i^m	t_i^p
x-assembly	2 hours	3 hours
y-production	2	1
z-production	2	1.5

The last column of Figure 22-10 shows the resulting numbers of move and production kanbans. Production areas will need to make numerous improvements before they are able to operate without shortages and stoppages with this reduced number of kanbans.

- Production of all parts is continuous.
- All operations required to complete a product are located in the same area, which improves communication and ensures that problems are immediately addressed.
- All parts of the production process have the same capacity and operate at the same speed. The entire process operates optimally.
- Inventory is reduced because move times are eliminated. The amount of floor space is also reduced.

The distinguishing feature of the JIT production system is its ability to identify and eliminate waste. When the end of the JIT journey is reached, all waste is eliminated from the production system. Then, the production system produces many products in low to medium volumes at the lowest possible cost, with the best possible quality, in the shortest possible time. Few companies reach zero inventory. For most, it is a target to aim for, a motivation for making improvements.

SITUATION 22.5

Physical Line Flow JIT System for a Product Family

THE FINAL ASSEMBLY LINE, x-assembly line, y-production area, and z-production area are studied to determine which equipment can be relocated into a special production line to produce products m31 and m32, assemblies x7, x12, x13, and x17, and parts y2, y7, y11, y13, z1, z3, and z5.

Equipment is organized into a physical line flow, usually a U-shaped production line (Figure 22-12 [A]). The four processes (final assembly, x-assembly, y-production, and z-production) form one production line and are connected by move and production kanbans. Initially, the same kanbans used in the kanban JIT system are used in the physical line flow JIT system. Because this is more inventory than necessary, the startup of the physical line flow system is easier.

Employees work inside the U-line and are trained to perform all operations in the four processes. This simplifies scheduling, improves communication, and allows operators to help each other. Another advantage of the U-line is that it uses less floor space than a straight line.

After employees are accustomed to the physical line flow JIT system and it has been operating properly for a time, management begins the process of reducing inventory by removing kanbans and reducing the size of kanban containers to force improvements. This continues until all problems or wastes are eliminated. Capacities and production speeds of the four processes will be perfectly balanced and no inventory will be needed between the processes. Figure 22-12 (B) shows the layout after numerous improvements have been made. When only one container, holding one unit, is needed between processes on the line, zero inventory is achieved and the JIT journey ends.

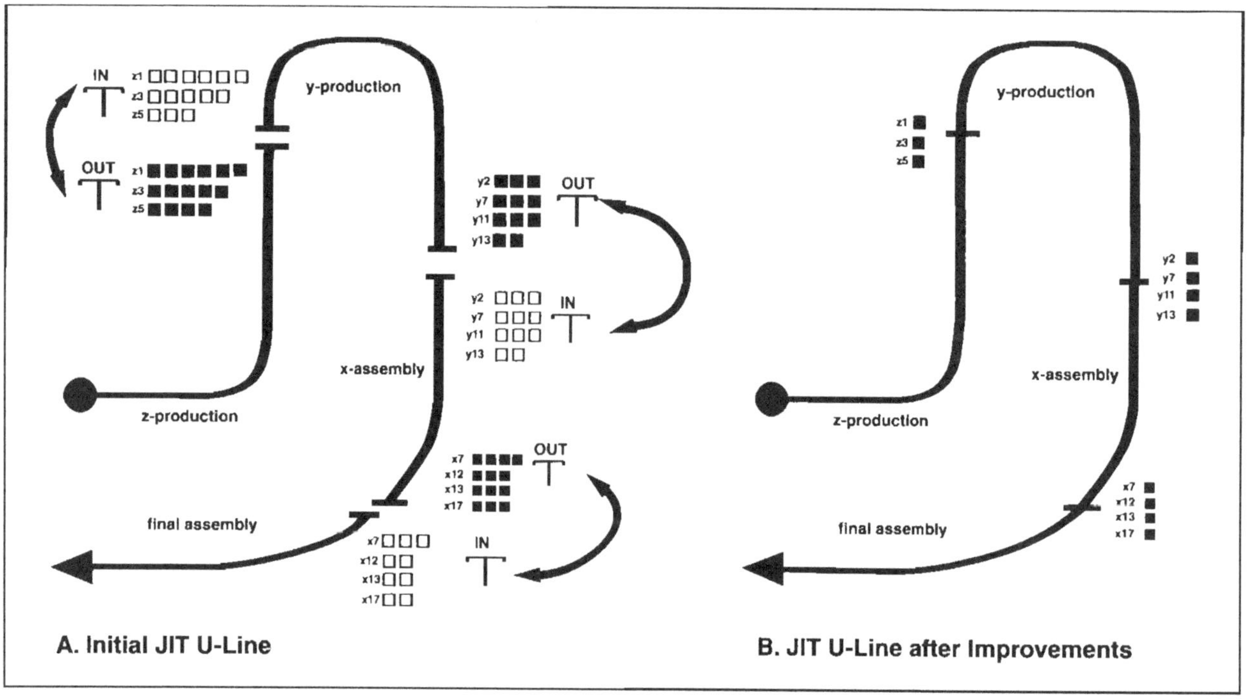

Figure 22-12 Layout and Material Flow for Physical Line Flow JIT in Situation 22.5

Manufacturing Levers

Manufacturing levers are set so that the JIT mechanism for identifying and eliminating waste operates to the fullest extent possible. This requires each lever to have an adult or higher level of manufacturing capability (Figure 22-1). Brief descriptions of each manufacturing lever follow, and more information is available in the large literature on just-in-time production.[3]

Human Resources

A JIT production system enables employees and equipment to contribute their utmost.

Operators are multiskilled. They operate several machines, participate in setups, do material handling, help with maintenance, take part in problem solving, do housekeeping, and perform quality control activities. The number of job classifications is small, and each job classification has a broad scope.

Managers are also multiskilled. They manage, provide training, facilitate problem solving, and make improvements.

Operators and managers receive a lot of training. They are compensated according to the number of skills they have mastered rather than the task they are currently doing.

Organization Structure and Controls

A JIT production system is usually a profit center. Line is more important than staff, organization structure is flat, and spans of control are wide. Competence at all levels in the company is continually improved through training, and decisions are made at the lowest possible level.

Teams are used extensively. Teams need not be self-managing. Companies with a JIT production system are learning organizations because they are always making improvements. Benchmarking is used to set targets and identify new and better practices (Chapter 14). Product engineering and process engineering work together in concurrent engineering programs to optimize product and process design (Chapter 15).

Control systems, such as accounting, capital appropriation (Chapter 17), compensation, individual and department performance measurement, vertical integration (Chapter 3), and supplier certification, differ from those used in other production systems. For example, customer-focused performance measures, such as actual cost and quality, delivery time and percentage on-time delivery, and ratio of actual to planned production, are most important in JIT. Financial performance measures such as ratios of direct labor, indirect labor, overhead to volume, and equipment utilization, are less important in JIT than other production systems.

Sourcing

Compared to other production systems, a JIT production system uses a small number of suppliers. JIT suppliers have high levels of manufacturing capability. JIT suppliers are partners over the long term. They share information on scheduling, cost, design, and quality. They make frequent deliveries of small orders, engage in problem solving and waste reduction, and participate in product design.

Production Planning and Control

Each area in the production process identifies its customers and suppliers. Each area produces in response to pull signals (two-bin or kanban) from its customers. MRP sets the capacity plan and master production schedule. Pull signals control activities on the factory floor.

The production planning and control lever is set so that the JIT mechanism to identify and eliminate waste operates to the fullest possible extent. Inventory is located on the factory floor. Management carefully reduces inventory in selected areas to identify wastes and force improvements.

Process Technology

A JIT production system tries to get the most out of its equipment and processes. Much of the improvement activity in JIT focuses on improving equipment reliability and process capability (Chapter 15). Whenever possible, equipment is arranged into U-shaped lines, as seen in Situation 22.2.

Short setup times are required because many different products are produced in low to medium volumes. Efficient housekeeping and workplace organization are important. Quality is very important. Statistical quality control techniques are used whenever possible for process control and problem solving.

Compared to a batch flow production system, JIT production is more continuous, so equipment is smaller, runs at slower speeds, and is less expensive.

Facilities

Facilities are medium-sized. The pace of production is steady but not as fast as an equipment-paced or continuous flow production system. Like process technology, facilities change constantly as improvements are made.

Manufacturing Outputs

Cost and Quality

A JIT production system is a line flow production system. It provides cost and quality at the levels associated with line flow production systems. JIT can do this because of its thoroughness at eliminating waste.

Performance

A JIT production system produces many products in low to medium volumes. In this respect, it is like a batch flow production system. Because it produces in low to medium volumes, the resources available to design new features and new processes are limited, so JIT provides performance at the same level as a batch flow production system.

This might seem surprising because companies, like Toyota, well known for JIT production, provide high levels of performance. In these companies, products manufactured by JIT production systems are so successful that demand increases and production volume changes from low-to-medium to medium-to-high. When demand increases, management changes a virtual line flow JIT production system to a physical line flow JIT production system. When demand further increases management changes a physical line flow JIT production system to an operator-paced line flow system. Because of all the improvements that have been made, the operator-paced line flow production system has a very high level of manufacturing capability. This high-capability production system provides the high level of performance. Situation 16.1 in Chapter 16 is an example.

Delivery

Delivery is provided at a high level because all operations required to produce a product are done on equipment arranged in a virtual or physical line. Like all line flow production systems, once production of a product starts, only a short time passes before the product is finished.

Flexibility and Innovativeness

A JIT production system produces many products in low to medium volumes. In this respect, it is like a batch flow production system. Because it produces many products, JIT provides flexibility and innovativeness at the same high levels as a batch flow production system. JIT can do this because of the high capabilities of its employees.

Endnotes

1. Ohno, T., *Toyota Production System: Beyond Large Scale Production*, Portland, OR: Productivity Press, p. 87, 1988.
2. Miltenburg, J., and Wijngaard, J., "Designing and Phasing In Just-in-Time Production Systems," *International Journal of Production Research*, Vol. 29, No. 1, pp. 115–131, 1991.
3. Five good books on just-in-time production are:
    - Hall, R., *Zero Inventories*, Homewood, IL.: Dow Jones-Irwin, 1983.
    - Monden, Y., *Toyota Production System*, Second Edition, Atlanta, GA: Industrial Engineering Press, 1993.
    - Ohno, T., *Toyota Production System: Beyond Large Scale Production*, Portland, OR: Productivity Press, 1988.
    - Sekine, K., *One-Piece Flow*, Portland, OR: Productivity Press, 1992.
    - Shingo, S., *A Study of the Toyota Production System*. Translated by A. Dillon. Portland, OR: Productivity Press, 1989.

CHAPTER 23

EQUIPMENT-PACED LINE FLOW PRODUCTION SYSTEM

Henry Ford developed the equipment-paced line flow production system in the 1920s, at his Rouge River factory in Detroit. Until that time, there were only two different production systems: job shop and batch flow. Ford's new system was a major innovation. It provided much higher levels of the cost, quality, and delivery manufacturing outputs (Figure 23-1). Almost immediately, customer expectations increased for lower cost, better quality, and faster delivery. Many companies were forced to change their production systems to the new equipment-paced line flow production system to meet these expectations. The transition was difficult for most companies.

We now have many years of experience with the equipment-paced line flow production system. Today, it is the easiest production system to design, manage, and operate, and the best production system to use.

Products and Volumes

An equipment-paced line flow production system is designed to produce several products in high volumes. Products are manufactured on specialized equipment using high volume tooling arranged in a line layout (Chapter 4). Compared to an operator-paced line flow or JIT production system, an equipment-paced line flow production system produces fewer products with higher, more regular volumes. The amount of product change that can be accommodated is limited to standard products with a small number of options.

Layout and Material Flow

An equipment-paced line flow production system produces several products, each with almost identical manufacturing requirements, on the same production line. The line speed or production rate, which is the speed or rate at which each machine on the line operates, is fast and cannot be varied. Either the line is running or it is stopped. A fixed number of operators are needed to run the line. If even one operator is missing, the line is stopped. Equipment and tooling are very specialized. They are designed to produce a small number of different products quickly, at low cost, and with high quality.

Competitive Advantage

It is a widely held belief that the equipment-paced line flow production system is the best production

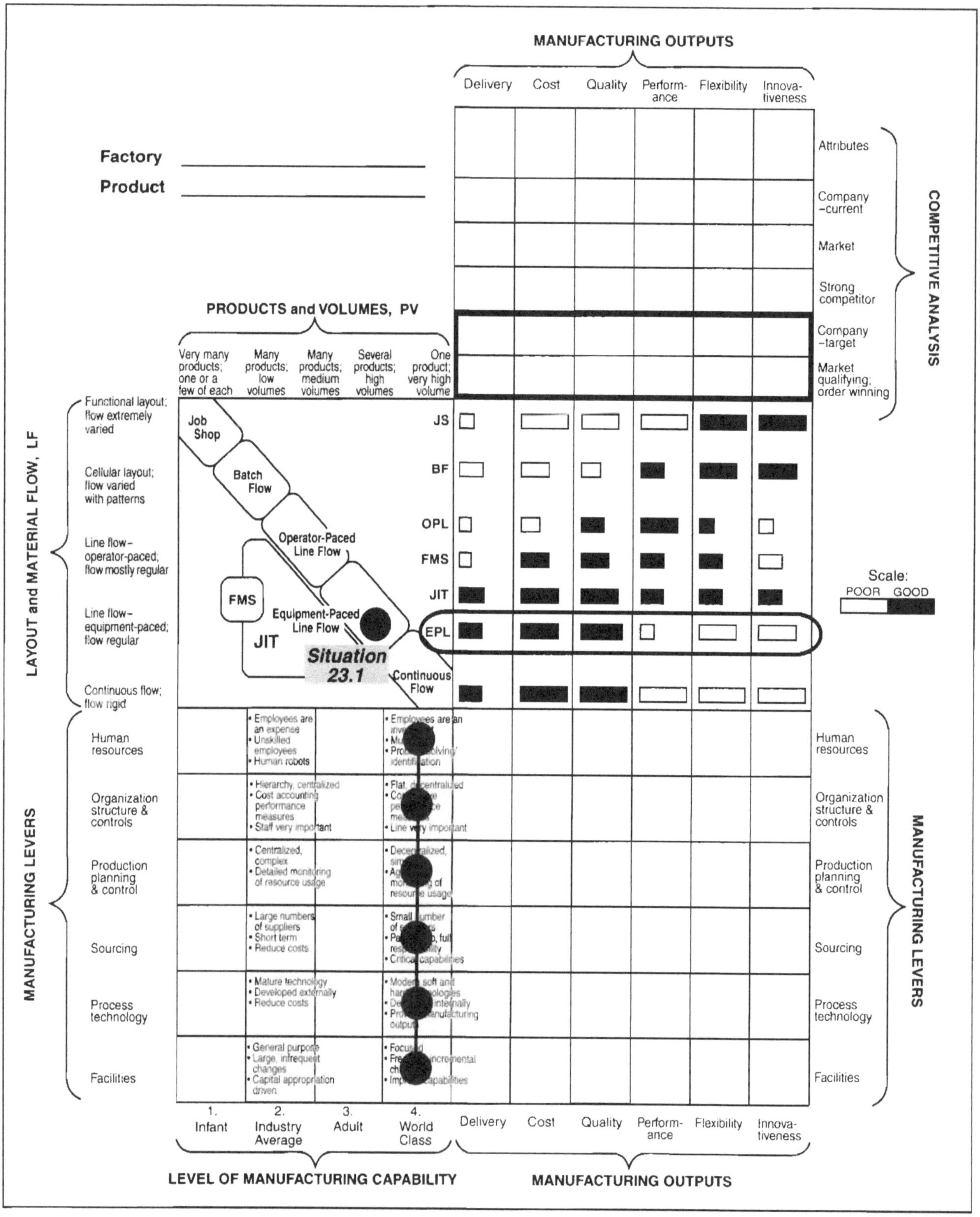

Figure 23-1 Equipment-Paced Line Flow Production System

system. It is the easiest system to design, manage, and operate, and it provides high levels of the cost, quality, and delivery outputs.

An equipment-paced line flow production system should be used whenever the following conditions hold:

- Customers need standard products with, at most, a small number of options. These needs will not change in the short term.
- Customers need high levels of the cost, quality, and delivery outputs.
- Products can be produced in sufficiently high volumes over their design life to adequately utilize expensive, specialized equipment.

Manufacturing Levers

Human Resources

Production operators in an equipment-paced line flow production system are not as skilled as those in a job shop, batch flow, JIT, or operator-paced line flow production system. The level of skill compares to a continuous flow production system. Detailed procedures and standards exist for all activities. Procedures and standards are necessary to keep costs low, maintain quality, and sustain line speed.

Operators perform the same production operations on each product. They are paid an hourly wage rate. A bonus scheme may also be used to persuade operators to arrive on time because any shortage of operators stops the production line. Numerous, large staff groups are needed to provide support services.

Organization Structure and Controls

An equipment-paced line flow production system is usually a cost center. Corporate influence on the production system in the areas of production scheduling, resource allocation, and capital expenditures is considerable. The production system is a high-volume business, and a centralized, bureaucratic organization structure manages it. The organization structure is hierarchical, with many levels in the hierarchy. It is similar to a continuous flow production system.

Staff groups manage product design, process engineering, production planning and control, maintenance, material handling, purchasing, quality control, and improvement activities. Close cooperation between product design engineers and process engineers ensures that products are easily produced by the specialized equipment on the production line. Even with close cooperation between these groups, it is difficult to make product design changes and introduce new products.

Several other issues are important in an equipment-paced line flow production system:

- Materials management ensures that material shortages do not stop the production line.
- Capacity planning ensures that capacity is available to meet customer orders without having to stop and restart the line excessively or having to carry excessive inventory.
- Staff is up to date on developments in process technology used on the line.

Sourcing

The production line produces a small number of products, so the number of purchased materials and parts is usually also small. These materials and parts are purchased in large volumes, at steady rates, over long periods, from a small number of suppliers. Consequently, the production system has considerable control over its suppliers. Supplier relationships are characterized by long-term contracts, sharing of responsibilities for quality and improvements, and participation in design activities.

Production Planning and Control

Schedules are planned far into the future and shared with customers and suppliers to avoid shortages. Once set, schedules do not change. Production is most often make-to-stock. Products are produced to a forecast and stored in finished goods inventory. Forecasting, scheduling, and material tracking are elaborate. Work-in-process inventory is low because the production line produces products quickly.

Purchased materials inventory depends on how much control the company has over its suppliers. With extensive control, purchased materials are scheduled to arrive exactly when needed. With limited control, large inventories are carried so that shortages do not stop the line. Purchased material inventory is also high when there are economies of scale for ordering or transporting large quantities of materials.

Process Technology

Equipment, fixtures, and tooling are very specialized, and automation is extensive. However, compared to a continuous flow production system, an equipment-paced line flow production system has less specialization and automation. The reason is the number of products produced. The equipment-paced line flow system produces several products or one product with several options on the same production line, while the continuous flow production system produces only one product on a production line.

The time to change the line from one product to another is sufficiently long that lengthy runs of each product are scheduled. This minimizes the production time lost because of setups. It also reduces quality problems that occur when production switches from one product to another. Most companies with an equipment-paced line flow production system have setup time reduction programs to make shorter production runs possible.

Process technology is important because process equipment produces most of the "value-added." An equipment-paced line flow production system is usually a technology leader. An important job for the process engineering department is keeping up to date on developments in process technology. Changes in technology are usually major and occur infrequently. When they occur, extensive changes are made to the line. This is also true for FMS and continuous flow production systems. Operator-paced, JIT, batch flow, and job shop production systems are different. In these systems, process technology changes are small and occur more frequently.

An equipment-paced line flow production system is capital intensive. Hard technologies are more important than soft technologies. Indirect costs, such as staff, are high. Of the direct costs, material cost is high, and direct labor is low.

Facilities

Facilities are large and seek economies of scale. Line speed or production rate is fast. Equipment on the production line is synchronized, so there are no bottlenecks. Equipment utilization and labor efficiency are high.

Manufacturing Outputs

Cost and Quality

An equipment-paced line flow production system produces several products in high volumes. High volume creates experience benefits provided learning occurs and improvements are made. Machines and fixtures are specialized and designed for high volume production. Operators are also specialized.

The combination of high volume and specialization generates low cost, high-quality products.

Performance

An equipment-paced line flow production system provides an average level of performance. There are two reasons for this.

- On the positive side, high volume justifies product design work to design new features and process improvements to produce products more efficiently.
- On the negative side, changing specialized equipment and retraining operators is expensive. Doing this on a regular basis, which is necessary to provide a high level of performance, is difficult.

Delivery

An equipment-paced line flow production system provides fast, reliable delivery. Machines on the production line are synchronized. Operators perform relatively simple tasks that are synchronized with machine operations. As a result, products are produced at a fast, steady rate.

Flexibility and Innovativeness

An equipment-paced line flow production system provides low levels of flexibility and innovativeness. Highly specialized machines, fixtures, and operators make it both expensive and difficult to change the existing product mix, make design changes, or introduce new products. Even small changes require large adjustments to the line. For example, it is not unusual for an equipment-paced line flow production system to require a one- or two-week shutdown period to make changes to introduce a new product.

Situation 23.1

Whirlpool Changes an Equipment-Paced Line Flow Production System

COMPETITION IN THE WASHING MACHINE business is keen. In 1950, there were about 150 washing machine manufacturers. By 1960, the number decreased to 75, and in 1970, there were only 25. In 1980, Whirlpool realized that the cost of its washing machines was too high.

Washing machine factories were organized into departments such as stamping, welding, fabrication, finishing, and assembly, according to the stages in the production process. Assembly used an equipment-paced line flow production system. Other departments used batch flow production systems. By 1980, this traditional strategy could no longer produce products with market qualifying levels of cost and quality.

To turn its situation around, Whirlpool developed a new manufacturing strategy. First, it concentrated all washing machine production in one factory. Second, it redesigned its products to be "customer friendly" and easy to manufacture. Third, it focused on people and processes.

The first element in Whirlpool's new strategy was its large factory in Clyde, Ohio. When the strategy was fully implemented, the factory was the largest, and perhaps, best washing machine factory in the world. It was two million square feet, employed 3,000 people, operated three shifts per day, and produced 14,000 washing machines per day. Twenty percent of production was exported. Productivity, measured as gross sales divided by number of employees, was 40 percent higher than industry average.

The new factory was organized by product. There were three product classes: premium, mid-line, and value. Each product-factory used an equipment-paced line flow production system (Figure 23-1). Products were designed to be easy to manufacture

SITUATION 23.1

Continued

on highly automated lines. Numerous adjustments to manufacturing levers were made to raise the level of manufacturing capability from industry average to world class. The factory defined world class as the capability "to compete with anyone in the world in the areas of quality, cost, and customer satisfaction."

The second element in Whirlpool's new strategy was designing "customer-friendly" products. A "customer-friendly" product was a washing machine with features that customers valued. For example, customers said they only wanted to make two trips to their washing machine.

- During the first trip, customers did two things. They put clothes, detergent, bleach, and fabric softener in the washing machine and pushed buttons to program the washing machine.
- The second trip was after washing was finished and water was drained away. This time, customers simply removed clothes from the washing machine and put them in the dryer.

The third element in Whirlpool's new strategy was "focus on people and processes." Focus on people and processes meant training employees and involving them in designing and improving processes. For example, initially, Whirlpool built only one production line. Employee input from that line was used to design and build the second line. Employee input from the first two lines was used to design and build the third line, and the same process was followed for the fourth line. The company had an employment security policy where employees did not lose their jobs because of improvements. The company also had a gain-sharing program where savings from improvements were shared with employees.

SITUATION 23.2

Television Manufacturer Fine-Tunes Production System

ABC ELECTRONICS PRODUCED 19- through 52-inch televisions at a factory in Europe. The factory was organized into three departments: fabrication, subassembly, and final assembly, according to the stages in the production process. The fabrication department used a batch flow production system, subassembly used an operator-paced line flow production system, and final assembly used an equipment-paced line flow production system. The factory actively made improvements. Fabrication and subassembly reduced setup times, improved housekeeping, and upgraded supplier relations. Final assembly installed a new planning and control system.

The final assembly department's equipment-paced line flow production system had two production lines. The smaller, slower line operated one shift per day, five days per week, and produced large televisions. The other line was newer and faster. It operated two shifts per day, five days per week, and produced regular and small televisions.

Human Resources in Final Assembly

Most assembly line operators were trained to work at one station only. A small number of relief operators could work at more than one station. They moved from station to station to relieve operators for short breaks. Lines moved at a constant speed, and operators had a fixed amount of time to complete their tasks.

Quality personnel took measurements and did checks at special stations on the lines. Maintenance personnel performed maintenance and repair activities. Material handling personnel brought parts to the line and removed empty containers. All employees received an hourly wage. No incentive wage plan was used.

Organization Structure and Controls in Final Assembly

The final assembly department was a cost center. Management was evaluated on the number of units produced, equipment utilization, labor efficiency, and actual costs compared to standard costs. It was most important to keep the lines running. Every effort was made to avoid breakdowns and minimize the times lines stopped to change from one size and model of television to another.

Organization structure was hierarchical. There were many staff groups: distribution, engineering, maintenance, material handling, production planning, purchasing, and quality. Each reported to its own general manager, who was responsible for similar groups in other departments, and also to the general manager of the final assembly department.

Sourcing in Final Assembly

High volumes of materials and parts were purchased from other departments and from outside suppliers. A large purchasing group managed this activity. Purchasing selected suppliers on the basis of low cost, satisfactory quality, and reliable delivery. Final assembly had considerable influence over its outside suppliers, but it had much less influence over the other departments that supplied it with parts.

Situation 23.2

Continued

Production Planning and Control in Final Assembly

Production planners, in close consultation with the sales department, scheduled the two production lines. A sophisticated MRP system planned quantities and delivery times for purchased materials and parts far into the future and conveyed schedules electronically to suppliers. Inventories of purchased materials and parts were small, as were work-in-process inventory and finished goods inventory.

Final assembly, in partnership with the distribution group, installed a bar code based system to provide timely information for planning and control. Bar code labels were attached to key parts of the television, and electronic readers scanned bar codes when parts were added to televisions on the production line. The status of each television was known at all times, even if it was taken off the line for rework. No television left the assembly department for the finished goods warehouse or shipping until the computer had accounted for it.

When a television passed the final bar code reading station, the computer released, from inventory, all parts necessary to build another television. This technique, called backflushing, helped the assembly department manage purchased parts inventory. Portable readers scanned bar codes on shipping cartons in the shipping area. The result was an accurate record of shipped orders and televisions still in finished goods inventory. Three peel-away labels were placed inside the television, which service representatives could use later if the set had to be repaired in the field.

Process Technology in Final Assembly

Equipment and tooling on the lines were very specialized and expensive. The time to change from one size and model of television to another was not excessively long, but production schedules still emphasized long runs of each product to minimize the production time lost because of setups. The process engineering group was always searching for new process technology that could produce televisions faster, cheaper, or with better quality. The group worked closely with the design engineering group to ensure that new products and design changes to existing products were done in a way that products were easy to produce.

Facilities in Final Assembly

The assembly department was large, modern, and clean. It was designed to achieve economies of scale. Televisions were produced at a fast rate. There were no bottlenecks. Equipment utilization and labor efficiency were high.

CHAPTER 24

CONTINUOUS FLOW PRODUCTION SYSTEM

Many producers of chemicals, food, lumber, metals, pharmaceuticals, plastics, and building materials use continuous flow production systems to produce very high volumes of standard products. In these cases, "the process is the product." The process produces all the value added. If anything goes wrong with the process, there is no product. For example, if a baking oven fails to hold its temperature, the bread or pastries moving through the oven on a conveyor belt will not bake properly.

Products and Volumes

A continuous flow production system produces one product, or a very small family of products, in very high volume. The product is produced on highly automated, specialized equipment (Figure 24-1).

The product is usually a commodity. A commodity is a product in the saturation stage of its product life cycle (Chapter 16). The product design, features, and specifications are standardized throughout the industry, so the "conformance to specifications" aspect of quality is crucial. All competitors produce identical products, so cost is the basis of competition.

Volume is so high that production is continuous, usually 24 hours per day, seven days per week, 52 weeks per year. Changes to product design and new product introductions are infrequent.

Layout and Material Flow

A continuous flow production system uses a line layout (Chapter 4). One product, or a very small family of products, each with identical manufacturing requirements, is produced by very specialized equipment and tooling, in a highly automated process, arranged in a line layout. Everything is very specialized, automated, and expensive.

Products are produced continuously at a very fast speed that cannot be varied. Either the production process is running or it is stopped. A small number of operators monitor the equipment in the production process.

Competitive Advantage

A continuous flow production system provides the lowest possible cost, highest possible quality, and fastest possible delivery. A continuous flow

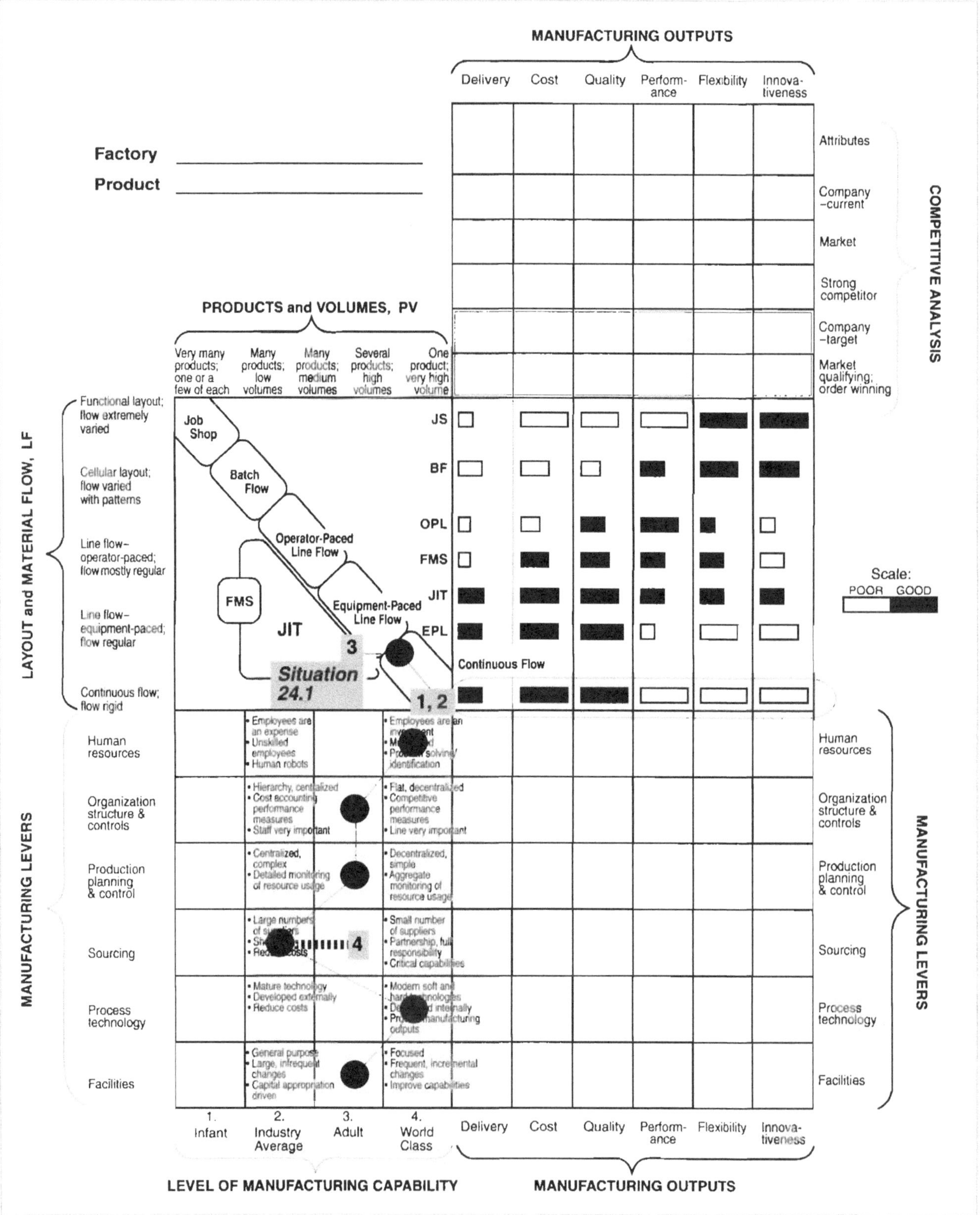

Figure 24-1 Continuous Flow Production System

production system is used whenever the following conditions hold:

- Customers require the best possible cost, quality, and delivery.
- Product design is very stable.
- Volume is high enough to keep a very expensive, highly automated, specialized process running continuously.

Only a small fraction of all products satisfy these conditions.

Manufacturing Levers

Human Resources

Production operators in a continuous flow production system are unskilled compared to those in other production systems. Their job is to monitor the highly automated production process to ensure that equipment operates within prescribed parameters. They may also track quality attributes on SPC charts and perform routine maintenance and housekeeping tasks.

All employees are paid an hourly wage rate. No incentive pay scheme is used, but bonuses may be awarded when high levels of production output are achieved.

Maintenance is a critical activity. A breakdown anywhere stops the entire production process. Maintenance personnel are responsible for preventive maintenance, making fast repairs when breakdowns occur, and maintaining spare parts.

Organization Structure and Controls

A continuous flow production system is usually a cost center. The high volume and rigid nature of the production system makes a centralized, bureaucratic organization structure best. The structure is hierarchical, with many levels in the hierarchy. Corporate influence is high in the areas of production scheduling, resource allocation, and capital expenditures. Management is evaluated on the number of units produced, equipment uptime, and actual costs compared to budget costs. Since keeping the production process running is most important, every effort is made to avoid breakdowns and raw material shortages.

Changes to the production process are expensive. A capital appropriation request to the corporation is required (Chapter 17). The request is accepted or rejected on the basis of estimated cost savings. The entire production process must be shut down to implement changes.

A continuous flow production system requires numerous staff departments to perform activities such as planning and scheduling production and maintenance, forecasting raw material requirements, tracking materials, making process improvements, and managing quality activities. Staff departments are often more influential than line departments. A quality department is responsible for all aspects of quality. This includes SPC activities in the production process, quality of raw materials, and projects for improving quality.

Sourcing

A continuous flow production system uses large volumes of a small number of raw materials, many of which are commodities. The production system has a great deal of control over its suppliers. Suppliers are selected on the basis of low cost, satisfactory quality, and reliable delivery.

Quantities and delivery times for raw materials are planned far into the future. Schedules are conveyed electronically to suppliers. The progress and delivery of purchase orders are tracked carefully.

Production Planning and Control

Production is make-to-stock. Products are produced to a forecast and stored in a large finished goods inventory, from which customer orders are filled. Work-in-process inventory is low. Raw material inventory is large so that shortages do not stop the production process. Raw material inventory is also large because purchase order quantities are large to achieve quantity discounts and minimize transportation costs.

Production schedules are planned far into the future. Changes to production schedules are possible, but there is usually a long period during which the schedule is frozen. Modern computerized systems are used to plan, control, and optimize all activities in the production system.

Process Technology

Equipment is highly specialized, tooling is high volume, and the process is highly automated. Everything is expensive. Changeover times are long. Consequently, one product, or a small family of very similar products, is produced. In the latter case, production runs are very long to minimize changeovers.

Process technology is very important because process equipment produces all of the value added. A continuous flow production system is a technology leader. An important job for the process engineering department is keeping up to date on developments in process technology. Technological change is revolutionary rather than incremental and takes the form of new, faster equipment and processes.

SPC is extensively used and is effective at maintaining high levels of quality throughout the process. Control charts and other SPC techniques are easy to apply because one product is produced continuously.

Additions to capacity are made in large pieces. A continuous flow production system is capital intensive. Indirect costs, such as staff, are high. Of the direct costs, material cost is high, and direct labor is low.

Facilities

Facilities are very large to achieve economies of scale. The production rate is very fast. There is no bottleneck machine because all machines have the same capacity and run at the same speed. A continuous flow production system produces high volumes of output, so it also produces large amounts of waste, some of which may be hazardous. The production system needs considerable resources to handle and treat waste.

Manufacturing Outputs

Cost and Quality

A continuous flow production system is designed to produce one product in very high volume. The production volume is so high that the process runs continuously, usually 24 hours per day, seven days per week, 52 weeks per year. Equipment is very specialized. Tooling is high volume. The process is highly automated.

The combination of high volume, specialization, and automation produces products with the lowest possible cost and the highest possible quality.

Performance

A continuous flow production system cannot consistently provide a high level of performance. A high level of performance requires a constant stream of product design changes, new products, and process changes. This is difficult for a continuous flow production system. It is very costly to modify specialized, automated equipment, retrain unskilled operators, stop production for a few weeks to implement changes, and so on.

These undertakings can be done from time to time, but not at the pace needed to provide a high level of performance on a regular basis.

Delivery

A continuous flow production system provides good delivery reliability and the fastest possible delivery time.

The production process produces one product continuously. The process runs at a very fast speed and is highly automated. Machines perform all operations. The result is the fastest possible delivery time. Delivery time reliability is high, provided maintenance is done well and suppliers are well managed.

Flexibility and Innovativeness

A continuous flow production system provides very low levels of flexibility and innovativeness.

The specialized machines are designed to run at one speed that cannot be varied. Changing product design or introducing a new product requires extensive modifications to specialized machines and tooling, retraining staff and unskilled operators, and a long shutdown to implement the changes.

Situation 24.1

Continuous Flow Production System in a Steel Plant

Problem[1]

The MGR steel plant was a successful minimill. The plant had an electric arc furnace, a continuous caster, and a rolling mill, all organized as a continuous flow production system. The plant produced two product families: lightweight steel bars for reinforcing concrete and lightweight structural shapes such as angles, rounds, and flats.

When the plant was built eight years ago, the capacity of the furnace was 250,000 tons per year, the capacity of the caster was 250,000 tons per year, and the capacity of the rolling mill was 500,000 tons per year. The plan was to add a second furnace and caster to balance the rolling mill after the plant gained more steelmaking experience and became profitable.

Some of the manufacturing levers in the continuous flow production system are examined next, starting with process technology.

Process Technology

The continuous flow production system began at the furnace where molten steel was produced, continued to the continuous caster where the molten steel was cast continuously into steel strands, and ended at the rolling mill where the steel strands were rolled into finished products. Because the MGR plant was new, it was a process technology follower. Each of these stages in the continuous process is examined next.

Furnace

An overhead crane picked up shredded scrap steel and loaded it into a charging bucket. Materials such as metal alloys and lime were also loaded, and the charging bucket was emptied into the electric arc furnace. Then, graphite electrodes were lowered into the furnace, and electrical power to the electrodes was turned on. An arc formed between the electrodes, and the resulting intense heat melted all the material in the furnace. The melted material was about 100 tons of steel and was called a heat.

SITUATION 24.1

Continued

Continuous caster

Once the steel in the furnace was melted, the furnace tilted, and the steel poured into a ladle. A ladle crane lifted the ladle of molten steel to the top of the continuous casting machine. The molten steel was released through a hole in the bottom of the ladle into a rectangular, trough-shaped dish called a tundish.

The tundish had four holes in its bottom. Molten steel flowed through the holes into molds. The molds oscillated to produce homogenous, billet-shaped strands of steel, approximately 15 cm $\times$ 15 cm in cross-section.

The strands flowed from the molds into water spray chambers where they cooled. Beyond the spray chambers, the strands solidified, were cut by automatic torches into standard lengths called billets, and moved through straighteners. Finally, the billets moved to a long cooling table.

The industry average time to cast a 100-ton heat was about two hours. The tundish and molds were cleaned after each heat, which took 12 minutes. During this time, the ladle crane lifted the empty ladle from above the tundish and lowered it to the ground. Then, the crane picked up a full ladle that had just been tapped and raised it up to the caster, thereby beginning the cycle again.

Rolling mill

Before being rolled into finished shapes, billets were reheated in a gas furnace. They were released individually from the furnace and moved through 15 rolling machines. These machines were sets of heavy rollers that used pressure to squeeze a hot billet into smaller and smaller sizes until the billet reached its final shape. The final shapes cooled on long racks and were cut and bound for shipping.

Changing from one product to another required changing some of the rollers in the rolling machines. The number of rollers that needed to be changed depended on whether the next product was a different shape or simply a different size of the product currently being rolled. The time to complete a changeover varied from 30 minutes to four hours. Planners scheduled long runs of each product shape and size to reduce the total time spent doing changeovers.

HUMAN RESOURCES

MGR's people were its greatest asset. MGR practiced participatory management and had a profit-sharing plan. An extensive training program was in place to raise the competency of all employees. Decisions were made at the lowest possible level in the company. MGR had never laid an employee off; but it had fired a few who did not fit in.

Organization Structure and Controls

Meetings and emails were discouraged in favor of phone calls and face-to-face conversations. Everyone was on a first-name basis, and employees were free to speak their minds. Offices and conference rooms were dispersed throughout the plant. The management structure was lean and flat, with only four levels from top to bottom. Production was king. Staff departments served production first and foremost.

Manufacturing Capability

The level of capability of the manufacturing levers in the continuous flow production system ranged from average to world class (Figure 24-1).

Employees participated in numerous improvement activities. The following program of improvements at the electric arc furnace increased the size of a heat from 100 tons every two hours, to 120 tons every 90 minutes. This increased capacity from 250,000 to 320,000 tons per year.

- More cooling was added to the electrical transformer.
- A new refractory brick was used to line the furnace.
- Welds were reinforced on the furnace shell.
- Two 20 cm rings were added to the top of each ladle to increase ladle size.

New technology, developed in-house, promised an additional increase in capacity to 400,000 tons within two years.

Employees made one improvement in the continuous caster. The life of the tundish was increased from five to 11 heats by changing the tundish's refractory brick liner. Production capacity increased from 250,000 to 270,000 tons per year because the tundish was relined less often. Employees were still working on two long-standing problems at the caster.

- From time to time, one of the four strands would clog or break out of its mold, which was very dangerous. When it occurred, the strand was quickly plugged off. This slowed production because, with fewer strands open, the molten

SITUATION 24.1

Continued

steel emptied from the tundish at a slower rate. After the heat was completed, the tundish and mold had to be cleaned.

- Water nozzles in the spray chamber were changed every three heats. Employees were still searching for ways to increase the life of the water nozzles.

The end result of all these improvements was that the continuous caster was a severe bottleneck. Its capacity was 270,000 tons per year. The capacity of the furnace was 320,000 tons and would soon be 400,000 tons. The capacity of the rolling mill was 520,000 tons. Management considered four proposals for increasing capacity at the continuous caster and further improving the production system.

Proposal 1

A group of managers had just returned from a trip to Japan to study a nonstop version of continuous casting. By carefully synchronizing existing equipment and adding one new piece of equipment, the Japanese had developed a casting procedure that permitted many heats to be cast consecutively, without stops to clean the tundish and the molds. Casting stopped after 11 heats when the refractory brick in the tundish wore out.

The new piece of equipment was a ladle platform, and it was set at the top of the caster. The platform consisted of a track and a car with positions for three ladles. The middle position was over the tundish and the other positions were on each side. Steel from a ladle in the middle position flowed into the tundish. Simultaneously, the electric arc furnace was tapped into another ladle, and the full ladle was raised to one of the empty positions on the car. The full ladle reached the car in time to slide over the tundish when needed but not early enough that the temperature in the ladle dropped below the casting temperature. When the ladle over the tundish was empty, it was rolled to an empty position, and the full ladle was rolled into place.

This system permitted long production runs provided all steel in the run had the same metallurgy. The system also reduced the scrap normally produced at the beginning and end of each heat. MGR estimated that its yield would increase from 88 to 95 percent. The system was expensive and required six weeks for implementation, during which time the plant had to be shut down.

Proposal 2

The chief engineer also had a proposal. Instead of a ladle platform, he proposed a system to make better use of the ladle crane to synchronize the furnace and the caster.

The ladle crane lifted a full ladle to the tundish and let it empty. Once emptied, the crane lowered the empty ladle to the ground and picked up a full ladle, which had just been tapped, and raised it to the caster. Lowering the empty ladle and raising the full ladle had to be done within the four minutes it took the tundish to empty.

The production superintendent did not like the proposal. He did not think that four minutes was enough time to do the crane work. Hurrying the ladle crane could be dangerous and, if a mistake in timing occurred, MGR would end up with a ladle filled with solid steel. Since he did not know of any other steel plant that operated this way, he did not think the idea would work.

Proposal 3

The comptroller and marketing manager also had a proposal. They thought MGR should increase the variety of shapes and sizes the plant produced and develop new markets in which to sell them. They thought demand for existing products was softening, and new products were needed to meet sales and profit objectives.

The comptroller and marketing manager recognized difficulties had to be overcome for their proposal to work. For example, it was difficult to forecast demand for each size and structural shape. Some new structural shapes had different metallurgies. These difficulties would make production scheduling harder and would increase finished goods inventory.

Proposal 4

The purchasing manager worried about the supply of scrap steel. Sometimes, it was difficult to find scrap steel. The price of scrap had fluctuated wildly in the previous year. Some minimills had purchased scrap yards to secure reliable sources of scrap steel, so perhaps MGR should do the same.

Solution

MGR must correct two problems in its continuous flow production system: the capacity imbalance between the electric arc

SITUATION 24.1

Continued

furnace, the continuous caster, and the rolling mill and the low level of manufacturing capability in the sourcing lever (Figure 24-1). Both problems are important.

CAPACITY IMBALANCE

Each process in a continuous process production system should have approximately the same capacity. Since the lowest capacity process determines how much the production system will produce, any process whose capacity exceeds the lowest capacity will have unused capacity.

Unused capacity increases cost because of the capital cost to purchase unused capacity and construct facilities in which to house it and the operating cost to maintain the unused capacity. A continuous process production system competes on the basis of low cost, so there is a strong incentive to use unused capacity or eliminate it.

MGR must increase the capacity of the continuous caster to bring it into line with the electric arc furnace and the rolling mill. Proposal 1 and proposal 2 are two ways to do this.

Proposal 1 moves MGR further down the diagonal of the PV-LF matrix (Figure 24-1). The proposal increases synchronization between the furnace and the caster. Material flow between these processes becomes more continuous. Simultaneously, production volume increases because production run sizes increase from five to 11 heats. Proposal 1 is a new technology with proven benefits. MGR is a technology follower and has enough manufacturing capability to implement the new technology. For all of these reasons, MGR should accept proposal 1.

Proposal 2 also moves MGR further down the diagonal of the PV-LF matrix. However, the proposal is a new, unproven technology, and since MGR is not a technology leader, the proposal must be rejected.

Proposal 3 increases the number of products and decreases volume because many new products will have low demands. Proposal 3 moves MGR to the left of the diagonal of the PV-LF matrix (Figure 24-1), which is a difficult product mix for a continuous flow production system, even one with a high level of manufacturing capability. Proposal 3 could only be accepted if MGR is prepared to change its production system to an equipment-paced line flow production system, but since it is not, the proposal must be rejected.

SOURCING

MGR has a good level of manufacturing capability in most levers (Figure 24-1). Human resources and process technology have world class levels of capability. This is due, in part, to eight years of work by employees to improve the furnace, caster, and rolling mill.

Sourcing has an industry average level of capability—the lowest capability of all levers in the production system. This lever will prevent the continuous flow production system from achieving adult and world class performance. Sourcing's level of capability should be raised to the adult level and higher.

The biggest difficulty in sourcing is securing a reliable supply of low cost scrap steel. This is an industry-wide problem, and MGR needs to act before it is too late. MGR should implement proposal 4 or some variation of it. For example, MGR can acquire one or more scrap yards or form partnerships with other suppliers of scrap steel.

In conclusion, MGR should implement proposal 1 and some variation of proposal 4. MGR should also focus improvement activities on increasing capacity in the continuous caster. MGR should address in other ways the concerns of the comptroller and marketing manager about keeping sales and profits high.

ENDNOTES

1. Adapted from Clark, K., "Chaparral Steel," Harvard Business School, Case Number 9-687-045, Boston, USA, and Radford, R., and Coughlan, P., "Steel Industry Technical Note," Ivey School of Business, Case Study Technical Note Number 9860013, London, Canada.

INDEX

ABOUT THE AUTHOR

John Miltenburg is professor of production and management science in the Michael DeGroote School of Business at McMaster University in Hamilton, Ontario, Canada. Before joining McMaster University in 1982 Dr. Miltenburg worked for General Motors. In 1988 and 1989, he was a visiting professor at the Eindhoven University of Technology in the Netherlands. In 1996 and 1997, he was a visiting professor at the Chinese University of Hong Kong.

Dr. Miltenburg has published 50 articles in scholarly journals and has written other professional articles. He served on the editorial boards of three journals. He has consulted for many leading companies. Much of the material in this book draws on his research and consulting work.

For Product Safety Concerns and Information please contact our EU representative GPSR@taylorandfrancis.com Taylor & Francis Verlag GmbH, Kaufingerstraße 24, 80331 München, Germany

* 9 7 8 1 5 6 3 2 7 3 1 7 9 *

T - #0046 - 230425 - C0 - 276/219/25 [27] - CB - 9781563273179 - Gloss Lamination